84468

National Party Conventions 1831-1996

Congressional Quarterly Inc.
Washington, D.C.

Cover illustration credits (clockwise from top right): Reuters; Andrew Innerarity/St. Petersburg
Times; John Cranford; Jonathan Salant; Library of Congress

Illustration credits: most of the photographs and engravings appearing in *National Party Conventions 1831-1996* were obtained from the collection of the Library of Congress. Other photos
and their sources were: William Jennings Bryan, pp. 60, 62, 66—National Portrait Gallery, Smith-
sonian Institution, Washington, D.C.; Thomas E. Dewey, pp. 90, 93—Collection of the New-York
Historical Society; Harry S. Truman, p. 93—Harry S. Truman Library.

Library of Congress Cataloging-in-Publication Data

National party conventions, 1831-1996.
     p.   cm.
     Includes bibliographical references and index.
     ISBN 1-56802-280-8 (alk. paper)
     1. Political conventions—United States—History.   2. Political parties—United
States—Platforms—History.   3. Presidential candidates—United States—Biography.
4. Vice-presidential candidates—United States—Biography.   I. Congressional Quarterly,
Inc.

JK2255.N377   1997
324.5′6′0973—dc21   97-20443

Contents

Preface

Perhaps the most recognizable image of the American political party is that of a cavernous hall filled with loyal delegates waving banners and cheering as a party leader or presidential nominee recites the party's cherished political beliefs. The national nominating convention is a uniquely American institution. Since the 1830s all major U.S. political parties and a host of prominent minor parties have chosen presidential and vice presidential candidates at national conventions. Through its adaptability and multiplicity of functions, the convention continues to evolve and remain an integral part of the presidential selection process.

The convention system, which has now been in continuous use for 165 years, was not mentioned in the Constitution. The Founders established the Electoral College as the sole mechanism in selecting the president. But the Founders also did not foresee the rise of political parties; and when competing parties developed in the nation's formative years, a nominating method had to be devised. In the early 19th century, party leaders first employed congressional caucuses to nominate presidential candidates. But as the desire for increased democracy swept the nation, the exclusive caucuses proved unsatisfactory and a way had to be found to involve mass citizen participation.

The new method turned out to be the convention and was initiated by the Anti-Masonic Party in September 1831. Its gathering was small by modern standards, attracting 116 delegates from 13 states. The delegates adopted an address to the people (a forerunner of the modern platform) and nominated William Wirt for the presidency. Although Wirt fared poorly in the general election and the Anti-Masonic Party failed to survive the decade, the success of the convention as a nominating mechanism led to its adoption by other parties.

The Democratic Party held its first convention in 1832 and without interruption has held a national convention every four years since then. The Democrats' gathering in Chicago in August 1996 was the party's 43rd (the party convened twice in 1860). The Republicans held their first convention in 1856, two years after the party's formation, and the August 1996 convention in San Diego was their 36th national meeting.

Through a century of massive political, social and technological changes, the survival of the convention is a tribute to both its adaptability and importance in the nomination of presidential candidates. Throughout its history, the convention has had a number of functions — foremost, the selection of a national ticket, the adoption of a platform, the discussion of party affairs and the building of party unity. While the conduct and setting of the convention have changed dramatically over the years, the major functions have remained unaltered.

Before the Civil War, conventions were held in relative obscurity. At most, several hundred delegates attended the early conventions. Delegate selection was often informal, and participation was open to anyone with the motivation to chance the nation's uncertain transportation system.

Improved transportation and communication provided conventions with greater national attention and placed them under closer scrutiny. The selection of delegates was formalized, and the drive for increased democratization produced the presidential primary, now the major method of delegate selection. In 1996, 42 states held either a Republican, Democratic or combined presidential primary.

Advances in radio and television enabled conventions in the post-World War II years to become media spectaculars. The thousands of delegates, spectators and media representatives who attended the Democratic and Republican conventions of 1996 offered a marked contrast to the relatively informal conventions of the 1830s.

The national party convention is on the verge of change once again. With presidential primaries stealing the suspense of who the eventual party nominee will be, television networks no longer provide gavel-to-gavel coverage of conventions. Party leaders now strive to avoid what were common occurrences of conventions past — the unscheduled interruptions by the delegates, the spontaneous demonstrations for candidates and the bitter floor fights over rules and platforms. Conventions have become, as evidenced by the smoothly run 1996 gatherings, carefully choreographed television presentations, timed to fill two or three hours each night and focused on the successful marketing of the party's presidential ticket.

About This Book

National Party Conventions 1831-1996 is an up-to-date collection of historical data and facts covering all major nominating conventions from the first Anti-Masonic convention in 1831 to the major national conventions of 1996 — the Republican convention that nominated former Senate majority leader Bob Dole of Kansas, the Reform Party's unusual two-stage convention that chose party founder and billionaire Ross Perot of Texas, and the Democratic convention that renominated President Bill Clinton.

The volume begins with a discussion of the presidential nominating process in the pre-convention years, from 1789 to 1828. It covers the origins of the American party system and the reliance on the congressional caucus during this period as the principal nominating method. The decline of the caucus and the rise of the convention system are also discussed.

The next section provides an overview of the functions and development of the national convention. It focuses on various aspects of the convention — delegate selection, party rules, credentials disputes, the platform and convention officers — as well as basic changes in the conduct of conventions. This section contains many useful tables and figures, such as the list of all officers and keynote speakers at Democratic and Republican national nominating conventions.

The heart of the volume is the third section, which describes the conventions of all parties that received at least 2 percent of the popular vote in any presidential election since 1831. Included are all Democratic, Republican and Whig conventions, as well as those of leading third parties.

Within each brief convention history are discussions of the contest for the presidential and vice presidential nominations, all significant roll calls and an overview of the party platform. Excerpts from the party's platform on leading issues of that particular campaign are included. A chronological table of national party convention highlights completes the section.

The following section augments the convention chronology with charts of key convention ballots, showing the vote of each state and territory on major roll calls at all Democratic, Republican and Whig conventions. Besides ballots for the presidential nominees, important votes on rules and credentials disputes are also provided.

The final section provides a variety of information on political parties and candidates. It includes historical profiles of all parties whose conventions are described in the convention chronology, as well as other parties, such as Green, Libertarian, New Alliance and Reform parties that are active today; a comprehensive roster of presidential and vice presidential nominees from 1831 to 1996 that lists minor as well as major party candidates; and a biographical directory of all presidential and vice presidential candidates who received electoral votes.

The book concludes with a bibliography, which provides the starting point for further reading about conventions and the nominating process, and a comprehensive index, which provides a quick way of locating a historical figure or party.

Pre-Convention Politics, 1789-1828

For more than a century and a half the United States has had an established two-party system. The Framers of the Constitution, however, never envisioned such a system. They in fact viewed the existence of political parties with suspicion.

In his Farewell Address, written in 1796, President George Washington warned the American people of "the danger of parties." He went on to state:

> There is an opinion that parties in free countries are useful checks upon the administration of the government, and serve to keep alive the spirit of liberty. This within certain limits is probably true; and in governments of a monarchical cast patriotism may look with indulgence, if not with favor, upon the spirit of party. But in those of the popular character, in governments purely elective, it is a spirit not to be encouraged.... A fire not to be quenched, it demands a uniform vigilance to prevent its bursting into a flame, lest, instead of warming, it should consume.

Other early American leaders shared Washington's suspicion of parties. Alexander Hamilton remarked in 1787, "[N]othing could be more illjudged than that intolerant spirit which has at all times characterized political parties." Two years later Thomas Jefferson declared: "If I could not go to heaven but with a party, I would not go there at all." Even a generation later, after the establishment of a U.S. party system, two early 19th-century presidents continued to speak out against the existence of political parties. Andrew Jackson, 12 years before he was elected president, wrote in 1816: "Now is the time to exterminate the monster called party spirit." In 1822, after his unopposed 1820 election victory, President James Monroe characterized parties as "the curse of the country."

Early American leaders were heavily influenced in their attitude by a dominant anti-party theme in European political philosophy, which equated parties with factions and viewed both negatively. Thomas Hobbes (1588-1679), David Hume (1711-1776) and Jean Jacques Rousseau (1712-1778) — three European philosophers whose views strongly influenced the Founders — regarded parties as threats to state government. In England there was no formal party system until the 1820s, several decades after the formation of parties in the United States. In colonial America there were no parties, and there were none in the Continental Congress or under the Articles of Confederation.

The Constitution did not provide authority for political parties or prohibitions against them. Historians have pointed out that most of the Framers had only a dim understanding of the function of political parties and thus were ambivalent, if not hostile, toward parties when they laid down the foundation of the new government. Nevertheless, the delegates to the Constitutional Convention and their successors in Congress ensured a role for parties in the government when they gave protection to civil rights and the right to organize. The Founders set up what they regarded as safeguards against excesses of party activity by providing an elaborate governmental system of checks and balances. The prevailing attitude of the convention was summed up by James Madison, who wrote in *The Federalist* that the "great object" of the new government was "to secure the public good and private rights against the danger of such a faction [party], and at the same time to preserve the spirit and the form of popular government."

Madison's greatest fear was that a party would become a tyrannical majority. This could be avoided, he believed, through the republican form of government that the proponents of the Constitution advocated. In *The Federalist* Madison wrote, "Among the numerous advantages promised by a well-constructed Union, none deserved to be more

Sources

Chambers, William N. *Political Parties in a New Nation: The American Experience, 1776-1809.* New York: Oxford University Press, 1963.

Key, V. O., Jr. *Politics, Parties and Pressure Groups.* 5th ed. New York: Thomas Y. Crowell, 1964.

Nichols, Roy F. *The Invention of the American Political Parties.* New York: Free Press, 1972.

Roseboom, Eugene H. *A History of Presidential Elections: From George Washington to Jimmy Carter.* 4th ed. New York: Macmillan, 1979.

Schlesinger, Arthur M., Jr. *History of U.S. Political Parties.* Vol. 1. 1973. Reprint. New York: Chelsea House, 1981.

Stanwood, Edward. *History of the Presidency.* Vol. 1. 1921. Reprint. New York: Kelley, 1975.

Stimpson, George W. *A Book about American Politics.* New York: Harper, 1952.

"[N]othing could be more illjudged than that intolerant spirit which has at all times characterized political parties."
—Alexander Hamilton, 1789

accurately developed than its tendency to break and control the violence of faction." A republic, as understood by Madison, was an elected body of wise, patriotic citizens, while a democracy was equated with mob rule. Madison dismissed the democratic form of government as a spectacle of "turbulence and contention."

Ironically, in this setting two competing parties grew up quickly. They developed as a result of public sentiment for and against adoption of the Constitution. The Federalist Party — a loose coalition of merchants, shippers, financiers and other business interests — favored the strong central government provided by the Constitution, while their opponents (at first called Anti-Federalists or Jeffersonians and later known as Democratic-Republicans) were intent upon preserving the sovereignty of the states. Underlying the controversy was the desire of the interests represented by the Federalists to create a government with power to guarantee the value of the currency (and thus protect the position of creditors) and the desire of the agrarians and frontiersmen who made up the Anti-Federalists to maintain easy credit conditions and the power of state legislatures to fend off encroachments by a remote federal government.

Unlike the Federalist Party, which was never more than a loose alliance of particular interests, the Anti-Federalists achieved a high degree of organization. The Federalists, in fact, never considered themselves a political party but rather a gentlemanly coalition of interests representing respectable society. What party management there was, they kept clandestine, a reflection of their own fundamental suspicion of parties.

There is no precise date for the beginning of parties, although both Thomas Jefferson and Alexander Hamilton (a Federalist) referred to the existence of a Jeffersonian republican "faction" in Congress as early as 1792.

While party organization became more formalized in the 1790s and early 1800s, particularly among the Jeffersonians, the parties never acquired nationally accepted names. The Jeffersonians most commonly referred to themselves as Republicans. Their opponents labeled them as Anti-Federalists, disorganizers, Jacobins (after the radical democrats in France) and Democrats — the latter an unflattering term in the early years of the Republic. To many Americans in the late 18th century, a democrat was considered a supporter of mob rule and revolution and often ideologically identified with the bloody French Revolution of 1789.

The designation Democrat-Republican was used by the Jeffersonians in several states but was never widely accepted as a party label. However, historians often refer to the Jeffersonians as the Democratic-Republicans, to avoid confusion with the later and unrelated Republican Party, founded in 1854.

Although the early American political leaders acknowledged the development of parties, they did not foresee the emergence of a two-party system. Rather, they often justified the existence of their own party as a reaction to an unacceptable opposition. Jefferson defended his party involvement as a struggle between good and evil: "[When] the principle of difference is as substantial and as strongly pronounced as between the republicans and the Monocrats of our country, I hold it as honorable to take a firm and decided part, and as immoral to pursue a middle line, as between the parties of Honest men, and Rogues, into which every country is divided."

Presidential Politics

The rise of parties forced an alteration in the presidential selection method envisioned by the creators of the Constitution. Delegates to the Constitutional Convention of 1787 had sought a presidential selection method in which the "spirit of party" would play no part. The Electoral College system they finally settled on was a compromise born of a basic distrust in the political abilities of the populace, the complexities of the separation of powers system and the diversity in the states — slavery in the South and rivalries between the big and small states.

Rather than have the people vote directly for president, the choice was to be entrusted to presidential "electors," who the Founders hoped would be wise leaders in the separate states, able to choose the one person best qualified to be president. Under the Electoral College system, states were to choose electors as they saw fit; the electors would meet in their separate states some time after their selection to record their votes for the next president.

While it seems odd that the leaders of a new democracy would choose to bypass the general populace, the decision was not so far out of line with conditions of the day as it might appear. The electors would merely be a somewhat more sophisticated version of the 18th-century electorate, which was quite different from the voting population of today. The Constitution left it to the states to determine voting requirements. In all states only men could vote. Many states also limited voting rights to property owners. Indeed, property qualifications had existed in all the colonies and endured in several states, although the exact requirements differed among states.

Some states allowed personal property or the payment of taxes as a substitute for holding real estate. By 1800 four states had established universal manhood suffrage. But property requirements of one sort or another were not abandoned by all the states until 1856. While they lasted, such requirements were restrictive, but their effect can be overstated. Because the United States was predominantly a middle-class society with fairly widespread ownership of property, such qualifications were not so significant a limit as they at first might appear. And since women and many men already were excluded from voting, restricting presidential selection to an elite group did not have the effect that it would today under universal suffrage.

Caucus System

While the Electoral College retained the power to *elect* the president, the state electors soon lost the authority to *nominate* the candidates and thus determine the field from which to choose a president. Strong political parties developed and removed the nomination process from the electors' hands. The parties created instead the first informal nominating device for choosing a president: a caucus of each party's members in Congress.

From 1796 until 1824, congressional caucuses — when a party had enough representatives to form one — chose almost all the candidates for president; the electors then chose from the party nominees. Only twice — in 1800 and 1824 — as a result of a failure of any candidate to receive a majority of electoral votes, were presidential elections decided by the House of Representatives, and even in those two cases political parties were instrumental in the election of the president.

Election of 1789

In the first presidential election, held in 1789 shortly after the ratification of the Constitution, the nominating and electing process centered in the Electoral College. Electors chosen in the various states were, under the Constitution, entitled to cast two votes and required to cast each vote for a different person. The individual receiving votes of a majority of the electors was named president and the person receiving the second highest total was named vice president.

There were no formal nominations in 1789, but public opinion centered on George Washington of Virginia for president. He received 69 electoral votes, the maximum possible. John Adams of Massachusetts was the leading second choice, although he did not enjoy the degree of unanimity that surrounded Washington. Adams easily won the vice presidency, receiving 34 electoral votes.

Election of 1792

The Federalists and Democratic-Republicans were emerging as competitive parties by the election of 1792. As a result, the Republic experienced the first modification in the presidential nominating process. No attempt was made to displace President Washington, but the Democratic-Republicans mounted a challenge to Vice President Adams. Meeting in Philadelphia in October 1792, a group of Democratic-Republican leaders from the Middle Atlantic states and South Carolina endorsed Gov. George Clinton of New York for the vice presidency, bypassing Sen. Aaron Burr of the same state. While Adams emerged victorious in the Electoral College, Clinton's endorsement by a meeting of party politicians was a milestone in the evolution of the presidential nominating process and a step away from the original Electoral College system.

Election of 1796

The election of 1796 brought further modifications in the nominating method, evidenced by the appearance of the congressional caucus.

There was no opposition to Thomas Jefferson as the Democratic-Republican presidential candidate, and he was considered the party's standard-bearer by a consensus of party leaders. A caucus of Democratic-Republican senators, however, was unable to agree on a running mate, producing a tie vote between Burr and Sen. Pierce Butler of South Carolina that ended with a walk-out by Butler's supporters. As a result, there was no formal Democratic-Republican candidate to run with Jefferson.

The Federalists held what historian Roy F. Nichols described as a "quasi caucus" of the party's members of Congress in Philadelphia in May 1796. The gathering chose Vice President Adams and Minister to Great Britain Thomas Pinckney of South Carolina as the Federalist candidates.

Presidents, 1789-1829

Term	President	Vice President
1789-93	George Washington (FED)	John Adams (FED)
1793-97	George Washington (FED)	John Adams (FED)
1797-1801	John Adams (FED)	Thomas Jefferson (D-R)
1801-05	Thomas Jefferson (D-R)	Aaron Burr (D-R)
1805-09	Thomas Jefferson (D-R)	George Clinton (D-R)
1809-13	James Madison (D-R)	George Clinton (D-R)
1813-17	James Madison (D-R)	Elbridge Gerry (D-R)
1817-21	James Monroe (D-R)	Daniel D. Tompkins (D-R)
1821-25	James Monroe (D-R)	Daniel D. Tompkins (D-R)
1825-29	John Q. Adams (D-R)	John C. Calhoun (D-R)

FED - Federalist; D-R - Democratic-Republican

Election of 1800

The election of 1800 was the first where both parties used the congressional caucus as the nominating body. Neither party, however, desired much publicity for the process, gathering in secret to deliberate. The proceedings were sketchily described by private correspondence and occasionally referred to in newspapers of the day. Unlike the public national conventions of later years, privacy was a hallmark of the early caucuses.

Although the actual dates of the 1800 caucuses are hazy, it is believed that both were held in May. The Democratic-Republican caucus was held in Marache's boardinghouse in Philadelphia, where 43 of the party's members of Congress selected Aaron Burr to run with Thomas Jefferson, the latter again the presidential candidate by consensus and not formally nominated by the caucus.

Federalist members of Congress met in the Senate chamber in Philadelphia and nominated President Adams and Gen. Charles Cotesworth Pinckney of South Carolina. Pinckney, the elder brother of the Federalist vice presidential candidate in 1796, was placed on the ticket at the insistence of Alexander Hamilton, who believed one of the South Carolina Pinckneys could win. Although the deliberations of the Federalist caucus were secret, the existence of the meeting was not. It was described by the local Democratic-Republican paper, the *Philadelphia Aurora*, as a "Jacobinical conclave." Further denunciations by the paper's author, Benjamin F. Bache, earned him a personal rebuke from the U.S. Senate.

Election of 1804

The 1804 election was the first one held after the 12th Amendment to the Constitution went into effect, requiring electors to cast separate votes for president and vice presi-

"If I could not go to heaven but with a party, I would not go there at all."

—Thomas Jefferson, 1789

"Among the numerous advantages promised by a well-constructed Union, none deserves to be more accurately developed than its tendency to break and control the violence of faction."

—James Madison, 1787

dent. The amendment was designed to avoid the unwieldy situation that had developed in 1800, when the two leading Democratic-Republican candidates, Jefferson and Burr, both received the same number of electoral votes. The unexpected tie vote threw the presidential election into the House of Representatives, where 36 ballots were cast before Jefferson finally won. With ratification of the amendment, parties in 1804 and thereafter specifically designated their presidential and vice presidential candidates.

The Democratic-Republicans retained the caucus system of nomination in 1804, as they did for the next two decades, and for the first time they publicly reported their deliberations. The party caucus was held in February and attracted 108 of the party's senators and representatives. President Jefferson was renominated by acclamation, but Vice President Burr was not considered for a second term. On the first nominating roll call publicly reported in American political history, New York's Gov. Clinton was chosen to run for vice president. He received 67 votes to easily defeat Sen. John Breckinridge of Kentucky, who collected 20 votes. To "avoid unpleasant discussions" no names were placed in nomination, and the vote was taken by written ballot.

Before adjourning, the caucus appointed a 13-member committee to conduct the campaign. A forerunner of party national committees, the new campaign group included members of both the House and Senate, but with no two individuals from the same state.

The Federalists dropped the congressional caucus as their nominating method. Federalist leaders in 1804 informally chose Charles Cotesworth Pinckney for president and Rufus King of New York for vice president. But the details of how they formulated this ticket are not known. There is no record in 1804 of any Federalist meeting to nominate candidates.

Election of 1808

The Democratic-Republican caucus was held in January 1808. For the first time a formal call was issued. Sen. Stephen R. Bradley of Vermont, the chairman of the 1804 caucus, issued the call to all 146 Democratic-Republicans in Congress and several Federalists sympathetic to the Democratic-Republican cause. His authority to call the caucus was questioned by several party leaders, but various reports indicate that 89 to 94 members of Congress attended.

As in 1804 the balloting was done without the formal placing of names in nomination. For president, Jefferson's handpicked successor, Secretary of State James Madison of Virginia, was an easy winner with 83 votes. Vice President Clinton and James Monroe of Virginia each received three votes. For vice president the caucus overwhelmingly renominated Clinton. He received 79 votes, while runner-up John Langdon of New Hampshire collected five. Even after the Democratic-Republicans renominated him for vice presi-

dent, Clinton's supporters continued to hope that the Federalists would nominate their man for president later in the year. But their hopes were dashed when the nomination ultimately went to Pinckney.

As in 1804 the Democratic-Republican caucus appointed a committee to conduct the campaign. Membership was expanded to 15 House and Senate members and it was formally called the "committee of correspondence and arrangement." The committee was authorized to fill any vacancies on the national ticket, should any occur.

Before adjournment a resolution was approved defending the caucus system as "the most practicable mode of consulting and respecting the interest and wishes of all." Later caucuses adopted similar resolutions throughout the history of the system.

The resolution was meant to stem the rumblings of opposition to the caucus system. Seventeen Democratic-Republican members of Congress signed a protest against Madison's selection and questioned the authority of the caucus as a nominating body. Vice President Clinton, himself selected by the caucus, wrote of his disapproval of the caucus system.

The Federalists in 1808 again altered their presidential selection process, holding a secret meeting of party leaders in August of that year to choose the ticket. The meeting, held in New York City, was initially called by the Federalist members of the Massachusetts legislature. Twenty-five to 30 party leaders from seven states, all north of the Potomac River except South Carolina, attended the national meeting. There was some discussion of choosing Vice President George Clinton, a dissident Democratic-Republican, for the presidency, but the meeting ultimately selected the Federalist candidates of 1804: Charles Cotesworth Pinckney and Rufus King.

Election of 1812

The Democratic-Republicans held their quadrennial nominating caucus in May 1812. Eighty-three of the party's 138 members of Congress attended, with the New England and New York delegations poorly represented. The New York delegation was sympathetic to the candidacy of the state's lieutenant governor, De Witt Clinton, who was maneuvering for the Federalist nomination, while New England was noticeably upset with the Madison foreign policy that was leading to war with England. President Madison was renominated with a near-unanimous total, receiving 82 votes. John Langdon of New Hampshire was chosen for vice president by a wide margin, collecting 64 votes to 16 for Gov. Elbridge Gerry of Massachusetts. But Langdon declined the nomination, citing his age (70) as the reason. In a second caucus, held in June, Gerry was a runaway winner with 74 votes.

In 1812, as four years earlier, the Federalists held a secret meeting in New York City. It was more than twice the size of the 1808 gathering, with 70 representatives from 11 states attending the three-day meeting in September. Delegates were sent to the conference by Federalist general committees, with all but nine of the delegates coming from the New England and Middle Atlantic states.

Debate centered on whether to run a separate Federalist ticket or to endorse the candidacy of De Witt Clinton, the nephew of George Clinton. The younger Clinton already had been nominated for the presidency by the New York Democratic-Republican caucus, and the Federalists ultimately adopted a resolution approving his candidacy and that of

Jared Ingersoll. Ingersoll was a Pennsylvania Federalist who was initially nominated for vice president by a party legislative caucus in that state.

Election of 1816

The Federalist Party was nearly extinct by 1816 and did not hold any type of meeting to nominate candidates for president and vice president. As a result, nomination by the Democratic-Republican caucus was tantamount to election. Only 58 members of Congress attended the first caucus in the House chamber. With the expectation of better attendance, a second caucus was held several days later in mid-March 1816 and drew 119 senators and representatives. By a vote of 65 to 54, Secretary of State James Monroe was nominated for president, defeating Secretary of War William H. Crawford of Georgia. Forty of Crawford's votes came from five states: Georgia, Kentucky, New Jersey, New York and North Carolina. The vice presidential nomination went to New York governor Daniel D. Tompkins, who easily outdistanced Pennsylvania governor Simon Snyder, 85 to 30. The nominations of Monroe and Tompkins revived a Virginia-New York alliance that extended back to the late 18th century. With the lone exception of 1812, every Democratic-Republican ticket from 1800 until 1824 was composed of a candidate from Virginia and a vice presidential candidate from New York.

While the collapse of the Federalists ensured Democratic-Republican rule, it also increased intraparty friction and spurred further attacks on the caucus system. Twenty-two Democratic-Republican members of Congress were absent from the second party caucus, and at least 15 were known to be opposed to the system. Historian Edward Stanwood wrote that there were mass meetings around the country to protest the caucus system. Opponents claimed that the writers of the Constitution did not envision the caucus, that presidential nominating should not be a function of Congress and that the caucus system encouraged candidates to curry the favor of Congress.

Election of 1820

The 1820 election came during the "Era of Good Feelings," a phrase coined by a Boston publication, the *Columbian Centinel,* to describe a brief period of virtual one-party rule in the United States. With only one candidate, President James Monroe, there was no need for a caucus. One was called, but fewer than 50 of the Democratic-Republicans' 191 members of Congress attended. The caucus voted unanimously to make no nominations and passed a resolution explaining that it was inexpedient to do so. Despite the fact that Monroe and Tompkins were not formally renominated, electoral slates were filed on their behalf. They both received nearly unanimous Electoral College victories.

Demise of the Caucus

In 1824 there was still only one party, but within this party there was an abundance of candidates for the presidency: Secretary of State John Quincy Adams of Massachusetts, Sen. Andrew Jackson of Tennessee, Secretary of War John C. Calhoun of South Carolina, House Speaker Henry Clay of Kentucky and Secretary of the Treasury William H. Crawford. It was generally assumed that Crawford was the strongest candidate among members of Congress and would

win a caucus if one were held; therefore, Crawford's opponents joined the growing list of caucus opponents.

In early February 1824, 11 Democratic-Republican members of Congress issued a call for a caucus to be held in the middle of the month. Their call was countered by 24 other members of Congress from 15 states who deemed it "inexpedient under existing circumstances" to hold a caucus. They claimed that 181 members of Congress were resolved not to attend if a caucus were held.

When the caucus convened in mid-February, only 66 members of Congress were present, with three-quarters of those attending from just four states — Georgia, New York, North Carolina and Virginia. As expected, Crawford won the presidential nomination, receiving 64 votes. Selected for vice president was Albert Gallatin of Pennsylvania, who received 57 votes. The caucus adopted a resolution defending its actions as "the best means of collecting and concentrating the feelings and wishes of the people of the Union upon this important subject." A committee was appointed to write an address to the people. As written, the text of the address viewed with alarm the "dismemberment" of the Democratic-Republican Party.

The caucus nomination proved to be an albatross for Crawford as his opponents denounced him as the candidate of "King Caucus." Reflecting the increasing democratization of American politics, other presidential candidates relied on nominations by state legislatures to legitimize their presidential ambitions. However, in an attempt to narrow the field, the candidates had to negotiate among themselves. Calhoun alone withdrew to become the vice presidential candidate of all the anti-caucus entries. Adams offered the vice presidency to Jackson as "an easy and dignified retirement to his old age." Jackson refused. Other maneuvers were equally unsuccessful, so that four presidential candidates remained in the field to collect electoral votes, subsequently throwing the election into the House of Representatives, where Adams won.

The election of 1828 proved to be a transitional one in the development of the presidential nominating process. The caucus was dead, but the national nominating convention was not yet born. Jackson was nominated by the legislature of his native Tennessee and in October 1825, three years before the election, accepted the nomination in a speech before the legislature. He accepted Vice President Calhoun as his running mate, after it was proposed in January 1827 by the *United States Telegraph,* a pro-Jackson paper in Washington. A Pennsylvania state convention paired President Adams with Secretary of the Treasury Richard Rush of Pennsylvania, a ticket that Adams' supporters in other states accepted. Both Jackson and Adams were endorsed by other legislatures, conventions and meetings.

"We must always have party distinctions."
—Martin Van Buren, 1827

Trend Toward Conventions

The birth of the national convention system came in 1831, seven years after the death of the caucus. The caucus system collapsed when a field of candidates appeared who would not acquiesce to the choice of one caucus-approved candidate. But other factors were present to undermine the caucus system. These included changes in voting procedures and an expansion of suffrage. Between 1800 and 1824 the proportion of states in which the electors were chosen by popular vote rather than by the state legislature increased from 4 out of 16 to 18 out of 24. In 1828 the popular vote reached 1.1 million, compared with fewer than 400,000 in 1824. A broader base of support than the congressional caucus became essential for presidential aspirants.

State legislatures, state conventions and mass meetings all emerged in the 1820s to challenge the caucus. The trend to democratization of the presidential nominating process, as evidenced by the expansion of suffrage and increased importance of the popular vote for president, led shortly to creation of the national nominating convention. The convention system, initiated by the Anti-Masons in 1831, was adopted by all the major parties before the end of the decade. *(Anti-Masons, pp. 25, 265)*

The birth of the national nominating convention was a milestone in the evolution of the presidential nominating process. Political scientist V. O. Key Jr. summarized some of the major forces that brought about the rise of the convention system:

> The destruction of the caucus represented more than a mere change in the method of nomination. Its replacement by the convention was regarded as the removal from power of self-appointed oligarchies that had usurped the right to nominate. The new system, the convention, gave, or so it was supposed, the mass of party members an opportunity to participate in nominations. These events occurred as the domestic winds blew in from the growing West, as the suffrage was being broadened, and as the last vestiges of the early aristocratic leadership were disappearing. Sharp alterations in the distribution of power were taking place, and they were paralleled by the shifts in methods of nomination.

With the establishment of the national convention came the re-emergence of the two-party system. Unlike the Founders, who were suspicious of competitive parties, some political leaders in the late 1820s and 1830s viewed the existence of opposing parties favorably. One of the most prominent of these men, Martin Van Buren, a leading organizer of Jackson's 1828 election victory and himself president after Jackson, had written in 1827: "We must always have party distinctions."

Nominating Conventions

Although the presidential nominating convention has been a target of criticism throughout its existence, it has survived to become a traditional fixture of American politics. The convention owes its longevity and general acceptance in large part to the multiplicity of functions that the convention uniquely combines.

The convention is a nominating body that the Democrats, Republicans and most of the other major parties have used for 165 years to choose their candidates for president and vice president. The convention also produces a platform containing the party's positions on campaign issues. Convention delegates form the organization's supreme governing body and as such they make major decisions on party affairs. Between conventions such decisions are made by the national committee with the guidance of the party chair.

The convention provides a forum for compromise among the diverse elements within a party, allowing the discussion and often the satisfactory solution of differing points of view. As the ultimate campaign rally, the convention also gathers together thousands of party leaders and rank-and-file members from across the country in an atmosphere that varies widely, sometimes encouraging sober discussion but often resembling a carnival. But even though the process has drawn heavy criticism, the convention has endured because it successfully performs a variety of actions.

The convention is an outgrowth of the American political experience. Nowhere is it mentioned in the Constitution nor has the authority of the convention ever been a subject of congressional legislation. Rather, the convention has evolved along with the presidential selection process. The convention has been the accepted nominating method of the major political parties since the election of 1832, but internal changes within the convention system have been massive since the early, formative years.

Convention Sites

Before the Civil War, conventions frequently were held in small buildings, even churches, and attracted only several hundred delegates and a minimum of spectators. Transportation and communications were slow, so most conventions were held in the late spring in a city with a central geographical location. Baltimore, Md., was the most popular convention city in this period, playing host to the first six Democratic conventions (1832 through 1852), two Whig conventions, one National Republican convention, and the 1831 Anti-Masonic gathering — America's first national nominating convention. With the nation's westward expansion, the heartland city of Chicago, Ill., emerged as the most frequent convention center. Since its first one in 1860, Chicago has been the site of 25 major party conventions (14 Republican, 11 Democratic). The Democrats held their national convention in Chicago as recently as 1996. The Republicans chose that year to meet in San Diego — the first time that California city hosted a national party convention.

Locating and Financing Conventions

Since 1976, presidential elections have been publicly funded. Early on, the newly created Federal Election Commission (FEC) ruled that host-city contributions to conventions are allowable, enabling the parties to far exceed the technical limit on convention spending. In 1988, for example, the FEC allotted the two major parties $9.2 million each in public funds for their conventions. The money came from an optional checkoff for publicly financing presidential campaigns on federal income tax forms. (Congress raised the original $1 checkoff to $3 per taxpayer, beginning in 1993.) In 1988, the Republicans, however, spent a total of $18 million on their New Orleans convention, while the Democrats spent $22.5 million in Atlanta. To attract the Democratic convention, Atlanta levied a special tax on hotel guests, which enabled the host committee to offer a package of $5 million in borrowed money. For both conventions, General Motors (with FEC permission) provided fleets of cars at an estimated cost of $350,000.

In 1992, the Democrats spent a record $38.6 million on their New York City meeting, according to political scientist Herbert E. Alexander. For the 1996 conventions, the FEC allotted the two major parties $12.4 million each in public funds, but the total spending for each party, according to Alexander, was at least $30 million. No authoritative breakdown of 1996 convention costs was available, but major outlays typically go for construction, administration, office space, convention committees and police and fire protection. Besides adequate hotel and convention hall facilities, safety of the delegates and other attendees is increasingly a major consideration in selection of a national party convention site. The island location of Miami Beach, for example, made it easier to contain protest demonstrators and reportedly was a factor in its selection by the Republicans in 1968 and by both parties in 1972. For the party that controls the White House, often the overriding factor in site selection is the president's personal preference — as in the GOP's decision to meet in 1992 at President George Bush's adopted home

Sites of Major Party Conventions, 1832-1996

The following chart lists the 21 cities selected as the sites of major party conventions and the number of conventions they have hosted from the first national gathering for the Democrats (1832) and the Republicans (1856) through the 1996 conventions. The Democrats have hosted a total of 43 conventions; the Republicans 36.

	Total Conventions	Democratic Conventions		Republican Conventions	
		Number	**Last Hosted**	**Number**	**Last Hosted**
Chicago, Ill.	25	11	1996	14	1960
Baltimore, Md.	10	9	1912	1	1864
Philadelphia, Pa.	7	2	1948	5	1948
St. Louis, Mo.	5	4	1916	1	1896
New York, N.Y.	5	5	1992	0	—
San Francisco, Calif.	4	2	1984	2	1964
Cincinnati, Ohio	3	2	1880	1	1876
Kansas City, Mo.	3	1	1900	2	1976
Miami Beach, Fla.	3	1	1972	2	1972
Cleveland, Ohio	2	0	—	2	1936
Houston, Texas	2	1	1928	1	1992
Atlanta, Ga.	1	1	1988	0	—
Atlantic City, N.J.	1	1	1964	0	—
Charleston, S.C.	1	1	1860	0	—
Dallas, Texas	1	0	—	1	1984
Denver, Colo.	1	1	1908	0	—
Detroit, Mich.	1	0	—	1	1980
Los Angeles, Calif.	1	1	1960	0	—
Minneapolis, Minn.	1	0	—	1	1892
New Orleans, La.	1	0	—	1	1988
San Diego, Calif.	1	0	—	1	1996

city of Houston, or the Democrats' decision to meet in Atlantic City in 1964, because President Lyndon Johnson wanted a site within helicopter distance of Washington, and convenient to New York City.

The national committees of the two parties select the sites about one year before the conventions are to take place.

Call of the Convention

The second major step in the quadrennial convention process follows several months after the site selection with announcement of the convention call, the establishment of the three major convention committees — credentials, rules and platform (resolutions) — the appointment of convention officers and finally the holding of the convention itself. While these basic steps have undergone little change during the past 165 years, there have been major alterations within the nominating convention system.

The call to the convention sets the date and site of the meeting and is issued early in each election year, if not before. The call to the first Democratic convention, held in 1832, was issued by the New Hampshire legislature. Early Whig conventions were called by party members in Congress. With the establishment of national committees later in the 19th century, the function of issuing the convention call fell to these new party organizations. Each national committee currently has the responsibility for allocating delegates to each state.

Delegate Selection

Both parties have modified the method of allocating delegates to the individual states and territories. From the beginning of the convention system in the 19th century, both the Democrats and Republicans distributed votes to the states based on their Electoral College strength. The first major deviation from this procedure was made by the Republicans after their divisive 1912 convention, in which President William Howard Taft won renomination over former president Theodore Roosevelt. Taft's nomination was due largely to almost solid support from the South — a region vastly over-represented in relation to its number of Republican voters. Before their 1916 convention the Republicans reduced the allocation of votes to the Southern states. At their 1924 convention the Republicans applied the first bonus system, by which states were awarded extra votes for supporting the Republican presidential candidate in the previous election. The concept of bonus votes, applied as a reward to the states for supporting the party ticket, has been used and expanded by both parties since that time.

The Democrats first used a bonus system in 1944, completing a compromise arrangement with Southern states after abolishing the party's controversial two-thirds nominating rule in 1936. Since then both parties have used various delegate-allocation formulas. At their 1972 convention the Republicans revised the formula and added more than 900 new delegate slots. The Ripon Society, an organization of liberal Republicans, sued to have the new rules overturned. They argued that, because of the extra delegates awarded to states that voted Republican in the previous presidential election, small Southern and Western states were favored at the expense of the more populous but less Republican Eastern states. The challenge failed when the Supreme Court in February 1976 refused to hear the case and thus let stand a U.S. Court of Appeals decision upholding the rules.

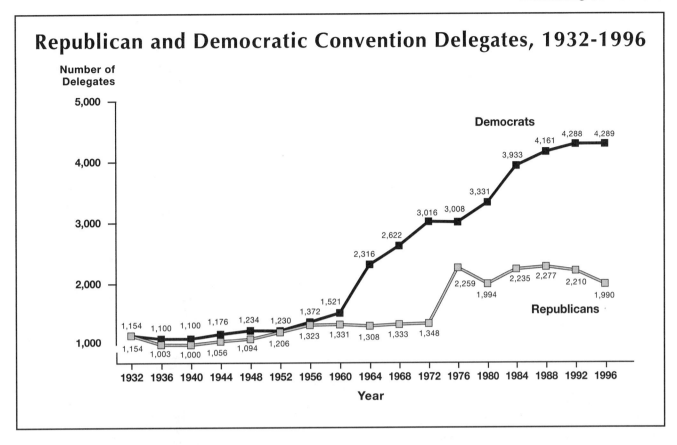

Republican and Democratic Convention Delegates, 1932-1996

Number of Delegates

Year

Democrats: 1,154 · 1,100 · 1,100 · 1,176 · 1,234 · 1,230 · 1,372 · 1,521 · 2,316 · 2,622 · 3,016 · 3,008 · 3,331 · 3,933 · 4,161 · 4,288 · 4,289

Republicans: 1,154 · 1,003 · 1,000 · 1,056 · 1,094 · 1,206 · 1,323 · 1,331 · 1,308 · 1,333 · 1,348 · 2,259 · 1,994 · 2,235 · 2,277 · 2,210 · 1,990

Only 116 delegates from 13 states attended the initial national nominating convention held by the Anti-Masons in 1831, but with the addition of more states and the adoption of increasingly complex voting-allocation formulas by the major parties, the size of conventions spiraled. The 1976 Republican convention had 2,259 delegates, while the Democrats in the same year had 3,075 delegates casting 3,008 votes. (The number of delegate votes was smaller than the number of delegates because Democratic Party rules provide for fractional voting.)

The expanded size of modern conventions in part reflected their democratization, with less command by a few party leaders and dramatic growth among youth, women and minority delegations. Increased representation by such groups was one of the major reasons given by the Republicans for the 60 percent increase in delegate strength authorized by the 1972 convention (and effective for the 1976 gathering). The Democrats adopted new rules in June 1978, expanding the number of delegates by 10 percent to provide extra representation for state and local officials. The new Democratic rules also required that women account for at least 50 percent of the delegates beginning with the 1980 convention. That party's national convention continued to grow throughout the next decade — from 3,933 delegates in 1984 to 4,289 in 1996. In 1996, 57 percent of the Democratic delegates were women; 33 percent were from minority groups.

In contrast, 1,990 delegates attended the 1996 Republican convention in San Diego. Unlike the Democrats, the Republican Party had no rules for the makeup of its convention delegates. Although 51 percent of the GOP registered voters in 1996 were women, only 39 percent of the convention delegates were women. However, while only 6 percent of registered Republican voters in 1996 were minorities, 8

percent of the Republican delegates were of minority groups.

With the increased size of conventions has come a formalization in the method of delegate selection, which at first was often haphazard and informal. At the Democratic convention in 1835, for example, Maryland had 188 delegates to cast the state's 10 votes. In contrast, Tennessee's 15 votes were cast by a traveling businessman who happened to be in the convention city at the time. While the number of delegates and the number of votes allocated tended to be equal or nearly so later in the 19th century, a few party bosses frequently exercised domination of national conventions.

Two basic methods of delegate selection were employed in the 19th century and continued to be used into the 20th: the caucus method, by which delegates were chosen by meetings at the local or state level, and the appointment method, by which delegates were appointed by the governor or a powerful state leader.

Presidential Primaries

A revolutionary new mechanism for delegate selection emerged during the early 1900s: the presidential primary election in which the voters directly elected convention delegates. Initiated in Florida in 1904, the presidential primary by 1912 was used by 13 states. In his first annual message to Congress the following year, President Woodrow Wilson advocated the establishment of a national primary to select presidential candidates: "I feel confident that I do not misinterpret the wishes or the expectations of the country when I urge the prompt enactment of legislation which will provide for primary elections throughout the country at which the voters of several parties may choose their nominees for the presidency without the intervention of nominating conventions." Wilson went on to suggest the retention of conven-

Democratic Conventions, 1832-1996

Year	City	Dates	Presidential Nominee	Vice Presidential Nominee	No. of Pres. Ballots
1832	Baltimore	May 21-23	Andrew Jackson	Martin Van Buren	1
1835	Baltimore	May 20-23	Martin Van Buren	Richard M. Johnson	1
1840	Baltimore	May 5-6	Martin Van Buren	—[1]	1
1844	Baltimore	May 27-29	James K. Polk	George M. Dallas	9
1848	Baltimore	May 22-25	Lewis Cass	William O. Butler	4
1852	Baltimore	June 1-5	Franklin Pierce	William R. King	49
1856	Cincinnati	June 2-6	James Buchanan	John C. Breckinridge	17
1860	Charleston	April 23-May 3	Deadlocked		57
	Baltimore	June 18-23	Stephen A. Douglas	Benjamin Fitzpatrick Herschel V. Johnson[2]	2
1864	Chicago	Aug. 29-31	George B. McClellan	George H. Pendleton	1
1868	New York	July 4-9	Horatio Seymour	Francis P. Blair	22
1872	Baltimore	July 9-10	Horace Greeley	Benjamin G. Brown	1
1876	St. Louis	June 27-29	Samuel J. Tilden	Thomas A. Hendricks	2
1880	Cincinnati	June 22-24	Winfield S. Hancock	William H. English	2
1884	Chicago	July 8-11	Grover Cleveland	Thomas A. Hendricks	2
1888	St. Louis	June 5-7	Grover Cleveland	Allen G. Thurman	1
1892	Chicago	June 21-23	Grover Cleveland	Adlai E. Stevenson	1
1896	Chicago	July 7-11	William J. Bryan	Arthur Sewall	5
1900	Kansas City	July 4-6	William J. Bryan	Adlai E. Stevenson	1
1904	St. Louis	July 6-9	Alton S. Parker	Henry G. Davis	1
1908	Denver	July 7-10	William J. Bryan	John W. Kern	1
1912	Baltimore	June 25-July 2	Woodrow Wilson	Thomas R. Marshall	46
1916	St. Louis	June 14-16	Woodrow Wilson	Thomas R. Marshall	1
1920	San Francisco	June 28-July 6	James M. Cox	Franklin D. Roosevelt	44
1924	New York	June 24-July 9	John W. Davis	Charles W. Bryan	103
1928	Houston	June 26-29	Alfred E. Smith	Joseph T. Robinson	1
1932	Chicago	June 27-July 2	Franklin D. Roosevelt	John N. Garner	4
1936	Philadelphia	June 23-27	Franklin D. Roosevelt	John N. Garner	Acclamation
1940	Chicago	July 15-18	Franklin D. Roosevelt	Henry A. Wallace	1
1944	Chicago	July 19-21	Franklin D. Roosevelt	Harry S. Truman	1
1948	Philadelphia	July 12-14	Harry S. Truman	Alben W. Barkley	1
1952	Chicago	July 21-26	Adlai E. Stevenson	John J. Sparkman	3
1956	Chicago	Aug. 13-17	Adlai E. Stevenson	Estes Kefauver	1
1960	Los Angeles	July 11-15	John F. Kennedy	Lyndon B. Johnson	1
1964	Atlantic City	Aug. 24-27	Lyndon B. Johnson	Hubert H. Humphrey	Acclamation
1968	Chicago	Aug. 26-29	Hubert H. Humphrey	Edmund S. Muskie	1
1972	Miami Beach	July 10-13	George McGovern	Thomas F. Eagleton R. Sargent Shriver[3]	1
1976	New York	July 12-15	Jimmy Carter	Walter F. Mondale	1
1980	New York	Aug. 11-14	Jimmy Carter	Walter F. Mondale	1
1984	San Francisco	July 16-19	Walter F. Mondale	Geraldine A. Ferraro	1
1988	Atlanta	July 18-21	Michael S. Dukakis	Lloyd Bentsen	1
1992	New York	July 13-16	Bill Clinton	Albert Gore Jr.	1
1996	Chicago	Aug. 26-29	Bill Clinton	Albert Gore Jr.	1

1. *The 1840 Democratic convention did not nominate a candidate for vice president.*

2. *The 1860 Democratic convention nominated Benjamin Fitzpatrick, who declined the nomination shortly after the convention adjourned. On June 25 the Democratic National Committee selected Herschel V. Johnson as the party's candidate for vice president.*

3. *The 1972 Democratic convention nominated Thomas F. Eagleton, who withdrew from the ticket on July 31. On Aug. 8 the Democratic National Committee selected R. Sargent Shriver as the party's candidate for vice president.*

tions for the purpose of declaring the results of the primaries and formulating the parties' platforms.

Before any action was taken on Wilson's proposal, the progressive spirit that spurred the growth of primaries died out. Not until after World War II, when widespread pressures for change touched both parties but especially the Democratic, was there a rapid growth in presidential primaries. In the mid-1980s some states reverted to the caucus method of delegate selection, but the revival trend soon abated. A record 44 primaries were held in 1996, including those in the District of Columbia and Puerto Rico.

In most states participation in the presidential primary is restricted to voters belonging to the party holding the primary. In some states, however, participation by voters outside the party is allowed by state-mandated open primaries, which override party rules to the contrary.

Democratic Rules in the 1980s and 1990s

In June 1982 the Democratic National Committee (DNC) adopted several changes in the presidential nominating process recommended by the party's Commission on Presidential Nominations, chaired by Gov. James B. Hunt Jr. of

Chief Officers and Keynote Speakers
At Democratic National Conventions, 1832-1996

Year	Chair National Committee	Temporary Chair	Permanent Chair	Keynote Speaker
1832		Robert Lucas, Ohio	Robert Lucas, Ohio	
1836		Andrew Stevenson, Va.	Andrew Stevenson, Va.	
1840		Isaac Hill, N.H.	William Carroll, Tenn.	
1844		Hendrick B. Wright, Pa.	Hendrick B. Wright, Pa.	
1848	Benjamin Hallet, Mass.	J.S. Bryce, La.	Andrew Stevenson, Va.	
1852	Robert M. McLane, Md.	Gen. Romulus M. Saunders, N.C.	John W. Davis, Ind.	
1856	David A. Smalley, Vt.	Samuel Medary, Ohio	John E. Ward, Ga.	
1860	August Belmont, N.Y.	Francis B. Flournoy, Ark.	Caleb Cushing, Mass.	
1864	August Belmont, N.Y.	William Bigler, Pa.	Horatio Seymour, N.Y.	
1868	August Belmont, N.Y.	Henry L. Palmer, Wis.	Horatio Seymour, N.Y.	
1872	Augustus Schell, N.Y.	Thomas Jefferson Randolph, Va.	James R. Doolittle, Wis.	
1876	Abram Stevens Hewitt, N.Y.	Henry M. Watterson, Ky.	John A. McClernand, Ill.	
1880	William H. Barnum, Conn.	George Hoadly, Ohio	John W. Stevenson, Ky.	
1884	William H. Barnum, Conn.	Richard B. Hubbard, Texas	William F. Vilas, Wis.	
1888	William H. Barnum, Conn.	Stephen M. White, Calif.	Patrick A. Collins, Mass.	
1892	William F. Harrity, Penn.	William C. Owens, Ky.	William L. Wilson, W.Va.	
1896	James K. Jones, Ark.	John W. Daniel, Va.	Stephen M. White, Calif.	
1900	James K. Jones, Ark.	Charles S. Thomas, Colo.	James D. Richardson, Tenn.	
1904	Thomas Taggart, Ind.	John Sharp Williams, Miss.	Champ Clark, Mo.	
1908	Norman E. Mack, N.Y.	Theodore A. Bell, Calif.	Henry D. Clayton, Ala.	
1912	William F. McCombs, N.Y.	Alton B. Parker, N.Y.	Ollie M. James, Ky.	
1916	Vance C. McCormick, Pa.	Martin H. Glynn, N.Y.	Ollie M. James, Ky.	
1920	George H. White, Ohio	Homer S. Cummings, Conn.	Joseph T. Robinson, Ark.	
1924	Clem Shaver, W.Va.	Pat Harrison, Miss.	Thomas J. Walsh, Mont.	
1928	John J. Raskob, Md.	Claude G. Bowers, Ind.	Joseph T. Robinson, Ark.	
1932	James A. Farley, N.Y.	Alben W. Barkley, Ky.	Thomas J. Walsh, Mont.	
1936	James A. Farley, N.Y.	Alben W. Barkley, Ky.	Joseph T. Robinson, Ark.	Alben W. Barkley, Ky.
1940	Edward J. Flynn, N.Y.	William B. Bankhead, Ala.	Alben W. Barkley, Ky.	William B. Bankhead, Ala.
1944	Robert E. Hannegan, Mo.	Robert S. Kerr, Okla.	Samuel D. Jackson, Ind.	Robert S. Kerr, Okla.
1948	J. Howard McGrath, R.I.	Alben W. Barkley, Ky.	Sam Rayburn, Texas	Alben W. Barkley, Ky.
1952	Stephen A. Mitchell, Ill.	Paul A. Dever, Mass.	Sam Rayburn, Texas	Paul A. Dever, Mass.
1956	Paul M. Butler, Ind.	Frank G. Clement, Tenn.	Sam Rayburn, Texas	Frank Clement, Tenn.
1960	Henry Jackson, Wash.	Frank Church, Idaho	LeRoy Collins, Fla.	Frank Church, Idaho
1964	John M. Bailey, Conn.	John O. Pastore, R.I.	John W. McCormack, Mass.	John O. Pastore, R.I.
1968	Lawrence F. O'Brien, Mass.	Daniel K. Inouye, Hawaii	Carl B. Albert, Okla.	Daniel K. Inouye, Hawaii
1972[1]	Lawrence F. O'Brien, Mass.		Lawrence F. O'Brien, Mass.	Reubin Askew, Fla.
1976	Robert S. Strauss, Texas		Lindy Boggs, La.	John Glenn, Ohio
				Barbara C. Jordan, Texas
1980	John C. White, Texas		Thomas P. O'Neill Jr., Mass.	Morris K. Udall, Ariz.
1984	Charles T. Manatt, Calif.		Martha Layne Collins, Ky.	Mario M. Cuomo, N.Y.
1988	Paul G. Kirk Jr., Mass.		Jim Wright, Texas	Ann W. Richards, Texas
1992	Ronald H. Brown, D.C.		Ann W. Richards, Texas	Bill Bradley, N.J.
				Zell Miller, Ga.
				Barbara C. Jordan, Texas
1996	Donald Fowler, S.C.		Thomas A. Daschle, S.D.	Evan Bayh, Ind.
			Richard A. Gephardt, Mo.	

1. A rule change eliminated the position of temporary chair.

North Carolina. The Hunt Commission, as it came to be known, suggested revisions to increase the power of party regulars and give the convention more freedom to act on its own. It was the fourth time in 12 years that the Democrats, struggling to repair their nominating process without repudiating earlier reforms, had rewritten their party rules. *(Changes in Democrats' Nominating Rules, box, p. 15)*

One major change in the Democrats' rules was the creation of a new group of "superdelegates," party and elected officials who would go to the 1984 convention uncommitted and would cast about 14 percent of the ballots. The DNC also adopted a Hunt Commission proposal to weaken the rule binding delegates to vote for their original presidential preference on the first convention ballot. But the new rule also allows a presidential candidate to replace any disloyal delegate with a more faithful one.

One of the most significant revisions was the Democrats' decision to relax proportional representation and end

Republican Conventions, 1856-1996

Year	City	Dates	Presidential Nominee	Vice Presidential Nominee	No. of Pres. Ballots
1856	Philadelphia	June 17-19	John C. Fremont	William L. Dayton	2
1860	Chicago	May 16-18	Abraham Lincoln	Hannibal Hamlin	3
1864	Baltimore	June 7-8	Abraham Lincoln	Andrew Johnson	1
1868	Chicago	May 20-21	Ulysses S. Grant	Schuyler Colfax	1
1872	Philadelphia	June 5-6	Ulysses S. Grant	Henry Wilson	1
1876	Cincinnati	June 14-16	Rutherford B. Hayes	William A. Wheeler	7
1880	Chicago	June 2-8	James A. Garfield	Chester A. Arthur	36
1884	Chicago	June 3-6	James G. Blaine	John A. Logan	4
1888	Chicago	June 19-25	Benjamin Harrison	Levi P. Morton	8
1892	Minneapolis	June 7-10	Benjamin Harrison	Whitelaw Reid	1
1896	St. Louis	June 16-18	William McKinley	Garret A. Hobart	1
1900	Philadelphia	June 19-21	William McKinley	Theodore Roosevelt	1
1904	Chicago	June 21-23	Theodore Roosevelt	Charles W. Fairbanks	1
1908	Chicago	June 16-19	William H. Taft	James S. Sherman	1
1912	Chicago	June 18-22	William H. Taft	James S. Sherman Nicholas Murray Butler[1]	1
1916	Chicago	June 7-10	Charles E. Hughes	Charles W. Fairbanks	3
1920	Chicago	June 8-12	Warren G. Harding	Calvin Coolidge	10
1924	Cleveland	June 10-12	Calvin Coolidge	Charles G. Dawes	1
1928	Kansas City	June 12-15	Herbert Hoover	Charles Curtis	1
1932	Chicago	June 14-16	Herbert Hoover	Charles Curtis	1
1936	Cleveland	June 9-12	Alfred M. Landon	Frank Knox	1
1940	Philadelphia	June 24-28	Wendell L. Willkie	Charles L. McNary	6
1944	Chicago	June 26-28	Thomas E. Dewey	John W. Bricker	1
1948	Philadelphia	June 21-25	Thomas E. Dewey	Earl Warren	3
1952	Chicago	July 7-11	Dwight D. Eisenhower	Richard M. Nixon	1
1956	San Francisco	Aug. 20-23	Dwight D. Eisenhower	Richard M. Nixon	1
1960	Chicago	July 25-28	Richard M. Nixon	Henry Cabot Lodge	1
1964	San Francisco	July 13-16	Barry Goldwater	William E. Miller	1
1968	Miami Beach	Aug. 5-8	Richard M. Nixon	Spiro T. Agnew	1
1972	Miami Beach	Aug. 21-23	Richard M. Nixon	Spiro T. Agnew	1
1976	Kansas City	Aug. 16-19	Gerald R. Ford	Robert Dole	1
1980	Detroit	July 14-17	Ronald Reagan	George Bush	1
1984	Dallas	Aug. 20-23	Ronald Reagan	George Bush	1
1988	New Orleans	Aug. 15-18	George Bush	Dan Quayle	1
1992	Houston	Aug. 17-20	George Bush	Dan Quayle	1
1996	San Diego	Aug. 12-15	Robert Dole	Jack Kemp	1

1. *The 1912 Republican convention nominated James S. Sherman, who died on Oct. 30. The Republican National Committee subsequently selected Nicholas Murray Butler to receive the Republican electoral votes for vice president.*

the ban on the "loophole" primary — winner take all by district. Proportional representation is the distribution of delegates among candidates to reflect their share of the primary or caucus vote. Mandated by party rules in 1980, it was blamed by some Democrats for the protracted primary fight between President Jimmy Carter and Sen. Edward M. Kennedy of Massachusetts. Because candidates needed only about 20 percent of the vote in most places to qualify for a share of the delegates, Kennedy was able to remain in contention. But while the system kept Kennedy going, it did nothing to help his chances of winning the nomination.

Although the Democrats' 1984 rules permitted states to retain proportional representation, they also allowed states to take advantage of two options that could help a front-running candidate build the momentum to wrap up the nomination early in the year.

One was a winner-take-more system. States could elect to keep proportional representation but adopt a winner bonus plan that would award the top vote-getter in each district one extra delegate.

The other option was a return to the loophole primary, which party rules outlawed in 1980 (with exemptions allowing Illinois and West Virginia to retain their loophole voting systems). In the loophole states, voters ballot directly for delegates, with each delegate candidate identified by presidential preference. Sometimes several presidential contenders win at least a fraction of the delegates in a given district, but the most common result is a sweep by the presidential frontrunner, even if he has less than an absolute majority. Loophole primaries aid the building of a consensus behind the front-runner, while still giving other candidates a chance to inject themselves back into the race by winning a major loophole state decisively.

The DNC retained the delegate-selection season adopted in 1978, a three-month period stretching from the second Tuesday in March to the second Tuesday in June. But, in an effort to reduce the growing influence of early states in the nominating process, the Democrats required Iowa and New Hampshire to move their highly publicized elections to late winter. Party rules maintained the privileged status of Iowa

Chief Officers and Keynote Speakers
At Republican National Conventions, 1856-1996

Year	Chair National Committee	Temporary Chair	Permanent Chair	Keynote Speaker
1856	Edwin D. Morgan, N.Y.	Robert Emmet, N.Y.	Henry S. Lane, Ind.	
1860	Edwin D. Morgan, N.Y.	David Wilmot, Pa.	George Ashmun, Mass.	
1864	Edwin D. Morgan, N.Y.	Robert J. Breckinridge, Ky.	William Dennison, Ohio	
1868	Marcus L. Ward, N.J.	Carl Schurz, Mo.	Joseph R. Hawley, Conn.	
1872	William Claflin, Mass.	Morton McMichael, Pa.	Thomas Settle, N.C.	
1876	Edwin D. Morgan, N.Y.	Theodore M. Pomeroy, N.Y.	Edward McPherson, Pa.	
1880	J. Donald Cameron, Pa.	George F. Hoar, Mass.	George F. Hoar, Mass.	
1884	Dwight M. Sabin, Minn.	John R. Lynch, Miss.	John B. Henderson, Mo.	
1888	B.F. Jones, Pa.	John M. Thurston, Neb.	Morris M. Estee, Calif.	
1892	James S. Clarkson, Iowa	J. Sloat Fassett, N.Y.	William McKinley Jr., Ohio	
1896	Thomas H. Carter, Mont.	Charles W. Fairbanks, Ind.	John M. Thurston, Neb.	
1900	Marcus A. Hanna, Ohio	Edward O. Wolcott, Colo.	Henry Cabot Lodge, Mass.	
1904	Henry C. Payne, Wis.	Elihu Root, N.Y.	Joseph G. Cannon, Ill.	
1908	Harry S. New, Ind.	Julius C. Burrows, Mich.	Henry Cabot Lodge, Mass.	
1912	Victor Rosewater, Neb.	Elihu Root, N.Y.	Elihu Root, N.Y.	
1916	Charles D. Hilles, N.Y.	Warren G. Harding, Ohio	Warren G. Harding, Ohio	
1920	Will H. Hays, Ind.	Henry Cabot Lodge, Mass.	Henry Cabot Lodge, Mass.	Henry Cabot Lodge, Mass.
1924	John T. Adams, Iowa	Theodore E. Burton, Ohio	Frank W. Mortdell, Wyo.	
1928	William M. Butler, Mass.	Simeon D. Fess, Ohio	George H. Moses, N.H.	
1932	Simeon D. Fess, Ohio	L. J. Dickinson, Iowa	Bertrand H. Snell, N.Y.	
1936	Henry P. Fletcher, Pa.	Frederick Steiwer, Ore.	Bertrand H. Snell, N.Y.	Frederick Steiwer, Ore.
1940	John Hamilton, Kan.	Harold E. Stassen, Minn.	Joseph W. Martin Jr., Mass.	Harold E. Stassen, Minn.
1944	Harrison E. Spangler, Iowa	Earl Warren, Calif.	Joseph W. Martin Jr., Mass.	Earl Warren, Calif.
1948	Carroll Reece, Tenn.	Dwight H. Green, Ill.	Joseph W. Martin Jr., Mass.	Dwight H. Green, Ill.
1952	Guy George Gabrielson, N.J.	Walter S. Hallanan, W.Va.	Joseph W. Martin Jr., Mass.	Douglas MacArthur
1956	Leonard W. Hall, N.Y.	William F. Knowland, Calif.	Joseph W. Martin Jr., Mass.	Arthur B. Langlie, Wash.
1960	Thruston B. Morton. Ky.	Cecil H. Underwood, W.Va.	Charles A. Halleck, Ind.	Walter H. Judd, Minn.
1964	William E. Miller, N.Y.	Mark O. Hatfield, Ore.	Thruston B. Morton, Ky.	Mark O. Hatfield, Ore.
1968	Ray C. Bliss, Ohio	Edward W. Brooke, Mass.	Gerald R. Ford, Mich.	Daniel J. Evans, Wash.
1972	Robert Dole, Kan.	Ronald Reagan, Calif.	Gerald R. Ford, Mich.	Richard G. Lugar, Ind. Anne L. Armstrong, Texas
1976	Mary Louise Smith, Iowa	Robert Dole, Kan.	John J. Rhodes, Ariz.	Howard H. Baker Jr., Tenn.
1980	Bill Brock, Tenn.	Nancy Landon Kassebaum, Kan.	John J. Rhodes, Ariz.	Guy Vander Jagt, Mich.
1984	Frank J. Fahrenkopf Jr., Nev.	Howard H. Baker Jr., Tenn.	Robert H. Michel, Ill.	Katherine Ortega, N.M.
1988	Lee Atwater, S.C.	Elizabeth Hanford Dole, N.C.	Robert H. Michel, Ill.	Thomas H. Kean, N.J.
1992	Richard N. Bond, N.Y.	Kay Bailey Hutchison, Texas	Robert H. Michel, Ill.	Phil Gramm, Texas
1996	Haley Barbour, Miss.	Christine Todd Whitman, N.J. George W. Bush, Texas	Newt Gingrich, Ga.	Susan Molinari, N.Y.

and New Hampshire before other states but mandated that their initial nominating rounds be held only eight days apart in 1984. Five weeks had intervened between the Iowa caucuses and New Hampshire primary in 1980.

The DNC also retained rules requiring primary states to set candidate filing deadlines 30 to 90 days before the election and limiting participation in the delegate selection process to Democrats only. This last rule eliminated crossover primaries where voters could participate in the Democratic primary without designating their party affiliation. African Americans and Hispanics won continued endorsement of affirmative action in the new party rules. Women gained renewed support for the equal division rule, which required state delegations at the national convention to be divided equally between men and women.

The Democratic Party's 1988 presidential nominating process remained basically the same as that used in 1984. The rules adopted by the national committee included only minor modifications suggested by the party's rules review panel, the Fairness Commission.

The bloc of uncommitted party and elected officials (superdelegates) was expanded slightly to 16 percent and rearranged to reserve more convention seats for members of Congress, governors and the DNC; the rules restricting participation in Democratic primaries and caucuses to Democrats only was relaxed so the open primaries in Wisconsin and Montana could be conducted with the approval of the national party; and the share of the vote a candidate must win in a primary or caucus to qualify for delegates was lowered from the 20 percent level used in most places in 1984 to 15 percent.

Only the rule regarding the 15 percent "threshold" spawned much debate during the rules-writing process, and though the discussion of the issue seldom was acrimonious, it did reveal a yawning chasm in the party on what the proper role of the national convention should be.

Political Party Organization and Rules

Political parties in the United States are loosely organized. Anyone of voting age can become a party member simply by signing up. Millions of Americans do just that, while many others shun formal partisan affiliations but think of themselves as Democrats or Republicans nonetheless.

Cowboy humorist Will Rogers used to get laughs by saying, "I am not a member of any organized party. I am a Democrat." But the same line could also be applied to the Republicans, even if they sometimes seemed to be less disorganized than their major rivals.

Both parties have the same fluidity of membership, with the rolls open to independents as well as to supporters of the other party. Formally registering as a Democrat or Republican has the advantage of permitting participation in the party's nominating primaries and caucuses. Most states bar crossover voting in the other party's elections, largely for fear that Democrats would try to nominate the weakest Republican candidates, and vice versa.

There is little evidence, however, that most rank-and-file voters are as concerned about parties as such. While almost 33 million Americans voted in primaries in 1992, a far greater number waited for the general election that November — the first U.S. election in which more than 100 million people voted. (But the number of voters in primaries and in the general election declined in 1996 — the second time since 1988 that the absolute number of voters declined in the general election for president.) And in 1995, for the first time ever, a plurality of voters surveyed by the Gallup poll identified themselves as other" (36 percent) rather than as Republican or Democratic (32 percent each).

Party Structure

Loose though it is, each major party has an organizational structure — a necessity for continuity as an institution, fund raising and conducting election campaigns. Congress has officially recognized the role of the parties and public funding is provided for their presidential nominating conventions. Some states also provide funding for election campaigns.

Beginning at the precinct or neighborhood level, a series of progressively larger units make up the national organization. Next up the line are city, county, legislative district, congressional district and, just below the national committee, the state organizations.

There is no "chain of command." Each unit is more or less independent. The national chair exerts influence mainly through prestige and force of personality, rather than through any specified powers. The national committee elects the chair, but the president actually designates the chair of the party controlling the White House. *(National Party Chairs, box, p. 22)*

With its 426 members, the DNC is more than twice the size of the 162-member Republican National Committee. Fifty-four members make up the DNC executive committee — the 9 officers, 20 regional representatives, 10 "at-large" members elected by the DNC and 15 others representing Democratic affiliates.

Since 1984 the Democrats have occupied their own $6.4 million national headquarters at 430 South Capitol Street, S.E., in Washington. Previous locations in New York and Washington (including the Watergate offices burglarized by the Republicans in 1972) were rented.

Besides the chair, eight other DNC officers are elected: five vice chairs, treasurer, secretary and national finance chair. Party organizations in the states and territories elect their DNC members for four-year terms, ending with the next convention. They are the state chair and the next highest-ranking member of the opposite sex. Another 200 votes are distributed on a population basis, with each state or territory guaranteed at least two, equally divided among men and women.

Other DNC members are two U.S. senators, two House members, two members of the College Democrats and three representatives each from among Democratic governors, mayors, state legislators, county officials, municipal officials, Young Democrats and the National Federation of Democratic Women.

The RNC elects four officers — the chair, co-chair, secretary and treasurer for two-year terms. The party owns its national headquarters at 310 First Street, S.E., in Washington. The Republicans maintain a large field staff and generally have more money than the Democrats to dispense to campaigns.

Because of their large sizes, the full national committees seldom meet more than a few times during the four years between the national conventions, which are the parties' supreme governing bodies. In both parties, the day-to-day work of the national organization is done by the chair and the headquarters staff, under direction of the executive committee.

Operating Rules

The most important rules of both major parties deal largely with the selection of delegates to the quadrennial national nominating conventions. While the Democrats in recent years have experimented widely with these rules, mainly to give more representation to women, youth and minorities, Republicans have left their rules largely unchanged. *(GOP Primary Rules, box, p. 16)*

Beginning with reforms proposed by Sen. George S. McGovern of South Dakota, who won the nomination himself in 1972, the Democratic Party attempted to "democratize" the process. A succession of commissions headed by Barbara A. Mikulski of Maryland (1972), Morley Winograd of Michigan (1976), Gov. James B. Hunt Jr. of North Carolina (1980) and Donald L. Fowler of South Carolina (1988), succeeded in gaining equal representation for women, requiring proportional representation of delegates among primary vote-getters and giving convention votes to "superdelegate" party and elected officials.

For the 1992 convention, Democrats for the first time in two decades did not have a special commission intensively examining the nominating process. Nevertheless, the DNC again changed the rules somewhat. In 1996 the Democratic Party left its rules unchanged. *(Democratic Rules in the 1980s and 1990s, p. 10)*

Changes in Democrats' Nominating Rules

Between 1972 and 1992 Democrats tinkered with their nominating rules every four years, producing a system that, if not better than before, was always different. In 1996, the party left its rules unchanged for the first time in 20 years. The following chart shows the ebb and flow of the Democratic Party's rules changes, with a "✔" indicating the years these major rules were in effect.

	1972	1976	1980	1984	1988	1992	1996
Timing: Restrict delegate-selection events to a three-month period (the "window").			✔	✔	✔	✔	✔
Conditions of Participation: Restrict participation in delegate-selection events to Democrats.		✔	✔	✔	✔	✔	✔
Proportional Representation: Ban all types of winner-take-all contests.				✔		✔	✔
Ban all types of winner-reward contests (where winner receives extra delegates).						✔	✔
Delegate Loyalty: Give candidates the right to approve delegates identifying with their candidacy.		✔	✔	✔	✔	✔	✔
Bind delegates to vote for their original presidential preference at convention on first ballot.			✔				
Party and Elected Officials: Expand each delegation to include pledged party and elected officials.				✔	✔	✔	✔	✔
Further expand each delegation to include uncommitted party and elected officials ("superdelegates").					✔	✔	✔
Demographic Representation: Encourage participation and representation of minorities and traditionally under-represented groups (affirmative action).				✔	✔	✔	✔	✔
Require delegations to be equally divided between men and women.			✔	✔	✔	✔	✔

Most party leaders, including Democratic National Chairman Paul G. Kirk Jr., wanted a threshold of at least 15 percent because they thought it would help steadily shrink the field of presidential candidates during the primary and caucus season and ensure that the convention would be a "ratifying" body that confirmed the choice of the party's voters.

But civil rights leader and presidential candidate Jesse L. Jackson saw it differently, as did a cadre of liberal activists. They wanted a convention that was more "deliberative," and they complained that getting one was virtually impossible under the system as it existed because it discriminated against long-shot candidates and produced an artificial consensus behind one candidate.

Most Democratic leaders were satisfied with the way the nominating process operated in 1984, and they felt it would be a disaster for the party to go through a free-wheeling, multi-ballot convention. Not since 1952 — at the begin-

ning of the television age — has a national party taken more than one ballot to nominate its candidate.

At the DNC meeting, some African American committee members joined with a few white liberal activists in proposing to eliminate the 15 percent threshold altogether. The proposal was rejected by voice vote. A second proposal to lower the threshold to 10 percent was defeated 92-178.

In 1990 the DNC made two basic changes that directly affected the delegate-selection process for the 1992 convention. One moved forward the officially sanctioned start of the presidential primary season by one week, from the second Tuesday in March to the first. This was an invitation to California to move its primary from June to March 3. (California declined in 1992, but in 1996 moved its primary from June to late March. This was part of a desire by both parties in 1992 to speed up the nomination contest and settle it by April or early May, so that united parties could organize their conventions with a focus on the November election.) The second

GOP Primary Rules

The Republican Party, wrote political scientist Nelson W. Polsby, "in many respects remains unreformed." Virtually anything has been permitted in the nominating process so long as it was not baldly discriminatory. And that has been the way GOP leaders have wanted it.

While the Democratic Party has a tightly crafted, nationalized set of rules that govern its nominating process, Republicans historically have shunned control by a central authority. The individual GOP state parties are given wide latitude to determine how their delegates are selected, with guidelines from the national party kept to a minimum.

The result has been a nominating procedure with a simplicity and continuity that the Democrats lack. A more homogeneous party than the Democrats, the Republicans have not felt the pressure for rules reform that had engulfed the Democrats. No major rules changes were made by the Republicans between 1974 and 1996.

Republicans, however, have not been able to operate totally in their own world. Campaign finance laws and the rising influence of mass media affected Republicans as well as Democrats. And in states where legislatures accommodated the Democrats and created a presidential primary, the Republicans were dragged along.

The Republican Party held 20 primaries in 1972, but over the next 24 years the number of primaries has steadily increased. In 1996 the party held a record 43 primaries, including those in the District of Columbia and Puerto Rico (the Democrats' record was 40 primaries in 1992). Primaries helped to select 85 percent of delegates to the GOP convention in 1996.

---

change banned winner-reward systems, which gave extra delegates to the winner of a primary or caucus. Fifteen states had used some form of winner-reward system in 1988.

The Democrats required all states in 1992 and thereafter to divide their publicly elected delegates proportionally among candidates who drew at least 15 percent of the primary or caucus vote.

The Democratic Party also continued to use superdelegates, expanding their number to 769 for the 1996 convention, or 18 percent of the 4,289 delegate votes.

During the 1972-1996 period the Republican Party followed an entirely different approach and made few changes in its nominating rules. While the Democratic rules were revised somewhat for each presidential cycle, the GOP rules remained stable. For the year 2000, however, the Republicans again changed their minds on the desirability of deciding the nomination contest by March or April; they provided a bonus for those states that choose their delegates to the 2000 GOP convention in May or June. *(GOP Primary Rules, box, above)*

Credentials Disputes

Before the opening of a convention the national committee compiles a temporary roll of delegates. The roll is referred to the convention's credentials committee, which holds hearings on the challenges and makes recommendations to the convention, the final arbiter of all disputes.

Some of the most bitter convention battles have concerned the seating of contested delegations. In the 20th century most of the heated credentials fights have concerned delegations from the South. In the Republican Party the challenges focused on the power of the Republican state organizations to dictate the selection of delegates. The issue was hottest in 1912 and 1952, when the party throughout most of the South was a skeletal structure whose power was restricted largely to selection of convention delegates. Within the Democratic Party the question of Southern credentials emerged after World War II on the volatile issues of civil rights and party loyalty. Important credentials challenges on these issues occurred at the 1948, 1952, 1964 and 1968 Democratic conventions.

There were numerous credentials challenges at the 1972 Democratic convention, but, unlike those at its immediate predecessors, the challenges involved delegations from across the nation and focused on violations of the party's newly adopted guidelines.

After their 1952 credentials battle, the Republicans established a contest committee within the national committee to review credentials challenges before the convention. After their divisive 1968 convention the Democrats also created a formal credentials procedure to review all challenges before the opening of the convention.

Equally important to the settlement of credentials challenges are the rules under which the convention operates. The Republican Party adopts a completely new set of rules at every convention. Although large portions of the existing rules are enacted each time, general revision is always possible.

After its 1968 convention the Democratic Party set out to reform itself and the convention system. The Commission on Rules and the Commission on Party Structure and Delegate Selection, both created by the 1968 convention, proposed many changes that were accepted by the national committee. As a result, a formal set of rules was adopted for the first time at the party's 1972 convention.

Controversial Rules

Although it did not have a formal set of rules before 1972, the Democratic Party operated with two controversial rules never used by the Republicans: the unit rule and the two-thirds nominating rule. The unit rule enabled the majority of a delegation, if authorized by its state party, to cast the entire vote of the delegation for one candidate or position. In use since the earliest Democratic conventions, the unit rule was abolished by the 1968 convention.

From their first convention in 1832 until the 1936 convention, the Democrats employed the two-thirds nominating rule, which required any candidate for president or vice president to win not just a simple majority but a two-thirds majority. Viewed as a boon to the South since it allowed that region a virtual veto power over any possible nominee, the rule was abolished with the stipulation that the South would receive an increased vote allocation at later conventions.

In its century of use the two-thirds rule frequently produced protracted, multi-ballot conventions, often giving the Democrats a degree of turbulence the Republicans, requiring only a simple majority, did not have. Between 1832 and 1932, seven Democratic conventions took more than 10 ballots to select a presidential candidate. In contrast, in their entire convention history, the Republicans have had just one convention that required more than 10 ballots to select a presidential candidate. *(Democrats' Two-Thirds Rule, box, right)*

One controversy that surfaced during the 1980 Democratic Party convention concerned a rule that bound delegates to vote on the first ballot for the candidates under whose banner they had been elected. Supporters of Sen. Kennedy had devoted their initial energies to prying the nomination from incumbent President Carter by defeating that rule. The final tally on the rule showed 1,936.42 delegates favoring the binding rule and 1,390.58 opposing it. Passage of the binding rule ensured Carter's renomination, and shortly after the vote Kennedy announced that his name would not be placed in nomination.

Convention Officers

Credentials, rules and platform are the three major convention committees, but each party has additional committees, including one in charge of convention arrangements.

Within the Republican Party the arrangements committee recommends a slate of convention officers to the national committee, which in turn refers the names to the committee on permanent organization for confirmation. The people the committee chooses are subject to the approval of the convention. In the Democratic Party, this function is performed by the rules committee.

In both the Democratic and Republican parties, the presiding officer during the bulk of the convention is the permanent chairman. Over the past quarter century the position usually has gone to the party's leader in the House of Representatives.

However, this loose precedent was broken in the Democratic Party by a rule adopted at the 1972 convention requiring that the presiding officer position alternate every four years between the sexes.

Party Platforms

The adoption of a party platform is one of the principal functions of a convention. The platform committee is charged with the responsibility of writing a party platform to be presented to the convention for its approval.

The main challenge before the platform committee is to write a platform all party candidates can use in their campaigns. For this reason, platforms often fit the description given them by Wendell L. Willkie, Republican presidential candidate in 1940: "fusions of ambiguity."

Despite the best efforts of platform-builders to resolve their differences in the comparative privacy of the committee room, they sometimes encounter so controversial a subject that it cannot be compromised. Under these conditions dissident committee members often submit a minority report to the convention floor. Open floor fights are not unusual and, like credentials battles, often reflect the strength of the various candidates.

When the party has an incumbent president, the platform often is drafted in the White House or at least has the approval of the president. Rarely does a party adopt a platform that is critical of an incumbent president of the same party. When Democratic delegates at their 1896 convention, inspired by William Jennings Bryan's "Cross of Gold" speech, repudiated President Grover Cleveland and his support for a gold standard for hard currency, and nominated Bryan for president on a "free silver" platform, they signaled a major sea change in American politics. A similar change took place

---

Democrats' Two-Thirds Rule

At their first convention in 1832, the Democrats adopted a rule requiring a two-thirds majority for nomination. Two presidential nominees— Martin Van Buren in 1844 and Champ Clark in 1912 — received majorities but failed to attain the two-thirds requirement.

On the first ballot in 1844 Van Buren received 146 of the 266 convention votes, 54.9 percent of the total. His total fell under a simple majority on succeeding roll calls and on the ninth ballot the nomination went to a dark-horse candidate, former governor James K. Polk of Tennessee.

In 1912 from the 10th through the 16th ballots Clark recorded a simple majority. He reached his peak on the 10th ballot, receiving 556 of the 1,094 convention votes, 50.8 percent of the total. The nomination, however, ultimately went to New Jersey governor Woodrow Wilson, who was selected on the 46th ballot.

At their 1936 convention, the Democrats voted to end the requirement for a two-thirds majority for nomination.

---

in 1948, when Democratic delegates led by Mayor Hubert Humphrey of Minneapolis overturned a recommendation by the platform committee and precipitated a walkout of Southern delegates by adopting a strong civil rights plank. Although overridden, President Harry S. Truman accepted the Humphrey plank—and won with it.

The first platform was adopted by the Democrats in 1840. It was a short document, fewer than 1,000 words. Since then the platforms with few exceptions have grown longer and longer, covering more issues and appealing to more and more interest groups. One of the exceptions to the growth trend was the 4,500-word Democratic platform of 1988 — about one-tenth the length of the 1984 platform. But by 1996 the Democrats' platform had grown again, to about 13,000 words, compared with about 28,000 words in its Republican counterpart.

The 1996 GOP platform was characterized by hard-line conservative stands on abortion and other social issues. Sen. Robert Dole, the party's nominee, sought to soften its stance and appeal to more middle-road non-party voters by giving prime time convention speaking slots to more moderate Republicans who publicly expressed disapproval with some of the platform, while affirming their support for a GOP victory in November.

Third Parties: Radical Ideas

Throughout American history, many daring and controversial political platforms adopted by third parties have been rejected as too radical by the major parties. Yet many of these proposals later have won popular acceptance and have made their way into the major party platforms — and into law. Ideas such as the abolition of slavery, prohibition, the graduated income tax, the popular election of senators, women's suffrage, minimum wages, Social Security and the 18-year-old vote were advocated by Populists, Progressives and other third parties long before they were finally accepted by the nation as a whole.

The radical third parties and their platforms have been anathema to the established wisdom of the day, denounced

Notable Credentials Fights

1848, Democratic. Two rival New York state factions, known as the Barnburners and the Hunkers, sent separate delegations. By a vote of 126 to 125, the convention decided to seat both delegations and split New York's vote between them. This compromise suited neither faction: the Barnburners bolted the convention; the Hunkers remained but refused to vote.

1860, Democratic. Dissatisfaction with the slavery plank in the party platform spurred a walkout by several dozen Southern delegates from the Charleston convention. When the tumultuous convention reconvened in Baltimore six weeks later, a credentials controversy developed on the status of the bolting delegates. The majority report of the credentials committee recommended that the delegates in question, except those from Alabama and Louisiana, be reseated. The minority report recommended that a larger majority of the withdrawing Charleston delegates be allowed to return. The minority report was defeated, 100-1/2 to 150, prompting a walkout by the majority of delegates from nine states.

1880, Republican. Factions for and against the candidacy of former president Ulysses S. Grant clashed on the credentials of the Illinois delegation. By a margin of 387 to 353, the convention rejected a minority report that proposed searing pro-Grant delegates elected at the state convention over other delegates elected at a congressional district caucus. Three other votes were taken on disputed credentials from different Illinois districts, but all were decided in favor of the anti-Grant forces by a similar margin. The votes indicated the weakness of the Grant candidacy. The nomination went to a dark-horse candidate, Rep. James A. Garfield of Ohio, on the 36th ballot.

1912, Republican. The furious struggle between President William Howard Taft and Theodore Roosevelt for the presidential nomination centered on credentials. The Roosevelt forces brought 72 delegate challenges to the floor of the convention, but the test of strength between the two candidates came on a procedural motion. By a vote of 567 to 507, the convention tabled a motion presented by the Roosevelt forces barring any of the delegates under challenge from voting on any of the credentials contests. This procedural vote clearly indicated Taft's control of the convention. All the credentials cases were settled in favor of the Taft delegates, and the presidential nomination ultimately went to the incumbent president.

1932, Democratic. Two delegations favorable to the front-runner for the presidential nomination, Franklin D. Roosevelt, came under challenge. However, in a show of strength, the Roosevelt forces won both contests: seating a Louisiana delegation headed by Sen. Huey P. Long by a vote of 638-3/4 to 514-1/4 and a Roosevelt delegation from Minnesota by an even wider margin, 658-1/4 to 492-3/4. Roosevelt won the nomination on the fourth ballot.

1952, Democratic. The refusal of three Southern states — Louisiana, South Carolina and Virginia — to agree to a party loyalty pledge brought their credentials into question. The Virginia delegation argued that the problem prompting the loyalty pledge was covered by state law. By a vote of 650-1/2 to 518, the convention approved the seating of the Virginia delegation. After Louisiana and South Carolina took positions similar to that of Virginia, they were seated by a voice vote.

1952, Republican. Sixty-eight delegates from three Southern states (Georgia, Louisiana and Texas) were the focal point of the fight for the presidential nomination between Gen. Dwight D. Eisenhower and Sen. Robert A. Taft of Ohio. The national committee, controlled by forces favorable to Taft, had voted to seat delegations friendly to the Ohio senator from these three states. But by a vote of 607 to 531 the convention seated the Georgia delegation favorable to Eisenhower. It seated the Eisenhower delegates from Louisiana and Texas without roll calls. The general went on to win the presidential nomination on the first ballot.

1968, Democratic. A struggle between the anti-Vietnam war forces, led by Sen. Eugene J. McCarthy of Minnesota, and the party regulars, headed by Vice President Hubert H. Humphrey, dominated the 17 cases considered by the credentials committee. Three of the cases, involving the Texas, Georgia and Alabama delegations, required roll calls on the convention floor. All were won by the Humphrey forces. By a vote of 1,368-1/4 to 956-3/4, the regular Texas delegation headed by Gov. John B. Connally was seated. A minority report to seat the entire Georgia delegation led by black leader Julian Bond was defeated, 1,043.55 to 1,415.45. And a minority report to seat a McCarthy-backed, largely black delegation from Alabama was also rejected, 880-3/4 to 1,607. Humphrey, having shown his strength during the credentials contests, went on to win an easy first ballot nomination.

1972, Democratic. The first test of strength at the convention between South Dakota senator George McGovern's delegates and party regulars came over credentials. Key challenges brought to the convention floor concerned the South Carolina, California and Illinois delegations. The South Carolina challenge was brought by the National Women's Political Caucus in response to alleged underrepresentation of women in the delegation. Although the caucus' position was supposedly supported by the McGovern camp, votes were withheld to avoid jeopardizing McGovern's chances of winning the important California contest. The caucus' challenge lost 1,429.05 to 1,555.75. The California challenge was of crucial importance to McGovern, since it involved 151 delegates initially won by the South Dakota senator in the state's winner-take-all primary, but stripped from him by the credentials committee. By a vote of 1,618.28 to 1,238.22, McGovern regained the contested delegates, thereby nailing down his nomination. With victory in hand, the dominant McGovern camp sought a compromise on the Illinois case, which pitted a delegation headed by Chicago's powerful mayor Richard Daley against an insurgent delegation composed of party reformers. Compromise was unattainable and with the bulk of McGovern delegates voting for the reformers, a minority report to seat the Daley delegates was rejected.

Major Platform Fights

1860, Democratic. A minority report on the slavery plank, stating that the decision on allowing slavery in the territories should be left to the Supreme Court, was approved, 165 to 138. The majority report (favored by the South) declared that no government — local, state or federal — could outlaw slavery in the territories. The acceptance of the minority report precipitated a walkout by several dozen Southern delegates and the eventual sectional split in the party.

1896, Democratic. The monetary plank of the platform committee, favoring free and unlimited coinage of silver at a ratio of 16 to 1 with gold, was accepted by the convention, which defeated a proposed gold plank, 626 to 303. During debate William Jennings Bryan made his famous "Cross of Gold" speech supporting the platform committee plank, bringing him to the attention of the convention and resulting in his nomination for president.

1908, Republican. A minority report, proposing a substitute platform, was presented by Sen. Robert M. La Follette of Wisconsin. Minority proposals included increased antitrust activities, enactment of a law requiring publication of campaign expenditures and popular election of senators. All the proposed planks were defeated by wide margins; the closest vote, on direct election of senators, was 114 for, 866 against.

1924, Democratic. A minority plank was presented that condemned the activities of the Ku Klux Klan, then enjoying a resurgence in the South and some states in the Midwest. The plank was defeated 542-7/20 to 543-3/20, the closest vote in Democratic convention history.

1932, Republican. A minority plank favoring repeal of the 18th Amendment (Prohibition) in favor of a state-option arrangement was defeated, 460-2/9 to 690-19/36.

1948, Democratic. An amendment to the platform, strengthening the civil rights plank by guaranteeing full and equal political participation, equal employment opportunity, personal security and equal treatment in the military service, was accepted, 651-1/2 to 582-1/2.

1964, Republican. An amendment offered by Sen. Hugh Scott of Pennsylvania to strengthen the civil rights plank by including voting guarantees in state as well as in federal elections and by eliminating job bias was defeated, 409 to 897.

1968, Democratic. A minority report on Vietnam called for cessation of the bombing of North Vietnam, halting of offensive and search-and-destroy missions by American combat units, a negotiated withdrawal of American troops and establishment of a coalition government in South Vietnam. It was defeated, 1,041-1/4 to 1,567-3/4.

1972, Democratic. By a vote of 1,852.86 to 999.34, the convention rejected a minority report proposing a government guaranteed annual income of $6,500 for a family of four. By a vote of 1,101.37 to 1,572.80, a women's rights plank supporting abortion rights was defeated.

1980, Democratic. The platform battle, one of the longest in party history, pitted President Jimmy Carter against his persistent rival, Sen. Edward M. Kennedy of Massachusetts. Stretching over 17 hours, the debate focused on Kennedy's economics plank, which finally was defeated by a voice vote. Yet Carter was forced to concede on so many specific points, including Kennedy's $12 billion anti-recession jobs programs, that the final document bore little resemblance to the draft initially drawn up by Carter's operatives.

1992, Democratic. A tax fairness plank offered by former senator Paul E. Tsongas of Massachusetts was defeated by a vote of 953 to 2,287. The plank called for a delay in any middle-class tax cut and tax credit for families with children until the deficit was under control.

---

as impractical, dangerous, destructive of moral virtues and even traitorous. They have been anti-establishment and more far-reaching in their proposed solutions to problems than the major parties have dared to be.

Major Parties: Broader Appeal

In contrast with the third parties, Democrats and Republicans traditionally have been much more chary of adopting radical platform planks. Trying to appeal to a broad range of voters, the two major parties have tended to compromise differences or to reject controversial platform planks.

The Democratic Party has been more ready than the Republicans to adopt once-radical ideas, but there is usually a considerable time lag between their origin in third parties and their eventual adoption in Democratic platforms. For example, while the Democrats by 1912 had adopted many of the Populist planks of the 1890s, the Bull Moose Progressives of that year already were way ahead of them in proposals for social legislation. Not until 1932 were many of the 1912 Progressive planks adopted by the Democrats.

Similarly, it was not until the 1960s that Democratic platforms incorporated many of the more far-reaching proposals originally put forward by the 1948 Progressive Party in that year.

Filling Vacancies

Starting with the Democratic convention of 1848, and the Republican Party's first national organizing meeting in 1856, both major parties have elected national committees to run the day-to-day business of the parties between conventions.

Since their beginning, one of the most important functions of national committees is to replace a candidate who dies or resigns after the convention adjourns, or after election day but before the electors cast their votes for president and vice president. This replacement power was assumed informally, but without controversy, at first; was granted by several national conventions during the Progressive Era (1900-1912); and was made part of both parties' permanent standing rules by the 1920s.

There have been four such vacancies.

In 1860, the Democratic designee for vice president, Sen. Benjamin Fitzpatrick of Alabama, declined the nomination after the ruinously chaotic Baltimore convention of that year finally adjourned. The national committee then nominated former Gov. Herschel V. Johnson of Georgia as Sen. Stephen A. Douglas' running mate.

Third Parties Usually Fade Rapidly

Most third party movements are like shooting stars, shining brightly in one election and then quickly disappearing. In the last century and a half, 11 third parties — plus independents John B. Anderson in 1980 and Ross Perot in 1992 — have drawn at least 5 percent of the popular vote in a presidential election. As of 1996 not one of the third parties was able to maintain its foothold in the electoral process. Four had disappeared by the next election, five others drew a smaller vote total and two merged with one of the major parties. It remained to be seen how the Reform Party would fare in the 2000 election.

Each of these significant third parties, except the Socialists in 1912, made its best showing in its first election. (The Socialists, led by Eugene V. Debs, first ran in 1900, winning just 0.62 percent of the vote.) The following chart lists each party's presidential candidate and the percentage of the vote the party received in its most successful race and in the following election. A dash (—) indicates that the party had disappeared.

Party (Candidate)	Year	Percentage of Vote	Next Election
Anti-Mason (William Wirt)	1832	7.8%	endorsed Whig
Free Soil (Martin Van Buren)	1848	10.1	4.9%
Whig-American (Millard Fillmore)	1856	21.5	—
Southern Democrats (John C. Breckinridge)	1860	18.1	—
Constitutional Union (John Bell)	1860	12.6	—
Populist (James B. Weaver)	1892	8.5	endorsed Democrat
Progressive (Bull Moose) (Theodore Roosevelt)	1912	27.4	0.2
Socialist (Eugene V. Debs)	1912	6.0	3.2
Progressive (Robert M. La Follette)	1924	16.6	—
American Independent (George C. Wallace)	1968	13.5	1.4
John B. Anderson	1980	6.6	endorsed Democrat
Ross Perot	1992	18.9	created Reform Party
Reform Party (Ross Perot)	1996	8.5	[1]

1. The Reform Party qualified for $30 million in federal matching funds for the 2000 election.

In 1872, the Democratic nominee for president, Horace Greeley, founder of the *New York Tribune*, died shortly after election day. (Republican Ulysses S. Grant had won the election.) Greeley's dispirited party's national committee declined to select a replacement candidate, and the Democratic electors voted for four different candidates.

In 1912, Vice President James S. Sherman of New York died in office the week before election day. The Republican convention of that year had authorized the national committee to fill vacancies, and the committee quickly replaced Sherman. His name remained on state ballots as President William Howard Taft's running mate, but the eight Republican electors voted, as recommended by the committee, for the replacement candidate, Nicholas Murray Butler of New York, president of Columbia University.

Finally, in 1972, the Democratic nominee for vice president, Sen. Thomas Eagleton of Missouri, resigned his candidacy after the convention adjourned. The nominee for president, Sen. George McGovern, recommended R. Sargent Shriver of Illinois, former head of the Peace Corps, as his replacement running mate, and Shriver was selected by a special meeting of an expanded national committee. *(Political Party Organization and Rules, box, p. 14)*

Communications and the Media

Major changes in the national nominating convention have resulted from the massive advances in transportation and communication technologies during the 20th century.

The revolution in transportation has affected the scheduling of conventions. In the 19th century, conventions were sometimes held a year or more before the election and at the latest were completed by late spring of the election year. With the ability of people to assemble quickly, conventions in recent years have been held later in the election year, usually in July or August. Advances in transportation also have affected site location. Geographic centrality is no longer a primary consideration in the selection of a convention city.

Radio coverage of conventions began in 1924; television coverage 16 years later. One of the first changes inspired by the media age was the termination of the custom that a presidential candidate not appear at the convention but accept

Chief Officers at Other National Party Conventions, 1831-1892

Year	Party	Temporary Chair	Chair
1831	Anti-Masonic		John C. Spencer, N.Y.
1831	National Republican	Abner Lacock, Pa.	James Barbour, Va.
1839	Whig	Isaac Bates, Mass.	James Barbour, Va.
1844	Whig	Andrew F. Hopkins, Ala.	Ambrose Spencer, N.Y.
1848	Whig	John A. Collier, N.Y.	John M. Morehead, N.C.
1852	Whig	George C. Evans, Maine	John G. Chapman, Md.
1843	Liberty		Leicester King
1848	Free Soiler		Charles Francis Adams, Mass.
1852	Free Soiler (Free Democrats)		Henry Wilson, Mass.
1856	American (Know-Nothing)		Ephraim Marsh
1860	Southern Democrat (Breckinridge Factor)		Caleb Cushing, Mass.
1860	Constitutional Union		Washington Hunt, N.Y.
1872	Liberal Republican	Stanley Matthews, Ohio	Carl Schurz, Mo.
1880	Greenback	Gilbert De La Matyr, Ind.	Richard Trevellick, Mich.
1888	Prohibition	H. A. Delano, Conn.	John P. St. John, Kans.
1892	Prohibition	John P. St. John, Kans.	Eli Ritter, Ind.
1892	People's (Populist)	C. H. Ellington, Ga.	H. L. Loricks, S.D.

his nomination in a ceremony several weeks later. Franklin D. Roosevelt was the first major party candidate to break this tradition when in 1932 he delivered his acceptance speech in person before the Democratic convention. Twelve years later Thomas E. Dewey became the first Republican nominee to give his acceptance speech to the convention. Since then the final activity of every Democratic and Republican convention has been the delivery of the acceptance speeches by the vice presidential and presidential nominees.

A second change was to cut back the frivolity and hoopla, and to emphasize the more important aspects of the convention process. Party leaders have also, in recent years, streamlined the schedule, with the assumption that the interest level of most of the viewing public for politics is limited. The result has been shorter speeches and generally fewer roll calls than at those conventions in the pre-television era.

Party leaders desire to put on a good show for the viewing public with the hope of winning votes for their party in November. The convention is a showcase, designed to present the party as both a model of democracy and an efficient, harmonious body. The schedule of convention activities is drawn up with an eye on the peak evening television viewing hours. There is an attempt to put the party's major selling points — the highly partisan keynote speech, the nominating ballots, and the candidates' acceptance speeches — on in prime time. (The effort to put acceptance speeches on in prime time has been especially strong since 1972, when

Democratic nominee George S. McGovern was forced to wait until 3 a.m. to make his speech.) Conversely, party leaders try to keep evidence of bitter party factionalism — such as explosive credentials and platform battles — out of the peak viewing period.

Both the Republicans and Democrats went to extraordinary lengths to turn their 1996 conventions into a tightly scripted, visually appealing television shows. But it seems that the harder the political parties try to win over American audiences, the less they have to show for their efforts. Many TV viewers voted with their remote controls — tuning out the 1996 conventions. Ratings for the three major networks' broadcasts of the conventions were off sharply from four years earlier.

In the media age the appearance of fairness is important, and in a sense this need to look fair and open has assisted the movement for party reform. Some influential party leaders, skeptical of reform of the convention, have found resistance difficult in the glare of television.

Before the revolution in the means of transportation and communication, conventions met in relative anonymity. Today conventions are held in all the privacy of a fishbowl, with every action and every rumor closely scrutinized. They have become media events and as such are targets for political demonstrations that can be not only an embarrassment to the party but a security problem as well.

In spite of its difficulties, the convention system has survived. As the nation has developed during the past century

National Party Chairs, 1848-1997

Name	State	Years of Service	Name	State	Years of Service
Democratic Party			**Republican Party (continued)**		
B. F. Hallett	Massachusetts	1848-52	Zachariah Chandler	Michigan	1876-79
Robert McLane	Maryland	1852-56	J. Donald Cameron	Pennsylvania	1879-80
David A. Smalley	Virginia	1856-60	Marshall Jewell	Connecticut	1880-83
August Belmont	New York	1860-72	D. M. Sabin	Minnesota	1883-84
Augustus Schell	New York	1872-76	B. F. Jones	Pennsylvania	1884-88
Abram S. Hewitt	New York	1876-77	Matthew S. Quay	Pennsylvania	1888-91
William H. Barnum	Connecticut	1877-89	James S. Clarkson	Iowa	1891-92
Calvin S. Brice	Ohio	1889-92	Thomas H. Carter	Montana	1892-96
William F. Harrity	Pennsylvania	1892-96	Mark A. Hanna	Ohio	1896-1904
James K. Jones	Arkansas	1896-1904	Henry C. Payne	Wisconsin	1904
Thomas Taggart	Indiana	1904-08	George B. Cortelyou	New York	1904-07
Norman E. Mack	New York	1908-12	Harry S. New	Indiana	1907-08
William F. McCombs	New York	1912-16	Frank H. Hitchcock	Massachusetts	1908-09
Vance C. McCormick	Pennsylvania	1916-19	John F. Hill	Maine	1909-12
Homer S. Cummings	Connecticut	1919-20	Victor Rosewater	Nebraska	1912
George White	Ohio	1920-21	Charles D. Hilles	New York	1912-16
Cordell Hull	Tennessee	1921-24	William R. Willcox	New York	1916-18
Clem Shaver	West Virginia	1924-28	Will Hays	Indiana	1918-21
John J. Raskob	Maryland	1928-32	John T. Adams	Iowa	1921-24
James A. Farley	New York	1932-40	William M. Butler	Massachusetts	1924-28
Edward J. Flynn	New York	1940-43	Hubert Work	Colorado	1928-29
Frank C. Walker	Pennsylvania	1943-44	Claudius H. Huston	Tennessee	1929-30
Robert E. Hannegan	Missouri	1944-47	Simeon D. Fess	Ohio	1930-32
J. Howard McGrath	Rhode Island	1947-49	Everett Sanders	Indiana	1932-34
William M. Boyle Jr.	Missouri	1949-51	Henry P. Fletcher	Pennsylvania	1934-36
Frank E. McKinney	Indiana	1951-52	John Hamilton	Kansas	1936-40
Stephen A. Mitchell	Illinois	1952-54	Joseph W. Martin Jr.	Massachusetts	1940-42
Paul M. Butler	Indiana	1955-60	Harrison E. Spangler	Iowa	1942-44
Henry M. Jackson	Washington	1960-61	Herbert Brownell Jr.	New York	1944-46
John M. Bailey	Connecticut	1961-68	B. Carroll Reece	Tennessee	1946-48
Lawrence F. O'Brien	Massachusetts	1968-69	Hugh D. Scott Jr.	Pennsylvania	1948-49
Fred Harris	Oklahoma	1969-70	Guy George Gabrielson	New Jersey	1949-52
Lawrence F. O'Brien	Massachusetts	1970-72	Arthur E. Summerfield	Michigan	1952-53
Jean Westwood	Utah	1972	C. Wesley Roberts	Kansas	1953
Robert Straus	Texas	1972-77	Leonard W. Hall	New York	1953-57
Kenneth Curtis	Maine	1977-78	H. Meade Alcorn Jr.	Connecticut	1957-59
John White	Texas	1978-81	Thruston B. Morton	Kentucky	1959-61
Charles Manatt	California	1981-85	William E. Miller	New York	1961-64
Paul Kirk	Massachusetts	1985-89	Dean Burch	Arizona	1964-65
Ronald H. Brown	Washington, D.C.	1989-93	Ray C. Bliss	Ohio	1965-69
David Wilhelm	Illinois	1993-94	Rogers C. B. Morton	Maryland	1969-71
Christopher Dodd (general chair)	Connecticut	1994-97	Robert Dole	Kansas	1971-73
			George Bush	Texas	1973-74
Donald Fowler	South Carolina	1994-97	Mary Louise Smith	Iowa	1974-77
Roy Romer (general chair)	Colorado	1997-	William Brock	Tennessee	1977-81
			Richard Richards	Utah	1981-83
Steven Grossman	Massachusetts	1997-	Paul Laxalt (general chair)	Nevada	1983-86
Republican Party			Frank Fahrenkopf Jr.	Nevada	1983-89
Edwin D. Morgan	New York	1856-64	Lee Atwater	South Carolina	1989-91
Henry J. Raymond	New York	1864-66	Clayton Yeutter	Nebraska	1991-92
Marcus L. Ward	New Jersey	1866-68	Rich Bond	New York	1992-93
William Claflin	Massachusetts	1868-72	Haley Barbour	Mississippi	1993-97
Edwin D. Morgan	New York	1872-76	Jim Nicholson	Colorado	1997-

Sources: Hugh A. Bone, *Party Committees and National Politics* (Seattle: University of Washington, 1958), 241-243; Congressional Quarterly, *The President, the Public, and the Parties,* 2nd ed. (Washington, D.C.: Congressional Quarterly, 1997), 21.

and a half, the convention has evolved as well, changing its form but retaining its variety of functions. Criticism has been leveled at the convention, but no substitute has yet been offered that would nominate a presidential ticket, adopt a party platform, act as the supreme governing body of the party, and serve as a massive campaign rally and propaganda forum. In addition to these functions, a convention is a place where compromise can take place — compromise often mandatory in a major political party that combines varying viewpoints.

Convention Chronology, 1831-1996

Sources: Convention Chronology

This section (pages 25 to 191) contains brief descriptions of all presidential nominating conventions of major American political parties and excerpts from party platforms. The chronology begins in 1831, when the Anti-Masonic Party held the first nominating convention in American history, and concludes with the Republican, Reform and Democratic party conventions of 1996.

The narrative includes conventions for all parties receiving at least 2 percent of the popular vote in the presidential election. Thus, conventions for the Socialist Party, which received at least 2 percent of the presidential popular vote in 1904, 1908, 1912, 1920 and 1932, are included. Socialist Party conventions for other presidential election years when the party received less than 2 percent of the popular vote do not appear.

The source most frequently consulted in preparing the narrative was Richard C. Bain and Judith H. Parris, *Convention Decisions and Voting Records*, (Washington, D.C.: Brookings Institution, 1973).

Ballot Vote Totals

Throughout the narrative, vote totals appear for significant ballots on platform disputes and procedural issues and for presidential and vice presidential balloting.

The source used for 1835-1972 vote totals was *Convention Decisions and Voting Records*. The sources for the 1976 through 1996 vote totals were *The Official Proceedings of the Democratic National Convention* and the Republican National Committee. Charts showing state-by-state voting on selected ballots appear in a separate section, "Key Convention Ballots," pages 195 to 260. *(See p. 194 for details on these charts.*

Platform Excerpts

The source for the party platform excerpts that appear in the convention chronology was Kirk H. Porter and Donald Bruce Johnson, *National Party Platforms, 1840-1972* (Urbana: University of Illinois Press, 1973). For the Democratic and Republican platform excerpts for 1976 to 1996, the official texts of the platforms adopted by the two parties were used.

In adopting the material from *National Party Platforms, 1840-1968*, Congressional Quarterly has added boldface subheadings to highlight the organization of the texts. For example, excerpts from the 1844 Democratic Party platform appear on page 30. The boldface headings — Appeal to the Masses, Internal Improvements, Government Spending, etc. — do not appear in the text of the party platform as it was published in *National Party Platforms, 1840-1972*. In all other respects, Congressional Quarterly has followed the style and typography of the platform texts appearing in *National Party Platforms, 1840-1968*. In excerpting the material from the Democratic and Republican platforms from 1976 to 1996, Congressional Quarterly has also edited the boldface subheadings from the original platform documents.

1831-32 Conventions

Presidential Candidates

William Wirt
Anti-Mason

Henry Clay
National Republican

Andrew Jackson
Democrat

Anti-Masons

In September 1831, the Anti-Masonic Party held the first national nominating convention in American history. One hundred sixteen delegates from 13 states, none south of Maryland, gathered in Baltimore. They selected the party's presidential and vice presidential candidates, adopted an address to the people (a precursor of the party platform) and established a national corresponding committee that created the framework for a national campaign organization.

Ironically, the Anti-Masons, whose keystone was opposition to Masonry, nominated a former Mason, William Wirt of Maryland, as their presidential standard-bearer. In spite of a rule requiring a three-fourths nominating majority, Wirt was an easy first-ballot winner and the nearly unanimous nominee of the convention.

He was not, however, the first choice of party leaders, who had been rebuffed in their earlier efforts to persuade Henry Clay and later Supreme Court Justice John McLean to take the presidential nomination. Wirt himself was not an enthusiastic candidate, stating that he saw nothing repugnant about Masonry and that if his views did not suit the convention, he would willingly withdraw from the ticket. The delegates supported Wirt and chose Amos Ellmaker of Pennsylvania as his vice presidential running mate.

National Republicans

In December 1831 the National Republicans held their national convention in Baltimore. The National Republicans were united primarily in their opposition to incumbent President Andrew Jackson. The idea of a convention had been proposed by an anti-Jackson committee in New York City and approved by the leading National Republican newspaper, the *National Intelligencer*. There was no uniform method of delegate selection, with state conventions, legislative caucuses and local meetings all being used.

One hundred sixty-eight delegates from 18 states attended the National Republican convention, although nearly one-quarter were late in arriving due to inclement winter weather. Without any pre-established rules, it was agreed that the roll calls would be taken by announcing each delegate's name. Henry Clay of Kentucky was the convention's unanimous choice for president, and former representative John Sergeant of Pennsylvania was selected without opposition for vice president. Letters accepting their nominations were received from both candidates.

There was no formal platform, although the convention adopted an address to the people that criticized Jackson for dividing a previously harmonious country.

In May 1832 a convention of young National Republicans met in Washington, D.C., and passed a series of resolutions calling for a protective tariff, federal support of internal improvements and recognition of the Supreme Court as the ultimate authority on constitutional questions. The last was a rebuke of Jackson for disregarding Supreme Court decisions concerning the Cherokee Indians. Other resolutions criticized Jackson's use of the spoils system in distributing patronage and his handling of foreign policy with Great Britain. Although not a formal platform, the resolutions adopted by the convention of young National Republicans were the most definitive discussion of issues during the 1832 campaign.

Democrats

The Democrats held their first national convention in Baltimore in late May 1832. Representatives from 23 states attended. The call for a Democratic national convention had been made by Jacksonian members of the New Hampshire legislature, and their proposal was approved by prominent members of President Andrew Jackson's administration. The convention was called to order by a member of the New Hampshire legislature, who explained the intent of the gathering in these words:

"...[The] object of the people of New Hampshire who called this convention was, not to impose on the people, as candidates for either of the two first offices of the government, any local favorite; but to concentrate the opinions of all the states.... They believed that the example of this convention would operate favorably in future elections; that

the people would be disposed, after seeing the good effects of this convention in conciliating the different and distant sections of the country, to continue this mode of nomination." *(Reprinted from* Convention Decisions and Voting Records, *by Richard C. Bain, p. 17.)*

The convention adopted two rules that Democratic conventions retained well into the 20th century. One based each state's convention vote on its electoral vote, an apportionment method unchanged until 1940.

A second rule established a two-thirds nominating majority, a controversial measure that remained a feature of Democratic conventions until 1936. The 1832 convention also adopted the procedure of having one person from each delegation announce the vote of his state.

The delegates did not formally nominate Jackson for the presidency. Instead they concurred in the various nominations he had received earlier from state legislatures. Jackson's choice for vice president, Martin Van Buren of New York, was easily nominated on the first ballot, receiving 208 of the 283 votes cast.

Instead of adopting a platform or address to the people, the convention decided that each state delegation should write its own report to its constituents. The convention also determined to establish in each state general corresponding committees that together would provide a nationwide organization for the campaign.

1835-36 Conventions

Presidential Candidates

Martin Van Buren
Democrat

William Henry Harrison
Whig

Daniel Webster
Whig

Hugh L. White
Whig

Democrats

The Democrats held their second national convention in Baltimore in May 1835. The early date had been set by President Jackson to prevent the emergence of opposition to his hand-picked successor, Vice President Martin Van Buren. Delegates from 22 states and two territories attended, and the size of the delegations was generally related to their distance from Baltimore. One hundred eighty-eight individuals were on hand from Maryland to cast the state's 10 votes, but only one person attended from Tennessee — a visiting businessman who cast 15 votes. Alabama, Illinois and South Carolina were unrepresented.

Two rival Pennsylvania delegations arrived, precipitating the first credentials dispute in convention history. It was decided to seat both delegations and let them share the Pennsylvania vote.

An effort to eliminate the rule requiring a two-thirds nominating majority initially passed by a margin of 231 to 210 (apparently counting individual delegates instead of state convention votes), but the two-thirds rule was reimposed by a voice vote. A question developed whether the nominating majority should be based on only the states represented or on all the states in the union. It was decided to base the majority on only those present.

Vice President Van Buren won the presidential nomination, winning all 265 votes. Richard M. Johnson of Kentucky barely reached the necessary two-thirds majority on the first vice presidential ballot, receiving 178 votes, just one vote more than the required minimum. *(Chart, p. 195)*

Johnson, famous as the alleged slayer of the Indian chief Tecumseh, had aroused some disapproval because of his personal life. Johnson had lived with a mulatto mistress by whom he had two daughters.

Once again the Democrats did not write a formal platform, although an address to the people was published in the party newspaper, *The Washington Globe.* Van Buren wrote a letter of acceptance in which he promised to "tread generally in the footsteps of President Jackson."

Whigs

During Jackson's second term, a new party, the Whigs, emerged as the Democrats' primary opposition. It con-

tained remnants of the short-lived National Republican Party, as well as anti-Jackson elements in the Democratic and Anti-Masonic parties. Although the Whigs were a rising political force, the party lacked national cohesion in 1836. Instead of holding a convention and nominating national candidates, the Whigs ran regional candidates nominated by state legislatures. It was the hope of Whig strategists that the regional candidates would receive enough electoral votes to throw the election into the House of Representatives, where the party could unite behind the leading prospect.

Sen. Daniel Webster of New Hampshire ran as the Whig candidate in Massachusetts; Sen. Hugh L. White of Tennessee was the party standard-bearer in the South; Gen. William Henry Harrison of Ohio was the Whig candidate in the rest of the country. The Whigs chose Francis Granger of New York as Harrison and Webster's running mate and John Tyler of Virginia to run with White.

1839-40 Conventions

Presidential Candidates

William Henry Harrison
Whig

Martin Van Buren
Democrat

Whigs

By 1839 the Whigs had established themselves as a powerful opposition party, unified enough to run a national candidate against the Democratic president, Martin Van Buren. The call for the Whigs' first national convention was issued by a group of party members in Congress. Nearly 250 delegates responded, gathering in Harrisburg, Pa., in December 1839.

Three candidates were in contention for the presidential nomination: Generals William Henry Harrison of Ohio and Winfield Scott of Virginia and Sen. Henry Clay of Kentucky. After long debate, it was decided that each state would ballot separately, then select representatives who would meet and discuss the views and results of their delegation meetings with representatives of the other states. The unit rule would be in effect, binding the entire vote of each state to the candidate who received a majority of the state's delegates.

The nominating rules agreed to by the convention strongly favored the forces opposed to Clay. First, they negated substantial Clay strength in state delegations in

which he did not hold a majority of the vote. Second, they permitted balloting in relative anonymity, so that delegates would be more likely to defect from the popular Kentuckian than they would if the balloting were public.

Clay led on the first ballot, but switches by Scott delegates on subsequent roll calls gave the nomination to Harrison. On the final ballot, Harrison received 148 votes to 90 for Clay and 16 for Scott. Harrison's vote was short of a two-thirds majority, but under Whig rules only a simple majority was needed to nominate.

To give the ticket factional and geographic balance, a friend of Clay, former Democrat John Tyler of Virginia, was the unanimous selection for vice president. The convention did not risk destruction of the tenuous unity of its anti-Democratic coalition by adopting a party platform or statement of principles.

Democrats

In May 1840 the Democrats held their national convention in Baltimore. The call once again was initiated by members of the New Hampshire legislature. Delegates from 21 states attended, while five states were unrepresented. Again, the size of the state delegations was largely determined by their distance from Baltimore. New Jersey sent 59 people to cast the state's eight votes, while only one delegate came from Massachusetts to decide that state's 14 votes.

To avoid a bitter dispute over the vice presidential nomination, the convention appointed a committee to recommend nominees for both spots on the ticket. The committee's recommendation that Van Buren be renominated for president was passed by acclamation. On the touchier problem of the vice presidency, the committee recommended that no nomination be made, a suggestion that was also agreed to by the convention. Dissatisfaction with the personal life of Vice President Johnson had increased, leading to the decision that state Democratic leaders determine who would run as the vice presidential candidate in their own states.

Before the nominating process had begun, the convention had approved the first party platform in American history. A platform committee was appointed "to prepare resolutions declaratory of the principles of the . . . party." The committee report was approved without discussion.

The first Democratic platform was a short document, fewer than 1,000 words long. Although brief by modern standards, the platform clearly emphasized the party's belief in a strict reading of the Constitution. It began by stating "that the federal government is one of limited powers" and spelled out in detail what the federal government could not do. The platform stated that the federal government did not have the power to finance internal improvements, assume state debts, charter a national bank or interfere with the rights of the states, especially relating to slavery. The platform criticized the abolitionists for stirring up the explosive slavery question. The Democrats urged the government to practice economy, supported President Van Buren's independent treasury plan and affirmed their belief in the principles expressed in the Declaration of Independence.

In addition to the platform, the convention adopted an address to the people, which was written by a separate committee. Much longer than the platform, the address discussed party principles, lauded Van Buren and Jackson for following these principles and warned of dire consequences if the opposition should be elected.

Following are excerpts from the Democratic platform of 1840:

Strict Construction. That the federal government is one of limited powers, derived solely from the constitution, and the grants of power shown therein, ought to be strictly construed by all the departments and agents of the government, and that it is inexpedient and dangerous to exercise doubtful constitutional powers.

Internal Improvements. That the constitution does not confer upon the general government the power to commence and carry on, a general system of internal improvements.

State Debts. That the constitution does not confer authority upon the federal government, directly or indirectly, to assume the debts of the several states, contracted for local internal improvements, or other state purposes; nor would such assumption be just or expedient.

Equality of Rights. That justice and sound policy forbid the federal government to foster one branch of industry to the detriment of another, or to cherish the interests of one portion to the injury of another portion of our common country — that every citizen and every section of the country, has a right to demand and insist upon an equality of rights and privileges, and to complete and ample protection of person and property from domestic violence, or foreign aggression.

Government Spending. That it is the duty of every branch of the government, to enforce and practice the most rigid economy, in conducting our public affairs, and that no more revenue ought to be raised, than is required to defray the necessary expenses of the government.

National Bank. That congress has no power to charter a national bank; that we believe such an institution one of deadly hostility to the best interests of the country, dangerous to our republican institutions and the liberties of the people, and calculated to place the business of the country within the control of a concentrated money power, and above the laws and the will of the people.

States' Rights, Slavery. That congress has no power, under the constitution, to interfere with or control the domestic institutions of the several states, and that such states are the sole and proper judges of everything appertaining to their own affairs, not prohibited by the constitution; that all efforts by abolitionists or others, made to induce congress to interfere with questions of slavery, or to take incipient steps in relation thereto, are calculated to lead to the most alarming and dangerous consequences, and that all such efforts have an inevitable tendency to diminish the happiness of the people, and endanger the stability and permanency of the union, and ought not to be countenanced by any friend to our political institutions.

Independent Treasury. That the separation of the moneys of the government from banking institutions, is indispensable for the safety of the funds of the government, and the rights of the people.

Democratic Principles. That the liberal principles embodied by Jefferson in the Declaration of Independence, and sanctioned in the constitution, which makes ours the land of liberty, and the asylum of the oppressed of every nation, have ever been cardinal principles in the democratic faith; and every attempt to abridge the present privilege of becoming citizens, and the owners of soil among us, ought to be resisted with the same spirit which swept the alien and sedition laws from our statute-book.

1843-44 Conventions

Presidential Candidates

James G. Birney
Liberty

Henry Clay
Whig

James K. Polk
Democrat

Liberty Party

The Liberty Party held its second national convention in Buffalo, N.Y., in August 1843. The party, born of the failure of the Whigs and the Democrats to make a strong appeal to abolitionist voters, had held its first national convention in April 1840 in Albany, N.Y. James G. Birney of Michigan, a former slave owner, was nominated for president and Thomas Earle of Ohio was chosen as his running mate. In the 1840 election the party polled 0.29 percent of the national popular vote.

At the 1843 convention, 148 delegates from 12 states assembled in Buffalo and renominated Birney for the presidency and chose Thomas Morris of Ohio as his running mate. The party platform was more than 3,000 words long, the lengthiest platform written by any party in the 19th century. In spite of its length, the platform discussed only one issue, slavery. In the 1844 election, the party received 2.3 percent of the national popular vote, its highest total in any presidential election. By 1848, most members of the party joined the newly formed Free Soil Party.

Following are excerpts from the Liberty Party platform of 1844:

Resolved. That the Liberty party ... will demand the absolute and unqualified divorce of the General Government from Slavery, and also the restoration of equality of rights, among men, in every State where the party exists, or may exist.

Therefore, Resolved, That we hereby give it to be distinctly understood, by this nation and the world, that, as abolitionists, considering that the strength of our cause lies in its righteousness — and our hope for it in our conformity to the LAWS of GOD, and our respect for the RIGHTS OF MAN, we owe it to the Sovereign Ruler of the Universe, as a proof of our allegiance to Him, in all our civil relations and offices, whether as private citizens, or as public functionaries sworn to support the Constitution of the United States, to regard and to treat the third clause of the second section of the fourth article of that instrument, whenever applied to the case of a fugitive slave, as utterly null and void, and consequently as forming no part of the Constitution of the United States, whenever we are called upon, or sworn, to support it.

Whigs

In a harmonious one-day session, the Whigs' national convention nominated for the presidency the party's former leader in Congress, Henry Clay. It was a final rebuff for President John Tyler from the party that had nominated him for the second spot on its ticket in 1840. Three years of bickering between the White House and Whig leaders in Congress had made Tyler, former Democrat, persona non grata in the Whig Party.

Delegates from every state were represented at the Whig convention, held in Baltimore on May 1, 1844. Clay was the unanimous nominee, and it was proposed that he be invited to address the convention the next day. However, the Kentuckian declined this opportunity to make the first acceptance speech in American political history, stating in a letter that he was unable to reconcile an appearance with his "sense of delicacy and propriety." *(Chart, p. 196)*

Three potential candidates for the vice presidency sent letters of withdrawal before balloting for second place on the ticket began. Unlike the convention four years earlier, the Whigs abandoned their relatively secret state caucus method of voting and adopted a public roll call, with the chair calling the name of each delegate. Theodore Frelinghuysen of New Jersey won a plurality of the convention vote for vice president on the first ballot and went on to gain, on the third ballot, the required majority.

After the nominations, several resolutions were adopted, including one that defined Whig principles and served as the party's first platform. It was a brief document, fewer than 100 words long, and the only clear difference between it and the platform adopted later by the Democratic convention was on the issue of distributing proceeds from the sale of public land. The Whigs favored distribution of these revenues to the states; the Democrats opposed it believing the proceeds should be retained by the federal government. In a continued reaction to the Jackson administration, the Whigs criticized "executive usurpations" and proposed a single-term presidency. The rest of the Whig platform called for government efficiency, "a well-regulated currency" and a tariff for revenue and the protection of American labor.

Westward territorial expansion, particularly the annexation of Texas, was not mentioned in the Whig platform, but it was an explosive issue by 1844 that made a significant impact on the Democratic convention.

Following are excerpts from the Whig platform of 1844:

> *Resolved*, That these principles may be summed as comprising, a well-regulated currency; a tariff for revenue to defray the necessary expenses of the government, and discriminating with special reference to protection of the domestic labor of the country; the distribution of the proceeds of the sales of the public lands; a single term for the presidency; a reform of executive usurpations; — and, generally — such an administration of the affairs of the country as shall impart to every branch of the public service the greatest practicable efficiency, controlled by a well regulated and wise economy.

Democrats

Delegates from every state except South Carolina assembled in Baltimore in late May 1844 for the Democratic convention. The front-runner for the presidential nomination was former president Martin Van Buren, whose status was threatened on the eve of the convention by his statement against the annexation of Texas. Van Buren's position jeopardized his support in the South, and with a two-thirds majority apparently necessary, dimmed his chances of obtaining the presidential nomination. The question of requiring a two-thirds nominating majority was debated in the early sessions of the convention, and by a vote of 148 to 118 the two-thirds majority rule, initially adopted by the party in 1832, was ratified. *(Chart, p. 195)*

Van Buren led the early presidential balloting, actually receiving a simple majority of the vote on the first ballot. On succeeding roll calls, however, his principal opponent, Lewis Cass of Michigan, gained strength and took the lead. But neither candidate approached the 178 votes needed for nomination.

With a deadlock developing, sentiment for a compromise candidate appeared. James K. Polk, former Speaker of the Tennessee House and former governor of Tennessee, emerged as an acceptable choice and won the nomination on the ninth ballot. It marked the first time in American history that a dark-horse candidate won a presidential nomination. *(Chart, p. 195)*

A friend of Van Buren, Sen. Silas Wright of New York, was the nearly unanimous nominee of the convention for vice president. But Wright refused the nomination, quickly notifying the delegates by way of Samuel Morse's new invention, the telegraph. After two more ballots, George M. Dallas of Pennsylvania was chosen as Polk's running mate.

Among its final actions, the convention appointed a central committee and recommended that a nationwide party organization be established — a forerunner of the national committee. The delegates did not adopt a platform but appointed a committee to draft resolutions.

The resulting document contained the same resolutions included in the party's 1840 platform, plus several new planks. The Democrats opposed the distribution of the proceeds from the sale of public lands; were against placing any restrictions on the executive veto power; and, to alleviate the sectional bitterness aroused by the prospect of Western expansion, recommended the annexation of both Texas and Oregon.

President Tyler, although abandoned by the major parties, wanted to remain in office. Friends and federal officeholders gathered in Baltimore at the same time as the Democrats and nominated Tyler. However, it became apparent that the president's national vote-getting appeal was limited, and he withdrew from the race in favor of the Democrat, Polk.

Following are excerpts from the Democratic resolutions of 1844:

Appeal to the Masses. That the American Democracy place their trust, not in factitious symbols, not in displays and appeals insulting to the judgment and subversive of the intellect of the people, but in a clear reliance upon the intelligence, patriotism, and the discriminating justice of the American masses.

That we regard this as a distinctive feature of our political creed, which we are proud to maintain before the world, as the great moral element in a form of government springing from and upheld by the popular will; and we contrast it with the creed and practice of Federalism, under whatever name or form, which seeks to palsy the will of the constituent, and which conceives no imposture too monstrous for the popular credulity.

Internal Improvements. That the Constitution does not confer upon the General Government the power to commence or carry on a general system of internal improvements.

State Debts. That the Constitution does not confer authority upon the Federal Government, directly or indirectly, to assume the debts of the several states.

Government Spending. That it is the duty of every branch of the government to enforce and practice the most rigid economy in conducting our public affairs, and that no more revenue ought to be raised than is required to defray the necessary expenses of the government.

National Bank. That Congress has no power to charter a United States Bank, that we believe such an institution one of deadly hostility to the best interests of the country, dangerous to our republican institutions and the liberties of the people.

States' Rights. That Congress has no power, under the Constitution, to interfere with or control the domestic institutions of the several States; and that such States are the sole and proper judges of everything pertaining to their own affairs, not prohibited by the Constitution; that all efforts, by abolitionists or others, made to induce Congress to interfere with questions of slavery, or to take incipient steps in relation thereto, are calculated to lead to the most alarming and dangerous consequences.

Public Lands. That the proceeds of the Public Lands ought to be sacredly applied to the national objects specified in the Constitution, and that we are opposed to the laws lately adopted, and to any law for the distribution of such proceeds among the States, as alike inexpedient in policy and repugnant to the Constitution.

Executive Veto Power. That we are decidedly opposed to taking from the President the qualified veto power by which he is enabled, under restrictions and responsibilities amply sufficient to guard the public interest.

Western Expansion. That our title to the whole of the Territory of Oregon is clear and unquestionable; that no portion of the same ought to be ceded to England or any other power, and that the reoccupation of Oregon and the reannexation of Texas at the earliest practicable period are great American measures, which this Convention recommends to the cordial support of the Democracy of the Union.

1848 Conventions

Presidential Candidates

Lewis Cass
Democrat

Zachary Taylor
Whig

Martin Van Buren
Free Soil

Democrats

Delegates from every state gathered in Baltimore in May 1848 for the Democratic Party's fifth national convention. A seating dispute between two rival New York delegations enlivened the early convention sessions. The conflict reflected a factional fight in the state Democratic Party between a more liberal anti-slavery faction, known as the Barnburners, and a more conservative faction, known as the Hunkers. By a vote of 126 to 125, the convention adopted a compromise by which both delegations were seated and shared New York's vote. However, this compromise satisfied neither of the contesting delegations. The Barnburners bolted the convention. The Hunkers remained but refused to vote. *(Chart, p. 196)*

Before the presidential balloting could begin, the convention had to decide whether to use the controversial two-thirds rule. Consideration of the rule preceded the credentials controversy, which brought an objection from New York delegates who wanted their seating dispute settled first. But, by a vote of 133 to 121, the convention refused to table the issue. A second vote on adoption of the two-thirds rule was approved, 176 to 78. *(Chart, p. 196)*

The front-runner for the presidential nomination was Sen. Lewis Cass of Michigan. Although Cass was from the North, his view that the existence of slavery in the territories should be determined by their inhabitants (a forerunner of Stephen Douglas' "popular sovereignty") was a position acceptable to the South.

Cass received 125 votes on the first ballot, more than double the total of his two principal rivals, James Buchanan of Pennsylvania and Levi Woodbury of New Hampshire. Cass' vote total steadily increased during the next three roll calls, and on the fourth ballot he received 179 votes and was nominated. His vote was actually short of a two-thirds majority of the allotted convention votes, but the chair ruled that, with New York not voting, the required majority was reduced. *(Chart, p. 196)*

The vice presidential nomination went on the second ballot to Gen. William O. Butler of Kentucky, who had 169 of the 253 votes cast. As in the earlier presidential balloting, Butler's two-thirds majority was based on votes cast rather than votes allotted. Butler's primary rival for the nomination was a military colleague, Gen. John A. Quitman of Mississippi.

One of the most significant acts of the convention was the formation of a national committee, with one member from each state, that would handle party affairs until the next convention four years later.

As in 1840 and 1844, the heart of the Democratic platform was a series of resolutions describing the party's concept of a federal government with limited powers. New resolutions emphasized Democratic opposition to a national bank and the distribution of land sales to the states, while applauding the independent treasury plan, the lower tariff bill passed in 1846 and the successful war against Mexico. An effort by William L. Yancey of Alabama to insert in the platform a plank on slavery that would prevent interference with the rights of slaveholders in states or territories was defeated, 216 to 36. The slavery plank written in the platform had the same wording as earlier versions in the 1840 and 1844 Democratic platforms. The plank was milder than Yancey's proposal, stating simply that Congress did not have the power to interfere with slavery in the states. The convention adopted the complete platform by a vote of 247 to 0.

Following are excerpts from the 1848 Democratic platform:

Mexican War. That the war with Mexico, provoked on her part by years of insult and injury, was commenced by her army crossing the Rio Grande, attacking the American troops, and invading our sister State of Texas; and that, upon all the principles of patriotism and laws of nations, it is a just and necessary war on our part, in which every American citizen should have shown himself on the side of his country, and neither morally nor physically, by word or by deed, have given "aid and comfort to the enemy."

Democratic Accomplishments. That the fruits of the great political triumph of 1844, which elected James K. Polk and George M. Dallas President and Vice President of the United States, have fulfilled the hopes of the Democracy of the Union — in defeating the declared purposes of their opponents to create a national bank; in preventing the corrupt and unconstitutional distribution of the land proceeds, from the common treasury of the Union, for local purposes; in protecting the currency and the labor of the country from ruinous fluctuations, and guarding the money of the people for the use of the people, by the establishment of the constitutional treasury; in the noble impulse given to the cause of free trade, by the repeal of the tariff in 1842 and the creation of the more equal, honest, and productive tariff of 1846.

Whigs

Whig delegates from every state except Texas gathered in Philadelphia in June 1848. Although the Lone Star state was unrepresented, a Texas Whig state convention had earlier given a proxy for its votes to the Louisiana delegates. There was debate in the convention about the legality of the proxy, but it was ultimately accepted by the delegates.

The battle for the Whig's presidential nomination involved three major contenders, the party's respected aging statesman, Henry Clay of Kentucky; and two generals — Zachary Taylor and Winfield Scott, both of Virginia — whose political appeal was significantly increased by their military exploits in the recently completed Mexican War. Taylor led throughout the balloting, taking the lead on the first ballot with 111 votes, compared with 97 for Clay and 43 for Scott. Taylor increased his lead on subsequent roll calls, winning the nomination on the fourth ballot with 171 of the 280 votes cast. *(Chart, p. 197)*

Millard Fillmore of New York and Abbott Lawrence of Massachusetts were the prime contenders for the vice presidential nomination. Fillmore led Lawrence, 115 to 109, on the first ballot and pulled away to win on the second ballot with 173 of the 266 votes cast.

A motion to make the presidential and vice presidential nominations unanimous failed when several delegates objected, doubting Taylor's support of Whig principles.

The Whig convention did not formally adopt a party platform, although a ratification meeting held in Philadelphia after the convention adopted a series of resolutions. The resolutions avoided a discussion of issues, instead lauding the party's presidential nominee, Zachary Taylor, and affirming his faithfulness to the tenets of the party.

Free Soilers

Anti-slavery Whigs, New York Barnburners and members of the Liberty Party gathered in Buffalo, N.Y., in August 1848 to form a new third party, the Free Soilers. While opposition to slavery was a common denominator of the various elements in the new party, the dissident Democrats and Whigs also were attracted to the Free Soil Party by the lack of influence they exerted in their former parties. The call for a Free Soil convention was made by the New York Barnburners at their state conclave in June 1848 and by a non-partisan gathering in Columbus, Ohio, the same month. The latter assembly, organized by Salmon P. Chase, was entitled a People's Convention of Friends of Free Territory and was designed to set the stage for a national Free Soil convention.

Four hundred sixty-five delegates from 18 states (including representatives from the slave states of Delaware, Maryland and Virginia) assembled in Buffalo for the birth of the Free Soil Party. Because of the large number of delegates, convention leaders determined that delegates from each state would select several members to form a Committee on Conference, which would conduct conven-

tion business. The rest of the delegates would sit in a large tent and listen to campaign oratory.

Martin Van Buren, the former Democratic president and a favorite of the Barnburners, was chosen as the new party's standard-bearer on the first ballot. Van Buren received 244 votes to defeat John P. Hale of New Hampshire, who had 181 votes. Hale had been nominated by the Liberty Party in October 1847, but with Van Buren's nomination he withdrew from the race. The vice presidential nomination went to a former Whig, Charles Francis Adams of Massachusetts.

The platform adopted by the Free Soil Party focused on the slavery issue, but its opposition to slavery was milder than earlier Liberty Party platforms. The Free Soilers also declared themselves on other issues besides slavery, further distinguishing themselves from the single-minded Liberty Party.

While the Free Soilers opposed the extension of slavery into the territories, they did not feel the federal government had the power to interfere with slavery in the states. Although this position was significantly stronger than the position adopted by the Democrats, it was milder than the all-out opposition to slavery expressed by the Liberty Party four years earlier.

The Free Soilers also adopted positions on a variety of other issues, supporting free land for settlers, a tariff for revenue purposes, cheap postage and federal spending for river and harbor improvements. Basically, the Free Soil platform expressed belief in a federal government with broader powers than that conceived by the Democrats.

Following are excerpts from the 1848 Free Soil Party platform:

Slavery. That Slavery in the several States of this Union which recognize its existence, depends upon the State laws alone, which cannot be repealed or modified by the Federal Government, and for which laws that Government is not responsible. We therefore propose no interference by Congress with Slavery within the limits of any State.

Resolved, THAT IT IS THE DUTY OF THE FEDERAL GOVERNMENT TO RELIEVE ITSELF FROM ALL RESPONSIBILITY FOR THE EXISTENCE OR CONTINUANCE OF SLAVERY WHEREVER THAT GOVERNMENT POSSESS CONSTITUTIONAL POWER TO LEGISLATE ON THAT SUBJECT, AND IS THUS RESPONSIBLE FOR ITS EXISTENCE.

Resolved, That the true, and, in the judgment of this Convention, the *only* safe means of preventing the extension of Slavery into territory now free, is to prohibit its existence in all such territory by *an act of Congress.*

Government Administration. That we demand CHEAP POSTAGE for the people; a retrenchment of the expenses and patronage of the Federal Government; the *abolition* of all *unnecessary* offices and salaries; and the election by the People of all civil officers in the service of the Government, so far as the same may be practicable.

Internal Improvements. That *river and harbor improvements,* when demanded by the safety and convenience of commerce with foreign nations, or among the several States, are objects of *national concern;* and that it is the duty of Congress, in the exercise of its constitutional powers, to provide therefor.

Homesteading. That the FREE GRANT TO ACTUAL SETTLERS, in consideration of the expenses they incur in making settlements in the wilderness, which are usually fully equal to their actual cost, and of the public benefits resulting therefrom, of reasonable portions of the public lands, under suitable limitations, is a wise and just measure of public policy, which will promote, in various ways, the interest of all the States of this Union; and we therefore recommend it to the favorable consideration of the American People.

Tariff. That the obligations of honor and patriotism require the earliest practical payment of the national debt,

and we are therefore in favor of such a tariff of duties as will raise revenue adequate to defray the necessary expenses of the Federal Government, and to pay annual installments of our debt and the interest thereon.

Party Motto. *Resolved,* That we inscribe on our banner, "FREE SOIL, FREE SPEECH, FREE LABOR, AND FREE MEN."

1852 Conventions

Presidential Candidates

Franklin Pierce
Democrat

Winfield Scott
Whig

John P. Hale
Free Soil

Democrats

In spite of the efforts of the major politicians of both parties, the explosive slavery question was fast becoming the dominant issue in American politics and was threatening the tenuous intersectional alliances that held together both the Democratic and Whig parties. Under the cloud of this volatile issue, the Democratic convention convened in Baltimore in June 1852.

The delegates were called to order by the party's first national chairman, Benjamin F. Hallett of Massachusetts. Hallett's first action was to limit the size of each state delegation to its electoral vote, dispatching members of oversized delegations to the rear of the hall. Retention of the two-thirds rule provoked little opposition, unlike the disputes at the 1844 and 1848 conventions, and an effort to table the rule was soundly beaten, 269 to 13.

With a degree of orderliness, the convention disposed of procedural matters, clearing the way for the presidential balloting. There were four major contenders for the nomination: Sen. Lewis Cass of Michigan, James Buchanan of Pennsylvania and William L. Marcy of New York — all three over 60 years old — and the rising young senator from Illinois, Stephen A. Douglas, 39. Each of the four challengers led at one point during the numerous ballots that followed.

Cass jumped in front initially, receiving 116 votes on the first ballot. Buchanan trailed with 93, while Marcy and Douglas were far back with 27 and 20 votes, respectively. Cass' vote dropped after the first few roll calls, but he was able to hold the lead until the 20th ballot, when Buchanan moved in front. Buchanan led for several roll calls, followed by Douglas, who edged into the lead on the 30th ballot,

only to be quickly displaced by Cass on the 32nd ballot. Marcy made his spurt between the 36th and 46th ballots, and took the lead on the 45th and 46th ballots. But in spite of the quick changes in fortune, none of the four contenders could win a simple majority of the votes, let alone the two-thirds required. *(Chart, p. 198)*

With a deadlock developing, on the 35th ballot the Virginia delegation introduced a new name, Franklin Pierce of New Hampshire. Although formerly a member of both houses of Congress, Pierce was little known nationally and not identified with any party faction. Pierce's relative anonymity made him an acceptable alternative in the volatile convention. Pierce received 15 votes on the 35th ballot and gradually gained strength on subsequent ballots, with the big break coming on the 49th roll call. Nearly unanimous votes for Pierce in the New England states created a bandwagon effect that resulted in his nomination on this ballot with 279 of the 288 votes cast. The 49 ballots took two days.

Beginning the vice presidential roll call, a spokesman for the Maine delegation suggested that second place on the ticket go to a representative of the South, specifically mentioning Sen. William R. King of Alabama. King moved into a strong lead on the first ballot with 125 votes and easily won nomination on the second roll call with 277 of the 288 votes cast.

The platform adopted by the Democratic convention contained the same nine resolutions that had been in all party platforms since 1840, detailing the Democratic concept of a limited federal government. The platform included a plank supporting the Compromise of 1850, the congressional solution to the slavery question. Actually, both the Whigs and Democrats endorsed the compromise of 1850. The major point of dispute between the two parties was over the issue of internal improvements, with the Whigs taking a broader view of federal power in this sphere.

Following are excerpts from the Democratic platform of 1852:

Compromise of 1850. *Resolved, . . .* the democratic party of the Union, standing on this national platform, will abide by and adhere to a faithful execution of the acts known as the compromise measures settled by the last Congress — "the act for reclaiming fugitives from service or labor" included; which act, being designed to carry out an express provision of the constitution, cannot, with fidelity thereto be repealed nor so changed as to destroy or impair its efficiency.

Resolved, That the democratic party will resist all attempts at renewing, in congress or out of it, the agitation of the slavery question, under whatever shape or color the attempt may be made.

Democratic Principles. That, in view of the condition of popular institutions in the Old World, a high and sacred duty is devolved, with increased responsibility upon the democratic party of this country, as the party of the people, to uphold and maintain the rights of every State, and thereby the Union of the States, and to sustain and advance among us constitutional liberty, by continuing to resist all monopolies and exclusive legislation for the benefit of the few at the expense of the many, and by a vigilant and constant adherence to those principles and compromises of the constitution, which are broad enough and strong enough to embrace and uphold the Union as it was, the Union as it is, and the Union as it shall be, in the full expansion of the energies and capacity of this great and progressive people.

Whigs

Although in control of the White House, the Whigs were more sharply divided by the Compromise of 1850 than were the Democrats. The majority of Northern Whigs in Congress opposed the Compromise, while most Southern members of the party favored it. Faced with widening division in their ranks, Whig delegates convened in Baltimore in June 1852. The call for this national convention had been issued by Whig members of Congress, and delegates from all 31 states attended.

The convention sessions were often lively and sometimes raucous. When asked to present its report the first day, the credentials committee responded that it was not ready to report and "didn't know when — maybe for days." A minister, invited to the hall to deliver a prayer to the convention, never had his chance. The delegates debated when the prayer should be delivered and finally decided to omit it.

A heated debate occurred on how many votes each state would be apportioned on the platform committee. By a vote of 149 to 144, the delegates adopted a plan whereby each state's vote on the committee would reflect its strength in the electoral college. Strong protests from Southern and small Northern states, however, brought a reversal of this decision, and although no formal vote was recorded, representation on the platform committee was changed so that each state received one vote.

The Northern and Southern wings of the Whig Party were nearly equally represented at the Baltimore convention, and the close split produced a prolonged battle for the party's presidential nomination. The two major rivals for the nomination, President Millard Fillmore and Winfield

Scott, had nearly equal strength. Ironically, the basic appeal of Fillmore of New York was among Southern delegates, who appreciated his support of the Compromise of 1850.

Although a native of Virginia, Scott was not popular in the South because of his ambivalence on the Compromise and the active support given him by a leading anti-slavery Northerner, Sen. William H. Seward of New York. Scott's strength was in the Northern and Western states. A third candidate in the field was Daniel Webster, the party's elder statesman, whose appeal was centered in his native New England.

On the first ballot, Fillmore received 133 votes, Scott had 132 and Webster collected 29. This nearly equal distribution of the vote between Fillmore and Scott continued with little fluctuation through the first two days of balloting. Midway through the second day, after the 34th ballot, a motion was made to adjourn. Although it was defeated by a vote of 126 to 76, other motions were made to adjourn throughout the rest of the session. Finally, amid increasing confusion, after the 46th ballot, delegates voted by a margin of 176 to 116 to adjourn. *(Chart, p. 199)*

Commotion continued the next day, with Southern delegates trying unsuccessfully to expel Henry J. Raymond, the editor of the *New York Times,* who was also a delegate by proxy. In an article, Raymond had charged collusion between party managers and Southern delegates, with the South getting its way on the platform while Scott received the presidential nomination.

Amid this uproar, the leaders of the Fillmore and Webster forces were negotiating. Fillmore was willing to release his delegates to Webster, if Webster could muster 41 votes on his own. As the balloting continued, it was apparent that Webster could not; and enough delegates defected to Scott to give the Mexican War hero a simple majority and the nomination on the 53rd ballot. On the final roll call, Scott received 159 votes, compared with 112 for Fillmore and 21 for Webster.

Several individuals placed in nomination for the vice presidency refused it immediately. The chairman of the convention finally declared Secretary of the Navy William A. Graham of North Carolina to be the unanimous selection. No formal roll-call vote was recorded.

For only the second time in their history, the Whigs adopted a party platform. Like their Democratic adversaries, the Whigs supported the Compromise of 1850 and perceived the federal government as having limited powers. Additional planks called for a tariff on imports to raise revenue and for an isolationist foreign policy that avoided "entangling alliances." The platform was adopted by a vote of 227 to 66, with all the dissenting votes cast by delegates from the North and West.

Following are excerpts from the Whig platform of 1852:

Strict Construction. The Government of the United States is of a limited character, and it is confined to the exercise of powers expressly granted by the Constitution, and such as may be necessary and proper for carrying the granted powers into full execution, and that all powers not granted or necessarily implied are expressly reserved to the States respectively and to the people.

Foreign Policy. That while struggling freedom everywhere enlists the warmest sympathy of the Whig party, we still adhere to the doctrines of the Father of his Country, as announced in his Farewell Address, of keeping ourselves free from all entangling alliances with foreign countries, and of never quitting our own to stand upon foreign ground, that our mission as a republic is not to propagate our opinions, or impose on other countries our form of government by artifice or force; but to teach, by example, and show by our success, moderation and justice, the blessings of self-government, and the advantages of free institutions.

Tariff. Revenue sufficient for the expenses of an economical administration of the Government in time of peace ought to be derived from a duty on imports, and not from direct taxation.

Internal Improvements. The Constitution vests in Congress the power to open and repair harbors, and remove obstructions from navigable rivers, whenever such improvements are necessary for the common defense, and for the protection and facility of commerce with foreign nations, or among the States, said improvements being, in every instance, national and general in their character.

Compromise of 1850. That the series of acts of the Thirty-first Congress, — the act known as the Fugitive Slave Law, included — are received and acquiesced in by the Whig Party of the United States as a settlement in principle and substance, of the dangerous and exciting question which they embrace; and, so far as they are concerned, we will maintain them, and insist upon their strict enforcement, until time and experience shall demonstrate the necessity of further legislation.

Free Democrats (Free Soilers)

After the 1848 election, the New York Barnburners returned to the Democratic Party, and the rest of the Free Soilers were ready to coalesce with either the Democrats or the Whigs. But the process of absorption was delayed by the Compromise of 1850. It was viewed as a solution to the slavery question by the two major parties but was regarded as a sellout by most anti-slavery groups.

Responding to a call for a national convention issued by a Cleveland, Ohio, anti-slavery meeting, delegates gathered in Pittsburgh in August 1852. Anti-slavery Whigs and remnants of the Liberty Party were in attendance at what was termed the Free Soil Democratic Convention.

John P. Hale of New Hampshire unanimously won the presidential nomination, and George W. Julian of Indiana was selected as his running mate.

Although the platform covered a number of issues, the document focused on the slavery question. The Free Soil Democrats opposed the Compromise of 1850 and called for the abolition of slavery. Like both major parties, the Free Democrats expressed the concept of a limited federal government, but they agreed with the Whigs that the government should undertake certain river and harbor improvements. The Free Democrats went beyond the other parties in advocating a homestead policy, extending a welcome to immigrants and voicing support for new republican governments in Europe and the Caribbean.

Following are excerpts from the Free Democratic platform of 1852:

Strict Construction. That the Federal Government is one of limited powers, derived solely from the Constitution, and the grants of power therein ought to be strictly construed by all the departments and agents of the Government, and it is inexpedient and dangerous to exercise doubtful constitutional powers.

Compromise of 1850. That, to the persevering and importunate demands of the slave power for more slave States, new slave Territories, and the nationalization of slavery, our distinct and final answer is — no more slave States, no slave Territory, no nationalized slavery, and no national legislation for the extradition of slaves.

That slavery is a sin against God and a crime against man, which no human enactment nor usage can make right; and that Christianity, humanity, and patriotism, alike demand its abolition.

That the Fugitive Slave Act of 1850 is repugnant to the Constitution, to the principles of the common law, to the spirit of Christianity, and to the sentiments of the civilized world. We therefore deny its binding force upon the American People, and demand its immediate and total repeal.

Homesteading. That the public lands of the United States belong to the people, and should not be sold to individuals nor granted to corporations, but should be held as a sacred trust for the benefit of the people, and should be granted in limited quantities, free of cost, to landless settlers.

Internal Improvements. That river and harbor improvements, when necessary to the safety and convenience of commerce with foreign nations or among the several States, are objects of national concern, and it is the duty of Congress in the exercise of its constitutional powers to provide for the same.

1856 Conventions
Presidential Candidates

John C. Fremont
Republican

Millard Fillmore
Know Nothing

James Buchanan
Democrat

Republicans

With the decline of the Whigs and the increasing importance of the slavery issue, there was room for a new political party. Officially born in 1854, the new Republican Party moved to fill the vacuum.

The party's first meeting was held in Pittsburgh in February 1856, with delegates from 24 states attending. United in their opposition to the extension of slavery and the policies of the Pierce administration, the gathering selected a national committee (with one representative from each state), which was empowered to call the party's first national convention.

The subsequent call was addressed not to Republicans but "to the people of the United States" who were opposed to the Pierce administration and the congressional compromises on slavery. Each state was allocated six delegates at the forthcoming convention, with three additional delegates for each congressional district.

When the first Republican National Convention assembled in Philadelphia in June 1856, the gathering was clearly sectional. There were nearly 600 delegates present, representing all the Northern states, the Border slave states of Delaware, Maryland, Virginia and Kentucky, and the District of Columbia. The territory of Kansas, symbolically important in the slavery struggle, was treated as a state and given full representation. There were no delegations from the remaining Southern slave states.

Under convention rules, the roll call was to proceed in alphabetical order, with each state allocated three times its electoral vote. In response to a question, the chair decided that a simple majority would be required and not the two-thirds majority mandated by the Democratic convention. This was an important rule that distinguished the conventions of the two major parties well into the 20th century.

Two major contenders for the Republican presidential nomination, Salmon P. Chase of Ohio and William H. Seward of New York, both withdrew before the balloting began. Another contender, Supreme Court Justice John McLean of Ohio, withdrew briefly, but then re-entered the race. However, McLean could not catch the front-runner, John C. Fremont of California. Although briefly a U.S.

senator, Fremont was most famous as an explorer, and he benefited from being free of any ideological identification.

The other contenders were all identified with one of the factions that had come to make up the new party. Fremont won a preliminary, informal ballot, receiving 359 votes to 190 for McLean. On the formal roll call, Fremont won easily, winning 520 of the 567 votes. *(Chart, p. 200)*

A preliminary, informal ballot was taken for the vice presidency as well. William L. Dayton, a former senator from New Jersey, led with 253 votes, more than twice the total received by an Illinois lawyer, Abraham Lincoln, who had served in the House of Representatives 1847-49. On the formal ballot, Dayton swept to victory with 523 votes. His nomination was quickly made unanimous.

The Republican platform was approved by a voice vote. It was a document with sectional appeal, written by Northern delegates for the North. Unlike the Democrats, the Republicans opposed the concept of popular sovereignty and believed that slavery should be prohibited in the territories. Specifically, the platform called for the admission of Kansas as a free state.

The Republicans also differed with the Democrats on the question of internal improvements, supporting the view that Congress should undertake river and harbor improvements. The Republican platform denounced the Ostend Manifesto, a document secretly drawn up by three of Pierce's ambassadors in Europe, that suggested the United States either buy or take Cuba from Spain. The Republicans termed the manifesto a "highwayman's plea, that 'might makes right.'"

Both parties advocated the building of a transcontinental transportation system, with the Republicans supporting the construction of a railroad.

Following are excerpts from the Republican platform of 1856:

Slavery. This Convention of Delegates, assembled in pursuance of a call addressed to the people of the United States, without regard to past political differences or divisions, who are opposed to the repeal of the Missouri Compromise; to the policy of the present Administration; to the extension of Slavery into Free Territory; in favor of the admission of Kansas as a Free State; of restoring the action of the Federal Government to the principles of Washington and Jefferson. . . .

That the Constitution confers upon Congress sovereign powers over the Territories of the United States for their government; and that in the exercise of this power, it is both the right and the imperative duty of Congress to prohibit in the Territories those twin relics of barbarism — Polygamy, and Slavery.

Cuba. That the highwayman's plea, that "might makes right," embodied in the Ostend Circular, was in every respect unworthy of American diplomacy, and would bring shame and dishonor upon any Government or people that gave it their sanction.

Transcontinental Railroad. That a railroad to the Pacific Ocean by the most central and practicable route is imperatively demanded by the interests of the whole country.

Internal Improvements. That appropriations by Congress for the improvement of rivers and harbors, of a national character, required for the accommodation and security of our existing commerce, are authorized by the Constitution, and justified by the obligation of the Government to protect the lives and property of its citizens.

American (Know-Nothings)

In addition to the Republicans, the American Party or Know-Nothings aspired to replace the Whigs as the nation's second major party. However, unlike the Republicans, the Know-Nothings were a national political organization, and the slavery issue that helped unite the Republicans divided the Know-Nothings. The main Know-Nothing concern was to place restrictions on the large number of European immigrants who arrived in the 1840s and 1850s.

The party held its first and only national convention in Philadelphia in February 1856. Several days before the convention began, the American Party's national council met and drew up the party platform. When the convention assembled, anti-slavery delegates objected to the platform, with its espousal of popular sovereignty, and called for the nomination of candidates who would outlaw slavery in the new territories. When their resolution was defeated, 141 to 59, these anti-slavery delegates — mainly from New England and Ohio — bolted the convention.

The remaining delegates nominated former president Millard Fillmore (1850-53) of New York for president. Fillmore was popular in the South for his support of compromise slavery measures during his administration and was nominated on the second ballot. Andrew Jackson Donelson of Tennessee was chosen as the vice presidential candidate.

In June 1856 several days before the Republican convention was scheduled to begin, the anti-slavery Know-Nothings assembled in New York and nominated Speaker of the House Nathaniel P. Banks of Massachusetts for the presidency and former governor William F. Johnston of Pennsylvania as his running mate. Banks, who actually favored Fremont's nomination, withdrew from the race when Fremont was chosen as the Republican candidate. Johnston bowed out in favor of Fremont's running mate, William L. Dayton, later in the campaign.

The Know-Nothing convention that had met earlier in Philadelphia adopted a platform similar to that of the Democrats on the slavery question. The document advocated non-interference in the affairs of the states and the concept of popular sovereignty for deciding slavery in the territories. Although also calling for economy in govern-

ment spending, the bulk of the Know-Nothing platform dealt with restricting immigrants. Among the nativistic planks were proposals that native-born citizens be given the first chance for all government offices, that the naturalization period for immigrants be extended to 21 years and that paupers and convicted criminals be kept from entering the United States.

Following are excerpts from the Know-Nothing platform of 1856:

Slavery, States' Rights. The unequalled recognition and maintenance of the reserved rights of the several states, and the cultivation of harmony and fraternal good-will between the citizens of the several states, and to this end, non-interference by Congress with questions appertaining solely to the individual states, and non-intervention by each state with the affairs of any other state.

The recognition of the right of the native-born and naturalized citizens of the United States, permanently residing in any territory thereof, to frame their constitutions and laws, and to regulate their domestic and social affairs in their own mode, subject only to the provisions of the federal Constitution, with the right of admission into the Union whenever they have the requisite population for one representative in Congress.

Nativism. *Americans must rule America;* and to this end, *native*-born citizens should be selected for all state, federal, or municipal offices of government employment, in preference to naturalized citizens. . . .

No person should be selected for political station (whether of native or foreign birth), who recognizes any alliance or obligation of any description to any foreign prince, potentate or power, who refuses to recognize the federal and state constitutions (each within its own sphere), as paramount to all other laws, as rules of particular [political] action.

A change in the laws of naturalization, making a continued residence of twenty-one years, of all not heretofore provided for, an indispensable requisite for citizenship hereafter, and excluding all paupers or persons convicted of crime from landing upon our shores.

Democrats

In June 1856 delegates from all 31 states gathered in Cincinnati, Ohio, for the party's seventh quadrennial convention. It was the first Democratic convention to be held outside Baltimore.

Roll-call votes were taken during the first two days on the establishment of a platform committee and on the method of ticket allocation for the galleries. The first close vote came on the credentials committee report concerning the seating of two contesting New York delegations. By a vote of 136 to 123, the convention agreed to a minority report seating both contending factions and splitting the state's vote between them.

Three men were in contention for the party's presidential nomination: President Franklin Pierce of New Hampshire, James Buchanan of Pennsylvania and Sen. Stephen A. Douglas of Illinois. All three had actively sought the nomination before. Ironically, Buchanan, who had spent the previous three years as ambassador to Great Britain, was in the most enviable position. Having been abroad, Buchanan had largely avoided the increasing slavery controversy that bedeviled his major rivals.

Buchanan led on the first ballot with 135-1/2 votes with Pierce receiving 122-1/2 and Douglas 33. As the balloting continued, Pierce lost strength, while both Buchanan and Douglas gained. After the 15th roll call, the vote stood:

Buchanan, 168-1/2, Douglas, 118-1/2, Pierce 3-1/2. *(Chart, p. 200)*

While the two front-runners had substantial strength, neither of them was a sectional candidate. Both received votes from Northern and Southern delegations. With the possibility of a stalemate looming, Douglas withdrew after the 16th ballot. On the 17th roll call, Buchanan received all 296 votes, and the nomination.

On the first ballot for the vice presidency, 11 different individuals received votes. Rep. John A. Quitman of Mississippi led with 59 votes, followed by Rep. John C. Breckinridge of Kentucky, with 50. At the beginning of the second ballot, the New England delegations cast a nearly unanimous vote for Breckinridge, creating a bandwagon effect that resulted in the nomination of the Kentuckian. Ironically, before the vice presidential balloting began, Breckinridge had asked that his name be withdrawn from consideration. Believing himself too young (he was 35), Breckinridge stated that "promotion should follow seniority."

In spite of his earlier demurrer, Breckinridge was in the convention hall and announced his acceptance of the nomination. It marked one of the few times in American political history that a candidate was present for his own nomination.

The party platform was considered in two segments, with the domestic and foreign policy sections debated separately. The theme of the domestic section, as in past platforms, was the Democrats' concept of a limited federal government. The unconstitutionality of a national bank, federal support for internal improvements and distribution of proceeds from the sale of public land were again mentioned.

Nearly one-third of the entire platform was devoted to the slavery question, with support for the various congressional compromise measures stressed. The Democratic position was underscored in a passage that was capitalized in the convention *Proceedings:* "non-interference by Congress with slavery in state and territory, or in the District of Columbia."

In another domestic area, the Democrats denounced the Know-Nothings for being un-American. The convention approved the domestic policy section of the platform by a vote of 261 to 35, with only the New York delegation voting in opposition.

The foreign policy section expressed a nationalistic and expansionist spirit that was absent from previous Democratic platforms.

There were six different foreign policy planks, each voted on separately. The first plank, calling for free trade, passed 210 to 29. The second, favoring implementation of the Monroe Doctrine, passed 240 to 21. The third plank, backing westward continental expansion, was approved 203 to 56. The fourth plank, which expressed sympathy with the people of Central America, grew out of the United States' dispute with Great Britain over control of that area. The plank was approved, 221 to 38. The fifth plank, calling for United States "ascendency in the Gulf of Mexico," passed 229 to 33. A final resolution, presented separately, called for the construction of roads to the Pacific Ocean. The resolution was at first tabled, 154 to 120, and a second vote to reconsider failed, 175 to 121. But when the resolution was raised a third time after the presidential nomination, it passed, 205 to 87.

Following are excerpts from the Democratic platform of 1856:

Slavery. That claiming fellowship with, and desiring the co-operation of all who regard the preservation of the Union under the Constitution as the paramount issue — and repudiating all sectional parties and platforms concerning domestic slavery, which seek to embroil the States and incite to treason and armed resistance to law in the Territories; and whose avowed purposes, if consummated, must end in civil war and disunion, the American Democracy recognize and adopt the principles contained in the organic laws establishing the Territories of Kansas and Nebraska as embodying the only sound and safe solution of the "slavery question" upon which the great national idea of the people of this whole country can repose in its determined conservatism of the Union — NON-INTERFERENCE BY CONGRESS WITH SLAVERY IN STATE AND TERRITORY, OR IN THE DISTRICT OF COLUMBIA.

Know-Nothings. ...the liberal principles embodied in the Declaration of Independence . . . makes ours the land of liberty and the asylum of the oppressed . . . every attempt to abridge the privilege of becoming citizens . . . ought to be resisted. . . .

Since the foregoing declaration was uniformly adopted by our predecessors in National Conventions, an adverse political and religious test has been secretly organized by a party claiming to be exclusively American, it is proper that the American Democracy should clearly define its relation thereto, and declare its determined opposition to all secret political societies, by whatever name they may be called.

Free Trade. That there are questions connected with the foreign policy of this country, which are inferior to no domestic question whatever. The time has come for the people of the United States to declare themselves in favor of free seas and progressive free trade. . . .

Latin America. [W]e should hold as sacred the principles involved in the Monroe Doctrine: their bearing and import admit of no misconstruction; they should be applied with unbending rigidity.

Gulf of Mexico. That the Democratic party will expect of the next Administration that every proper effort be made to insure our ascendency in the Gulf of Mexico.

Transcontinental Roads. That the Democratic party recognizes the great importance, in a political and commercial point of view, of a safe and speedy communication, by military and postal roads, through our own territory, between the Atlantic and Pacific coasts. . . .

Whigs

On the verge of extinction, the Whig Party held its last national convention in September 1856. Delegates assembled in Baltimore from 21 states and endorsed the Know-Nothing ticket of Fillmore and Donelson.

However, the Whigs adopted their own platform. It avoided specific issues, instead calling for preservation of the Union. The platform criticized both the Democrats and Republicans for appealing to sectional passions and argued for the presidential candidacy of the former Whig, Millard Fillmore.

Following are excerpts from the Whig platform of 1856:

Preserving the Union. That the Whigs of the United States are assembled here by reverence for the Constitution, and unalterable attachment to the National Union, and a fixed determination to do all in their power to preserve it for themselves and posterity. They have no new principles to announce — no new platform to establish, but are content broadly to rest where their fathers have rested upon the Constitution of the United States, wishing no safer guide, no higher law.

1860 Conventions

Presidential Candidates

Stephen A. Douglas
Democrat

John C. Breckinridge
Southern Democrat

Abraham Lincoln
Republican

John Bell
Constitutional Union

Democrats

Rarely in American history has there been a convention as tumultuous as the one that assembled in Charleston, S.C., in April 1860. The Democrats met at a time when their party was threatened by sectional division, caused by the explosive slavery question. The issue had grown increasingly inflammatory during the 1850s, and, because of rising emotions, the chances of a successful compromise solution decreased.

From the outset of the convention, there was little visible effort to obtain party unity. Parliamentary squabbling with frequent appeals to the chair marked the early sessions. Before the presidential balloting even began, 27 separate roll calls on procedural and platform matters were taken.

A bitter dispute between Northern and Southern delegates over the wording of the platform's slavery plank precipitated a walkout by several dozen Southern delegates. Both the majority and minority reports submitted to the convention called for a reaffirmation of the Democratic platform of 1856. In addition, however, the majority report (favored by the South) declared that no government — local, state or federal — could outlaw slavery in the territories. The minority report took a more moderate position, stating that the decision on allowing slavery in the territories should be left to the Supreme Court.

After a day of debate, the convention agreed, by a vote of 152 to 151, to recommit both reports to the platform committee. Basically, the vote followed sectional lines, with Southern delegates approving recommittal. However, the revised majority and minority reports subsequently presented to the convention were similar to the originals.

An amendment by Benjamin F. Butler of Massachusetts, to endorse the 1856 platform without any mention of slavery, was defeated, 198 to 105. After two procedural roll calls, the delegates voted, 165 to 138, to accept the minority report. The vote followed sectional lines, with the Northern delegates victorious. *(Chart, p. 201)*

Unhappy with the platform and unwilling to accept it, 45 delegates from nine states bolted the convention. The majority of six Southern delegations withdrew (Alabama,

Mississippi, Florida, Texas, South Carolina and Louisiana), along with scattered delegates from three other states (Arkansas, Delaware and North Carolina).

With the size of the convention reduced, chairman Caleb Cushing of Massachusetts made an important decision. He ruled that the two-thirds nominating majority would be based on the total votes allocated (303) rather than the number of delegates present and voting. Although Cushing's ruling was approved by a vote of 141 to 112, it countered precedents established at the 1840 and 1848 Democratic conventions, when the nominating majority was based on those present and voting.

Cushing's ruling made it nearly impossible for any candidate to amass the necessary two-thirds majority. Particularly affected was the front-runner, Sen. Stephen A. Douglas of Illinois, whose standing in the South had diminished with his continued support of popular sovereignty. Douglas moved into a big lead on the first ballot, receiving 145-1/2 votes to 42 for Sen. Robert M. T. Hunter of Virginia and 35-1/2 for James Guthrie of Kentucky. Despite his large lead over the rest of the field, Douglas was well short of the 202 votes needed for nomination and, with his limited sectional appeal, had little chance of gaining the needed delegates.

After three days of balloting and 57 presidential roll calls, the standing of the three candidates had undergone little change. Douglas led with 151-1/2 votes, followed by Guthrie with 65-1/2 and Hunter with 16. The delegates, in session for 10 days and wearied by the presidential deadlock, voted 194-1/2 to 55-1/2 to recess for six weeks and reconvene in Baltimore. This marked the first and only time that a major party adjourned its convention and moved it from one city to another.

Reconvening in Baltimore in June, the delegates were faced with another sticky question: whether or not to seat the delegates who had bolted the Charleston convention. The majority report presented by the credentials committee reviewed each case individually and recommended that the bolting Southern delegates, except those from Alabama and Louisiana, be reseated. The minority report recommended that a larger majority of the withdrawing Charleston delegates be reseated. The minority report was defeated, 150 to 100-1/2. Ten more roll calls followed on various aspects of the credentials dispute, but they did not change the result of the first vote. *(Chart, p. 201)*

The convention vote on credentials produced a new walkout, involving the majority of delegates from Virginia, North Carolina, Tennessee, Maryland, Kentucky, Missouri, Arkansas, California and Oregon, and anti-Douglas delegates from Massachusetts. With the presidential balloting ready to resume, less than two-thirds of the original convention was present.

On the first ballot, Douglas received 173-1/2 of the 190-1/2 votes cast. On the second ballot, his total increased to 190-1/2, but it was obviously impossible for him to gain two-thirds (202) of the votes allocated (303). After the second roll call, a delegate moved that Douglas, having obtained a two-thirds majority of the votes cast, be declared the Democratic presidential nominee. The motion passed unanimously on a voice vote. *(Chart, p. 201)*

The convention left the selection of the vice presidential candidate to a caucus of the remaining Southern delegates. They chose Sen. Benjamin Fitzpatrick of Alabama, who received all 198-1/2 votes cast on the vice presidential roll call.

Shortly after the convention adjourned, Fitzpatrick declined the nomination. For the first time in American history, a national committee was called upon to fill a vacancy on the ticket. By a unanimous vote of committee members, the former governor of Georgia, Herschel V. Johnson, was chosen to be Douglas' running mate.

The Democratic platform, in addition to the controversial slavery plank, provided a reaffirmation of the 1856 platform, with its proposals for a limited federal government but an expansionist foreign policy. The 1860 platform added planks that continued the expansionist spirit, calling for the construction of a transcontinental railroad and acquisition of the island of Cuba.

Following are excerpts from the 1860 Democratic platform:

Slavery. Inasmuch as difference of opinion exists in the Democratic party as to the nature and extent of the powers of a territorial legislature, and as to the powers and duties of Congress, under the Constitution of the United States, over the institution of slavery within the Territories, *Resolved,* That the Democratic party will abide by the decision of the Supreme Court of the United States upon these questions of Constitutional law.

Transcontinental Railroad. That one of the necessities of the age, in a military, commercial, and postal point of view, is speedy communication between the Atlantic and Pacific States; and the Democratic party pledge such Constitutional Government aid as will insure the construction of a Railroad to the Pacific coast, at the earliest practicable period.

Cuba. That the Democratic party are in favor of the acquisition of the Island of Cuba on such terms as shall be honorable to ourselves and just to Spain.

Southern Democrats (Breckinridge Faction)

A small group of Southern delegates that bolted the Charleston convention met in Richmond, Va., in early June. They decided to delay action until after the resumed Democratic convention had concluded. In late June they met in Baltimore with bolters from the regular Democratic convention. There were representatives from 19 states among the more than 200 delegates attending, but most of

the 58 Northern delegates were officeholders in the Buchanan administration. Vice President John C. Breckinridge of Kentucky won the presidential nomination, and Sen. Joseph Lane of Oregon was chosen as his running mate.

The platform adopted by the Southern Democrats was similar to the one approved by the Democratic convention at Charleston. The bolters reaffirmed the Democrats' 1856 platform, which called for the construction of a transcontinental railroad and acquisition of Cuba. But on the controversial slavery issue, the rump assemblage adopted the Southerners' plank defeated at the Charleston convention. The failure to reach agreement on this one issue, the most disruptive sectional split in the history of American political parties, presaged the Civil War.

Following are excerpts from the platform adopted by the Southern (or Breckinridge faction) Democrats in 1860:

Resolved, that the platform adopted by the Democratic party at Cincinnati be affirmed, with the following explanatory resolutions:

1. That the Government of a Territory organized by an act of Congress is provisional and temporary, and during its existence all citizens of the United States have an equal right to settle with their property in the Territory, without their rights, either of person or property, being destroyed or impaired by Congressional or Territorial legislation.

2. That it is the duty of the Federal Government, in all its departments, to protect, when necessary, the rights of persons and property in the Territories, and wherever else its constitutional authority extends.

Republicans

With their major opposition split along sectional lines, the Republicans gathered for their convention in Chicago in a mood of optimism. The Democrats had already broken up at Charleston before the Republican delegates convened in May 1860.

The call for the convention was addressed not only to faithful party members but to other groups that shared the Republicans' dissatisfaction with the policies of the Buchanan administration. The call to the convention particularly emphasized the party's opposition to any extension of slavery into the territories.

Delegates from all the Northern states and the territories of Kansas and Nebraska, the District of Columbia, and the slave states of Maryland, Delaware, Virginia, Kentucky, Missouri and Texas assembled at Chicago's new 10,000-seat convention hall, known as the Wigwam. A carnival-like atmosphere enveloped Chicago, with bands marching through the streets and thousands of enthusiastic Republicans ringing the overcrowded convention hall.

Inside, the delegates' first debate concerned the credentials report. The question was raised whether the represented Southern states should be allocated votes reflecting their electoral college strength, when there were very few Republicans in these states. By a vote of 275-1/2 to 171-1/2, the convention recommitted the credentials report for the purpose of scaling down the vote allocation of the Southern states.

A second debate arose over what constituted a nominating majority. The rules committee recommended that the nominating majority reflect the total electoral vote of all the states in the Union. The minority report argued that, since all the states were not represented, the nominating majority suggested by the rules committee would in fact require nearly a two-thirds majority. The minority report recommended instead that nominations be based on a simple majority of votes allocated for the states represented. The minority report passed, 349-1/2 to 88-1/2.

Sen. William H. Seward of New York was the front-runner for the presidential nomination and led on the first ballot. Seward received 173-1/2 votes to lead runner-up Abraham Lincoln of Illinois, who had 102. Sen. Simon Cameron of Pennsylvania followed with 50-1/2 votes, Salmon P. Chase of Ohio with 49 and Edward Bates of Missouri with 48. *(Chart, p. 202)*

With the packed galleries cheering their native son, Lincoln closed the gap on the second roll call. After two ballots, the voting stood: Seward, 184-1/2; Lincoln, 181; Chase, 42-1/2; Bates, 35. Lincoln, who had gained national prominence two years earlier as a result of his debates on slavery with Democrat Stephen A. Douglas in the 1858 campaign for the U.S. Senate, emerged as the candidate of the anti-Seward forces. On the third ballot, he won the nomination. When the third roll call was completed, Lincoln's vote total stood at 231-1/2, 1-1/2 votes short of a majority. But Ohio quickly shifted four votes to Lincoln, giving him the nomination. After changes by other states, the final vote was Lincoln, 340; Seward, 121-1/2.

The primary contenders for the vice presidential nomination were Sen. Hannibal Hamlin of Maine and Cassius M. Clay of Kentucky. Hamlin assumed a strong lead on the first ballot, receiving 194 votes to 100-1/2 for Clay. On the second roll call, an increased vote for Hamlin from states in his native New England created a bandwagon for the Maine senator. Hamlin won the nomination on the second ballot with 367 votes, far outdistancing Clay, who received 86. After the roll call was completed, Hamlin's nomination was declared unanimous.

About half of the platform adopted by the Republican convention dealt with the slavery question. Unlike the Democrats, the Republicans clearly opposed the extension of slavery into the territories. However, the Republican platform also expressed support for states' rights, which served as a rebuke to radical abolitionism.

The Republican and Democratic platforms again were opposed on the question of internal improvements. The Republicans supported river and harbor improvements, while the Democrats, by reaffirming their 1856 platform, opposed any federal support for internal improvements. Both parties favored construction of a transcontinental railroad and opposed restrictions on immigration.

However, on two major issues, the Republicans went beyond the Democrats, advocating a protective tariff and homestead legislation.

Following are excerpts from the 1860 Republican platform:

Slavery. That the new dogma that the Constitution, of its own force, carries slavery into any or all of the territories of the United States, is a dangerous political heresy, at variance with the explicit provisions of that instrument itself, with contemporaneous exposition, and with legislative and judicial precedent; is revolutionary in its tendency, and subversive of the peace and harmony of the country.

That the normal condition of all the territory of the United States is that of freedom.... we deny the authority of Congress, of a territorial legislature, or of any individuals, to give legal existence to slavery in any territory of the United States.

States' Rights. That the maintenance inviolate of the rights of the states, and especially the right of each state to order and control its own domestic institutions according to its own judgment exclusively, is essential to that balance of powers on which the perfection and endurance of our political fabric depends; and we denounce the lawless invasion by armed force of the soil of any state or territory, no matter under what pretext, as among the gravest of crimes.

Tariff. That, while providing revenue for the support of the general government by duties upon imports, sound policy requires such an adjustment of these imports as to encourage the development of the industrial interests of the whole country.

Transcontinental Railroad. That a railroad to the Pacific Ocean is imperatively demanded by the interests of the whole country; that the federal government ought to render immediate and efficient aid in its construction; and that, as preliminary thereto, a daily overland mail should be promptly established.

Constitutional Union

At the invitation of a group of Southern Know-Nothing congressmen, the remnants of the 1856 Fillmore campaign, conservative Whigs and Know-Nothings, met in Baltimore in May 1860 to form the Constitutional Union Party.

The chief rivals for the presidential nomination were former Sen. John Bell of Tennessee and Gov. Sam Houston of Texas. Bell won on the second ballot, and Edward Everett of Massachusetts was selected as his running mate.

The Constitutional Union Party saw itself as a national unifying force in a time of crisis. The brief platform did not discuss issues, instead denouncing the sectionalism of the existing parties and calling for national unity.

Following are excerpts from the 1860 Constitutional Union platform:

Whereas, Experience has demonstrated that Platforms adopted by the partisan Conventions of the country have had the effect to mislead and deceive the people, and at the same time to widen the political divisions of the country, by the creation and encouragement of geographical and sectional parties; therefore

Resolved, that it is both the part of patriotism and of duty to *recognize* no political principle other than THE CONSTITUTION OF THE COUNTRY, THE UNION OF THE STATES, AND THE ENFORCEMENT OF THE LAWS.

1864 Conventions
Presidential Candidates

Abraham Lincoln
Republican

George McClellan
Democrat

Republicans (Union Party)

Although elements in the Republican Party were dissatisfied with the conduct of the Civil War, President Lincoln was in firm control of his party's convention, which met in Baltimore in June 1864. As with previous Republican conventions, the call was not limited to the party faithful. Democrats in support of the Lincoln war policy were encouraged to attend, and the name "Union Party" was used to describe the wartime coalition.

Delegates were present from all the Northern states, the territories, the District of Columbia and the slave states of Arkansas, Florida, Louisiana, Tennessee, South Carolina and Virginia. Credentials disputes occupied the early sessions. The credentials committee recommended that all the Southern states except South Carolina be admitted, but denied the right to vote. A minority report, advocating voting privileges for the Tennessee delegation, was passed, 310 to 151. A second minority report favoring voting privileges for Arkansas and Louisiana was approved, 307 to 167. However, the credentials committee recommendation that Florida and Virginia be denied voting rights, and South Carolina be excluded entirely, were accepted without a roll call.

Although dissatisfaction with the administration's war policy had spawned opposition to Lincoln, the boomlets for such presidential hopefuls as Treasury Secretary Salmon P. Chase petered out. The Lincoln forces controlled the convention, and the president was easily renominated on the first ballot. Lincoln received 494 of the 516 votes cast, losing only Missouri's 22 votes, which were committed to Gen. Ulysses S. Grant. After the roll call, Missouri moved that the vote be made unanimous. *(Chart, p. 203)*

Lincoln did not publicly declare his preference for a vice presidential running mate, leaving the selection to the convention. The main contenders included the incumbent vice president, Hannibal Hamlin of Maine; the former senator and military governor of Tennessee, Democrat Andrew Johnson; and former senator Daniel S. Dickinson of New York. Johnson led on the first ballot with 200 votes, followed by Hamlin with 150 and Dickinson with 108. After completion of the roll call, a switch to Johnson by the

Kentucky delegation ignited a surge to the Tennessean that delivered him 492 votes and the nomination.

The Republican (Union) platform was approved without debate. Unlike the Democrats, who criticized the war effort and called for a quick, negotiated peace, the Republicans favored a vigorous prosecution of the war until the South surrendered unconditionally. The Republicans called for the eradication of slavery, with its elimination embodied in a constitutional amendment.

Although the Republican document focused on the Civil War, it also included planks encouraging immigration, urging the speedy construction of a transcontinental railroad and reaffirming the Monroe Doctrine.

Following are excerpts from the Republican (Union) platform of 1864:

Resolved ... we pledge ourselves, as Union men, animated by a common sentiment and aiming at a common object, to do everything in our power to aid the Government in quelling by force of arms the Rebellion now raging against its authority, and in bringing to the punishment due to their crimes the Rebels and traitors arrayed against it.

Resolved, That we approve the determination of the Government of the United States not to compromise with Rebels, or to offer them any terms of peace, except such as may be based upon an unconditional surrender of their hostility and a return to their just allegiance to the Constitution and laws of the United States, and that we call upon the Government to maintain this position and to prosecute the war with the utmost possible vigor to the complete suppression of the Rebellion, in full reliance upon the self-sacrificing patriotism, the heroic valor and the undying devotion of the American people to the country and its free institutions.

Resolved, That as slavery was the cause, and now constitutes the strength of this Rebellion, and as it must be, always and everywhere, hostile to the principles of Republican Government, justice and the National safety demand its utter and complete extirpation from the soil of the Republic ... we are in favor, furthermore, of such an amendment to the Constitution, to be made by the people in conformity with its provisions, as shall terminate and forever prohibit the existence of Slavery within the limits of the jurisdiction of the United States.

Resolved, That the thanks of the American people are due to the soldiers and sailors of the Army and Navy, who have periled their lives in defense of the country and in vindication of the honor of its flag.

Democrats

The Democrats originally scheduled their convention for early summer but postponed it until late August to gauge the significance of military developments.

The party, badly split during the 1860 campaign, no longer had the Southern faction with which to contend. But while there was no longer a regional split, new divisions arose over the continuing war. There was a large peace faction, known as the Copperheads, that favored a quick, negotiated peace with the South. Another faction supported the war but criticized its handling by the Lincoln administration. A third faction supported Lincoln's conduct of the war and defected to support the Republican president.

Although factionalized, the Democratic delegates who assembled in Chicago were optimistic about their party's chances. The war-weary nation, they thought, was ready to vote out the Lincoln administration if there was not a quick change in Northern military fortunes.

Although the border states were represented at the Democratic convention, the territories and seceded Southern states were not. In spite of the party's internal divisions, there was little opposition to the presidential candidacy of Gen. George B. McClellan of New Jersey. The former commander of the Union Army won on the first ballot, receiving 174 of the 226 votes cast. Former governor Thomas H. Seymour of Connecticut trailed with 38 votes. A switch to McClellan by several Ohio delegates prompted shifts by other delegations and brought his total to 202-1/2. Clement Vallandigham, a leader of the Copperhead faction, moved that McClellan's nomination be made unanimous.

Eight candidates were placed in nomination for the vice presidency. James Guthrie of Kentucky led Rep. George H. Pendleton of Ohio, the favorite of the Copperheads, on the first ballot, 65-1/2 to 55. However, shifts to Pendleton by Illinois, Kentucky and New York after completion of the roll call created a bandwagon that led quickly to his unanimous nomination. In the convention hall at the time of his selection, Pendleton made a short speech of acceptance. *(Chart, p. 203)*

The platform adopted by the Democrats reflected the views of the Copperhead faction. The Lincoln administration's conduct of the Civil War was denounced, with particular criticism of the use of martial law and the abridgement of state and civil rights. The platform called for an immediate end to hostilities and a negotiated peace. The "sympathy" of the party was extended to soldiers and sailors involved in the war. Besides a criticism of the war and its conduct by the Lincoln administration, there were no other issues discussed in the platform.

Following are excerpts from the Democratic platform of 1864:

Resolved, That this convention does explicitly declare, as the sense of the American people, that after four years of failure to restore the Union by the experiment of war, during which, under the pretense of a military necessity of war-power higher than the Constitution, the Constitution itself has been disregarded in every part, and public liberty and private right alike trodden down, and the material prosperity of the country essentially impaired, justice, humanity, liberty, and the public welfare demand that immediate efforts be made for a cessation of hostilities, with a view of an ultimate convention of the States, or other peaceable means, to the end that, at the earliest practicable moment, peace may be restored on the basis of the Federal Union of the States.

Resolved, That the sympathy of the Democratic party is heartily and earnestly extended to the soldiery of our army and sailors of our navy, who are and have been in the field and on the sea under the flag of our country, and, in the events of its attaining power, they will receive all the care, protection, and regard that the brave soldiers and sailors of the republic have so nobly earned.

1868 Conventions
Presidential Candidates

Ulysses S. Grant
Republican

Horatio Seymour
Democrat

Republicans

The "National Union Republican Party," as the political organization was termed in its platform, held its first postwar convention in Chicago in May 1868. Delegations from the states of the old Confederacy were accepted; several included blacks.

The turbulent nature of postwar politics was evident in the fact that Gen. Ulysses S. Grant, the clear front-runner for the Republican nomination, had been considered a possible contender for the Democratic nomination barely a year earlier. Less than six months before the convention, the basically apolitical Grant had broken with Andrew Johnson, who had become president following the assassination of Abraham Lincoln in 1865.

Grant's was the only name placed in nomination, and on the ensuing roll call he received all 650 votes.

While the presidential race was cut and dried, the balloting for vice president was wide open, with 11 candidates receiving votes on the initial roll call. Sen. Benjamin F. Wade of Ohio led on the first ballot with 147 votes, followed by Gov. Reuben E. Fenton of New York with 126, Sen. Henry Wilson of Massachusetts with 119 and Speaker of the House Schuyler Colfax of Indiana with 115.

Over the next four ballots, Wade and Colfax were the front-runners, with Colfax finally moving ahead on the fifth ballot. His lead over Wade at this point was only 226 to 207, but numerous vote shifts after the roll call quickly pushed the Indiana representative over the top and gave him the nomination. After all the vote changes, Colfax's total stood at 541, followed by Fenton with 69 and Wade with 38.

Not surprisingly, the platform adopted by the Republicans differed sharply with the Democrats over reconstruction and Johnson's presidency. The Republican platform applauded the radical reconstruction program passed by Congress and denounced Johnson as "treacherous" and deserving of impeachment. The Republican platform approved of voting rights for black men in the South but determined that this was a subject for each state to decide in the rest of the nation.

The two parties also differed on their response to the currency question. While the Democrats favored a "soft-money" policy, the Republicans supported a continued "hard-money" approach, rejecting the Democratic proposal that the economic crisis could be eased by an increased supply of greenbacks.

Following are excerpts from the Republican platform of 1868:

Reconstruction. We congratulate the country on the assured success of the reconstruction policy of Congress, as evinced by the adoption, in the majority of the States lately in rebellion, of constitutions securing equal civil and political rights to all, and regard it as the duty of the Government to sustain those constitutions, and to prevent the people of such States from being remitted to a state of anarchy or military rule.

The guaranty by Congress of equal suffrage to all loyal men at the South was demanded by every consideration of public safety, of gratitude, and of justice, and must be maintained; while the question of suffrage in all the loyal States properly belongs to the people of those States.

President Andrew Johnson. We profoundly deplore the untimely and tragic death of Abraham Lincoln, and regret the accession of Andrew Johnson to the Presidency, who has acted treacherously to the people who elected him and the cause he was pledged to support; has usurped high legislative and judicial functions; has refused to execute the laws; has used his high office to induce other officers to ignore and violate the laws; has employed his executive powers to render insecure the property, the peace, the liberty, and life of the citizen; has abused the pardoning power; has denounced the National Legislature as unconstitutional; has persistently and corruptly resisted, by every means in his power, every proper attempt at the reconstruction of the States lately in rebellion; has perverted the public patronage into an engine of wholesale corruption; and has been justly impeached for high crimes and misdemeanors, and properly pronounced guilty thereof by the vote of thirty-five senators.

Currency. We denounce all forms of repudiation as a national crime; and national honor requires the payment of the public indebtedness in the utmost good faith to all creditors at home and abroad, not only according to the letter, but the spirit of the laws under which it was contracted.

Democrats

Reunited after the Civil War, the Democratic Party held its first postwar convention in New York's newly constructed Tammany Hall. It was no accident that convention proceedings began on July 4, 1868. The Democratic National Committee had set the date, and its chairman, August Belmont of New York, opened the first session with a harsh criticism of Republican reconstruction policy and the abridgement of civil rights.

Delegates from Southern states were voting members of the convention, but an effort to extend representation to the territories was defeated, 184 to 106.

Before the presidential balloting began, the convention chairman ruled that, as at the 1860 Charleston assembly, a nominating majority would be based on two-thirds of the total votes allocated (317) and not votes cast. On the opening ballot, the party's vice presidential candidate four years earlier, George H. Pendleton of Ohio, took the lead. Pendleton, although popular in the economically depressed Midwest because of his plan to inflate the currency by printing more greenbacks, had little appeal in the Eastern states. Nonetheless, he led on the first ballot with 105 votes. President Andrew Johnson was next, with 65 votes. Johnson's vote was largely complimentary and declined after the first roll call. Pendleton, however, showed increased strength, rising to a peak of 156-1/2 votes on the eighth ballot. But Pendleton's total was well short of the 212 votes required to nominate, and his total steadily decreased after the eighth roll call. *(Chart, p. 204)*

The collapse of the Pendleton and Johnson candidacies produced a boom for Gen. Winfield Scott Hancock of Pennsylvania. Opponents of Hancock attempted to break his surge by calling for adjournment after the 16th ballot. Although the move for adjournment was defeated, 174-1/2 to 142-1/2, the Hancock boom began to lose momentum. The Civil War general peaked at 144-1/2 votes on the 18th ballot, well short of a two-thirds majority.

With Hancock stymied, a new contender, Sen. Thomas A. Hendricks of Indiana, gained strength. Hendricks' vote rose to 132 on the 21st ballot, and the trend to the Indiana senator continued on the 22nd ballot until the roll call reached Ohio. However, Ohio shifted its entire vote to Horatio Seymour, the permanent chairman of the convention and a former governor of New York. Seymour declined to be a candidate, and so announced to the convention, but Ohio did not change its vote, and friends of Seymour hustled the reluctant candidate from the hall. The bandwagon had begun, and when the vote switches were completed, Seymour had received all 317 votes.

The vice presidential nomination went to Gen. Francis P. Blair Jr. of Missouri, a former Republican, who was unanimously selected on the first ballot. The names of several other candidates were placed in nomination, but the announcement of Blair's candidacy created a bandwagon that led to the withdrawal of the others.

The Democratic platform was accepted by a voice vote without debate. The platform began by declaring the questions of slavery and secession to be permanently settled by the Civil War. Several planks criticized the Republican reconstruction program, passed by the party's Radical wing in Congress. The Radicals themselves were scathingly denounced for their "unparalleled oppression and tyranny." The Democratic platform expressed its support for Andrew Johnson's conduct as president and decried the attempts to impeach him.

For the first time, the question of the coinage and printing of money was discussed in the party platform. Two planks were included that could be generally interpreted as supporting Pendleton's inflationary greenback plan.

On the tariff issue, the Democrats called for a tariff that would primarily raise revenue but also protect American industry.

Following are excerpts from the Democratic platform of 1868:

Reconstruction. . . .we arraign the Radical party for its disregard of right, and the unparalleled oppression and tyranny which have marked its career.

Instead of restoring the Union, it has, so far as in its power, dissolved it, and subjected ten States, in time of profound peace, to military despotism and negro supremacy.

President Andrew Johnson. That the President of the United States, Andrew Johnson, in exercising the power of his high office in resisting the aggressions of Congress upon the Constitutional rights of the States and the people, is entitled to the gratitude of the whole American people; and in behalf of the Democratic party, we tender him our thanks for his patriotic efforts in that regard.

Currency. . . .where the obligations of the government do not expressly state upon their face, or the law under which they were issued does not provide, that they shall be paid in coin, they ought, in right and in justice, to be paid in the lawful money of the United States. . . . One currency for the government and the people, the laborer and the office-holder, the pensioner and the soldier, the producer and the bond-holder.

1872 Conventions
Presidential Candidates

Horace Greeley
Liberal Republican, Democrat

Ulysses S. Grant
Republican

Liberal Republicans

The short-lived Liberal Republican Party grew out of grievances that elements in the Republican Party had with the policies of the Grant administration. There was particular dissatisfaction with the "carpetbag" governments in the South, support for extensive civil service reform and a general distaste for the corrupt administration of President Ulysses S. Grant.

The idea for the Liberal Republican movement originated in Missouri, where, in the 1870 state elections, a coalition of reform Republicans and Democrats swept to victory. In January 1872 a state convention of this new coalition issued the call for a national convention to be held that May in Cincinnati, Ohio.

Without a formal, nationwide organization, the delegate selection process was haphazard. Some of the delegates were self-appointed, but generally the size of each delegation reflected twice a state's electoral vote.

Three separate groups — reformers, anti-Grant politicians and a coalition of four influential newspaper editors known as "the Quadrilateral" — vied for control of the convention. For the presidential nomination, the reformers favored either Charles Francis Adams of Massachusetts or Sen. Lyman Trumbull of Illinois. The professional politicians were inclined to Supreme Court Justice David Davis of Illinois or Horace Greeley of New York. The newspaper editors opposed Davis.

On the first ballot, Adams led with 203 votes, followed by Greeley with 147, Trumbull with 110, Gov. B. Gratz Brown of Missouri with 95 and Davis with 92-1/2. After the roll call, Brown announced his withdrawal from the race and his support for Greeley. For the next five ballots, Greeley and Adams battled for the lead. But on the sixth ballot, the professional politicians were able to ignite a stampede for Greeley that resulted in his nomination.

Many of the reform-minded delegates, disgusted with the selection of the New York editor, left the convention. The vice presidential nomination went on the second ballot to a Greeley supporter, Gov. Brown of Missouri.

The platform adopted by the Liberal Republicans differed with the one later accepted by the Republicans on three main points: reconstruction, civil service reform and the tariff.

The Liberal Republicans called for an end to reconstruction with its "carpetbag" governments, a grant of universal amnesty to southern citizens and a return to home rule in the South. The Liberal Republicans sharply criticized the corruption of civil service under the Grant administration and labeled its reform one of the leading issues of the day. The civil service plank advocated a one-term limit on the presidency.

The presence of delegates supporting both protection and free trade led to a tariff plank that frankly stated the party's position on the issue should be left to local determination.

Following are excerpts from the Liberal Republican platform of 1872:

Reconstruction. We demand the immediate and absolute removal of all disabilities imposed on account of the Rebellion, which was finally subdued seven years ago, believing that universal amnesty will result in complete pacification in all sections of the country.

Local self-government, with impartial suffrage, will guard the rights of all citizens more securely than any centralized power. The public welfare requires the supremacy of the civil over the military authority, and freedom of person under the protection of the *habeas corpus.*

Civil Rights. We recognize the equality of all men before the law, and hold that it is the duty of Government in its dealings with the people to mete out equal and exact justice to all of whatever nativity, race, color, or persuasion, religious or political.

Civil Service Reform. The Civil Service of the Government has become a mere instrument of partisan tyranny and personal ambition and an object of selfish greed. It is a scandal and reproach upon free institutions and breeds a demoralization dangerous to the perpetuity of republican government. We therefore regard such thorough reforms of the Civil Service as one of the most pressing necessities of the hour; that honesty, capacity, and fidelity constitute the only valid claim to public employment; that the offices of the Government cease to be a matter of arbitrary favoritism and patronage, and that public station become again a post of honor. To this end it is imperatively required that no President shall be a candidate for re-election.

Tariff.. . . recognizing that there are in our midst honest but irreconcilable differences of opinion with regard to the respective systems of Protection and Free Trade, we remit the discussion of the subject to the people in their Congress Districts, and to the decision of Congress thereon, wholly free of Executive interference or dictation.

Homesteading. We are opposed to all further grants of lands to railroads or other corporations. The public domain should be held sacred to actual settlers.

Democrats

The Democratic convention that met in Baltimore in July 1872 was one of the most bizarre in American political history. In sessions totaling only six hours, the delegates endorsed the decisions on candidates and platform made at a convention one month earlier by the Liberal Republicans. The Democratic convention merely rubber-stamped the creation of a coalition of Liberal Republicans and the core of the Democratic Party. *(Chart, p. 206)*

This new coalition was established with little dissent. When it came time for the presidential balloting, nominating speeches were not allowed. On the subsequent roll call, Greeley, the nominee of the Liberal Republicans, received 686 of the allotted 732 votes. It was an ironic choice, because in earlier decades Greeley, as editor of *The New York Tribune,* had been a frequent critic of the Democratic Party. More than anything else, however, Greeley's selection underscored the lack of strong leadership in the post-Civil War Democratic Party.

In similar fashion, the convention endorsed the nomination of B. Gratz Brown for vice president. Brown, the governor of Missouri and the choice of the Liberal Republicans, was the early unanimous nominee of the Democrats, with 713 votes.

By a vote of 574 to 158, the delegates agreed to limit debate on the platform to one hour. Except for a brief introduction, the Democrats approved the same platform that had been adopted by the Liberal Republicans a month earlier. Key planks called for an end to reconstruction and complete amnesty for Southern citizens, a return to a federal government with limited powers, civil service reform and the halt of grants of public land to railroads and other corporations. Ironically, the platform also favored a hard-money policy, a reversal of the Democrats' soft-money stand in 1868. Although there was some objection to the point-by-point acceptance of the Liberal Republican platform, it was adopted by a vote of 671 to 62. *(For platform excerpts, see the Liberal Republicans section, p. 46)*

Republicans

With the reform wing of the Republican Party already having bolted, the remaining elements of the party gathered in relative harmony in Philadelphia in June 1872. President Ulysses S. Grant was renominated without opposition, receiving all 752 votes cast. *(Chart, p. 206)*

The only contest at the convention centered around the vice presidential nomination, with the incumbent, Schuyler Colfax of Indiana, and Sen. Henry Wilson of Massachusetts the two major rivals. Wilson took a slim plurality over Colfax on the first roll call, 364-1/2 to 321-1/2, but a vote shift by Virginia after completion of the roll gave Wilson the necessary majority with 399-1/2 votes.

Without debate or opposition, the platform was adopted. It lauded the 11 years of Republican rule, noting the success of reconstruction, the hard-money policy and the homestead program. A tariff plank called for a duty on imports to raise revenue as well as to protect American business.

The platform also included several progressive planks, including a recommendation that the franking privilege be abolished, an extension of rights to women and a call for federal and state legislation that would ensure equal rights for all races throughout the nation. The last plank was a significant change from the 1868 platform, which called for black suffrage in the South but left the decision on black voting rights to the individual states elsewhere.

Following are excerpts from the Republican platform of 1872:

Reconstruction. We hold that Congress and the President have only fulfilled an imperative duty in their measures for the suppression of violent and treasonable organizations in certain lately rebellious regions, and for the protection of the ballot-box, and therefore they are entitled to the thanks of the nation.

Civil Rights. Complete liberty and exact equality in the enjoyment of all civil, political, and public rights should be established and effectually maintained throughout the Union, by efficient and appropriate State and Federal legislation. Neither the law nor its administration should admit any discrimination in respect of citizens by reason of race, creed, color, or previous condition of servitude.

Civil Service Reform. Any system of the civil service under which the subordinate positions of the government are considered rewards for mere party zeal is fatally demoralizing, and we therefore favor a reform of the system by laws which shall abolish the evils of patronage, and make honesty, efficiency, and fidelity the essential qualifications for public positions, without practically creating a life-tenure of office.

Tariff.. . .revenue . . . should be raised by duties upon importations, the details of which should be so adjusted as to aid in securing remunerative wages to labor, and to promote the industries, prosperity, and growth of the whole country.

Homesteading. We are opposed to further grants of the public lands to corporations and monopolies, and demand that the national domain be set apart for free homes for the people.

Women's Rights. The Republican party is mindful of its obligations to the loyal women of America for their noble devotion to the cause of freedom. Their admission to wider fields of usefulness is viewed with satisfaction, and the honest demand of any class of citizens for additional rights should be treated with respectful consideration.

1876 Conventions

Presidential Candidates

Rutherford B. Hayes
Republican

Samuel J. Tilden
Democrat

Republicans

The Republican convention assembled in Cincinnati, Ohio, in mid-June 1876. The call to the convention extended the olive branch to the dissident Liberal Republicans, who in large measure had rejoined their original party.

One of the highlights of the early sessions was a speech by the prominent black leader Frederick Douglass, who lambasted the Republicans for freeing the slaves without providing means for their economic or physical security.

A dispute developed over the seating of two contesting Alabama delegations. It was a candidate-oriented dispute, with the majority report favoring a delegation strongly for House Speaker James G. Blaine of Maine. The minority report supported a delegation pledged to Sen. Oliver P. Morton of Indiana. In the subsequent roll call, the convention decided in favor of the Blaine delegation by a vote of 369 to 360.

The presidential race was contested by the champions of the three nearly equal wings of the party. The Radicals were led by senators Roscoe Conkling of New York and Morton; the Half-Breeds, by Blaine; and the reformers, by former treasury secretary Benjamin H. Bristow of Kentucky.

A fiery nominating speech for Blaine, delivered by Col. Robert G. Ingersoll, referred to the House Speaker as the "plumed knight," an appellation that stuck with Blaine the rest of his political career. Although it was a compelling speech, its effect was reduced by a failure in the hall's lighting system, which forced an early adjournment.

Nonetheless, when balloting commenced the next morning, Blaine had a wide lead, receiving 285 votes on the first ballot, compared with 124 for Morton, 113 for Bristow and 99 for Conkling. *(Chart, p. 208)*

In the middle of the second ballot, a procedural dispute arose over the legality of the unit rule. Three delegates in the Pennsylvania delegation wished to vote for another candidate and appealed to the chair. The chair ruled that their votes should be counted, even though Pennsylvania was bound by the state convention to vote as a unit. The ruling of the chair was upheld on a voice vote, but subsequent debate brought a roll call on reconsidering

the decision. The motion to reconsider passed, 381 to 359. However, by a margin of 395 to 353, another roll call upheld the power of the convention chairman to abolish the unit rule.

Although the vote had long-range significance for future Republican conventions, in the short run it provided a slight boost for Blaine, who gained several delegates in Pennsylvania. On the next four ballots, Blaine retained his large lead but could not come close to the necessary 379 votes needed for nomination. The only candidate to show increased strength was Gov. Rutherford B. Hayes of Ohio, who jumped from 68 votes on the fourth roll call to 104 on the fifth.

On the sixth ballot, however, Blaine showed renewed strength, rising to 308 votes, while Hayes assumed second place with 113. The House Speaker continued to gain on the seventh ballot, but the anti-Blaine forces quickly and successfully united behind Hayes. The Ohio governor, a viable compromise choice who had not alienated any of the party factions, won the nomination with 384 votes to 351 for Blaine.

Five candidates were placed in nomination for the vice presidency. However, Rep. William A. Wheeler of New York was so far in the lead that the roll call was suspended after South Carolina voted, and Wheeler was declared the nominee by acclamation.

Platform debate centered on the party's immigration plank. A Massachusetts delegate proposed deletion of the plank, which called for a congressional investigation of oriental immigration. The delegate argued that the plank was inconsistent with the Republican principle that favored the equality of all races. However, by a vote of 518 to 229, the plank was retained as written.

The Republican platform included a scathing denunciation of the Democratic Party, but only on the issues of currency and tariff was it markedly different from the opposition. The Republicans, unlike the Democrats, favored complete payment of Civil War bonds in hard money as quickly as possible. While the Democrats supported a tariff for revenue purposes only, the Republicans implied that the tariff should protect American industry as well as raise revenue.

As in past platforms, the Republicans called for the extension of civil rights, civil service reform, increased rights for women, the abolition of polygamy and the distribution of public land to homesteaders. A new plank proposed that a constitutional amendment be passed forbidding the use of federal funds for non-public schools.

Following are excerpts from the Republican platform of 1876:

Currency. In the first act of congress, signed by President Grant, the national government ... solemnly pledged its faith "to make provisions at the earliest practicable period, for the redemption of the United States notes in coin." Commercial prosperity, public morals, and the national credit demand that this promise be fulfilled by a continuous and steady progress to specie payment.

Tariff. The revenue necessary for current expenditures and the obligations of the public debt must be largely derived from duties upon importations, which, so far as possible, should be so adjusted as to promote the interests of American labor and advance the prosperity of the whole country.

Immigration. It is the immediate duty of congress fully to investigate the effects of the immigration and importation of Mongolians on the moral and material interests of the country.

Education. The public school system of the several states is the bulwark of the American republic; and, with a view to its security and permanence, we recommend an amendment to the constitution of the United States, forbidding the application of any public funds or property for the benefit of any school or institution under sectarian control.

Democratic Party. We therefore note with deep solicitude that the Democratic party counts, as its chief hope of success, upon the electoral vote of a united South, secured through the efforts of those who were recently arrayed against the nation; and we invoke the earnest attention of the country to the grave truth, that a success thus achieved would reopen sectional strife and imperil national honor and human rights.

We charge the Democratic party with being the same in character and spirit as when it sympathized with treason; with making its control of the house of representatives the triumph and opportunity of the nation's recent foes; with reasserting and applauding in the national capitol the sentiments of unrepentant rebellion; with sending Union soldiers to the rear, and promoting Confederate soldiers to the front; with deliberately proposing to repudiate the plighted faith of the government; with being equally false and imbecile upon the over-shadowing financial question; with thwarting the ends of justice, by its partisan mismanagements and obstruction of investigation; with proving itself, through the period of its ascendency in the lower house of Congress, utterly incompetent to administer the government; — and we warn the country against trusting a party thus alike unworthy, recreant, and incapable.

Democrats

America's rapid westward expansion was typified by the site of the Democratic Party's 1876 convention — St. Louis, Mo. It marked the first time that a national convention was held west of the Mississippi River.

The Democratic delegates assembled in late June. The one procedural matter debated was a proposal that the two-thirds rule be abolished at the 1880 convention and that the Democratic National Committee include such a recommendation in its next convention call. A move to table the proposal was defeated, 379 to 359. However, the national committee took no action on the proposal.

Two governors, Samuel J. Tilden of New York and Thomas A. Hendricks of Indiana, were the principal contenders for the presidential nomination, with Tilden having a substantial lead in delegates as the convention opened. Ironically, Tilden's most vocal opposition came from his own New York delegation, where John Kelly of Tammany Hall spearheaded an effort to undermine Tilden's candidacy. Tilden's reform moves as governor had alienated Tammany Hall, and several times during the convention, Kelly took the floor to denounce Tilden.

Nonetheless, Tilden had a substantial lead on the first ballot, receiving 401-1/2 votes to 140-1/2 for Hendricks. Although short of the 492 votes needed to nominate, Tilden moved closer when Missouri switched its votes to him after the first roll call. The movement to Tilden continued on the second ballot, and he finished the roll call with 535 votes, more than enough to ensure his nomination. *(Chart, p. 207)*

Hendricks, the runner-up for the presidential nomination, was the nearly unanimous choice of the delegates for the vice presidency. Hendricks received 730 votes, with the other eight votes not being cast.

The Democratic platform was an unusual one. Rather than being arranged in usual fashion with a series of numbered planks, it was written in paragraph form in language unusually powerful for a party platform. The theme of the document was the need for reform, and nearly half the paragraphs began with the phrase, "Reform is necessary...."

Debate focused on the party's stand on the currency issue. The majority report proposed repeal of the Resumption Act of 1875, a hard-money measure that called for the payment of Civil War bonds in coin. A minority report sponsored by delegates from five eastern states proposing deletion of this position was defeated, 550 to 219. A second minority report, introduced by Midwestern delegates, favored a more strongly worded opposition to the Resumption Act. It too was defeated, 505 to 229, with Midwestern delegations providing the bulk of the minority vote. The platform as a whole was approved, 651 to 83, again with most of the dissenting votes coming from the Midwest.

Besides the currency proposal, the platform called for extensive civil service reform, a tariff for revenue purposes only, restrictions on Chinese immigration and a new policy on the distribution of public land that would benefit the homesteaders and not the railroads. In addition to its reform theme, the platform was filled with sharp criticisms of Republican rule.

Following are excerpts from the Democratic platform of 1876:

Civil Service Reform. Reform is necessary in the civil service. Experience proves that efficient economical conduct of the government is not possible if its civil service be subject to change at every election, be a prize fought for at the ballot-box, be an approved reward of party zeal instead of posts of honor assigned for proved competency and held for fidelity in the public employ; that the dispensing of patronage should neither be a tax upon the time of our public men nor an instrument of their ambition. Here again, profession falsified in the performance attest that the party in power can work out no practical or salutary reform. Reform is necessary even more in the higher grades of the public service. President, Vice-President, judges, senators, representatives, cabinet officers — these and all others in authority are the people's servants. Their offices are not a private perquisite; they are a public trust. When the annals of this Republic show disgrace and censure of a Vice-

President; a late Speaker of the House of Representatives marketing his rulings as a presiding officer; three Senators profiting secretly by their votes as law-makers; five chairmen of the leading committees of the late House of Representatives exposed in jobbery; a late Secretary of the Treasury forcing balances in the public accounts; a late Attorney-General misappropriating public funds; a Secretary of the Navy enriched and enriching friends by a percentage levied off the profits of contractors with his department; an Ambassador to England censured in a dishonorable speculation; the President's Private Secretary barely escaping conviction upon trial for guilty complicity in frauds upon the revenue; a Secretary of War impeached for high crimes and misdemeanors — the demonstration is complete, that the first step in reform must be the people's choice of honest men from another party, lest the disease of one political organization infect the body politic, and lest by making no change of men or parties, we get no change of measures and no real reform.

Currency. We denounce the improvidence which, in eleven years of peace, has taken from the people in Federal taxes thirteen times the whole amount of the legal-tender notes and squandered four times their sum in useless expense, without accumulating any reserve for their redemption. We denounce the financial imbecility and immorality of that party, which, during eleven years of peace, has made no advance toward resumption, no preparation for resumption, but instead has obstructed resumption by wasting our resources and exhausting all our surplus income, and while annually professing to intend a speedy return to specie payments, has annually enacted fresh hindrances thereto. As such hindrance we denounce the resumption clause of the act of 1875 and we here demand its repeal.

Tariff. We denounce the present tariff levied upon nearly four thousand articles as a masterpiece of injustice, inequality and false pretense, which yields a dwindling and not a yearly rising revenue, has impoverished many industries to subsidize a few.... We demand that all custom-house taxation shall be only for revenue.

Homesteading. Reform is necessary to put a stop to the profligate waste of public lands and their diversion from actual settlers by the party in power, which has squandered two hundred millions of acres upon railroads alone, and out of more than thrice that aggregate has disposed of less than a sixth directly to the tillers of the soil.

Immigration. ... we denounce the policy which thus discards the liberty-loving German and tolerates the revival of the coolie-trade in Mongolian women for immoral purposes, and Mongolian men held to perform servile labor contracts, and demand such modification of the treaty with the Chinese Empire, or such legislation within constitutional limitations, as shall prevent further importation or immigration of the Mongolian race.

1880 Conventions

Presidential Candidates

James A. Garfield
Republican

James B. Weaver
Greenback

Winfield Hancock
Democrat

Republicans

The Republicans gathered in Chicago beginning June 2, 1880, for their seventh quadrennial nominating convention. For the first time, the convention call was addressed only to Republicans and not more broadly to others who sympathized with party principles.

The convention was divided into two factions. One, headed by Sen. Roscoe Conkling of New York, favored the nomination of former president Ulysses S. Grant for a third term. The anti-Grant faction, although not united around one candidate, included the eventual nominee, Rep. James A. Garfield of Ohio, among its leaders.

Pre-convention skirmishing focused on the selection of a temporary chairman. The Grant forces desired one from their own ranks who would uphold the unit rule — a rule important to Grant, because he had the support of a majority of delegates in several large states. However, the Grant strategy was blocked, and a temporary chairman neutral to both sides was chosen by the Republican National Committee, leaving the ultimate decision on the unit rule to the convention.

A test of strength between the two factions came early in the convention on an amended motion by Conkling directing the credentials committee to report to the convention prior to the rules committee. Conkling's amended motion was defeated, 406 to 318.

In spite of the defeat of the amended motion, much time was spent debating delegate credentials. More than 50 cases were presented in committee, and seven of them came to the floor for a vote. Five of the cases featured seating disputes among delegates selected in district caucuses and those chosen for the same seats in state conventions. In each case — involving delegates from the states of Illinois, Kansas and West Virginia — the convention supported the claim of the delegates elected at the district level.

The Illinois credentials fight produced the only candidate-oriented division, with the Grant forces favoring the seating of the delegates selected at the state convention. But by a margin of 387 to 353, the convention voted to seat the delegates selected in the district caucuses. Three other votes were taken on disputed credentials from different Illinois districts, but all were decided in favor of the anti-Grant forces by a similar margin. *(Chart, p. 210)*

The majority report of the rules committee advocated that the controversial unit rule not be used. A motion by the Grant forces that the presidential nominations begin without passage of the rules committee report was defeated, 479 to 276. The vote was a key setback for the supporters of the former president, as the majority report was subsequently adopted by acclamation.

While the Grant forces suffered defeat on adoption of the unit rule, their candidate assumed the lead on the first ballot for president, with 304 votes. Sen. James G. Blaine of Maine followed closely with 284, and Treasury Secretary John Sherman of Ohio, the candidate nominated by Rep. Garfield, trailed with 93 votes.

Ballot after ballot was taken throughout the day, but after the 28th roll call, the last of the night, there was little change in the vote totals of the leading candidates. Grant led with 307 votes; Blaine had 279, and Sherman, 91.

When balloting resumed the next morning, Sherman's vote total jumped to 116, the biggest gain among the contenders, but still well behind Grant and Blaine. Grant gained votes on the 34th ballot, rising to a new high of 312, but on the same roll call a boom for Garfield began, with the Ohio representative collecting 16 votes from Wisconsin. Garfield protested that he was not a candidate but was ruled out of order by the chairman.

The Ohio representative continued to gain on the 35th ballot, his vote total rising to 50. On the next ballot, Garfield won the nomination, receiving the votes of nearly all the anti-Grant delegates. At the end of the roll call, Garfield had 399 votes; Grant, 306, and Blaine, 42, with nine votes distributed among other candidates.

Four men were placed in nomination for the vice presidency, but Chester A. Arthur of New York was the easy winner on the first ballot. Arthur, the former collector of the port of New York, received 468 votes to 193 for former representative Elihu B. Washburne of Illinois. Most of Arthur's support came from delegates who had backed Grant.

The Republican platform was passed by a voice vote without debate. For the first time, the platform included planks that clearly called for the exercise of federal power, emphasizing that the Constitution was "a supreme law, and not a mere contract." This philosophy contrasted with the Democratic platform, which favored home rule and government decentralization.

The two parties also differed on the tariff issue. The Republicans favored a revenue tariff that would also protect American industry, while the Democrats explicitly called for a revenue tariff only.

In its original form, the Republican platform did not include a civil service plank. An amendment from the floor, however, calling for a "thorough, radical and complete" reform of the civil service, was passed by a voice vote.

Following are excerpts from the Republican platform of 1880:

Federal Power. The Constitution of the United States is a supreme law, and not a mere contract. Out of confederated States it made a sovereign nation. Some powers are denied to the Nation, while others are denied to the States; but the boundary between the powers delegated and those reserved is to be determined by the National and not by the State tribunal.

The work of popular education is one left to the care of the several States, but it is the duty of the National Government to aid that work to the extent of its constitutional power. The intelligence of the Nation is but the aggregate of the intelligence in the several States, and the destiny of the Nation must be guided, not by the genius of any one State, but by the aggregate genius of all.

Tariff. We affirm the belief, avowed in 1876, that the duties levied for the purpose of revenue should so discriminate as to favor American labor....

Civil Service Reform. The Republican party, ... adopts the declaration of President Hayes that the reform of the civil service should be thorough, radical and complete.

Chinese Immigration. ... the Republican party, regarding the unrestricted immigration of the Chinese as a matter of grave concernment ... would limit and restrict that immigration by the enactment of such just, humane and reasonable laws and treaties as will produce that result.

Greenback Party

A coalition of farmer and labor groups met in Chicago beginning June 9, 1880, to hold the second national Greenback Party convention. The party's first convention was held four years earlier, but it was not until 1880 that the Greenback Party received more than 2 percent of the popular vote. The party held its third and final convention four years later, but was unable in 1884 to attain 2 percent of the popular vote.

The 1880 convention attracted representatives of the various Greenback Party factions, as well as 44 delegates from the Socialist Labor Party. Rep. James B. Weaver of Iowa was nominated for the presidency, and B. J. Chambers of Texas was chosen as his running mate.

The platform adopted was far broader than the one conceived by the Greenbacks at their first convention in 1876. That year they focused solely on the currency issue. For the agrarian interests, currency planks remained that called for the unlimited coinage of silver and gold and the issuance of currency by the federal government and not private banks. Also adopted for the farm elements were planks advocating increased public land for settlers, denouncing large monopolies and proposing that Congress control passenger and freight rates.

Included for the labor groups were proposals for an eight-hour day, the abolition of child labor, the improvement of working conditions and the curtailment of Chinese immigration.

The Greenback platform also included planks that favored a graduated income tax and women's suffrage.

Following are excerpts from the Greenback platform of 1880:

Currency. ... All money, whether metallic or paper, should be issued and its volume controlled by the Government, and not by or through banking corporations, and when so issued should be a full legal-tender for all debts, public and private.

That the bonds of the United States should not be refunded, but paid as rapidly as practicable, according to contract. To enable the Government to meet these obligations, legal-tender currency should be substituted for the notes of the National banks, the National banking system abolished, and the unlimited coinage of silver, as well as gold, established by law.

Labor. That labor should be so protected by National and State authority as to equalize the burdens and insure a just distribution of its results; the eight-hour law of Congress should be enforced, the sanitary condition of industrial establishments placed under rigid control; the competition of contract labor abolished, a bureau of labor statistics established, factories, mines, and workshops inspected, the employment of children under fourteen years of age forbidden, and wages paid in cash.

Chinese Immigration. Slavery being simply cheap labor, and cheap labor being simple slavery, the importation and presence of Chinese serfs necessarily tends to brutalize and degrade American labor.

Homesteading. Railroad and land grants forfeited by reason of non-fulfillment of contract should be immediately reclaimed by the Government, and henceforth the public domain reserved exclusively as homes for actual settlers.

Regulation of Monopolies. It is the duty of Congress to regulate inter-state commerce. All lines of communication and transportation should be brought under such legislative control as shall secure moderate, fair and uniform rates for passenger and freight traffic.

We denounce as destructive to prosperity and dangerous to liberty, the action of the old parties in fostering and sustaining gigantic land, railroad, and money corporations and monopolies, invested with, and exercising powers belonging to the Government, and yet not responsible to it for the manner of their exercise.

Income Tax. All property should bear its just proportion of taxation, and we demand a graduated income tax.

Women's Suffrage. That every citizen of due age, sound mind, and not a felon, be fully enfranchised, and that this resolution be referred to the States, with recommendation for their favorable consideration.

Democrats

The Democrats held their 13th quadrennial nominating convention in Cincinnati, Ohio, in late June 1880. Credentials disputes enlivened the early sessions, with two competing New York delegations the focus of attention. The challenging group, controlled by Tammany Hall, requested 20 of New York's 70 votes. But by a margin of 457 to 205-1/2, the convention refused the request.

Samuel J. Tilden, the Democratic standard-bearer in 1876 and the narrow loser in that controversial election, was not a candidate in 1880, although he did not officially notify his supporters of this fact until the presidential balloting had begun. Tilden's indecision, however, had long before opened the door for other prospective candidates.

On the first ballot, Gen. Winfield Scott Hancock of Pennsylvania, a candidate for the nomination in both 1868 and 1876, led with 171 votes, followed by Sen. Thomas F. Bayard of Delaware with 153-1/2 and former representative

Henry G. Payne of Ohio (who served as a stalking horse for the Tilden forces), with 81. *(Chart, p. 209)*

Tilden's declaration of non-candidacy was announced before the second ballot, and the Tilden forces shifted their strength to House Speaker Samuel J. Randall of Pennsylvania. Nonetheless, Hancock was the big gainer on the second ballot, his vote total jumping to 320. Randall followed with 128-1/2, and Bayard slipped to third place with 112. Although Hancock was well short of the 492 votes needed for nomination, Wisconsin began a string of vote switches to Hancock that resulted in the military leader's selection. After all the changes, Hancock received 705 of the 738 votes cast.

The vice presidential nomination went by acclamation to former representative William H. English of Indiana, the only candidate.

The platform was accepted without debate or opposition. Its style of short, sharp phrases contrasted with the 1876 platform, which was written in flowing sentences built around the theme of the necessity of reform.

The 1880 platform called for decentralization of the federal government with increased local government, currency based on hard money, a tariff for revenue only, civil service reform and an end to Chinese immigration. The platform saved its harshest language to describe the party's reaction to the controversial election of 1876, which it labeled "the great fraud."

Following are excerpts from the Democratic platform of 1880:

Government Centralization. Opposition to centralization and to that dangerous spirit of encroachment which tends to consolidate the powers of all departments in one, and thus to create whatever be the form of government, a real despotism. No sumptuary laws; separation of Church and State, for the good of each; common schools fostered and protected.

Currency. Home rule; honest money, consisting of gold and silver, and paper convertible into coin on demand.

Tariff. . . . a tariff for revenue only.

Civil Service Reform. We execrate the course of this administration in making places in the civil service a reward for political crime, and demand a reform by statute which shall make it forever impossible for a defeated candidate to bribe his way to the seat of the usurper by billeting villains upon the people.

Chinese Immigration. No more Chinese immigration, except for travel, education, and foreign commerce, and that even carefully guarded.

Election of 1876. The great fraud of 1876-77, by which, upon a false count of the electoral voters of two States, the candidate defeated at the polls was declared to be President, and for the first time in American history, the will of the people was set aside under a threat of military violence, struck a deadly blow at our system of representative government. The Democratic party, to preserve the country from the horrors of a civil war, submitted for the time in firm and patriotic faith that the people would punish this crime in 1880. This issue precedes and dwarfs every other. It imposes a more sacred duty upon the people of the Union than ever addressed the conscience of a nation of free men.

1884 Conventions

Presidential Candidates

James G. Blaine
Republican

Grover Cleveland
Democrat

Republicans

The Republicans gathered in Chicago in June 1884 for their convention. For the first time, the call to the convention prescribed how and when delegates should be selected, an effort to avoid the credentials disputes that had besieged the convention four years earlier.

The assassination of President James A. Garfield three years earlier had opened up the Republican presidential race, and the party war horse, James G. Blaine of Maine, emerged as the front-runner for the nomination. However, there was strong opposition to Blaine from several candidates, including the incumbent president, Chester A. Arthur of New York.

The first test between the two sides was over the choice of a temporary chairman. The Blaine forces supported former senator Powell Clayton of Arkansas, while the anti-Blaine coalition favored a black delegate from Mississippi, John R. Lynch. Lynch won by a vote of 424 to 384. *(Chart, p. 212)*

A motion by the Blaine forces to adjourn after the presidential nominating speeches was also beaten, 412 to 391. But on the first ballot Blaine assumed the lead with 334-1/2 votes, followed by President Arthur with 278 and Sen. George F. Edmunds of Vermont with 93. Most of Arthur's strength was in the South, where the administration's patronage power had great effect.

Blaine gained votes on the next two ballots, his total rising to 375 on the third ballot, while Arthur dropped slightly to 274. After this roll call, the anti-Blaine forces tried to force adjournment but were defeated, 458 to 356. On the fourth ballot, Blaine received the nomination, winning 541 votes to 207 for Arthur and 41 for Edmunds.

Sen. John A. Logan of Illinois was the only person placed in nomination for vice president. Logan, who earlier had been in contention for the presidential nomination, received 779 of the 820 votes in the convention for second place on the ticket.

The party platform was adopted without dissent, and on major issues was little different from the planks presented by the Democrats. The Republicans proposed a tariff that would both protect American industry and raise revenue, called for civil service reform, advocated restric-

tions on Chinese immigration and favored increased availability of public lands for settlers. In addition, the Republicans adopted features of the Greenback Party platform, calling for government regulation of railroads and an eight-hour work day.

Following are excerpts from the Republican platform of 1884:

Tariff. We . . . demand that the imposition of duties on foreign imports shall be made, not "for revenue only," but that in raising the requisite revenues for the government, such duties shall be so levied as to afford security to our diversified industries and protection to the rights and wages of the laborer; to the end that active and intelligent labor, as well as capital, may have its just reward, and the laboring man his full share in the national prosperity.

Chinese Immigration. . . . . we denounce the importation of contract labor, whether from Europe or Asia, as an offense against the spirit of American institutions; and we pledge ourselves to sustain the present law restricting Chinese immigration, and to provide such further legislation as is necessary to carry out its purposes.

Labor. We favor the establishment of a national bureau of labor; the enforcement of the eight hour law.

Regulation of Railroads. The principle of public regulation of railway corporations is a wise and salutary one for the protection of all classes of the people; and we favor legislation that shall prevent unjust discrimination and excessive charges for transportation, and that shall secure to the people, and the railways alike, the fair and equal protection of the laws.

Democrats

The 1884 Democratic convention was held in Chicago in July. For the first time, the party extended delegate voting rights to the territories and the District of Columbia.

A debate over the unit rule highlighted the first day of the convention. Delegates from Tammany Hall, a minority of the New York delegation, presented an amendment to the temporary rules designed to abolish the unit rule. All the New York delegates were bound by their state convention to vote as a unit. However, the national convention defeated the amendment by a vote of 463 to 332, thus limiting the power of the Tammany delegates.

A resolution was passed opening the position of party chairman to individuals who were not members of the Democratic National Committee. Another resolution, to eliminate the two-thirds rule at future conventions, was put to a vote, but the roll call was suspended when it became apparent the resolution would not pass.

Several peculiarities were evident during the presidential nominating speeches. Sen. Thomas A. Hendricks of Indiana, the favorite of the Hoosier delegation, nominated former senator Joseph E. McDonald as the state's favorite son in a speech listing attributes that easily could have described Hendricks. Two seconding speeches for Gov. Grover Cleveland of New York were delivered by Tammany delegates who actually used the time to denounce him.

In spite of the opposition within his own delegation, Cleveland was the front-runner for the nomination and had a big lead on the first ballot. Cleveland received 392 votes, easily outdistancing Sen. Thomas F. Bayard of Delaware, who had 170. Former senator Allen G. Thurman of Ohio was next, with 88. Hendricks received one vote but protested to the convention that he was not a candidate.

A boom for Hendricks was undertaken on the second ballot, with the Indiana delegation shifting its support from McDonald to Hendricks. However, Cleveland also gained and continued to hold a large lead over the rest of the field. After two roll calls, these vote totals stood: Cleveland, 475; Bayard, 151-1/2; Hendricks, 123-1/2; Thurman, 60. With the New York governor holding a majority of the vote, North Carolina switched to Cleveland, and this started a bandwagon that gave him the required two-thirds majority. After the shifts, Cleveland received 683 of the 820 votes in the convention. *(Chart, p. 211)*

Over the objections of the Indiana delegation, Hendricks was nominated for the vice presidency. The Indiana leaders were a bit upset that Hendricks did not receive the presidential nomination but did contribute to his nearly unanimous total for second place on the ticket. When the roll call was completed, Hendricks had received all but four votes.

The Democratic platform of 1884 was one of the longest documents adopted by the party in the 19th century. The platform was about 3,000 words long, with the first third devoted to a description of alleged Republican failures.

The platform straddled the increasingly important tariff issue. In 1880 the Democrats clearly favored a revenue tariff only, but the 1884 document called for both revenue and protection of American industry.

A minority report introduced by Benjamin F. Butler, former governor of Massachusetts, focused on the tariff issue. Butler advocated a duty on imports that would hit harder at luxury items and less on necessities than the tariff favored by the majority report and would ensure more protection for American labor. The minority report was defeated, 721-1/2 to 96-1/2.

Butler, a former Republican and, earlier in 1884, nominated for president by the Greenback and Anti-Monopoly parties, also introduced substitute planks on labor, monopoly, public corporations, currency and civil service reform. These other planks were defeated by a voice vote, and the platform as written was adopted by acclamation.

Following are excerpts from the Democratic platform of 1884:

Tariff. Knowing full well, ... that legislation affecting the operations of the people should be cautious and conservative in method, not in advance of public opinion, but reponsive to its demands, the Democratic party is pledged to revise the tariff in a spirit of fairness to all interests.

But in making reduction in taxes, it is not proposed to injure any domestic industries, but rather to promote their healthy growth. From the foundation of this Government, taxes collected at the Custom House have been the chief source of Federal Revenue. Such they must continue to be. Moreover, many industries have come to rely upon legislation for successful continuance, so that any change of law must be at every step regardful of the labor and capital thus involved. The process of reform must be subject in the execution to this plain dictate of justice....

Sufficient revenue to pay all the expenses of the Federal Government ... can be got, under our present system of taxation, from the custom house taxes on fewer imported articles, bearing heaviest on articles of luxury, and bearing lightest on articles of necessity.

Civil Liberties — Civil Service Reform. We oppose sumptuary laws which vex the citizen and interfere with individual liberty; we favor honest Civil Service Reform, and the compensation of all United States officers by fixed salaries; the separation of Church and State; and the diffusion of free education by common schools, so that every child in the land may be taught the rights and duties of citizenship.

Chinese Immigration. [W]e ... do not sanction the importation of foreign labor, or the admission of servile races, unfitted by habits, training, religion, or kindred, for absorption into the great body of our people, or for the citizenship which our laws confer. American civilization demands that against the immigration or importation of Mongolians to these shores our gates be closed.

1888 Conventions

Presidential Candidates

Clinton B. Fisk
Prohibitionist

Grover Cleveland
Democrat

Benjamin Harrison
Republican

Prohibition

The Prohibition Party held its fifth national convention in Indianapolis in late May 1888. The party had held conventions since the 1872 campaign, but not until 1888 did the Prohibitionists receive at least 2 percent of the popular vote. *(Prohibition Party, p. 273)*

The 1888 convention selected Clinton B. Fisk of New Jersey for president and John A. Brooks of Missouri as his running mate. While the platform focused on the need for prohibition, planks were included that covered other issues. The Prohibition Party favored a tariff that would both protect American industry and raise revenue, supported the extension of voting rights, favored immigration restrictions and proposed the abolition of polygamy.

Following are excerpts from the Prohibition Party platform of 1888:

Prohibition. That the manufacture, importation, exportation, transportation and sale of alcoholic beverages should be made public crimes, and prohibited as such.

Tariff. That an adequate public revenue being necessary, it may properly be raised by import duties; but import duties should be so reduced that no surplus shall be accumulated in the Treasury, and that the burdens of taxation shall be removed from foods, clothing and other comforts and necessaries of life, and imposed on such articles of import as will give protection both to the manufacturing employer and producing laborer against the competition of the world.

Democrats

When the Democratic convention assembled in St. Louis in early June 1888, the party, for the first time since the outset of the Civil War, was in control of the White House. There was no contest for the presidential nomination, with the incumbent, Grover Cleveland, renominated by acclamation. However, the death of Vice President Thomas A. Hendricks in 1885 left open the second place on the ticket.

Former senator Allen G. Thurman of Ohio was the favorite for the vice presidential nomination and won easily on the first ballot with 684 votes. Gov. Isaac P. Gray of

Indiana had 101 votes, and Gen. John C. Black of Illinois trailed with 36. After the nomination of the 75-year-old Thurman, red bandannas were strung up around the hall. The bandanna was Thurman's political symbol, used extensively in his public habit of pinching snuff.

The platform was adopted by acclamation. It reaffirmed the Democratic platform written four years earlier, but in addition lauded the policies of President Cleveland and the achievements of Democratic rule, opposed the existing protective tariff and supported legislation to modify it and proposed a reformation of tax laws. A plank introduced from the floor favoring Irish home rule was included in the platform.

Following are excerpts from the Democratic platform of 1888:

Tariff. The Democratic party of the United States, in National Convention assembled, renews the pledge of its fidelity to Democratic faith and reaffirms the platform adopted by its representatives in the Convention of 1884, and indorses the views expressed by President Cleveland in his last annual message to Congress as the correct interpretation of that platform upon the question of Tariff reduction; and also indorses the efforts of our Democratic Representatives in Congress to secure a reduction of excessive taxation....

Resolved, That this convention hereby indorses and recommends the early passage of the bill for the reduction of the revenue now pending in the House of Representatives.

Tax Reform. All unnecessary taxation is unjust taxation.... Every Democratic rule of governmental action is violated when through unnecessary taxation a vast sum of money, far beyond the needs of an economical administration, is drawn from the people and the channels of trade, and accumulated as a demoralizing surplus in the National Treasury.... The Democratic remedy is to enforce frugality in public expense and abolish needless taxation.

Federal Power. Chief among its principles of party faith are the maintenance of an indissoluble Union of free and indestructible States, now about to enter upon its second century of unexampled progress and renown; devotion to a plan of government regulated by a written Con-

stitution, strictly specifying every granted power and expressly reserving to the States or people the entire
ungranted residue of power.

Republicans

The Republicans assembled for their convention in
Chicago in late June 1888. Not only was the party out of
the White House for the first time since the Civil War, but
a perennial contender for the presidential nomination,
James G. Blaine, had taken himself out of the running.
Although this encouraged a number of candidates to seek
the nomination, none came near to mustering the needed
majority as the balloting for president began.

The 832 convention votes were distributed among 14
candidates, with Sen. John Sherman of Ohio leading the
field with 229 votes. Circuit Judge Walter Q. Gresham of
Indiana followed with 107 votes, while four other candidates received more than 70 votes. During the rest of the
day, two more ballots were taken, with little appreciable
change in the strength of the candidates. After the third
roll call, Sherman led with 244 votes, followed by Gresham
with 123 and former governor Russell A. Alger of Michigan
with 122.

The unexpected withdrawal from the race of Chauncey
Depew of New York, the favorite of that state's delegation,
prompted a call for adjournment after the third ballot. The
motion passed, 531 to 287.

When balloting resumed the next morning, the biggest
gainer was former Sen. Benjamin Harrison of Indiana. Although Sherman still held the lead with 235 votes on the
fourth ballot, Harrison's vote total had leaped from 94
votes on the third to 216 on the fourth. There was little
change on the fifth ballot, taken on a Saturday, and after
the roll call the delegates approved, 492 to 320, a motion to
adjourn until Monday. The motion was generally supported by delegates opposed to Harrison.

When the convention reconvened, both Sherman and
Harrison showed small gains — Sherman rising to 244
votes and Harrison to 231. On the next roll call, the seventh, Harrison took the lead for the first time, thanks
largely to a shift of votes from delegates previously holding
out for Blaine. Harrison led, 279 to 230, and the trend to
the Indianan accelerated to a bandwagon the next ballot.
Harrison easily achieved a majority on the eighth roll call,
winning 544 votes to 118 for Sherman.

Three individuals were placed in nomination for vice
president, but former representative Levi P. Morton of
New York was the runaway winner on the first ballot.
Morton received 592 votes to easily outdistance Rep. Wil-
liam Walter Phelps of New Jersey, 119 votes, and William
O. Bradley of Kentucky, 103.

The platform sharply differed from that of the Democrats on the important tariff issue, strongly supporting the
protective tariff and opposing the legislation favored by the

Democrats. Like the Democrats, the Republicans called for
a reduction in taxes, specifically recommending repeal of
taxes on tobacco and on alcohol used in the arts and for
mechanical purposes. In other areas, the Republicans favored the use of both gold and silver as currency, strongly
opposed the Mormon practice of polygamy and called for
veterans' pensions.

Following are excerpts from the Republican platform
of 1888:

Tariff. We are uncompromisingly in favor of the
American system of protection; we protest against its destruction as proposed by the President and his party. They
serve the interests of Europe; we will support the interests
of America. . . . The protective system must be maintained.
Its abandonment has always been followed by general
disaster to all interests, except those of the usurer and the
sheriff. We denounce the Mills bill as destructive to the
general business, the labor and the farming interests of the
country, and we heartily indorse the consistent and patriotic action of the Republican Representatives in Congress in
opposing its passage.

Tax Reform. The Republican party would effect all
needed reduction of the National revenue by repealing the
taxes upon tobacco, which are an annoyance and burden to
agriculture, and the tax upon spirits used in the arts, and
for mechanical purposes, and by such revision of the tariff
laws as will tend to check imports of such articles as are
produced by our people, the production of which gives
employment to our labor, and releases from import duties
those articles of foreign production (except luxuries), the
like of which cannot be produced at home. If there shall
remain a larger revenue than is requisite for the wants of
the government we favor the entire repeal of internal taxes
rather than the surrender of any part of our protective
system at the joint behests of the whiskey trusts and the
agents of foreign manufacturers.

Currency. The Republican party is in favor of the use
of both gold and silver as money, and condemns the policy
of the Democratic Administration in its efforts to demone-
tize silver.

Veterans' Benefits. The gratitude of the Nation to
the defenders of the Union cannot be measured by laws. . . .
We denounce the hostile spirit shown by President Cleveland in his numerous vetoes of measures for pension relief,
and the action of the Democratic House of Representatives
in refusing even a consideration of general pension legislation.

Polygamy. The political power of the Mormon
Church in the Territories as exercised in the past is a
menace to free institutions too dangerous to be longer
suffered. Therefore we pledge the Republican party to
appropriate legislation asserting the sovereignty of the
Nation in all Territories where the same is questioned, and
in furtherance of that end to place upon the statute books
legislation stringent enough to divorce the political from the
ecclesiastical power, and thus stamp out the attendant
wickedness of polygamy.

1892 Conventions

Presidential Candidates

Benjamin Harrison
Republican

Grover Cleveland
Democrat

James B. Weaver
Populist

Republicans

Although President Benjamin Harrison was unpopular with various elements in the Republican Party, administration forces were in control of the convention that assembled in early June 1892 in Minneapolis, Minn. A Harrison supporter, former representative William McKinley of Ohio, was elected without opposition as the convention's permanent chairman.

A question concerning the credentials of six Alabama delegates resulted in a protracted debate on whether the six delegates in question could vote on their own case. The situation was resolved when the Alabama delegates voluntarily abstained from voting. The minority report, which proposed seating the six Alabama delegates on the original roll, was defeated, 463 to 423-1/2, and the majority report was subsequently adopted, 476 to 365-1/2. The two votes were candidate-oriented, with the winning side in each case composed largely of Harrison voters.

Harrison's chances of renomination were so strong that two other possibilities, James G. Blaine and William McKinley, never publicly announced as candidates for the presidency. Harrison won easily on the first ballot, receiving 535-1/6 votes to 182-1/6 for Blaine and 182 for McKinley. McKinley was in the ironic position of presiding over the convention at the same time he was receiving votes on the presidential ballot. The Ohioan withdrew briefly as permanent chairman and moved that Harrison's nomination be made unanimous. The motion was withdrawn after objections but placed McKinley publicly on the Harrison bandwagon. *(Chart, p. 214)*

While the Republican Party had an incumbent vice president in Levi P. Morton, the New York delegation supported Whitelaw Reid, the former editor of *The New York Tribune* and ambassador to France. With Morton making little effort to retain his position, Reid was nominated by acclamation, the first time a Republican convention had dispensed with a roll call in choosing a member of its national ticket.

The platform was adopted by a voice vote, and on only two major issues did it differ from that of the Democrats. The Republicans supported a protective tariff, clearly diverging from the Democrats, who supported import duties for revenue only. The Republicans also included a plank that sympathized with the prohibition effort, while the Democrats announced their opposition "to all sumptuary laws."

Both parties favored a bimetallic currency, with gold and silver of equal value, and supported the construction of a canal across Nicaragua. In addition, the Republicans advocated an expansionist foreign policy.

Following are excerpts from the Republican platform of 1892:

Tariff. We reaffirm the American doctrine of protection. We call attention to its growth abroad. We maintain that the prosperous condition of our country is largely due to the wise revenue legislation of the Republican congress.

We believe that all articles which cannot be produced in the United States, except luxuries, should be admitted free of duty, and that on all imports coming into competition with the products of American labor, there should be levied duties equal to the difference between wages abroad and at home.

Currency. The American people, from tradition and interest, favor bi-metallism, and the Republican party demands the use of both gold and silver as standard money, with such restrictions and under such provisions, to be determined by legislation, as will secure the maintenance of the parity of values of the two metals so that the purchasing and debt-paying power of the dollar, whether of silver, gold, or paper, shall be at all times equal. The interests of the producers of the country, its farmers and its workingmen, demand that every dollar, paper or coin, issued by the government, shall be as good as any other.

Foreign Policy. We reaffirm our approval of the Monroe doctrine and believe in the achievement of the manifest destiny of the Republic in its broadest sense.

Central American Canal. The construction of the Nicaragua Canal is of the highest importance to the American people, both as a measure of National defense and to build up and maintain American commerce, and it should be controlled by the United States Government.

Prohibition. We sympathize with all wise and legitimate efforts to lessen and prevent the evils of intemperance and promote morality.

Democrats

One of the strangest conventions in party annals was held by the Democrats in Chicago in late June 1892. Much of the disturbance was due to stormy weather, with the accompanying noise and leaks in the roof frequently interrupting the proceedings. Inside the hall, the discomfort of the delegates was increased by the vocal opposition of 600 Tammany Hall workers to the renomination of former president Grover Cleveland of New York.

Although Cleveland was a solid favorite for renomination, he was opposed by his home state delegation. The Tammany forces engineered an early state convention that chose a delegation committed to Gov. David B. Hill. But in spite of the hostility of the New York delegation, Cleveland was able to win renomination on the first ballot, receiving 617-1/3 votes to 114 for Hill and 103 for Gov. Horace Boies of Iowa. *(Chart, p. 214)*

Four individuals were placed in nomination for the vice presidency, with Adlai E. Stevenson of Illinois assuming the lead on the first ballot. Stevenson, a former representative and later assistant postmaster general during Cleveland's first administration, led former governor Isaac P. Gray of Indiana, 402 to 343. After the first roll call was completed, Iowa switched to Stevenson, starting a bandwagon that led quickly to his nomination. After all the switches had been tallied, Stevenson was the winner with 652 votes, followed by Gray with 185.

The platform debate centered around the tariff plank. The plank, as originally written, straddled the issue. But a sharply worded substitute proposed from the floor, calling for a tariff for revenue only, passed easily, 564 to 342. The currency section called for stable money, with the coinage of both gold and silver in equal amounts. The platform also included a plank that called for the construction of a canal through Nicaragua.

Following are excerpts from the Democratic platform of 1892:

> **Tariff.** We denounce Republican protection as a fraud, a robbery of the great majority of the American people for the benefit of the few. We declare it to be a fundamental principle of the Democratic party that the Federal Government has no constitutional power to impose and collect tariff duties, except for the purpose of revenue only, and we demand that the collection of such taxes shall be limited to the necessities of the Government when honestly and economically administered.

> **Currency.** . . . We hold to the use of both gold and silver as the standard money of the country, and to the coinage of both gold and silver without discriminating against either metal or charge for mintage, but the dollar unit of coinage of both metals must be of equal intrinsic and exchangeable value, or be adjusted through international agreement or by such safeguards of legislation as shall insure the maintenance of the parity of the two metals and the equal power of every dollar at all times in the markets and in the payment of debts; and we demand that all paper currency shall be kept at par with and redeemable in such coin.

> **Central American Canal.** For purposes of national defense and the promotion of commerce between the States, we recognize the early construction of the Nicaragua Canal and its protection against foreign control as of great importance to the United States.

> **Prohibition.** We are opposed to all sumptuary laws, as an interference with the individual rights of the citizen.

> **Federal Power.** . . . we solemnly declare that the need of a return to these fundamental principles of free popular government, based on home rule and individual liberty, was never more urgent than now, when the tendency to centralize all power at the Federal capital has become a menace to the reserved rights of the States that strikes at the very roots of our Government under the Constitution as framed by the fathers of the Republic.

Prohibition

The Prohibition Party's sixth convention was held in Cincinnati in late June 1892 and nominated John Bidwell of California for president and James B. Cranfill of Texas as his running mate. While the Prohibition Party continued to run a national ticket through the 1972 election, 1892 marked the last year that the party received more than 2 percent of the popular vote.

Although beginning and ending with calls for prohibition, the 1892 platform as a whole was a reform-minded document, favoring women's suffrage and equal wages for women, an inflated currency and the nationalization of railroad, telegraph, and other public corporations.

Following are excerpts from the Prohibition platform of 1892:

> **Prohibition.** . . . We declare anew for the entire suppression of the manufacture, sale, importation, exportation and transportation of alcoholic liquors as a beverage by Federal and State legislation, and the full powers of Government should be exerted to secure this result. Any party that fails to recognize the dominant nature of this issue in American politics is undeserving of the support of the people.

> **Women's Rights.** No citizen should be denied the right to vote on account of sex, and equal labor should receive equal wages, without regard to sex.

> **Currency.** The money of the country should consist of gold, silver, and paper, and be issued by the General Government only, and in sufficient quantity to meet the demands of business and give full opportunity for the employment of labor. To this end an increase in the volume of money is demanded, and no individual or corporation should be allowed to make any profit through its issue. It should be made a legal tender for the payment of all debts, public and private. Its volume should be fixed at a definite sum per capita and made to increase with our increase in population.

> **Tariff.** Tariff should be levied only as a defense against foreign governments which levy tariff upon or bar out our products from their markets, revenue being incidental.

> **Government Nationalization.** Railroad, telegraph, and other public corporations should be controlled by the Government in the interest of the people.

People's Party (Populists)

The most successful of the 19th century farmer-labor coalitions was the People's Party, commonly known as the Populists, which formally organized as a political party at a convention in Cincinnati in May 1891. Further organization was accomplished at a convention in St. Louis the next February, from which emanated the call to the party's first national nominating convention, to be held that summer in Omaha, Neb. The election of 1892 was the only one in which the Populists received more than 2 percent of the national vote. Four years later the party endorsed the Democratic ticket, and from 1900 through 1908 the Populists ran separate tickets, but failed to receive 2 percent of the popular vote. *(People's Party-Populists, p. 271)*

The call to the 1892 convention specified procedures

for the selection of delegates and set the size of the convention at 1,776 delegates. Thirteen hundred to fourteen hundred delegates actually assembled in Omaha for the Populist convention, which opened July 2. The field for the presidential nomination was reduced by the death early in 1892 of Southern agrarian leader Leonidas L. Polk of North Carolina and the refusal of Judge Walter Q. Gresham of Indiana to seek the nomination. First place on the ticket went to former representative James B. Weaver of Iowa, who defeated Sen. James H. Kyle of South Dakota, 995 to 275.

James G. Field of Virginia won the vice presidential nomination over Ben Terrell of Texas by a vote of 733 to 554. The ticket bridged any sectional division, pairing a former Union general (Weaver) with a former Confederate major (Field).

On July 4 the delegates enthusiastically adopted the platform. It contained few ideas that were not contained in the earlier platforms of other farmer-labor parties. But the document adopted by the Populists brought these proposals together into one forcefully written platform. More than half the platform was devoted to the preamble, which demanded widespread reform and sharply criticized the two major parties. It attacked the Democrats and Republicans for waging "a sham battle over the tariff," while ignoring more important issues.

The remainder of the platform was divided into three major parts that discussed finance, transportation and land policy. The Populists proposed that the currency be inflated, with the unlimited coinage of silver and a substantial increase in the circulating medium to at least $50 per capita. The Populists' currency plank was sharply different from those of the two major parties, which favored a stable, bimetallic currency.

The Populists also went well beyond the two major parties in advocating the nationalization of the railroads and telegraph and telephone companies. Both the Populists and Democrats advocated land reform, although the proposals received greater emphasis in the Populist platform.

The Populists included a call for a graduated income tax and expanded government power.

Although not considered part of the platform, supplementary resolutions were passed that favored the initiative and referendum, a limit of one term for the president, the direct election of senators, the secret ballot and additional labor-oriented proposals that called for improvement in working conditions.

Following are excerpts from the Populist platform of 1892:

Preamble. The conditions which surround us best justify our co-operation; we meet in the midst of a nation brought to the verge of moral, political, and material ruin. Corruption dominates the ballot-box, the Legislatures, the Congress, and touches even the ermine of the bench. The people are demoralized; most of the states have been compelled to isolate the voters at the polling places to prevent universal intimidation and bribery. The newspapers are largely subsidized or muzzled, public opinion silenced, business prostrated, homes covered with mortgages, labor impoverished, and the land concentrating in the hands of capitalists. The urban workmen are denied the right to organize for self-protection; imported pauperized labor beats down their wages, a hireling standing army, unrecognized by our laws, is established to shoot them down, and they are rapidly degenerating into European conditions. The fruits of the toil of millions are boldly stolen to build up colossal fortunes for a few, unprecedented in the history of mankind; and the possessors of these, in turn despise the Republic and endanger liberty. From the same prolific womb of governmental injustice we breed the two great classes — tramps and millionaires....

We have witnessed for more than a quarter of a century the struggles of the two great political parties for power and plunder, while grievous wrongs have been inflicted upon the suffering people. We charge that the controlling influence dominating both these parties have permitted the existing dreadful conditions to develop without serious effort to prevent or restrain them. Neither do they now promise us any substantial reform. They have agreed together to ignore, in the coming campaign, every issue but one. They propose to drown the outcries of a plundered people with the uproar of a sham battle over the tariff, so that capitalists, corporations, national banks, rings, trusts, watered stock, the demonetization of silver and the oppressions of the usurers may all be lost sight of. They propose to sacrifice our homes, lives, and children on the altar of mammon; to destroy the multitude in order to secure corruption funds from the millionaires.

...We believe that the power of government — in other words, of the people — should be expanded (as in the case of the postal service) as rapidly and as far as the good sense of an intelligent people and the teachings of experience shall justify, to the end that oppression, injustice and poverty, shall eventually cease in the land.

While our sympathies as a party of reform are naturally upon the side of every proposition which will tend to make men intelligent, virtuous and temperate, we nevertheless regard these questions, important as they are, as secondary to the great issues now pressing for solution, and upon which not only our individual prosperity, but the very existence of free institutions depend; and we ask all men to first help us to determine whether we are to have a republic to administer, before we differ as to the conditions upon which it is to be administered, believing that the forces of reform this day organized will never cease to move forward, until every wrong is remedied, and equal rights and equal privileges securely established for all the men and women of this country.

Currency. We demand free and unlimited coinage of silver and gold at the present legal ratio of 16 to 1.

We demand that the amount of circulating medium be speedily increased to not less than $50 per capita.

We demand that postal savings banks be established by the government for the safe deposit of the earnings of the

---

Explanatory Note

This section on the history of party nominating conventions includes conventions for parties receiving at least 2 percent of the popular vote in the presidential election. The Socialist Party, for example, received at least 2 percent of the popular vote in 1904, 1908, 1912, 1916, 1920 and 1932; the Socialist Party conventions for these years are included in this section. The Socialist Party conventions for other years when the party received less than 2 percent of the vote are not included. (*Additional details on this section, p. 24*).

people and to facilitate exchange.

Transportation. Transportation being a means of exchange and a public necessity, the government should own and operate the railroads in the interest of the people. The telegraph and telephone, like the post office system, being a necessity for the transmission of news, should be owned and operated by the government in the interest of the people.

Land. The land, including all the natural sources of wealth, is the heritage of the people, and should not be monopolized for speculative purposes, and alien ownership of land should be prohibited. All land now held by railroad and other corporations in excess of their actual needs, and all lands now owned by aliens, should be reclaimed by the government and held for actual settlers only.

1896 Conventions

Presidential Candidates

William McKinley
Republican

William J. Bryan
Democrat

Republicans

The currency issue, which spawned several third-party efforts in the late 19th century, emerged as the dominant issue of contention between the Republican and Democratic parties in the campaign of 1896. The forces in favor of the gold standard were firmly in control of the Republican convention that was held in St. Louis in early June 1896.

Actually, the convention was less a forum for the discussion of issues than a showcase for the political acumen of Mark Hanna of Ohio. Hanna, William McKinley's campaign manager, had been intensely courting delegates across the country, especially in the South, for more than a year before the convention. Before the rap of the opening gavel, Hanna had amassed a majority of the delegates for the popular Ohio governor.

The first evidence of McKinley strength came on a credentials question. A minority report was introduced claiming the credentials committee had held hearings on only two of 160 cases and proposing that the committee resume hearings. A maneuver to squelch the minority report was made when a delegate moved to cut off debate. With the McKinley forces providing most of the majority, the motion passed, 551-1/2 to 359-1/2.

Four other candidates in addition to McKinley were in contention for the presidential nomination, but McKinley was the runaway winner on the first ballot. He received 661-1/2 votes to 84-1/2 for the runner-up, House Speaker Thomas B. Reed of Maine. *(Chart, p. 216)*

There were two serious contenders for the vice presidential nomination: Garret A. Hobart, a McKinley sup-

porter and former state legislator from New Jersey, and Henry Clay Evans, a former candidate for governor of Tennessee. Hobart won, winning 523-1/2 votes on the first ballot to 287-1/2 for Evans.

As at the Democratic convention, the platform debate centered around the currency issue. The gold forces, firmly in control of the Republican convention, produced a majority report that called for maintenance of the gold standard until the time when bimetallism could be effected by an international agreement. This plank did not satisfy the silver minority. Led by Sen. Henry M. Teller of Colorado, a minority plank was introduced favoring the unlimited coinage of silver and gold at the ratio of 16 to 1. Teller's plank, similar to the currency plank adopted later by the Democrats, was defeated, 818-1/2 to 105-1/2. A second roll call on adoption of the majority plank resulted in another decisive defeat for the silver forces. The majority plank carried, 812-1/2 to 110-1/2.

With the decisive defeat of the minority plank, Teller led a walkout by 24 silver delegates, including the entire Colorado and Idaho delegations and members of the Montana, South Dakota and Utah delegations. The rest of the platform was adopted by a voice vote.

The currency plank that caused the commotion was buried deep in the middle of the Republican platform. The document began with a denunciation of Democratic rule and proceeded into a discussion of the merits of a protective tariff. A tariff for revenue purposes only was advocated in the Democratic platform, but the issue in the Republican document was clearly considered to be of secondary importance.

The Republican platform was also distinguishable from that of the Democrats in recommending a more expansionistic foreign policy, proposing stricter immigration restrictions and, for the first time, specifically denouncing the practice of lynching.

Following are excerpts from the Republican platform of 1896:

Currency. The Republican party is unreservedly for sound money.... We are unalterably opposed to every measure calculated to debase our currency or impair the credit of our country. We are therefore opposed to the free coinage of silver, except by international agreement with the leading commercial nations of the earth, which agreement we pledge ourselves to promote, and until such agreement can be obtained the existing gold standard must be maintained.

Tariff. We renew and emphasize our allegiance to the policy of protection, as the bulwark of American industrial independence, and the foundation of American development and prosperity.... Protection and Reciprocity are twin measures of American policy and go hand in hand. Democratic rule has recklessly struck down both, and both must be re-established. Protection for what we produce; free admission for the necessaries of life which we do not produce; reciprocal agreement of mutual interests, which gain open markets for us in return for our open markets for others. Protection builds up domestic industry and trade and secures our own market for ourselves; reciprocity builds up foreign trade and finds an outlet for our surplus.

Foreign Policy. Our foreign policy should be at all times firm, vigorous and dignified, and all our interests in the western hemisphere should be carefully watched and guarded.

The Hawaiian Islands should be controlled by the United States, and no foreign power should be permitted to interfere with them. The Nicaragua Canal should be built, owned and operated by the United States. And, by the purchase of the Danish Islands we should secure a much needed Naval station in the West Indies.... We therefore, favor the continued enlargement of the navy, and a complete system of harbor and sea-coast defenses.

Immigration. For the protection of the equality of our American citizenship and of the wages of our workingmen, against the fatal competition of low priced labor, we demand that the immigration laws be thoroughly enforced, and so extended as to exclude from entrance to the United States those who can neither read nor write.

Lynching. We proclaim our unqualified condemnation of the uncivilized and preposterous [barbarous] practice well known as lynching, and the killing of human beings suspected or charged with crime without process of law.

Democrats

The Democratic convention that assembled in Chicago in July 1896 was dominated by one issue — currency. A delegate's viewpoint on this single issue influenced his position on every vote taken. Generally, the party was split along regional lines, with Eastern delegations favoring a hard-money policy with maintenance of the gold standard, and most Southern and Western delegations supporting a soft-money policy with the unlimited coinage of silver.

Division in the convention was apparent on the first day, when the silver forces challenged the national committee's selection of Gov. David B. Hill of New York as temporary chairman. The pro-silver delegates put up Sen. John W. Daniel of Virginia for the post, and Daniel won easily, 556 to 349. His victory indicated the dominance of the

silver forces and presaged their ability to control the convention.

Two sets of credentials challenges were next on the agenda. By a voice vote, the convention agreed to seat a Nebraska delegation headed by a young silver supporter, William Jennings Bryan. And, by a vote of 558 to 368, the convention defeated a recommendation to seat Michigan delegates supported by the hard-money-dominated national committee.

With their lack of strength apparent, the gold forces declined to run a candidate for president. However, the silver delegates could not initially coalesce behind one candidate, and 14 individuals received votes on the first ballot. Rep. Richard P. "Silver Dick" Bland of Missouri was the pacesetter, with 235 votes, followed by Bryan, a former House member, with 137 and Robert E. Pattison, former Pennsylvania governor, with 97. Bryan, 36 years old, earlier had electrified the convention during the platform debate on currency, with his memorable "Cross of Gold" speech, which had elevated him to the position of a major contender. *(Chart, p. 215)*

On the next two roll calls, both candidates showed gains. Bland's total climbed to 291 on the third ballot and Bryan's rose to 219. Bryan continued to gain on the next ballot and assumed the lead over Bland, 280 to 241. The movement to Bryan accelerated on the fifth ballot, and he won the nomination easily, receiving 652 of the 930 convention votes. Although Bryan was the nearly unanimous choice of the silver forces, 162 gold delegates indicated their dissatisfaction with the proceedings by refusing to vote.

With Bryan declining to indicate a preference for vice president, 16 candidates received votes for the office on the first ballot. The Nebraska delegation, following Bryan's example, declined to participate in the vice-presidential balloting.

Former representative John C. Sibley of Pennsylvania took the lead on the first ballot with 163 votes, followed by Ohio editor and publisher John R. McLean with 111, and Maine shipbuilder Arthur Sewall with 100.

Bland spurted into the lead on the second ballot with 294 votes, followed by McLean and Sibley. After the roll call, Sibley withdrew, and on the third ballot the race between Bland and McLean tightened. The Missourian led, 255 to 210, but he too withdrew after the roll call. Sewall emerged as McLean's major competitor on the fourth ballot, and with the withdrawal of the Ohio journalist from the race, the nomination was Sewall's on the fifth ballot. Actually, Sewall's vote total of 602 on the final roll call was less than two-thirds of the convention vote, but with 251 disgruntled gold delegates refusing to vote, the required majority was reduced to only those voting.

Not surprisingly, the platform debate centered around the currency plank. The Eastern delegations proposed that, until silver coinage could be arranged by international agreement, the gold standard should be maintained. The Southern and Western delegations countered by demanding that the unlimited coinage of silver should begin without requiring a delay to reach an international agreement. Bryan managed the platform debate for the silver forces and scheduled himself as the final speaker, an enviable position from which to make a deep impression on the emotion-packed convention.

Bryan made the most of his opportunity, ending his dramatic speech with the famous peroration: "You shall not press down upon the brow of labor this crown of thorns, you shall not crucify mankind upon a cross of gold." The gold plank was defeated, 626 to 303. Although the speech was a key factor in Bryan's nomination, it was not influential in defeating the gold plank, which was already doomed to defeat. *(Chart, p. 215)*

A resolution commending the Cleveland administration was also defeated, 564 to 357, and after several attempts to modify the currency plank were rejected by voice votes, the platform as a whole was adopted, 622 to 307.

Following are excerpts from the Democratic platform of 1896:

Currency. We demand the free and unlimited coinage of both silver and gold at the present legal ratio of 16 to 1 without waiting for the aid or consent of any other nation.

Railroads. The absorption of wealth by the few, the consolidation of our leading railroad systems, and the formation of trusts and pools require a stricter control by the Federal Government of those arteries of commerce. We demand the enlargement of the powers of the Interstate

Commerce Commission and such restriction and guarantees in the control of railroads as will protect the people from robbery and oppression.

No Third Term. We declare it to be the unwritten law of this Republic, established by custom and usage of 100 years, and sanctioned by the examples of the greatest and wisest of those who founded and have maintained our Government that no man should be eligible for a third term of the Presidential office.

Federal Power. During all these years the Democratic Party has resisted the tendency of selfish interests to the centralization of governmental power, and steadfastly maintained the integrity of the dual scheme of government established by the founders of this Republic of republics. Under its guidance and teachings the great principle of local self-government has found its best expression in the maintenance of the rights of the States and in its assertion of the necessity of confining the general government to the exercise of the powers granted by the Constitution of the United States.

1900 Conventions

Presidential Candidates

William McKinley
Republican

William J. Bryan
Democrat

Republicans

Surface harmony was the hallmark of the Republican conclave held in Philadelphia in June 1900. The Colorado delegation, which had walked out of the 1896 convention, was honored by having one of its members, Sen. Edward O. Wolcott, chosen as temporary chairman.

There was no opposition to President William McKinley, and he won all 926 votes on the first roll call. However, the death of Vice President Garret A. Hobart in 1899 had left the second spot on the ticket open. McKinley did not have a preference and asked his campaign manager, Mark Hanna, not to influence the convention. McKinley's hands-off policy worked to the advantage of the popular governor of New York and hero of the Spanish-American War, Theodore Roosevelt, whom Hanna disliked. *(Chart, p. 217)*

Roosevelt's popularity, coupled with the desire of New York boss Thomas C. Platt to eliminate a powerful state rival, enabled the 41-year-old governor to clinch the nomination before balloting began. On the vice presidential roll call, Roosevelt received all but one vote. The single uncast vote came from Roosevelt's New York delegation, which

cast 71 of its 72 votes for Roosevelt.

The Republicans adopted a platform that applauded the four years of Republican rule and credited McKinley's policies with improving business conditions and winning the Spanish-American War. The platform defended postwar expansionism and called for increased foreign trade and the creation of a Department of Commerce.

As in 1896, the Republican platform opposed the unlimited coinage of silver and supported maintenance of the gold standard. On the tariff issue, the Republicans continued to laud the protective duty on imports.

Following are excerpts from the Republican platform of 1900:

Foreign Trade, Panama Canal. We favor the construction, ownership, control and protection of an Isthmian Canal by the Government of the United States. New markets are necessary for the increasing surplus of our farm products. Every effort should be made to open and obtain new markets, especially in the Orient, and the Administration is warmly to be commended for its successful efforts to commit all trading and colonizing nations to the policy of the open door in China.

International Expansion. In accepting by the Treaty of Paris the just responsibility of our victories in the Spanish war, the President and the Senate won the undoubted approval of the American people. No other course was possible than to destroy Spain's sovereignty throughout the West Indies and in the Philippine Islands. That course created our responsibility before the world, and with the unorganized population whom our intervention had freed from Spain, to provide for the maintenance of law and order, and for the establishment of good government and for the performance of international obligations. Our authority could not be less than our responsibility; and whenever sovereign rights were extended it became the high duty of the Government to maintain its authority, to put down armed insurrection and to confer the blessings of liberty and civilization upon all the rescued peoples.

Antitrust. We recognize the necessity and propriety of the honest co-operation of capital to meet new business conditions and especially to extend our rapidly increasing foreign trade, but we condemn all conspiracies and combinations intended to restrict business, to create monopolies, to limit production, or to control prices; and favor such legislation as will effectively restrain and prevent all such abuses, protect and promote competition and secure the rights of producers, laborers, and all who are engaged in industry and commerce.

Currency. We renew our allegiance to the principle of the gold standard and declare our confidence in the wisdom of the legislation of the Fifty-sixth Congress, by which the parity of all our money and the stability of our currency upon a gold basis has been secured....

We declare our steadfast opposition to the free and unlimited coinage of silver.

Tariff. We renew our faith in the policy of Protection to American labor. In that policy our industries have been established, diversified and maintained. By protecting the home market competition has been stimulated and production cheapened.

Democrats

The Democrats opened their 1900 convention in Kansas City, Mo., on July 4, and showed a degree of party harmony not evident at their convention four years earlier. After the party factionalism of 1896, the delegates made a conscious effort to display a unified front — an effort aided by the decline of the controversial silver issue. The discovery of new gold deposits in North America and the subsequent increase in currency had lessened the divisive impact of the silver issue.

William Jennings Bryan, the Democratic standard-bearer in 1896, was renominated without opposition, receiving all 936 votes. The harmony in the convention was evident when former New York senator David B. Hill, a leader of the gold forces four years earlier, gave a seconding speech for Bryan. *(Chart, p. 217)*

Seven names were placed in nomination for the vice presidency. However, two withdrew before the balloting began. Adlai E. Stevenson of Illinois, vice president under Grover Cleveland, led on the first roll call with 559-1/2 votes, followed by Hill, who received 200 votes in spite of withdrawing from the race before the voting started. After completion of the ballot, a series of vote switches resulted in Stevenson's unanimous nomination.

The platform was adopted without floor debate. The major theme of the document was anti-imperialism, although an attack on trusts and a discussion of the currency question also were emphasized.

The anti-imperialism section was placed at the begin-

ning of the platform and was labeled the most important issue of the campaign. The delegates enthusiastically accepted the plank, which forcefully criticized American international expansion after the Spanish-American War. The platform asserted "that no nation can long endure half republic and half empire" and denounced increasing U.S. militarism. The Democratic position sharply differed from the one advocated by the Republicans, whose platform defended postwar expansionism.

After the anti-imperialism section was a sharp attack on monopolies, the most detailed antitrust section that had yet appeared in a Democratic platform. The plank called for more comprehensive antitrust legislation and more rigid enforcement of the laws already enacted. Although the Republicans also condemned monopolies, the issue received a mere one-sentence mention in their platform.

With the decline of the silver issue, the necessity of a pro-silver plank was a matter of debate in the resolutions committee. However, Bryan threatened to withdraw his candidacy if a plank calling for the unlimited coinage of silver was not included in the platform. By a majority of one vote, the resolutions committee included the silver plank, and it was accepted without dissent by the convention. The Democratic position set up another distinction with the Republicans, who, as four years earlier, favored maintenance of the gold standard.

In addition to the anti-imperialism, antitrust and currency sections of the platform, the Democrats proposed the creation of a Department of Labor, favored the direct election of senators and, unlike the Republicans, supported the construction and ownership of a Nicaraguan canal. The Republican platform advocated construction and ownership of a canal across the Isthmus of Panama.

Following are excerpts from the Democratic platform of 1900:

Anti-imperialism. We hold that the Constitution follows the flag, and denounce the doctrine that an Executive or Congress deriving their existence and their powers from the Constitution can exercise lawful authority beyond it or in violation of it. We assert that no nation can long endure half republic and half empire, and we warn the American people that imperialism abroad will lead quickly and inevitably to despotism at home....

We are not opposed to territorial expansion when it takes in desirable territory which can be erected into States in the Union, and whose people are willing and fit to become American citizens. We favor trade expansion by every peaceful and legitimate means. But we are unalterably opposed to seizing or purchasing distant islands to be governed outside the Constitution, and whose people can never become citizens....

The importance of other questions, now pending before the American people is no wise diminished and the Democratic party takes no backward step from its position on them, but the burning issue of imperialism growing out of the Spanish war involves the very existence of the Republic and the destruction of our free institutions. We regard it as the paramount issue of the campaign....

We oppose militarism. It means conquest abroad and intimidation and oppression at home. It means the strong arm which has ever been fatal to free institutions.... This republic has no place for a vast military establishment, a sure forerunner of compulsory military service and conscription. When the nation is in danger the volunteer soldier is his country's best defender.

Antitrust. We pledge the Democratic party to an unceasing warfare in nation, State and city against private monopoly in every form. Existing laws against trusts must be enforced and more stringent ones must be enacted....

Tariff laws should be amended by putting the products of trusts upon the free list, to prevent monopoly under the plea of protection.

Currency. We reaffirm and indorse the principles of the National Democratic Platform adopted at Chicago in 1896, and we reiterate the demand of that platform for an American financial system made by the American people for themselves, and which shall restore and maintain a bimetallic price-level, and as part of such system the immediate restoration of the free and unlimited coinage of silver and gold at the present legal ratio of 16 to 1, without waiting for the aid or consent of any other nation.

1904 Conventions

Presidential Candidates

Eugene V. Debs
Socialist

Theodore Roosevelt
Republican

Alton B. Parker
Democrat

Socialists

The Socialist Party held its first national nominating convention in Chicago in early May 1904 and nominated Eugene V. Debs of Indiana for president and Benjamin Hanford of New York as his running mate. Debs ran in 1900 as the presidential candidate of two socialist groups, the Social Democratic Party and a moderate faction of the Socialist Labor Party.

The bulk of the platform was devoted to the philosophy of the international Socialist movement, with its belief in the eventual demise of capitalism and the ultimate achievement of a classless, worker-oriented society. To hasten the creation of a Socialist society, the platform favored many reforms advocated by the Populists and earlier agrarian-labor movements: the initiative, referendum and recall; women's suffrage; tax reform, including the graduated income tax; the public ownership of transportation, communication and exchange; and various labor benefits, including higher wages and shorter hours.

Following are excerpts from the Socialist platform of 1904:

> To the end that the workers may seize every possible advantage that may strengthen them to gain complete control of the powers of government, and thereby the sooner establish the cooperative commonwealth, the Socialist Party pledges itself to watch and work, in both the economic and the political struggle, for each successive immediate interest of the working class; for shortened days of labor and increases of wages; for the insurance of the workers against accident, sickness and lack of employment; for pensions for aged and exhausted workers; for the public ownership of the means of transportation, communication and exchange; for the graduated taxation of incomes, inheritances, franchises and land values, the proceeds to be applied to the public employment and improvement of the conditions of the workers; for the complete education of children, and their freedom from the workshop; for the prevention of the use of the military against labor in the settlement of strikes; for the free administration of justice; for popular government, including initiative, referendum, proportional representation, equal suffrage of men and women, municipal home rule, and the recall of officers by their constituents; and for every gain or advantage for the workers that may be wrested from the capitalist system, and that may relieve the suffering and strengthen the hands of labor. We lay upon every man elected to any executive or legislative office the first duty of striving to procure whatever is for the workers' most immediate interest, and for whatever will lessen the economic and political powers of the capitalist, and increase the like powers of the worker.

Republicans

President Theodore Roosevelt was totally in command of the Republican convention held in Chicago in June 1904. His most dangerous potential rival for the nomination, Sen. Mark Hanna of Ohio, had died in February, leaving the field clear for Roosevelt.

The rather trivial matter of most interest before the presidential balloting began was Hawaii's vote allocation. The rules committee recommended that the votes of the territory be reduced from six to two. A substitute amendment proposed that Hawaii retain its six votes for the 1904 convention but that its vote allocation be reviewed by the national committee for future conventions. The substitute was accepted by the narrow margin of 495 to 490.

Roosevelt's nomination caused less commotion. On the first ballot, he received all 994 votes. The party leadership favored Sen. Charles W. Fairbanks of Indiana for the vice presidency. Although the Georgia, Illinois, Missouri and

Nebraska delegations noted that they preferred other candidates, Fairbanks was nominated by acclamation.

The party platform was adopted without dissent. In the document the Republicans charted little new ground, instead detailing the benefits of Republican rule and restating old positions. America's expansionistic foreign policy was praised, as was the protective tariff and the gold standard.

A display of Roosevelt theatrics followed the adoption of the platform. The convention chairman was instructed to read a message from the secretary of state to the American consul in Morocco: "We want either Perdicaris alive or Raisuli dead." The message referred to an alleged American citizen, Ion Perdicaris, who had been captured by the Moroccan chieftain, Raisuli. The American ultimatum read to the convention followed the dispatch of several ships to Morocco. The reading of the message roused the delegates, as it was no doubt intended to do.

Following are excerpts from the Republican platform in 1904:

Shipbuilding. We ... favor legislation which will encourage and build up the American merchant marine, and we cordially approve the legislation of the last Congress which created the Merchant Marine Commission to investigate and report upon this subject.

Monopoly. Combinations of capital and of labor are the results of the economic movement of the age, but neither must be permitted to infringe upon the rights and interests of the people. Such combinations, when lawfully formed for lawful purposes, are alike entitled to the protection of the laws, but both are subject to the laws and neither can be permitted to break them.

Democrats

William Jennings Bryan, after two unsuccessful campaigns for the presidency, was not a candidate for the Democratic nomination in 1904. However, he was present at the party's convention in St. Louis that July and was a prominent factor in the proceedings.

Bryan's first appearance before the convention came during a credentials dispute, featuring a challenge by Bryan supporters in Illinois to the state delegation approved by the credentials committee. Bryan spoke in behalf of his supporters, but their minority report was beaten, 647 to 299.

Bryan appeared again to second the presidential nomination of Sen. Francis M. Cockrell of Missouri, one of eight candidates nominated. Much of his speech, however, was devoted to criticizing the conservative front-runner, Alton B. Parker, chief justice of the New York Court of Appeals, while boosting more progressive candidates. In spite of Bryan's opposition, Parker came within nine votes of receiving the necessary two-thirds majority on the first ballot. Parker had 658 votes, followed by Rep. William Randolph Hearst of New York, with 200, and Cockrell, who trailed with 42. Although Hearst had progressive credentials, Bryan hesitated to support him and jeopardize his own leadership of the progressive wing of the party.

With Parker so close to victory, Idaho shifted its votes to the New York judge, prompting enough switches by other states to give Parker 679 votes and the nomination. Hearst, with his strength in the Middle West and West, finished with 181 votes. *(Chart, p. 218)*

With the nomination in hand, Parker stunned the convention by sending a telegram to the New York delega-

tion, announcing his support of the gold standard and advising the convention to select a new candidate if they found his position unacceptable. Parker supporters drafted a response stating that there was nothing to preclude his nomination, because the platform was silent on the currency issue.

Bryan, ill with a fever in his hotel but still a supporter of the silver cause, rose from his sickbed to join several Southern leaders on the floor of the convention in denouncing Parker's telegram and the drafted response. Nonetheless, the response recommended by the Parker forces was approved, 794 to 191, with opposition principally from the Middle West and West.

For vice president, the convention chose former West Virginia senator Henry G. Davis. He nearly achieved a two-thirds majority on the first ballot, receiving 654 votes. With Davis' nomination so near, a motion to declare him the vice presidential candidate was approved. Davis, at age 80, was the oldest candidate ever put on a national ticket by a major party. He was a man of great wealth, and the Democrats hoped that he would give freely to their campaign.

Although the platform was accepted without debate by a voice vote, there was maneuvering behind the scenes to meet the objections of Bryan. The initial platform draft before the resolutions committee included a plank that declared that recent gold discoveries had removed the currency question as a political issue. Bryan found this plank objectionable and successfully fought in the resolutions committee for its deletion. Bryan was less successful in having an income tax plank included but was able to get a more strongly worded antitrust resolution.

Unlike the Democratic platform of 1900, which focused on anti-imperialism, anti-monopoly and currency, the 1904 platform covered about two dozen topics with nearly equal emphasis.

The Democrats and Republicans disagreed on one new issue: federal support for private shipping firms. The Democrats opposed government assistance; the Republicans favored it. But on other issues the platform of the Democrats, like that of the Republicans, broke little new ground, instead restating positions that had been included in earlier Democratic platforms. There was a continued attack on American imperialism and a call for a smaller Army. There were planks that urged less international involvement and more emphasis on domestic improvements.

Following are excerpts from the Democratic platform of 1904:

Roosevelt Administration. The existing Republican administration has been spasmodic, erratic, sensational, spectacular and arbitrary. It has made itself a satire upon the Congress, courts, and upon the settled practices and usages of national and international law ... the necessity of reform and the rescue of the administration of Government from the headstrong, arbitrary and spasmodic methods which distract business by uncertainty, and pervade the public mind with dread, distrust and perturbation.

Shipbuilding. We denounce the ship subsidy bill recently passed by the United States Senate as an iniquitous appropriation of public funds for private purposes and a wasteful, illogical and useless attempt to overcome by subsidy the obstructions raised by Republican legislation to the growth and development of American commerce on the sea.

We favor the upbuilding of a merchant marine without new or additional burdens upon the people and without bounties from the public treasury.

1908 Conventions

Presidential Candidates

Eugene V. Debs
Socialist

William H. Taft
Republican

William J. Bryan
Democrat

Socialists

The Socialists met in Chicago in May 1908 and renominated the ticket that had represented the party four years earlier: Eugene V. Debs of Indiana for president and Benjamin Hanford of New York as his running mate.

The platform was divided into several major sections, including a discussion of principles, and topics entitled general demands, industrial demands and political demands. The Socialists' goal was the creation of a classless society, and in pursuance of this goal the movement was identified as a party of the working class.

Among the general demands were proposals for public works programs to aid the unemployed and public ownership of land, means of transportation and communication and monopolies.

Industrial demands included calls for reduced working hours, the abolition of child labor and more effective inspections of working areas.

The section on political demands began with a restatement of earlier positions, with a call for tax reform, women's suffrage and the initiative, referendum and recall. However, the section also included more radical demands, such as the abolition of the Senate, the amendment of the Constitution by popular vote, the direct election of all judges and the removal of power from the Supreme Court to declare legislation passed by Congress unconstitutional.

Following are excerpts from the Socialist platform of 1908:

Public Works Projects. The immediate government relief for the unemployed workers by building schools, by reforesting of cutover and waste lands, by reclamation of arid tracts, and the building of canals, and by extending all other useful public works. All persons employed on such works shall be employed directly by the government under an eight hour work day and at the prevailing union wages. The government shall also loan money to states and municipalities without interest for the purpose of carrying on public works. It shall contribute to the funds of labor organizations for the purpose of assisting their unemployed members, and shall take such other measures within its power as will lessen the widespread misery of the workers caused by the misrule of the capitalist class.

Public Ownership. The collective ownership of railroads, telegraphs, telephones, steamship lines and all other means of social transportation and communication, and all land.

The collective ownership of all industries which are organized on a national scale and in which competition has virtually ceased to exist.

Labor. The improvement of the industrial condition of the workers.

(a) By shortening the workday in keeping with the increased productiveness of machinery.

(b) By securing to every worker a rest period of not less than a day and a half in each week.

(c) By securing a more effective inspection of workshops and factories.

(d) By forbidding the employment of children under sixteen years of age.

(e) By forbidding the interstate transportation of the products of child labor, of convict labor and of all uninspected factories.

(f) By abolishing official charity and substituting in its place compulsory insurance against unemployment, illness, accident, invalidism, old age and death.

Tax Reform. The extension of inheritance taxes, graduated in proportion to the amount of the bequests and the nearness of kin.

A graduated income tax.

Women's Suffrage. Unrestricted and equal suffrage for men and women. . . .

Senate. The abolition of the senate.

Constitutional and Judicial Reforms. The abolition of the power usurped by the supreme court of the United States to pass upon the constitutionality of legislation enacted by Congress. National laws to be repealed or abrogated only by act of Congress or by a referendum of the whole people.

That the constitution be made amendable by majority vote.

That all judges be elected by the people for short terms, and that the power to issue injunctions shall be curbed by immediate legislation.

Republicans

The Republicans held their convention in Chicago in June 1908. Although President Roosevelt declined to be a candidate for re-election, his choice for the presidency, Secretary of War William Howard Taft, was assured of nomination before the convention began.

Two hundred and twenty-three of the 980 seats at the convention were contested, but all the challenges were settled before the convention assembled. However, a dispute arose over the vote-allocation formula for the next convention. An amendment to the rules committee report proposed that the vote allocation be based on population rather than the electoral vote, as was currently in effect. Essentially, the amendment would have reduced the power of the Southern delegations. But a combination of Southern delegates and Taft supporters from other states defeated the amendment, 506 to 471. *(Chart, p. 220)*

Seven names were placed in nomination for the presidency, but Taft was a landslide winner on the first ballot, receiving 702 votes. Sen. Philander C. Knox of Pennsylvania was a distant runner-up with 68 votes.

For vice president, the convention selected Rep. James S. Sherman, a conservative New Yorker. Sherman won 816 votes on the first ballot, easily outdistancing former New Jersey governor Franklin Murphy, who had 77 votes.

The Wisconsin delegation, led by Sen. Robert M. La Follette, introduced a detailed minority report to the party platform. The Wisconsin proposals were considered in several separate sections. The first section included proposals for the establishment of a permanent tariff commission, the creation of a Department of Labor and the limitation of an eight-hour day for government workers. It was defeated, 952 to 28.

The second section recommended legislation to require the publication of campaign contributions. It was defeated, 880 to 94. Further sections of the minority report proposed the physical valuation of railroad property to help determine reasonable rates, and the direct election of senators. The railroad reform plank was beaten, 917 to 63, while the senatorial election plank was rejected, 866 to 114. After these votes, the majority report on the platform was adopted by a voice vote.

The platform approved by the delegates applauded the benefits of Republican rule, noting that under the party's guidance the United States had become the wealthiest nation on Earth. The principle of a protective tariff was applauded, as was the gold standard, an expansionist foreign policy and support for America's merchant marine.

Following are excerpts from the Republican platform of 1908:

Party Differences. In history, the difference between Democracy and Republicanism is that the one stood for debased currency, the other for honest currency; the one for free silver, the other for sound money; the one for free trade, the other for protection; the one for the contraction of American influence, the other for its expansion; the one has been forced to abandon every position taken on the great issues before the people, the other has held and vindicated all.

The present tendencies of the two parties are even more marked by inherent differences. The trend of Democracy is toward socialism, while the Republican party stands for a wise and regulated individualism. . . . Ultimately Democracy would have the nation own the people, while Republicanism would have the people own the nation.

Democrats

The Democratic convention of 1908 was held in July in Denver, Colo. — the first convention held by a major party in a Western state. The convention was dominated by the Bryan forces, who regained control of the party after the conservative Alton B. Parker's landslide defeat in 1904.

Bryan's strength was evident on the first roll-call vote, concerning a Pennsylvania credentials dispute. The majority report claimed there were voting irregularities in five Philadelphia districts and urged the seating of Bryan delegates in place of those elected. By a vote of 604-1/2 to 386-1/2, the convention defeated the minority report, which argued for the delegates initially elected in the primary. The majority report then passed by a voice vote.

Bryan's presidential nomination was never in doubt. He was an easy winner on the first ballot, receiving 888-1/2 votes to 59-1/2 for Judge George Gray of Delaware and 46 for Gov. John A. Johnson of Minnesota. *(Chart, p. 219)*

Bryan left the choice of his running mate to the delegates. Although four names were placed in nomination, former Indiana gubernatorial candidate John W. Kern was chosen by acclamation. *The New York Times* sarcastically described the consistency of the Bryan-Kern ticket: "For a man twice defeated for the Presidency was at the head of it, and a man twice defeated for governor of his state was at the tail of it."

The platform adopted by the convention was tailored to Bryan's liking and had as its theme, "Shall the people rule?" The first portion of the document criticized Republican rule, specifically denouncing government overspending, a growing Republican-oriented bureaucracy and an unethical link between big business and the Republican Party characterized by large, unreported campaign contributions.

Meeting three weeks after the Republicans, the Democrats adopted most of the minority planks rejected earlier by the Republicans. Included in the Democratic platform were calls for the physical valuation of railroads, the creation of a Department of Labor, eight-hour work days for government employees, the direct election of senators and a prohibition against corporate campaign contributions and individual contributions over "a reasonable amount." The two parties continued to disagree on support of the American merchant marine, the nature of tariff revision and the direction of foreign policy, particularly regarding the lands acquired after the Spanish-American War.

The Democratic platform restated the party's support of a lower tariff, more extensive antitrust legislation with more rigid enforcement, a graduated income tax, increased power for the Interstate Commerce Commission to regulate railroads, telephone and telegraph companies, and a recommendation of prompt independence for the Philippines.

The Democrats included a plank abhorring Roosevelt's attempt to create a "dynasty," a direct reference to the outgoing president's hand-picking his war secretary, William Howard Taft, as the next Republican presidential candidate.

Following are excerpts from the Democratic platform of 1908:

Appeal to the Masses. The conscience of the nation is now aroused to free the Government from the grip of those who have made it a business asset of the favor-seeking corporations. It must become again a people's government, and be administered in all its departments according to the Jeffersonian maxim, "equal rights to all; special privileges to none."

"Shall the people rule?" is the overshadowing issue which manifests itself in all the questions now under discussion.

Campaign Contributions. We demand Federal legislation forever terminating the partnership which has existed between corporations of the country and the Republican party under the expressed or implied agreement that in return for the contribution of great sums of money wherewith to purchase elections, they should be allowed to continue substantially unmolested in their efforts to encroach upon the rights of the people....

We pledge the Democratic party to the enactment of a law prohibiting any corporation from contributing to a campaign fund and any individual from contributing an amount above a reasonable maximum, and providing for the publication before election of all such contributions.

Labor. Questions of judicial practice have arisen especially in connection with industrial disputes. We deem that the parties to all judicial proceedings should be treated with rigid impartiality, and that injunctions should not be issued in any cases in which injunctions would not issue if no industrial dispute were involved....

We favor the eight hour day on all Government work.

We pledge the Democratic party to the enactment of a law by Congress, as far as the Federal jurisdiction extends, for a general employer's liability act covering injury to body or loss of life of employes.

We pledge the Democratic party to the enactment of a law creating a Department of Labor, represented separately in the President's Cabinet, in which Department shall be included the subject of mines and mining.

1912 Conventions

Presidential Candidates

| Eugene V. Debs | William H. Taft | Woodrow Wilson | Theodore Roosevelt |
| Socialist | Republican | Democrat | Progressive |

Socialists

Eugene V. Debs of Indiana was nominated by the Socialists in 1912 to make his fourth run for the presidency. The convention, which met in Indianapolis in May, chose Emil Seidel of Wisconsin as his running mate.

The platform adopted by the Socialists was similar to the one written four years earlier, with calls for increased worker benefits, public works jobs for the unemployed, public ownership of land and the means of transportation and communication, tax reform, widespread political reform and a social insurance program.

The Socialists also added new proposals, advocating public ownership of the banking and currency system, the introduction of minimum wage scales, the elimination of the profit system in government contracts, an increase in corporation taxes and the direct election of the president and vice president.

Following are excerpts from the Socialist platform of 1912:

Social Insurance. By abolishing official charity and substituting a non-contributory system of old age pensions, a general system of insurance by the State of all its members against unemployment and invalidism and a system of compulsory insurance by employers of their workers, without cost to the latter, against industrial diseases, accidents and death.

Government Contracts. By abolishing the profit system in government work and substituting either the direct hire of labor or the awarding of contracts to cooperative groups of workers.

Minimum Wage. By establishing minimum wage scales.

Tax Reform. The adoption of a graduated income tax, the increase of the rates of the present corporation tax and the extension of inheritance taxes, graduated in proportion to the value of the estate and to nearness of kin — the proceeds of these taxes to be employed in the socialization of industry.

Banking and Currency. The collective ownership and democratic management of the banking and currency system.

Direct Election of President. The election of the President and Vice-President by direct vote of the people.

Republicans

The 1912 Republican convention was one of the most tumultuous ever. It was held in Chicago in June and served as a fiery culmination to the bitter contest between President William Howard Taft and former president Theodore Roosevelt for the party's presidential nomination.

Roosevelt had overwhelmed Taft in the presidential primaries, but Roosevelt's popular strength was more than offset by Taft's control of the national committee and Southern delegations. Taft supporters held 37 of 53 seats on the national committee, an edge that the incumbent president's managers used to advantage in settling seating disputes. Two hundred and fifty-four of the 1,078 convention seats were contested before the national committee, and 235 were settled in favor of Taft delegates. Although a number of Roosevelt challenges were made with little justification, the dispensation of the challenges showed Taft's control of the convention organization.

With the conservative Republicans united behind Taft, Roosevelt faced the additional problem of sharing support from the progressive wing of the party with another candidate, Sen. Robert M. La Follette of Wisconsin. La Follette had only 41 delegates; but, angered by Roosevelt's bid to control the progressive forces, refused to withdraw as a candidate.

The first skirmish at the convention was over the choice of a temporary chairman. The Taft forces favored Sen. Elihu Root of New York, while the Roosevelt delegates supported Gov. Francis E. McGovern of Wisconsin.

On a prolonged roll call, during which the vote of each delegate was taken individually, Root defeated McGovern, 558 to 501. *(Chart, p. 222)*

With the contest for the temporary chairmanship settled, the battle shifted to credentials. Virtually shut out in the settlement of credentials cases by the national committee, the Roosevelt forces brought 72 delegate challenges to the floor of the convention. Before consideration of the cases, the Roosevelt leaders moved that none of the challenged delegates (favorable to Taft) be allowed to vote on any of the credentials contests. However, a motion to table this proposal carried, 567 to 507, and the challenged delegates were allowed to vote on all cases except their own. Although the Taft forces were clearly in control of the convention, four credentials cases were presented for a vote, and all were decided in favor of the Taft delegates. The rest of the contests were settled by voice votes.

At this point, Roosevelt, who had dramatically come to Chicago to direct his forces, advised his delegates to abstain from voting but to remain in the convention as a silent protest to what he regarded as steamroller tactics. In the convention hall itself, the pro-Roosevelt galleries emphasized the feelings of their leader by rubbing sandpaper and blowing horns to imitate the sounds of a steamroller.

Only two names were placed in nomination for the presidency — Taft's and La Follette's. Taft was nominated by Warren G. Harding of Ohio, who himself would be president less than a decade later but at the time was merely a former lieutenant governor. With most of the Roosevelt delegates abstaining, Taft won easily on the first ballot with 556 votes. Roosevelt received 107 votes and La Follette 41, while 348 delegates were present and did not vote.

Vice President James S. Sherman was easily renominated, collecting 596 votes to 21 for the runner-up, Sen. William E. Borah of Idaho. However, 352 delegates were present but refused to vote, and 72 others were absent. In recognition of Sherman's failing health, the convention passed a resolution empowering the national committee to fill any vacancy on the ticket that might occur.

Although the Roosevelt delegates had remained in the convention hall as a silent protest to the renomination of Taft and Sherman, the groundwork for the creation of a Roosevelt-led third party had begun as soon as the credentials contests were settled in favor of Taft. Before the Republican convention even began its presidential balloting, Roosevelt announced that he would accept the nomination of the "honestly elected majority" of the Republican convention or a new progressive party. The next day, June 22, after final adjournment of the Republican convention, many of the Roosevelt delegates assembled in a Chicago auditorium to hear their leader announce his availability as a candidate of an honestly elected progressive convention. Gov. Hiram Johnson of California was named temporary chairman of the new party, and planning was begun to hold a national convention later in the summer.

As in 1908, a progressive minority report to the platform was submitted. However, instead of taking individual votes on the various planks, the convention tabled the whole report by a voice vote. Subsequently, the majority report was accepted by a vote of 666 to 53, with 343 delegates present but not voting.

The platform lauded the accomplishments of the McKinley, Roosevelt and Taft administrations but contained few major positions different from the Democrats'. The Republican platform included, however, new planks favoring judicial reform and legislation publicizing campaign contributions and outlawing corporate campaign donations.

Following are excerpts from the Republican platform of 1912:

Tariff. The protective tariff is so woven into the fabric of our industrial and agricultural life that to substitute for it a tariff for revenue only would destroy many industries and throw millions of our people out of employment. The products of the farm and of the mine should receive the same measure of protection as other products of American labor.

Campaign Contributions. We favor such additional legislation as may be necessary more effectually to prohibit corporations from contributing funds, directly or indirectly, to campaigns for the nomination or election of the President, the Vice-President, Senators, and Representatives in Congress.

We heartily approve the recent Act of Congress requiring the fullest publicity in regard to all campaign contributions, whether made in connection with primaries, conventions, or elections.

Judicial Reform. That the Courts, both Federal and State, may bear the heavy burden laid upon them to the complete satisfaction of public opinion, we favor legislation to prevent long delays and the tedious and costly appeals which have so often amounted to a denial of justice in civil cases and to a failure to protect the public at large in criminal cases.

Democrats

For the first time since 1872, the Democratic convention was held in Baltimore. The delegates, who assembled in the Maryland city in June, one week after the Republicans began their convention in Chicago, had a number of presidential candidates to choose from, although House Speaker Champ Clark of Missouri and Gov. Woodrow Wilson of New Jersey were the major contenders.

Once again, William Jennings Bryan had a major impact on the proceedings of a Democratic convention. His first appearance came in opposition to the national committee's selection of Judge Alton B. Parker of New York, the party's standard-bearer in 1904, as temporary chairman. Bryan nominated Sen. John W. Kern of Indiana for the post. In declining to be a candidate for temporary chairman, Kern recommended that Parker also withdraw as a candidate. But when Parker refused, Kern nominated Bryan for the post. Parker won on the roll call that followed, 579 to 508, with most of the Wilson delegates voting for Bryan, the Clark delegates splitting their support and delegates for other candidates favoring Parker. *(Chart, p. 221)*

The defeat of Bryan produced an avalanche of telegrams from across the country, with a contemporary estimate of more than 100,000 flooding the delegates in Baltimore. Most of the telegrams were written by progressives and served to weaken the candidacy of the more conservative Clark.

In an attempt to appease Bryan, Parker urged members of the platform committee to select the Nebraskan as their chairman. Bryan, however, refused this overture. Subsequently, the platform committee announced that, by a margin of 41 to 11, the committee had voted to delay presentation of the platform until after selection of the candidates.

The Wilson forces won their first key vote on a question involving the unit rule. The vote specifically concerned the Ohio delegation, where district delegates, elected for Wilson, were bound by the state convention to vote for Gov. Judson Harmon of Ohio. By a vote of 565-1/2 to 491-1/3, the convention approved the right of the district delegates to vote for Wilson.

The Wilson forces won another test on a credentials dispute concerning the South Dakota delegation. The credentials committee recommended seating a delegation pledged to Clark; but the convention, by a vote of 639-1/2 to 437, supported the minority report, which called for seating delegates pledged to Wilson.

Bryan reappeared before the presidential balloting and introduced a resolution opposing the nomination of any candidate "who is the representative of or under obligation to J. Pierpont Morgan, Thomas F. Ryan, August Belmont, or any other member of the privilege-hunting and favor-seeking class." Bryan's resolution passed easily, 883 to 202-1/2.

Six names were placed in nomination for the presidency. Clark led on the first ballot with 440-1/2 votes, followed by Wilson with 324, Harmon with 148 and Rep. Oscar W. Underwood of Alabama with 117-1/2. Under the two-thirds rule, 730 votes were needed to nominate. *(Chart, p. 221)*

For nine ballots, there was little change in the vote totals, but on the 10th roll call New York shifted its 90 votes from Harmon to Clark. Expecting a quick triumph, the Clark forces unleashed an hour-long demonstration. However, their celebration was premature. While Clark had 556 votes, a majority, his total was well short of the two-thirds majority required by the rules.

The 10th ballot proved to be the high-water mark for Clark. On succeeding roll calls, he slowly began to lose strength. During the 14th ballot, Bryan received permission to address the convention again, this time to explain his vote. "The Great Commoner" announced that he could not support a candidate endorsed by the Tammany-con-

trolled New York delegation and, although bound earlier by state primary results to support Clark, was now switching his vote to Wilson. Most of the Nebraska delegation followed Bryan in voting for Wilson. After the 14th ballot, the vote totals stood: Clark, 553; Wilson, 361; Underwood, 111.

There were long intervals between other major vote switches. On the 20th ballot, Kansas shifted 20 of its votes from Clark to Wilson. On the 28th ballot, after a weekend recess, Indiana's favorite son, Gov. Thomas R. Marshall, withdrew in favor of Wilson. The slow trend in favor of the New Jersey governor finally enabled Wilson to pass Clark on the 30th roll call, 450 to 455; Underwood remained a distant third with 121-1/2 votes. *(Chart, p. 221)*

The convention adjourned for the evening after the 42nd ballot, but the Wilson momentum continued the next day. Illinois switched its 58 votes to Wilson on the 43rd ballot, giving him a simple majority with 602 votes. Clark continued to decline, slipping to 329 votes.

Wilson showed slight gains on the next two ballots, but the big break came on the 46th roll call, when Underwood withdrew. This was followed by the withdrawal of Clark and the other remaining candidates. Wilson received 990 votes on the 46th ballot, followed by Clark with 84.

Clark's failure to win the nomination marked the first occasion since 1844 that a candidate achieved a simple majority of the votes, without subsequently winning the necessary two-thirds majority. The 46 roll calls also represented the highest number of presidential ballots taken at any convention, Republican or Democratic, since 1860.

Wilson preferred Underwood as his running mate, but the Alabama representative was not interested in second place on the ticket. On the vice presidential roll call that followed, nine candidates received votes, led by Marshall with 389 votes and Gov. John Burke of North Dakota with 304-2/3. Marshall lengthened his lead over Burke on the second ballot, 644-1/2 to 386-1/3. After the roll call was completed, a New Jersey delegate moved that Marshall's nomination be made unanimous, and the motion passed.

The Democratic platform was approved without debate before selection of the vice presidential candidate. The platform restated a number of positions included in earlier party documents. It blamed the high cost of living on the protective tariff and the existence of trusts, and it called for a lower, revenue-only tariff and the passage of stronger antitrust legislation. The tariff issue was one of the major areas on which there was a marked difference between the parties, as the Republicans continued to support a protective tariff.

As in 1908, planks were included favoring the publicizing of campaign contributions and calling for the prohibition of corporate contributions and a limit on individual contributions.

The Democrats' labor plank was also virtually a restatement of the party's position four years earlier, supporting creation of a Department of Labor, a more limited use of injunctions, the guaranteed right of workers to organize and passage of an employees' compensation law. In contrast to the Democrats' support of employers' liability, the Republicans advocated workmen's compensation legislation.

Unlike the Republicans, the Democrats called for federal legislation to regulate the rates of railroad, telegraph, telephone and express companies based on valuation by the Interstate Commerce Commission. A plank was also included in the Democratic platform calling for the ratification of constitutional amendments establishing a graduated income tax and the direct election of senators — issues on which the Republican platform was silent. Imperialism was again denounced, as it had been in every Democratic platform since 1900.

New planks advocated a single-term presidency, the extension of presidential primaries to all states, reform of the judicial system to eliminate delays and cut expenses in court proceedings, and the strengthening of the government's pure food and public health agencies.

Following are excerpts from the Democratic platform of 1912:

Single-term Presidency. We favor a single Presidential term, and to that end urge the adoption of an amendment to the Constitution making the President of the United States ineligible to reelection, and we pledge the candidates of this Convention to this principle.

Presidential Primaries. The movement toward more popular government should be promoted through legislation in each State which will permit the expression of the preference of the electors for national candidates at presidential primaries.

Judicial Reform. We recognize the urgent need of reform in the administration of civil and criminal law in the United States, and we recommend the enactment of such legislation and the promotion of such measures as will rid the present legal system of the delays, expense, and uncertainties incident to the system as now administered.

States' Rights. Believing that the most efficient results under our system of government are to be attained by the full exercise by the States of their reserved sovereign powers, we denounce as usurpation the efforts of our opponents to deprive the States of any of the rights reserved to them, and to enlarge and magnify by indirection the powers of the Federal government.

Progressives

Early in August 1912 the bolting Roosevelt forces assembled in Chicago and nominated their leader to guide a new party, the Progressives. More than 2,000 delegates, representing every state except South Carolina, gathered for the three-day convention. It was a diverse assembly that matched the Populists in crusading idealism and included, for the first time, women as well as men politicians and social workers as well as businessmen.

While the delegates enthusiastically sang "Onward, Christian Soldiers" and "The Battle Hymn of the Republic" and cheered the appearance of Roosevelt before the convention, there was some dissension caused by the party's racial policy.

During the campaign for the Republican presidential nomination, Taft had the support of party organizations in the South, which included blacks. As a result, Roosevelt directed his appeal strictly to white leaders in the region. Describing Southern black delegates as uneducated and purchasable, Roosevelt insisted that only "lily white" delegations from the South be seated at the Progressive convention, but he allowed blacks to be included in delegations from other states. Although there was no floor debate on this policy, a number of liberal delegates were dissatisfied with Roosevelt's decision.

Both Roosevelt and his handpicked choice for vice president, Gov. Hiram W. Johnson of California, were nominated by acclamation. Jane Addams, a Chicago social worker and leader in the women's rights movement, gave evidence of the role of women in the Progressive Party by delivering a seconding speech for Roosevelt.

Like the nominations of the Progressive standard-bearers, the party platform was adopted by acclamation. But the voice vote hid the dissatisfaction felt by Midwestern and Western Progressives over the antitrust plank. Most of the Progressives from these regions favored the busting of trusts through enforcement of the Sherman Anti-trust Act. Roosevelt, however, favored government regulation rather than trust-busting.

The platform approved by the convention included the trust-busting position. However, Roosevelt and his close advisers deleted the section in the official report. While there was obvious disagreement in the party on this issue, there was no floor debate or roll-call vote on the subject.

With the theme "A Covenant with the People," the platform argued for increased democratization coupled with more people-oriented federal programs. The party favored nationwide presidential primaries, the direct election of senators, the initiative, referendum and recall and women's suffrage. Additionally, the Progressives proposed that state laws ruled unconstitutional be submitted to a vote of the state electorate.

The platform also advocated congressional reforms: the registration of lobbyists, the publicizing of committee hearings except in foreign affairs, and the recording of committee votes.

Like the Democrats, the Progressives favored creation of a Department of Labor and a more limited use of labor injunctions, but additionally the new party called for a prohibition of child labor and convict contract labor.

The Progressives went beyond both major parties in proposing the union of government health agencies into a single national health service and the creation of a social insurance system that would assist both the elderly and workers who were ill or unemployed. To help support their proposed federal programs, the Progressives recommended passage of the income tax amendment and establishment of a graduated inheritance tax.

Having adopted their platform and selected their candidates, the delegates to the Progressive convention adjourned by singing the "Doxology."

Following are excerpts from the Progressive platform of 1912:

Electoral Reform. In particular, the party declares for direct primaries of the nomination of State and National officers, for nation-wide preferential primaries for candidates for the presidency; for the direct election of United States Senators by the people; and we urge on the States the policy of the short ballot, with responsibility to the people secured by the initiative, referendum and recall.

Women's Suffrage. The Progressive party, believing that no people can justly claim to be a true democracy which denies political rights on account of sex, pledges itself to the task of securing equal suffrage to men and women alike.

Judicial Reform. That when an Act, passed under the police power of the State, is held unconstitutional under the State Constitution, by the courts, the people, after an ample interval for deliberation, shall have an opportunity to vote on the question whether they desire the Act to become law, notwithstanding such decision.

Campaign Contributions. We pledge our party to legislation that will compel strict limitation of all campaign contributions and expenditures, and detailed publicity of both before as well as after primaries and elections.

Congressional Reform. We pledge our party to

legislation compelling the registration of lobbyists; publicity of committee hearings except on foreign affairs, and recording of all votes in committee....

National Health Service. We favor the union of all the existing agencies of the Federal Government dealing with the public health into a single national health service without discrimination against or for any one set of therapeutic methods, school of medicine, or school of healing with such additional powers as may be necessary to enable it to perform efficiently such duties in the protection of the public from preventable diseases as may be properly undertaken by the Federal authorities, including the executing of existing laws regarding pure food, quarantine and cognate subjects, the promotion of vital statistics and the extension of the registration area of such statistics, and cooperation with the health activities of the various States and cities of the Nation.

Social Insurance. The protection of home life against the hazards of sickness, irregular employment and old age through the adoption of a system of social insurance adapted to American use....

Antitrust Action. We therefore demand a strong National regulation of inter-State corporations ... we urge the establishment of a strong Federal administrative commission of high standing, which shall maintain permanent active supervision over industrial corporations engaged in inter-State commerce, or such of them as are of public importance, doing for them what the Government now does for the National banks, and what is now done for the railroads by the Inter-State Commerce Commission.

Income and Inheritance Taxes. We believe in a graduated inheritance tax as a National means of equalizing the obligations of holders of property to Government, and we hereby pledge our party to enact such a Federal law as will tax large inheritances, returning to the States an equitable percentage of all amounts collected.

We favor the ratification of the pending amendment to the Constitution giving the Government power to levy an income tax.

Tariff. We demand tariff revision because the present tariff is unjust to the people of the United States. Fair dealing toward the people requires an immediate downward revision of those schedules wherein duties are shown to be unjust or excessive....

The Democratic party is committed to the destruction of the protective system through a tariff for revenue only — a policy which would inevitably produce widespread industrial and commercial disaster.

Republicans and Democrats. Political parties exist to secure responsible government and to execute the will of the people.

From these great tasks both of the old parties have turned aside. Instead of instruments to promote the general welfare, they have become the tools of corrupt interests which use them impartially to serve their selfish purposes. Behind the ostensible government sits enthroned an invisible government owing no allegiance and acknowledging no responsibility to the people.

To destroy this invisible government, to dissolve the unholy alliance between corrupt business and corrupt politics is the first task of the statesmanship of the day.

States' Rights. The extreme insistence on States' rights by the Democratic party in the Baltimore platform demonstrates anew its ability to understand the world into which it has survived or to administer the affairs of a union of States which have in all essential respects become one people.

1916 Conventions

Presidential Candidates

Charles E. Hughes
Republican

Woodrow Wilson
Democrat

Republicans

The Republicans and Progressives both held their conventions in Chicago in early June 1916. Leaders of both parties were ready to negotiate to heal the split that had divided the Republican Party in 1912.

Before the convention began, the Republican National Committee already had effected reform in the vote-allocation formula. To meet the objection raised in 1912 that the South was overrepresented, the national committee adopted a new method of vote allocation that considered a state's Republican voting strength as well as its electoral vote. Under the new formula, the Southern states lost 78 delegate seats, or more than a third of their 1912 total.

But while the Republicans were willing to make some

internal reforms, most party leaders were adamantly opposed to nominating the hero of the Progressives, Theodore Roosevelt. Before the presidential balloting began, the Republican convention approved by voice vote the selection of a five-man committee to meet jointly with representatives of the Progressive convention, with the hope of finding a course of action that would unify the two parties.

However, the Republican representatives reported back that the Progressives, while desiring unity with the Republicans, firmly favored the nomination of Roosevelt. The Republican convention chairman, Sen. Warren G. Harding of Ohio, instructed the conferees to continue negotiations but allowed the presidential balloting to begin.

Charles Evans Hughes, a Supreme Court justice and former governor of New York, was the front-runner for the Republican nomination. Hughes did not actively seek the nomination and remained on the Supreme Court during the pre-convention period. But he was viewed by many party leaders as an ideal compromise candidate, because of his progressive credentials and lack of involvement in the divisive 1912 campaign.

However, some conservative party leaders felt Hughes was too progressive and sought other candidates. Seventeen men received votes on the first ballot, led by Hughes with 253-1/2. Next were Sen. John W. Weeks of Massachusetts with 105 votes and former senator Elihu Root of New York with 103. Five of the other vote recipients had at least 65 votes each. The justice widened his lead on the second ballot, receiving 328-1/2 votes to 98-1/2 for Root. After the second roll call the convention voted 694-1/2 to 286-1/2 to recess for the evening. Most of the votes for adjournment came from delegates outside the Hughes column. *(Chart, p. 224)*

While the Republican convention was in recess, the joint committee of Republicans and Progressives continued to negotiate. The Republican members proposed Hughes as a compromise candidate, but in a message from his home in Oyster Bay, N.Y., Roosevelt stunned both parties by suggesting the name of Henry Cabot Lodge, a conservative senator from Massachusetts.

The Progressive delegates reacted defiantly to this recommendation by nominating Roosevelt by acclamation and selecting John M. Parker of Louisiana as his running mate. Roosevelt, however, immediately scotched the enthusiasm of the Progressive delegates by conditionally declining the nomination. Roosevelt informed the convention that he would support Hughes if the latter's positions on major issues were acceptable.

When the Republican convention reconvened the next day, the opposition to Hughes had evaporated. The New Yorker received 949-1/2 of the 987 convention votes on the third ballot, and his nomination was subsequently declared unanimous.

Charles W. Fairbanks of Indiana, vice president under Roosevelt, was the convention's choice to fill out the Republican ticket. Fairbanks won on the first ballot by 863 votes to 108 for former Nebraska senator Elmer J. Burkett.

The Wisconsin delegation again presented its own minority platform report, which included planks that denounced "dollar diplomacy" and called for women's suffrage, a referendum before any declaration of war and constitutional amendments to establish the initiative, referendum and recall. The minority report was defeated and the majority report was approved by voice votes.

The adopted platform harshly criticized the policies of the Wilson administration. In foreign policy, the Republicans denounced the Wilson government for "shifty expedients" and "phrase making" and promised "strict and honest neutrality." The platform condemned the administration for its intervention in Mexico and non-involvement in the Philippines. The Republicans also called for a stronger national defense.

The two parties continued to disagree on the tariff issue, with the Republicans criticizing the lower (Democratic-passed) Underwood tariff and arguing for a higher, protective tariff. The Republican platform lauded the party's efforts in passing antitrust and transportation rate regulation, but it criticized the Democrats for harassing business.

Following are excerpts from the Republican platform of 1916:

Foreign Policy. We desire peace, the peace of justice and right, and believe in maintaining a strict and honest neutrality between the belligerents in the great war in Europe. We must perform all our duties and insist upon all our rights as neutrals without fear and without favor. We believe that peace and neutrality, as well as the dignity and influence of the United States, cannot be preserved by shifty expedients, by phrase making, by performances in language, or by attitudes ever changing in an effort to secure votes or voters.

National Defense. We must have a Navy so strong and so well proportioned and equipped, so thoroughly ready and prepared, that no enemy can gain command of the sea and effect a landing in force on either our Western or our Eastern coast. To secure these results we must have a coherent continuous policy of national defense, which even in these perilous days the Democratic party has utterly failed to develop, but which we promise to give to the country.

Merchant Marine. We are utterly opposed to the Government ownership of vessels as proposed by the Democratic party, because Government-owned ships, while effectively preventing the development of the American Merchant Marine by private capital, will be entirely unable to provide for the vast volume of American freights and will leave us more helpless than ever in the hard grip of foreign syndicates.

Tariff. The Republican party stands now, as always, in the fullest sense for the policy of tariff protection to American industries and American labor.

Business. The Republican party firmly believes that all who violate the laws in regulation of business, should be individually punished. But prosecution is very different from persecution, and business success, no matter how honestly attained, is apparently regarded by the Democratic party as in itself a crime. Such doctrines and beliefs choke enterprise and stifle prosperity. The Republican party believes in encouraging American business as it believes in and will seek to advance all American interests.

Women's Suffrage. The Republican party, reaffirming its faith in government of the people, by the people, for the people, as a measure of justice to one-half the adult people of this country, favors the extension of the suffrage to women, but recognizes the right of each state to settle this question for itself.

Democrats

The Democratic convention of 1916 was held in St. Louis in mid-June. The delegates were nearly unanimous in their support for President Woodrow Wilson, who was renominated by the vote of 1,092 to 1 — the lone dissenting vote coming from an Illinois delegate who disapproved of a motion to nominate Wilson by acclamation. With Wilson's approval, Vice President Thomas R. Marshall was renominated by acclamation.

For the first time in more than two decades, William Jennings Bryan was not a major convention force. Bryan was defeated in his bid to be a delegate-at-large from Nebraska and attended the convention as a reporter. He was invited to address the delegates and echoed the theme stressed by other speakers, that Wilson would keep the nation out of war.

Wilson was the recognized leader of the Democratic Party, but the pacifistic theme, emphasized by Bryan and other convention orators, struck a responsive chord among the delegates that was mildly alarming to Wilson and his managers. They initially had planned to accent the theme of Americanism and national unity.

The wording of the national unity plank was a matter of debate within the platform committee. The Democratic senators from Missouri warned that Wilson's strongly worded plank might offend German-American citizens. Nonetheless, the Wilson plank was retained and placed prominently near the beginning of the platform.

The only section of the platform brought to a floor vote was the plank on women's suffrage. The majority plank favored extending the vote to women, while a minority plank advocated leaving the matter to the individual states. The minority plank was defeated, 888-1/2 to 181-1/2. The rest of the platform was then adopted by a voice vote. The Democratic position on women's suffrage contrasted with that of the Republicans, who proposed leaving the matter up to the individual states. *(Chart, p. 223)*

The platform's inclusion of national unity and military preparedness planks was a contrast with earlier Democratic platforms around the turn of the century, which had consistently denounced imperialism and denied the need for a stronger military. Even though spurred by the war in Europe, the new planks were a notable change.

The rest of the platform focused on the progressive reforms of the Wilson administration, particularly in tariff, banking, labor and agriculture. Wilson himself was lauded as "the greatest American of his generation."

Noticeably absent from the platform were two planks in the party's document four years earlier: a call for a single-term presidency and a defense of states' rights.

Following are excerpts from the Democratic platform of 1916:

National Unity. In this day of test, America must show itself not a nation of partisans but a nation of patriots. There is gathered here in America the best of the blood, the industry and the genius of the whole world, the elements of a great race and a magnificent society to be welded into a mighty and splendid Nation. Whoever, actuated by the purpose to promote the industry of a foreign power, in disregard of our own country's welfare or to injure this government in its foreign relations or cripple or destroy its industries at home, and whoever by arousing prejudices of a racial, religious or other nature creates discord and strife among our people so as to obstruct the wholesome process of unification, is faithless to the trust which the privileges of citizenship repose in him and is disloyal to his country.

Military Preparedness. We therefore favor the maintenance of an army fully adequate to the requirements of order, of safety, and of the protection of the nation's rights, the fullest development of modern methods of sea-coast defence and the maintenance of an adequate reserve of citizens trained to arms and prepared to safeguard the people and territory of the United States against any danger of hostile action which may unexpectedly arise; and a fixed policy for the continuous development of a navy, worthy to

support the great naval traditions of the United States and fully equal to the international tasks which this Nation hopes and expects to take a part in performing.

Tariff. We reaffirm our belief in the doctrine of a tariff for the purpose of providing sufficient revenue for the operation of the government economically administered, and unreservedly endorse the Underwood tariff law as truly exemplifying that doctrine.

Women's Suffrage. We recommend the extension of the franchise to the women of the country by the States upon the same terms as to men.

Socialists

The Socialists did not hold a convention in 1916 but did nominate candidates and adopt a platform. The candidates were chosen in a unique mail referendum. With Eugene V. Debs' refusal to run, the presidential nomination went to Allan L. Benson of New York. George R. Kirkpatrick of New Jersey was selected as his running mate.

More than half of the Socialist platform was devoted to criticizing the United States' preparations for war. The Socialists opposed the war in Europe and viewed the American drive for preparedness as an effort by ruling capitalists to protect the system and their profits.

The Socialist platform specifically advocated no increase in military appropriations, a national referendum on any declaration of war, the shifting of the power to make foreign policy from the president to Congress, the abandonment of the Monroe Doctrine and immediate independence for the Philippines.

The rest of the platform was divided into sections entitled political demands, industrial demands and collective ownership. The proposals in these sections paralleled earlier Socialist platforms, although there was a new plank, advocating lending by the federal government to local governments, which was an early expression of the concept of revenue-sharing.

Following are excerpts from the Socialist platform of 1916:

Militarism and Preparedness. The working class must recognize militarism as the greatest menace to all efforts toward industrial freedom, and regardless of political or industrial affiliations must present a united front in the fight against preparedness and militarism.... The war in Europe, which diminished and is still diminishing the remote possibility of European attack upon the United States, was nevertheless seized upon by capitalists and by unscrupulous politicians as a means of spreading fear throughout the country, to the end that, by false pretenses, great military establishments might be obtained. We denounce such "preparedness" as both false in principle, unnecessary in character and dangerous in its plain tendencies toward militarism.

Foreign Policy. We, therefore, demand that the power to fix foreign policies and conduct diplomatic negotiations shall be lodged in congress and shall be exercised publicly, the people reserving the right to order congress, at any time, to change its foreign policy.

Referendum on War. That no war shall be declared or waged by the United States without a referendum vote of the entire people, except for the purpose of repelling invasion.

Federal Loans to Local Governments. The government shall lend money on bonds to counties and municipalities at a nominal rate of interest for the purpose of taking over or establishing public utilities and for building or maintaining public roads or highways and public schools.

1920 Conventions

Presidential Candidates

Eugene V. Debs
Socialist

Warren G. Harding
Republican

James M. Cox
Democrat

Socialists

The Socialists held their convention in New York in May and for the fifth time nominated Eugene V. Debs of Indiana for president. It was one of the strangest candidacies in American political history, because at the time Debs was serving a 10-year prison term in the Atlanta federal penitentiary for his outspoken opposition to the American war effort. Seymour Stedman of Ohio was chosen as his running mate.

The Socialist platform was again a distinctive document, going far beyond the platforms of the two major parties in the radical nature of the reforms proposed. The platform characterized the war policies and peace proposals of the Wilson administration as "despotism, reaction and oppression unsurpassed in the annals of the republic." It called for the replacement of the "mischievous" League of Nations with an international parliament. It favored recognition of both the newly established Irish Republic and the Soviet Union.

The Socialists continued to advocate extensive tax reform and included new calls for a tax on unused land and a progressive property tax on wartime profits that would help pay off government debts. The platform warned that the continuing militaristic mood of both major parties could lead to another war.

The Socialists continued to recommend extensive labor benefits, but for the first time they specifically mentioned migratory workers as needing government assistance.

Following are excerpts from the Socialist platform of 1920:

League of Nations. The Government of the United States should initiate a movement to dissolve the mischievous organization called the "League of Nations" and to create an international parliament, composed of democratically elected representatives of all nations of the world based upon the recognition of their equal rights, the principles of self determination, the right to national existence of colonies and other dependencies, freedom of international trade and trade routes by land and sea, and universal disarmament, and be charged with revising the Treaty of Peace on the principles of justice and conciliation.

Labor. Congress should enact effective laws to abolish child labor, to fix minimum wages, based on an ascertained cost of a decent standard of life, to protect migratory and unemployed workers from oppression, to abolish detective and strike-breaking agencies and to establish a shorter work-day in keeping with increased industrial productivity.

Blacks. Congress should enforce the provisions of the Thirteenth, Fourteenth and Fifteenth Amendments with reference to the Negroes, and effective federal legislation should be enacted to secure the Negroes full civil, political, industrial and educational rights.

Republicans

In mid-June, Republicans met for the fifth straight time in Chicago for their quadrennial convention. For the first time, women were on the floor in large numbers as delegates. With the constitutional amendment granting women the vote on the verge of passage, Republicans, especially in the Midwest and West, were quick to include women in their delegations.

The Republicans, like the Democrats two weeks later, entered their convention with no clear front-runner for the presidential nomination. Three candidates were at the top of the list, but two of them, Maj. Gen. Leonard Wood of New Hampshire and Sen. Hiram Johnson of California, split the party's progressive wing, while the third entry, Gov. Frank Lowden of Illinois, ran poorly in the presidential primaries and was accused of campaign spending irregularities.

The names of 11 men were placed in nomination for the presidency, but none came close during the first day of balloting to the 493 votes needed to nominate. Wood led on the initial roll call with 287-1/2 votes, trailed by Lowden with 211-1/2 and Johnson with 133-1/2. Sen. Warren G. Harding of Ohio, who had not campaigned for the nomination as extensively as the three pacesetters, placed sixth with 65-1/2 votes. Wood, Lowden and Johnson all gained strength during the first three ballots. *(Chart, p. 226)*

After the third roll call, the Johnson delegates moved for adjournment but were defeated, 701-1/2 to 275-1/2. On the fourth ballot, Wood's vote total rose to 314-1/2, well short of a majority but the highest mark attained yet by any candidate. At this point, Harding stood in fifth place with 61-1/2 votes. Although a motion to adjourn had been soundly defeated after the previous roll call, the permanent chairman, Sen. Henry Cabot Lodge of Massachusetts, entertained a new motion to adjourn and declared it passed on a closely divided voice vote.

The adjournment gave Republican leaders a chance to confer and discuss the various presidential possibilities. Much is made in history books about Harding's selection that night in the legendary "smoke-filled room," when Harding was allegedly interviewed at 2 o'clock by Republican leaders and, answering their questions satisfactorily, was chosen as the nominee. The authenticity of the meeting has been questioned, as has the power of the politicians who made the designation. But, nonetheless, it was clear that Harding was a viable compromise choice who was both acceptable to the conservative party leadership and could be nominated by the delegates.

Harding's vote total rose slowly in the next day's balloting until the ninth ballot, when a large shift, primarily of Lowden delegates, boosted the Ohio senator's vote from 133 to 374-1/2. This was the highest total for any candidate to this point and started a bandwagon that produced Harding's nomination on the 10th ballot. After the various switches, the final vote stood: Harding, 692-1/5; Wood, 156, and Johnson, 80-4/5, with the rest of the vote scattered.

Immediately after Harding's nomination, the vice presidential balloting began. After the nomination of Sen. Irvine L. Lenroot of Wisconsin, a delegate from Oregon rose and, standing on his chair, nominated Gov. Calvin Coolidge of Massachusetts. An enthusiastic demonstration followed, showing the wide delegate support for Coolidge. The governor, who had risen to national prominence less than a year earlier with his handling of a Boston police strike, was a runaway winner on the one vice presidential ballot. Coolidge received 674-1/2 votes to Lenroot's 146-1/2.

The Wisconsin delegation again presented a detailed minority report to the platform. It included planks that opposed entry into the League of Nations under the terms of the proposed treaty, objected to compulsory military service, called for the quick conclusion of peace negotiations and normalization of foreign relations and recommended a bonus for servicemen to match the wages of wartime civilian workers.

In domestic reforms, the Wisconsin report advocated the election of federal judges and the passage of a constitutional amendment that would establish the initiative, referendum and recall. The entire minority report was rejected by a voice vote, and the platform as written was adopted in a similar manner.

The platform began by denouncing the Wilson administration for being completely unprepared for both war and peace. It went on to criticize Wilson for establishing an "executive autocracy" by arrogating to himself power that belonged to other branches of government.

The platform included a League of Nations plank that intentionally straddled the controversial issue, applauding the Republican-controlled Senate for defeating Wilson's League but pledging the party "to such agreements with the other nations of the world as shall meet the full duty of America to civilization and humanity."

To help cut federal spending, the Republicans favored consolidating some departments and bureaus and establishing an executive budget.

Both parties continued to differ on the tariff, with the Democrats reiterating their belief in a revenue tariff and the Republicans restating their support of a protective tariff.

Following are excerpts from the Republican platform of 1920:

League of Nations. The Republican party stands for agreement among the nations to preserve the peace of the world. . . .

The covenant signed by the President at Paris failed signally . . . and contains stipulations, not only intolerable for an independent people, but certain to produce the injustice, hostility and controversy among nations which it proposed to prevent.

. . . we pledge the coming Republican administration to such agreements with the other nations of the world as shall meet the full duty of America to civilization and humanity, in accordance with American ideals, and without surrendering the right of the American people to exercise its judgment and its power in favor of justice and peace.

Democrats

San Francisco was the host city for the 1920 Democratic convention, marking the first time a convention of one of the major parties was held west of the Rockies. Not only was the site a new one, but when the convention opened in late June, for the first time in a generation the Democratic Party had no recognized leader such as Cleveland, Bryan or Wilson.

President Woodrow Wilson had some hope of a third nomination, but his failing health and skidding popularity made this an unrealistic prospect. But Wilson's refusal to endorse another candidate prevented the emergence of any presidential hopeful as a front-runner for the nomination. In all, 24 candidates received votes on the first presidential roll call, but none approached the 729 votes needed for nomination. William Gibbs McAdoo, Wilson's son-in-law and former treasury secretary, led with 266 votes, in spite of having withdrawn from the race several days before the convention began. Attorney General A. Mitchell Palmer, famed for his efforts during the "Red Scare," followed closely with 254 votes. Two governors, Ohio's James M. Cox and New York's Alfred E. Smith, trailed with 134 and 109 votes respectively. *(Chart, p. 225)*

Another ballot was taken before evening adjournment, with the top four candidates retaining the same order and nearly the same vote.

During the next day's balloting, Cox gained steadily and passed both McAdoo and Palmer. When the majority of McAdoo and Palmer delegates successfully carried a motion to recess after the 16th ballot, Cox held the lead with 454-1/2 votes. McAdoo was next with 337 votes and Palmer trailed with 164-1/2.

Six more ballots were taken during the evening session, and although Cox's lead narrowed, he still led McAdoo after the 22nd ballot, 430 to 372-1/2. In the next day's balloting, McAdoo gradually gained ground until he finally passed Cox on the 30th ballot, 403-1/2 to 400-1/2. After completion of the roll call, the motion was made to eliminate the lowest candidate on each succeeding ballot until a nominee had been selected. This drastic proposal to shorten the convention was defeated, 812-1/2 to 264.

Balloting continued without interruption through the 36th roll call. McAdoo still led with 399 votes, but his margin over Cox was reduced to 22 votes, and Palmer with 241 votes achieved his highest total since the 11th ballot.

A candidate was finally nominated during the evening session of the convention's third day of presidential balloting. The Palmer revival fizzled quickly, with most of his delegates going to either McAdoo or Cox. The Ohio governor regained the lead on the 39th ballot, when the majority of the Indiana delegation shifted from McAdoo to Cox. After this roll call, Cox led McAdoo, 468-1/2 to 440, Palmer having slipped to 74. Cox continued to gain, and a last-ditch effort by McAdoo delegates to force an adjournment failed, 637 to 406. Cox's vote total reached 699-1/2 votes on the 44th ballot, and, with victory imminent, a motion was adopted to declare the Ohio governor the unanimous nominee of the convention. *(Chart, p. 225)*

Cox's choice for the vice presidential nomination was Franklin Delano Roosevelt of New York, the 38-year-old assistant secretary of the Navy. Roosevelt was nominated by acclamation.

William Jennings Bryan attended the convention and proposed five planks as amendments to the platform. Only his plank endorsing prohibition, however, was submitted for a roll-call vote, and it was soundly beaten, 929-1/2 to 155-1/2. A counterproposal by a New York delegate, recognizing the legality of the prohibition amendment to the Constitution but favoring the manufacture of beer and light wines for home use, was also defeated, 724-1/2 to 356. The platform finally adopted did not discuss the prohibition question.

Bryan's four other planks covered a wide range of issues. He favored establishing a national newspaper, reducing from two-thirds to a simple majority the vote needed to approve treaties in the Senate, expressed opposition to peacetime universal compulsory military training and recommended that interstate companies reveal the difference between the cost and selling price of their products. All four planks were defeated by voice votes.

One other amendment, calling for the recognition of Irish independence, came to the floor for a roll-call vote. It was beaten, 674 to 402-1/2. Included instead was a milder plank sympathizing with the Irish struggle for independence. Subsequently, the delegates approved by voice vote the entire platform as it was first written.

Although the delegates were unwilling to renominate Wilson, the platform was largely devoted to praise of his leadership and legislation passed during his presidency. The platform reflected Wilson's thinking by placing the League of Nations plank prominently at the beginning and supporting the president's call for American membership. The plank did allow for reservations to the treaty, but none that would prevent American participation in the League.

Following are excerpts from the Democratic platform of 1920:

League of Nations. The Democratic Party favors the League of Nations as the surest, if not the only, practicable means of maintaining the permanent peace of the world and terminating the insufferable burden of great military and naval establishments....

We commend the President for his courage and his high conception of good faith in steadfastly standing for the covenant agreed to by all the associated and allied nations at war with Germany, and we condemn the Republican Senate for its refusal to ratify the treaty merely because it was the product of Democratic statesmanship, thus interposing partisan envy and personal hatred in the way of the peace and renewed prosperity of the world....

We advocate the immediate ratification of the treaty without reservations which would impair its essential integrity, but do not oppose the acceptance of any reservations making clearer or more specific the obligations of the United States to the league associates.

Irish Independence. The great principle of national self-determination has received constant reiteration as one of the chief objectives for which this country entered the war and victory established this principle.

Within the limitations of international comity and usage, this Convention repeats the several previous expressions of the sympathy of the Democratic Party of the United States for the aspirations of Ireland for self-government.

1924 Conventions

Presidential Candidates

Calvin Coolidge
Republican

John W. Davis
Democrat

Robert M. La Follette
Progressive

Republicans

The Republicans gathered for their convention in Cleveland, Ohio, in June. For the first time, a convention was broadcast by radio. Also for the first time, Republican Party rules were changed to elect women to the national committee, with one man and one woman to be chosen from each state and territory.

Unlike the Democratic marathon that began two weeks later in New York, there was surface harmony at the Republican convention. President Calvin Coolidge's success in the spring primaries, and his ability to defuse the corruption issue, eliminated any major opposition. Coolidge was easily nominated on the first ballot, receiving 1,065 votes. Sen. Robert M. La Follette of Wisconsin was a distant second with 34 votes, while Sen. Hiram W. Johnson of California collected the remaining 10. *(Chart, p. 227)*

The vice presidential nomination was a confused matter. Eight candidates were nominated, and on the first ballot former Illinois governor Frank O. Lowden led with 222 votes. Although Lowden publicly stated that he would not accept the nomination, he received a majority of the vote on the second roll call. A recess was taken to see if Lowden had changed his mind, but when it was certain that he had not the delegates resumed balloting.

On the third roll call, former budget bureau director Charles G. Dawes received 682-1/2 votes to win nomination. Secretary of Commerce Herbert Hoover was second with 234-1/2 votes.

As was its custom throughout the early 20th century, the Wisconsin delegation proposed a detailed minority report to the platform. Proposals included government ownership of railroads and water power, an increased excess profits tax and reduced taxes on individuals with low incomes. The Wisconsin platform was rejected without a roll-call vote.

The platform that was adopted lauded the economy in government shown by the Republican administration and promised a reduction in taxes.

The Democrats and Republicans continued to differ on the tariff issue, with the Republicans again defending the protective tariff. The Ku Klux Klan was not mentioned in the Republican platform, nor was it discussed on the floor. The controversial organization was the subject of a divisive floor fight at the Democratic convention.

The Republican platform criticized the corruption found to exist in the Harding administration, but it also denounced efforts "to besmirch the names of the innocent and undermine the confidence of the people in the government under which they live."

In the area of foreign policy, the Republicans opposed membership in the League of Nations, although favoring participation in the World Court. While applauding the return of peace and reflecting the nation's increasing mood of isolationism, the Republicans opposed cutbacks in the Army and Navy.

Following are excerpts from the Republican platform of 1924:

Corruption. We demand the speedy, fearless and impartial prosecution of all wrong doers, without regard for political affiliations; but we declare no greater wrong can be committed against the people than the attempt to destroy their trust in the great body of their public servants. Admitting the deep humiliation which all good citizens share that our public life should have harbored some dishonest men, we assert that these undesirables do not represent the standard of our national integrity.

Taxes. We pledge ourselves to the progressive reduction of taxes of all the people as rapidly as may be done with due regard for the essential expenditures for the government administered with rigid economy and to place our tax system on a sound peace time basis.

League of Nations. This government has definitely refused membership in the league of nations or to assume any obligations under the covenant of the league. On this we stand.

Military. There must be no further weakening of our regular army and we advocate appropriations sufficient to provide for the training of all members of the national guard, the citizens' military training camps, the reserve officers' training camps and the reserves who may offer themselves for service. We pledge ourselves for service. We pledge ourselves to round out and maintain the navy to the full strength provided the United States by the letter and spirit of the limitation of armament conference.

War Profiteering. . . .should the United States ever again be called upon to defend itself by arms the president be empowered to draft such material resources and such services as may be required, and to stabilize the prices of services and essential commodities, whether used in actual warfare or private activities.

Republican Philosophy. The prosperity of the American nation rests on the vigor of private initiative which has bred a spirit of independence and self-reliance. The republican party stands now, as always, against all attempts to put the government into business.

American industry should not be compelled to struggle against government competition. The right of the government to regulate, supervise and control public utilities and public interests, we believe, should be strengthened, but we are firmly opposed to the nationalization or government ownership of public utilities.

Democrats

The 1924 Democratic convention in New York's old Madison Square Garden was the longest in American history. From the opening gavel on June 24 through final adjournment on July 10, the convention spanned 17 days. The reason for the convention's unprecedented length was an almost unbreakable deadlock between the party's rural and urban factions that extended the presidential balloting for a record 103 roll calls. *(Chart, pp. 228-229)*

Gov. Alfred E. Smith of New York was the candidate of the urban delegates, while William Gibbs McAdoo of California led the rural forces. But beyond any ideological differences between the two candidates was a bitter struggle between the urban and rural wings for control of the party. Smith, a Roman Catholic of Irish ancestry and an opponent of Prohibition and the Ku Klux Klan, embodied characteristics loathed by the rural leaders. McAdoo, a Protestant, a supporter of Prohibition and tolerant of the Ku Klux Klan, was equally unacceptable to the urban forces. Without a strong leader to unite the two factions, and with the two-thirds rule in effect, a long deadlock was inevitable.

Besides Smith and McAdoo, 14 other candidates were nominated. The most memorable speech was delivered by Franklin Delano Roosevelt, who, in nominating Smith, referred to him as "the happy warrior," a description that remained with Smith the rest of his career.

Presidential balloting commenced on Monday, June 30. McAdoo led on the first roll call with 431-1/2 votes, followed by Smith with 241, with 733 votes needed for nomination. Through the week, 77 ballots were taken, but none of the candidates approached the required two-thirds majority. At the end of the week, after the 77th ballot, McAdoo led with 513 votes; Smith had 367; John W. Davis of New York, the eventual nominee, was a distant third with 76-1/2, an improvement of 45-1/2 votes over his first-ballot total. McAdoo had reached the highest total for any candidate, 530 votes, on the 69th ballot.

William Jennings Bryan, making his last appearance at a Democratic convention, as a delegate from Florida, was given permission to explain his opposition to Smith during the 38th ballot. But Bryan's final convention oration was lost in a chorus of boos from the urban forces who found his rural philosophy increasingly objectionable.

After the 66th ballot, the first of a series of proposals was introduced to break the deadlock. It was recommended that the convention meet in executive session and listen to each of the candidates. This received majority approval, 551 to 538, but a two-thirds majority was needed to change the rules. A second proposal, to invite Smith alone to address the convention, also fell short of the necessary two-thirds, although achieving a majority, 604-1/2 to 473.

After the 73rd ballot, it was recommended that the lowest vote-getter be dropped after each roll call until only five candidates remained, a proposal to be in effect for one day only. This recommendation was defeated, 589-1/2 to 496. A more drastic motion, to adjourn after the 75th ballot and reconvene two weeks later in Kansas City, was decisively beaten, 1,007.3 to 82.7. The delegates did agree, however, to have representatives of each candidate hold a conference over the weekend.

Balloting resumed on Monday, July 7, with the 78th roll call. After the 82nd ballot, a resolution was passed, 985 to 105, releasing all delegates from their commitments.

McAdoo's vote dropped sharply as the balloting progressed, and for the first time, on the 86th roll call, Smith passed him, 360 to 353-1/2. A boom for Sen. Samuel M. Ralston of Indiana, which had begun on the 84th ballot, petered out on the 93rd roll call when Ralston quit the race. At the time of his withdrawal, Ralston was in third place with 196-1/4 votes.

After the ballot, Roosevelt announced that Smith was willing to withdraw from the race if McAdoo would also. McAdoo rejected this suggestion. McAdoo did regain the lead from Smith on the 94th ballot, 395 to 364-1/2, but with victory beyond reach, released his delegates after the 99th ballot.

Davis was the principal beneficiary of the McAdoo withdrawal, moving into second place on the 100th ballot and gaining the lead on the next roll call with 316 votes. Most of Smith's strength moved to Alabama's anti-Klan, anti-Prohibition senator, Oscar W. Underwood, who took second place on the 101st ballot with 229-1/2 votes. Underwood, however, could not keep pace with Davis, who stretched his lead on the next two ballots. After the 103rd ballot, Davis' total stood at 575-1/2 votes to 250-1/2 for the Alabama senator.

Before the next ballot could begin, Iowa switched its vote to Davis, causing other shifts that brought Davis the nomination. After the changes had been recorded, Davis had 844 votes to 102-1/2 for Underwood. The West Virginian's nomination was then declared unanimous.

The core of Davis' vote had come from the rural delegates; urban delegates gave him the necessary votes to win the nomination. After nine days of balloting, the Democrats had a presidential candidate.

The party leadership preferred Gov. Charles W. Bryan of Nebraska, William Jennings Bryan's younger brother, as Davis' running mate. Bryan trailed Tennessee labor leader George L. Berry on the first ballot, 263-1/2 to 238, but vote switches begun by Illinois after the roll call brought Bryan the nomination. After the changes Bryan had 740 votes, barely beyond the two-thirds majority necessary.

The discord evident in the presidential and vice presidential balloting had its roots in the spirited platform battle that preceded the nominations. The first subject of debate was the League of Nations, with the majority report recommending that American entry be determined by a national referendum. The minority plank argued that this was an unwieldy solution that would put the issue aside. Instead, the minority report favored entry into the League of Nations and World Court without reservation. The minority position was rejected, 742-1/2 to 353-1/2. Nonetheless, the Democrats differed markedly in their position from the Republicans, who flatly opposed membership in the League, although favoring participation in the World Court.

The League of Nations debate proved to be merely a warmup for the controversial religious liberties plank. The focus of debate was the Ku Klux Klan, which was opposed by name in the minority report but was not mentioned in the majority report. In one of the closest votes in convention history, the minority plank was defeated, 543-3/20 to 543-7/20. The vote closely followed factional lines, with most rural delegates opposing condemnation of the Klan and urban delegates supporting the minority plank.

The rest of the platform stressed Democratic accomplishments during the Wilson presidency, in contrast to Republican corruption. Democratic links with the common man were emphasized, while the Republicans were denounced as the party of the rich. The Democratic platform advocated increased taxes on the wealthy in contrast to the Republicans, who promised a reduction in taxes.

The Democrats continued to advocate a low tariff that would encourage competition. A plank demanding states' rights appeared in the platform, but there were also calls for government regulation of the anthracite coal industry, federal support of the American merchant marine and legislation that would restrict and publicize individual campaign contributions.

There were planks favoring a cutback in the American military, a national referendum before any declaration of war (except outright aggression against the United States) and the drafting of resources as well as men during wartime. The anti-militaristic planks were a return to the position the party had held earlier in the 20th century.

Following are excerpts from the Democratic platform of 1924:

Republican Corruption. Such are the exigencies of partisan politics that republican leaders are teaching the strange doctrine that public censure should be directed against those who expose crime rather than against criminals who have committed the offenses. If only three cabinet officers out of ten are disgraced, the country is asked to marvel at how many are free from taint. Long boastful that it was the only party "fit to govern," the republican party has proven its inability to govern even itself. It is at war with itself. As an agency of government it has ceased to function.

Income Tax. The income tax was intended as a tax upon wealth. It was not intended to take from the poor any part of the necessities of life. We hold that the fairest tax with which to raise revenue for the federal government is the income tax. We favor a graduated tax upon incomes, so adjusted as to lay the burdens of government upon the taxpayers in proportion to the benefits they enjoy and their ability to pay.

Campaign Contributions. We favor the prohibition of individual contributions, direct and indirect, to the campaign funds of congressmen, senators or presidential candidates, beyond a reasonable sum to be fixed in the law, for both individual contributions and total expenditures, with requirements for full publicity.

States' Rights. We demand that the states of the union shall be preserved in all their vigor and power. They constitute a bulwark against the centralizing and destructive tendencies of the republican party.

Anti-militarism. We demand a strict and sweeping reduction of armaments by land and sea, so that there shall be no competitive military program or naval building. Until international agreements to this end have been made we advocate an army and navy adequate for our national safety....

War is a relic of barbarism and it is justifiable only as a measure of defense.

War Profiteering. In the event of war in which the manpower of the nation is drafted, all other resources should likewise be drafted. This will tend to discourage war by depriving it of its profits.

Progressives

Under the sponsorship of the Conference of Progressive Political Action, representatives of various liberal, labor and agrarian groups met in Cleveland on July 4 to launch the Progressive Party and ratify the ticket of Wisconsin senator Robert M. La Follette for president and Montana senator Burton K. Wheeler for vice president. The conference earlier had designated La Follette as its presidential nominee and had given him the power to choose his running mate. The national ticket of the Progressives crossed party lines, joining a Republican, La Follette, with a Democrat, Wheeler. The ticket was endorsed by the Socialists, who supported the Progressive candidates rather than run a separate national ticket.

In large part the Progressive platform advocated measures that had been proposed earlier by the Populists, Socialists and Progressives before World War I. The key issue, as viewed by the La Follette Progressives, was "the control of government and industry by private monopoly." The platform favored the government ownership of railroads and water power, rigid federal control over natural resources, the outlawing of injunctions in labor disputes, a cutback in military spending, tax reform and political reform — including the direct election of the president, a national referendum before a declaration of war (except in cases of invasion), election of federal judges and congressional power to override the Supreme Court.

Following are excerpts from the Progressive platform of 1924:

Anti-monopoly. The great issue before the American people today is the control of government and industry by private monopoly.

For a generation the people have struggled patiently, in the face of repeated betrayals by successive administrations, to free themselves from this intolerable power which has been undermining representative government.

Through control of government, monopoly has steadily extended its absolute dominion to every basic industry.

In violation of law, monopoly has crushed competition, stifled private initiative and independent enterprise....

The equality of opportunity proclaimed by the Declaration of Independence and asserted and defended by Jefferson and Lincoln as the heritage of every American citizen has been displaced by special privilege for the few, wrested from the government of the many.

Tax Reform. We ... favor a taxation policy providing for immediate reductions upon moderate incomes, large increases in the inheritance tax rates upon large estates to prevent the indefinite accumulation by inheritance of great fortunes in a few hands, taxes upon excess profits to penalize profiteering, and complete publicity, under proper safeguards, of all Federal tax returns.

Court Reform. We favor submitting to the people, for their considerate judgment, a constitutional amendment providing that Congress may by enacting a statute make it effective over a judicial vote.

We favor such amendment to the constitution as may be necessary to provide for the election of all Federal

Judges, without party designation, for fixed terms not exceeding ten years, by direct vote of the people.

National Referendums. Over and above constitutions and statutes and greater than all is the supreme sovereignty of the people, and with them should rest the final decision of all great questions of national policy. We favor such amendments to the Federal Constitution as may be necessary to provide for the direct nomination and election of the President, to extend the initiative and referendum to the federal government, and to insure a popular referendum for or against war except in cases of actual invasion.

1928 Conventions

Presidential Candidates

Herbert Hoover
Republican

Alfred E. Smith
Democrat

Republicans

The Republicans held their convention in Kansas City, Mo., in mid-June 1928. Nearly a year earlier, President Calvin Coolidge had declared his intention not to seek re-election with a typically brief statement: "I do not choose to run for President in 1928." While some business leaders hoped that Coolidge would be open to a draft, the taciturn incumbent made no effort to encourage them. The vacuum caused by Coolidge's absence was quickly filled by Commerce Secretary Herbert Hoover of California, whose success in the spring primaries solidified his position as the front-runner.

Hoover's strength was evident on the first roll call of the convention, a credentials challenge to 18 Hoover delegates from Texas. In a vote that revealed candidate strength, the move to unseat the Hoover delegates was defeated, 659-1/2 to 399-1/2. In the presidential balloting that followed, he gained more votes to win the nomination easily on the first ballot. Hoover's vote total was swelled before the balloting began by the withdrawal of his principal opponent, former Illinois governor Frank O. Lowden, who declared in a letter that he could not accept the party platform's stand on agriculture. Six names were placed in nomination, but Hoover was a landslide winner, receiving 837 of the 1,089 convention votes. Lowden finished second with 74 votes. *(Chart, p. 230)*

Sen. Charles Curtis of Kansas was virtually unopposed for the vice presidential nomination, receiving 1,052 votes.

Although Wisconsin's prominent progressive leader, Robert M. La Follette, had died in 1925, his state's delegation again presented a minority platform. The report was presented by Sen. Robert M. La Follette Jr., who had taken over his father's Senate seat. Among the planks of the Wisconsin report were proposals favoring enactment of the McNary-Haugen farm bill, government operation of major water power projects, increased income taxes on the rich and liberalization of Prohibition. No vote was taken on the Wisconsin proposals.

A resolution favoring repeal of Prohibition was tabled by a voice vote.

A separate agricultural resolution was proposed that advocated the basic provisions of the McNary-Haugen bill (twice vetoed by Coolidge), without mentioning the controversial bill by name. On a roll-call vote, the resolution was defeated, 807 to 277, with support centered in the farm states but with most Hoover delegates voting against it.

The platform as originally written was adopted by a voice vote. The platform promised continued prosperity and government economy. The belief in a protective tariff was reiterated. The document concluded with a plank entitled "home rule," which expressed the party's belief in self-reliance and strong local government.

Following are excerpts from the Republican platform of 1928:

Tariff. We reaffirm our belief in the protective tariff as a fundamental and essential principle of the economic life of this nation.... However, we realize that there are certain industries which cannot now successfully compete with foreign producers because of lower foreign wages and a lower cost of living abroad, and we pledge the next Republican Congress to an examination and where necessary a revision of these schedules to the end that American labor in these industries may again command the home market, may maintain its standard of living, and may count upon steady employment in its accustomed field.

Outlaw War. We endorse the proposal of the Secretary of State for a multilateral treaty proposed to the principal powers of the world and open to the signatures of all nations, to renounce war as an instrument of national policy and declaring in favor of pacific settlement of international disputes, the first step in outlawing war.

Agriculture. We promise every assistance in the reorganization of the market system on sounder and more economical lines and, where diversification is needed, Government financial assistance during the period of transition.

The Republican Party pledges itself to the enactment of legislation creating a Federal Farm Board clothed with the necessary powers to promote the establishment of a farm marketing system of farmer-owned and controlled stabilization corporations or associations to prevent and control surpluses through orderly distribution....

We favor, without putting the Government into business, the establishment of a Federal system of organization for co-operative and orderly marketing of farm products.

Prohibition. The people through the method provided by the Constitution have written the Eighteenth Amendment into the Constitution. The Republican Party pledges itself and its nominees to the observance and vigorous enforcement of this provision of the Constitution.

Republican Philosophy. There is a real need of restoring the individual and local sense of responsibility and self-reliance; there is a real need for the people once more to grasp the fundamental fact that under our system of government they are expected to solve many problems themselves through their municipal and State governments, and to combat the tendency that is all too common to turn to the Federal Government as the easiest and least burdensome method of lightening their own responsibilities.

Democrats

The Democratic convention was held in late June in Houston, Texas, the first time since 1860 that the party's nominating convention had been conducted in a Southern city. The rural and urban wings of the party, which had produced the fiasco in Madison Square Garden four years earlier, wanted no more bloodletting. This explained the acceptance of Houston as the convention site by the urban forces, whose presidential candidate, Gov. Alfred E. Smith of New York, was the front-runner for the nomination. Smith's path to the nomination was largely unobstructed, thanks to the decision of William Gibbs McAdoo not to run. McAdoo, the rural favorite in 1924, feared the possibility of another bitter deadlock that would destroy party unity.

The convention broke with tradition by bypassing politicians and selecting Claude G. Bowers of Indiana, a historian and an editorial writer for *The New York World*, as temporary chairman.

When it came time for the selection of a presidential candidate, Franklin Delano Roosevelt once again placed Smith's name in nomination. On the roll call that followed, the New York governor came within 10 votes of the required two-thirds. Ohio quickly switched 44 of its votes to Smith, and the switch pushed "the happy warrior" over the top. When the vote switches were completed, Smith had received 849-1/6 of the 1,100 convention votes. No other candidate's vote had totaled more than 100. *(Chart, p. 230)*

Senate Minority Leader Joseph T. Robinson of Arkansas had little opposition for the vice presidency and was nominated on the first ballot with 914-1/6 votes. Sen. Alben W. Barkley of Kentucky finished a distant second with 77 votes. After a vote switch, Robinson had 1,035-1/6 votes. As a "dry" Protestant from the South, Robinson balanced the ticket. He was the first Southerner to be nominated for national office by either major party since the Civil War.

For the first time since 1912, there were no roll-call votes on amendments to the Democratic platform. A minority plank was introduced calling for the party's complete support of Prohibition, but there was no effort to force a roll-call vote. The platform included a milder Prohibition plank that promised "an honest effort to enforce the 18th Amendment (Prohibition)." On the surface there was little difference from the Republican plank, which pledged "vigorous enforcement" of Prohibition. But in a telegram read to the convention shortly before its final adjournment, Smith negated the effect of the milder plank by declaring there should be "fundamental changes in the present provisions for national Prohibition." Smith's statement was disappointing to many "dry" delegates and lessened whatever enthusiasm they felt for the New York governor. No other issues were discussed, and the platform as written was approved by a voice vote.

Agriculture, the most depressed part of the economy in the 1920s, received more space in the platform than any other issue. The Democrats opposed federal subsidies to farmers, but they advocated government loans to cooperatives and the creation of a federal farm board that would operate similarly to the Federal Reserve Board. While the Republican platform also favored creation of a farm board, as a whole it called for more initiative by the farmers themselves and less direct government help than did the Democratic platform.

Since the late 19th century, Democratic platforms had favored a low tariff. The 1928 tariff plank represented a change, expressing as much interest in ensuring competition and protecting the American wage-earner as in raising revenue. Instead of being consistently low, tariff rates were to be based on the difference between the cost of production in the United States and abroad. As a result of the Democrats' altered stand on the tariff, the positions of the two parties on this issue were the closest they had been in a generation.

The Democrats' 1928 platform did not mention the League of Nations, in contrast to the Republicans, who restated their opposition to the League. Both parties called for maintenance of American military strength until international disarmament agreements could be reached. A section of the Democratic foreign policy plank questioned the extent of presidential power in the area of international affairs. President Coolidge was specifically criticized for authorizing American military intervention in Nicaragua without congressional approval.

An unemployment plank was included in the Democratic platform that proposed the creation of public works jobs in times of economic hardship.

As was the case with most Democratic platforms since the early 19th century, there was a defense of states' rights and a plank that recognized education as an area of state responsibility. The Democrats made no mention of civil rights in contrast to the Republicans, who, as in 1920, proposed federal anti-lynching legislation.

Following are excerpts from the Democratic platform of 1928:

Prohibition. Speaking for the national Democracy, this convention pledges the party and its nominees to an honest effort to enforce the eighteenth amendment.

Agriculture. Farm relief must rest on the basis of an economic equality of agriculture with other industries. To give this equality a remedy must be found which will include among other things:

(a) Credit aid by loans to co-operatives on at least as

favorable a basis as the government aid to the merchant marine.

(b) Creation of a federal farm board to assist the farmer and stock raiser in the marketing of their products, as the Federal Reserve Board has done for the banker and business man.

Presidential War Power. Abolition of the practice of the president of entering into and carrying out agreements with a foreign government, either de facto or de jure, for the protection of such government against revolution or foreign attack, or for the supervision of its internal affairs, when such agreements have not been advised and consented to by the Senate, as provided in the Constitution of the United States, and we condemn the administration for carrying out such an unratified agreement that requires us to use our armed forces in Nicaragua.

Tariff. Duties that will permit effective competition, insure against monopoly and at the same time produce a fair revenue for the support of government. Actual difference between the cost of production at home and abroad, with adequate safeguard for the wage of the American laborer must be the extreme measure of every tariff rate.

Unemployment and Public Works. We favor the adoption by the government, after a study of this subject, of a scientific plan whereby during periods of unemployment appropriations shall be made available for the construction of necessary public works and the lessening, as far as consistent with public interests, of government construction work when labor is generally and satisfactorily employed in private enterprise.

Education. We believe with Jefferson and other founders of the Republic that ignorance is the enemy of freedom and that each state, being responsible for the intellectual and moral qualifications of its citizens and for the expenditure of the moneys collected by taxation for the support of its schools, shall use its sovereign right in all matters pertaining to education.

1932 Conventions

Presidential Candidates

Norman Thomas
Socialist

Herbert Hoover
Republican

Franklin D. Roosevelt
Democrat

Socialists

The Socialist Party held its convention in Milwaukee, Wis., in May and renominated the same ticket that had represented the party in 1928: Norman Thomas of New York for president and James H. Maurer of Pennsylvania for vice president. Aided by the deepening economic depression, the Socialists received more than 2 percent of the popular vote for the first time since 1920. The party continued to run a national ticket until 1956, but 1932 was the last election in which the Socialists received at least 2 percent of the vote.

By a vote of 117 to 64, the convention adopted a resolution supporting the efforts of the Soviet Union to create a Socialist society. An attempt to oust Morris Hillquit as national chairman of the party was beaten, 108 to 81.

The Socialist platform of 1932 contained a number of proposals that had been set forth in earlier party platforms, such as public ownership of natural resources and the means of transportation and communication, increased taxes on the wealthy, an end to the Supreme Court's power to rule congressional legislation unconstitutional and a reduction in the size and expenditures of the military.

The platform also advocated United States recognition of the Soviet Union and American entry into the League of Nations. Repeal of Prohibition was recommended, as was the creation of a federal marketing system that would buy and market farm commodities.

To meet the hardship of the Depression, the Socialists listed a series of proposals, which included the expenditure of $10 billion for unemployment relief and public works projects.

Following are excerpts from the Socialist platform of 1932:

Unemployment Relief. 1. A Federal appropriation of $5,000,000,000 for immediate relief for those in need to supplement State and local appropriations.

2. A Federal appropriation of $5,000,000,000 for public works and roads, reforestation, slum clearance, and decent homes for the workers, by Federal Government, States and cities.

3. Legislation providing for the acquisition of land, buildings, and equipment necessary to put the unemployed to work producing food, fuel, and clothing and for the erection of houses for their own use.

4. The 6-hour day and the 5-day week without reduction of wages.

5. A comprehensive and efficient system of free public employment agencies.

6. A compulsory system of unemployment compensation with adequate benefits, based on contributions by the Government and by employers.

7. Old-age pensions for men and women 60 years of age and over.

8. Health and maternity insurance.

Republicans

As the incumbent party during the outset of the Depression, the Republicans bore the major political blame for the worsening economy. In a subdued mood, the party gathered in Chicago in June 1932 for its national convention.

Republican leaders did not view their electoral prospects optimistically for the fall election, but saw no realistic alternative to President Herbert Hoover.

Hoover was easily if unenthusiastically renominated, receiving 1,126-1/2 of the 1,154 convention votes. The highlight of the presidential balloting was the attempt by former Maryland senator Joseph I. France, who ran in several spring primaries, to gain the rostrum and nominate former president Coolidge. France's dramatic plan, however, was foiled by convention managers, who refused him permission to speak and had him escorted from the hall. *(Chart, p. 232)*

Vice President Charles Curtis had stiff opposition in his bid for renomination. The incumbent was seriously challenged by Maj. Gen. James G. Harbord of New York and the national commander of the American Legion, Hanford MacNider of Iowa. Curtis was short of a majority after the first ballot, but Pennsylvania quickly shifted its 75 votes to the vice president and this pushed him over the top. With the vote standing at Curtis, 634-1/4; MacNider, 182-3/4, and Harbord, 161-3/4, Curtis' renomination was made unanimous.

The major platform controversy surrounded the Prohibition plank. The majority plank, supported by Hoover, was ambiguous. It called for the enforcement of Prohibition but advocated a national referendum that would permit each state to determine whether or not it wanted Prohibition. A more clear-cut minority plank favored repeal of Prohibition. The minority proposal was defeated, however, 690-19/36 to 460-2/9. Following this roll call, the rest of the platform was approved by a voice vote.

The document approved by the Republicans was the longest in the party's history — nearly 9,000 words. It blamed the United States' continued economic problems on a worldwide depression, but lauded Hoover's leadership in meeting the crisis. The Republicans saw reduced government spending and a balanced budget as keys to ending the Depression. The party platform viewed unemployment relief as a matter for private agencies and local governments to handle.

The Republicans continued their support of a protective tariff. On the agricultural issue, the party proposed acreage controls to help balance supply and demand.

The final plank of the Republican platform urged party members in Congress to demonstrate party loyalty by supporting the Republican program. The plank warned that the party's strength was jeopardized by internal dissent.

Following are excerpts from the Republican platform of 1932:

Unemployment Relief. The people themselves, by their own courage, their own patient and resolute effort in the readjustments of their own affairs, can and will work out the cure. It is our task as a party, by leadership and a wise determination of policy, to assist that recovery. . . .

True to American traditions and principles of government, the administration has regarded the relief problem as one of State and local responsibility. The work of local agencies, public and private has been coordinated and enlarged on a nation-wide scale under the leadership of the President.

Government Spending. We urge prompt and drastic reduction of public expenditure and resistance to every appropriation not demonstrably necessary to the performance of government, national or local.

Agriculture. The fundamental problem of American agriculture is the control of production to such volume as will balance supply with demand. In the solution of this problem the cooperative organization of farmers to plan production, and the tariff, to hold the home market for American farmers, are vital elements. A third element equally as vital is the control of the acreage of land under cultivation, as an aid to the efforts of the farmer to balance production.

Prohibition. We . . . believe that the people should have an opportunity to pass upon a proposed amendment the provision of which, while retaining in the Federal Government power to preserve the gains already made in dealing with the evils inherent in the liquor traffic, shall allow the States to deal with the problem as their citizens may determine, but subject always to the power of the Federal Government to protect those States where prohibition may exist and safeguard our citizens everywhere from the return of the saloon and attendant abuses.

Democrats

With the nation in the midst of the Great Depression, the Democratic Party had its best chance for victory since 1912. The delegates assembled in Chicago in late June 1932, confident that the convention's nominee would defeat President Hoover.

Gov. Franklin D. Roosevelt of New York entered the convention with a majority of the votes, but was well short of the two-thirds majority needed for nomination. Ironically, his principal opponent was the man he had nominated for the presidency three times, former New York governor Alfred E. Smith.

Roosevelt's strength was tested on several key roll calls before the presidential balloting began. Two of the votes involved credentials challenges to Roosevelt delegations from Louisiana and Minnesota. By a vote of 638-3/4 to 514-1/4, the delegates seated the Roosevelt forces from Louisiana, headed by Sen. Huey P. Long. And by a wider margin of 658-1/4 to 492-3/4 the convention seated the Roosevelt delegates from Minnesota. *(Chart, p. 231)*

After settlement of the credentials cases, the battleground shifted to the selection of the permanent convention chairman. The Roosevelt forces backed Sen. Thomas J. Walsh of Montana, who was recommended by the committee on permanent organization. The Smith and other anti-Roosevelt factions coalesced behind Jouett Shouse of Kansas, chairman of the executive committee of the Democratic National Committee, who was recommended for permanent chairman by the national committee. But by a vote of 626 to 528, the Roosevelt forces won again, and Walsh assumed the gavel as permanent chairman.

The Roosevelt managers considered challenging the two-thirds rule; but, realizing that a bruising fight could alienate some of their own delegates, particularly in the South, they dropped the idea. Instead, the report of the rules committee recommended that a change in the two-thirds rule be delayed until the 1936 convention.

The presidential balloting began in the middle of an all-night session. After a motion to adjourn was defeated, 863-1/2 to 281-1/2, the first roll call began at 4:30 a.m. Roosevelt received a clear majority of 666-1/4 votes on the first ballot, compared with 201-3/4 for Smith and 90-1/4 for House Speaker John Nance Garner of Texas. Seven hundred and seventy votes were necessary for nomination. *(Chart, p. 231)*

Roosevelt gained slightly on the second ballot, advancing to 677-3/4 votes, while Smith dropped to 194-1/4 and Garner remained constant. Of side interest was the shift of Oklahoma's votes from its governor to Will Rogers, the state's famous humorist.

There were few changes on the next roll call, and at 9:15 a.m. the delegates agreed to adjourn. The vote totals after three ballots: Roosevelt, 682.79; Smith, 190-1/4; Garner, 101-1/4.

When balloting resumed the next evening, William Gibbs McAdoo of California quickly launched the bandwagon for Roosevelt by announcing that his state's 44 votes were switching from Garner to the New York governor. Other states followed California's lead, and when the fourth ballot was completed Roosevelt had 945 votes and the nomination. With the Smith vote holding at 190-1/2, no effort was made to make the nomination unanimous.

Although it is not clear whether there was a formal deal struck before the fourth ballot between the Garner and Roosevelt forces, the Texas representative was the unanimous choice of the convention for vice president. Forty states seconded his nomination, and no roll call was taken.

In an effort to break what he described as "absurd traditions," Roosevelt flew from Albany to Chicago to accept the presidential nomination personally. (Previously, a major party candidate would be formally notified of his nomination in a ceremony several weeks after the convention.) In his speech of acceptance, Roosevelt struck a liberal tone and issued his memorable pledge of "a new deal for the American people."

The platform adopted by the convention was not a blueprint for the New Deal to follow. It was fewer than 2,000 words long, the party's shortest platform since 1888, and less than one-fourth as long as the document adopted by the Republicans. It blamed the Depression on the "disastrous policies" practiced by the Republicans but made few new proposals, instead forcefully restating positions that had appeared in earlier party platforms.

The Democrats advocated a balanced budget with a cut of at least 25 percent in federal spending and called for removal of the federal government from competition with private enterprise in all areas except public works and natural resources.

The Democratic platform, unlike its Republican counterpart, advocated extensive unemployment relief and public works projects, regulation of holding companies and securities exchanges, "a competitive tariff for revenue" and the extension of farm cooperatives.

The plank that sparked the most enthusiasm among the delegates was the call for the repeal of Prohibition. A milder plank favored by "dry" delegates was resoundingly defeated, 934-3/4 to 213-3/4.

The only measure added from the floor of the convention favored "continuous responsibility of government for human welfare, especially for the protection of children." It was approved by a standing vote.

Following are excerpts from the Democratic platform of 1932:

Government Spending. We advocate an immediate and drastic reduction of governmental expenditures by abolishing useless commissions and offices, consolidating departments and bureaus, and eliminating extravagance to accomplish a saving of not less than twenty-five percent in the cost of the Federal Government. And we call upon the Democratic Party in the states to make a zealous effort to achieve a proportionate result.

We favor maintenance of the national credit by a federal budget annually balanced on the basis of accurate executive estimates within revenues, raised by a system of taxation levied on the principle of ability to pay.

Unemployment Relief, Public Works Projects. We advocate the extension of federal credit to the states to provide unemployment relief wherever the diminishing resources of the states makes it impossible for them to provide for the needy; expansion of the federal program of necessary and useful construction effected with a public interest, such as adequate flood control and waterways.

We advocate the spread of employment by a substantial reduction in the hours of labor, the encouragement of the shorter week by applying that principle in government service; we advocate advance planning of public works.

We advocate unemployment and old-age insurance under state laws.

Prohibition. We advocate the repeal of the Eighteenth Amendment. To effect such repeal we demand that the Congress immediately propose a Constitutional Amendment to truly represent [sic] the conventions in the states called to act solely on that proposal; we urge the enactment of such measures by the several states as will actually promote temperance, effectively prevent the return of the saloon, and bring the liquor traffic into the open under complete supervision and control by the states.

Agriculture. Extension and development of the Farm Cooperative movement and effective control of crop surpluses so that our farmers may have the full benefit of the domestic market.

The enactment of every constitutional measure that will aid the farmers to receive for their basic farm commodities prices in excess of cost.

1936 Conventions

Presidential Candidates

Alfred M. Landon
Republican

Franklin D. Roosevelt
Democrat

William Lemke
Union

Republicans

The Republican convention, held in Cleveland in early June, was an unusually harmonious gathering for a party out of power. There were only two roll-call votes on the convention floor, for president and vice president, and both were one-sided.

The only matter of debate was the vote allocation for Alaska, Hawaii and the District of Columbia. By a voice vote, the convention approved the minority report of the rules committee, which sliced the vote for these three from six to three votes apiece.

Former president Herbert Hoover received an enthusiastic reception when he spoke, but by that time Kansas governor Alfred M. Landon had the presidential nomination sewed up. Landon, one of the few Republican governors to be re-elected during the Depression, received 984 votes on the first ballot, compared with 19 for Sen. William E. Borah of Idaho. *(Chart, p. 233)*

Before the balloting began, Landon had sent a telegram to the convention that expressed his agreement with the "word and spirit" of the party platform but elaborated his position on several points. The Kansan advocated the passage of a constitutional amendment to ensure women and children safe working conditions and to establish guidelines for wages and hours in the event that legislation passed by Congress was ruled unconstitutional. Landon's message also proposed extending the civil service to include all workers in federal departments and agencies below the rank of assistant secretary, and it defined "sound currency" as currency that could be exchanged for gold. Landon's pronouncements were met with 30 minutes of cheering.

For vice president, the convention selected Col. Frank Knox of Illinois, publisher of *The Chicago Daily News*. Knox, who earlier had campaigned energetically, if not successfully, for the presidential nomination, received all 1,003 votes on the first ballot.

The Republican platform, which began with the sentence, "America is in peril," focused on the alleged threat of New Deal policies to American constitutional govern-ment. The platform assailed the Roosevelt administration for "dishonoring American traditions" and promised to protect local self-government and the power of the Supreme Court.

The Republicans promised a balanced budget, reduced federal expenditures, a "sound currency," a more discriminating public works program and the administration of unemployment relief by "non-political local agencies" that would be financed jointly by the various states and the federal government.

The Republicans shared with the Democrats the belief in an isolationist foreign policy and the concepts of social security, unemployment insurance and crop control.

Following are excerpts from the Republican platform of 1936:

Roosevelt's 'New Deal.' America is in peril. The welfare of American men and women and the future of our youth are at stake. We dedicate ourselves to the preservation of their political liberty, their individual opportunity and their character as free citizens, which today for the first time are threatened by Government itself. . . .

The powers of Congress have been usurped by the President.

The integrity and authority of the Supreme Court have been flouted.

The rights and liberties of American citizens have been violated.

Regulated monopoly has displaced free enterprise.

The New Deal Administration constantly seeks to usurp the rights reserved to the States and to the people.

Unemployment Relief. The return of responsibility for relief administration to nonpolitical local agencies familiar with community problems. . . .

Undertaking of Federal public works only on their merits and separate from the administration of relief.

Government Spending, Currency. Balance the budget — not by increasing taxes but by cutting expenditures, drastically and immediately. . . .

We advocate a sound currency to be preserved at all hazards.

The first requisite to a sound and stable currency is a balanced budget.

Foreign Policy. We pledge ourselves to promote and maintain peace by all honorable means not leading to foreign alliances or political commitments.

Obedient to the traditional foreign policy of America and to the repeatedly expressed will of the American people, we pledge that America shall not become a member of the League of Nations nor of the World Court nor shall America take on any entangling alliances in foreign affairs.

Democrats

The 1936 Democratic convention, held in Philadelphia in late June, was one of the most harmonious in party history. There were no floor debates, and, for the first time since 1840, there were no roll-call votes.

The only matter that required discussion — elimination of the century-old two-thirds rule — was settled in the rules committee. There, by a vote of 36 to 13, the committee agreed to abrogate the rule, which had been a controversial part of Democratic conventions since 1832. To mollify the South, which was particularly threatened by elimination of the two-thirds rule, the rules committee added a provision that would include consideration of a state's Democratic voting strength in determining its future convention vote allocation. The rules committee report was approved by a voice vote.

Both President Franklin D. Roosevelt and Vice President John Nance Garner were renominated by acclamation, but more than a full day of oratory was expended in eulogizing the Democratic standard-bearers. Roosevelt was seconded by delegates from each of the states and territories — more than 50 separate speakers. Seventeen delegates spoke on behalf of Garner.

Both Roosevelt and Garner personally accepted their nominations in ceremonies at the University of Pennsylvania's Franklin Field. Before a crowd estimated as large as 100,000, Roosevelt electrified his listeners with a speech that blasted his adversaries among the rich as "economic royalists" and included the sentence: "This generation of Americans has a rendezvous with destiny."

As in 1932 the platform adopted by the Democrats was a short one, about 3,000 words. The document paid lip service to the concept of a balanced budget and reduced government spending, but it supported continuation of the extensive federal programs undertaken by the Roosevelt administration.

The platform did not, as many in past years had, mention states' rights; this reflected the party's changing view toward federal power. To counter what was viewed as obstructionism by the Supreme Court, the Democrats suggested the possibility of passing a "clarifying amendment" to the Constitution that would enable Congress and state legislatures to enact bills without the fear of an unfavorable decision from the Supreme Court.

The foreign policy plank recognized the isolationist mood of the period, calling for neutrality in foreign disputes and the avoidance of international commitments that would draw the United States into war.

Following are excerpts from the Democratic platform of 1936:

Federal Power. The Republican platform proposes to meet many pressing national problems solely by action of the separate States. We know that drought, dust storms, floods, minimum wages, maximum hours, child labor, and working conditions in industry, monopolistic and unfair business practices cannot be adequately handled exclusively by 48 separate State legislatures, 48 separate State administrations, and 48 separate State courts. Transactions and activities which inevitably overflow State boundaries call for both State and Federal treatment.

We have sought and will continue to seek to meet these problems through legislation within the Constitution.

If these problems cannot be effectively solved by legislation within the Constitution, we shall seek such clarifying amendment as will assure to the legislatures of the several States and to the Congress of the United States, each within its proper jurisdiction, the power to enact those laws which the State and Federal legislatures, within their respective spheres, shall find necessary, in order adequately to regulate commerce, protect public health and safety and safeguard economic security. Thus we propose to maintain the letter and spirit of the Constitution.

Government Spending. We are determined to reduce the expenses of government. We are being aided therein by the recession in unemployment. As the requirements of relief decline and national income advances, an increasing percentage of Federal expenditures can and will be met from current revenues, secured from taxes levied in accordance with ability to pay. Our retrenchment, tax and recovery programs thus reflect our firm determination to achieve a balanced budget and the reduction of the national debt at the earliest possible moment.

Foreign Policy. We reaffirm our opposition to war as an instrument of national policy, and declare that disputes between nations should be settled by peaceful means. We shall continue to observe a true neutrality in the disputes of others; to be prepared resolutely to resist aggression against ourselves; to work for peace and to take the profits out of war; to guard against being drawn, by political commitments, international banking or private trading, into any war which may develop anywhere.

Union Party

With the support of Father Charles E. Coughlin and his National Union for Social Justice, on June 19, 1936, Rep. William Lemke of North Dakota, a Republican, declared his presidential candidacy on the newly formed Union Party ticket. Thomas O'Brien, a Boston railroad union lawyer, was announced as Lemke's running mate. The fledgling political organization had a brief existence, running a national ticket only in the 1936 election. *(Union Party, p. 277)*

The Union Party was basically an extension of Coughlin's organization, and the Lemke-O'Brien ticket was endorsed at the National Union for Social Justice convention in August by a vote of 8,152 to 1.

The Union Party platform reportedly was written by Coughlin, Lemke and O'Brien at the Roman Catholic priest's church in Royal Oak, Mich. It was a brief document, fewer than 1,000 words, that contained 15 points similar to the 16-point program favored by Coughlin's National Union. The primary distinctions between the Union Party and the two major parties were in currency expansion, civil service reform and restrictions on wealth. The Union Party called for the creation of a central bank, regulated by Congress, that would issue currency to help pay off the federal debt and refinance agricultural and home mortgage indebtedness. The Union Party platform also proposed extending the civil service to all levels of the federal government and advocated placing restrictions on annual individual income coupled with a ceiling on gifts and inheritances. The new party differed from the Socialists by emphasizing that private property should not be confiscated.

Following are excerpts from the Union Party platform of 1936:

Currency Expansion. Congress and Congress alone shall coin and issue the currency and regulate the value of all money and credit in the United States through a central bank of issue.

Immediately following the establishment of the central bank of issue Congress shall provide for the retirement of all tax-exempt, interest-bearing bonds and certificates of indebtedness of the Federal Government and shall refinance all the present agricultural mortgage indebtedness for the farmer and all the home mortgage indebtedness for the farmer and all the home mortgage indebtedness for the city owner by the use of its money and credit which it now gives to the private bankers.

Civil Service Reform. Congress shall so legislate that all Federal offices and positions of every nature shall be distributed through civil-service qualifications and not through a system of party spoils and corrupt patronage.

Restrictions on Wealth. Congress shall set a limitation upon the net income of any individual in any one year and a limitation of the amount that such an individual may receive as a gift or as an inheritance, which limitation shall be executed through taxation.

Foreign Policy. Congress shall establish an adequate and perfect defense for our country from foreign aggression either by air, by land, or by sea, but with the understanding that our naval, air, and military forces must not be used under any consideration in foreign fields or in foreign waters either alone or in conjunction with any foreign power. If there must be conscription, there shall be a conscription of wealth as well as a conscription of men.

1940 Conventions
Presidential Candidates

Wendell L. Willkie
Republican

Franklin D. Roosevelt
Democrat

Republicans

The Republican convention was held in Philadelphia in late June, and it culminated one of the most successful of all campaign blitzes. Wendell L. Willkie, an Indiana native who had never before run for public office, was nominated by the Republicans to run for president. A Democrat until 1938, Willkie had gained fame as a defender of private enterprise in opposition to Roosevelt's public power projects. Although Willkie had broad personal appeal, he and his well-financed group of political "amateurs" did not launch their presidential bid until late spring and missed the presidential primaries. Willkie's momentum came from his rapid rise in the Republican preference polls, as he soared from only 3 percent in early May to 29 percent six weeks later.

At the Republican convention, 10 names were placed in nomination for the presidency. Willkie's principal rivals were Manhattan District Attorney Thomas E. Dewey, making his first presidential bid at age 38, and Sen. Robert A. Taft of Ohio. On the first ballot, Dewey led with 360 votes, followed by Taft with 189 and Willkie with 105. Five hundred and one votes were needed for nomination. *(Chart, p. 234)*

After the first roll call, Dewey steadily lost strength, while Willkie and Taft gained. Willkie assumed the lead on the fourth ballot, passing both Dewey and Taft. Willkie's vote was 306, while Taft moved into second place with 254. Dewey dropped to third with 250.

On the fifth ballot, the contest narrowed to just Willkie and Taft, as both candidates continued to gain — Willkie jumping to 429 votes and Taft to 377. The shift of Michigan's votes to Willkie on the sixth ballot started a bandwagon for the Indianan that pushed him over the top. When the roll call was completed, Willkie was nominated with 655 votes, and a motion to make his nomination unanimous was adopted.

As his running mate, Willkie favored Senate Minority Leader Charles L. McNary of Oregon. McNary, a supporter of some New Deal measures, was opposed by Rep. Dewey Short of Missouri, a vocal anti-New Dealer. McNary, however, was able to win easily on a single ballot, receiving 890 votes to 108 for Short.

The Republican platform was adopted without debate, although an Illinois member of the platform committee commented that his state would have preferred a stronger anti-war plank. As it was, the Republican foreign policy plank sharply criticized the Roosevelt administration for not adequately preparing the nation's defense. However, the rest of the plank was similar to the one adopted three weeks later by the Democrats at the convention: opposing involvement in war but stressing national defense, and advocating aid to the Allies that would not be "inconsistent with the requirements of our own national defense."

In domestic affairs, the Republicans lambasted the extension of federal power under the New Deal and promised cuts in government spending and the reduction of federal competition with private enterprise. The Republican platform agreed with the concept of unemployment relief and social security initiated by the Roosevelt administration, but it proposed the administration of these programs by the states and not the federal government.

The Republicans attacked Roosevelt's monetary measures and advocated currency reforms that included congressional control.

The platform also proposed new amendments to the Constitution that would provide equal rights for men and women and would limit a president to two terms in office.

Following are excerpts from the Republican platform of 1940:

Foreign Policy. The Republican Party is firmly opposed to involving this Nation in foreign war. . . .

The Republican Party stands for Americanism, preparedness and peace. We accordingly fasten upon the New Deal full responsibility for our unpreparedness and for the consequent danger of involvement in war. . . .

Our sympathies have been profoundly stirred by invasion of unoffending countries and by disaster to nations whole [whose] ideals most closely resemble our own. We favor the extension to all peoples fighting for liberty, or whose liberty is threatened, of such aid as shall not be in violation of international law or inconsistent with the requirements of our own national defense.

Unemployment Relief. We shall remove waste, discrimination, and politics from relief — through administration by the States with federal grants-in-aid on a fair and nonpolitical basis, thus giving the man and woman on relief a larger share of the funds appropriated.

Currency. The Congress should reclaim its constitutional powers over money, and withdraw the President's arbitrary authority to manipulate the currency, establish bimetallism, issue irredeemable paper money, and debase the gold and silver coinage. We shall repeal the Thomas Inflation Amendment of 1933 and the (foreign) Silver Purchase Act of 1934, and take all possible steps to preserve the value of the Government's huge holdings of gold and reintroduce gold into circulation.

Women's Rights. We favor submission by Congress to the States of an amendment to the Constitution providing for equal rights for men and women.

No Third Term. To insure against the overthrow of our American system of government we favor an amendment to the Constitution providing that no person shall be President of the United States for more than two terms.

Democrats

At the time of both major party conventions in the summer of 1940, Hitler's forces were moving quickly and relentlessly across Western Europe. International events assumed a major importance in political decisions. President Franklin D. Roosevelt, who gave evidence before 1940 that he would not seek a third term, became increasingly receptive to the idea of a draft as the Democratic convention drew nearer. The threat to American security caused by the awesomely successful Nazi military machine, coupled with Roosevelt's inability to find an adequate New Deal-style successor, seemed to spur F.D.R.'s decision to accept renomination.

The Democratic convention was held in Chicago in mid-July. On the second night of the convention, a message from Roosevelt was read stating that he did not desire to run for re-election and urging the delegates to vote for any candidate they wished. Although worded in a negative way, the message did not shut the door on a draft. The delegates reacted, however, by sitting in stunned silence until a Chicago city official began shouting over the public address system, "We want Roosevelt." The cheerleading galvanized the delegates into an hour-long demonstration.

Presidential balloting was held the next day. Roosevelt won easily on the first roll call, although two members of his administration, Vice President John Nance Garner and Postmaster General James A. Farley of New York, ran against him. Roosevelt received 945-13/30 of the 1,100 votes. Farley had 72-9/10 and Garner had 61. *(Chart, p. 233)*

While the delegates were satisfied to have Roosevelt at the top of the ticket again, many balked at his choice for vice president, Agriculture Secretary Henry A. Wallace of Iowa. Wallace, a leading liberal in the administration and a former Republican, was particularly distasteful to conservative Democrats. Many delegates were expecting Roosevelt to leave the vice presidential choice to the convention and were unhappy to have the candidate dictated to them.

It took a personal appearance at the convention by the president's wife, Eleanor Roosevelt, and a threat by F.D.R. that he would not accept the presidential nomination without his hand-picked running mate, to steer the delegates toward Wallace. In spite of the pressure by the Roosevelt forces, the vote was scattered among 13 candidates on the vice presidential ballot. Wallace, though, was able to obtain a slim majority, 626-11/30 votes to 329-3/5 for the runner-up, House Speaker William B. Bankhead of Alabama. Because of the displeasure of many of the delegates, Wallace was asked not to address the convention.

The convention closed by hearing a radio address by Roosevelt, who stated that he had not wanted the nomination but accepted it because the existing world crisis called for personal sacrifice.

The party platform was adopted without a roll call, although there was an amendment presented by a Minnesota representative that opposed any violation of the two-term tradition. It was rejected by a voice vote. The platform as adopted was divided into three sections. The first discussed American military preparedness and foreign policy; the second detailed the New Deal's benefits for various segments of the economy (agriculture, labor, business); the third listed New Deal welfare measures, ranging from unemployment relief to low-cost housing.

As a concession to the party's isolationist wing, the first section contained the administration's promise not to participate in foreign wars or fight in foreign lands, except in case of an attack on the United States. The plank stressed the need of a strong national defense to discourage aggression, but also pledged to provide to free nations (such as Great Britain) material aid "not inconsistent with the interests of our own national self-defense."

An electric power plank was included in the second section of the platform as a direct result of the Republicans' selection of Wendell L. Willkie, a former utilities executive, as their presidential candidate. The Democrats argued in favor of the massive public power projects constructed during the New Deal and criticized private utilities such as the one formerly headed by Willkie.

The third section of the platform drew a sharp distinction from the Republicans on the issue of unemployment relief, opposing any efforts to turn the administration of relief over to the states or local governments.

Following are excerpts from the Democratic platform of 1940:

Democratic Achievements. Toward the modern fulfillment of the American ideal, the Democratic Party, during the last seven years, has labored successfully:

1. *To strengthen democracy by defensive preparedness against aggression, whether by open attack or secret infiltration;*

2. *To strengthen democracy by increasing our economic efficiency; and*

3. *To strengthen democracy by improving the welfare of the people.*

Foreign Policy. We will not participate in foreign wars, and we will not send our army, naval or air forces to fight in foreign lands outside of the Americas, except in case of attack....

Weakness and unpreparedness invite aggression. We must be so strong that no possible combination of powers would dare to attack us. We propose to provide America with an invincible air force, a navy strong enough to protect all our seacoasts and our national interests, and a fully-equipped and mechanized army.

Unemployment Relief. We shall continue to recognize the obligation of Government to provide work for deserving workers who cannot be absorbed by private industry.

We are opposed to vesting in the states and local authorities the control of Federally-financed work relief. We believe that this Republican proposal is a thinly disguised plan to put the unemployed back on the dole.

Electric Power. The nomination of a utility executive by the Republican Party as its presidential candidate raises squarely the issue, whether the nation's water power shall be used for all the people or for the selfish interests of a few. We accept that issue.

1944 Conventions

Presidential Candidates

Thomas E. Dewey
Republican

Franklin D. Roosevelt
Democrat

Republicans

For the first time since 1864, the nation was at war during a presidential election year. The Republicans held their convention first, meeting in Chicago in late June 1944. With a minimum of discord, the delegates selected a national ticket and adopted a platform. Gov. Thomas E. Dewey of New York, the front-runner for the presidential nomination, was the nearly unanimous selection when his last two rivals, Gov. John W. Bricker of Ohio and former Minnesota governor Harold E. Stassen, both withdrew from the race before the roll call. On the single ballot, Dewey received 1,056 of the 1,057 votes cast. The one dissenting vote was cast by a Wisconsin delegate for Gen. Douglas MacArthur. *(Chart, p. 235)*

As Dewey's running mate, the delegates unanimously selected Gov. Bricker, an isolationist and party regular, who received all 1,057 votes cast. During the nominating speeches, Rep. Charles A. Halleck of Indiana made the unusual move of recommending his state's first choice for vice president, William L. Hutcheson, for secretary of labor.

Dewey came to Chicago personally to accept the nomination, becoming the first Republican presidential candidate to break the tradition of waiting to accept the nomination in a formal notification ceremony. The thrust of Dewey's speech was an attack on the Roosevelt administration, which he referred to as "stubborn men grown old and tired and quarrelsome in office."

The platform was approved without dissent. The international section was written in a guarded tone. It favored "responsible participation by the United States in post-war cooperative organization" but declared that any agreement must be approved by a two-thirds vote of the Senate. The Republicans favored the establishment of a postwar Jewish state in Palestine.

The domestic section of the platform denounced the New Deal's centralization of power in the federal government, with its increased government spending and deficits. The Republicans proposed to stabilize the economy through the encouragement of private enterprise.

The platform restated several of the planks included four years earlier, among which were the call for an equal rights amendment, a two-term limitation on the president and the return of control over currency matters from the president to Congress.

The Republicans adopted a civil rights plank that

called for a congressional investigation of the treatment of blacks in the military, passage of a constitutional amendment to eliminate the poll tax and legislation that would outlaw lynching and permanently establish a Fair Employment Practice Commission.

Following are excerpts from the Republican platform of 1944:

Postwar International Organization. We favor responsible participation by the United States in post-war cooperative organization among sovereign nations to prevent military aggression and to attain permanent peace with organized justice in a free world.

Such organization should develop effective cooperative means to direct peace forces to prevent or repel military aggression. Pending this, we pledge continuing collaboration with the United Nations to assure these ultimate objectives....

We shall sustain the Constitution of the United States in the attainment of our international aims; and pursuant to the Constitution of the United States any treaty or agreement to attain such aims made on behalf of the United States with any other nation or any association of nations, shall be made only by and with the advice and consent of the Senate of the United States provided two-thirds of the Senators present concur.

Israel. In order to give refuge to millions of distressed Jewish men, women and children driven from their homes by tyranny, we call for the opening of Palestine to their unrestricted immigration and land ownership, so that in accordance with the full intent and purpose of the Balfour Declaration of 1917 and the Resolution of a Republican Congress in 1922, Palestine may be constituted as a free and democratic Commonwealth. We condemn the failure of the President to insist that the mandatory of Palestine carry out the provision of the Balfour Declaration and of the mandate while he pretends to support them.

New Deal. Four more years of New Deal policy would centralize all power in the President, and would daily subject every act of every citizen to regulation by his henchmen; and this country could remain a Republic only in name. No problem exists which cannot be solved by American methods. We have no need of either the communistic or the fascist technique.

...The National Administration has become a sprawling, overlapping bureaucracy. It is undermined by executive abuse of power, confused lines of authority, duplication of effort, inadequate fiscal controls, loose personnel practices and an attitude of arrogance previously unknown in our history.

Economy. We reject the theory of restoring prosperity through government spending and deficit financing.

We shall promote the fullest stable employment through private enterprise.

Civil Rights. We pledge an immediate Congressional inquiry to ascertain the extent to which mistreatment, segregation and discrimination against Negroes who are in our armed forces are impairing morale and efficiency, and the adoption of corrective legislation.

We pledge the establishment by Federal legislation of a permanent Fair Employment Practice Commission.

The payment of any poll tax should not be a condition of voting in Federal elections and we favor immediate submission of a Constitutional amendment for its abolition.

We favor legislation against lynching and pledge our sincere efforts in behalf of its early enactment.

Agriculture. An American market price to the American farmer and the protection of such price by means of support prices, commodity loans, or a combination thereof, together with such other economic means as will assure an income to agriculture that is fair and equitable in comparison with labor, business and industry. We oppose subsidies as a substitute for fair markets.

Serious study of and search for a sound program of crop insurance with emphasis upon establishing a self-supporting program.

Democrats

President Franklin Delano Roosevelt, who four years earlier did not make a final decision about accepting a third nomination until the last moment, clearly stated his intention to run for a fourth term a week before the 1944 convention was to open in Chicago. In a message to Democratic National Chairman Robert E. Hannegan of Missouri released July 11, Roosevelt declared that while he did not desire to run, he would accept renomination reluctantly as a "good soldier."

The early sessions of the convention were highlighted by approval of the rules committee report and settlement of a credentials challenge. The rules committee mandated the national committee to revamp the convention's vote-allocation formula in a way that would take into account Democratic voting strength. This measure was adopted to appease Southern delegates, who in 1936 were promised an increased proportion of the convention vote in return for elimination of the two-thirds rule. No action had been taken to implement the pledge in the intervening eight years.

The credentials dispute involved the Texas delegation, which was represented by two competing groups. By a voice vote, the convention agreed to seat both groups.

Vice President Henry A. Wallace enlivened the presidential nominations by appearing before the convention to urge Roosevelt's renomination. Wallace termed the president the "greatest liberal in the history of the U.S." In the balloting that followed, Roosevelt easily defeated Sen. Harry F. Byrd of Virginia, who was supported by some conservative Southern delegates unhappy with the domestic legislation favored by the New Deal. The final tally: Roosevelt, 1,086; Byrd, 89; former postmaster general James A. Farley, 1. *(Chart, p. 235)*

Roosevelt accepted the nomination in a radio address delivered from the San Diego Naval Base, where he had stopped off en route to a wartime conference.

The real drama of the convention, the selection of the vice presidential nominee, came next. Roosevelt had been ambivalent about the choice of his running mate, encouraging several people to run but not publicly endorsing any of them. The president wrote an ambiguous letter to the convention chairman, which was read to the delegates. Roosevelt stated that if he were a delegate himself he would vote for Wallace's renomination, but that the ultimate choice was the convention's and it must consider the pros and cons of its selection.

In another message, written privately for National Chairman Hannegan, Roosevelt declared that he would be happy to run with either Missouri senator Harry S. Truman or Supreme Court Justice William O. Douglas. Most of the party bosses preferred Truman to the more liberal alternatives, Wallace and Douglas. Truman originally was slated to nominate former South Carolina senator and Supreme Court Justice James F. Byrnes for vice president. But, spurred by his political advisers, Roosevelt telephoned Truman in Chicago and urged him to accept the nomination. Truman reluctantly agreed.

Roosevelt's final preference for Truman was not publicly announced, and 12 names were placed before the convention. Wallace led on the first roll call with 429-1/2 votes, followed by Truman with 319-1/2. Favorite sons and other hopefuls shared the remaining votes cast.

Truman passed Wallace on the second ballot, 477-1/2 to 473, and, immediately after completion of the roll call, Alabama began the bandwagon for the Missouri senator by switching its votes to him. When all the shifts had been made, Truman was an easy winner with 1,031 votes, while Wallace finished with 105.

The platform adopted by the convention was a short one, only 1,360 words. The first third of the platform lauded the accomplishments of Roosevelt's first three terms. The rest of the document outlined the party's proposals for the future. In foreign affairs, the Democrats advocated the creation of a postwar international organization that would have adequate forces available to prevent future wars. The party also called for American membership in an international court of justice. The Democrats joined their Republican opponents in favoring the establishment of an independent Jewish state in Palestine.

The domestic section of the platform proposed a continuation of New Deal liberalism, with passage of an equal rights amendment for women, price guarantees and crop insurance for farmers and the establishment of federal aid to education that would be administered by the states.

A minority report concerning foreign policy called for the establishment of an international air force to help keep peace. The proposal was rejected, however, when the platform committee chairman indicated that the existence of an air force was included in the majority report's call for "adequate forces" to be at the disposal of the proposed international organization.

Following are excerpts from the Democratic platform of 1944:

Postwar International Organizations. That the world may not again be drenched in blood by international outlaws and criminals, we pledge:

To join with the other United Nations in the establishment of an international organization based on the principle of the sovereign equality of all peace-loving states, open to membership by all such states, large and small, for the prevention of aggression and the maintenance of international peace and security.

To make all necessary and effective agreements and arrangements through which the nations would maintain adequate forces to meet the needs of preventing war and of making impossible the preparation for war and which would have such forces available for joint action when necessary.

Such organization must be endowed with power to employ armed forces when necessary to prevent aggression and preserve peace.

Israel. We favor the opening of Palestine to unrestricted Jewish immigration and colonization, and such a policy as to result in the establishment there of a free and democratic Jewish commonwealth.

Women's Rights. We favor legislation assuring equal pay for equal work, regardless of sex.

We recommend to Congress the submission of a Constitutional amendment on equal rights for women.

Education. We favor Federal aid to education administered by the states without interference by the Federal Government.

Agriculture. Price guarantees and crop insurance to farmers with all practical steps:

To keep agriculture on a parity with industry and labor.

To foster the success of the small independent farmer.

To aid the home ownership of family-sized farms.

To extend rural electrification and develop broader domestic and foreign markets for agricultural products.

Civil Rights. We believe that racial and religious minorities have the right to live, develop and vote equally with all citizens and share the rights that are guaranteed by our Constitution. Congress should exert its full constitutional powers to protect those rights.

1948 Conventions

Presidential Candidates

Thomas E. Dewey
Republican

Harry S. Truman
Democrat

J. Strom Thurmond
States' Rights

Henry A. Wallace
Progressive

Republicans

The Republican convention was held in Philadelphia in late June. As in 1944, New York governor Thomas E. Dewey entered the convention as the front-runner for the nomination. But unlike four years earlier, when he was virtually handed the nomination, Dewey was contested by several candidates, including Ohio senator Robert A. Taft and former Minnesota governor Harold E. Stassen.

In all, seven names were placed in nomination, with 548 votes needed to determine a winner. Dewey led on the first roll call with 434 votes, followed by Taft with 224 and Stassen with 157. Each of the other candidates received fewer than 100 votes. *(Chart, p. 237)*

On the second roll call, Dewey moved closer to the nomination, receiving 515 votes. Taft and Stassen continued to trail, with 274 and 149 votes respectively. At this point, the anti-Dewey forces requested a recess, which was agreed to by the confident Dewey organization.

Unable to form a coalition that could stop Dewey, all his opponents withdrew before the third ballot. On the subsequent roll call, the New York governor was the unanimous choice of the convention, receiving all 1,094 votes.

Dewey's choice for vice president was California governor Earl Warren, who was nominated by acclamation. Warren had been a favorite-son candidate for the presidency and agreed to take second place on the ticket only after receiving assurances that the responsibilities of the vice presidency would be increased if Dewey were elected.

The Republican platform was adopted without dissent. The wording of the platform was unusually positive for a party out of the White House. The failures of the Truman administration were dismissed in a short paragraph, with the rest of the document praising the accomplishments of the Republican 80th Congress and detailing the party's proposals for the future.

One of the major issues of the 1948 campaign was the controversial Taft-Hartley labor law, a measure supported by the Republicans, but which most Democratic leaders felt should be repealed. The Republicans were silent on national health insurance, and the party's housing position stressed private initiative rather than federal legislation. As in 1944

the Republicans opposed the poll tax and segregation in the military and favored legislation to outlaw lynching.

The Republican platform accepted the concept of a bipartisan foreign policy. Paragraphs were inserted that supported the Marshall Plan for European recovery, the United Nations and recognition of Israel.

Following are excerpts from the Republican platform of 1948:

Civil Rights. This right of equal opportunity to work and to advance in life should never be limited in any individual because of race, religion, color, or country of origin. We favor the enactment and just enforcement of such Federal legislation as may be necessary to maintain this right at all times in every part of this Republic. . . .

Lynching or any other form of mob violence anywhere is a disgrace to any civilized state, and we favor the prompt enactment of legislation to end this infamy. . . .

We favor the abolition of the poll tax as a requisite to voting.

We are opposed to the idea of racial segregation in the armed services of the United States.

Housing. Housing can best be supplied and financed by private enterprise; but government can and should encourage the building of better homes at less cost. We recommend Federal aid to the States for local slum clearance and low-rental housing programs only where there is a need that cannot be met either by private enterprise or by the States and localities.

Labor. Here are some of the accomplishments of this Republican Congress: a sensible reform of the labor law, protecting all rights of Labor while safeguarding the entire community, against those breakdowns in essential industries which endanger the health and livelihood of all. . . .

We pledge continuing study to improve labor-management legislation in the light of experience and changing conditions. . . .

We favor equal pay for equal work regardless of sex.

Internal Security. We pledge a vigorous enforcement of existing laws against Communists and enactment of such new legislation as may be necessary to expose the treasonable activities of Communists and defeat their objective of establishing here a godless dictatorship controlled from abroad.

Foreign Policy. We are proud of the part that Republicans have taken in those limited areas of foreign policy in which they have been permitted to participate. We shall invite the Minority Party to join us under the next Republican Administration in stopping partisan politics at the water's edge.

United Nations. We believe in collective security against aggression and in behalf of justice and freedom. We shall support the United Nations as the world's best hope in this direction, striving to strengthen it and promote its effective evolution and use. The United Nations should progressively establish international law, be freed of any veto in the peaceful settlement of international disputes, and be provided with the armed forces contemplated by the Charter.

Israel. We welcome Israel into the family of nations and take pride in the fact that the Republican Party was the first to call for the establishment of a free and independent Jewish Commonwealth.

Democrats

The Democratic delegates were in a melancholy mood when they gathered in Philadelphia in mid-July 1948. Franklin D. Roosevelt was dead; the Republicans had regained control of Congress in 1946; Roosevelt's successor, Harry S. Truman, appeared unable to stem massive defections of liberals and Southern conservatives from the New Deal coalition.

The dissatisfaction of Southern delegates with policies of the national party was a prominent feature of the 1948 convention. Although the national committee had been mandated by the 1944 convention to devise a new vote allocation procedure that would appease the South, the redistribution of votes for the 1948 convention merely added two votes to each of the 36 states that backed Roosevelt in the 1944 election. This did not appreciably bolster Southern strength.

As the convention progressed, Southern displeasure focused on the civil rights issue. The Mississippi delegation included in its credentials anti-civil-rights resolutions that bound the delegation to bolt the convention if a states' rights plank was not included in the platform. The Mississippi resolutions also denied the power of the national convention to require the Democratic Party of Mississippi to support any candidate who favored President Truman's civil rights program or any candidate who failed to denounce that program.

A minority report was introduced that recommended the Mississippi delegation not be seated. This proposal was defeated by a voice vote, and, in the interest of party harmony, no roll-call vote was taken. However, in an unusual move, several delegations, including those of California and New York, asked that they be recorded in favor of the minority report.

Joined by several other Southern states, Texas presented a minority proposal to the rules committee report, which favored re-establishment of the two-thirds rule. The minority proposal, however, was beaten by a voice vote.

When the presidential balloting began, the entire Mississippi delegation and 13 members of the Alabama delegation withdrew in opposition to the convention's stand on civil rights. However, their withdrawal in no way jeopardized the nomination of Truman. Some party leaders had earlier flirted with the possibility of drafting Gen. Dwight D. Eisenhower or even Supreme Court Justice William O.

Douglas. But the lack of interest of these two men in the Democratic nomination left the field clear for Truman.

The incumbent won a clear majority on the first ballot, receiving 926 votes to 266 for Georgia senator Richard B. Russell, who received the votes of more than 90 percent of the remaining Southern delegates. Among the states of the Old Confederacy, Truman received only 13 votes, all from North Carolina. After several small vote switches, the final tally stood: Truman, 947-1/2; Russell, 263. *(Chart, p. 236)*

Veteran Kentucky senator Alben W. Barkley, the convention's keynoter, was nominated by acclamation for vice president.

Truman appeared before the convention to accept the nomination and aroused the dispirited delegates with a lively speech attacking the Republican Congress. Referring to it as the "worst 80th Congress," Truman announced that he would call a special session so that the Republicans could pass the legislation they said they favored in their platform.

The Democratic platform was adopted by a voice vote, after a heated discussion of the civil rights section. As presented to the convention by the platform committee, the plank favored equal rights for all citizens but was couched in generalities such as those in the 1944 plank. Southern delegates wanted a weaker commitment to civil rights, and various Southern delegations offered three different amendments.

One, presented by former governor Dan Moody of Texas and signed by 15 members of the platform committee, was a broadly worded statement that emphasized the power of the states. A second amendment, sponsored by two Tennessee members of the platform committee, was a brief, emphatic statement declaring the rights of the states. The third amendment, introduced by the Mississippi delegation as a substitute for the Moody amendment, specifically listed the powers of the states to maintain segregation. The Moody amendment was beaten, 924 to 310, with nearly all the support limited to the South. The other two amendments were rejected by voice vote. *(Chart, p. 236)*

Northern liberals countered by proposing to strengthen the civil rights plank. Introduced by former representative Andrew J. Biemiller of Wisconsin and championed by Mayor Hubert H. Humphrey of Minneapolis, the amendment commended Truman's civil rights program and called for congressional action to guarantee equal rights in voting participation, employment opportunity, personal security and military service. The Biemiller amendment was passed, 651-1/2 to 582-1/2, with delegations from the larger Northern states supporting it. Delegations from the South were in solid opposition and were joined by delegates from Border and small Northern states. *(Chart, p. 236)*

The rest of the platform lauded Truman's legislative program and blamed the Republican Congress for obstructing beneficial legislation. In the New Deal tradition, the platform advocated the extension of social security, raising of the minimum wage, establishment of national health insurance and the creation of a permanent flexible price support system for farmers. Congress was blamed for obstructing passage of federal aid to education, comprehensive housing legislation and funding for the Marshall Plan to help rebuild Europe. The Republicans were also criticized for crippling reciprocal trade agreements, passage of the Taft-Hartley Act and even the rising rate of inflation.

The development of the Cold War with the communist world produced a new issue, internal security, on which the two major parties differed sharply. While the Republican position stressed the pursuit of subversives, the Democrats placed more emphasis on the protection of individual rights.

In foreign affairs, the Democratic platform called for the establishment of a United Nations military force, international control of the atomic bomb and recognition of the state of Israel.

Following are excerpts from the Democratic platform of 1948:

Civil Rights. We highly commend President Harry S Truman for his courageous stand on the issue of civil rights.

We call upon the Congress to support our President in guaranteeing these basic and fundamental American Principles: (1) the right of full and equal political participation; (2) the right to equal opportunity of employment; (3) the right of security of person; (4) and the right of equal treatment in the service and defense of our nation.

Housing. We shall enact comprehensive housing legislation, including provisions for slum clearance and low-rent housing projects initiated by local agencies. This nation is shamed by the failure of the Republican 80th Congress to pass the vitally needed general housing legislation as recommended by the President. Adequate housing will end the need for rent control. Until then, it must be continued.

Social Security, Health Insurance. We favor the extension of the Social Security program established under Democratic leadership, to provide additional protection against the hazards of old age, disability, disease or death. We believe that this program should include:

Increases in old-age and survivors' insurance benefits by at least 50 percent, and reduction of the eligibility age for women from 65 to 60 years; extension of old-age and survivors' and unemployment insurance to all workers not now covered; insurance against loss of earnings on account of illness or disability; improved public assistance for the needy.

Labor. We advocate the repeal of the Taft-Hartley Act. It was enacted by the Republican 80th Congress over the President's veto....

We favor the extension of the coverage of the Fair Labor Standards Act as recommended by President Truman, and the adoption of a minimum wage of at least 75 cents an hour in place of the present obsolete and inadequate minimum of 40 cents an hour.

We favor legislation assuring that the workers of our nation receive equal pay for equal work, regardless of sex.

United Nations. We will continue to lead the way toward curtailment of the use of the veto. We shall favor such amendments and modifications of the charter as experience may justify. We will continue our efforts toward the establishment of an international armed force to aid its authority. We advocate the grant of a loan to the United Nations recommended by the President, but denied by the Republican Congress, for the construction of the United Nations headquarters in this country.

Disarmament. We advocate the effective international control of weapons of mass destruction, including the atomic bomb, and we approve continued and vigorous efforts within the United Nations to bring about the successful consummation of the proposals which our Government has advanced.

Israel. We pledge full recognition to the State of Israel. We affirm our pride that the United States under the leadership of President Truman played a leading role in the adoption of the resolution of November 29, 1947, by the United Nations General Assembly for the creation of a Jewish State.

Internal Security. We shall continue vigorously to enforce the laws against subversive activities, observing at all times the constitutional guarantees which protect free speech, the free press and honest political activity. We shall strengthen our laws against subversion to the full extent necessary, protecting at all times our traditional individual freedoms.

States' Rights (Dixiecrats)

Provoked by the Democratic convention's adoption of a strong civil rights plank, Gov. Fielding L. Wright of Mississippi invited other Southern Democrats to meet in Birmingham, Ala., on July 17 to select a regional ticket that would reflect Southern views.

It was a disgruntled group that gathered in Birmingham, just three days after the close of the Democratic convention. Placards on the floor of the convention hall identified 13 states, yet there were no delegates from Georgia, Kentucky or North Carolina, and Virginia was represented by four University of Virginia students and an Alexandria woman who was returning home from a trip south. Most major Southern politicians shied away from the bolters, fearing that involvement would jeopardize their standing with the national party and their seniority in Congress.

Former Alabama governor Frank M. Dixon vocalized the anti-civil-rights mood of the gathering with a keynote address charging that Truman's civil rights program would "reduce us to the status of a mongrel, inferior race, mixed in blood, our Anglo-Saxon heritage a mockery."

As its standard-bearers, the convention chose Gov. J. Strom Thurmond of South Carolina for president and Gov. Wright for vice president. Thurmond's acceptance speech touched on another grievance of bolting Southern Democrats: their decreasing power within the Democratic Party. Thurmond warned: "If the South should vote for Truman this year, we might just as well petition the Government to give us a colonial status."

The platform adopted by the Dixiecrats was barely 1,000 words long, but it forcefully presented the case for states' rights. The platform warned that the tendency toward greater federal power ultimately would establish a totalitarian police state.

The Dixiecrats saved their most vitriolic passages to describe the civil rights plank adopted by the Democratic convention. They declared their support for segregation and charged that the plank adopted by the Democrats was meant "to embarrass and humiliate the South."

The platform also charged the national Democratic Party with ingratitude, claiming that the South had supported the Democratic ticket with "clock-like regularity" for nearly 100 years, but that now the national party was being dominated by states controlled by the Republicans.

Following are excerpts from the States' Rights platform of 1948:

States' Rights. We believe that the protection of the American people against the onward march of totalitarian government requires a faithful observance of Article X of the American Bill of Rights which provides that: "The powers not delegated to the United States by the Constitution, nor prohibited by it to the states, are reserved to the states respectively, or to the people."

Civil Rights. We stand for the segregation of the races and the racial integrity of each race; the constitutional right to choose one's associates; to accept private employment without governmental interference, and to earn one's living in any lawful way. We oppose the elimination of segregation employment by Federal bureaucrats called for by the misnamed civil rights program. We favor home rule, local self-government and a minimum interference with individual rights.

We oppose and condemn the action of the Democratic convention in sponsoring a civil rights program calling for the elimination of segregation, social equality by Federal fiat, regulation of private employment practices, voting and local law enforcement.

We affirm that the effective enforcement of such a program would be utterly destructive of the social, economic and political life of the Southern people, and of other localities in which there may be differences in race, creed or national origin in appreciable numbers.

Progressives

On Dec. 29, 1947, former vice president Henry A. Wallace announced his presidential candidacy at the head of a new liberal party. Officially named the Progressive Party at its convention in Philadelphia in late July 1948, the new party was composed of some liberal Democrats as well as more radical groups and individuals that included some communists.

Nearly 3,200 delegates nominated Wallace for the presidency and Democratic senator Glen H. Taylor of Idaho as his running mate. The colorful Taylor and his family regaled the delegates with their rendition of "When You Were Sweet Sixteen."

On the final night of the convention, 32,000 spectators assembled to hear Wallace deliver his acceptance speech at Shibe Park. The Progressive standard-bearer expressed his belief in "progressive capitalism," which would place "human rights above property rights," and envisioned "a new frontier ... across the wilderness of poverty and sickness."

Former Roosevelt associate Rexford G. Tugwell chaired the 74-member platform committee that drafted a detailed platform, about 9,000 words in length, that was adopted by the convention. The platform denounced the two major parties as champions of big business and claimed the new party to be the true "political heirs of Jefferson, Jackson and Lincoln." However, many political observers and opponents of the Progressives dismissed the new party as a Communist-front organization.

Although numerous positions taken by the Progressives in 1948 were considered radical, many were later adopted or seriously considered by the major parties.

The foreign policy plank advocated negotiations between the United States and the Soviet Union ultimately leading to a peace agreement, and it sharply criticized the "anti-Soviet hysteria" of the period. The platform called for repeal of the draft, repudiation of the Marshall Plan, worldwide disarmament featuring abolition of the atomic bomb, amnesty for conscientious objectors imprisoned in World War II, recognition and aid to Israel, extension of United Nations humanitarian programs and the establishment of a world legislature.

In the domestic area, the Progressives opposed internal security legislation, advocated the 18-year-old vote, favored the creation of a Department of Culture, called for food stamp and school hot lunch programs and proposed a federal housing plan that would build 25 million homes in 10 years and subsidize low-income housing.

The Progressives also reiterated the proposals of earlier third parties by favoring the direct election of the president and vice president, extensive tax reform, stricter control of monopolies and the nationalization of the principal means of communication, transportation and finance.

The Progressives joined the Democrats and Republicans in proposing strong civil rights legislation and an equal rights amendment for women.

Following are excerpts from the Progressive platform of 1948:

Soviet Union. The Progressive Party ... demands negotiation and discussion with the Soviet Union to find areas of agreement to win the peace.

Disarmament. The Progressive Party will work through the United Nations for a world disarmament agreement to outlaw the atomic bomb, bacteriological warfare, and all other instruments of mass destruction; to destroy existing stockpiles of atomic bombs and to establish United Nations controls, including inspection, over the production of atomic energy; and to reduce conventional armaments drastically in accordance with resolutions already passed by the United Nations General Assembly.

World Legislation. The only ultimate alternative to war is the abandonment of the principle of the coercion of sovereignties by sovereignties and the adoption of the principle of the just enforcement upon individuals of world federal law, enacted by a world federal legislature with limited but adequate powers to safeguard the common defense and the general welfare of all mankind.

Draft. The Progressive Party calls for the repeal of the peacetime draft and the rejection of Universal Military Training.

Amnesty. We demand amnesty for conscientious objectors imprisoned in World War II.

Internal Security. We denounce anti-Soviet hysteria as a mask for monopoly, militarism, and reaction....

The Progressive Party will fight for the constitutional rights of Communists and all other political groups to express their views as the first line in the defense of the liberties of a democratic people.

Civil Rights. The Progressive Party condemns segregation and discrimination in all its forms and in all places....

We call for a Presidential proclamation ending segregation and all forms of discrimination in the armed services and Federal employment.

We demand Federal anti-lynch, anti-discrimination, and fair-employment-practices legislation, and legislation abolishing segregation in interstate travel.

We call for immediate passage of anti-poll tax legislation, enactment of a universal suffrage law to permit all citizens to vote in Federal elections, and the full use of Federal enforcement powers to assure free exercise of the right to franchise.

Food Stamps, School Lunches. We also call for assistance to low-income consumers through such programs as the food stamp plan and the school hot-lunch program.

Housing. We pledge an attack on the chronic housing shortage and the slums through a long-range program to build 25 million new homes during the next ten years. This program will include public subsidized housing for low-income families.

Nationalization. As a first step, the largest banks, the railroads, the merchant marine, the electric power and gas industry, and industries primarily dependent on government funds or government purchases such as the aircraft, the synthetic rubber and synthetic oil industries must be placed under public ownership.

Youth Vote. We call for the right to vote at eighteen.

1952 Conventions

Presidential Candidates

Dwight D. Eisenhower
Republican

Adlai E. Stevenson
Democrat

Republicans

For the third straight time, both major parties held their conventions in the same city. In 1952 the site was Chicago; the Republicans met there in early July two weeks before the Democrats. The battle for the presidential nomination pitted the hero of the party's conservative wing, Sen. Robert A. Taft of Ohio, against the favorite of most moderate and liberal Republicans, Gen. Dwight D. Eisenhower. The general, a Texas native, had resigned as supreme commander of the North Atlantic Treaty Organization (NATO) less than six weeks before the convention to pursue the nomination actively.

As in 1912, when Taft's father had engaged in a bitter struggle with Theodore Roosevelt for the nomination, the outcome of the presidential race was determined in preliminary battles over convention rules and credentials.

The first confrontation came on the issue of the voting rights of challenged delegates. The Taft forces proposed adoption of the 1948 rules, which would have allowed contested delegates to vote on all credentials challenges except their own. The Eisenhower forces countered by proposing what they called a "fair play amendment," which would seat only those contested delegates who were approved by at least a two-thirds vote of the national committee. At stake were a total of 68 delegates from Georgia, Louisiana and Texas, with the large majority of the challenged delegates in favor of Taft. The Taft forces introduced a substitute to the "fair play amendment," designed to exempt seven delegates from Louisiana. On the first test of strength between the two candidates, the Eisenhower forces were victorious, as the substitute amendment was defeated, 658 to 548. The "fair play amendment" was subsequently approved by a voice vote. *(Chart, p. 239)*

The second confrontation developed with the report of the credentials committee. The Eisenhower forces presented a minority report concerning the contested Georgia, Louisiana and Texas seats. After a bitter debate, a roll-call vote was taken on the Georgia challenge, with the Eisenhower forces winning again, 607 to 531.

The Louisiana and Texas challenges were settled in

favor of the Eisenhower forces without a roll-call vote. The favorable settlement of the credentials challenges increased the momentum behind the Eisenhower candidacy.

Before the presidential balloting began, a non-partisan debate was held on a proposal to add state chairmen to the national committee from states recording Republican electoral majorities and to remove the requirement that women hold one of each state's seats on the national committee. The proposal was primarily intended to decrease Southern influence on the national committee. But the major opposition was raised by a number of women delegates who objected to the rule change; however, their effort to defeat it was rejected by voice vote.

Five men were nominated for the presidency, but on completion of the first roll call Eisenhower had 595 votes and was within nine votes of victory. Taft was a strong second with 500 votes. However, before a second ballot could begin, Minnesota switched 19 votes from favorite son Harold E. Stassen to Eisenhower, giving the latter the nomination. After a series of vote changes, the final tally stood: Eisenhower, 845; Taft, 280; other candidates, 81. The general's nomination was subsequently made unanimous.

Eisenhower's choice as a running mate, 39-year-old senator Richard M. Nixon of California, was nominated by acclamation. Eisenhower promised in his acceptance speech to lead a "crusade" against "a party too long in power."

The 6,000-word platform was adopted by a voice vote. The document included a sharp attack on the Democrats, charging the Roosevelt and Truman administrations with "violating our liberties ... by seizing powers never granted," "shielding traitors" and attempting to establish "national socialism." The foreign policy section, written by John Foster Dulles, supported the concept of collective security but denounced the Truman policy of containment and blamed the administration for the communist takeover of China. The Republican platform advocated increased national preparedness.

As well as castigating the Democrats for an incompetent foreign policy, the Republicans denounced their opposition for laxness in maintaining internal security. A plank asserted: "There are no Communists in the Republican Party."

On most domestic issues the platform advocated a reduction in federal power. The civil rights plank proposed federal action to outlaw lynching, poll taxes and discriminatory employment practices. However, unlike the plank four years earlier, the Republican position included a paragraph that declared the individual states had primary responsibility for their own domestic institutions. On a related issue of states' rights, the Republicans, as in 1948, favored state control of tideland resources.

Following are excerpts from the Republican platform of 1952:

Democratic Failures. We charge that they have arrogantly deprived our citizens of precious liberties by seizing powers never granted.

We charge that they work unceasingly to achieve their goal of national socialism. . . .

We charge that they have shielded traitors to the Nation in high places, and that they have created enemies abroad where we should have friends.

We charge that they have violated our liberties by turning loose upon the country a swarm of arrogant bureaucrats and their agents who meddle intolerably in the lives and occupations of our citizens.

We charge that there has been corruption in high places, and that examples of dishonesty and dishonor have shamed the moral standards of the American people.

We charge that they have plunged us into war in Korea without the consent of our citizens through their authorized representatives in the Congress, and have carried on the war without will to victory. . . .

Tehran, Yalta and Potsdam were the scenes of those tragic blunders with others to follow. The leaders of the Administration in power acted without the knowledge or consent of Congress or of the American people. They traded our overwhelming victory for a new enemy and for new oppressions and new wars which were quick to come.

. . . And finally they denied the military aid that had been authorized by Congress and which was crucially needed if China were to be saved. Thus they substituted on our Pacific flank a murderous enemy for an ally and friend.

Internal Security. By the Administration's appeasement of Communism at home and abroad it has permitted Communists and their fellow travelers to serve in many key agencies and to infiltrate our American life. . . .

There are no Communists in the Republican Party. We have always recognized Communism to be a world conspiracy against freedom and religion. We never compromised with Communism and we have fought to expose it and to eliminate it in government and American life.

Civil Rights. We believe that it is the primary responsibility of each State to order and control its own domestic institutions, and this power, reserved to the states, is essential to the maintenance of our Federal Republic. However, we believe that the Federal Government should take supplemental action within its constitutional jurisdiction to oppose discrimination against race, religion or national origin.

We will prove our good faith by:

Appointing qualified persons, without distinction of race, religion or national origin, to responsible positions in the Government.

Federal action toward the elimination of lynching.

Federal action toward the elimination of poll taxes as a prerequisite to voting.

Appropriate action to end segregation in the District of Columbia.

Enacting Federal legislation to further just and equitable treatment in the area of discriminatory employment practices. Federal action should not duplicate state efforts to end such practices; should not set up another huge bureaucracy.

Labor. We favor the retention of the Taft-Hartley Act. . . .We urge the adoption of such amendments to the Taft-Hartley Act as time and experience show to be desirable, and which further protect the rights of labor, management and the public.

Democrats

The Democrats held their 1952 convention in Chicago in late July. The convention lasted six days, the longest by either party in the post-World War II years. The proceedings were enlivened by disputes over credentials and a party loyalty pledge and a wide-open race for the presidential nomination.

The legitimately selected Texas delegation, dominated by the Dixiecrat wing of the state party, was challenged by a delegation loyal to the national party, but chosen in a rump assembly. Without a roll-call vote, the convention approved the credentials of the Dixiecrat-oriented delegates, although their seating was protested by Northern liberals.

The Dixiecrat bolt of 1948 resulted in the introduction of a party loyalty pledge at the 1952 convention. The resolution, introduced by Sen. Blair Moody of Michigan, proposed that no delegate be seated who would not assure the credentials committee that he would work to have the Democratic national ticket placed on the ballot in his state under the party's name. This resolution was aimed at several Southern states that had listed the Thurmond-Wright ticket under the Democratic Party label on their state ballots in 1948.

Sen. Spessard L. Holland of Florida introduced a substitute resolution that simply declared it would be "honorable" for each delegate to adhere to the decisions reached in the convention. Holland's resolution, however, was defeated and Moody's was approved, both by voice votes.

The report of the credentials committee listed three Southern states — Louisiana, South Carolina and Virginia — that declined to abide by the Moody resolution. The question of their seating rights came to a head during the roll call for presidential nominations, when Virginia questioned its own status in the convention. A motion to seat the Virginia delegation in spite of its non-observance of the resolution was presented for a vote. Although not agreeing to the pledge, the chairman of the Virginia delegation indicated that the problem prompting the Moody resolution was covered by state law. After a long, confusing roll call, interrupted frequently by demands to poll individual delegates, the motion to seat the Virginia delegation passed, 650-1/2 to 518. *(Chart, p. 238)*

After efforts to adjourn were defeated, the Louisiana and South Carolina delegations offered assurances similar to those presented by Virginia and were seated by a voice vote.

Eleven names were placed in nomination for the presidency, although the favorite of most party leaders, Illinois governor Adlai E. Stevenson, was a reluctant candidate. Stevenson expressed interest only in running for re-election as governor, but a draft-Stevenson movement developed and gained strength quickly as the convention proceeded.

Sen. Estes Kefauver of Tennessee, a powerful vote-getter in the primaries, was the leader on the first ballot, with 340 votes. He was followed by Stevenson with 273, Sen. Richard B. Russell of Georgia, the Southern favorite, with 268, and W. Averell Harriman of New York with 123-1/2.

The second ballot saw gains by the three front-runners, with Kefauver's vote rising to 362-1/2, Stevenson's to 324-1/2 and Russell's to 294. A recess was taken during which Harriman and Massachusetts' favorite son, Gov. Paul A. Dever, both withdrew in favor of Stevenson.

The Illinois governor won a narrow majority on the third ballot, receiving 617-1/2 of the 1,230 convention votes. Kefauver finished with 275-1/2 and Russell with 261. The selection of Stevenson represented the first success for a presidential draft movement of a reluctant candidate since the nomination of James A. Garfield by the Republicans in 1880. *(Chart, p. 238)*

For vice president, Stevenson chose Sen. John J. Sparkman of Alabama, who was nominated by acclamation.

Although a reluctant candidate, Stevenson promised the delegates a fighting campaign but warned: "Better we lose the election than mislead the people; and better we lose than misgovern the people."

The Democratic platform was adopted without the rancor that had accompanied consideration of the party platform four years earlier. The document was approved by a voice vote, although both the Georgia and Mississippi delegations asked that they be recorded in opposition.

The platform promised extension and improvement of New Deal and Fair Deal policies that had been proposed and enacted over the previous 20 years. The party's foremost goal was stated to be "peace with honor," which could be achieved by support for a strengthened United Nations, coupled with the policy of collective security in the form of American assistance for allies around the world. The peaceful use of atomic energy was pledged, as were efforts to establish an international control system. However, the platform also promised the use of atomic weapons, if needed, for national defense.

The civil rights plank was nearly identical to the one that appeared in the 1948 platform. Federal legislation was called for to guarantee equal rights in voting participation, employment opportunity and personal security.

The platform called for extending and changing the social security system. A plank favored elimination of the work clause so that the elderly could collect benefits and still work.

Political reform was recommended that would require the disclosure of campaign expenses in federal elections.

The Democrats and Republicans took different stands on several major domestic issues. The Democrats favored repeal of the Taft-Hartley Act; the Republicans proposed to retain the act but make modifications where necessary. The Democrats advocated closing tax loopholes and, after defense needs were met, reducing taxes. The Republicans called for tax reduction based on a cut in government spending. In education, the Democrats favored federal assistance to state and local units; the Republicans viewed education solely as the responsibility of local and state governments.

The Democrats favored continuation of federal power projects, while the Republicans opposed "all-powerful federal socialistic valley authorities."

Both parties favored a parity price program for farmers. The Democrats advocated a mandatory price support program for basic agricultural products at not less than 90 percent of parity, and the Republicans proposing a program that would establish "full parity prices for all farm products."

Following are excerpts from the Democratic platform of 1952:

Atomic Energy. In the field of atomic energy, we pledge ourselves:

(1) to maintain vigorous and non-partisan civilian administrations, with adequate security safeguards;

(2) to promote the development of nuclear energy for peaceful purposes in the interests of America and mankind;

(3) to build all the atomic and hydrogen firepower needed to defend our country, deter aggression, and promote world peace;

(4) to exert every effort to bring about bona fide international control and inspection of all atomic weapons.

Civil Rights. We will continue our efforts to eradicate discrimination based on race, religion or national origin. . . .

We are proud of the progress that has been made in securing equality of treatment and opportunity in the Nation's armed forces and the civil service and all areas under Federal jurisdiction. . . .

At the same time, we favor Federal legislation effectively to secure these rights to everyone:

(1) the right to equal opportunity for employment;

(2) the right to security of persons;

(3) the right to full and equal participation in the Nation's political life, free from arbitrary restraints.

Agriculture. We will continue to protect the producers of basic agricultural commodities under the terms of a mandatory price support program at not less than ninety percent of parity. We continue to advocate practical methods for extending price supports to other storables and to the producers of perishable commodities, which account for three-fourths of all farm income.

Campaign Finance. We advocate new legislation to provide effective regulation and full disclosure of campaign expenditures in elections to Federal office, including political advertising from any source.

Labor. We strongly advocate the repeal of the Taft-Hartley Act.

Tax Reform. We believe in fair and equitable taxation. We oppose a Federal general sales tax. We adhere to the principle of ability to pay. We have enacted an emergency excess profits tax to prevent profiteering from the defense program and have vigorously attacked special tax privileges. . . . As rapidly as defense requirements permit, we favor reducing taxes, especially for people with lower incomes. . . .

Justice requires the elimination of tax loopholes which favor special groups. We pledge continued efforts to the elimination of remaining loopholes.

Social Security. We favor the complete elimination of the work clause for the reason that those contributing to the Social Security program should be permitted to draw benefits, upon reaching the age of eligibility, and still continue to work.

Education. Local, State and Federal governments have shared responsibility to contribute appropriately to the pressing needs of our educational system. We urge that Federal contributions be made available to State and local units which adhere to basic minimum standards.

The Federal Government should not dictate nor control educational policy.

1956 Conventions
Presidential Candidates

Adlai E. Stevenson
Democrat

Dwight D. Eisenhower
Republican

Democrats

Both parties held their conventions in August, the latest date ever for the Republicans and the latest for the Democrats since the wartime convention of 1864. For the first time since 1888 the date of the Democratic convention preceded that of the Republicans. The Democrats met in mid-August in Chicago with an allotment of 1,372 votes, the largest in party history. The increased allotment was the result of a new distribution formula, which for the first time rewarded states for electing Democratic governors and senators in addition to supporting the party's presidential candidate.

A provision of the convention call handled the party loyalty question, a thorny issue at the 1952 convention, by assuming that, in the absence of a challenge, any delegate would be understood to have the best interests of the party at heart. Another provision of the call threatened any national committeeman who did not support the party's national ticket with removal from the Democratic National Committee.

In an unusual occurrence, nominating speeches were delivered by a past and a future president for men who would not attain the office themselves. Sen. John F. Kennedy of Massachusetts placed Adlai E. Stevenson's name in nomination, while former president Harry S. Truman seconded the nomination of New York governor W. Averell Harriman. Truman criticized Stevenson as a "defeatist," but was countered by Eleanor Roosevelt, who appeared before the convention in support of the former Illinois governor.

In spite of the oratorical byplay, Stevenson was in good position to win the nomination before the convention even began, having eliminated his principal rival, Sen. Estes Kefauver of Tennessee, in the primaries. Stevenson won a majority on the first ballot, receiving 905-1/2 votes to easily defeat Harriman, who had 210. Sen. Lyndon B. Johnson of Texas finished third, with 80 votes. Upon completion of the roll call, a motion was approved to make Stevenson's nomination unanimous. *(Chart, p. 240)*

In an unusual move, Stevenson announced that he would not personally select his running mate but would

leave the choice to the convention. Stevenson's desire for an open selection was designed to contrast with the expected cut-and-dried nature of the upcoming Republican convention. But the unusual move caught both delegates and prospective candidates off guard.

Numerous delegations passed on the first ballot, and upon completion of the roll call votes were scattered among 13 different candidates. When the vote totals were announced at the end of the roll call, Kefauver led with 483-1/2 votes, followed by Kennedy with 304, Sen. Albert A. Gore of Tennessee with 178, Mayor Robert F. Wagner of New York City with 162-1/2 and Sen. Hubert H. Humphrey of Minnesota with 134-1/2. Six hundred eighty-seven votes were needed to nominate.

With a coalition that included most of the Southern and Eastern delegates, Kennedy drew into the lead on the second ballot. After the roll call but before the chair recognized vote changes, the totals stood: Kennedy, 618; Kefauver, 551-1/2; Gore, 110-1/2. Kentucky, the first state to be recognized, shifted its 30 votes to Kennedy, leaving the 39-year-old senator fewer than 40 votes short of the nomination.

But Gore was recognized next and began a bandwagon for Kefauver by withdrawing in favor of his Tennessee colleague. Other states followed Gore's lead, and at the conclusion of the vote shifts Kefauver had a clear majority. The final tally was Kefauver, 755-1/2 and Kennedy, 589. Kennedy moved that his opponent's nomination be made unanimous.

Ironically, Kefauver won a majority of the votes in only two states in his home region, Tennessee and Florida. His strength lay in Midwestern and Western delegations.

As in 1948 platform debate focused on the civil rights issue. A Minnesota member of the platform committee introduced a minority report that advocated a civil rights plank stronger than that in the majority report. The plank presented by the platform committee pledged to carry out Supreme Court decisions on desegregation, but not through the use of force. The party promised to continue to work for equal rights in voting, employment, personal security and education. The Minnesota substitute was more specific, as it favored federal legislation to achieve equal voting rights and employment opportunities and to guarantee personal safety. The minority plank also favored more rigid enforcement of civil rights legislation. Although several states clamored for a roll-call vote, the chair took a voice vote, which went against the Minnesota substitute.

The entire platform was the longest yet approved by a Democratic convention, about 12,000 words. The document was divided into 11 sections, the first dealing with defense and foreign policy and the remainder with domestic issues.

The platform described President Eisenhower as a "political amateur ... dominated ... by special privilege." It applauded the legislative accomplishments of the Democratic Congress elected in 1954 and proposed a continuation of the social and economic legislation begun during the New Deal.

The foreign policy of the Eisenhower administration was criticized in a plank that accused the Republicans of cutting funds for the military in an attempt to balance the budget. The Democrats declared that the United States must have the strongest military in the world to discourage aggression by America's enemies. The foreign policy plank also pledged to strengthen the United Nations as a peacekeeping organization and promised to work diligently for worldwide disarmament.

The platform blamed the Republicans for allowing big business to dominate the economy and promised tax relief and other government assistance to help small business. The Democrats advocated repeal of the Taft-Hartley Act, as the party had done in every platform since 1948, and favored an increase in the minimum wage. Tax reductions were proposed for lower-income taxpayers, and an increase of at least $200 in the personal tax exemption was recommended.

For farmers, the Democrats proposed price supports at 90 percent of parity on basic crops, as opposed to the Republican program of flexible price supports.

For the first time since the beginning of the New Deal, the Democratic platform mentioned the importance of states' rights. The party also reiterated its position on education, which advocated federal assistance, but stated that ultimate control of the schools lay in the hands of state and local governments.

In political reform the platform proposed restrictions on government secrecy and repeated the party's call for the passage of an equal rights amendment.

Following are excerpts from the Democratic platform of 1956:

Foreign Policy. *The Failure at Home.* Political considerations of budget balancing and tax reduction now come before the wants of our national security and the needs of our Allies. The Republicans have slashed our own armed strength, weakened our capacity to deal with military threats, stifled our air force, starved our army and weakened our capacity to deal with aggression of any sort save by retreat or by the alternatives, "massive retaliation" and global atomic war. Yet, while our troubles mount, they tell us our prestige was never higher, they tell us we were never more secure.

Disarmament. To eliminate the danger of atomic war, a universal, effective and enforced disarmament system must be the goal of responsible men and women everywhere. So long as we lack enforceable international control of weapons, we must maintain armed strength to avoid war. But technological advances in the field of nuclear weapons make disarmament an ever more urgent problem. Time and distance can never again protect any nation of the world.

Labor. We unequivocally advocate repeal of the Taft-Hartley Act. The Act must be repealed because State "right-to-work" laws have their genesis in its discriminatory anti-labor provisions....

The Taft-Hartley Act has been proven to be inadequate, unworkable and unfair. It interferes in an arbitrary manner with collective bargaining, causing imbalance in the relationship between management and labor.

Agriculture. Undertake immediately by appropriate action to endeavor to regain the full 100 percent of parity the farmers received under the Democratic Administrations. We will achieve this by means of supports on basic commodities at 90 percent of parity and by means of commodity loans, direct purchases, direct payments to producers, marketing agreements and orders, production adjustments, or a combination of these, including legislation, to bring order and stability into the relationship between the producer, the processor and the consumer.

Education. We are now faced with shortages of educational facilities that threaten national security, economic prosperity and human well-being. The resources of our States and localities are already strained to the limit. Federal aid and action should be provided, within the traditional framework of State and local control.

Tax Reform. We favor realistic tax adjustments, giving first consideration to small independent business and the small individual taxpayer. Lower-income families need tax relief; only a Democratic victory will assure this. We favor an increase in the present personal tax exemption of $600 to a minimum of at least $800.

Government Secrecy. *Freedom of Information.* During recent years there has developed a practice on the part of Federal agencies to delay and withhold information which is needed by Congress and the general public to make important decisions affecting their lives and destinies. We believe that this trend toward secrecy in Government should be reversed and that the Federal Government should return to its basic tradition of exchanging and promoting the freest flow of information possible in those unclassified areas where secrets involving weapons development and bona fide national security are not involved.

States' Rights. While we recognize the existence of honest differences of opinion as to the true location of a Constitutional line of demarcation between the Federal Government and the States, the Democratic Party expressly recognizes the vital importance of the respective States in our Federal Union. The Party of Jefferson and Jackson pledges itself to continued support of those sound principles of local government which will best serve the welfare of our people and the safety of our democratic rights.

Civil Rights. We are proud of the record of the Democratic Party in securing equality of treatment and opportunity in the nation's armed forces, the Civil Service, and in all areas under Federal jurisdiction. The Democratic Party pledges itself to continue its efforts to eliminate illegal discriminations of all kinds, in relation to (1) full rights to vote, (2) full rights to engage in gainful occupations, (3) full rights to enjoy security of the person, and (4) full rights to education in all publicly supported institutions.

Recent decisions of the Supreme Court of the United States relating to segregation in publicly supported schools and elsewhere have brought consequences of vast importance to our Nation as a whole and especially to communities directly affected. We reject all proposals for the use of force to interfere with the orderly determination of these matters by the courts.

Republicans

The Republicans opened their convention in San Francisco three days after the close of the Democratic convention in Chicago. In contrast to the turbulent convention of their adversaries, the Republicans' renomination of Dwight D. Eisenhower and Richard M. Nixon was a formality. The only possible obstacle to Eisenhower's candidacy was his health, but by August 1956 his recovery from a heart attack and an ileitis operation was complete enough to allow him to seek a second term. On the convention's single roll call for president, Eisenhower received all 1,323 votes.

What drama occurred at the Republican convention surrounded the vice presidential nomination. Several weeks before the opening of the convention, former Minnesota governor Harold Stassen, the disarmament adviser to Eisenhower, had begun a movement to replace Vice President Nixon with Massachusetts governor Christian A. Herter. However, with lack of interest from party leaders, this movement petered out. At the convention both Herter and Stassen gave nominating speeches for Nixon. During the roll call, a commotion was caused by a Nebraska delegate, who attempted to nominate "Joe Smith." After some discussion, it was determined that "Joe Smith" was a fictitious individual, and the offending delegate was escorted from the hall. On the one ballot for vice president, a unanimous vote was recorded for Nixon.

While no opposition to the platform was expressed on the floor of the convention, several Southern delegates were unhappy with the civil rights plank and withdrew from the convention. The plank in question listed advances in desegregation under the Republican administration, voiced acceptance of the Supreme Court ruling on school desegregation and pledged to enforce existing civil rights statutes.

The platform as a whole was slightly longer than the Democratic document and was dedicated to Eisenhower and "the youth of America." Unlike the Democratic platform, which began with a discussion of foreign policy and national defense, the first issue pursued by the Republicans was the economy.

The Eisenhower administration was praised for balancing the budget, reducing taxes and halting inflation. The platform promised continued balanced budgets, gradual reduction of the national debt and cuts in government spending consistent with the maintenance of a strong military. Two measures favored by the Democrats, tax relief for small businesses and tax reductions for low-income and middle-income families, were both mentioned as secondary economic goals in the Republican platform.

The labor plank advocated revision but not repeal of the Taft-Hartley Act. The agricultural section favored elimination of price-depressing surpluses and continuation of the flexible price-support program. As they had for the past quarter century, the Republicans joined the Democrats in recommending passage of an equal rights amendment.

The foreign policy section of the Republican platform praised the Eisenhower administration for ending the Korean War, stemming the worldwide advance of communism and entering new collective security agreements. The plank also emphasized the necessity of a bipartisan foreign policy. The "preservation" of Israel was viewed as an "important tenet of American foreign policy," a notable difference from the Democratic platform, which took a more even-handed approach toward both Israel and the Arab states.

The national defense section emphasized the United States' possession of "the strongest striking force in the world," a rebuttal to Democratic charges that the Republicans had jeopardized the efficiency of the armed forces in

an effort to balance the budget.

Following are excerpts from the Republican platform of 1956:

Economy. We pledge to pursue the following objectives:

Further reductions in Government spending as recommended in the Hoover Commission Report, without weakening the support of a superior defense program or depreciating the quality of essential services of government to our people.

Continued balancing of the budget, to assure the financial strength of the country which is so vital to the struggle of the free world in its battle against Communism; and to maintain the purchasing power of a sound dollar, and the value of savings, pensions and insurance.

Gradual reduction of the national debt.

Then, insofar as consistent with a balanced budget, we pledge to work toward these additional objectives:

Further reductions in taxes with particular consideration for low and middle income families.

Initiation of a sound policy of tax reductions which will encourage small independent businesses to modernize and progress.

Labor. Revise and improve the Taft-Hartley Act so as to protect more effectively the rights of labor unions, management, the individual worker, and the public. The protection of the right of workers to organize into unions and to bargain collectively is the firm and permanent policy of the Eisenhower Administration.

Agriculture. This program must be versatile and flexible to meet effectively the impact of rapidly changing conditions. It does not envision making farmers dependent upon direct governmental payments for their incomes. Our objective is markets which return full parity to our farm and ranch people when they sell their products.

Civil Rights. The Republican Party accepts the decision of the U.S. Supreme Court that racial discrimination in publicly supported schools must be progressively eliminated. We concur in the conclusion of the Supreme Court that its decision directing school desegregation should be accomplished with "all deliberate speed" locally through Federal District Courts. The implementation order of the Supreme Court recognizes the complex and acutely emotional problems created by its decision in certain sections of our country where racial patterns have been developed in accordance with prior and longstanding decisions of the same tribunal.

We believe that true progress can be attained through intelligent study, understanding, education and good will. Use of force or violence by any group or agency will tend only to worsen the many problems inherent in the situation. This progress must be encouraged and the work of the courts supported in every legal manner by all branches of the Federal Government to the end that the constitutional ideal of equality before the law, regardless of race, creed or color, will be steadily achieved.

Foreign Policy. The advance of Communism has been checked, and, at key points, thrown back. The once-monolithic structure of International Communism, denied the stimulant of successive conquests, has shown hesitancy both internally and abroad.

National Defense. We *have* the strongest striking force in the world — in the air — on the sea — and a magnificent supporting land force in our Army and Marine Corps.

Israel. We regard the preservation of Israel as an important tenet of American foreign policy. We are determined that the integrity of an independent Jewish State shall be maintained. We shall support the independence of

Israel against armed aggression. The best hope for peace in the Middle East lies in the United Nations. We pledge our

continued efforts to eliminate the obstacles to a lasting peace in this area.

1960 Conventions

Presidential Candidates

John F. Kennedy
Democrat

Richard M. Nixon
Republican

Democrats

For the first time, a national political convention was held in Los Angeles. More than 4,000 delegates and alternates converged on the California metropolis in July to select the Democratic standard-bearers for 1960. The delegate allocation method had been changed since 1956 by the Democratic National Committee, from a formula that included Democratic voting strength to a system that emphasized population only. No states lost seats, but the new formula tended to strengthen populous Northern states.

The early sessions of the convention dealt with rules and credentials. The convention rules, approved without debate, included the compromise loyalty pledge adopted by the 1956 convention. The only credentials dispute involved two contesting delegations from the Commonwealth of Puerto Rico. By a voice vote, the convention agreed to seat both delegations while splitting the vote of the Commonwealth.

The front-runner for the presidential nomination was Massachusetts senator John F. Kennedy, whose success in the primaries and support from many of the party's urban leaders put him on the verge of a nominating majority. His principal rival was Senate Majority Leader Lyndon B. Johnson of Texas, although the favorite of the convention galleries was Adlai E. Stevenson, the party's unsuccessful standard-bearer in 1952 and 1956. Johnson challenged Kennedy to a debate, which was held before a joint gathering of the Massachusetts and Texas delegations. Coming the day before the balloting, the debate had little effect on the ultimate outcome.

Nine men were nominated, but Kennedy received a clear majority on the first ballot. At the end of the roll call, the Massachusetts senator had 806 votes, to easily outdistance Johnson, who received 409. Sen. Stuart Symington of Missouri was a distant third with 86 votes, and Stevenson followed with 79-1/2. A motion to make Kennedy's nomination unanimous was approved by a voice vote. Kennedy's selection marked the first time since 1920 that a senator

had been nominated for the presidency by Democrats or Republicans and the first time since 1928 that a Roman Catholic had been represented on a national ticket of one of the two major parties. *(Chart, p. 241)*

Kennedy surprised some supporters and political observers by choosing his erstwhile adversary, Lyndon Johnson, as his running mate. A motion to nominate Johnson by acclamation was approved by a voice vote.

Kennedy delivered his acceptance speech to 80,000 spectators at the Los Angeles Coliseum. He envisioned the United States as "on the edge of a new frontier — the frontier of the 1960s — a frontier of unknown opportunities and perils — a frontier of unfulfilled hopes and threats," adding that this "new frontier . . . is not a set of promises — it is a set of challenges."

The Democratic platform was easily the longest yet written by the party, about 20,000 words. The platform itself was approved by a voice vote, although the civil rights and fiscal responsibility planks were debated on the convention floor, and roll-call votes had been taken in committee.

Regional hearings had been held by subcommittees of the 108-member platform committee in the spring, but votes on controversial issues were not taken by the full committee until the convention. A plank that urged elimination of the immigration quota system was approved, 66 to 28, with opposition led by Sen. James O. Eastland of Mississippi. An agricultural plank recommending price supports at 90 percent of parity was passed, 66 to 22, with opponents claiming that it was a restatement of the liberal program proposed by the National Farmers Union. A motion to reconsider the plank was defeated, 38 to 32. An Eastland motion to delete condemnation of "right-to-work" laws was defeated without a recorded vote.

The civil rights plank caused the greatest controversy. Sen. Sam J. Ervin Jr. of North Carolina introduced motions to delete portions that proposed establishing a Fair Employment Practices Commission, continuing the Civil

Rights Commission as a permanent agency, granting the attorney general the power to file civil injunction suits to prevent discrimination, and setting 1963 as the deadline for the initiation of school desegregation plans. Ervin's motions were defeated by a voice vote, and the entire plank was approved, 66 to 24.

Delegates from nine Southern states signed a statement that repudiated the civil rights plank. Led by Georgia Democratic Chairman James H. Gray and Ervin, these nine states introduced a minority report on the convention floor calling for elimination of the platform's civil rights plank. After an hour's debate, the minority report was rejected by a voice vote.

A minority amendment introduced by the Virginia delegation, proposing that the fiscal responsibility plank include a planned schedule for reduction of the national debt, also was rejected by a voice vote.

As approved by the convention, the platform began with a discussion of foreign policy. The Democrats blamed the Republican administration for allowing the United States military strength to deteriorate. The national defense plank declared there was a "missile gap, space gap, and limited-war gap," and promised to improve America's military position so that it would be second to none. The Democrats recommended creation of "a national peace agency for disarmament planning and research." The money saved by international disarmament, the plank stated, could be used to attack world poverty.

Foreign military aid was viewed as a short-range necessity that should be replaced by economic aid "as rapidly as security considerations permit." At the same time, the platform proposed that development programs be placed on a "long-term basis to permit more effective planning."

The Democrats' economic plank called for an average national growth rate of 5 percent annually. Economic growth at this rate would create needed tax revenue, the Democrats believed, which — coupled with cuts in government waste, closing of tax loopholes and more extensive efforts to catch tax evaders — would help balance the budget. The Democrats promised to use measures such as public works projects and temporary tax cuts to combat recessions or depressions.

The platform promised an increase in the minimum wage to $1.25 an hour and pledged to extend coverage to include more workers. There was a pledge to amend the Social Security program so the elderly could continue working without sacrificing basic benefits.

Equal rights legislation was favored, although the platform did not call for passage of a constitutional amendment of 1960.

Following are excerpts from the Democratic platform of 1960:

National Defense. Our military position today is measured in terms of gaps — missile gap, space gap, limited-war gap....

This is the strength that must be erected:

1. Deterrent military power such that the Soviet and Chinese leaders will have no doubt that an attack on the United States would surely be followed by their own destruction.

2. Balanced conventional military forces which will permit a response graded to the intensity of any threats of aggressive force.

3. Continuous modernization of these forces through intensified research and development, including essential programs now slowed down, terminated, suspended or neglected for lack of budgetary support.

Disarmament. This requires a national peace agency for disarmament planning and research to muster the scientific ingenuity, coordination, continuity, and seriousness of purpose which are now lacking in our arms control efforts....

As world-wide disarmament proceeds, it will free vast resources for a new international attack on the problem of world poverty.

Immigration. The national-origins quota system of limiting immigration contradicts the founding principles of this nation. It is inconsistent with our belief in the rights of man. This system was instituted after World War I as a policy of deliberate discrimination by a Republican Administration and Congress....

Foreign Aid. Where military assistance remains essential for the common defense, we shall see that the requirements are fully met. But as rapidly as security considerations permit, we will replace tanks with tractors, bombers with bulldozers, and tacticians with technicians.

Civil Rights. We believe that every school district affected by the Supreme Court's school desegregation decision should submit a plan providing for at least first-step compliance by 1963, the 100th anniversary of the Emancipation Proclamation....

For this and for the protection of all other Constitutional rights of Americans, the Attorney General should be empowered and directed to file civil injunction suits in Federal courts to prevent the denial of any civil right on grounds of race, creed or color.

Economy. We Democrats believe that our economy can and must grow at an average rate of 5 percent annually, almost twice as fast as our average annual rate since 1953. We pledge ourselves to policies that will achieve this goal without inflation....

The policies of a Democratic Administration to restore economic growth will reduce current unemployment to a minimum.

Tax Reform. We shall close the loopholes in the tax laws by which certain privileged groups legally escape their fair share of taxation.

Among the more conspicuous loopholes are depletion allowances which are inequitable, special consideration for recipients of dividend income, and deductions for extravagant "business expenses" which have reached scandalous proportions.

Labor. We pledge to raise the minimum wage to $1.25 an hour and to extend coverage to several million workers not now protected.

Agriculture. The Democratic Administration will work to bring about full parity income for farmers in all segments of agriculture by helping them to balance farm production with the expanding needs of the nation and the world.

Measures to this end include production and marketing quotas measured in terms of barrels, bushels and bales, loans on basic commodities at not less than 90 percent of parity, production payments, commodity purchases, and marketing orders and agreements.

Government Spending. The Democratic Party believes that state and local governments are strengthened — not weakened — by financial assistance from the Federal Government. We will extend such aid without impairing local administration through unnecessary Federal interference or red tape.

Republicans

On July 25, 10 days after the close of the Democratic convention, the Republican convention opened in Chicago.

Although Vice President Richard M. Nixon had a lock on the presidential nomination, the party's two major figures four years later, Arizona senator Barry Goldwater and New York governor Nelson A. Rockefeller, both had major roles in convention activities.

Both Goldwater and Rockefeller announced that they did not want their names placed in nomination, but the Arizona delegation disregarded Goldwater's request and nominated him anyway. In a convention speech, the Arizona senator withdrew his name and went on to advise conservative Republicans to work within the party: "Let's grow up conservatives.... If we want to take this party back — and I think we can someday — let's get to work."

On the roll call that followed, Nixon was a nearly unanimous choice, receiving 1,321 votes to 10 for Goldwater (all from Louisiana). On a voice vote, Nixon's nomination was made unanimous.

Nixon reportedly wanted Rockefeller as his running mate, but was unable to persuade the New Yorker to join the ticket. The Republican standard-bearer subsequently turned to United Nations Ambassador Henry Cabot Lodge Jr., a former senator from Massachusetts who had been beaten for re-election by John Kennedy in 1952. On the vice presidential ballot, Lodge received all but one vote. The lone dissenter, a Texas delegate, initially abstained but switched his vote to Lodge at the end of the roll call.

In his acceptance speech, Nixon promised to campaign in all 50 states and rebutted a theme in Kennedy's acceptance speech. "Our primary aim must be not to help government, but to help people — to help people attain the life they deserve," said Nixon.

Much of the drama of the 1960 Republican convention surrounded the party platform. And the highlight of the platform maneuvering was a late-night meeting involving Nixon and Rockefeller, held at Rockefeller's New York City apartment two days before the opening of the convention. The meeting, a secret to most of Nixon's closest aides, resulted in a 14-point agreement between the two Republican leaders on major issues contained in the platform. The agreement, informally dubbed the "compact of Fifth Avenue," was issued by Rockefeller, who declared that the meeting was held at Nixon's insistence.

Half of the 14 points dealt with national security and foreign policy. The other half discussed domestic issues, including government reorganization, civil rights, agriculture, economic growth and medical care for the elderly. Although not markedly different in wording from the draft of the platform committee, the "compact" expressed a tone of urgency that was not evident in the draft.

The Nixon-Rockefeller agreement was made with the knowledge of the platform committee chairman, Charles H. Percy of Illinois, but was greeted with hostility by many members of the committee and by party conservatives. Goldwater termed the "compact" a "surrender" and the "Munich of the Republican Party" that would ensure the party's defeat that fall.

The two issues of greatest controversy were civil rights and national defense. The original civil rights plank, drafted by the platform committee, did not express support for civil rights demonstrations or promise federal efforts to gain job equality for blacks. The Nixon-Rockefeller agreement did both. Nixon threatened to wage a floor fight if the stronger civil rights plank was not inserted in the platform. By a vote of 50 to 35, the platform committee agreed to reconsider the original civil rights plank; by a margin of 56 to 28, the stronger plank was approved.

With the approval of both Rockefeller and President Dwight D. Eisenhower, several changes were made in the national security plank that emphasized the necessity of quickly upgrading America's armed forces. The platform committee approved reconsideration of the original defense plank by a voice vote, and the whole platform was adopted unanimously.

With disagreements resolved in the committee, there were neither minority reports nor floor fights. The convention approved the platform by a voice vote.

In its final form, the Republican platform was shorter than its Democratic counterpart, although still nearly 15,000 words in length. The foreign policy section asserted that the nation's greatest task was "to nullify the Soviet conspiracy." The platform claimed that America's military strength was second to none but, in line with the Nixon-Rockefeller "compact," indicated that improvements were needed in some parts of the armed forces.

The Republicans joined their Democratic opposition in favoring a workable disarmament program but did not advocate a phaseout of foreign military aid, as did the Democrats. However, the Republicans proposed a change in the funding of foreign aid that emphasized "the increasing use of private capital and government loans, rather than outright grants."

The Republicans agreed with the Democrats that the nation should experience more rapid economic growth but did not adopt the 5 percent annual growth rate favored by the Democrats. The Republicans stressed the virtues of a balanced budget and regarded free enterprise, rather than massive government programs, as the key to economic growth.

As in 1956, the two parties differed on farm price supports. The Republicans supported a program of flexible support payments, while the Democrats recommended setting price supports at 90 percent of parity.

Both parties proposed allowing individuals to work beyond their mandatory retirement age, although the Democrats tied their proposal to amendment of the Social Security program.

The Republicans did not urge elimination of the immigration quota system, as did their opponents, but they favored overhaul of the system to allow an increase in immigration.

On the issue of equal rights, the Republicans continued to favor passage of a constitutional amendment. The Democrats had backed away from this position, which they had held in earlier platforms, instead proposing the passage of equal rights legislation in Congress.

As they had since the beginning of the New Deal, the Republican and Democratic platforms differed noticeably as to the extent and desirability of federal spending. The Democrats viewed federal assistance to state and local governments as beneficial. The Republicans believed the federal government could help meet the problems of urban growth, but that state and local governments should administer all the programs they could best handle.

Following are excerpts from the Republican platform of 1960:

National Defense. The future of freedom depends heavily upon America's military might and that of her allies. Under the Eisenhower-Nixon Administration, our military might has been forged into a power second to none....

The strategic imperatives of our national defense policy are these:

A second-strike capability, that is, a nuclear retaliatory power that can survive surprise attack, strike back, and destroy any possible enemy.

Highly mobile and versatile forces, including forces deployed, to deter or check local aggressions and "brush fire wars" which might bring on all-out nuclear war.

National determination to employ all necessary military capabilities so as to render any level of aggression unprofitable. Deterrence of war since Korea, specifically, has been the result of our firm statement that we will never again permit a potential aggressor to set the ground rules for his aggression; that we will respond to aggression with the full means and weapons best suited to the situation....

Disarmament. We are similarly ready to negotiate and to institute realistic methods and safeguards for disarmament, and for the suspension of nuclear tests. We advocate an early agreement by all nations to forego nuclear tests in the atmosphere, and the suspension of other tests as verification techniques permit.

Immigration. The annual number of immigrants we accept be at least doubled.

Obsolete immigration laws be amended by abandoning the outdated 1920 census data as a base and substituting the 1960 census.

The guidelines of our immigration policy be based upon judgment of the individual merit of each applicant for admission and citizenship.

Foreign Aid. Agreeable to the developing nations, we would join with them in inviting countries with advanced economies to share with us a proportionate part of the capital and technical aid required. We would emphasize the increasing use of private capital and government loans, rather than outright grants, as a means of fostering independence and mutual respect.

Civil Rights. *Voting.* We pledge:

Continued vigorous enforcement of the civil rights laws to guarantee the right to vote to all citizens in all areas of the country....

Public Schools. We pledge:

The Department of Justice will continue its vigorous support of court orders for school desegregation....

We oppose the pretense of fixing a target date 3 years from now for the mere submission of plans for school desegregation. Slow-moving school districts would construe it as a three-year moratorium during which progress would cease, postponing until 1963 the legal process to enforce compliance. We believe that each of the pending court actions should proceed as the Supreme Court has directed and that in no district should there be any such delay.

Employment. We pledge:

Continued support for legislation to establish a Commission on Equal Job Opportunity to make permanent and to expand with legislative backing the excellent work being performed by the President's Committee on Government Contracts....

Housing. We pledge:

Action to prohibit discrimination in housing constructed with the aid of federal subsidies.

Public Facilities and Services. We pledge:

Removal of any vestige of discrimination in the operation of federal facilities or procedures which may at any time be found....

Economy. We reject the concept of artificial growth forced by massive new federal spending and loose money policies. The only effective way to accelerate economic growth is to increase the traditional strengths of our free economy — initiative and investment, productivity and efficiency....

Agriculture. Use of price supports at levels best fitted to specific commodities, in order to widen markets, ease production controls, and help achieve increased farm family income.

Government Reorganization. The President must continue to be able to reorganize and streamline executive operations to keep the executive branch capable of responding effectively to rapidly changing conditions in both foreign and domestic fields....

Two top positions should be established to assist the President in, (1) the entire field of National Security and International Affairs, and (2) Governmental Planning and Management, particularly in domestic affairs.

Government Spending. Vigorous state and local governments are a vital part of our federal union. The federal government should leave to state and local governments those programs and problems which they can best handle and tax sources adequate to finance them. We must continue to improve liaison between federal, state and local governments. We believe that the federal government, when appropriate, should render significant assistance in dealing with our urgent problems of urban growth and change. No vast new bureaucracy is needed to achieve this objective.

1964 Conventions

Presidential Candidates

Barry Goldwater
Republican

Lyndon B. Johnson
Democrat

Republicans

Division between the party's conservative and moderate wings, muted during the Eisenhower administration, exploded at the Republicans' July 13-16 convention in San Francisco.

Although Sen. Barry Goldwater of Arizona, the hero of Republican conservatives, had a commanding lead as the convention opened, he was vigorously challenged by Pennsylvania governor William W. Scranton, the belated leader of the moderate forces. Two days before the presidential balloting, a letter in Scranton's name was sent to Goldwater. It charged the Goldwater organization with regarding the delegates as "little more than a flock of chickens whose necks will be wrung at will." The message continued, describing Goldwater's political philosophy as a "crazy-quilt collection of absurd and dangerous positions." The letter concluded by challenging the Arizona senator to a debate before the convention. Although the message was written by Scranton's staff without his knowledge, the Pennsylvania governor supported the substance of the letter. Goldwater declined the invitation to debate.

Although seven names were placed in nomination for the presidency, the outcome was a foregone conclusion. Goldwater was an easy winner on the first ballot, receiving 883 of the 1,308 votes. Scranton was a distant second with 214 votes; New York governor Nelson A. Rockefeller followed with 114. Scranton moved that Goldwater's nomination be made unanimous, and his motion was approved by a voice vote. Support for the major moderate candidates, Scranton and Rockefeller, was centered in the Northeast. Goldwater had an overwhelming majority of the delegates from other regions. *(Chart, p. 242)*

As his running mate, Goldwater selected the Republican national chairman, Rep. William E. Miller of New York. On disclosing his choice of Miller, Goldwater stated that "one of the reasons I chose Miller is that he drives Johnson nuts." On the vice presidential roll call, the conservative New York representative received 1,305 votes, with three delegates from Tennessee abstaining. A Roman Catholic, Miller became the first member of that faith ever to run on a Republican national ticket.

Goldwater's acceptance speech was uncompromising and did not attempt to dilute his conservatism in an effort to gain votes: "Anyone who joins us in all sincerity we welcome. Those who do not care for our cause, we don't expect to enter our ranks in any case. And let our Republicanism so focused and so dedicated not be made fuzzy and futile by unthinking and stupid labels. I would remind you that extremism in the defense of liberty is no vice. And let me remind you also that moderation in the pursuit of justice is no virtue."

By a voice vote, the convention adopted the party platform, but not before the moderate forces waged floor fights on three issues — extremism, civil rights and control of nuclear weapons. Within the platform committee, 70 to 80 different amendments were presented, but when the platform reached the floor the moderates concentrated on these three specific issues.

Extremism was the first issue considered, with Sen. Hugh Scott of Pennsylvania introducing an amendment that specifically denounced efforts of the John Birch Society, the Ku Klux Klan and the Communist Party to infiltrate the Republican Party. Rockefeller spoke on behalf of the amendment but was booed throughout his speech. Rockefeller argued that a "radical, high-financed, disciplined minority" was trying to take over the Republican Party, a minority "wholly alien to the middle course . . . the mainstream." The amendment was rejected on a standing vote, by a margin estimated at two to one.

A second amendment on extremism, proposed by Michigan governor George W. Romney, condemned extremist groups but not by name. The Romney amendment was similarly rejected on a standing vote by about the same margin. Scott introduced a civil rights amendment adding additional pledges to the existing plank, including more manpower for the Justice Department's Civil Rights Division; a statement of pride in Republican support of the 1964 Civil Rights Act; requirements for first-step compliance with school desegregation by all school districts in one year; voting guarantees to state as well as federal elections, and promises to eliminate job bias. The platform's brief plank on civil rights called for "full implementation and faithful execution" of the 1964 act, but it also stated that "the elimination of any such discrimination is a matter of heart, conscience and education as well as of equal rights under law." On a roll-call vote, the Scott amendment was defeated, 897 to 409. The pattern of the vote closely followed the presidential ballot, with support for the amendment centered in the Northeast. *(Chart, p. 242)*

Romney offered a brief, alternative civil rights plank that pledged action at the state, local and private levels to eliminate discrimination in all fields. It was defeated by a voice vote.

Scott proposed another amendment, declaring the president to have sole authority to control the use of nuclear weapons. This contrasted with Goldwater's position advocating that North Atlantic Treaty Organization (NATO) commanders be given greater authority in the use of tactical nuclear weapons. The Scott amendment was rejected on a standing vote.

In its final form, the Republican platform was barely half as long as its Democratic counterpart. The Republican platform was divided into four sections, the first two enumerating Democratic failures in foreign policy and domestic affairs. The last two sections detailed Republican proposals.

The Republicans were suspicious of any détente with the communist world, instead calling for "a dynamic strategy of victory . . . for freedom." The platform contended that American military strength was deteriorating and promised the establishment of a military force superior to that of the nation's enemies. The Republicans expressed distrust of the 1963 nuclear test ban treaty and vowed to "never unilaterally disarm America." The platform promised to revitalize NATO, which was viewed as a keystone of Republican foreign policy.

Concerning specific trouble spots around the world, the platform demanded removal of the Berlin Wall, pledged to "move decisively to assure victory in South Vietnam" and promised to recognize a Cuban government in exile as well as to supply assistance to Cuban guerrilla freedom fighters.

Coupled with the anti-communism of the foreign policy sections was the central theme of the domestic sections — the need to trim the power of the federal government and to relocate it in state and local governments. This conservative philosophy was evident in various domestic planks.

The Republicans promised a reduction of at least $5 billion in federal spending and pledged to end budget deficits. A proposal was made to cut federal income taxes and to transfer the excise tax and several other federal tax sources from the federal government to state and local governments. The Republicans also recommended that state and local tax payments be credited against federal income taxes.

The platform favored a reduction of federal involvement in school financing and advocated passage of a constitutional amendment to allow prayer in public schools. A plank was included that urged passage of legislation to curb the flow of obscene materials through the mails.

The "one person, one vote" ruling of the Supreme Court brought the recommendation by the Republicans that a constitutional amendment be passed to allow states with bicameral legislatures to use a measurement other than population.

Following are excerpts from the Republican platform of 1964:

Peace. This Administration has sought accommodations with Communism without adequate safeguards and compensating gains for freedom. It has alienated proven allies by opening a "hot line" first with a sworn enemy rather than with a proven friend, and in general pursued a risky path such as began at Munich a quarter century ago. . . .

The supreme challenge to this policy is an atheistic imperialism — Communism.

Our nation's leadership must be judged by — indeed, American independence and even survival are dependent upon — the stand it takes toward Communism.

That stand must be: victory for freedom. There can be no peace, there can be no security, until this goal is won.

National Defense. This Administration has adopted policies which will lead to a potentially fatal parity of power with Communism instead of continued military superiority for the United States.

It has permitted disarmament negotiations to proceed without adequate consideration of military judgment — a procedure which tends to bring about, in effect, a unilateral curtailment of American arms rendered the more dangerous by the Administration's discounting known Soviet advances in nuclear weaponry.

It has failed to take minimum safeguards against possible consequences of the limited nuclear test ban treaty, including advanced underground tests where permissible and full readiness to test elsewhere should the need arise. . . .

. . . we will regularly review the status of nuclear weaponry under the limited nuclear test ban to assure this nation's protection. We shall also provide sensible, continuing reviews of the treaty itself. . . .

We will maintain a superior, not merely equal, military capability as long as the Communist drive for world domination continues. It will be a capability of balanced force, superior in all its arms, maintaining flexibility for effective performance in the rapidly changing science of war.

Republicans will never unilaterally disarm America.

Berlin. We will demand that the Berlin Wall be taken down prior to the resumption of any negotiations with the Soviet Union on the status of forces in, or treaties affecting, Germany.

Cuba. We Republicans will recognize a Cuban government in exile; we will support its efforts to regain the independence of its homeland; we will assist Cuban freedom fighters in carrying on guerrilla warfare against the Communist regime; we will work for an economic boycott by all nations of the free world in trade with Cuba; and we will encourage free elections in Cuba after liberty and stability are restored.

Vietnam. We will move decisively to assure victory in South Vietnam. While confining the conflict as closely as possible, America must move to end the fighting in a reasonable time and provide guarantees against further aggression. We must make it clear to the Communist world that, when conflict is forced with America, it will end only in victory for freedom.

United Nations. This Administration has failed to provide forceful, effective leadership in the United Nations.

It has weakened the power and influence of this world organization by failing to demand basic improvements in its procedures and to guard against its becoming merely a form of anti-Western insult and abuse.

Federal Power. Humanity is tormented once again by an age-old issue — is man to live in dignity and freedom under God or to be enslaved — are men in government to serve, or are they to master, their fellow men? . . .

1. Every person has the right to govern himself, to fix his own goals, and to make his own way with a minimum of governmental interference.

2. It is for government to foster and maintain an

environment of freedom encouraging every individual to develop to the fullest his God-given powers of mind, heart and body; and, beyond this, government should undertake only needful things, rightly of public concern, which the citizen cannot himself accomplish.

We Republicans hold that these two principles must regain their primacy in our government's relations, not only with the American people, but also with nations and peoples everywhere in the world.

Economy. In furtherance of our faith in the individual, we also pledge prudent, responsible management of the government's fiscal affairs to protect the individual against the evils of spendthrift government — protecting most of all the needy and fixed-income families against the cruelest tax, inflation — and protecting every citizen against the high taxes forced by excessive spending, in order that each individual may keep more of his earning for his own and his family's use.

Tax Reform. In furtherance of our faith in limited, frugal and efficient government we also pledge: credit against Federal taxes for specified State and local taxes paid, and a transfer to the States of excise and other Federal tax sources, to reinforce the fiscal strength of State and local governments so that they may better meet rising school costs and other pressing urban and suburban problems such as transportation, housing water systems and juvenile delinquency....

Civil Rights. Full implementation and faithful execution of the Civil Rights Act of 1964, and all other civil rights statutes, to assure equal rights and opportunities guaranteed by the Constitution to every citizen; ... continued opposition to discrimination based on race, creed, national origin or sex. We recognize that the elimination of any such discrimination is a matter of heart, conscience, and education, as well as of equal rights under law.

Education. To continue the advancement of education on all levels, through such programs as selective aid to higher education, strengthened State and local tax resources, including tax credits for college education, while resisting the Democratic efforts which endanger local control of schools; to help assure equal opportunity and a good education for all, while opposing Federally-sponsored "inverse discrimination," whether by the shifting of jobs, or the abandonment of neighborhood schools, for reasons of race;....

School Prayer. Support of a Constitutional amendment permitting those individuals and groups who choose to do so to exercise their religion freely in public places, provided religious exercises are not prepared or prescribed by the state or political subdivision thereof and no person's participation therein is coerced, thus preserving the traditional separation of church and state;....

Obscenity. Enactment of legislation, despite Democratic opposition, to curb the flow through the mails of obscene materials which has flourished into a multimillion dollar obscenity racket;....

Medical Care for Elderly. Full coverage of all medical and hospital costs for the needy elderly people, financed by general revenues through broader implementation of Federal-State plans, rather than the compulsory Democratic scheme covering only a small percentage of such costs, for everyone regardless of need;....

Reapportionment. Support of a Constitutional amendment, as well as legislation, enabling States having bicameral legislatures to apportion one House on bases of their choosing, including factors other than population;....

Democrats

In late August in Atlantic City, N.J., the Democratic

convention nominated President Lyndon B. Johnson for a full term in the White House. The proceedings were stage-managed by the president and were met with little visible dissent on the convention floor. The four-day event Aug. 24-27 was a political triumph for the veteran politician from Texas, who less than a year earlier had been the assassinated John F. Kennedy's vice president.

The Democratic convention was larger than any previous convention of an American political party, with 5,260 delegates and alternates. A new vote-allocation formula was in effect that combined consideration of a state's electoral vote with its support for the Kennedy-Johnson ticket in 1960. While no states lost votes from four years earlier, many of the larger states gained significantly. As a result, there were 2,316 votes at the 1964 convention, compared with 1,521 in 1960.

With no controversy surrounding either the party nominee or platform, attention focused on the credentials challenge brought by the integrated Mississippi Freedom Democratic Party against the all-white delegation sent by the regular state party. By a voice vote, the convention approved a compromise negotiated by Minnesota senator Hubert H. Humphrey. The settlement called for seating of the Mississippi regulars, provided they signed a written pledge to back the national ticket and urged the state's presidential electors to do likewise. It also proposed the seating of Democrats as delegates at large, and the remainder of the delegation as honored guests; and it stipulated that at future conventions delegations would be barred from states that allowed racial discrimination in voting. Although the convention approved this solution, the Freedom Democrats rejected the compromise, and all but four members of the regular Mississippi delegation refused to sign the pledge and left the convention.

The convention also approved a recommendation requiring the Alabama delegation to sign a personal loyalty oath, the result of the state party's placing "unpledged" (anti-Johnson) electors on the Alabama ballot. Eleven Alabama members signed the loyalty oath; the remaining 42 delegates and alternates withdrew from the convention.

The roll-call vote for president was dispensed with, and Johnson was nominated by acclamation. Immediately after his selection, Johnson made the unprecedented move of appearing before the delegates to announce his choice for vice president, Humphrey. Johnson had tried to make his selection as suspenseful and dramatic as possible. Although most observers felt Humphrey would be the choice, earlier that day Johnson had called both the Minnesota senator and Connecticut senator Thomas J. Dodd to the White House. However, at this meeting Johnson invited Humphrey to be on the ticket, and later that night the delegates nominated Humphrey by acclamation. (The 1964 Democratic convention was only the second in party history in which there were no roll-call votes — the other time was 1936.)

On the final day of the convention, the two nominees delivered their acceptance speeches. Humphrey frequently referred to the Republican candidate, Sen. Goldwater, as "the temporary Republican spokesman," and listed major legislation supported by a majority of both parties in the Senate, "but not Sen. Goldwater."

The emotional highlight of the convention was the appearance of Attorney General Robert F. Kennedy, who introduced a film about the presidency of his late brother.

By a voice vote, the convention approved the party platform. Following the trend toward longer and longer documents, the platform was 22,000 words in length. Although the document was adopted without debate on the convention floor, several roll-call votes were taken in the platform committee. By a vote of 53 to 16, the committee rejected a proposal by Sen. Joseph S. Clark of Pennsylvania to strengthen the disarmament plank. Clark's proposal called for further disarmament "under world law," wording that the committee majority did not want to include.

By a margin of 39 to 38, the platform committee pledged to support a constitutional amendment giving the District of Columbia representation in Congress. On another roll-call vote (52 to 19), the committee promised to repeal the Taft-Hartley Act provision permitting state right-to-work laws.

Without a recorded vote, the committee adopted another provision by Sen. Clark proposing revision of congressional rules and procedures to "assure majority rule after reasonable debate and to guarantee that major legislative proposals of the President can be brought to a vote after reasonable consideration in committee." The proposal was a reference to the Senate cloture rule, requiring a two-thirds vote to cut off debate, and to the power of the House Rules Committee to keep legislation from the floor.

The entire platform was a wide-ranging document designed to appeal to as many segments of the electorate as possible. Self-described as a "covenant of unity," the platform was written in a moderate tone to contrast with the unqualified conservatism expressed in the Republican platform.

The latter three-quarters of the Democratic platform was a section entitled "An Accounting of Stewardship, 1961-1964," which described the accomplishments of the Kennedy-Johnson administration in 38 areas of public policy. The first quarter of the platform discussed the party's position on major issues of the day, from peace and national defense to civil rights, the economy, agriculture, natural resources, urban affairs, federal power and government reform, and extremism.

In view of the militant anti-communism of Sen. Goldwater and the Republican platform, the Democrats viewed peace and national defense as winning issues with a majority of the electorate. The Democrats claimed that the world was closer to peace than in 1960, due in part to the United States' overwhelming nuclear superiority and internal splits in the communist world, as well as the success of international negotiations such as those resulting in the nuclear test ban treaty. But, in an allusion to Goldwater's stance, the platform warned that recklessness by a president in foreign policy could result in nuclear disaster. The Democratic platform included a provision rejected by the Republicans, insisting that control of nuclear weapons must be kept in the hands of the president.

While peace and national defense were stressed by the Democrats, the Republican platform concentrated on the need to limit the power of the federal government. On this issue, the Democratic platform contained a recommendation to help state and local governments develop new revenue sources. But the Democratic plank also included an assertion that contradicted the Republicans' criticism of expanding federal power: "No government at any level can properly complain of violation of its power, if it fails to meet its responsibilities."

Neither party had a civil rights plank containing specifics. The difference was wording, with the Democrats promising "fair, effective enforcement" of the 1964 Civil Rights Act, but precluding the use of quotas in combating racial discrimination. The Republicans pledged "full implementation and faithful execution" of civil rights laws.

An effort at the Republican convention to have the party platform condemn specific "extremist" groups failed, although the issue was hotly debated on the convention floor. Without dissent, the Democratic platform included a provision that condemned extremism of the right and left, especially the Communist Party, the Ku Klux Klan and the John Birch Society.

The two parties differed in their opinion of the health of the economy. The Republicans blamed their opposition for inflation and continuing unemployment and promised a reduction of at least $5 billion in federal spending. The Democrats countered by claiming the Kennedy-Johnson administration had engineered "the longest and strongest peacetime prosperity in modern history."

Following are excerpts from the Democratic platform of 1964:

Peace. At the start of the third decade of the nuclear age, the preservation of peace requires the strength to wage war and the wisdom to avoid it. The search for peace requires the utmost intelligence, the clearest vision, and a strong sense of reality.... Battered by economic failures, challenged by recent American achievements in space, torn by the Chinese-Russian rift, and faced with American strength and courage — international Communism has lost its unity and momentum.

National Defense. Specifically, we must and we will:
—Continue the overwhelming supremacy of our Strategic Nuclear Forces.
—Strengthen further our forces for discouraging limited wars and fighting subversion.
—Maintain the world's largest research and development effort, which has initiated more than 200 new programs since 1961, to ensure continued American leadership in weapons systems and equipment....
Control of the use of nuclear weapons must remain solely with the highest elected official in the country — the President of the United States....
The complications and dangers in our restless, constantly changing world require of us consummate understanding and experience. One rash act, one thoughtless decision, one unchecked reaction — and cities could become smouldering ruins and farms parched wasteland.

Civil Rights. The Civil Rights Act of 1964 deserves and requires full observance by every American and fair, effective enforcement if there is any default....
True democracy of opportunity will not be served by establishing quotas based on the same false distinctions we seek to erase, nor can the effects of prejudice be neutralized by the expedient of preferential practices.

Extremism. We condemn extremism, whether from the Right or Left, including the extreme tactics of such organizations as the Communist Party, the Ku Klux Klan and the John Birch Society.

Federal Power. The Democratic Party holds to the belief that government in the United States — local, state and federal — was created in order to serve the people. Each level of government has appropriate powers and each has specific responsibilities. The first responsibility of government at every level is to protect the basic freedoms of the people. No government at any level can properly complain of violation of its power, if it fails to meet its responsibilities.
The federal government exists not to grow larger, but to enlarge the individual potential and achievement of the people.
The federal government exists not to subordinate the states, but to support them.

Economy. In 42 months of uninterrupted expansion

under Presidents Kennedy and Johnson, we have achieved the longest and strongest peacetime prosperity in modern history. . . .

It is the national purpose, and our commitment, that every man or woman who is willing and able to work is entitled to a job and to a fair wage for doing it.

1968 Conventions

Presidential Candidates

Richard M. Nixon
Republican

Hubert H. Humphrey
Democrat

George C. Wallace
American Independent

Republicans

The Republican convention, held in Miami Beach, Fla., Aug. 5-8, had a surface tranquility that the later Democratic convention lacked. Only two roll-call votes were taken on the convention floor, to nominate presidential and vice presidential candidates.

There was only one challenge seriously considered by the credentials committee, and that involved a single delegate. By a 32-32 vote, the committee defeated an unexpectedly strong attempt to overturn the preconvention decision to seat Rep. H. R. Gross of Iowa rather than a Des Moines housewife. The full convention approved the report of the credentials committee without a roll-call vote.

The report of the rules committee was approved without comment. It contained recommendations to prohibit discrimination in the selection of future convention delegates and to add the Republican state chairmen as members of the Republican National Committee.

Twelve names were placed in nomination for the presidency, although the contest was clearly among three candidates: the front-runner, former vice president Richard M. Nixon, and two governors, Nelson A. Rockefeller of New York and Ronald Reagan of California. The ideological gulf between the more liberal Rockefeller and the more conservative Reagan made it difficult for them to agree on a common strategy to stop Nixon, even when Reagan abandoned his favorite-son status for active candidacy two days before the balloting.

To head off the defection to Reagan of his more conservative supporters, Nixon seemed to take a sharp tack to the right the day before the balloting. He told Southern delegations he would not run an administration that would "ram anything down your throats," that he opposed school busing, that he would appoint "strict constitutionalists" to the Supreme Court and that he was critical of federal intervention in local school board affairs.

Nixon won the nomination on the first ballot, receiving 692 votes (25 more than necessary) to easily outdistance

Rockefeller, who had 277, and Reagan, who had 182. After vote switches, the final totals were Nixon, 1,238, Rockefeller, 93, and Reagan, 2. In a brief speech to the convention, Reagan moved that Nixon's nomination be made unanimous, but his motion was never put to a vote. (*Chart, p. 244*)

In his selection of a running mate, Nixon surprised many observers by tapping Maryland governor Spiro T. Agnew. Agnew, who had delivered the major nominating speech for Nixon, had, ironically, been one of Rockefeller's earliest and strongest supporters. But the Maryland governor ceased his active support of Rockefeller in March, irked by the New York governor's indecision about entering the race, and, at the beginning of convention week, announced his support for Nixon.

In addition to Agnew, the name of Michigan governor George Romney also was placed in nomination for vice president. Agnew was an easy winner, receiving 1,119 votes to 186 for Romney, who made no effort to withdraw his name. After completion of the roll call, a Romney motion to make Agnew's nomination unanimous was approved.

The delegates approved without debate the 1968 Republican platform, which steered a careful middle course between conservatives and liberals on domestic policy and between "doves" and "hawks" on the touchy Vietnam issue. The 11,500-word document was somewhat more liberal in tone than that of 1960 and was far removed from the militantly conservative tone of the 1964 document.

A major floor fight on the platform was averted when platform committee members, led by Senate Minority Leader Everett McKinley Dirksen of Illinois, substituted for the original hard-line war plank new language stressing the need for de-Americanization of both the military and civilian efforts in Vietnam. Both "hawks" and "doves" decided to go along with the revised version.

As originally written, the plank criticized the Johnson administration for not leaving key Vietnam decisions to the military and for the administration's policy of military gradualism. Both Nixon and Rockefeller backers opposed the strong language, and a compromise Vietnam plank was accepted. As well as advocating the de-Americanization of the war, it proposed concentrating on protection of the South Vietnamese population rather than on capturing territory, and on efforts to strengthen local forces and responsibility.

While the platform endorsed continued negotiations with Hanoi, it remained silent on the important issues of a bombing pause and of a possible Saigon coalition that would include the communists. During platform committee deliberations, Sen. Jacob K. Javits of New York offered a plank to bring the National Liberation Front into the negotiations, but the suggestion was rejected overwhelmingly.

In its discussion of national defense, the platform criticized the administration for failure to develop superior new weaponry. The document indicated that, when the Vietnam War was over, a reduced defense budget might make possible increased federal spending on social welfare programs. But it neither suggested how much more spending nor recommended any substantial increases in the near future.

The platform treated rioting and crime in militant fashion: "We will not tolerate violence!" The crime plank criticized the Johnson administration for not taking effective action against crime and pledged "an all-out federal-state-local crusade."

It was in the cities plank that the party, in a short statement, mentioned civil rights legislation. The statement simply pledged: "Energetic, positive leadership to enforce statutory and constitutional protections to eliminate discrimination." It was seen as an endorsement of the recently enacted open housing law, in addition to other federal civil rights statutes. The platform did not endorse any new civil rights legislation. However, the Republicans endorsed high-priority objectives of civil rights groups, such as increased food for the poor and job-training programs.

In its youth plank, the Republicans made two specific proposals. First, the party urged the states to lower the voting age to 18 but did not endorse proposals for a constitutional amendment similarly to lower the federal voting age. Second, the plank advocated action to shorten the period in which young men were eligible for the draft and proposed to develop eventually a voluntary force.

Following are excerpts from the Republican platform of 1968:

Vietnam. The Administration's Vietnam policy has failed — militarily, politically, diplomatically, and with relation to our own people.

We condemn the Administration's breach of faith with the American people respecting our heavy involvement in Vietnam. Every citizen bitterly recalls the Democrat campaign oratory of 1964: "We are not about to send American boys 9-10,000 miles away from home to do what Asian boys ought to be doing for themselves." The Administration's failure to honor its own words has led millions of Americans to question its credibility.

The entire nation has been profoundly concerned by hastily-extemporized, undeclared land wars which embroil massive U.S. Army forces thousands of miles from our shores. It is time to realize that not every international conflict is susceptible of solution by American ground forces....

We pledge to adopt a strategy relevant to the real problems of the war, concentrating on the security of the population, on developing a greater sense of nationhood,

and on strengthening the local forces. It will be a strategy permitting a progressive de-Americanization of the war, both military and civilian....

We pledge a program for peace in Vietnam — neither peace at any price nor a camouflaged surrender of legitimate United States or allied interests — but a positive program that will offer a fair and equitable settlement to all, based on the principle of self-determination, our national interests and the cause of long-range world peace.

We will sincerely and vigorously pursue peace negotiations as long as they offer any reasonable prospect for a just peace. We pledge to develop a clear and purposeful negotiating position.

National Defense. Grave errors, many now irretrievable, have characterized the direction of our nation's defense.

A singular notion — that salvation for America lies in standing still — has pervaded the entire effort. Not retention of American superiority but parity with the Soviet Union has been made the controlling doctrine in many critical areas. We have frittered away superior military capabilities, enabling the Soviets to narrow their defense gap, in some areas to outstrip us, and to move to cancel our lead entirely by the early Seventies.

China. Improved relations with Communist nations can come only when they cease to endanger other states by force or threat. Under existing conditions, we cannot favor recognition of Communist China or its admission to the United Nations.

Israel. The fact of a growing menace to Israel is undeniable. Her forces must be kept at a commensurate strength both for her protection and to help keep the peace of the area. The United States, therefore, will provide countervailing help to Israel, such as supersonic fighters, as necessary for these purposes.

Crime. Fire and looting, causing millions of dollars of property damage, have brought great suffering to home owners and small businessmen, particularly in black communities least able to absorb catastrophic losses. The Republican Party strongly advocates measures to alleviate and remove the frustrations that contribute to riots. We simultaneously support decisive action to quell civil disorder, relying primarily on state and local governments to deal with these conditions.

America has adequate peaceful and lawful means for achieving even fundamental social change if the people wish it. *We will not tolerate violence!*

Lawlessness is crumbling the foundations of American society....

We must re-establish the principle that men are accountable for what they do, that criminals are responsible for their crimes, that while the youth's environment may help to explain the man's crime, it does not excuse that crime.

The present Administration has:

—Refused to sanction the use of either the court-supervised wiretapping authority to combat organized crime or the revised rules of evidence, both made available by Congress.

—Failed to deal effectively with threats to the nation's internal security by not prosecuting identified subversives....

For the future, we pledge an all-out, federal-state-local crusade against crime, including:

—Leadership by an Attorney General who will restore stature and respect to that office....

—Enactment of legislation to control indiscriminate availability of firearms, safeguarding the right of responsible citizens to collect, own and use firearms for legitimate purposes, retaining primary responsibility at the state level, with such federal laws as necessary to better enable the states to meet their responsibilities.

Economy. Under the Johnson-Humphrey Administration we have had economic mismanagement of the highest order. . . .

Such funds as become available with the termination of the Vietnam war and upon recovery from its impact on our national defense will be applied in a balanced way to critical domestic needs and to reduce the heavy tax burden.

Democrats

While violence flared in the streets and thousands of police and guards imposed security precautions unprecedented at presidential nominating conventions, the 1968 Democratic convention met Aug. 26-29 in Chicago to nominate Hubert H. Humphrey of Minnesota for the presidency and to endorse the controversial Vietnam policies of the Johnson-Humphrey administration.

Twin themes — physical force to keep order and political force to overrule minority sentiment in the Democratic Party — were apparent throughout the convention.

The physical force, supplied by 11,900 Chicago police, 7,500 Army regulars, 7,500 Illinois National Guardsmen and 1,000 FBI and Secret Service agents, was exerted to keep vociferous Vietnam War critics away from the convention headquarters hotels and the International Amphitheatre where official sessions were held. A security ring several blocks wide guarded the amphitheatre, itself surrounded by a barbed wire fence and multiple security checkpoints for entering delegates, newsmen and guests. No violence erupted in the amphitheatre area, but near the downtown hotels there were days of bitter demonstrations that ended with repeated police use of tear gas. At the end of convention week, the Chicago police announced that 589 persons had been arrested during the disturbances, with more than 119 police and 100 demonstrators injured.

The political force was exerted by the Johnson administration organization backing Vice President Humphrey, whose supporters enjoyed clear control of convention proceedings from start to end. In a distinct minority were the anti-war factions that rallied around the candidacies of Senators Eugene J. McCarthy of Minnesota and George McGovern of South Dakota. The McCarthy forces mounted a series of challenges to the Humphrey faction — on credentials, rules, the platform and finally the nomination itself.

In the first business of the convention, the Humphrey and McCarthy forces joined to ban the unit rule, rejecting by voice vote a motion by the Texas delegation to retain the rule through the 1968 convention.

However, as expected, the brief moments of unity between the opposing sides ended when the convention moved on to consider credentials challenges. The two sides split on the question of adjournment, with the Humphrey forces defeating by a vote of 1,701-1/2 to 875 a motion to delay consideration of credentials until the second session.

The credentials committee had considered an unprecedented number of challenges, involving delegates from 15 states. Although McCarthy supported almost all the challenges, his candidacy was not always the paramount issue. In the case of the disputed Southern delegations, racial imbalance, the party loyalty issue, or a combination of both, were more important. Of the 17 different challenges, McCarthy supported all but one (in Wisconsin); McGovern backed all the Southern challenges; Humphrey supported only the Mississippi challenge publicly.

In a historic move, the convention by a voice vote seated a new loyalist Democratic faction from Mississippi and unseated the delegation of the traditionally segregationist, conservative regular party.

The credentials committee decided all other challenges in favor of the regular delegations, but minority reports were filed for the Alabama, Georgia, North Carolina and Texas challengers. The North Carolina case was decided by a voice vote supporting the regular delegation, but the other three cases were settled by roll-call votes.

The first state to be considered was Texas, and, by a vote of 2,368-1/4 to 956-3/4, the convention approved the seating of the regular delegation led by Gov. John B. Connally. The rival McCarthy-supported Texas faction was led by Sen. Ralph Yarborough. *(Chart, p. 243)*

The Georgia case was considered next, with the credentials committee recommending that both rival delegations be seated and the Georgia vote split evenly between them. However, both delegations found this to be an unsatisfactory solution and presented reports to have their entire delegation seated alone. A minority report to seat the challenging Loyal National Democrats, led by black state representative Julian Bond, was defeated 1,415.45 to 1,043.55. A minority report to seat the regular delegation, hand-picked by Gov. Lester G. Maddox and Democratic state chairman James H. Gray, was rejected by a voice vote. The solution recommended by the credentials committee was subsequently approved by a voice vote.

The Alabama case involved three competing factions: the regulars, the largely black National Democratic Party of Alabama (NDPA) and the integrated Alabama Independent Democratic Party (AIDP), created solely to run a slate of presidential electors loyal to the national party against the third-party candidacy of Alabama governor George C. Wallace. The credentials committee proposed seating all members of the regular delegation who would sign a loyalty pledge and replacing those who would not sign with loyal members of the AIDP delegation. However, the McCarthy-backed NDPA introduced a minority report to seat its entire delegation. By a vote of 1,607 to 880-3/4, the convention rejected this minority report and by a voice vote approved the recommendation of the credentials committee.

The remainder of the credentials committee report was approved, including a resolution instructing the Democratic National Committee to include, in the call for the 1972 convention, encouragement to state parties to ensure that all Democrats in each state have a "meaningful and timely" opportunity to participate in delegate selection.

McCarthy, McGovern and other liberal factions won their greatest breakthrough on convention rules, obtaining abolition of a mandatory unit rule for the 1968 convention, and, by a vote of 1,351-1/4 to 1,209, obtaining elimination of the unit rule at every level of party activity leading up to and including the 1972 convention. Many Humphrey-pledged delegates also backed the unit rule change. Also a part of this successful minority report was the requirement that the delegate-selection process in 1972 be public and held within the calendar year of the convention.

A proposal to add state chairmen and state Young Democratic presidents to the Democratic National Committee was defeated, 1,349-1/4 to 1,125-3/4.

On Wednesday night, on the third day of the convention, while nominations and balloting for president took place at the amphitheatre, the worst violence of the convention broke out downtown, and television screens carried pictures of phalanxes of Chicago police advancing on demonstrators.

At the same time, hundreds of Chicago mayor Richard

J. Daley's workers were brought into the galleries with apparent improper credentials. Some delegates, apparently refusing to show their credentials to the omnipresent security guards, were physically ejected from the convention floor. The McCarthy and McGovern forces charged "atrocities" and tried to adjourn the convention for two weeks. House Majority Leader Carl Albert of Oklahoma, the convention chairman, refused to accept their motions.

In addition to Humphrey, McCarthy and McGovern, only two other candidates were placed in nomination — the Rev. Channing E. Phillips of the District of Columbia, who became the first black ever nominated for the presidency at a national convention, and North Carolina governor Dan K. Moore. Telegrams were read from President Johnson and Massachusetts senator Edward M. Kennedy, each stating that he did not choose to be nominated.

The emotional highlight of the session was provided by McGovern's nominator, Connecticut senator Abraham A. Ribicoff, who charged that "with George McGovern as president of the United States we wouldn't have to have Gestapo tactics in the streets of Chicago."

Humphrey was an easy winner on the first ballot, receiving 1,759-1/4 votes to 601 for McCarthy, 146-1/2 for McGovern and 67-1/2 for Phillips. Humphrey's winning majority included the bulk of party moderates, big-city organizations of the North (including Daley's) and Southern conservatives. In a tumultuous ending to one of the wildest nights in American politics, Chairman Albert gaveled through a motion to make the nomination unanimous (despite major opposition on the floor) and adjourned the session. *(Chart, p. 243)*

As his running mate, Humphrey chose Maine senator Edmund S. Muskie. Julian Bond's name also was placed in nomination, but Bond, then 28, withdrew, explaining that he was under the "legal age" to be president (the constitutional minimum is 35). Before the end of the first ballot, Albert recognized Mayor Daley, who moved that Muskie be declared the vice presidential nominee by acclamation. With the convention in a particularly unruly state, the Daley motion was quickly adopted. At the time the roll call was suspended, Muskie already had received 1,942-1/2 votes, a majority. Bond was a distant second with 48-1/2.

A filmed tribute to the late New York senator Robert F. Kennedy preceded the vice presidential nomination. Kennedy had been a presidential candidate until his assassination in June after winning the California primary. The tribute to Kennedy evoked a long, standing ovation and the singing of "The Battle Hymn of the Republic."

The 18,000-word platform, adopted by a voice vote, was a document that met the demands of the Democratic Party's liberals word for word in almost every section except that which dealt with United States policy in Vietnam. At one point during the platform-writing sessions, it appeared that Humphrey might assent to a plank calling for a halt in U.S. bombing of North Vietnam. But President Johnson reportedly sent personal instructions that the plank should support administration policy.

The administration plank, approved by a 62-35 vote in the platform committee, supported a bombing halt only when it "would not endanger the lives of our troops in the field," did not call for a reduction in search-and-destroy missions or a withdrawal of troops until the end of the war, and advocated a new government in Saigon only after the war had ended. The minority plank, drafted by McCarthy and McGovern, called for an immediate halt to the bombing, reduction of offensive operations in the South Vietnamese countryside, a negotiated troop withdrawal and encouragement of the South Vietnamese government to negotiate with communist insurgents.

The bitterness created by the Vietnam issue and Humphrey's march toward the nomination finally erupted when the convention managers attempted to force debate and voting on the Vietnam plank at 2 a.m., when most television viewers were already asleep. Albert, in violation of convention rules, refused to recognize a motion from a McCarthy backer to adjourn. But a few minutes later, when the convention could not be brought to order, Albert recognized a similar motion from Mayor Daley.

Nearly three hours of debate were held the next afternoon. On the subsequent roll call, the minority plank was defeated, 1,567-3/4 to 1,041-1/4. After the result was announced, members of the New York delegation and others slipped on black armbands and sang "We Shall Overcome." *(Chart, p. 243)*

Unlike the Republican platform, which called for decreased United States involvement in Vietnam, Democrats adopted a plan that called for a continued strong American war effort. Although the Democrats agreed with Republicans that the South Vietnamese eventually should take over their nation's defense, they gave no indication that an expanded Vietnamese role could lead to U.S. troop reductions in the near future.

While promising to reduce waste in military spending, the Democrats stated that the nation "must and will maintain a strong and balanced defense establishment adequate to the task of security and peace." The platform said there "must be no doubt" about U.S. capability to meet either nuclear or more limited challenges.

Crime was one of the leading domestic issues. The platform contained a strongly worded but rather unspecific plank on crime, a plank containing fewer detailed proposals than its Republican counterpart. The Democratic crime plank was entitled "Justice and Law," in a deliberate effort to avoid use of such phrases as "law and order," which were in the Republican plank and which some observers felt had connotations of overly suppressive tactics, particularly in black ghettos.

The Democratic plank did not mention the role of the attorney general. The Republicans said they would seek an attorney general who would "restore stature and respect to that office." Nor did the Democrats, unlike the Republicans, mention implementation of the federal wiretapping authority granted by the Safe Streets Act, or prosecution of subversives.

Both parties pledged further efforts to control the indiscriminate sale of firearms, but neither party was specific. Democratic liberals had tried unsuccessfully within the platform committee to strengthen the gun control section.

The Democratic platform contained a more specific endorsement of open housing than did the Republican document. Both platforms urged better job opportunities, housing and food programs for the poor, and the Democrats also promised reforms in existing welfare programs.

The Democrats, like the Republicans, called for tax reform, but their goals were more pointed. The platform asked for a minimum income tax for wealthy persons based on total income regardless of source and committed the party to seeking decreased rates for lower-income families and an increase in the minimum standard deduction.

The Democrats supported a constitutional amendment to permit 18-year-old voting and recommended a draft lottery and better community representation on draft boards.

Reform of the electoral college was favored, so that it would accurately reflect the will of the voters.

Following are excerpts from the Democratic platform of 1968:

Vietnam. Recognizing that events in Vietnam and the negotiations in Paris may affect the timing and the actions we recommend we would support our Government in the following steps:

Bombing — Stop all bombing of North Vietnam when this action would not endanger the lives of our troops in the field; this action should take into account the response from Hanoi.

Troop Withdrawal — Negotiate with Hanoi an immediate end or limitation of hostilities and the withdrawal from South Vietnam of all foreign forces — both United States and allied forces, and forces infiltrated from North Vietnam.

Election of Postwar Government — Encourage all parties and interests to agree that the choice of the postwar government of South Vietnam should be determined by fair and safeguarded elections, open to all major political factions and parties prepared to accept peaceful political processes. We would favor an effective international presence to facilitate the transition from war to peace and to assure the protection of minorities against reprisal.

Interim Defense and Development Measures — Until the fighting stops, accelerate our efforts to train and equip the South Vietnamese army so that it can defend its own country and carry out cutbacks of U.S. military involvement as the South Vietnamese forces are able to take over their larger responsibilities. We should simultaneously do all in our power to support and encourage further economic, political and social development and reform in South Vietnam, including an extensive land reform program. We support President Johnson's repeated offer to provide a substantial U.S. contribution to the post-war reconstruction of South Vietnam as well as to the economic development of the entire region, including North Vietnam. Japan and the European industrial states should be urged to join in this post-war effort.

National Defense. We must and will maintain a strong and balanced defense establishment adequate to the task of security and peace. There must be no doubt about our strategic nuclear capacity, our capacity to meet limited challenges, and our willingness to act when our vital interests are threatened. . . .

We face difficult and trying times in Asia and in Europe. We have responsibilities and commitments we cannot escape with honor.

China. The immediate prospects that China will emerge from its self-imposed isolation are dim. But both Asians and Americans will have to coexist with the 750 million Chinese on the mainland. We shall continue to make it clear that we are prepared to cooperate with China whenever it is ready to become a responsible member of the international community. We would actively encourage economic, social and cultural exchange with mainland China as a means of freeing that nation and her people from their narrow isolation.

Israel. As long as Israel is threatened by hostile and well-armed neighbors, we will assist her with essential military equipment needed for her defense, including the most advanced types of combat aircraft.

Crime. In fighting crime we must not foster injustice. Lawlessness cannot be ended by curtailing the hard-won liberties of all Americans. The right of privacy must be safeguarded. Court procedures must be expedited. Justice delayed is justice denied.

A respect for civil peace requires also a proper respect for the legitimate means of expressing dissent. A democratic society welcomes criticism within the limits of the law.

Freedom of speech, press, assembly and association, together with free exercise of the franchise, are among the legitimate means to achieve change in a democratic society. But when the dissenter resorts to violence, he erodes the institutions and values which are the underpinnings of our democratic society. We must not and will not tolerate violence.

Tax Reform. We support a proposal for a minimum income tax for persons of high income based on an individual's total income regardless of source, in order that wealthy persons will be required to make some kind of income tax contribution, no matter how many tax shelters they use to protect their incomes.

We also support a reduction of the tax burden on the poor by lowering the income tax rates at the bottom of the tax scale and increasing the minimum standard deduction. No person or family below the poverty level should be required to pay federal income taxes.

Electoral Reform. We fully recognize the principle of one man, one vote in all elections. We urge that due consideration be given to the question of Presidential primaries throughout the nation. We urge reform of the electoral college and election procedures to assure that the votes of the people are fully reflected.

American Independent Party

Former Alabama governor George C. Wallace declared his third-party presidential candidacy on Feb. 8, 1968. The vehicle for his candidacy was his personally created American Independent Party. No convention was held by the party to ratify his selection. (A descendant of the 1968 Wallace campaign, the American Party ran a national ticket in 1972 but received less than 2 percent of the vote.)

On Feb. 14 Wallace announced the choice of former Georgia governor Marvin Griffin as his "interim" vice presidential running mate, but he made clear that an official candidate would be chosen later in the campaign. Griffin's tentative candidacy was necessary to allow the American Independent Party to get on the ballot in several states.

On Oct. 3 Wallace announced his choice of retired Air Force general Curtis E. LeMay, an Ohio native, as his official running mate.

Ten days later, Wallace released the text of his party's platform. The document generally took a harder line toward domestic and international problems than did the Democratic and Republican platforms.

Wallace favored termination of the Vietnam War through negotiations but added that, if negotiations failed, the United States should seek a military solution.

As expected, the emphasis of the platform on domestic issues centered on returning control of local affairs to the states and communities, with the federal government serving in an assisting role rather than an authoritarian manner.

To curb the interference of the federal government in local affairs, Wallace advocated adoption of a constitutional amendment under which federal district judges would stand for election periodically and higher judges, including Supreme Court justices, would be required to be periodically reconfirmed by the Senate. Wallace further proposed, in essence, repeal of the open housing provision of the 1968 Civil Rights Act and to "absolutely prohibit the agencies and agents of the Federal Government from intruding into and seeking to control the affairs of the local school systems of the states, counties and cities of the nation." He further pledged to "cooperate with the administrators of our institutions of higher learning now in the hands of revolutionaries. We must support these officials in the restoration of order on their campuses and we must assure that no assistance, financial or otherwise, from the federal level be given to those seeking to disrupt and destroy these great institutions."

In a section entitled "Crime and Disorder," Wallace pledged to give his full support to law enforcement agencies at every level of government, to "insist on fair and equal treatment for all persons before the bar of justice," to appoint an attorney general "interested in the enforcement rather than the disruption of the legal processes," and to oppose federal legislation requiring gun registration.

Wallace also promised to seek an immediate increase in Social Security benefits, to increase agricultural support prices to 90 percent of parity and to seek legislation increasing maximum support to 100 percent of parity.

Following are excerpts from the American Independent Party platform of 1968:

Vietnam. We earnestly desire that the conflict be terminated through peaceful negotiations and we will lend all aid, support, effort, sincerity and prayer to the efforts of our negotiators. Negotiation will be given every reasonable and logical chance for success and we will be patient to an extreme in seeking an end to the war through this means. If it becomes evident that the enemy does not desire to negotiate in good faith, that our hopes of termination of hostilities are not being realized and that the lives and safety of our committed troops are being further endangered, we must seek a military conclusion.

National Defense. We propose an intensive and immediate review of the policies, practices and capabilities of the Department of Defense with a view to reestablishing sound principles of logic and reasoning to the decisions and directives of that agency and to eliminating from its ranks all of those who have been party to the dissemination and promulgation of the false doctrines of security and the coercion, intimidation and punishment of all who would oppose or disagree with them.

Middle East. Should arms continue to be introduced . . . by foreign powers to such an extent as to endanger the peace in this part of the world, we must take steps to assure that a balance of force is brought to exist. We will join with other nations of the free world in providing the means whereby this balance of force will continue and the threat of aggression of one nation against another is made less likely.

United Nations. We will not abandon the United Nations Organization unless it first abandons us. It should be given fair opportunity at resolving international disputes, however, we will not subordinate the interest of our nation to the interest of any international organization. We feel that in this organization, as in any other, participating members should bear proportionate shares of the cost of operation and we will insist on financial responsibility on the part of the member nations.

Crime. Lawlessness has become commonplace in our present society. The permissive attitude of the executive and judiciary at the national level sets the tone for this moral decay. The criminal and anarchist who preys on the decent law abiding citizen is rewarded for his misconduct through never ending justification and platitudes from those in high places who seem to have lost their concern for that vast segment of America that so strongly believes in law and order. . . .

We will appoint as Attorney General a person interested in the enforcement rather than the disruption of legal processes and restore that office to the dignity and stature it deserves and requires.

Economy. We will review and propose revisions to our present tax structure so as to ease the load of the small income citizen and to place upon all their rightful share of the tax burden. . . .

We will eliminate the favorable treatment now accorded the giant, non-tax paying foundations and institutions and require these organizations to assume their rightful responsibility as to the operation of our government. . . .

We propose to rely heavily upon a competitive market structure rather than upon prices administered or fixed by bureaucratic procedures.

Federal Power. The Federal Government, in derogation and flagrant violation of this Article [X] of the Bill of Rights, has in the past three decades seized and usurped many powers not delegated to it, such as, among others: the operation and control of the public school system of the several states; the power to prescribe the eligibility and qualifications of those who would vote in our state and local elections; the power to intrude upon and control the farmer in the operation of his farm; the power to tell the property owner to whom he can and cannot sell or rent his property; and, many other rights and privileges of the individual citizen, which are properly subject to state or local control, as distinguished from federal control. The Federal Government has forced the states to reapportion their legislatures, a prerogative of the states alone. The Federal Government has attempted to take over and control the seniority and apprenticeship lists of the labor unions; the Federal Government has adopted so-called "Civil Rights Acts," particularly the one adopted in 1964, which have set race against race and class against class, all of which we condemn.

The Judiciary. In the period of the past three decades, we have seen the Federal judiciary, primarily the Supreme Court, transgress repeatedly upon the prerogatives of the Congress and exceed its authority by enacting judicial legislation, in the form of decisions based upon political and sociological considerations, which would never have been enacted by the Congress. We have seen them, in their solicitude for the criminal and lawless element of our society, shackle the police and other law enforcement agencies; and, as a result, they have made it increasingly difficult to protect the law-abiding citizen from crime and criminals. This is one of the principal reasons for the turmoil and the near revolutionary conditions which prevail in our country today, and particularly in our national capital. The Federal judiciary, feeling secure in their knowledge that their appointment is for life, have far exceeded their constitutional authority, which is limited to interpreting or construing the law.

It shall be our policy and our purpose, at the earliest possible time, to propose and advocate and urge the adoption of an amendment to the United States Constitution whereby members of the Federal judiciary at District level be required to face the electorate on his record at periodical intervals; and, in the event he receives a negative vote upon such election, his office shall thereupon become vacant, and a successor shall be appointed to succeed him.

With respect to the Supreme Court and the Courts of Appeals I [George Wallace] would propose that this amendment require reconfirmation of the office holder by the United States Senate at reasonable intervals.

1972 Conventions

Presidential Candidates

George McGovern
Democrat

Richard M. Nixon
Republican

Democrats

Massive reforms in convention rules and delegate se-lection procedures made the 1972 Democratic convention, held in Miami Beach, Fla., July 10-13, significantly differ-ent from the violence-plagued assembly in Chicago four years earlier.

Two special commissions created by the 1968 conven-tion drafted the reforms. The Commission on Rules, chaired by Rep. James G. O'Hara of Michigan, composed the first set of rules ever written on Democratic convention procedure. Among the reforms that the Democratic Na-tional Committee adopted were:

● A new vote-allocation formula based nearly equally on electoral college strength and the Democratic vote in recent presidential elections.

● An expansion of the convention rules, platform and credentials committees so that their make-up would reflect state population differences rather than the previous method of allocating two seats to each state.

● The assurance that women and men be equally repre-sented on committees and among convention officers.

● The requirement that the meetings and votes of all convention committees be open to the public.

● The requirement that the reports and minority views of all the committees be released at specified dates before the opening of the convention.

● The banning of floor demonstrations for candidates.

● The arrangement of the states and territories for roll calls in random sequence determined by lot rather than in the traditional alphabetical order.

The Commission on Party Structure and Delegate Se-lection, first chaired by Sen. George McGovern of South Dakota and later by Rep. Donald M. Fraser of Minnesota, formulated 18 guidelines to be met by the states in the delegate-selection process. With the approval of these guidelines by the Democratic National Committee, they became part of the 1972 convention call, thus requiring the states to be in full compliance with the guidelines before they would be seated.

Among the important features of the 18 guidelines were the elimination of the unit rule; the restriction that no

more than 10 percent of a state's delegation be named by its state committee; the requirement that all steps in the delegate-selection process be publicly advertised and held in easily accessible public places within the calendar year of the convention; the requirement that women, youth and minority groups be included in delegations "in reasonable relationship" to their presence in the state's population; and the establishment of a detailed, public method of hearing delegate challenges.

The reforms encouraged an unprecedented number of challenges. The credentials committee opened hearings in Washington, D.C., two weeks before the start of the con-vention, faced with 82 challenges from 30 states and one territory. A total of 1,289 delegates were challenged, repre-senting more than 40 percent of the convention delegates. More than four-fifths of the challenges were filed on grounds of non-compliance with reform commission guide-lines regarding adequate representation of women, youth and minorities.

The most controversial challenges involved the Cali-fornia delegation and the part of the Illinois delegation controlled by Mayor Richard J. Daley of Chicago.

The credentials committee, in a move that surprised supporters of McGovern, a candidate for the presidential nomination, upheld a challenge of California's winner-take-all primary law, stripping McGovern of 151 of the 271 delegate votes he had won in the primary.

The committee voted 72 to 66 to award the 151 con-vention seats to Sen. Hubert H. Humphrey of Minnesota and seven other candidates in proportion to their share of the popular ballots cast in the state's June primary. Al-though McGovern was clearly the front-runner for the nomination, the decision, if not overturned by the full convention, threatened his chances of being selected.

In a tense and dramatic balloting session the next day, the committee voted 71 to 61 to unseat Daley and 58 of his Chicago delegates. The committee decided to replace the 59 delegates on grounds that the procedures under which the Daley delegates had been selected violated five of the party's reform guidelines. Most of the Illinois delegates challenging Daley supported McGovern.

Although the losing sides in both the California and Illinois decisions appealed their cases, the courts ruled that the party conventions decide their claims.

The emotional credentials challenges were considered on the first night of the convention. Twenty-three challenges from 15 states were brought to the convention floor, but the spotlight was on the California and Illinois cases. A key preliminary vote took place on a challenge to the South Carolina delegation brought by the National Women's Political Caucus. The challenge, seeking to increase the number of women in the state delegation, was rejected by a vote of 1,555.75 to 1,429.05. *(Chart, p. 246)*

The outcome of the vote could have set an important precedent on what constituted a majority on subsequent challenges. Anti-McGovern forces had hoped to get a ruling from the chair allowing an absolute majority of 1,509 delegates to prevail rather than a simple majority of delegates actually voting.

Convention Chairman Lawrence F. O'Brien (also chairman of the Democratic National Committee) had announced earlier that a majority would consist of one-half plus one of the number of eligible voters. The rules provided that no delegates could vote on their own credentials challenges.

Because the winning total on the South Carolina vote exceeded by a wide margin both the eligible majority and the absolute majority of the convention's 3,016 votes, the anti-McGovern coalition was unable to force a test of what constituted a majority. Thus the vote, although it rejected the position of South Carolina challengers favorable to McGovern, set the stage for returning the 151 California delegates to McGovern. The McGovern forces subsequently won the crucial California challenge, 1,618.28 to 1,238.22.

Immediately after the vote on the California challenge, a Wallace delegate from Florida appealed the ruling of the chair that allowed 120 McGovern delegates from California to vote on their state's other 151 delegates. The appeal was rejected, 1,689.52 to 1,162.23.

Former Nebraska governor Frank B. Morrison, a McGovern supporter, proposed a compromise solution for the Illinois case that would seat both the Daley delegates and the insurgent challengers, while splitting the vote between them. The Morrison proposal asked for suspension of the rules — a parliamentary procedure requiring a two-thirds majority. The motion to suspend the rules was rejected by 1,473.08 nays to 1,411.05 yeas.

The minority report, which asked for seating of the Daley delegates alone, was defeated 1,486.04 to 1,371.56. The vote seated a group, a majority of which supported McGovern, headed by Chicago alderman William Singer and black activist Jesse Jackson. *(Chart, p. 246)*

No other roll-call votes were needed to resolve the remaining credentials challenges. After the settlement of all the delegate contests, the convention had a composition unlike that of any previous major party convention. The 1972 Democratic assembly was the largest in major party history, with 3,203 delegates casting 3,016 votes. Unlike the situation in 1968, most delegates were chosen in state primary elections rather than in state conventions or caucuses. Nearly two-thirds of the delegates to the 1972 convention were selected in primaries, while only 41 percent had been elected by the primary system four years earlier.

There were also large increases in the number of women, youth and racial minorities at the 1972 convention. The proportion of women delegates rose from 13 percent in 1968 to 40 percent in 1972; the number of youth delegates

(30 and under) dramatically jumped from 2.6 percent in 1968 to 21 percent four years later; and black delegates made up 15 percent of the 1972 convention, compared with 5.5 percent in 1968. But while women, youth and blacks were better represented than at earlier conventions, there was a lower level of participation by elected party officials. Only 30 of the 255 Democratic U.S. House members were present in Miami Beach.

The report of the rules committee was approved on the second day of the convention by a voice vote. The report proposed the abolition of winner-take-all primaries in 1976; the abolition of cross-over voting by Republicans in future Democratic presidential primaries; the selection of a woman as chairman of the 1976 convention, with the job rotating between the sexes thereafter; the creation of a special fund in the Democratic National Committee to subsidize the expenses of poor delegates at future national conventions and other party councils, and the appointment of a commission to make "appropriate revisions" in the reform guidelines.

Although the delegates overwhelmingly accepted these reforms, they balked at approving the party charter drafted by the rules committee. The new charter, the first ever written for a major party, was intended to free the national party of four-year presidential election cycles and to broaden public involvement in major national policy questions. But the charter was opposed by some party leaders, particularly members of Congress, who viewed the document as shifting power from elected politicians to the grass-roots level. By a vote of 2,408.45 to 195.10, the convention approved a compromise resolution to delay consideration of the charter until a proposed midterm policy conference in 1974. The compromise also enlarged the Democratic National Committee and revised its membership to reflect Democratic strength in the various states.

The settlement of the California challenge on the opening night of the convention in favor of the McGovern forces effectively locked up the presidential nomination for the South Dakota senator. The next day, two of his major rivals in the primaries, Senators Humphrey and Muskie, withdrew from the race. In the balloting on the third day of the convention, McGovern was an easy winner on the first roll call. Before switches, McGovern had received 1,728.35 votes to 525 for Sen. Henry M. Jackson of Washington, 381.7 for Gov. Wallace of Alabama and 151.95 for Rep. Shirley Chisholm of New York. After vote changes, McGovern's vote total rose to 1,864.95, but no attempt was made to make his nomination unanimous. *(Chart, p. 247)*

With McGovern's first choice for vice president, Sen. Edward M. Kennedy of Massachusetts, rebuffing all overtures, McGovern selected Sen. Thomas F. Eagleton of Missouri. The vice presidential balloting was prolonged by the nomination of six other candidates, and, by the time the roll call was suspended, votes were distributed among more than 70 different "candidates." Eagleton received 1,741.81 votes, a majority. He was followed by Frances T. "Sissy" Farenthold, a women's rights leader from Texas, who had 404.04 votes, Sen. Mike Gravel of Alaska with 225.38 and former Massachusetts governor Endicott Peabody with 107.26. On the motion of Farenthold, the roll call was suspended and Eagleton was nominated by acclamation.

Because of the long vice presidential roll call, it was nearly 3 a.m. before McGovern was able to deliver his acceptance speech. In it he stressed the anti-war theme that was a basic part of his campaign and implored the nation to "come home" to its founding ideals.

Barely 10 days after selection of the Democratic ticket,

on July 25, Eagleton disclosed that he voluntarily had hospitalized himself three times between 1960 and 1966 for "nervous exhaustion and fatigue." McGovern strongly supported his running mate at the time, but in the following days, his support for the Missouri senator began to wane. After a meeting with McGovern on July 31, Eagleton withdrew from the ticket. It marked the first time since 1860 that a major party candidate had withdrawn from a national ticket after the convention had adjourned.

On Aug. 5 McGovern announced that his choice to replace Eagleton was R. Sargent Shriver of Maryland, U.S. ambassador to France and the former director of the Peace Corps and the Office of Economic Opportunity. The newly enlarged Democratic National Committee formally nominated Shriver in an Aug. 8 meeting in Washington. The new vice presidential candidate received 2,936 of the 3,013 votes cast, with the Missouri vote going to Eagleton and four of Oregon's votes to former senator Wayne Morse.

The 1972 Democratic platform was probably the most liberal and the longest (about 25,000 words) ever offered by a major political party. The platform was more a collection of independent reform proposals than a unified plan of action. Its recommendations, largely written by separate subject-area task forces, did not translate into a compact program for Congress to consider or for a president to propose. But the platform's common themes reflected the changes in the party since 1968 and set it off from all other Democratic platforms of the previous generation.

The convention made no concessions to the views of Wallace, even though he made a dramatic appearance at the podium in a wheelchair to urge adoption of minority planks his supporters had offered. Wallace was partially paralyzed from gunshot wounds he had received two months earlier in Laurel, Md., while campaigning for the Democratic presidential nomination.

The Wallace-supported planks called for a constitutional amendment to outlaw busing, tax reform, reintroduction of the death penalty, cutbacks in foreign aid, popular election of federal judges and Senate reconfirmation of Supreme Court justices, a school prayer amendment and support for the right to own guns. They were rejected by voice votes.

Twenty separate minority planks were considered by the convention, but only two were adopted, both by voice vote. One strengthened the American commitment to Israel by adding language promising "a military force in Europe and at sea in the Mediterranean ample to deter the Soviet Union from putting unbearable pressure on Israel." The second endorsed "allocation of federal surplus lands to American Indians on a priority basis."

Two roll-call votes were taken on other planks. The National Welfare Rights Organization sponsored a measure requiring the federal government to guarantee every family of four an annual income of $6,500. This proposal lost, 1,852.86 to 999.34. The other roll call was on a minority plank supporting the right of women to control their reproductive lives without legal interference. Offered by pro-abortion groups, it was defeated 1,572.80 to 1,101.37.

Two other significant minority planks were rejected by voice votes. One was a tax reform measure pushed by Sen. Fred Harris of Oklahoma, which had the slogan, "Take the rich off welfare." The other was a "gay rights" plank endorsing the repeal of all laws regarding voluntary sex acts performed by adults in private.

The platform session demonstrated the firm control McGovern had over the proceedings of the convention. The two minority planks added to the platform were the only

proposed additions that McGovern did not specifically oppose. He asked his delegates to support the pro-Israel plank and told them to vote their consciences on the Indian issue.

Planks dealing with domestic issues composed more than four-fifths of the platform. The domestic planks recommended little significant expansion of the size and scope of the federal government. With the major exception of health insurance, the platform sought to restructure society by shifting money and political power to the underprivileged, not by developing federal agencies to alter their lives.

The platform endorsed income redistribution through tax reforms and a guaranteed annual income. It sought expansion of minority-group rights in all political and federal government affairs. To solve the financial crisis at local levels, it endorsed general revenue sharing with local control over use of the money. All this represented a departure from the statist liberalism that had dominated Democratic platforms since the New Deal of the 1930s.

The foreign policy planks broke with the Cold War rhetoric of 1968 and previous years. While endorsing the concept of a strong national defense, the platform devoted more space to peace in Indochina, improved relations with the communist world and less help for non-communist totalitarian regimes. Only four years earlier, the Democrats had given considerable space to warnings against Soviet and Chinese expansion and to praise for the North Atlantic Treaty Organization. The 1968 platform called for scrutiny of wasteful defense spending practices, but the 1972 document made military cuts a major campaign promise and a source of financing for domestic programs.

The platform's position on the Vietnam War was blunt and unequivocal. As "the first order of business" of a Democratic administration, the platform pledged "immediate and complete withdrawal of all U.S. forces in Indochina." The plank also promised an end to military aid to the Saigon regime but pledged economic assistance to Vietnam to help the nation emerge from the war. Amnesty for war resisters was recommended after the return of American prisoners of war.

Following are excerpts from the Democratic platform of 1972:

Foreign Policy. The next Democratic Administration should:

• End American participation in the war in Southeast Asia.

• Re-establish control over military activities and reduce military spending, where consistent with national security.

• Defend America's real interests and maintain our alliances, neither playing world policeman nor abandoning old and good friends.

• Not neglect America's relations with small third-world nations in placing reliance on great power relationships.

• Return to Congress, and to the people, a meaningful role in decisions on peace and war, and

• Make information public, except where real national defense interests are involved.

Vietnam. We believe that war is a waste of human life. We are determined to end forthwith a war which has cost 50,000 American lives, $150 billion of our resources, that has divided us from each other, drained our national will and inflicted incalculable damage to countless people. We will end that war by a simple plan that need not be kept secret: The immediate total withdrawal of all Americans from Southeast Asia.

Military Spending. Military strength remains an essential element of a responsible international policy.

America must have the strength required for effective deterrence.

But military defense cannot be treated in isolation from other vital national concerns. Spending for military purposes is greater by far than federal spending for education, housing, environmental protection, unemployment insurance or welfare. Unneeded dollars for the military at once add to the tax burden and pre-empt funds from programs of direct and immediate benefit to our people. Moreover, too much that is now spent on defense not only adds nothing to our strength but makes us less secure by stimulating other countries to respond.

Vietnam Amnesty. To those who for reasons of conscience refused to serve in this war and were prosecuted or sought refuge abroad, we state our firm intention to declare an amnesty, on an appropriate basis, when the fighting has ceased and our troops and prisoners of war have returned.

Federal Power. The new Democratic Administration can begin a fundamental re-examination of all federal domestic social programs and the patterns of service delivery they support. Simply advocating the expenditure of more funds is not enough, although funds are needed, for billions already have been poured into federal government programs like urban renewal, current welfare and aid to education, with meager results. The control, structure and effectiveness of every institution and government grant system must be fully examined and these institutions must be made accountable to those they are supposed to serve.

Economy. The heart of a program of economic security based on earned income must be creating jobs and training people to fill them. Millions of jobs — real jobs, not make-work — need to be provided. Public service employment must be greatly expanded in order to make the government the employer of last resort and guarantee a job for all.

Tax Reform. The cost of government must be distributed more fairly among income classes. We reaffirm the long-established principle of progressive taxation — allocating the burden according to ability to pay — which is all but a dead letter in the present tax code.

Poverty. The next Democratic Administration must end the present welfare system and replace it with an income security program which places cash assistance in an appropriate context with all of the measures outlined above, adding up to an earned income approach to ensure each family an income substantially more than the poverty level defined in the area. Federal income assistance will supplement the income of working poor people and assure an adequate income for those unable to work.

Crime. There must be laws to control the improper use of hand guns. Four years ago a candidate for the presidency was slain by a hand gun. Two months ago, another candidate for that office was gravely wounded. Three out of four police officers killed in the line of duty are slain with hand guns. Effective legislation must include a ban on sale of hand guns known as Saturday night specials which are unsuitable for sporting purposes.

Free Expression and Privacy. The new Democratic Administration should bring an end to the pattern of political persecution and investigation, the use of high office as a pulpit for unfair attack and intimidation and the blatant efforts to control the poor and to keep them from acquiring additional economic security or political power.

The epidemic of wiretapping and electronic surveillance engaged in by the Nixon Administration and the use of grand juries for purposes of political intimidation must be ended. The rule of law and the supremacy of the Constitution, as these concepts have traditionally been understood, must be restored.

Rights of Women. Women historically have been denied a full voice in the evolution of the political and social institutions of this country and are therefore allied with all underrepresented groups in a common desire to form a more humane and compassionate society. The Democratic Party pledges the following:

●A priority effort to ratify the Equal Rights Amendment. . . .

●Appointment of women to positions of top responsibilities in all branches of the federal government, to achieve an equitable ratio of women and men.

School Busing. We support the goal of desegregation as a means to achieve equal access to quality education for all our children. There are many ways to desegregate schools: School attendance lines may be redrawn; schools may be paired; larger physical facilities may be built to serve larger, more diverse enrollments; magnet schools or educational parks may be used. Transportation of students is another tool to accomplish desegregation. It must continue to be available according to Supreme Court decisions to eliminate legally imposed segregation and improve the quality of education for all children.

Agriculture. We will resist a price ceiling on agriculture products until farm prices reach 110 percent of parity, based on the 1910-14 ratios, and we will conduct a relationship between the prices of raw commodities and retail prices;

We will end farm program benefits to farm units larger than family-size. . . .

Presidential Elections. We favor a Constitutional change to abolish the Electoral College and to give every voter a direct and equal voice in Presidential elections. The amendment should provide for a runoff election, if no candidate received more than 40 percent of the popular vote.

Republicans

Six weeks after the Democratic convention, the Republicans gathered in the same Miami Beach convention hall. The Aug. 21-23 convention, precisely programmed to make the most of free prime time, was a gigantic television spectacular from start to finish. The main business of the convention, the nomination of President Richard Nixon and Vice President Spiro T. Agnew to a second term, was a carefully planned ritual.

The selection of Miami Beach as the convention city provided as much drama as the convention itself. Initially the Republicans had chosen San Diego, Calif., as the host city, but the reluctance of that city to provide necessary facilities on schedule, coupled with the revelation that the International Telephone and Telegraph Corp. had pledged as much as $400,000 in local contributions, led the Republican National Committee to move the convention to Miami Beach.

Despite the preliminary organizational problems, the atmosphere of the convention itself was almost euphoric, and the sessions proceeded with dispatch. The five sessions lasted only 16 hours and 59 minutes, compared with the 32 hours and 18 minutes of the Democratic convention.

The one debate, which lasted only an hour, occurred over the adoption of new procedures for selecting national convention delegates. The Republican National Committee's preconvention rules committee approved a 1976 delegate-allocation plan initiated by Sen. John G. Tower of Texas and Rep. Jack F. Kemp of New York. The plan emphasized a state's Republican presidential vote in awarding bonus delegates. It was viewed as especially beneficial to small Southern and Western states. The convention rules committee amended the Tower-Kemp plan to make it more palatable to larger states by adding some bonus delegates for states electing Republican governors and members of Congress.

However, Rep. William A. Steiger of Wisconsin introduced a different plan, weighted more toward states electing Republican governors and members of Congress — a plan that would work to the advantage of the larger states. The debate on the contrasting plans focused on the question of whether states should be rewarded chiefly for delivering their electoral votes to a Republican presidential candidate or whether the bonus should be based to some extent on gubernatorial and congressional contests.

The dispute was in part a battle between liberals and conservatives. Final victory for the conservatives was achieved on a 910-to-434 roll-call vote that defeated the Steiger amendment. The reallocation formula adopted by the delegates would expand the 1976 convention to more than 2,000 delegates, compared with the 1,348 who went to Miami Beach in 1972.

The struggle over the delegate-allocation formula was the only sign of party division at the convention. Nixon was renominated on the third night of the convention, receiving 1,347 of the 1,348 votes. The only opposing vote was cast reluctantly by a delegate from New Mexico for Rep. Paul N. McCloskey Jr. of California, whose anti-war challenge of the president had fizzled after the year's first primary in New Hampshire. *(Chart, p. 245)*

One measure of the unity that surrounded the festive proceedings was the appearance of Gov. Nelson A. Rockefeller of New York to deliver Nixon's nominating speech. Rockefeller had become a loyal supporter of the president after having been his chief rival for the Republican nomination in 1960 and 1968.

Agnew was nominated the next night with 1,345 votes. There were two abstentions and one waggish vote for newscaster David Brinkley.

In his acceptance speech, Nixon combined a review of his first four years with promises for the next four and indirect but highly partisan attacks on his Democratic opponent, George McGovern. Nixon stressed that the choice in the upcoming election was "not between radical change and no change, the choice . . . is between change that works and change that won't work."

The Republican platform provoked little discussion on the convention floor and was approved by a voice vote. Two amendments were offered. The first, which would have pledged a prohibition on deficit federal spending, was defeated by voice vote. The second, advocating self-determination for American Indians, was approved by voice vote with the consent of the platform committee chairman, Rep. John J. Rhodes of Arizona.

The document, approximately 20,000 words long, was generally moderate in its proposals and conservative in language, in contrast to the Democrats' liberal platform.

The actual drafting of the Republican platform was heavily influenced by the White House, and platform committee sessions were held behind closed doors. In contrast, the Democrats held 10 regional hearings around the country, drafted their platform in public and were required by party rules to produce a final version at least 10 days before the convention opened.

The Republican platform was sharply critical not only of McGovern's new leadership of the Democratic Party but also of the Kennedy and Johnson administrations of the "nightmarish" 1960s.

The contrast with the Democratic platform on domestic affairs was stark. The Democrats advocated income redistribution through tax reform and a guaranteed annual income. The Republicans mentioned tax reform but did not include specifics. They rejected the guaranteed income plan.

Both parties called for a reduction in property taxes, although the Republicans made no mention of the value-added tax, a revenue measure the Nixon administration was said to be considering.

The Democrats advocated an immediate end to economic controls; the Republicans proposed to remove the controls "once the economic distortions spawned in the late 1960s are repaired."

The Democrats supported a federally financed and administered national health insurance system, while the Republicans supported a national health insurance plan financed by employers and employees as well as the federal government.

The Republicans opposed busing children to achieve racial balance in schools. The Democrats, however, viewed busing as "another tool" to bring about desegregation. The Republicans supported voluntary school prayer, an issue the Democrats did not mention.

The Republicans opposed legislation on gun control, while the Democrats endorsed a ban on the sale of handguns. The Republicans opposed the legalization of marijuana; the Democrats did not mention the subject in their platform.

Both parties took similar positions on several controversial social issues. The Republicans and Democrats both supported the Equal Rights Amendment to the Constitution, but neither platform specifically mentioned abortion or the rights of homosexuals.

Major differences between the parties were evident in national defense and foreign affairs. The Republicans chided the Democrats for proposing "meat-ax slashes" in the defense budget and charged that their proposals were "worse than misguided; they are dangerous." The Republicans rejected what they described as "a whimpering 'come back America' retreat to isolationism."

The continuing Vietnam War highlighted the foreign policy section. The Republican platform took a swipe at the Democrats by promising that the Nixon administration would not abandon the South Vietnamese or "go begging to Hanoi." If negotiations with North Vietnam failed, the platform promised continuation of the administration's Vietnamization program, gradually phasing out American involvement in the war. But before the remaining United States troops would be withdrawn, the Republicans declared, there must be a return of prisoners of war and an accounting of those missing in action. The Republicans opposed any form of amnesty.

The Republicans pledged to maintain an adequate nuclear deterrent, to help other nations develop the capability to defend themselves, to honor treaty commitments and to defend American interests but limit involvement when American interests were not at stake.

The Democrats had taken a stronger stand than in previous platforms against what they considered misguided American support for repressive regimes throughout the world. In addition, the Democrats argued for re-examination of the hostile United States policy toward Cuba.

Following are excerpts from the Republican platform of 1972:

Foreign Policy. Historians may well regard these years as a golden age of American diplomacy. Never before

121

has our country negotiated with so many nations on so wide a range of subjects — and never with greater success.

Vietnam. We will continue to seek a settlement of the Vietnam War which will permit the people of Southeast Asia to live in peace under political arrangements of their own choosing. We take specific note of the remaining major obstacle to settlement — Hanoi's demand that the United States overthrow the Saigon government and impose a Communist-dominated government on the South Vietnamese. We stand unequivocally at the side of the President in his effort to negotiate honorable terms, and in his refusal to accept terms which would dishonor this country.

Military Spending. To the alarm of free nations everywhere, the New Democratic Left now would undercut our defenses and have America retreat into virtual isolation, leaving us weak in a world still not free of aggression and threats of aggression. We categorically reject this slash-now, beg-later approach to defense policy....

We draw a sharp distinction between prudent reductions in defense spending and the meat-ax slashes with which some Americans are not beguiled by the political opposition.

Vietnam Amnesty. We are proud of the men and women who wear our country's uniform, especially of those who have borne the burden of fighting a difficult and unpopular war. Here and now we reject all proposals to grant amnesty to those who have broken the law by evading military service. We reject the claim that those who fled are more deserving, or obeyed a higher morality, than those next in line who served in their places.

Economy. We have already removed some temporary controls on wages and prices and will remove them all once the economic distortions spawned in the late 1960s are repaired. We are determined to return to an unfettered economy at the earliest possible moment.

We affirm our support for the basic principles of capitalism which underline the private enterprise system of the United States. At a time when a small but dominant faction of the opposition Party is pressing for radical economic schemes which so often have failed around the world, we hold that nothing has done more to help the American people achieve their unmatched standard of living than the free enterprise system.

Tax Reform. We reject the deceitful tax "reform" cynically represented as one that would soak the rich, but in fact one that would sharply raise the taxes of millions of families in middle-income brackets as well. We reject as well the lavish spending promised by the opposition Party which would more than double the present budget of the United States Government. This, too, would cause runaway inflation or force heavy increases in personal taxes.

Gun Control. [We pledge to] safeguard the right of responsible citizens to collect, own and use firearms for legitimate purposes, including hunting, target shooting and self-defense. We will strongly support efforts of all law enforcement agencies to apprehend and prosecute to the limit of the law all those who use firearms in the commission of crimes.

Women's Rights. Continued ... support of the Equal Rights Amendment to the Constitution, our Party being the first national party to back this Amendment.

School Busing. We are irrevocably opposed to busing for racial balance. Such busing fails its stated objective — improved learning opportunities — while it achieves results no one wants — division within communities and hostility between classes and races. We regard it as unnecessary, counter-productive and wrong.

School Prayer. We reaffirm our view that voluntary prayer should be freely permitted in public places — particularly, by school children while attending public schools — provided that such prayers are not prepared or prescribed by the state or any of its political subdivisions and that no person's participation is coerced, thus preserving the traditional separation of church and state.

Education. Our efforts to remedy ancient neglect of disadvantaged groups will continue in universities as well as in society at large, but we distinguish between such efforts and quotas. We believe the imposition of arbitrary quotas in the hiring of faculties or the enrollment of students has no place in our universities; we believe quotas strike at the essence of the university.

Health. To assure access to basic medical care for all our people, we support a program financed by employers, employees and the Federal Government to provide comprehensive health insurance coverage, including insurance against the cost of long-term and catastrophic illnesses and accidents and renal failure which necessitates dialysis, at a cost which all Americans can afford....

We oppose nationalized compulsory health insurance. This approach would at least triple in taxes the amount the average citizen now pays for health and would deny families the right to choose the kind of care they prefer. Ultimately it would lower the overall quality of health care for all Americans.

Welfare. Perhaps nowhere else is there a greater contrast in policy and philosophy than between the Administration's remedy for the welfare ills and the financial orgy proposed by our political opposition....

We flatly oppose programs or policies which embrace the principle of a government-guaranteed income. We reject as unconscionable the idea that all citizens have the right to be supported by the government, regardless of their ability or desire to support themselves and their families.

1976 Conventions

Presidential Candidates

Jimmy Carter
Democrat

Gerald R. Ford
Republican

Democrats

Jimmy Carter, whose presidential primary campaign flouted Democratic Party regulars, brought the party's diverse elements together July 12-15 in a show of unaccustomed unity.

The four-day 1976 convention in New York City was the party's most harmonious in 12 years and a stark contrast to the bitter and divisive conventions of 1968 and 1972.

The spirit of harmony was evident in the committee reports. No credentials challenges were carried to the convention floor and just one minority plank to the platform was offered. Only the rules committee report sparked much debate, and it was muted compared with the emotional struggles in the previous two conventions.

The lack of a spirited competition for the presidential nomination was an important factor in the absence of credentials challenges. However, the groundwork for the harmonious atmosphere had been established months earlier, when the Democratic National Committee adopted new delegate-selection and convention rules.

The delegate selection rules abolished the implicit quota system that had been the basis of most challenges in 1972. The only basis for a challenge in 1976 was the violation of a state's delegate selection or affirmative action plan to ensure the fair representation of minorities. Since all states had their plans approved by the national committee's Compliance Review Commission, the Credentials Committee was not weighing the fairness of the plan, but merely whether the state party had implemented it. In reverse of the 1972 system, the burden of proof was on the challenging individual or group, not on the state parties.

The task of challengers was further impeded by the action of the national committee in October 1975, raising the petition requirement for convention minority reports from 10 percent to 25 percent of Credentials Committee members.

The stringent new rules had an effect on the demographic composition of the convention. A post-convention survey by the national committee indicated that 36 percent of the delegates in 1976 were women, compared with 38

percent in 1972; 7 percent were black compared with 15 percent four years earlier and 14 percent were youths, compared with 21 percent in 1972.

The first roll call of the convention came on a Rules Committee minority report that would have permitted extended debate on the platform. The measure was promoted by party liberals, who complained that the restrictive convention rules cut off their chance for full debate. They urged platform debate on a maximum of three issues for a total of one hour, if at least 300 delegates from 10 states signed a petition for such issues. The proposal called for debate only; no votes would have been taken.

Carter delegates, though, were nearly unanimous in their opposition, fearing that adoption of the minority report would unduly lengthen the proceedings. The convention rejected the minority report by a vote of 735 to 1,957-1/2.

Liberals had better luck when the rules relating to future conventions were considered. By voice votes, they won approval of majority reports to establish the party's new Judicial Council as an arbiter of party rules and to eliminate the controversial loophole primary.

A loophole primary permitted election of delegates on a winner-take-all basis at the congressional district level. Carter and Democratic National Chairman Robert S. Strauss both favored the minority report, which called simply for review of the loophole primary by the newly established Commission on the Role and Future of Presidential Primaries, headed by Michigan state chairman Morley Winograd.

Liberals argued that this was not enough. They claimed that the loophole primary violated the party charter, which required proportional representation. Their position prevailed in the rules committee by a razor-thin margin of 58-1/2 to 58-1/4.

Although Carter managers were unhappy with the majority report, they did not press for a roll call and it was approved by voice vote.

But the convention rejected on roll-call votes liberal amendments to mandate the size and agenda of the party's

1978 mid-term conference and to lower the minority report requirement at future conventions.

The minority report on the 1978 conference would have required a prescribed agenda that included the discussion of policy matters. It also would have mandated a conference of at least 2,000 delegates, two-thirds of them elected at the congressional district level. On the roll call the proposal ran ahead 1,240 to 1,128, but it failed because of convention rules requiring a constitutional majority of 1,505 votes.

Another roll call came on the unsuccessful attempt by liberal delegates to have the minority report requirement at future conventions lowered from 25 percent to 15 percent of convention committee members. It was rejected, 1,249 to 1,354-1/2.

Potentially the most explosive of the rules issues, regarding a "female quota" at future conventions, was settled in behind-the-scenes meetings between Carter and representatives of the women's caucus.

At a Rules Committee meeting in Washington, D.C., in late June, the women's caucus had demanded equal representation with men in state delegations at future conventions. The Carter forces balked at this. Carter's views prevailed in the rules committee, which urged each state to promote equal division between the sexes but left the implementation of the rule to each state party. The women's caucus filed a minority report.

Both sides expressed a willingness to compromise, and in New York City July 11 and 12 Carter met with representatives of the women's caucus. They reached a compromise that encouraged — but did not require — equal representation for women at the party's mid-term conference and at future conventions. Language was inserted calling for the national committee to "encourage and assist" state parties in achieving equal division.

The compromise also included agreements between Carter and the women on other questions. Carter promised to establish an independent women's division in the party outside the realm of the chairman and pledged full party representation for women. The candidate promised to work for the ratification of the Equal Rights Amendment and pledged high government positions for women.

With acceptance of this compromise by the women's caucus, the minority report was withdrawn and the compromise language on equal division was worked into the majority report.

Balloting for president came on July 14, the third day of the convention, but it was merely a formality. Carter had locked up the nomination over a month earlier when he won the June 8 Ohio primary, a victory that prompted a cascade of endorsements and stymied his remaining opposition. Besides Carter, three other names were placed in nomination: Rep. Morris K. Udall of Arizona, Carter's most persistent primary challenger; Gov. Edmund G. Brown Jr. of California; and anti-abortion crusader Ellen McCormack. The proceedings, though, turned into a love-feast as Udall before the balloting and Brown afterwards appeared at the convention to declare their support for Carter.

On the presidential roll call, Carter received 2,238-1/2 of the convention's 3,008 votes, topping the needed majority little more than halfway through the balloting with the vote from Ohio. Udall finished second with 329-1/2 votes, followed by Brown with 300-1/2, Gov. George C. Wallace of Alabama with 57 and McCormack with 22. The rest of the vote was scattered. After completion of the roll call — and vote switches in California, Rhode Island and Louisiana —

a motion to make the nomination unanimous was approved by voice vote. *(Chart, p. 248)*

The following morning Carter announced that his choice for vice president was Sen. Walter F. Mondale of Minnesota. Carter noted that it was a difficult decision, admitting that he had changed his mind three times in the previous 30 days.

In explaining his choice, Carter cited Mondale's experience and political philosophy, his concept of the presidency and the preparation Mondale had made for his interview with Carter. Most of all, Carter emphasized compatibility, saying, "It's a very sure feeling that I have."

Mondale was one of seven prospective running mates Carter had personally interviewed. At his home in Plains, Ga., Carter had interviewed, besides Mondale, Sens. Edmund S. Muskie (Maine) and John Glenn (Ohio). At the New York convention he interviewed Sens. Henry M. Jackson (Wash.), Frank Church (Idaho) and Adlai E. Stevenson III (Ill.) and Rep. Peter W. Rodino Jr. (N.J.). Rodino withdrew his name from consideration shortly after his interview.

Like the presidential roll call the previous night, the balloting for vice president on July 15 was a formality. Mondale had only one declared opponent, Gary Benoit, a Massachusetts college student and a Wallace delegate. Two others were nominated but withdrew — Rep. Ronald V. Dellums of California and Vietnam War resister Fritz Efaw of Oklahoma.

Dellums, a black legislator from Oakland, appeared personally to withdraw his name and used the opportunity to plead with Carter to pay attention to the needs of minorities at home and to Third World aspirations abroad.

On the roll call, Mondale swamped his rivals, receiving 2,817 votes, more than 90 percent of the convention total. Retiring House Speaker Carl Albert (Okla.) finished a distant second with 36 votes, all cast as a complimentary gesture by his home state delegation. Rep. Barbara C. Jordan (Texas), the black congresswoman from Houston, followed with 28 votes, an apparent tribute to her dramatic keynote address.

Following the balloting, Mondale delivered his acceptance speech and succeeded in arousing the delegates with a partisan oratorical style reminiscent of his Minnesota mentor, Sen. Hubert H. Humphrey.

"We have just lived through the worst scandal in American history," Mondale declared, "and are now led by a president who pardoned the person who did it." His reference to the Watergate affair and to the Nixon pardon brought the delegates to their feet.

Carter's acceptance speech, unlike Mondale's, was not a rousing one in the traditional sense. But Carter was able to begin his address before 11 p.m., in the prime television slot that Strauss had promised as a contrast to George McGovern's nearly unheard 3 a.m. acceptance speech in 1972.

Like less-heralded Carter addresses earlier in the campaign, the acceptance speech ranged across a variety of issues and featured at least a few lines for those at different ends of the political spectrum. For the right, there were criticisms of wasteful federal bureaucracy, a call for a balanced budget and praise for business competition with "minimal intrusion of government in our free economic system."

For the left, there were endorsements of national health insurance, reform of the tax structure and further efforts to end discrimination by race and sex.

There was populism, with partisan overtones: "I see no reason why big-shot crooks should go free and the poor ones go to jail."

There were appeals to humanism: "We should make major investments in people, not in buildings and weapons. The poor, the aged, the weak and the afflicted must be treated with respect and with compassion and with love."

Throughout the acceptance speech was Carter's familiar emphasis on competence — a competent American people, a need for competence in the federal bureaucracy and derision for an incompetent Republican administration. "We can have an American government," Carter said, "that has turned away from scandal and corruption and official cynicism and is once again as decent and competent as our people."

"Love must be translated into simple justice," Carter said at one point, dropping his voice almost to a velvety whisper and holding the attention of the audience. A few moments later, he called for "full involvement by those who know what it is to suffer from discrimination," raising his voice almost to a shout and drawing loud applause. Then he added quietly, "and they'll be in the government if I'm elected."

The 1976 platform had been carefully constructed by the Carter forces at platform committee meetings in Washington, D.C., in June. The 90-page document was something of a throwback to earlier years — a broad statement of party goals rather than a list of legislative programs and controversial stands on issues.

The platform and the care with which it was written reflected the Democrats' determination to avoid the platform fights and issues that proved costly to the party in the previous two elections. The 1968 Vietnam plank approved on the convention floor had split the party so badly that many antiwar Democrats refused to support nominee Hubert H. Humphrey. The 1972 platform, probably the longest (about 25,000 words) and most liberal ever offered by a major party, covered too many issues in elaborate detail. It provided Republicans with free ammunition, such as the damaging charge that Democrats in 1972 favored "amnesty, acid and abortion."

Unlike 1972, when there was sharp, divisive debate on 20 minority planks, only one minority plank — on revising the 1939 Hatch Act to allow federal employees to run for political office and participate in partisan campaigns — was presented to the delegates in Madison Square Garden. It was approved by the Carter forces and was adopted by a voice vote after minimal debate.

Major goals outlined in the rest of the platform included the following:

- A target of 3 percent unemployment within four years.
- A phased-in national health insurance system to be supported through payroll deductions and other federal tax revenues.
- Gradual replacement of federal-state welfare systems with a federal system of income maintenance for recipients who accepted jobs or job training.
- "Full and complete pardon" for Vietnam War resisters, and case-by-case judgment for military deserters.
- Prohibitions against control of multiple energy resources by major oil companies.
- Strategic arms limitation agreements with the Soviet Union "emphasizing mutual reductions."

Following are excerpts from the Democratic platform of 1976:

Economy. To meet our goals we must set annual targets for employment, production and price stability; the Federal Reserve must be made a full partner in national economic decisions and become responsive to the economic goals of Congress and the President; credit must be generally available at reasonable interest rates; tax spending and credit policies must be carefully coordinated with our economic goals, and coordinated within the framework of national economic planning.

Full Employment. We have met the goals of full employment with stable prices in the past and can do it again. The Democratic Party is committed to the right of all adult Americans willing, able and seeking work to have opportunities for useful jobs at living wages. To make that commitment meaningful, we pledge ourselves to the support of legislation that will make every responsible effort to reduce adult unemployment to 3 percent within 4 years.

Consistent and coherent economic policy required federal anti-recession grant programs to state and local government, accompanied by public employment, public works projects and direct stimulus to the private sector. In each case, the programs should be phased in automatically when unemployment rises and phased out as it declines.

Inflation. At times, direct government involvement in wage and price decisions may be required to ensure price stability. But we do not believe that such involvement requires a comprehensive system of mandatory controls at this time.

Tax Reform. We pledge the Democratic Party to a complete overhaul of the present tax system, which will review all special tax provisions to ensure that they are justified and distributed equitably among our citizens. A responsible Democratic tax reform program could save over $5 billion in the first year with larger savings in the future.

We will strengthen the internal revenue tax code so that high income citizens pay a reasonable tax on all economic income.

We will reduce the use of unjustified tax shelters in such areas as oil and gas, tax-loss farming, real estate and movies.

We will seek and eliminate provisions that encourage uneconomic corporate mergers and acquisitions.

Government Reform. The Democratic Party is committed to the adoption of reforms such as zero-based budgeting, mandatory reorganization timetables, and sunset laws which do not jeopardize the implementation of basic human and political rights.

An Office of Citizen Advocacy should be established as part of the executive branch, independent of any agency, with full access to agency records and with both the power and the responsibility to investigate complaints.

We support the revision of the Hatch Act so as to extend to federal workers the same political rights enjoyed by other Americans as a birthright, while still protecting the Civil Service from political abuse.

We call for legislative action to provide for partial public financing on a matching basis of the congressional elections, and the exploration of further reforms to insure the integrity of the electoral process.

Health. We need a comprehensive national health insurance system with universal and mandatory coverage. Such a national health insurance system should be financed by a combination of employer-employee shared payroll taxes and general tax revenues. Consideration should be given to developing a means of support for national health insurance that taxes all forms of economic income.

Welfare Reform. We should move toward replacement of our existing inadequate and wasteful system with a simplified system of income maintenance, substantially financed by the federal government, which includes a requirement that those able to work be provided with appropriate available jobs or job training opportunities. Those persons who are physically able to work (other than mothers with dependent children) should be required to accept appropriate available jobs or job training.

As an interim step, and as a means of providing immediate federal fiscal relief to state and local governments, local governments should no longer be required to bear the burden of welfare costs. Further, there should be a phased reduction in the states' share of welfare costs.

Civil Rights and Liberties. ... [W]e pledge vigorous federal programs and policies of compensatory opportunity to remedy for many Americans the generations of injustice and deprivation; and full funding of programs to secure the implementation and enforcement of civil rights.

We seek ratification of the Equal Rights Amendment, to insure that sex discrimination in all its forms will be ended, implementation of Title IX, and elimination of discrimination against women in all federal programs.

We pledge effective and vigorous action to protect citizens' privacy from bureaucratic and technological intrusions, such as wiretapping and bugging without judicial scrutiny and supervision; and a full and complete pardon for those who are in legal or financial jeopardy because of their peaceful opposition to the Vietnam War, with deserters to be considered on a case-by-case basis.

We fully recognize the religious and ethical nature of the concerns which many Americans have on the subject of abortion. We feel, however, that it is undesirable to attempt to amend the U.S. Constitution to overturn the Supreme Court decision in this area.

Education. Mandatory transportation of students beyond their neighborhoods for the purpose of desegregation remains a judicial tool of last resort for the purpose of achieving school desegregation. The Democratic Party will be an active ally of those communities which seek to enhance the quality as well as the integration of educational opportunities. We encourage a variety of other measures, including the redrawing of attendance lines, pairing of schools, use of the "magnet school" concept, strong fair housing enforcement, and other techniques for the achievement of racial and economic integration.

The Party reaffirms its support of public school education. The Party also renews its commitment to the support of a constitutionally acceptable method of providing tax aid for the education of all pupils in non-segregated schools in order to insure parental freedom in choosing the best education for their children.

Housing. We support direct federal subsidies and low interest loans to encourage the construction of low and moderate income housing.

Cities. Federal policies and programs have inadvertently exacerbated the urban crisis. Within the framework of a new partnership of federal, state and local governments, and the private sector, the Democratic Party is pledged to the development of America's first national urban policy.

The Democratic Party recognizes that a number of major, older cities — including the nation's largest city — have been forced to undertake even greater social responsibilities, which have resulted in unprecedented fiscal crises. There is a national interest in helping such cities in their present travail, and a new Democratic President and the Congress shall undertake a massive effort to do so.

Criminal Justice. [W]e support a major reform of the criminal justice system, but we oppose any legislative effort to introduce repressive and anti-civil libertarian measures in the guise of reform of the criminal code.

Gun Control. Handguns simplify and intensify violent crime. Ways must be found to curtail the availability of these weapons. The Democratic Party must provide the

leadership for a coordinated federal and state effort to strengthen the presently inadequate controls over the manufacture, assembly, distribution and possession of handguns and to ban Saturday night specials.

Furthermore, since people and not guns commit crimes, we support mandatory sentencing for individuals convicted of committing a felony with a gun.

The Democratic Party, however, affirms the right of sportsmen to possess guns for purely hunting and target-shooting purposes.

Transportation. ... [W]e will work to expand substantially the discretion available to states and cities in the use of federal transportation money, for either operating expenses or capital programs on the modes of transportation which they choose. A greater share of Highway Trust Fund money should also be available on a flexible basis.

Energy. The Democratic energy platform begins with a recognition that the federal government has an important role to play in insuring the nation's energy future, and that it must be given the tools it needs to protect the economy and the nation's consumers from arbitrary and excessive energy price increases and help the nation embark on a massive domestic energy program focusing on conservation, coal conversion, exploration and development of new technologies to insure an adequate short-term and long-term supply of energy for the nation's needs.

The pricing of new natural gas is in need of reform. We should narrow the gap between oil and natural gas prices with new natural gas ceiling prices that maximize production and investment while protecting the economy and the consumer.

Strip mining legislation designed to protect and restore the environment, while ending the uncertainty over the rules governing future coal mining, must be enacted.

The huge reserves of oil, gas and coal on federal territory, including the outer continental shelf, belong to all the people. The Republicans have pursued leasing policies which give the public treasury the least benefit and the energy industry the most benefit from these public resources. Consistent with environmentally sound practices, new leasing procedures must be adopted to correct these policies, as well as insure the timely development of existing leases.

U.S. dependence on nuclear power should be kept to the minimum necessary to meet our needs. We should apply stronger safety standards as we regulate its use. And we must be honest with our people concerning its problems and dangers as well as its benefits.

When competition inadequate to insure free markets and maximum benefit to American consumers exists, we support effective restrictions on the right of major companies to own all phases of the oil industry.

We also support the legal prohibition against corporate ownership of competing types of energy, such as oil and coal. We believe such "horizontal" concentration of economic power to be dangerous both to the national interest and to the functioning of the competitive system.

Establishment of a more orderly system for setting energy goals and developing programs for reaching those goals should be undertaken. The current proliferation of energy jurisdictions among many executive agencies underscores the need for a more coordinated system. Such a system should be undertaken, and provide for centralization of overall energy planning in a specific executive agency and an assessment of the capital needs for all priority programs to increase production and conservation of energy.

Environment. The Democratic Party's strong commitment to environmental quality is based on its conviction that environmental protection is not simply an aesthetic goal, but is necessary to achieve a more just society. Cleaning up air and water supplies and controlling the proliferation of dangerous chemicals is a necessary part of a successful national health program. Protecting the worker from workplace hazards is a key element of our full employment program.

Federal environmental anti-pollution requirement programs should be as uniform as possible to eliminate economic discrimination. A vigorous program with national minimum environmental standards fully implemented, recognizing basic regional differences, will ensure that states and workers are not penalized by pursuing environmental programs.

Foreign Policy. Eight years of Nixon-Ford diplomacy have left our nation isolated abroad and divided at home. Policies have been developed and applied secretly and arbitrarily by the executive department from the time of secret bombing in Cambodia to recent covert assistance in Angola. They have been policies that relied on ad hoc, unilateral maneuvering, and a balance-of-power diplomacy suited better to the last century than to this one. They have disdained traditional American principles which once earned the respect of other peoples while inspiring our own. Instead of efforts to foster freedom and justice in the world, the Republican administration has built a sorry record of disregard for human rights, manipulative interference in the internal affairs of other nations, and, frequently, a greater concern for our relations with totalitarian adversaries than with our democratic allies. . .

We will. . .actively seek to limit the dangers inherent in the international development of atomic energy and in the proliferation of nuclear weapons.

The United States should not provide aid to any government — anywhere in the world — which uses secret police, detention without charges, and torture to enforce its powers. Exceptions to this policy should be rare, and the aid provided should be limited to that which is absolutely necessary. The United States should be open and unashamed in its exercise of diplomatic efforts to encourage the observance of human rights in countries which receive American aid.

National Defense. To this end, our strategic nuclear forces must provide a strong and credible deterrent to nuclear attack and nuclear blackmail. Our conventional forces must be strong enough to deter aggression in areas whose security is vital to our own. In a manner consistent with these objectives, we should seek those disarmament and arms control agreements which will contribute to mutual reductions in both nuclear and conventional arms.

. . . [W]ith the proper management, with the proper kind of investment of defense dollars, and with the proper choice of military programs, we believe we can reduce present defense spending by about $5-billion to $7-billion.

In order to provide for a comprehensive review of the B1 test and evaluation program, no decision regarding B-1 production should be made prior to February 1977.

Détente. Our task is to establish U.S.-U.S.S.R. relations on a stable basis, avoiding excesses of both hope and fear. Patience, a clear sense of our own priorities, and a willingness to negotiate specific firm agreements in areas of mutual interest can return balance to relations between the United States and the Soviet Union.

However, in the area of strategic arms limitation, the U.S. should accept only such agreements that would not over-all limit the U.S. to levels of intercontinental strategic forces inferior to the limits provided for the Soviet Union.

United Nations. The heat of debate at the General Assembly should not obscure the value of our supporting United Nations involvement in keeping the peace and in the increasingly complex technical and social problems — such as pollution, health, economic development and population growth — that challenge the world community.

Middle East. We shall continue to seek a just and lasting peace in the Middle East. The cornerstone of our policy is a firm commitment to the independence and security of the State of Israel.

We will continue our consistent support of Israel, including sufficient military and economic assistance to maintain Israel's deterrent strength in the region, and the maintenance of U.S. military forces in the Mediterranean adequate to deter military intervention by the Soviet Union.

We will avoid efforts to impose on the region an externally devised formula for settlement, and will provide support for initiatives toward settlement, based on direct face-to-face negotiation between the parties and normalization of relations and a full peace within secure and defensible boundaries.

Asia. We remain a Pacific power with important stakes and objectives in the region, but the Vietnam War has taught us the folly of becoming militarily involved where our vital interests were not at stake.

We reaffirm our commitment to the security of the Republic of Korea, both in itself and as a key to the security of Japan. However, on a prudent and carefully planned basis, we can redeploy, and gradually phase out, the U.S. ground forces, and can withdraw the nuclear weapons now stationed in Korea without endangering that support, as long as our tactical air and naval forces in the region remain strong.

Latin America. We must make clear our revulsion at the systematic violations of basic human rights that have occurred under some Latin American military regimes.

We pledge support for a new Panama Canal treaty, which insures the interests of the United States in that waterway, recognizes the principles already agreed upon, takes into account the interests of the Canal work force, and which will have wide hemispheric support.

Relations with Cuba can only be normalized if Cuba refrains from interference in the internal affairs of the United States, and releases all U.S. citizens currently detained in Cuban prisons and labor camps for political reasons. We can move towards such relations if Cuba abandons its provocative international actions and policies.

Republicans

After four boisterous, raucous and sometimes tearful days, Republicans ended their 1976 national convention on a positive note absent during most of a gathering characterized by strident attacks on the Democrats and the Congress they controlled.

The Republican delegates arrived in Kansas City for the Aug. 16-19 convention more evenly split than they had been since 1952, when Dwight D. Eisenhower edged Sen. Robert A. Taft of Ohio (1939-53) for the GOP nomination. Both President Gerald R. Ford, breaking with tradition, and former California governor Ronald Reagan arrived in town three days before the balloting to continue their pursuit of delegates.

Ford, relying heavily on the prestige of the presidency that sometimes had failed to produce results during the seven-month campaign, invited a number of wavering delegates to his hotel suite in the new Crown Center Hotel while Reagan also courted delegates personally.

Campaign strategists and conservative supporters pursued other maneuvers that either fizzled or could not break Ford's scanty but solid delegate margin. Early in the week, conservative House members tried unsuccessfully to convince New York's senator James L. Buckley, Cons-R, to seek the nomination in an effort to draw off enough votes to deny Ford a first-ballot victory.

By a margin of 111 votes on Aug. 17, the Reagan forces

lost the first and probably the most important roll call of the convention. The vote came on a Reagan-sponsored amendment to the rules committee report that would have required all presidential candidates to name their running mates before the presidential balloting the next night.

The idea of a test vote on the vice presidential question was sprung by Reagan's campaign manager, John Sears, barely a week before the convention, when on Aug. 9 he appeared before the rules committee and urged that the proposal be included as Section C of Rule 16. The amendment was clearly aimed at throwing Ford on the defensive, because Reagan had designated Sen. Richard S. Schweiker of Pennsylvania as his running mate on July 26. Under the proposal, failure of a candidate to comply would have freed all delegates from any commitments to vote for him.

The Reagan proposal was handily defeated in the preconvention rules committee, where Ford supporters predominated. But Sears was publicly confident that the Reagan forces could carry the issue on the convention floor. Victory on the rules question, he predicted, would be a steppingstone to Reagan's nomination.

The convention debate and vote on Rule 16C was the focal point of the Aug. 17 session and was treated as such by many in the gallery and on the floor, who interrupted the proceedings several times with loud chanting. Vociferous cheers and boos erupted from the Ford and Reagan sections of the hall as speeches were delivered for or against their positions.

Supporters of the proposals characterized it as a "right-to-know" amendment. "A presidential candidate must tell us who's on his team before we are expected to join him," argued former Missouri representative Thomas B. Curtis, the sponsor of the amendment. "The delegates have the right to be consulted for a day of decision that will have an impact for years to come."

Speakers against the amendment countered that it was solely a maneuver of the Reagan forces and that any vice presidential selection reform should be deliberately considered on its merits.

Reagan forces held the lead throughout the early going on the roll-call vote, but they lost the advantage about halfway through when New York voted against the amendment.

The deficit of the Reagan backers increased after Ohio went 7-90 against and Pennsylvania 14-89 against. The Pennsylvania result was a clear indication that state leaders in the Ford campaign remained in control of the delegation, despite Schweiker's effort to woo their support.

Reagan strength near the end of the roll call tightened the count, but Florida and Mississippi, which had passed when first called, cast heavy votes against the amendment. Florida's 28-38 vote against sealed the amendment's defeat. Mississippi, under the unit rule, cast its entire 30 votes against the Reagan proposal, padding the Ford margin.

The final court stood at 1,069 in favor of the amendment and 1,180 against, with 10 abstentions. The vote was the first tangible evidence of Ford strength at the convention and paved the way for his nomination. *(Chart, p. 249)*

None of the other parts of the rules committee report were debated, including the controversial "justice resolution" (Rule 18) that bound delegates elected in primary states according to state law. Fearing a defection of "closet" Reagan delegates in several primary-state delegations, Ford leaders had pushed for the amendment. In contrast to their attitude toward Rule 16C, the Reagan forces did not order a fight on the "justice resolution,"

although it was extensively debated in committee deliberations. After the roll-call vote on Rule 16C, the rules committee report was adopted by a voice vote.

Whatever enthusiasm the Reagan supporters had lost after their defeat on the vice presidential rule had returned by presidential nominating night, Aug. 18.

Two and one-half hours of the six-hour session were consumed in demonstrations. Reagan's supporters were by far the most boisterous. But it was the Californian's last hurrah.

On the presidential roll call, Reagan, bolstered by the votes in California and some Deep South states, took a healthy lead. But, as everyone expected, Ford's strength in the big Northeastern states — New York, New Jersey, Pennsylvania, Connecticut, Ohio — and others such as Minnesota and Illinois pushed Ford ahead.

There was a pause as the Virginia delegation was individually polled. Then West Virginia, voting 20 to 8 in favor of Ford, put the president over the top.

The final vote was 1,187 for Ford, 1,070 for Reagan, one vote from the New York delegation for Commerce Secretary Elliot L. Richardson and one abstention. *(Chart, p. 249)*

On a voice vote the convention made the nomination unanimous.

Ford added to the partisan style of the Republican ticket the next day by selecting Sen. Robert Dole of Kansas as his running mate after Reagan ruled out his acceptance of the second spot. While little mentioned during speculation about Ford's vice presidential choice, Dole, a former chairman of the Republican National Committee, was seen as an effective gut fighter who would allow Ford to keep his campaign style presidential in the battle against Carter.

Vice President Nelson A. Rockefeller nominated his own potential successor, telling the crowd that the Kansas senator not only could stand the heat of political battle, but also could "really dole it out." Rockefeller, unpopular with conservatives, had not sought to continue in the job he had gained through appointment in 1974.

On the vice presidential roll call, Dole received 1,921 of the convention's 2,259 votes. Sen. Jesse A. Helms of North Carolina, a hero of the conservatives, finished a distant second with 103 votes. The remaining votes were scattered among 29 other "candidates."

Ford's acceptance speech concentrated on his record since taking office in mid-1974. The president took credit for cutting inflation in half, increasing employment to a record level and bringing the country to peace.

He touched several times on the restoration of confidence in the White House and the return of personal integrity to the executive branch of government. His administration, Ford said, had been "open, candid and forthright" from the beginning.

Needling his Democratic challenger, Jimmy Carter, Ford asserted to applause: "My record is one of specifics, not smiles."

For the future, Ford promised continued economic recovery, less "impudence" from bureaucracy and a balanced federal budget by 1978. He listed a host of other proposals ranging from tax reform to a sane nuclear policy.

"We will build on performance, not promises; experiences, not expediency; real progress instead of mysterious plans to be revealed in some dim and distant future," Ford said in another reference to Carter.

While primarily positive in tone, Ford's speech did rebuke the Democratic Congress for its passage of bills he had vetoed and its obstruction of his proposals to revise tax rules, restrict busing and overhaul criminal laws.

"My friends, Washington is not the problem — their Congress is the problem," he argued.

Ford diverged from his prepared text to issue a direct challenge to Carter. "I'm ready, eager to go before the American people and debate the real issues face to face with Jimmy Carter," the president said. "The American people have the right to know first-hand exactly where both of us stand."

The 1976 Republican platform was a conservative document, combining restrained compliments toward the Ford administration with frequent and slashing attacks on the Democratic Congress.

Ford and Reagan both praised the platform. Although neither side was entirely happy with the final document, both were willing to compromise to avoid splitting the party.

By the time the convention got around to debating the platform the night of Aug. 17, an expected bitter struggle between Ford and Reagan forces had been deflated by the earlier vote on rules. The arena, which had been packed two hours earlier, held a somewhat smaller crowd after midnight. Many Ford delegates in particular, confident that they had won the main event, left while members of the platform committee presented the 65-page document.

Two minority planks were offered, in accordance with platform committee rules that required petitions signed by 25 percent of the members. The first, sponsored by Ann F. Peckham of Wisconsin, called for deleting all platform references to abortion. The committee-approved section supported a constitutional amendment "to restore protection of the right to life of unborn children."

The 12-minute debate on the abortion plank did not split along Ford-Reagan lines. Supporters of the minority report argued that abortion was not a suitable topic for a party document. Opponents insisted that the anti-abortion language should be retained. The minority report was defeated clearly by voice vote, and the language stayed in.

The second minority report, a six-paragraph addition to the foreign policy section, was sponsored by 34 Reagan supporters on the platform committee. Without mentioning names, it criticized President Ford and Secretary of State Henry A. Kissinger for losing public confidence, making secret international agreements and discouraging the hope of freedom for those who did not have it — presumably captive nations.

Many of Ford's supporters, including Rep. John B. Anderson of Illinois and Senate Minority Leader Hugh Scott of Pennsylvania, earlier had expressed strong opposition to the "morality in foreign policy" plank, as it came to be called. Ford's floor leader, Sen. Robert P. Griffin of Michigan, and Rep. David C. Treen of Louisiana sought compromise language in informal negotiations on the floor. But the Reagan forces, led by Sen. Helms, were adamant.

Not wishing to offend the Reagan contingent further, Ford's supporters decided not to fight. Sen. Roman L. Hruska of Nebraska, chairman of the foreign policy subcommittee, announced from the podium that there would be no organized opposition to the plank. It was passed by voice vote. The convention then approved the platform.

The document reflected the nearly equal influence of President Ford and Ronald Reagan at the convention. It was a traditional Republican blueprint for limited government — a clear contrast with the Democratic platform.

Ordinarily, the platform of the party holding the White House heaps praise on the incumbent president and boasts of the way he has led the nation. This Republican platform did not. With Ford embroiled in a contest for the nomination, the platform writers chose to mention him by name only a few times. Richard Nixon was never mentioned. There were only vague references to Watergate.

The platform's foreign policy planks, over which Ford and Reagan clashed most strongly, praised the record of "two Republican administrations." But they also repeated some of Reagan's campaign criticisms of current foreign policy. Kissinger, a favorite target of the party's conservative wing, was not mentioned.

The domestic planks boasted of reductions in inflation and steered clear of direct government initiatives to reduce unemployment. The president was commended for vetoing 40 bills that would have increased federal spending.

The platform concentrated most of its fire on Congress. The Republicans barely acknowledged their opponent for national leadership, Jimmy Carter. The platform mentioned Carter only once, on the first page.

Following are excerpts from the Republican Party platform of 1976:

Republican Philosophy. — As a general rule we believe that government action should be taken first by the government that resides as close to you as possible. Governments tend to become less responsive to your needs the farther away they are from you. Thus, we prefer local and state government to national government, and decentralized national government wherever possible. The Democrats' Platform repeats the same thing on every page: More government, more spending, more inflation. Compare. This Republican Platform says exactly the opposite — less government, less spending, less inflation. In other words, we want you to retain more of your own money; money that represents the worth of your labors, to use as you see fit for the necessities and conveniences of life.

Economy. We believe it is of paramount importance that the American people understand that the number one destroyer of jobs is inflation.

Republicans hope every American realizes that if we are to permanently eliminate high unemployment, it is essential to protect the integrity of our money. That means putting an end to deficit spending.

Wage and price controls are not the solution to inflation. They attempt to treat only the symptom — rising prices — not the cause. Historically, controls have always been a dismal failure, and in the end they create only shortages, black markets and higher prices. For these reasons the Republican Party strongly opposes any reimposition of such controls, on a standby basis or otherwise.

Sound job creation can only be accomplished in the private sector of the economy. Americans must not be fooled into accepting government as the employer of last resort.

No nation can spend its way into prosperity; a nation can only spend its way into bankruptcy.

Tax Reform. Simplification should be a major goal of tax reform.

When balanced by expenditure reductions, the personal exemption should be raised to $1,000.

Agriculture. We oppose government-controlled grain reserves, just as we oppose federal regulations that are unrealistic in farm practices, such as those imposed by the Occupational Safety and Health Administration (OSHA) and the Environmental Protection Agency (EPA).

We firmly believe that when the nation asks our farmers to go all out to produce as much as possible for world-wide markets, the government should guarantee them unfettered access to those markets. Our farmers should not be singled out by export controls.

Government Reform. There must be functional re-alignment of government, instead of the current arrangement by subject areas or constituencies.

Revenue Sharing is an effort to reverse the trend toward centralization. Revenue Sharing must continue without unwarranted federal strictures and regulations.

Block grant programs should be extended to replace many existing categorical health, education, child nutrition and social programs.

While we oppose a uniform national primary, we encourage the concept of regional presidential primaries, which would group those states which voluntarily agree to have presidential primaries in a geographical area on a common date.

... [W]e oppose "federal post card registration." The possibilities could not only cheapen our ballot, but in fact threaten the entire electoral process.

We offer these proposals of far-reaching reform:

Public accountability demands that [congressmen] publicly vote on increases on the expenses of their office.

—Elimination of proxy voting which allows Members [of Congress] to record votes in committee without being present for the actual deliberations or vote on a measure.

—Full public disclosure of financial interests by Members [of Congress] and divestiture of those interests which present conflicts of interest.

—Improved lobby disclosure legislation so that the people will know how much money is being spent to influence public officials.

Criminal Justice. Each state should have the power to decide whether it wishes to impose the death penalty for certain crimes. All localities are urged to tighten their bail practices and to review their sentencing and parole procedures.

Gun Control. We support the right of citizens to keep and bear arms. We oppose federal registration of firearms. Mandatory sentences for crimes committed with a lethal weapon are the only effective solution to this problem.

Education. We believe that segregated schools are morally wrong and unconstitutional. However, we oppose forced busing to achieve racial balances in our schools. We believe there are educational advantages for children in attending schools in their own neighborhoods and that the Democrat-controlled Congress has failed to enact legislation to protect this concept.

If Congress continues to fail to act, we would favor consideration of an amendment to the Constitution forbidding the assignment of children to schools on the basis of race.

Local communities wishing to conduct non-sectarian prayers in their public schools should be able to do so. We favor a constitutional amendment to achieve this end.

Health. We support extension of catastrophic illness protection to all who cannot obtain it. We should utilize our private health insurance system to assure adequate protection for those who do not have it. Such an approach will eliminate the red tape and high bureaucratic costs inevitable in a comprehensive national program.

The Republican Party opposes compulsory national health insurance.

Civil Rights and Liberties. The Republican Party reaffirms its support for ratification of the Equal Rights Amendment. Our Party was the first national party to endorse the E.R.A. in 1940. We continue to believe its ratification is essential to insure equal rights for all Americans.

The Republican Party favors a continuance of the public dialogue on abortion and supports the efforts of those who seek enactment of a constitutional amendment to restore protection of the right to life for unborn children.

Labor. Union membership as a condition of employment has been regulated by state law under Section 14(b) of the Taft-Hartley Act. This basic right should continue to be determined by the states. We oppose strikes by federal employees, the unionization of our military forces and the legalization of common-situs picketing.

Employees of the federal government should not engage in partisan politics. The Civil Service System must remain nonpartisan and nonpolitical. The Hatch Act now protects federal employees; we insist that it be uniformly administered.

Welfare Reform. We oppose federalizing the welfare system; local levels of government are most aware of the needs of their communities.

We also oppose the guaranteed annual income concept or any programs that reduce the incentive to work.

Those features of the present law, particularly the food stamp program, that draw into assistance programs people who are capable of paying for their own needs should be corrected. The humanitarian purpose of such programs must not be corrupted by eligibility loopholes.

Cities. The Republican programs of revenue sharing and block grants for community development and manpower have already immensely helped our cities and counties. We favor extension of revenue sharing and the orderly conversion of categorical grants into block grants.

Housing. To continue to encourage home ownership which now encompasses 64 per cent of our families, we support the deductibility of interest on home mortgages and property taxes.

Transportation. In keeping with the local goal setting in transportation, the Republican Party applauds the system under which state and local governments can divert funds from interstate highway mileage not essential to interstate commerce or national defense to other, more pressing community needs, such as urban mass transit.

Energy. One fact should now be clear: We must reduce sharply our dependence on other nations for energy and strive to achieve energy independence at the earliest possible date. We cannot allow the economic destiny and international policy of the United States to be dictated by the sovereign powers that control major portions of the world's petroleum supplies.

We must immediately eliminate price controls on oil and newly-discovered natural gas in order to increase supply, and to provide the capital that is needed to finance further exploration and development of domestic hydrocarbon reserves.

At this critical time, the Democrats have characteristically resorted to political demagoguery seeking short-term political gain at the expense of the long-term national interest. They object to the petroleum industry making any profit. The petroleum industry is an important segment of our economy and is entitled to reasonable profits to permit further exploration and development.

Now, the Democrats proposed to dismember the American oil industry. We vigorously oppose such divestiture of oil companies — a move which would surely result in higher energy costs, inefficiency and under-capitalization of the industry.

The uncertainties of governmental regulation regarding the mining, transportation and use of coal must be removed and a policy established which will assure that governmental restraints, other than proper environmental controls, do not prevent the use of coal. Mined lands must be returned to beneficial use.

Uranium offers the best intermediate solution to America's energy crisis. We support accelerated use of nuclear energy through processes that have been proven safe.

Environment. We are in complete accord with the recent Supreme Court decision on air pollution that allows the level of government closest to the problem and the solution to establish and apply appropriate air quality standards.

We are determined to preserve land use planning as a unique responsibility of state and local government.

Foreign Policy. We recognize and commend that great beacon of human courage and morality, Alexander Solzhenitsyn, for his compelling message that we must face the world with no illusions about the nature of tyranny. Ours will be a foreign policy that keeps this ever in mind.

Ours will be a foreign policy which recognizes that in international negotiations we must make no undue concessions; that in pursuing détente we must not grant unilateral favors with only the hope of getting future favors in return.

Agreements that are negotiated, such as the one signed in Helsinki, must not take from those who do not have freedom the hope of one day gaining it.

Finally, we are firmly committed to a foreign policy in which secret agreements, hidden from our people, will have no part.

National Defense. A superior national defense is the fundamental condition for a secure America and for peace and freedom for the world. Military strength is the path to peace. A sound foreign policy must be rooted in a superior defense capability, and both must be perceived as a deterrent to aggression and supportive of our national interests.

As a necessary component of our long-range strategy, we will produce and deploy the B-1 bomber in a timely manner, allowing us to retain air superiority.

Security assistance programs are important to our allies and we will continue to strengthen their efforts at self-defense.

Asia. The United States is indisputably a Pacific power. Japan will remain the main pillar of our Asian policy. United States troops will be maintained in Korea so long as there exists the possibility of renewed aggression from North Korea.

We recognize that there is a wide divergence of opinion concerning Vietnam, but we pledge that American troops will never again be committed for the purpose of our own defense, or the defense of those to whom we are committed by treaty or other solemn agreements, without the clear purpose of achieving our stated diplomatic and military objectives.

The United States will fulfill and keep its commitments, such as the mutual defense treaty with the Republic of China.

Latin America. By continuing its policies of exporting subversion and violence, Cuba remains outside the Inter-American family of nations. We condemn attempts by the Cuban dictatorship to intervene in the affairs of other nations; and, as long as such conduct continues, it shall remain ineligible for admission to the Organization of American States.

The United States intends that the Panama Canal be preserved as an international waterway for the ships of all nations. This secure access is enhanced by a relationship which commands the respect of Americans and Panamanians and benefits the people of both countries. In any talks with Panama, however, the United States negotiators should in no way cede, dilute, forfeit, negotiate or transfer any rights, power, authority, jurisdiction, territory or property that are necessary for the protection and security of the United States and the entire Western Hemisphere.

Middle East. Our policy must remain one of decisive support for the security and integrity of Israel.

At the same time, Republican Administrations have succeeded in reestablishing communication with the Arab countries, and have made extensive progress in our diplomatic and commercial relations with the more moderate Arab nations.

Because we have such fundamental interests in the Middle East, it will be our policy to continue our efforts to maintain the balance of power in the Mediterranean region.

Détente. American foreign policy must be based upon a realistic assessment of the Communist challenge in the world. It is clear that the perimeters of freedom continue to shrink throughout the world in the face of the Communist challenge.

Thus our relations with the Soviet Union will be guided by solid principles. We will maintain our strategic and conventional forces; we will oppose the deployment of Soviet power for unilateral advantages or political and territorial expansion; we will never tolerate a shift against us in the strategic balance; and we will remain firm in the face of pressure, while at the same time expressing our willingness to work on the basis of strict reciprocity toward new agreements which will help achieve peace and stability.

United Nations. The political character of the United Nations has become complex. With 144 sovereign members, the U.N. experiences problems associated with a large, sometimes cumbersome and diverse body.

The United States does not wish to dictate to the U.N., yet we do have every right to expect and insist that scrupulous care be given to the rights of all members. Steamroller techniques for advancing discriminatory actions will be opposed.

The United States will continue to be a firm supporter and defender of any nation subjected to such outrageous assaults. We will not accept ideological abuses in the United States.

1980 Conventions

Presidential Candidates

Jimmy Carter
Democrat

Ronald Reagan
Republican

John B. Anderson
Independent

Republicans

Ronald Reagan, the 69-year-old former California governor, was installed as the Republican presidential nominee at the party's national convention in Detroit, but his moment of glory nearly was overshadowed by an unusual flap over the number-two spot. The choosing of Reagan's running mate provided the only suspense at the GOP convention, held July 14-17, 1980, in Detroit's Joe Louis Arena.

Who would fill the number-one spot had been determined long before when Reagan won 28 out of the 34 Republican presidential primaries and eliminated all of his major rivals. The last to withdraw — George Bush — was tapped by Reagan July 16 as his ticket mate in a dramatic post-midnight appearance before the delegates.

For most of the evening of July 16, it looked as though Gerald R. Ford would occupy the second spot on the ticket, which would have made him the first former president to run for vice president. Private polls reportedly had shown that Ford was the only Republican who would enhance Reagan's chances in November. And a number of Republicans had described the combination as a "dream ticket." Groups described as "friends of Ronald Reagan" and "friends of Gerald Ford" had met four times to "discuss" the possibility of forging a Reagan-Ford ticket.

The Ford group consisted of former secretary of state Henry A. Kissinger, former chairman of the Council of Economic Advisers Alan Greenspan, and Ford aides Robert Barnett and John Marsh. The Reagan group was the nucleus of his primary campaign staff: Edwin Meese, campaign director, and Richard Wirthlin, Reagan's pollster. Reagan and Ford first discussed Ford's joining the ticket at a meeting July 15, although no formal offer was made, according to a source close to Reagan. " 'I want you to think this over and then we'll discuss it tomorrow,' " the source quoted Reagan as telling Ford.

The pair met again the following day to continue their discussions, but nothing was resolved. When the convention reconvened at 6:30 p.m., reports began swirling about the floor, many of them spawned by Ford himself, who in two televised interviews gave strong indications that he

would accept the second spot if certain conditions were met.

In an interview with Walter Cronkite of CBS about 7:30 p.m., Ford said, "I would not go to Washington and be a figurehead vice president. If I go to Washington I have to be there in the belief that I would play a meaningful role." Later, in an interview with Barbara Walters of ABC, Ford said he did not want the job unless his role would be "nonceremonial, constructive and responsive." Such an arrangement, he said, would require a "far different structure" from the duties performed by other vice presidents. Asked whether it would be difficult to be a vice president again after having had the top job, Ford said, "Not at all. I'd be more interested in substance than glamor."

Ford declined to spell out what his conditions for taking the job would be, but descriptions of his requirements would have made him in effect co-president with Reagan. The discussions reportedly centered around providing a role for Ford somewhat akin to the White House chief of staff's. In this kind of post he would have had responsibility for agencies such as the Office of Management and Budget, the National Security Council, the domestic policy staff and the Council of Economic Advisers.

Ford further fed the speculation, offering a simple solution to the temporary problem that would have been posed by the 12th Amendment to the Constitution. The amendment would have had the effect of prohibiting the members of the electoral college from California from voting for both Reagan and Ford because both were California residents. The amendment says that the electors from any state must vote for at least one person who is not from that state.

However, nothing in the Constitution would have excluded two residents of the same state from serving as president and vice president or prevented electors from states other than their home state from voting for those two individuals. Ford said Reagan's lawyers had researched the residency question and determined that legally there would be no problem if the former president changed his residence to Michigan, which he represented in the House for 25 years, or to Colorado, where he owned a home.

But Ford expressed reservations about how such a move might be interpreted. "I think it could create in the minds of the American people that we're trying to do something a little cute," he said. "Well, I've never done that in politics. I've got a good reputation and I'm worried about it.... I think it would be construed to be to some extent a gimmick."

As the evening of July 16 wore on, the speculation heightened. "The expectation, as it is presently being reported is it's going through," Gov. William G. Milliken of Michigan said of the Ford candidacy. "I have it on very reliable sources within the Ford camp that it is put together," said Gov. Pierre S. "Pete" du Pont of Delaware.

About 9:15 p.m. Reagan telephoned Ford to ask him to make up his mind whether he wanted the vice president's job. Meanwhile, convention officials proceeded to call the roll of the states. When Reagan received enough votes to become the official nominee, the arena erupted into a cheering, hornblowing, flag-waving, foot-stomping, band-playing demonstration. The noise abated a bit while the roll call was finished, but continued for more than an hour.

But at about 11:15 p.m. the Reagan-Ford arrangement fell apart. Ford went to Reagan's suite in the Detroit Plaza Hotel and the two men agreed that it would be better for Ford to campaign for the GOP ticket rather than be a member of it. "His [Ford's] instinct told him it was not the thing to do," Reagan said later.

When it became apparent that efforts to persuade Ford to join the ticket had failed, Reagan turned to Bush, a moderate with proven vote-getting ability. The Reagan camp refused to acknowledge that Bush was the second choice, even though it was widely perceived that way. "There was everybody else and then the Ford option," Edwin Meese, Reagan's chief of staff, said later.

Bush had been Reagan's most persistent competitor through the long primary season, but he won only six primaries — Michigan, Massachusetts, Connecticut, Pennsylvania, the District of Columbia and Puerto Rico. Bush was one of the vice presidential possibilities favored by those in the party who believed that Reagan had to reach outside the GOP's conservative wing if he were to have broad appeal in November.

Bush supporters said that his background would balance the ticket geographically and that his extensive government service would overcome criticism that Reagan did not have any Washington experience. Bush served from 1967 to 1971 in the U.S. House from Texas and had been ambassador to the United Nations, head of the U.S. liaison office in Peking and director of the Central Intelligence Agency.

Bush's first appearance at the convention earlier had produced a rousing demonstration from supporters throughout the hall, but his strongest support on the floor was in delegations from the Midwest and Northeast, such as New Jersey and the states where he won primary victories.

Reagan's choice of the moderate George Bush was viewed as his first major choice between political pragmatism and ideological purity. Throughout the primary season, Reagan had drawn a large measure of his support from the right wing of the Republican Party and had pledged himself to support conservative economic, social and defense policies. During the convention, Sen. Jesse Helms of North Carolina, the most vocal leader of the GOP's right wing, masterminded the rightward tilt of the party plat-form to reflect conservative viewpoints. Helms, concerned about the nomination of a moderate such as Bush, threatened to place his own name in nomination to put pressure on the GOP standard-bearers to abide by conservative and "moral" principles. In the end, Helms supported the Reagan-Bush ticket but warned that it had better support the party's conservative platform. Though Helms was not nominated for vice president, his supporters nonetheless gave him 54 votes. He finished second behind Bush, who got 1,832 votes.

The Republican Party's 1980 platform was more a blueprint for victory in November than a definitive statement of party views. Rather than slug it out over specifics, the party's moderate and conservative wings agreed to blur their differences to appear united, to broaden the party's appeal and to smooth Reagan's way to the White House.

Platform writers veered from traditional Republican positions on a few issues. On others they went out of their way to embrace policies that meshed with Reagan's views more than their own. For the most part, they managed to fashion a policy statement that pleased no party faction entirely but with which all could live reasonably.

Overwhelmingly, platform committee members agreed the document should be consistent with Reagan's positions. Thus, though one media poll found delegates overwhelmingly in favor of resuming a peacetime draft, the platform bowed to the view of its nominee and stated its opposition to a renewal of the draft "at this time." In the same manner, the party's platform took no position on ratification of the Equal Rights Amendment (ERA) to the Constitution. Since 1940 Republican platforms had supported an ERA amendment. Reagan, however, opposed ratification, and ERA opponents far outnumbered the amendment's supporters on the platform committee. Yet Reagan, in a gesture to moderates, suggested that the platform not take a position on the issue, and the committee agreed.

Most of the platform document consisted of policy statements on which most Republicans agreed. There were calls for tax cuts, pleas for less government regulation and harsh criticisms of the Carter administration. In two areas, however, the platform took a particularly hard-line position. The platform supported a constitutional amendment that would outlaw abortion and called on a Reagan administration to appoint federal judges who opposed abortion. On defense, platform writers took an already hard-line plank that had been drafted by party staff and moved it sharply to the right. The platform called for massive increases in defense spending and scoffed at the Carter administration's proposed strategic arms limitation treaty (SALT II).

On the other hand, to pick up votes from organized labor, blacks and the poor, the platform made some new overtures to those traditionally non-Republican groups. It pledged to strengthen enforcement of the civil rights laws, made overtures to U.S. workers put out of their jobs by competition from foreign imports and promised to save America's inner cities.

The platform was adopted by the convention July 15 without change, but not before an attempt was made to reopen on the floor one of its more controversial sections. Although party moderates such as Sens. Charles H. Percy, Illinois, Charles McC. Mathias Jr., Maryland, and Jacob K. Javits, New York, made little secret of their unhappiness with the platform's failure to reaffirm the party's support for ratification of the ERA, they were particularly chagrined by the section suggesting that Reagan appoint federal judges who oppose abortion. Percy called the section "the worst plank I have ever seen in any platform by the Republican Party." The moderates July 14 sought to round up support for reopening the platform on the floor, but their efforts failed. In caucuses held early July 15, a number of state delegations including New York and Illinois voted down motions to change the platform's position on abortion.

Nonetheless, as Chairman John J. Rhodes, Ariz., proposed that the convention adopt the platform, Hawaii delegate John Leopold leaped onto a chair to seek Rhodes' recognition. When Rhodes ordered the Hawaii delegation's microphone turned on, Leopold said the group unanimously proposed a motion to suspend the convention rules to permit delegates to "discuss" the platform on the floor. If the rules were suspended, Leopold told reporters, he intended to propose that the language on federal judges be deleted. Not to allow floor discussion of the platform, he said, would be to "railroad" the document through the convention.

Rhodes explained that under convention rules a majority of the members of six state delegations was required to bring a motion to suspend the rules to a vote. He asked if a majority of the delegates from any other state supported Leopold's motion. Only Rep. Silvio O. Conte, chairman of the Massachusetts delegation, rose. But rather than announce support for Leopold's motion, Conte stated only that a majority of his delegation supported a recorded vote on the platform, something Leopold had not proposed. To the applause of many of the delegates, Rhodes then declared that Leopold's motion had failed. The platform subsequently was approved by voice vote.

Ronald Reagan received the Republican nomination on the first ballot. *(Chart, p. 251)*

In his acceptance speech, Reagan combined sharp jabs at the alleged shortcomings of the Carter administration with a reaffirmation of his own conservative credo. Reagan cited three grave threats to the nation's existence — "a disintegrating economy, a weakened defense and an energy policy based on the sharing of scarcity." The culprits, Reagan contended, were President Carter and the Democratic Congress. He said they had preached that the American people needed to tighten their belts. "I utterly reject that view," he declared. Reagan was especially critical of the Democratic administration's conduct of foreign policy. He ridiculed it as weak, vacillating and transparently hypocritical.

Following are excerpts from the Republican Party platform of 1980:

Taxes. . . . [W]e believe it is essential to cut personal tax rates out of fairness to the individual. . . .

Therefore, the Republican Party supports across-the-board reductions in personal income tax rates, phased in over three years, which will reduce tax rates from the range of 14 to 70 percent to a range of from 10 to 50 percent.

. . . Republicans will move to end tax bracket creep caused by inflation. We support tax indexing to protect taxpayers from the automatic tax increases caused when cost-of-living wage increases move them into higher tax brackets.

Welfare. We pledge a system that will:
- provide adequate living standards for the truly needy;
- end welfare fraud by removing ineligibles from the welfare rolls, tightening food stamp eligibility requirements, and ending aid to illegal aliens and the voluntarily unemployed;
- strengthen work incentives, particularly directed at the

productive involvement of able-bodied persons in useful community work projects;
- provide educational and vocational incentives to allow recipients to become self-supporting; and
- better coordinate federal efforts with local and state social welfare agencies and strengthen local and state administrative functions.

We oppose federalizing the welfare system; local levels of government are most aware of the needs in their communities. We support a block grant program that will help return control of welfare programs to the states.

Black Americans. During the next four years we are committed to policies that will:
- encourage local governments to designate specific enterprise zones within depressed areas that will promote new jobs, new and expanded businesses and new economic vitality;
- open new opportunities for black men and women to begin small businesses of their own by, among other steps, removing excessive regulations, disincentives for venture capital and other barriers erected by the government;
- bring strong, effective enforcement of federal civil rights statutes, especially those dealing with threats to physical safety and security which have recently been increasing; and
- ensure that the federal government follows a non-discriminatory system of appointments . . . with a careful eye for qualified minority aspirants.

Women's Rights. We acknowledge the legitimate efforts of those who support or oppose ratification of the Equal Rights Amendment.

We reaffirm our Party's historic commitment to equal rights and equality for women.

We support equal rights and equal opportunities for women, without taking away traditional rights of women such as exemption from the military draft. We support the enforcement of all equal opportunity laws and urge the elimination of discrimination against women.

We reaffirm our belief in the traditional role and values of the family in our society. . . . The importance of support for the mother and homemaker in maintaining the values of this country cannot be over-emphasized.

Abortion. While we recognize differing views on this question among Americans in general — and in our own Party — we affirm our support of a constitutional amendment to restore protection of the right to life for unborn children. We also support the Congressional efforts to restrict the use of taxpayers' dollars for abortion.

Education. . . . [T]he Republican Party supports deregulation by the federal government of public education, and encourages the elimination of the federal Department of Education.

We support Republican initiatives in the Congress to restore the right of individuals to participate in voluntary, non-denominational prayer in schools and other public facilities.

. . . [W]e condemn the forced busing of school children to achieve arbitrary racial quotas. . . . It [busing] has failed to improve the quality of education, while diverting funds from programs that could make the difference between success and failure for the poor, the disabled, and minority children.

[W]e reaffirm our support for a system of educational assistance based on tax credits that will in part compensate parents for their financial sacrifices in paying tuition at the elementary, secondary, and post-secondary level.

Health. Republicans unequivocally oppose socialized medicine, in whatever guise it is presented by the Democratic Party. We reject the creation of a national health service and all proposals for compulsory national health insurance.

Older Americans. Social Security is one of this nation's most vital commitments to our senior citizens. We commit the Republican Party to first save, and then strengthen, this fundamental contract between our government and its productive citizens.

... [W]e proudly reaffirm our opposition to mandatory retirement and our long-standing Republican commitment to end the Democrats' earnings limitation upon Social Security benefits. In addition, the Republican Party is strongly opposed to the taxation of Social Security benefits and we pledge to oppose any attempts to tax these benefits.

Crime. We believe that the death penalty serves as an effective deterrent to capital crime and should be applied by the federal government and by states which approve it as an appropriate penalty for certain major crimes.

We believe the right of citizens to keep and bear arms must be preserved. Accordingly, we oppose federal registration of firearms. Mandatory sentences for commission of armed felonies are the most effective means to deter abuse of this right.

Foreign Competition. The Republican Party recognizes the need to provide workers who have lost their jobs because of technological obsolescence or imports the opportunity to adjust to changing economic conditions. In particular, we will seek ways to assist workers threatened by foreign competition.

The Republican Party believes that protectionist tariffs and quotas are detrimental to our economic well-being. Nevertheless, we insist that our trading partners offer our nation the same level of equity, access, and fairness that we have shown them.

Training and Skills. ... [T]he success of federal employment efforts is dependent on private sector participation. It must be recognized as the ultimate location for unsubsidized jobs, as the provider of means to attain this end, and as an active participant in the formulation of employment and training policies on the local and national level.

We urge a reduction of payroll tax rates, a youth differential for the minimum wage, and alleviation of other costs of employment until a young person can be a productive employee.

Fairness to the Employer. The Republican Party declares war on government overregulation.

While we recognize the role of the federal government in establishing certain minimum standards designed to improve the quality of life in America, we reaffirm our conviction that these standards can best be attained through innovative efforts of American business without the federal government mandating the methods of attainment.

OSHA. OSHA should concentrate its resources on encouraging voluntary compliance by employers and monitoring situations where close federal supervision is needed and serious hazards are most likely to occur. OSHA should be required to consult with, advise, and assist businesses in coping with the regulatory burden before imposing any penalty for non-compliance. Small businesses and employers with good safety records should be exempt from safety inspections, and penalties should be increased for those with consistently poor performance.

Agriculture. Republicans will ensure that:
• international trade is conducted on the basis of fair and effective competition and that all imported agricultural products meet the same standards of quality that are required of American producers. ...
• the future of U.S. agricultural commodities is protected from the economic evils of predatory dumping by other producing nations and that the domestic production of these commodities ... is preserved.

... We believe that agricultural embargoes are only symbolic and are ineffective tools of foreign policy. ... The Carter grain embargo should be terminated immediately.

Big Government. The Republican Party reaffirms its belief in the decentralization of the federal government and in the traditional American principle that the best government is the one closest to the people. There, it is less costly, more accountable, and more responsive to people's needs. ...

Energy. We are committed to ... a strategy of aggressively boosting the nation's energy supplies; stimulating new energy technology and more efficient energy use; restoring maximum feasible choice and freedom in the marketplace for energy consumers and producers alike; and eliminating energy shortages and disruptions. ...

Republicans support a comprehensive program of regulatory reform, improved incentives, and revision of cumbersome and overly stringent Clean Air Act regulations.

We support accelerated use of nuclear energy through technologies that have been proven efficient and safe.

We reject unequivocally punitive gasoline and other energy taxes designed to artificially suppress energy consumption.

A Republican policy of decontrol, development of our domestic energy resources, and incentives for new supply and conservation technologies will substantially reduce our dependence on imported oil.

Republicans will move toward making available all suitable federal lands for multiple use purposes including exploration and production of energy resources.

Environment. We believe that a healthy environment is essential to the present and future well-being of our people, and to sustainable national growth.

At the same time, we believe that it is imperative that environmental laws and regulations be reviewed, and where necessary, reformed to ensure that the benefits achieved justify the costs imposed.

Balanced Budget. If federal spending is reduced as tax cuts are phased in, there will be sufficient budget surpluses to fund the tax cuts, and allow for reasonable growth in necessary program spending.

... We believe a Republican President and a Republican Congress can balance the budget and reduce spending through legislative actions, eliminating the necessity for a Constitutional amendment to compel it. However, if necessary, the Republican Party will seek to adopt a Constitutional amendment to limit federal spending and balance the budget, except in time of national emergency as determined by a two-thirds vote of Congress.

Inflation. The Republican Party believes inflation can be controlled only by fiscal and monetary restraint, combined with sharp reductions in the tax and regulatory disincentives for savings, investments, and productivity. Therefore, the Republican Party opposes the imposition of wage and price controls and credit controls.

National Security. Republicans commit themselves to an immediate increase in defense spending to be applied judiciously to critically needed programs. We will build toward a sustained defense expenditure sufficient to close the gap with the Soviets. Republicans approve and endorse a national strategy of peace through strength. ... The general principles and goals of this strategy would be:
• to inspire, focus, and unite the national will and determination to achieve peace and freedom;
• to achieve overall military and technological superiority over the Soviet Union;
• to create a strategic and civil defense which would protect the American people against nuclear war at least as well as the Soviet population is protected;
• to accept no arms control agreement which in any way jeopardizes the security of the United States or its allies, or

which locks the United States into a position of military inferiority;

● to reestablish effective security and intelligence capabilities;

● to pursue positive nonmilitary means to roll back the growth of communism;

● to help our allies and other non-Communist countries defend themselves against Communist aggression; and

● to maintain a strong economy and protect our overseas sources of energy and . . . raw materials.

Nuclear Forces. . . . We reject the mutual-assured-destruction (MAD) strategy of the Carter Administration. . . . We propose, instead, a credible strategy which will deter a Soviet attack by the clear capability of our forces to survive and ultimately to destroy Soviet military targets.

A Republican Administration will strive for early modernization of our theater nuclear forces so that a seamless web of deterrence can be maintained against all levels of attack, and our credibility with our European allies is restored.

National Intelligence. A Republican Administration will seek adequate safeguards to ensure that past abuses will not recur, but we will seek the repeal of ill-considered restrictions sponsored by Democrats, which have debilitated U.S. intelligence capabilities while easing the intelligence collection and subversion efforts of our adversaries.

Defense Manpower and the Draft. The Republican Party is not prepared to accept a peacetime draft at this time. . . . We will not consider a peacetime draft unless a well-managed, Congressionally-funded, full-scale effort to improve the all-volunteer force does not meet expectations.

Arms Control. The Republican approach to arms control has been . . . based on three fundamental premises:

● first, before arms control negotiations may be undertaken, the security of the United States must be assured by the funding and deployment of strong military forces sufficient to deter conflict at any level or to prevail in battle should aggression occur;

● second, negotiations must be conducted on the basis of strict reciprocity of benefits — unilateral restraint by the U.S. has failed to bring reductions by the Soviet Union; and

● third, arms control negotiations, once entered, represent an important political and military undertaking that cannot be divorced from the broader political and military behavior of the parties.

U.S.-Soviet Relations. Republicans believe that the United States can only negotiate with the Soviet Union from a position of unquestioned principle and unquestioned strength.

A Republican Administration will continue to seek to negotiate arms reductions in Soviet strategic weapons, in Soviet bloc force levels in Central Europe, and in other areas that may be amenable to reductions or limitations. We will pursue hard bargaining for equitable, verifiable, and enforceable agreements.

We reaffirm our commitment to press the Soviet Union to implement the United Nations Declaration on Human Rights and the Helsinki Agreements which guarantee rights such as the free interchange of information and the right to emigrate.

NATO and Western Europe. A Republican Administration, as one of its highest priorities and in close concert with our NATO partners, will . . . ensure that the United States leads a concerted effort to rebuild a strong, confident Alliance. . . .

In pledging renewed United States leadership, cooperation, and consultation, Republicans assert their expectation that each of the allies will bear a fair share of the common defense effort and that they will work closely together in support of common Alliance goals.

Middle East, Persian Gulf. With respect to an ultimate peace settlement, Republicans reject any call for involvement of the PLO as not in keeping with the long-term interests of either Israel or the Palestinian Arabs. The imputation of legitimacy to organizations not yet willing to acknowledge the fundamental right to existence of the State of Israel is wrong.

The sovereignty, security, and integrity of the State of Israel is a moral imperative and serves the strategic interests of the United States. Republicans reaffirm our fundamental and enduring commitment to this principle.

While reemphasizing our commitment to Israel, a Republican Administration will pursue close ties and friendship with moderate Arab states.

The Americas. We deplore the Marxist Sandinista takeover of Nicaragua and the Marxist attempts to destabilize El Salvador, Guatemala, and Honduras. We do not support United States assistance to any Marxist government in this hemisphere and we oppose the Carter Administration aid program for the government of Nicaragua. However, we will support the efforts of the Nicaraguan people to establish a free and independent government.

Asia and the Pacific. A new Republican Administration will restore a strong American role in Asia and the Pacific. We will make it clear that any military action which threatens the independence of America's allies and friends will bring a response sufficient to make its cost prohibitive to potential adversaries.

China. We will strive for the creation of conditions that will foster the peaceful elaboration of our relationship with the People's Republic of China.

At the same time, we deplore the Carter Administration's treatment of Taiwan, our long-time ally and friend. We pledge that our concern for the safety and security of the 17 million people of Taiwan will be constant.

Africa. The Republican Party supports the principle and process of self-determination in Africa. We reaffirm our commitment to this principle and pledge our strong opposition to the effort of the Soviet Union . . . to subvert this process.

Foreign Aid. No longer should American foreign assistance programs seek to force acceptance of American governmental forms. The principal consideration should be whether or not extending assistance to a nation or group of nations will advance America's interests and objectives.

Decisions to provide military assistance should be made on the basis of U.S. foreign policy objectives. Such assistance to any nation need not imply complete approval of a regime's domestic policy.

International Economic Policy. Under a Republican Administration, our international economic policy will be harmonized with our foreign and defense policies to leave no doubt as to the strategy and purpose of American policy.

Republicans will conduct international economic policy in a manner that will stabilize the value of the dollar at home and abroad.

The Republican Party believes the United States must adopt an aggressive export policy. Trade, especially exporting, must be high on our list of national priorities. The Republicans will . . . promote trade to ensure the long-term health of the U.S. economy.

Democrats

President Jimmy Carter emerged victorious from a deeply divided Democratic National Convention unsure whether his plea for unity to supporters of rival Sen. Edward M. Kennedy of Massachusetts had succeeded. Kennedy had been Carter's main opponent in his quest for renomination throughout the spring primary season. When it became apparent that Kennedy had not won in the primaries and caucuses the delegate support he needed, he turned his efforts to prying the nomination away from the president at the convention.

Kennedy's presence was strong throughout the convention week and expressions of support for the senator sometimes upstaged those for the incumbent president. Chants of "We want Ted" rocked off the walls of New York's Madison Square Garden during the convention's four days, Aug. 11-14. And their echo faintly followed the president as he left the podium following his acceptance speech. It was a stark reminder that Carter, even though he had captured the nomination and engaged in a series of reconciliation gestures with his rival, still faced the difficult task of rallying a divided party behind his candidacy.

Kennedy's efforts to wrest the nomination from Carter centered around a convention rule that bound delegates to vote on the first ballot for the candidates under whose banner they were elected. When the convention opened, Carter could count 315 more votes than he needed for the nomination — votes that he had won in nominating caucuses and presidential primaries. As a result, Kennedy's only chance to gain the nomination was to defeat the binding rule.

In the week before the convention, negotiators for Carter and Kennedy agreed to one hour of debate on the rules question to begin at 6:30 p.m. Monday, Aug. 11. Kennedy forces had wanted a Tuesday night rules vote, which would have given them an extra day to lobby delegates. But they settled instead for the Monday night debate, which enabled them to argue their case before a prime-time nationwide television audience.

Opponents of the binding rule tried to present a broad-based front. Arguing against the rule on the convention floor were a Carter delegate, two Kennedy backers and two leading uncommitted delegates — New York governor Hugh L. Carey and prominent Washington attorney Edward Bennett Williams, the chief spokesman of the Committee for an Open Convention.

They argued that political conditions had changed since the delegates were elected months earlier and that to bind them would break with a century and a half of Democratic tradition. "For the first time in 150 years, delegates to the national convention are being asked to deliver their final freedom of choice, and to vote themselves into bondage to a candidate," Williams contended. To adopt the binding rule, other speakers added, would make the delegates little more than robots.

But most Carter supporters scoffed at that contention, stressing that delegates were free to vote their conscience on all roll calls but the one for president. Passage of the rule was simply fair play, they added. It had been adopted in 1978 without opposition by the party's last rules review commission and the Democratic National Committee. Only when it was apparent that Carter was winning, claimed Atlanta mayor Maynard Jackson, did the Kennedy camp want to change the rules to allow a "fifth ball, a fourth out or a tenth inning."

When the measure finally came to a vote, Carter forces turned back the attempt to overturn the proposed rule. The vote was 1,936.418 to 1,390.580 against Kennedy's position. *(Chart, p. 250)*

Shortly after the vote, Kennedy ended his nine-month challenge to the president by announcing that his name

would not be placed in nomination Aug. 13. Passage of the binding rule assured Carter's renomination.

In addition to its binding-rule objection, the Kennedy camp filed four other minority rules reports, but all were withdrawn before the Aug. 11 session. Three originally had been filed in response to Carter efforts to streamline the convention schedule. At its July meeting in Washington, D.C., the convention rules committee approved proposals to increase the number of signatures required on nominating petitions for president, vice president and convention chairman; to limit to two the number of speakers on each side of each issue of debate; and to allow every roll call, except for president and vice president, to be conducted by telephone while convention business proceeded.

In return for Kennedy's withdrawal of the minority reports, the Carter camp did consent to raise the number of speakers on each side of each issue to three. They also agreed to a Kennedy proposal to add a platform accountability rule that would require each presidential candidate to submit his written views on the party platform along with his pledge to carry it out. The statement would have to be presented shortly after convention consideration of the platform was completed. The Kennedy proposal also called for the candidates' statements to be distributed and read to the delegates.

Despite the loss on the binding rule, the Kennedy camp succeeded in molding the party platform more to their liking. The final document was filled with so many concessions to the Kennedy forces that it won only a half-hearted endorsement from the president. The platform battle, one of the longest in party history, filled 17 hours of debate and roll calls that stretched over two days, Aug. 12 and 13.

Most of Carter's concessions and outright defeats came on the economic and human needs sections of the 40,000-word document. It was these revisions that Carter rejected — as diplomatically as possible — in a statement issued several hours after the debate wound to a close.

In the debate on social issues, Carter lost two roll-call votes — one on adoption of Kennedy's plank calling for jobs to be "our single highest domestic priority," and the other supporting Medicaid funding for abortions. The president also lost a voice vote on a minority report to withhold all party funds and campaign assistance to candidates who did not support the then-pending Equal Rights Amendment to the Constitution.

The only victory posted by Carter in the human needs chapter was over a Kennedy minority report calling for a single, comprehensive national health insurance plan with gradually phased-in benefits. That report was defeated on a 1,409.9-to-1,623.8 vote that came at the start of the platform debate.

It had been clear since the platform was drafted in late June that the economic plank, which contained the major Carter-Kennedy differences, would be the focus of dispute. When the hour for debate arrived, it was evident that the control Carter had exercised the previous evening on the question of binding delegates had evaporated.

Before the convention began, Carter had yielded to Kennedy language on several issues, including one of the senator's four minority economic reports. That report asserted that a policy of high interest rates and unemployment should not be used to fight inflation. White House domestic affairs adviser Stuart E. Eizenstat announced Aug. 10 that Carter would go along with that amendment — but none of the others in the economy section — because it stated a broad goal while the others called for specific legislation.

The marathon platform debate reached its high point on Tuesday evening, Aug. 12, when Kennedy addressed the delegates on behalf of his minority report on the economic chapter. Kennedy's speech provided the Democratic convention with its most exciting moments. The address, which sparked a 40-minute emotional demonstration when it was over, called for Democratic unity and laced into the Republican nominee, Ronald Reagan.

Kennedy defended his liberal ideology, supporting national health insurance and federal spending to restore deteriorated urban areas. He lashed out at Reagan's proposal for a massive tax cut, labeling it as beneficial only to the wealthy. "For all those whose cares have been our concern the work goes on, the cause endures, the hope still lives and the dream shall never die," concluded Kennedy. Buoyed by the Kennedy oratory, the convention went on to pass by voice vote three liberal Kennedy platform planks on the economy, thereby rejecting the more moderate versions favored by Carter.

The first of the Kennedy-sponsored planks was a statement pledging that fairness would be the overriding principle of the Democrats' economic policy and that no actions would be taken that would "significantly increase" unemployment. The convention next approved a Kennedy plank seeking a $12 billion anti-recession jobs program, a $1 billion rail renewal plan and an expanded housing program for low- and moderate-income families. The final Kennedy economic plank was a statement of opposition to fighting inflation through a policy of high interest rates and unemployment. Carter had agreed to this plank the day before the convention opened.

Carter floor managers realized that it would be difficult to block passage of the Kennedy economic proposals. After the senator's emotion-filled speech, Carter advisers — realizing their position could not prevail — quickly sought to change from a roll call to a voice vote on the economic planks.

During the floor demonstration that followed Kennedy's speech, a series of telephone calls ricocheted between the podium and the senator's campaign trailer located off the convention floor. The negotiations involved how many elements of the Kennedy program would be accepted by voice vote. In the end, Carter prevailed on only one of Kennedy's economic minority reports, the call for an immediate wage and price freeze followed by controls.

Prior to the 1980 convention, Democratic presidential nominees had been able to gloss over their distaste for objectionable portions of the platform. But Kennedy made that difficult to do. In his carefully worded statement following the platform debate, Carter did not flatly reject any of Kennedy's amendments, but he did not embrace them either.

Of Kennedy's $12 billion anti-recession jobs program, Carter said he would "accept and support the intent" of the program but he refused to commit himself to a specific dollar amount. Responding to Kennedy language that placed a jobs program above all other domestic priorities, Carter wrote, "We must make it clear that to achieve full employment, we must also be successful in our fight against inflation."

Carter treated two women's issues the same way. Responding to adopted language that endorsed federal funding for abortion, the president repeated his personal opposition but said he would be guided by court decisions on the

questions. He also reiterated his support for ratification of the Equal Rights Amendment but did not directly comment on the platform language adopted on the floor that prevented the Democratic Party from giving campaign funds to candidates who did not back the amendment.

Carter concluded his statement with the unity refrain that had become the hallmark of every official White House comment on the platform since the drafting process began: "The differences within our party on this platform are small in comparison with the differences between the Republican and Democratic Party platforms." Kennedy apparently agreed. And shortly after Carter's renomination Aug. 13, Kennedy issued a statement endorsing the platform and pledging his support for Carter. In the final moments before adjournment, Kennedy made a stiff and brief appearance on the platform with Carter, Vice President Walter F. Mondale and a host of Democratic officeholders. But the coolness of his appearance — accompanied by the warmest reception of the night — left questionable the commitment of the senator and his supporters to work strenuously for Carter's re-election.

Carter won the Democratic nomination with 2,123 votes compared with Kennedy's 1,150.5. Other candidates split 54.5 votes. *(Chart, p. 250)*

In his acceptance speech, Carter alluded to the convention's divisions. He led off with praise for Kennedy's tough campaign, thanks for his concessions during the convention and an appeal for future help. "Ted, your party needs — and I need — you, and your idealism and dedication working for us." Carter spent much of the speech characterizing Reagan's programs as a disastrous "fantasy world" of easy answers. He avoided detailed comments on the economic issues over which he and Kennedy had split, confining himself to statements that he wanted jobs for all who needed them.

As expected, Mondale was renominated for vice president. Two other party members had their names placed in nomination so they could raise the issues of homosexual rights and Carter's decision to reinstitute draft registration. Activist Patricia Simon of Newton, Mass., withdrew after delivering a plea that "we be known as a party of peace." The other candidate was Melvin Boozer of Washington, D.C. Boozer, a number of favorite sons and others received only a smattering of votes and Mondale was nominated by acclamation before that roll call had been completed.

The vice president's acceptance speech set delegates chanting "Not Ronald Reagan" as Mondale reeled off a list of liberal values and programs that, he said, most Americans agreed with. Mondale was one of the few speakers to unequivocally praise Carter's record, which he did at some length. The speech ended with a warning not to "let anyone make us less than what we can be."

Following are excerpts from the Democratic Party platform of 1980:

Employment. We specifically reaffirm our commitment to achieve all the goals of the Humphrey-Hawkins Full Employment Act within the currently prescribed dates in the Act, especially those relating to a joint reduction in unemployment and inflation. Full employment is important to the achievement of a rising standard of living, to the pursuit of sound justice, and to the strength and vitality of America.

Anti-Recession Assistance. A Democratic anti-recession program must recognize that Blacks, Hispanics, other minorities, women, and older workers bear the brunt of recession. We pledge a $12 billion anti-recession jobs program, providing at least 800,000 additional jobs, including full funding of the counter-cyclical assistance program for the cities, a major expansion of the youth employment and training program to give young people in our inner cities new hope, expanded training programs for women and displaced homemakers to give these workers a fair chance in the workplace, and new opportunities for the elderly to contribute their talents and skills.

Tax Reductions. We commit ourselves to targeted tax reductions designed to stimulate production and combat recession as soon as it appears so that tax reductions will not have a disproportionately inflationary effect. We must avoid untargeted tax cuts which would increase inflation.

Federal Spending. Spending restraint must be sensitive to those who look to the federal government for aid and assistance, especially to our nation's workers in times of high unemployment. At the same time, as long as inflationary pressures remain strong, fiscal prudence is essential to avoid destroying the progress made to date in reducing the inflation rate.

Fiscal policy must remain a flexible economic tool. We oppose a Constitutional amendment requiring a balanced budget.

Interest Rates. . . . [W]e must continue to pursue a tough anti-inflationary policy which will lead to an across-the-board reduction in interest rates on loans.

In using monetary policy to fight inflation, the government should be sensitive to the special needs of areas of our economy most affected by high interest rates.

Expanding American Exports. To create new markets for American products and strengthen the dollar, we must seek out new opportunities for American exports; help establish stable, long-term commercial relationships between nations; offer technical assistance to firms competing in world markets; promote reciprocal trading terms for nations doing business here; and help ensure that America's domestic retooling is consistent with new opportunities in foreign trade.

We must intensify our efforts to promote American exports and to ensure that our domestic industries and workers are not affected adversely by unfair trade practices, such as dumping. . . . We must ensure that our efforts to lower tariff barriers are reciprocated by our trading partners. We recognize the superior productivity of American agriculture and the importance of agricultural exports to the balance of trade.

Worker Protection. The Democratic Party will not pursue a policy of high interest rates and unemployment as the means to fight inflation. We will take no action whose effect will be a significant increase in unemployment, no fiscal action, no monetary action, no budgetary action. The Democratic Party remains committed to policies that will not produce high interest rates or high unemployment.

OSHA protections should be properly administered, with the concern of the worker being the highest priority; legislative or administrative efforts to weaken OSHA's basic worker protection responsibilities are unacceptable.

We will continue to oppose a sub-minimum wage for youth and other workers and to support increases in the minimum wage so as to ensure an adequate income for all workers.

Small Business. . . . [T]he Democratic Party commits itself to the first comprehensive program for small business in American history. That program will include the following measures:

. . . Allocation of a fair percentage of federal research funds to small business.

Protection of small and independent business against takeover by giant conglomerates.

Continued efforts to end federal regulations which reinforce barriers to entry by new and small firms, and which thereby entrench the dominance of market leaders.

A review of regulations and requirements which impose unnecessary burdens upon smaller firms. We will adopt regulatory requirements to meet the needs of smaller firms, where such action will not interfere with the objectives of the regulation.

Minority Business. The Democratic Party pledges itself to advance minority businesses, including Black, Hispanic, Asian/Pacific Americans, Native Americans and other minorities to:

● Increase the overall level of support and the overall level of federal procurement so that minority groups will receive additional benefits and opportunities.

● Triple the 1980 level of federal procurement from minority-owned firms as we have tripled the 1977 levels in the past three years.

● Increase substantially the targeting of Small Business Administration loans to minority-owned businesses.

● Increase ownership of small businesses by minorities, especially in those areas which have traditionally been closed to minorities, such as communications and newspapers.

● Expand management, technical, and training assistance for minority firms, and strengthen minority capital development. . . .

Women and the Economy. The Democratic Party . . . commits itself to strong steps to close the wage gap between men and women, to expand child care opportunities for families with working parents, to end the tax discrimination that penalizes married working couples, and to ensure that women can retire in dignity.

We will strictly enforce existing anti-discrimination laws with respect to hiring, pay and promotions. We will adopt a full employment policy, with increased possibilities for part-time work. . . . [W]e will ensure that women in both the public and private sectors are not only paid equally for work which is identical to that performed by men, but are also paid equally for work which is of comparable value to that performed by men.

Consumer Protection. Over the next four years, we must continue to guarantee and enhance the basic consumer rights to safety, to information, to choice and to a fair hearing.

We must continue our support of basic health, safety, environmental and consumer protection regulatory programs. . . .

Human Needs. While we recognize the need for fiscal restraint . . . we pledge as Democrats that for the sole and primary purpose of fiscal restraint alone, we will *not* support reductions in the funding of any program whose purpose is to serve the basic human needs of the most needy in our society — programs such as unemployment, income maintenance, food stamps, and efforts to enhance the educational, nutritional or health needs of children.

Health. The answer to runaway medical costs is not, as Republicans propose, to pour money into a wasteful and inefficient system. The answer is not to cut back on benefits for the elderly and eligibility for the poor. The answer is to enact a comprehensive, universal national health insurance plan.

To meet the goals of a program that will control costs and provide health coverage to every American, the Democratic Party pledges to seek a national health insurance program. . . .

Social Security. The Democratic Party will oppose any effort to tamper with the Social Security system by cutting or taxing benefits as a violation of the contract the

American government has made with its people. We hereby make a covenant with the elderly of America that as we have kept the Social Security trust fund sound and solvent in the past, we shall keep it sound and solvent in the years ahead.... We oppose efforts to raise the age at which Social Security benefits will be provided.

Finally, the Democratic Party vehemently opposes all forms of age discrimination and commits itself to eliminating mandatory retirement.

Welfare Reform. As a means of providing immediate federal fiscal relief to state and local governments, the federal government will assume the local government's burden of welfare costs. Further, there should be a phased reduction in the states' share of welfare costs in the immediate future.

We strongly reject the Republican Platform proposal to transfer the responsibility for funding welfare costs entirely to the states. Such a proposal would not only worsen the fiscal situation of state and local governments, but would also lead to reduced benefits and services to those dependent on welfare programs. The Democratic policy is exactly the opposite — to provide greater assistance to state and local governments for their welfare costs and to improve benefits and services....

Education. ... [W]e will continue to support the Department of Education and assist in its all-important educational enterprise....

... The federal government and the states should be encouraged to equalize or take over educational expenses, relieving the overburdened ... taxpayer.

The Democratic Party continues to support programs aimed at achieving communities integrated both in terms of race and economic class.... Mandatory transportation of students beyond their neighborhoods for the purpose of desegregation remains a judicial tool of last resort.

The Party reaffirms its support of public school education and would not support any program or legislation that would create or promote economic, sociological or racial segregation.

The Party accepts its commitment to the support of a constitutionally acceptable method of providing tax aid for the education of all pupils in schools which do not racially discriminate, and excluding so-called segregation academies.

Equal Rights Amendment. ... [T]he Democratic Party must ensure that ERA at last becomes the 27 Amendment to the Constitution. We oppose efforts to rescind ERA in states which have already ratified the amendment, and we shall insist that past recissions are invalid.

Civil Rights and Liberties. We oppose efforts to undermine the Supreme Court's historic mandate of school desegregation, and we support affirmative action goals to overturn patterns of discrimination in education and employment.

Our commitment to civil rights embraces not only a commitment to legal equality, but a commitment to economic justice as well. It embraces a recognition of the right of every citizen ... to a fair share in our economy.

We call for passage of legislation to charter the purposes, prerogatives, and restraints on the Federal Bureau of Investigation, the Central Intelligence Agency, and other intelligence agencies of government with full protection for the civil rights and liberties of American citizens living at home or abroad. Under no circumstances should American citizens be investigated because of their beliefs.

Abortion. The Democratic Party recognizes reproductive freedom as a fundamental human right. We therefore oppose government interference in the reproductive decisions of Americans, especially those government programs or legislative restrictions that deny poor Americans their

right to privacy by funding or advocating one or a limited number of reproductive choices only. Specifically, the Democratic Party opposes ... restrictions on funding for health services for the poor that deny poor women especially the right to exercise a constitutionally-guaranteed right to privacy.

Tax Reform. Capital formation is essential both to control inflation and to encourage growth. New tax reform efforts are needed to increase savings and investment, promote the principle of progressive taxation, close loopholes, and maintain adequate levels of federal revenue.

Gun Control. The Democratic Party affirms the right of sportsmen to possess guns for purely hunting and target-shooting purposes. However, handguns simplify and intensify violent crime.... The Democratic Party supports enactment of federal legislation to strengthen the presently inadequate regulations over the manufacture, assembly, distribution, and possession of handguns and to ban "Saturday night specials."

Energy. We must make energy conservation our highest priority, not only to reduce our dependence on foreign oil, but also to guarantee that our children and grandchildren have an adequate supply of energy.

Major new efforts must be launched to develop synthetic and alternative renewable energy sources.

The Democratic Party regards coal as our nation's greatest energy resource. It must play a decisive role in America's energy future.

Oil exploration on federal lands must be accelerated, consistent with environmental protections.

Offshore energy leasing and development should be conditioned on full protection of the environment and marine resources.

Solar energy use must be increased, and strong efforts, including continued financial support, must be undertaken to make certain that we achieve the goal of having solar energy account for 20% of our total energy by the year 2000.

A stand-by gasoline rationing plan must be adopted for use in the event of a serious energy supply interruption.

... Through the federal government's commitment to renewable energy sources and energy efficiency, and as alternative fuels become available in the future, we will retire nuclear power plants....

We must give the highest priority to dealing with the nuclear waste disposal problem.... [E]fforts to develop a safe, environmentally sound nuclear waste disposal plan must be continued and intensified.

Environment. We must move decisively to protect our countryside and our coastline from overdevelopment and mismanagement. ... [P]rotection must be balanced with the need to properly manage and utilize our land resources during the 1980s.

We must develop new and improved working relationships among federal, state, local, tribal, and territorial governments and private interests, to manage effectively our programs for increased domestic energy production and their impact on people, water, air, and the environment in general.

Grain Embargo. Recognizing the patriotic sacrifices made by the American farmer during the agricultural embargo protesting the invasion of Afghanistan, we commend the agricultural community's contribution in the field of foreign affairs. Except in time of war or grave threats to national security, the federal government should impose no future embargoes on agricultural products.

Foreign Policy. The Democratic Administration sought to reconcile ... two requirements of American foreign policy — principle and strength.... We have tried to make clear the continuing importance of American strength in a world of change. Without such strength, there is a genuine risk that global change will deteriorate into anarchy to be exploited by our adversaries' military power. Thus, the revival of American strength has been a central pre-occupation of the Democratic Administration.

The use of American power is necessary as a means of shaping not only a more secure, but also a more decent world. . . . [W]e must pursue objectives that are moral, that make clear our support for the aspirations of mankind and that are rooted in the ideals of the American people.

That is why the Democrats have stressed human rights. That is why America once again has supported the aspirations of the vast majority of the world's population for greater human justice and freedom.

. . . In meeting the dangers of the coming decade the United States will consult closely with our Allies to advance common security and political goals. As a result of annual summit meetings, coordinated economic policies and effective programs of international energy conservation have been fashioned.

. . . [W]e must continue to improve our relations with the Third World by being sensitive to their legitimate aspirations. The United States should be a positive force for peaceful change in responding to ferment in the Third World.

Our third objective must be peace in the Middle East. . . . Our nation feels a profound moral obligation to sustain and assure the security of Israel. . . . Israel is the single democracy, the most stable government, the most strategic asset and our closest ally in the region.

To fulfill this imperative, we must move towards peace in the Middle East. Without peace, there is a growing prospect, indeed inevitability, that this region will become radicalized, susceptible to foreign intrusion, and possibly involved in another war. Thus, peace in the Middle East also is vital for our national security interests. . . . Our goal is to make the Middle East an area of stability and progress in which the United States can play a full and constructive role.

National Security. Our fourth major objective is to strengthen the military security of the United States and our Allies at a time when trends in the military balance have become increasingly adverse. America is now, and will continue to be, the strongest power on earth. It was the Democratic Party's greatest hope that we could, in fact, reduce our military effort. But realities of the world situation, including the unremitting buildup of Soviet military forces, required that we begin early to reverse the decade-long decline in American defense efforts.

Arms Control. . . . [T]he Democrats have been and remain committed to arms control, especially to strategic arms limitations, and to maintain a firm and balanced relationship with the Soviet Union.

To avoid the danger to all mankind from an intensification of the strategic arms competition, and to curb a possible acceleration of the nuclear arms race while awaiting the ratification of the SALT II Treaty, we endorse the policy of continuing to take no action which would be inconsistent with its object and purpose, so long as the Soviet Union does likewise.

Arms control and strategic arms limitation are of crucial importance to us and to all other people. The SALT II Agreement is a major accomplishment of the Democratic Administration. It contributes directly to our national security, and we will seek its ratification at the earliest feasible time.

National Unity Campaign

Rep. John B. Anderson of Illinois, a Republican, declared himself an independent candidate for the presidency April 24, 1980, after it became clear that he could not obtain his party's presidential nomination. Anderson cre-ated the National Unity Campaign as the vehicle for his third-party candidacy. No party convention was held to select Anderson or to ratify the selection.

On Aug. 25 Anderson announced he had tapped former Wisconsin governor Patrick J. Lucey, a Democrat, to be his running mate. The selection of Lucey was seen as a move by Anderson to attract liberal Democrats disgruntled by President Jimmy Carter's renomination. Anderson's choice of a running mate and the Aug. 30 release of a National Unity Campaign platform helped establish him as a genuine contender in the presidential race.

The 317-page platform put forth specific proposals on a variety of national issues, emphasizing domestic questions. The positions taken generally were fiscally conservative and socially liberal, remaining true to Anderson's "wallet on the right, heart on the left" philosophy.

The platform made clear that Anderson's primary goal was to restore the nation's economic health by adopting fiscal and tax policies that would "generate a substantial pool of investment capital," which then would be used to increase productivity and create jobs. Anderson proposed countercyclical revenue sharing to direct federal funds to areas hardest hit by the election year recession. He rejected mandatory wage and price controls as a cure for inflation, proposing instead a program under which the government would encourage labor and management to work toward agreement on proper levels for wages and prices and use tax incentives to encourage compliance with the standards set. In contrast to both Carter and Reagan, Anderson opposed tax cuts for individuals. He also criticized constitutional amendments to balance the federal budget, saying that while the budget should be balanced "in ordinary times," it could be expected to run a deficit in times of "economic difficulty."

Anderson's energy policy made reducing oil imports the top priority. His platform proposed a 50-cent-a-gallon excise tax on gasoline to discourage consumption, with the revenue to be used to cut Social Security taxes. Anderson favored the decontrol of oil prices begun under Carter and proposed a 40-mile-per-gallon fuel economy standard for new autos.

For American cities, Anderson proposed using about 90 percent of alcohol and tobacco taxes to help build mass transit systems and fight deterioration of public facilities. He also favored offering tax incentives to encourage businesses to locate in blighted urban areas.

In foreign policy, Anderson emphasized strengthening alliances with Western Europe and Japan, resisting Soviet expansion while negotiating "whenever possible" and respecting the sovereignty of Third World nations. His platform supported human rights and humanitarian aid for refugees and disaster victims abroad. He pledged to support the Middle East peace process but opposed the creation of a Palestinian state between Israel and Jordan or U.S. recognition of the Palestine Liberation Organization until the PLO recognized Israel's right to exist.

On defense issues, Anderson opposed development of the MX missile, B-1 bomber and neutron bomb, criticized the arms race and opposed a peacetime draft registration. He pledged to seek ratification of the SALT II treaty negotiated with the Soviet Union, saying that "essential equivalence" existed between U.S. and Soviet missile forces. He opposed a strategy of nuclear superiority, emphasizing instead the beefing up of conventional military forces.

Anderson finished the 1980 presidential race a distant

third behind Jimmy Carter with 5,719,722 votes, 6.6 percent.

Following are excerpts from the National Unity Campaign platform of 1980:

Economy. We will construct a Wage-Price Incentives Program. Our administration will invite labor and management leaders to agree upon fair and realistic guidelines and to determine appropriate tax-based incentives to encourage compliance....

In the absence of sharp and prolonged increases in the rate of inflation, we will oppose mandatory wage and price standards.

Youth Unemployment. To deal with the critical problem of youth unemployment, particularly among minorities, we propose: enactment of the proposed Youth Act of 1980 to provide over $2 billion a year for job training and state and local educational programs designed to improve the employability of disadvantaged and out-of-school youth; increased funding for youth career intern programs; a youth opportunity wage incentive that would exempt eligible youths and employers from Social Security taxes during the first months of employment.

Gasoline Tax. We would couple decontrol of oil and gas prices with an excise tax of 50 cents per gallon on gasoline, the full revenues of that tax being returned to individuals through reductions in payroll taxes and increased Social Security benefits.... We will employ tax credits and other incentives to promote substitution of nonpetroleum energy for oil, adoption of energy-efficient systems in industry and elsewhere, improvements in transportation and energy production technologies, and development of less wasteful structures for home and commerce.

Nuclear Power. ... [W]e will act on the recommendations of the Rogovin and Kemeny Commissions to make certain that installation of any future plants is preceded by demonstration of satisfactory standards and action on the nuclear waste question. We will assess nuclear power in light of its dependence on public subsidy and of the possibility that slower growth in demand may enable us to phase in other energy supplies in preference to nuclear systems.

Cities. ... [A]n Anderson-Lucey Administration will propose an Urban Reinvestment Trust Fund. Funded through ... revenues from the Federal alcohol and tobacco excise taxes and phased in over three years, it will disburse approximately $3.9 billion annually. It will be used for upgrading, repair and replacement of [urban] capital plant and equipment.

Within our distressed older cities, there are zones of devastation, blighted by crime, arson and population flight.... We favor legislation that would create "enterprise zones" in these areas, by lowering corporate, capital gains, payroll and property taxes and by furnishing new tax incentives....

Environment. We will guard and consolidate the achievements in every field of environmental protection and preservation. We will insist, however, that economic impact studies, assessing not only direct costs but employment and energy implications, accompany proposals for major changes in environmental standards.

Social Issues. We are committed to ratification of the Equal Rights Amendment. We oppose government intrusion in the most intimate of family decisions — the right to bear or not to bear children — and will fight against any constitutional amendment prohibiting abortion. We support public funding of family planning services and other efforts to enable women to find ... alternatives to abortion.

National Defense and Arms Control. In strategic forces, we will maintain a stable balance by preserving essential equivalence with the Soviet Union. To meet an evolving threat to our deterrent, we will modernize and diversify our strategic arsenal.

The growing concern over the threat to fixed, land-based missiles poses an urgent problem to both the United States and the Soviet Union. Economically, environmentally and strategically, the ... cure proposed by the Carter Administration — the MX system — is unsound.

Arms control agreements must enhance our basic security and must not compromise our ability to protect our national interests. Agreements must preserve and reinforce the stability of the strategic balance.... Arms control must be based on adequate, effective verification.

The Western alliance should proceed with its plans to modernize its theater nuclear arsenal; at the same time, we should keep open the possibility of negotiations with the Soviet Union to limit theater nuclear forces.

We favor ... a short-term ... nuclear test ban treaty between the United States, the Soviet Union and the United Kingdom....

For a more effective defense, we will rely heavily on collective security arrangements with our principal allies in NATO and Japan. We will work to reinforce and enhance our historic partnership with our Western European allies.

We will propose to Moscow supplementary measures that could make possible the ratification of the SALT II Treaty and the start of SALT III negotiations. These proposals will respond to concerns expressed in the U.S. Senate regarding such issues as verification and future force reductions.

Middle East. The establishment and maintenance of peace in the Middle East will be an urgent objective.... A lasting settlement must encompass the principles affirmed in the Camp David accords.

Our administration will support the recognition of Palestinian rights as embodied in the Camp David accords, but will oppose the creation of a Palestinian state between Israel and Jordan.

The United States will not recognize or negotiate with the Palestine Liberation Organization unless that organization repudiates terrorism, explicitly recognizes Israel's right to exist in peace and accepts U.N. Security Council Resolutions 242 and 338....

China. ... [T]he Anderson-Lucey Administration would work to discourage antagonism between Russia and China. We should not become an arms supplier to China. We should work for better understanding by China's leaders of the consequences of nuclear war, of measures that should be taken to guard against accidental war and of ways to make the nuclear balance more stable.

Finally, our administration would abide by both the letter and spirit of the Taiwan Relations Act. We would maintain our contacts with Taiwan but would not establish official relations with its government.

1984 Conventions

Presidential Candidates

Walter F. Mondale
Democrat

Ronald Reagan
Republican

Democrats

Ending a long and difficult nomination campaign with a display of party unity and a historic vice presidential choice, Walter F. Mondale used the 1984 Democratic convention to sound the opening themes of his challenge to President Ronald Reagan: family, fairness, the flag and the future.

Accepting their nominations July 19 before cheering, flag-waving delegates at the San Francisco convention, the presidential candidate and his running mate, Rep. Geraldine A. Ferraro of New York, served notice that they would hold Reagan to account for his policies in their uphill battle to capture the White House. "Here is the truth about the [nation's] future," Mondale told the Democrats as they wrapped up their four-day convention. "We are living on borrowed money and borrowed time."

The spectacle of Mondale and Ferraro, with their families, celebrating with delegates in the jammed Moscone Center capped a week in which the Democrats came together to choose their ticket and shore up party unity. Toward that end, the convention succeeded to a greater degree than had seemed possible when the former vice president was battling Sen. Gary Hart of Colorado and the Rev. Jesse Jackson in the primaries and caucuses. There was little acrimony over consideration of the party platform. And, once Mondale was nominated, the three rivals seemed to put aside their most visible differences.

The 56-year-old Minnesotan had been the apparent winner since the final round of primaries on June 5, when he took New Jersey, which gave him the 1,967 pledged delegates needed to take the nomination. Mondale finished the convention balloting with nearly 1,000 votes more than Hart, his closest competitor, yet he was by no means the overwhelming choice. He polled 2,191 votes — about 56 percent of a possible 3,933. *(Chart, p. 253)*

Fears that radical and homosexual elements in San Francisco would stage massive confrontations in the streets outside the convention center — evoking memories of the party's 1968 catastrophe in Chicago — did not materialize. Except for a few minor clashes between crowds and the police, there were no violent incidents. Several hundred thousand homosexuals and labor union members marched

peacefully in separate demonstrations July 15, and protestors representing a variety of causes gathered throughout convention week in the giant parking lot across the street from the convention center.

The Democratic unity displayed in San Francisco — so different from the 1980 convention, when the struggle between President Jimmy Carter and Sen. Edward M. Kennedy of Massachusetts left the party torn and battered — was due largely to delegates' deeply felt antipathy to the policies of the Reagan administration. The unusual harmony was also due, at least in part, to Gov. Mario M. Cuomo of New York, who electrified delegates with his keynote address on the opening night, July 16. In an eloquent appeal for family values and compassion for the poor, he set the tone for the rest of the convention. His speech was rivaled in intensity only by Ferraro's nomination by acclamation July 19 and an impassioned speech given by Jackson on July 17.

Speaking forcefully but without dramatic oratorical flourishes, and repeatedly interrupted by emotional applause, Cuomo combined an appeal to Democratic traditions with specific attacks on the domestic and foreign policies of the Reagan administration. Noting Reagan's reference to America as "a shining city on a hill," Cuomo said that "the hard truth is that not everyone is sharing in this city's splendor and glory. There is despair, Mr. President, in the faces that you don't see, in the places that you don't visit in your shining city."

The product of weeks of intensive work by the candidate and a team of advisers, Mondale's acceptance speech July 19 was a carefully drawn outline for his campaign against Reagan. Although the former vice president had been criticized for lacking speech-making flair during the nomination campaign, he repeatedly brought delegates to their feet during his address.

To introduce Mondale, the party turned to Kennedy, one of its most effective practitioners of rousing oratory. Kennedy's booming voice filled the hall with denunciations of Reagan and the Republican Party, which he called a "cold citadel of privilege."

"By his choice of Geraldine Ferraro, Walter Mondale has already done more for this country in one short day than Ronald Reagan has done in four long years in office," he said, as delegates cheered and stomped their feet.

Shortly before Mondale's address, aides had passed out thousands of small American flags to delegates, so the crowd was a sea of red, white and blue when the former vice president arrived on the podium.

Pledging a government of "new realism" that would combine strong but conciliatory foreign policies with tough economic initiatives, Mondale vowed in his address to squeeze the budget and raise taxes to reduce soaring deficits, then approaching $200 billion a year. "Let's tell the truth. . . . Mr. Reagan will raise taxes, and so will I," Mondale said. "He won't tell you. I just did."

To Ferraro, the first woman put on the national ticket by a major party, her nomination by acclamation was a special honor. Quoting the late Rev. Martin Luther King Jr., she said that " 'Occasionally in life there are moments which cannot be completely explained in words. Their meaning can only be articulated by the inaudible language of the heart.' Tonight is such a moment for me. My heart is filled with pride."

The platform adopted at the convention created few divisions in the party, but few candidates were enthusiastic about using it in their fall campaigns. Adopted in an emphatic but seldom angry four-hour debate July 17, the platform drew heavily from Mondale's campaign themes. It also contained significant contributions from Hart and Jackson.

The process of assembling the platform was an important exercise for the party. In four months of hearings and drafting sessions, the Democrats invited dozens of interest groups to weave their goals and ideals into the platform. The variegated document became a symbol of the party's all-inclusive philosophy, as it grew to roughly 45,000 words after countless pressure groups had their say.

The final draft was loyal to traditional Democratic ideology, with commitments to unions, blacks, feminists, the poor, environmentalists and other liberal constituencies. But it also included new ideas from the party's younger generation, especially on economic policy. The platform did not call for major new social spending, making it economically more conservative than Democratic documents of the previous 50 years. But in its support for homosexual rights, the availability of abortions and other social issues, it was more liberal than earlier platforms.

The platform's central theme was an attack on the Reagan administration. The document indicted the president's record on topics ranging from budget deficits to civil rights to arms control, and it laid out what Democrats proposed as an alternative.

Besides giving a voice to the various interest groups that composed the Democratic Party, the 1984 platform also was a vehicle designed to unite the three presidential contenders. Negotiations continued up to the last minute on the five minority planks presented to the convention delegates July 17 by Jackson and Hart. But Mondale's forces demonstrated a firm grip on the delegates, soundly defeating Jackson planks on defense spending, "no first use" of nuclear weapons and runoff primaries. Mondale accepted Hart's plank restricting the use of U.S. troops overseas. Mondale also compromised on a Jackson plank outlining the party's affirmative action policy.

One person conspicuously absent from the convention platform debate was Ferraro, who chaired the committee that produced the document. Ferraro was to run the program July 17 — until Mondale asked her to be his running mate. When asked why Ferraro was not handling the plat-

form, Mondale quipped, "There's been a somewhat altered change in Mrs. Ferraro's professional plans over the next eight years."

The debate on the five minority planks was lackluster compared with the heated platform struggles between Carter and Kennedy at the 1980 convention. The first sign that Mondale would surmount the Jackson challenges came on the "no-first-use" plank. After a brief debate, it was defeated, with 1,405.7 delegates voting for it and 2,216.3 against. *(Chart, p. 252)*

As adopted by the platform committee June 23, the document said a Democratic president would "move toward" a policy in which the United States would not initiate a nuclear attack. Jackson supporters said it was "morally and militarily insane" even to consider using nuclear weapons, but Mondale's backers said the arms control language in the platform was strong enough. Also, Mondale argued that the North Atlantic Treaty Organization's conventional forces needed to be strengthened before the United States could adopt a "no-first-use" stance.

In contrast to the opposition to Jackson's national security planks, Hart's "peace plank" was readily accepted by Mondale. Delegates adopted it, 3,271.8 to 351.2. The plank delineated conditions under which a Democratic president would not "hazard American lives or engage in unilateral military involvement" abroad. It was dubbed the Persian Gulf—Central America plank, because the underlying message was that U.S. troops should not be sent to those regions unless American objectives were clear and diplomatic efforts had been exhausted.

Mondale's supporters opposed the plank when the platform committee considered it in June. At that time they said the plank would put a Democratic president "in a political or diplomatic straitjacket." But Mondale softened his stand in San Francisco. By accepting the plank, Mondale also hoped to distinguish Democratic foreign policy from Reagan's "saber-rattling" international agenda, as one Mondale supporter put it.

Jackson's two other minority reports dealt with issues of special interest to his black constituency: runoff primaries in the South and affirmative action. His call to abolish runoff primaries was defeated, but a compromise version of the affirmative action plank was accepted.

Ten Southern states used runoff primaries when no candidate received a majority in the first primary. Jackson claimed these second elections diluted minority voting strength because white voters often reverted to racial loyalty when a runoff choice was between a white and a black candidate. Supporters of second primaries argued that they prevented the nomination of fringe candidates who could receive a plurality in first-round primaries when more credible candidates split the vote. There also was strong sentiment against Jackson's plank from conservative Southerners who did not want the national party dictating their state election procedures.

Mondale's language pledged to eliminate discriminatory barriers to full voting rights. It also promised an indepth study of runoff primaries and other voting practices that could discriminate against minorities.

The other dispute was whether the platform should reject the use of quotas to overturn discrimination in employment and education. As adopted in June, the platform specifically rejected quotas but called for affirmative action goals and timetables to end discrimination in hiring, promotions and education.

Following are excerpts from the Democratic platform of 1984:

Budget Deficits. ...The Democratic Party is pledged to reducing these intolerable deficits. We will reassess defense expenditures; create a tax system that is both adequate and fair; control skyrocketing health costs without sacrificing quality of care; and eliminate other unnecessary expenditures.

We oppose the artificial and rigid Constitutional restraint of a balanced budget amendment. Further we oppose efforts to call a federal constitutional convention for this purpose.

Defense Spending. ...As Democrats, we believe in devoting the needed resources to ensure our national security. But military might cannot be measured solely by dollars spent. American military strength must be secured at an affordable cost. We will reduce the rate of increase in defense spending. Through careful reevaluation of proposed and existing weapons, we will stop throwing away money on unworkable or unnecessary systems; through military reform we will focus defense expenditure on the most cost-effective military policies. We will insist that our allies contribute fairly to our collective security, and that the Department of Defense reduces its scandalous procurement waste.

Tax Reform. We will cap the effect of the Reagan tax cuts for wealthy Americans and enhance the progressivity of our personal income tax code, limiting the benefits of the third year of the Reagan tax cuts to the level of those with incomes of less than $60,000. We will partially defer indexation while protecting average Americans. We will close loopholes, eliminate the preferences and write-offs, exemptions, and deductions which skew the code toward the rich and toward unproductive tax shelters. Given the fact that there has been a veritable hemorrhage of capital out of the federal budget, reflected in part by the huge budget deficit, there must be a return to a fair tax on corporate income. Under the Reagan Administration, the rate of taxation on corporations has been so substantially reduced that they are not contributing their fair share to federal revenues. We believe there should be a 15% minimum corporate tax. In addition, our tax code has facilitated the transfer of capital from the United States to investments abroad, contributing to plant closing without notice in many communities and loss of millions of jobs. We will toughen compliance procedures to reduce the $100 billion annual tax evasion....

Controlling Domestic Spending. Social Security is one of the most important and successful initiatives in the history of our country, and it is an essential element of the social compact that binds us together as a community. There is no excuse — as the Reagan Administration has repeatedly suggested — for slashing Social Security to pay for excesses in other areas of the budget. We will steadfastly oppose such efforts, now and in the future.

It is rather in the area of health care costs that reform is urgently needed. By 1988, Medicare costs will rise to $106 billion; by the turn of the century, the debt of the trust fund may be as great as $1 trillion. In the Republican view, the problem is the level of benefits which senior citizens and the needy receive. As Democrats, we will protect the interests of health care beneficiaries. The real problem is the growing cost of health care services.

We propose to control these costs, and to demand that the health care industry become more efficient in providing care to all Americans, both young and old. We will limit what health care providers can receive as reimbursement, and spur innovation and competition in health care delivery....

Education. We call for the immediate restoration of the cuts in funding of education programs by the Reagan Administration, and for a major new commitment to education. We will create a partnership for excellence among federal, state and local governments. We will provide incentives to local school districts to concentrate on science, math, communications and computer literacy; to provide access to advanced technology....

Vocational education should be overhauled to bring instructional materials, equipment, and staff up to date with the technology and practices for the workplace and target assistance to areas with large numbers of disadvantaged youth. We will pay special attention to the needs of the handicapped....

Bilingual education enables children to achieve full competence in the English language and the academic success necessary to their full participation in the life of our nation....

We will make certain that higher education does not become a luxury affordable only by the children of the rich. In our America, no qualified student should be deprived of the ability to go on to college because of financial circumstance.

Job Training. The Democratic Party must give our young people new skills and new hope; we must work hand in hand with the private sector if job training is to lead to jobs. Specifically, targeted efforts are needed to address the urgent problem of unemployment among minority teenagers. We must provide job training for those who have dropped out of school, and take every step to expand educational opportunity for those still in school. We must recognize the special needs of the over-age 50 worker and the displaced homemaker. Through education, training and retraining we must reduce these dangerously high levels of unemployment.

We must provide an opportunity for workers, including those dislocated by changing technologies, to adapt to new opportunities; we must provide workers with choices as to which skills they wish to acquire. We know that Americans want to work. We are committed to ensuring that meaningful job training is available — for our students, for housewives returning to the workplace, and for those displaced by changing patterns of technology or trade....

Housing. First, we must intensify our commitment to the adequate operation, management, and rehabilitation of the current inventory of government-assisted housing. This housing stock is not one, but the only option for the least fortunate among our lower income families and senior citizens. It is the right thing to do and it makes economic sense to preserve our own economic investment.

Second, we must maintain and expand the flow of mortgage capital. The American dream of home ownership will fall beyond the reach of this generation and future ones if government fails to help attract new sources of capital for housing....

Trade. ...The reality of the 1980s is that the international economy is the arena in which we must compete. The world economy is an integrated economy; the challenge for our political leadership is to assure that the new arena is in fact a fair playing field for American businesses and consumers. We are committed to pursuing industrial strategies that effectively and imaginatively blend the genius of the free market with vital government partnership and leadership. As Democrats, we will be guided by the following principles and policies.

— We need a vigorous, open and fair trade policy that builds America's competitive strength and that allows our nation to remain an advanced, diversified economy while promoting full employment and raising living standards in the United States and other countries of the world; opens overseas markets for American products; strengthens the international economic system; assists adjustment to foreign competition; and recognizes the legitimate interests of American workers, farmers and businesses.

— We will pursue international negotiations to open markets and eliminate trade restrictions, recognizing that the growth and stability of the Third World depends on its ability to sell its products in international markets. High technology, agriculture and other industries should be brought under the General Agreement on Trade and Tariffs. Moreover, the developing world is a major market for U.S. exports, particularly capital goods. As a result, the U.S. has a major stake in international economic institutions that support growth in the developing world.

— We recognize that the growth and development of the Third World is vital both to global stability and to the continuing expansion of world trade. The U.S. presently sells more to the Third World than to the European Community and Japan combined. If we do not buy their goods, they cannot buy ours, nor can they service their debt. Consequently, it is important to be responsive to the issues of the North/South dialogue such as volatile commodity prices, inequities in the functioning of the international financial and monetary markets, and removal of barriers to the export of Third World goods.

— If trade has become big business for the country, exports have become critical to the economic health of a growing list of American industries. In the future, national economic policy will have to be set with an eye to its impact on U.S. exports. The strength of the dollar, the nature of the U.S. tax system, and the adequacy of export finance all play a role in making U.S. exports internationally competitive.

— The United States continues to struggle with trade barriers that affect its areas of international strength. Subsidized export financing on the part of Europe and Japan has also created problems for the United States, as has the use of industrial policies in Europe and Japan. In some cases, foreign governments target areas of America's competitive strength. In other cases, industrial targeting has been used to maintain industries that cannot meet international competition — often diverting exports to the American market and increasing the burden of adjustment for America's import-competing industries. We will ensure that timely and effective financing can be obtained by American businesses through the Export-Import Bank, so that they can compete effectively against subsidized competitors from abroad.

— A healthy U.S. auto industry is essential to a strong trade balance and economy. That industry generates a large number of American jobs and both develops and consumes new technology needed for economic vitality. We believe it is a sound principle of international trade for foreign automakers which enjoy substantial sales in the United States to invest here and create jobs where their markets are. We also believe U.S. automakers need to maintain high volume small car production in the U.S. With the U.S. auto companies' return to profitability (despite continued unemployment in the auto sector), we urge expanded domestic investment to supply consumers with a full range of competitive vehicles. We support efforts by management and labor to improve auto quality and productivity, and to restrain prices.

— Where foreign competition is fair, American industry should compete without government assistance. Where competition is unfair, we must respond powerfully. We will use trade law and international negotiations to aid U.S. workers, farmers, and business injured by unfair trade practices.

Agriculture. . . . The Democratic Party pledges action. We must solve the immediate farm crisis through a combination of humanitarian aid programs abroad, aggressive promotion of farm exports, and a fair moratorium on

farm debt and foreclosure by federal credit agencies to family farm borrowers being forced out of business through no fault of their own, until a long-term program addressing the farm credit crisis can be put into place. Beginning next January with the writing of a new long-term farm bill, the Democratic Party pledges to rebuild a prosperous system of family farms and ranches. We will forge a new agreement on a farm and food policy that assures a fair deal for family farmers, consumers, taxpayers, conservationists, and others with a direct stake in the organizational structure of the food economy. . . .

Finally, we must reverse the annual decrease in the value and volume of U.S. farm exports which has occurred in each year of Ronald Reagan's term. Our farm exports are vital to the nation's prosperity and provide a major part of total farm income. We must restore the ability of U.S. farm products to compete in world markets, and increase worldwide demand for American agricultural products. To do this, we must make major changes in Ronald Reagan's economic policies, and correct his grossly distorted currency exchange rates, which have caused American competitiveness in international trade to decline. We must also resist efforts to lower commodity price supports; such action would only lower farm income without addressing the economic policies which are the root cause of declining competitiveness of U.S. farm products in world markets.

Energy. . . . America is blessed with abundant coal and natural gas, substantial supplies of oil, and plentiful reserves of uranium. Although very costly to process, vast supplies of oil shales and tar sands represent future energy sources. Significant contributions to our energy supply can be made by utilizing renewable resources and indigenous energy, such as active and passive solar systems, windpower, geothermal and ocean thermal power, and the recovery of gas from agricultural waste, coal mines, and garbage dumps. These proven energy sources, as well as more experimental energy systems, should be encouraged for the positive environmental and economic contribution they can make to our energy security.

We will insist on the highest possible standards of safety and protection of public health with respect to nuclear power, including siting, design, operation, evacuation plans, and waste disposal procedures. We will require nuclear power to compete fairly in the marketplace. We will reexamine and review all federal subsidies to the nuclear industry, including the Price-Anderson Act's limits on the liability of the industry which will be considered for reauthorization in the next Congress. A Democratic Administration will give the Nuclear Regulatory Commission the integrity, competence, and credibility it needs to carry out its mandate to protect the public health and safety. We will expand the role of the public in NRC procedures.

We will ensure that no offshore oil and gas exploration will be taken up that is inconsistent with the protection of our fisheries and coastal resources.

Hazardous Wastes. Thousands of dump sites across America contain highly dangerous poisons that can threaten the health and safety of families who live nearby or who depend on water supplies that could be contaminated by the poisons. Although Congress has established the Superfund for emergency cleanup of these dangerous sites, President Reagan refuses to use it vigorously. The Democratic Party is committed to enforcing existing laws, to dramatically increasing Superfund resources to clean up all sites that threaten public health, and to assuring that everyone whose health or property is damaged has a fair opportunity to force the polluters to pay for the damage. This increased support should be financed at least in part through new taxes on the generation of hazardous wastes, so companies have an economic incentive to reduce the volume and toxicity of their dangerous wastes. . . .

Clean Air and Water. The Democratic Party supports a reauthorized and strengthened Clean Air Act. Statutory requirements for the control of toxic air pollutants should be strengthened, with the environmental agency required to identify and regulate within three years priority air pollutants known or anticipated to cause cancer and other serious diseases. The Democratic Party calls for an immediate program to reduce sulfur dioxide emissions by 50% from 1980 levels within the next decade. Our effort should be designed to reduce environmental and economic damage from acid rain while assuring such efforts do not cause regional economic dislocations....

The Democratic Party is committed to strengthening the Clean Water Act to curb both direct and indirect discharge of toxic pollutants into our nation's waters, and supports a strengthened Environmental Protection Agency to assure help to American cities in providing adequate supplies of drinking water free of toxic chemicals and other contaminants....

Environmental Protection Agency. The Democratic Party opposes the Reagan Administration's budget cuts, which have severely hampered the effectiveness of our environmental programs. The Environmental Protection Agency should receive a budget that exceeds in real dollars the agency's purchasing power when President Reagan took office, since the agency's workload has almost doubled in recent years.

Public Lands. The Democratic Party believes in retaining ownership and control of our public lands, and in managing those lands according to the principles of multiple use and sustained yield, with appropriate environmental standards and mitigation requirements to protect the public interest. The Democratic Party supports the substantial expansion of the National Wilderness Preservation System, with designations of all types of ecosystems, including coastal areas, deserts, and prairies as well as forest and alpine areas.

Separation of Church and State. The current Administration has consistently sought to reverse in the courts or overrule by constitutional amendment a long line of Supreme Court decisions that preserve our historic commitment to religious tolerance and church/state separation. The Democratic Platform affirms its support of the principles of religious liberty, religious tolerance and church/state separation and of the Supreme Court decisions forbidding violation of those principles. We pledge to resist all efforts to weaken those decisions....

Affirmative Action. The Democratic Party firmly commits itself to protect the civil rights of every citizen and to pursue justice and equal treatment under the law for all citizens. The Party reaffirms its longstanding commitment to the eradication of discrimination in all aspects of American life through the use of affirmative action goals, timetables, and other verifiable measurements to overturn historic patterns and historic burdens of discrimination in hiring, training, promotions, contract procurement, education, and the administration of all Federal programs....

Equal Rights for Women. A top priority of a Democratic Administration will be ratification of the unamended Equal Rights Amendment.... The Democratic Party defines nondiscrimination to encompass both equal pay for equal work *and* equal pay for work of comparable worth, and we pledge to take every step, including enforcement of current law and amending the Constitution to include the unamended ERA, to close the wage gap.

Abortion. The Democratic Party recognizes reproductive freedom as a fundamental human right. We therefore oppose government interference in the reproductive decisions of Americans, especially government interference which denies poor Americans their right to privacy by funding or advocating one or a limited number of reproductive choices only....

Unions. This nation established a labor policy more than a generation ago whose purpose is to encourage collective bargaining and the right of workers to organize to obtain this goal. The Democratic Party is committed to extending the benefit of this policy to all workers and to removing the barriers to its administration. To accomplish this, the Democratic Party supports: the repeal of Section 14B of the National Labor Relations Act; labor law reform legislation; a prohibition on the misuse of federal bankruptcy law to prevent the circumvention of the collective bargaining process and the destruction of labor-management contracts; and legislation to allow building trades workers the same peaceful picketing rights currently afforded industrial workers....

Voting Rights Act. A Democratic President and Administration pledge to eliminate any and all discriminatory barriers to full voting rights, whether they be at-large requirements, second-primaries, gerrymandering, annexation, dual registration, dual voting or other practices. Whatever law, practice, or regulation discriminates against the voting rights of minority citizens, a Democratic President and Administration will move to strike it down....

Homosexual Rights. ... All groups must be protected from discrimination based on race, color, sex, religion, national origin, language, age, or sexual orientation. We will support legislation to prohibit discrimination in the workplace based on sexual orientation. We will assure that sexual orientation *per se* does not serve as a bar to participation in the military....

National Health Insurance. ... As Democrats we believe that quality health care is a necessity for everyone. We reaffirm our commitment to the long-term goal of comprehensive national health insurance and view effective health care cost containment as an essential step toward that goal. Health cost containment must be based on a strong commitment to quality of service delivery and care. We also pledge to return to a proper emphasis on basic scientific research and meeting the need for health professionals — areas devastated by the Reagan Administration.

Gun Control. We support tough restraints on the manufacture, transportation, and sale of snubnosed handguns, which have no legitimate sporting use and are used in a high proportion of violent crimes.

Arms Control. ... A Democratic President will propose an early summit with regular, annual summits to follow, with the Soviet leaders, and meetings between senior civilian and military officials, in order to reduce tensions and explore possible formal agreements.... A new Democratic Administration will implement a strategy for peace which makes arms control an integral part of our national security policy. We must move the world back from the brink of nuclear holocaust and set a new direction toward an enduring peace, in which lower levels of military spending will be possible. Our ultimate aim must be to abolish all nuclear weapons in a world safe for peace and freedom....

The first practical step is to take the initiative, on January 20, 1985, to challenge the Soviets to halt the arms race quickly. As President Kennedy successfully did in stopping nuclear explosions above ground in 1963, a Democratic President will initiate temporary, verifiable, and mutual moratoria, to be maintained for a fixed period during negotiations so long as the Soviets do the same, on the testing of underground nuclear weapons and anti-satellite weapons; on the testing and deployment of all weapons in space; on the testing and deployment of new strategic ballistic missiles now under development; and on the deployment of nuclear-armed, sea-launched cruise missiles.

These steps should lead promptly to the negotiation of a comprehensive, mutual and verifiable freeze on the testing, production, and deployment of all nuclear weapons. Building on this initiative, the Democratic President will update and resubmit the SALT II Treaty to the Senate for its advice and consent....

Defense Policy. The Reagan Administration measures military might by dollars spent. The Democratic Party seeks prudent defense based on sound planning and a realistic assessment of threats. In the field of defense policy, the Democratic Administration will work with our NATO and other allies to ensure our collective security, especially by strengthening our conventional defenses so as to reduce our need to rely on nuclear weapons, and to achieve this at increased spending levels, with funding to continue at levels appropriate to our collective security, with the firm hope that successful steps to reduce tensions and to obtain comprehensive and verifiable arms control agreements will guarantee our nation both military security and budgetary relief ... [and] oppose a peacetime military draft or draft registration....

A Democratic President will be prepared to apply military force when vital American interests are threatened, particularly in the event of an attack upon the United States or its immediate allies. But he or she will not hazard American lives or engage in unilateral military involvement:
- Where our objectives are not clear;
- Until all instruments of diplomacy and non-military leverage, as appropriate, have been exhausted;
- Where our objectives threaten unacceptable costs or unreasonable levels of military force;
- Where the local forces supported are not working to resolve the causes of conflict;
- Where multilateral or allied options for the resolution of conflict are available....

The Middle East. The Democratic Party believes that the security of Israel and the pursuit of peace in the Middle East are fundamental priorities for American foreign policy. Israel remains more than a trusted friend, a steady ally, and a sister democracy. Israel is strategically important to the United States, and we must enter into meaningful strategic cooperation.

The Democratic Party opposes this Administration's sales of highly advanced weaponry to avowed enemies of Israel, such as AWACS aircraft and Stinger missiles to Saudi Arabia. While helping to meet the legitimate defensive needs of states aligned with our nation, we must ensure Israel's military edge over any combination of Middle East confrontation states. The Democratic Party opposes any consideration of negotiations with the PLO, unless the PLO abandons terrorism, recognizes the state of Israel, and adheres to U.N. Resolutions 242 and 338.

Jerusalem should remain forever undivided with free access to the holy places for people of all faiths. As stated in the 1976 and 1980 platforms, the Democratic Party recognizes and supports the established status of Jerusalem as the capital of Israel. As a symbol of this stand, the U.S. Embassy should be moved from Tel Aviv to Jerusalem.

Central America. A Democratic President ... will approach Central American policy in the following terms:
— First, there must be unequivocal support for the Contadora process and for the efforts by those countries to achieve political solutions to the conflicts that plague the Central American region.
— Second, there must be a commitment on the part of the United States to reduce tensions in the region. We must terminate our support for the *contras* and other paramilitary groups fighting in Nicaragua. We must halt those U.S. military exercises in the region which are being conducted for no other real purpose than to intimidate or provoke the Nicaraguan government or which may be used as a pretext for deeper U.S. military involvement in the area. And, we must evidence our firm willingness to work for a demilitarized Central America, including the mutual withdrawal of all foreign forces and military advisers from the region. A Democratic President will

seek a multilateral framework to protect the security and independence of the region which will include regional agreements to bar new military bases, to restrict the numbers and sophistication of weapons being introduced into Central America, and to permit international inspection of borders. This diplomatic effort can succeed, however, only if all countries in Central America, including Nicaragua, will agree to respect the sovereignty and integrity of their neighbors, to limit their military forces, to reject foreign military bases (other than those provided for in the Panama Canal Treaties), and to deny any external force or power the use of their territories for purposes of subversion in the region. The viability of any security agreement for Central America would be enhanced by the progressive development of pluralism in Nicaragua. To this end, the elections proposed for November [1984] are important; how they are conducted will be an indication of Nicaragua's willingness to move in the direction of genuine democracy.
— Third, there must be a clear, concise signal to indicate that we are ready, willing and able to provide substantial economic resources, through the appropriate multilateral channels, to the nations of Central America, as soon as the Contadora process achieves a measure of success in restoring peace and stability in the region. In the meantime, of course, we will continue to provide humanitarian aid and refugee relief assistance. The Democratic Administration will work to help churches and universities which are providing sanctuary and assistance to Guatemalan, Haitian, and Salvadoran refugees, and will give all assistance to such refugees as is consistent with U.S. law.
— Fourth, a Democratic President will support the newly elected President of El Salvador in his efforts to establish civilian democratic control, by channeling U.S. aid through him and by conditioning it on the elimination of government-supported death squads and on progress toward his objectives of land reform, human rights, and serious negotiations with contending forces in El Salvador, in order to achieve a peaceful democratic political settlement of the Salvadoran conflict.
— Fifth, a Democratic President will not use U.S. armed forces in or over El Salvador or Nicaragua for the purpose of engaging in combat unless:
1) Congress has declared war or otherwise authorized the use of U.S. combat forces, or
2) the use of U.S. combat forces is necessary to meet a clear and present danger of attack upon the U.S., its territories or possessions or upon U.S. embassies or citizens, consistent with the War Powers Act.

Republicans

A jubilant Republican Party wound up its Aug. 20-23 convention in Dallas, Texas, confident that President Ronald Reagan and Vice President George Bush would be the "winning team" in November. With the ticket's renomination certain beforehand, the 33rd Republican National Convention was more a celebration than a business meeting of GOP activists. Behind the cheering and display of party unity, however, ran a current of dissent: Moderates, who were greatly outnumbered, voiced unhappiness with the party's direction and its platform.

During convention week, speaker after speaker criticized the Democrats, saying they represented a legacy of "malaise" from Jimmy Carter's administration and promised only a future of fear. Reagan, too, emphasized that theme in his 55-minute acceptance speech. To repeated interruptions of applause and cheers, he drew sharp differences between Republicans and Democrats and between himself and the Democratic presidential nominee, Walter F. Mondale. "The choices this year are not just between two different personalities or between two political parties," Reagan said. "They are between two different visions of the future, two fundamentally different ways of governing — their government of pessimism, fear and limits . . . or ours of hope, confidence and growth."

In his acceptance speech, Bush vigorously touted the Reagan administration's record. "Under this president, more lands have been acquired for parks, more for wilderness," he said. "The quality of life is better — and that's a fact." In foreign affairs, Bush said, ". . . there is new confidence in the U.S. leadership around the world. . . . Because our president stood firm in defense of freedom, America has regained respect throughout the world. . . ."

Speakers in previous sessions had sought to make the same points. They tried to link former vice president Mondale to the policies and problems of the administration in which he had served. "Carter-Mondale" became their shorthand for a list of evils: inflation, high interest rates, foreign policy failures and sagging national spirit.

GOP leaders also were anxious to portray the Democratic ticket and the party's leadership as out of step with most Democrats. They gave the spotlight to Democrats-turned-Republicans and issued one of their warmest welcomes to Jeane J. Kirkpatrick, the U.S. representative to the United Nations, whom one party leader referred to as an "enlightened Democrat." Kirkpatrick delivered a foreign policy speech during the opening session.

Yet this convention was clearly a Republican event, with the administration firmly in control and many of its members on hand. The party's leaders also made clear they were making a pitch for women voters, in response to the candidacy of Rep. Geraldine A. Ferraro, D-N.Y., Mondale's running mate.

Conditions outside the hall were almost as controlled as events inside. Police were ever present, but demonstrations by and large were tepid. One major reason was the record-breaking heat: It prompted some protesters to leave town and delegates and the press to stay in the air-conditioned indoors.

The opening ceremonies Aug. 20 were a mix of the patriotic and the political. About 50 young people carrying flags and wearing smocks decorated with red, white and blue elephants lined the interior of the hall; delegates then sang "The Star-Spangled Banner" and recited the pledge of allegiance.

The evening session was the GOP's "ladies' night." Four of the six speakers were women, including Katherine D. Ortega, the U.S. treasurer, and Kirkpatrick. Although Ortega was billed as the keynote speaker, it was Democrat Kirkpatrick who received the most sustained and vigorous applause from the delegates. Kirkpatrick had harsh words for her fellow Democrats, charging that they "treat foreign affairs as an afterthought." She asserted that the Carter administration "did not seem to notice much, care much, or do much" about a host of international problems.

The highlight of the Aug. 21 evening session was a speech by former president Gerald R. Ford. Delegates gave Ford and his wife, Betty, a rousing welcome. Ford wasted no time attacking the Democratic nominee, telling delegates: "Mondale wants this election to be a 'referendum on the future.' I can't blame him for wanting to forget the past, the four years of Carter-Mondale from 1977 through 1980. Who wants to remember four years of roaring inflation, skyrocketing interest rates and so-called 'malaise'?"

Before Reagan and Bush were renominated on the evening of Aug. 22, Sen. Barry Goldwater of Arizona addressed the convention. Goldwater, the party's presidential nominee in 1964, said he wanted to talk to the delegates about "freedom." He opened his speech with a slogan from his campaign 20 years earlier: "Let me remind you," he said, "extremism in the defense of liberty is no vice." Goldwater charged that the Democrats at their convention "turned their backs on our own heritage. Indeed, they would have us ashamed of our freedom and our ability to defend it. To me, the worst part was that they said nicer things about the Soviet Union than about our own military services."

The delegates moved to renominate Reagan and Bush. Although the outcome came as no surprise, there was an unusual joint roll call on the nominations, with Reagan receiving 2,233 votes and Bush, 2,231. *(Chart, p. 254)*

On the final night of the converntion, Reagan and Bush came to the hall to claim their nominations. With standing room only in the 17,000-seat arena, guests were lined up three deep in some places for an evening of balloons, speeches and patriotic music.

Earlier, after spirited debate, the 106-member platform committee adopted a 1984 campaign document that conformed in virtually all respects to the themes Reagan had sounded during his first term in office. The convention itself ratified the 30,000-word platform with no debate Aug. 21. On almost every aspect of public policy, the document stood in stark contrast to the platform the Democrats had adopted in San Francisco.

However, in its strong stand against tax increases and its criticism of the independent Federal Reserve Board, the Republican platform went further than the White House wanted. Administration representatives led by former transportation secretary Drew Lewis sought to soften the tax plank, but, while they succeeded in modifying some of the language, they were unable to alter it substantially. The tax section of the Republican platform pledged that the party would continue efforts to lower tax rates and would support tax reform that "will lead to a fair and simple tax system." The platform said the party believed that a "modified flat tax — with specific exemptions for such items as mortgage interest — is a most promising approach."

Taxes had mushroomed as an election issue when Democratic presidential nominee Walter F. Mondale said in his acceptance speech at the Democratic National Convention that, regardless of who won in November, tax increases would be necessary in 1985 to combat record federal budget deficits. Mondale also accused Reagan of having a secret plan to raise taxes.

Despite an hour-long debate, the GOP platform committee had refused to endorse the proposed Equal Rights Amendment (ERA) — which Reagan opposed — or compromise language stating that the Republicans respected those who supported the amendment. The committee also turned aside challenges by party moderates to language endorsing voluntary prayer in public schools and opposing federal financing for abortions under any circumstances. Some moderate delegates had considered trying to offer a minority plank on the ERA stating respect for differing Republican views on the issue. But moderates determined that they lacked support to bring a floor challenge and did not pursue this.

The platform included the following major points:

● Unqualified opposition to tax increases, which were dismissed as a "misguided effort to balance the budget."

● A call for passage by Congress of a constitutional amendment to require a balanced federal budget.

● Support for a constitutional convention to write a balanced budget amendment if Congress failed to act on the issue.

● Criticism of Federal Reserve Board policies as "destabilizing," and a suggestion that the gold standard "may be a useful mechanism" for achieving the goal of stable prices.

● Support for the administration's policy in Central America, specifically its support of the government in El Salvador.

● A pledge of party support for putting the United States in a superior military position in the world, although the term "military superiority" that appeared in the 1980 platform was not used in 1984.

● A call for repealing the windfall profits tax on oil.

● Support for abolition of the Department of Energy.

● Opposition to quotas to remedy discrimination because they "are the most insidious form of discrimination against the innocent."

● Support for a constitutional amendment to ban abortion and reaffirmation of a statement in the 1980 platform that Reagan should appoint federal judges who opposed abortion.

● Support for the right of students to engage in voluntary school prayer.

A multi-section chapter entitled "Security for the Individual" covered the environment, education, individual rights and "our constitutional system." On the environment, the platform said the party "endorses a strong effort to control and clean up toxic wastes." It asserted further that the GOP "supports the continued commitment to clean air and clean water. This support includes the implementation of meaningful clean air and clean water acts."

The 1980 platform had called for abolition of the Department of Education, which Congress created in 1979 at the urging of President Carter. The 1984 GOP platform stated that education was a "local function, a state responsibility and a federal concern. The federal role should be limited." However, it stopped short of urging that the federal department be disbanded.

In the section on individual rights, the platform devoted several paragraphs to GOP support for women's rights. In one section, the document stated, "President Reagan believes, as do we, that all members of our party are free to work individually for women's progress." At another point, the platform called for "assuring that women have equal opportunity, security and real choices for the promising future." But while it called for "equal pay for equal work," the document said that "with equal emphasis, we oppose the concept of 'comparable worth.' We believe that the free-market system can determine the value of jobs better than any government authority."

On the issue of abortion, the platform picked up language from the 1980 document advocating a constitutional amendment to ban abortion and supporting a ban on federal funding for abortion. An amendment that called for support of federal funding for abortions in the case of rape or incest was rejected.

In the foreign affairs area, the Republicans took dead aim at the Democrats. The platform declared that the Soviet Union's "globalist ideology and its leadership obsessed with military power make it a threat to freedom and peace on every continent. The Carter-Mondale Administration ignored that threat, and the Democratic candidates underestimate it today. The Carter-Mondale illusion that the Soviet leaders share our ideals and aspirations is not only false but a profound danger to world peace." The platform added that Republicans "reaffirm our belief that

Soviet behavior at the negotiating table cannot be divorced from Soviet behavior elsewhere."

This section was similar in tone to the 1980 platform, which declared "the premier challenge facing the United States, its allies and the entire globe is to check the Soviet Union's global ambitions." Although the 1984 campaign document did not contain the call for outright U.S. "military superiority" that appeared in the 1980 platform, the notion that the United States should be the superior power in the world ran through the chapter. The platform also stated that the Republicans "enthusiastically" supported the development of "non-nuclear, space-based defensive systems" designed to protect the United States from incoming missiles, as proposed by Reagan in 1983.

Following are excerpts from the Republican platform of 1984:

Economic Policy. Our most important economic goal is to expand and continue the economic recovery and move the nation to full employment without inflation. We therefore oppose any attempts to increase taxes, which would harm the recovery and reverse the trend to restoring control of the economy to individual Americans. We favor reducing deficits by continuing and expanding the strong economic recovery brought about by the policies of this Administration and by eliminating wasteful and unnecessary government spending....

To assure workers and entrepreneurs the capital required to provide jobs and growth, we will further expand incentives for personal saving. We will expand coverage of the Individual Retirement Account, especially to homemakers, and increase and index the annual limits on IRA contributions. We will increase the incentives for savings by moving toward the reduction of taxation of interest income. We will work for indexation of capital assets and elimination of the double taxation of dividends to increase the attractiveness of equity investments for small investors.

We oppose withholding on dividend and interest income. It would discourage saving and investment, create needless paperwork, and rob savers of their due benefits. A higher personal savings rate is key to deficit control. We therefore oppose any disincentives to thrift.

History has proven again and again that wage and price controls will not stop inflation. Such controls only cause shortages, inequities, and ultimately high prices. We remain firmly opposed to the imposition of wage and price controls.

We are committed to bringing the benefits of economic growth to all Americans. Therefore, we support policies which will increase opportunities for the poorest in our society to climb the economic ladder. We will work to establish enterprise zones in urban and rural America; we will work to enable those living in government-owned or subsidized housing to purchase their homes....

Tax Policy. The Republican Party pledges to continue our efforts to lower tax rates, change and modernize the tax system, and eliminate the incentive-destroying effects of graduated tax rates. We therefore support tax reform that will lead to a fair and simple tax system and believe a modified flat tax — with specific exemptions for such items as mortgage interest — is a most promising approach.

For families, we will restore the value of personal exemptions, raising it to a minimum of $2,000 and indexing to prevent further erosion. We will preserve the deduction for mortgage interest payments. We will propose an employment income exclusion to assure that tax burdens are not shifted to the poor....

Balancing the Budget. The congressional budget process is bankrupt. Its implementation has not brought spending under control, and it must be thoroughly reformed. We will work for the constitutional amendment requiring a balanced federal budget passed by the Republican Senate but blocked by the Democrat-controlled House and denounced by the Democrat Platform. If Congress fails to act on this issue, a constitutional convention should be convened to address only this issue in order to bring deficit spending under control.

The President is denied proper control over the federal budget. To remedy this, we support enhanced authority to prevent wasteful spending, including a line-item veto....

Monetary Policy. Just as our tax policy has only laid the groundwork for a new era of prosperity, reducing inflation is only the first step in restoring a stable currency. A dollar now should be worth a dollar in the future. This allows real economic growth without inflation and is the primary goal of our monetary policy.

The Federal Reserve Board's destabilizing actions must therefore stop. We need coordination between fiscal and monetary policy, timely information about Fed decisions, and an end to the uncertainties people face in obtaining money and credit. The Gold Standard may be a useful mechanism for realizing the Federal Reserve's determination to adopt monetary policies needed to sustain price stability.

Minimum Wage. There are still federal statutes that keep Americans out of the workforce. Arbitrary minimum wage rates, for example, have eliminated hundreds of thousands of jobs and, with them, the opportunity for young people to get productive skills, good work habits, and a weekly paycheck. We encourage the adoption of a youth opportunity wage to encourage employers to hire and train inexperienced workers....

Energy. We will complete America's energy agenda. Natural gas should be responsibly decontrolled as rapidly as possible so that families and businesses can enjoy the full benefits of lower prices and greater production, as with decontrolled oil. We are committed to the repeal of the confiscatory windfall profits tax, which has forced the American consumer to pay more for less and left us vulnerable to the energy and economic stranglehold of foreign producers.

While protecting the environment, we should permit abundant American coal to be mined and consumed. Environmentally sound development of oil and natural gas on federal properties (which has brought the taxpayers $20 billion in revenue in the last four years) should continue. We believe that as controls have been lifted from the energy marketplace, conservation and alternative sources of energy, such as solar, wind, and geothermal, have become increasingly cost-effective....

We now have a sound, long-term program for disposal of nuclear waste. We will work to eliminate unnecessary regulatory procedures so that nuclear plants can be brought on line quickly, efficiently, and safely. We call for an energy policy, the stability and continuity of which will restore and encourage public confidence in the fiscal stability of the nuclear industry.

We are committed to the termination of the Department of Energy. President Reagan has succeeded in abolishing that part which was telling Americans what to buy, where to buy it, and at what price — the regulatory part of DOE. Then he reduced the number of bureaucrats by 25 percent. Now is the time to complete the job.

Agriculture Policy. ... Republicans are very much aware of the devastating impact which high interest rates have had, and continue to have, on the viability of America's farmers and ranchers. We also realize that, unless interest rates decline significantly in the near future, the character of American agriculture and rural life will be tragically changed. For these reasons, we pledge to pursue every possible course of action, including the consideration of temporary interest rate reductions, to ensure the Ameri-

can farmer or rancher is not a patient that dies in the course of a successful economic operation....

Republicans are cognizant that there are many well-managed, efficient, farm and ranch operations which face bankruptcy and foreclosure. The foreclosures and resulting land sales will jeopardize the equity positions of neighboring farms and ranches, compounding financial problems in agriculture. Republicans pledge to implement comprehensive Farmers Home Administration and commercial farm and ranch debt restructuring procedures, including the establishment of local community farm and ranch finance committees, which shall advise borrowers, lenders, and government officials regarding debt restructuring alternatives and farmer and rancher eligibility....

Our farmers and ranchers must have full access to world markets and should not have to face unfair export subsidies and predatory dumping by other producing nations without redress. Republicans believe that unfair trade practices and non-tariff barriers are so serious that a comprehensive renegotiation of multilateral trade arrangements must be undertaken to revitalize the free, fair, and open trade critical to worldwide economic growth.

The Republican Party is unalterably opposed to the use of embargoes of grain or other agricultural products as a tool of foreign policy....

Trade Policy.... We are committed to a free and open international trading system. All Americans benefit from the free flow of goods, services and capital, and the efficiencies of a vigorous international market. We will work with all of our international trading partners to eliminate barriers to trade, both tariff and non-tariff. As a first step, we call on our trading partners to join in a new round of trade negotiations to revise the General Agreement on Tariffs and Trade in order to strengthen it. And we further call on our trading partners to join us in reviewing trade with totalitarian regimes....

Housing. We reaffirm our commitment to the federal-tax deductibility of mortgage interest payments. In the States, we stand with those working to lower property taxes that strike hardest at the poor, the elderly, and large families. We stand, as well, with Americans earning possession of their homes through "sweat-equity" programs.

We will, over time, replace subsidies and welfare projects with a voucher system, returning public housing to the free market.

Despite billions of dollars poured into public housing developments, conditions remain deplorable for many low-income Americans who live in them. These projects have become breeding grounds for the very problems they were meant to eliminate. Their dilapidated and crumbling structures testify to decades of corrupt or incompetent management by poverty bureaucrats.

Some residents of public housing developments have reversed these conditions by successfully managing their own housing units through creative self-help efforts.... The Republican Party therefore supports the development of programs which will lead to homeownership of public housing developments by current residents.

We strongly believe in open housing. We will vigorously enforce all fair housing laws and will not tolerate their distortion into quotas and controls.

Welfare.... Because there are different reasons for poverty, our programs address different needs and must never be replaced with a unitary income guarantee. That would betray the interests of the poor and the taxpayers alike.

We will employ the latest technology to combat welfare fraud in order to protect the needy from the greedy.

Whenever possible, public assistance must be a transition to the world of work, except in cases, particularly with the aged and disabled, where that is not appropriate. In other cases, it is long overdue.

Remedying poverty requires that we sustain and broaden economic recovery, hold families together, get government's hand out of their pocketbooks, and restore the work ethic.

Environment. ... The Republican Party endorses a strong effort to control and clean up toxic wastes. We have already tripled funding to clean up hazardous waste dumps, quadrupled funding for acid rain research, and launched the rebirth of the Chesapeake Bay.

...The Republican Party supports the continued commitment to clean air and clean water. This support includes the implementation of meaningful clean air and clean water acts. We will continue to offer leadership to reduce the threat to our environment and our economy from acid rain, while at the same time preventing economic dislocation. ...

We will be responsible to future generations, but at the same time, we must remember that quality of life means more than protection and preservation. Quality of life also means a good job, a decent place to live, accommodation for a growing population, and the continued economic and technological development essential to our standard of living. ...

Education. We believe that education is a local function, a State responsibility, and a federal concern. The federal role in education should be limited. It includes helping parents and local authorities ensure high standards, protecting civil rights, and ensuring family rights. ...

We have enacted legislation to guarantee equal access to school facilities by student religious groups. Mindful of our religious diversity, we reaffirm our commitment to the freedoms of religion and speech guaranteed by the Constitution of the United States and firmly support the rights of students to openly practice the same, including the right to engage in voluntary prayer in schools. ...

While much has been accomplished, the agenda is only begun. We must complete the block-grant process begun in 1981. We will return revenue sources to State and local governments to make them independent of federal funds and of the control that inevitably follows.

The Republican Party believes that developing the individual dignity and potential of disabled Americans is an urgent responsibility. To this end, the Republican Party commits itself to prompt and vigorous enforcement of the rights of disabled citizens, particularly those rights established under the Education for All Handicapped Children Act, Section 504 of the Rehabilitation Act of 1973, and the Civil Rights of Institutionalized Persons Act. We insist on the highest standards of quality for services supported with federal funds.

In education, as in other activities, competition fosters excellence. We therefore support the President's proposal for tuition tax credits. We will convert the Chapter One grants to vouchers, thereby giving poor parents the ability to choose the best schooling available. Discrimination cannot be condoned, nor may public policies encourage its practice. Civil rights enforcement must not be twisted into excessive interference in the education process.

Crime and Gun Control. ... Republicans respect the authority of State and local law enforcement officials. The proper federal role is to provide strong support and coordination for their efforts and to vigorously enforce federal criminal laws. By concentrating on repeat offenders, we are determined to take career criminals off the street.

The best way to deter crime is to increase the probability of detection and to make punishment certain and swift. As a matter of basic philosophy, we advocate preventive rather than merely corrective measures. Republicans advocate sentencing reform and secure, adequate prison construction. We concur with the American people's approval of capital punishment where appropriate and will ensure that it is carried out humanely.

Republicans will continue to defend the constitutional right to keep and bear arms. When this right is abused and armed felonies are committed, we believe in stiff, mandatory sentencing. ...

Discrimination. Just as we must guarantee opportunity, we oppose attempts to dictate results. We will resist efforts to replace equal rights with discriminatory quota systems and preferential treatment. Quotas are the most insidious form of discrimination: reverse discrimination against the innocent. We must always remember that, in a free society, different individual goals will yield different results. ...

Women's Rights. The Republican Party has an historic commitment to equal rights for women. Republicans pioneered the right of women to vote, and our party was the first major party to advocate equal pay for equal work, regardless of sex.

President Reagan believes, as do we, that all members of our party are free to work individually for women's progress. As a party, we demand that there be no detriment to that progress or inhibition of women's rights to full opportunity and advancement within this society.

With women comprising an increasing share of the work force, it is essential that the employment opportunities created by our free market system be open to individuals without regard to their sex, race, religion, or ethnic origin. We firmly support an equal opportunity approach which gives women and minorities equal access to all jobs — including the traditionally higher-paying technical, managerial, and professional positions — and which guarantees that workers in those jobs will be compensated in accord with the laws requiring equal pay for equal work under Title VII of the Civil Rights Act.

We are creating an environment in which individual talents and creativity can be tapped to the fullest, while assuring that women have equal opportunity, security, and real choices for the promising future. For all Americans, we demand equal pay for equal work. With equal emphasis, we oppose the concept of "comparable worth." We believe that the free market system can determine the value of jobs better than any government authority.

Protecting the Handicapped. We are committed to enforcing statutory prohibitions barring discrimination against any otherwise qualified handicapped individuals, in any program receiving federal financial assistance, solely by reason of their handicap.

We recognize the need for watchful care regarding the procedural due process rights of persons with handicaps both to prevent their placement into inappropriate programs or settings and to ensure that their rights are represented by guardians or other advocates, if necessary.

For handicapped persons who need care, we favor family-based care where possible, supported by appropriate and adequate incentives. We increased the tax credit for caring for dependents or spouses physically or mentally unable to care for themselves. We also provided a deduction of up to $1,500 per year for adopting a child with special needs that may otherwise make adoption difficult.

Labor Unions. We reaffirm the right of all individuals freely to form, join, or assist labor organizations to bargain collectively, consistent with State laws and free from unnecessary government involvement. We support the fundamental principle of fairness in labor relations. We will continue the Reagan Administration's "open door" policy toward organized labor and its leaders. We reaffirm our long-standing support for the right of States to enact "Right-to-Work" laws under section 14(b) of the Taft-Hartley Act.

Campaign Reform. The holding of public office in our country demands the highest degree of commitment to integrity, openness, and honesty by candidates running for all elective offices. Without such a commitment, public confidence rapidly erodes. Republicans, therefore, reaffirm our commitment to the fair and consistent application of financial disclosure laws. We will continue our support for full disclosure by all high officials of the government and candidates in positions of public trust. This extends to the financial holdings of spouses or dependents, of which the official has knowledge, financial interest, or benefit. We will continue to hold all public officials to the highest ethical standards and will oppose the inconsistent application of those standards on the basis of gender....

... In light of the inhibiting role federal election laws and regulations have had, Congress should consider abolishing the Federal Election Commission....

Abortion. The unborn child has a fundamental individual right to life which cannot be infringed. We therefore reaffirm our support for a human life amendment to the Constitution, and we endorse legislation to make clear that the Fourteenth Amendment's protections apply to unborn children. We oppose the use of public revenues for abortion and will eliminate funding for organizations which advocate or support abortions....

We applaud President Reagan's fine record of judicial appointments, and we reaffirm our support for the appointment of judges at all levels of the judiciary who respect traditional family values and the sanctity of innocent human life....

Foreign Policy. The supreme purpose of our foreign policy must be to maintain our freedom in a peaceful international environment in which the United States and our allies and friends are secure against military threats, and democratic governments are flourishing in a world of increasing prosperity.

This we pledge to our people and to future generations: we shall keep the peace by keeping our country stronger than any potential adversary....

Central America. Today, democracy is under assault throughout [Central America]. Marxist Nicaragua threatens not only Costa Rica and Honduras, but also El Salvador and Guatemala. The Sandinista regime is building the largest military force in Central America, importing Soviet equipment, Eastern bloc and PLO advisers, and thousands of Cuban mercenaries. The Sandinista government has been increasingly brazen in its embrace of Marxism-Leninism. The Sandinistas have systematically persecuted free institutions, including synagogue and church, schools, the private sector, the free press, minorities, and families and tribes throughout Nicaragua. We support continued assistance to the democratic freedom fighters in Nicaragua. Nicaragua cannot be allowed to remain a Communist sanctuary, exporting terror and arms throughout the region. We condemn the Sandinista government's smuggling of illegal drugs into the United States as a crime against American society and international law.

The heroic effort to build democracy in El Salvador has been brutally attacked by Communist guerrillas supported by Cuba and the Sandinistas. Their violence jeopardizes improvements in human rights, delays economic growth, and impedes the consolidation of democracy. El Salvador is nearer to Texas than Texas is to New England, and we cannot be indifferent to its fate. In the tradition of President Truman's postwar aid to Europe, President Reagan has helped the people of El Salvador defend themselves. Our opponents object to that assistance, citing concern for human rights. We share that concern, and more than that, we have taken steps to help curb abuses. We have firmly and actively encouraged human rights reform, and results have been achieved. In judicial reform, the murderers of the American nuns in 1980 have been convicted and sentenced; and in political reform, the right to vote has been exercised by 80 percent of the voters in the fair, open elections of 1982 and 1984. Most important, if the Communists seize power there, human rights will be extinguished, and tens of thousands will be driven from their homes. We, therefore, support the President in his determination that the Salvadoran people will shape their own future.

The Soviet Union. Stable and peaceful relations with the Soviet Union are possible and desirable, but they depend upon the credibility of American strength and determination.... Our policy of peace through strength encourages freedom-loving people everywhere and provides hope for those who look forward one day to enjoying the fruits of self-government....

We hold a sober view of the Soviet Union. Its globalist ideology and its leadership obsessed with military power make it a threat to freedom and peace on every continent.... Republicans reaffirm our belief that Soviet behavior at the negotiating table cannot be divorced from Soviet behavior elsewhere. Over-eagerness to sign agreements with the Soviets at any price, fashionable in the Carter-Mondale Administration, should never blind us to this reality. Any future agreement with the Soviets must require full compliance, be fully verifiable, and contain suitable sanctions for non-compliance.... We insist on full Soviet compliance with all treaties and executive agreements.

We seek to deflect Soviet policy away from aggression and toward peaceful international conduct. To that end, we will seek substantial reductions in nuclear weapons, rather than merely freezing nuclear weapons at their present dangerous level. We will continue multilateral efforts to deny advanced Western technology to the Soviet war machine.

Europe. ... We would be in mortal danger were Western Europe to come under Soviet domination. Fragmenting NATO is the immediate objective of the Soviet military buildup and Soviet subversion.... To keep the peace, the Reagan-Bush Administration is offsetting the Soviet military threat with the defensive power of the Alliance. We are deploying Pershing II and Cruise missiles. Remembering the Nazi Reich, informed voters on both sides of the Atlantic know they cannot accept Soviet military superiority in Europe.

The Middle East. ... Lebanon is still in turmoil, despite our best efforts to foster stability in that unhappy country. With the Syrian leadership increasingly subject to Soviet influence, and the Palestine Liberation Organization and its homicidal subsidiaries taking up residence in Syria, U.S. policy toward the region must remain vigilant and strong. Republicans reaffirm that the United States should not recognize or negotiate with the PLO so long as that organization continues to promote terrorism, rejects Israel's right to exist, and refuses to accept U.N. Resolutions 242 and 338.

The bedrock of that protection remains, as it has for over three decades, our moral and strategic relationship with Israel. We are allies in the defense of freedom. Israel's strength, coupled with United States assistance, is the main obstacle to Soviet domination of the region. The sovereignty, security, and integrity of the state of Israel are moral imperatives. We pledge to help maintain Israel's qualitative military edge over its adversaries.

We recognize that attacks in the U.N. against Israel are but thinly disguised attacks against the United States, for it is our shared ideals and democratic way of life that are their true target. Thus, when a U.N. agency denied Israel's right to participate, we withheld our financial support until that action was corrected. And we have worked behind the scenes and in public in other international organizations to defeat discriminatory attacks against our ally.

... We pledge continued support to Egypt and other moderate regimes against Soviet and Libyan subversion, and we look to them to contribute to our efforts for a long-term settlement of the region's destructive disputes.

We believe that Jerusalem should remain an undivided

city with free and unimpeded access to all holy places by people of all faiths.

China and Taiwan. . . . In keeping with the pledge of the 1980 Platform, President Reagan has continued the process of developing our relationship with the People's Republic of China. We commend the President's initiatives to build a solid foundation for the long-term relations between the United States and the People's Republic, emphasizing peaceful trade and other policies to promote regional peace. Despite fundamental differences in many areas, both nations share an important common objective: opposition to Soviet expansionism.

At the same time, we specifically reaffirm our concern for, and our moral commitment to, the safety and security of the 18 million people on Taiwan. We pledge that this concern will be constant, and we will continue to regard any attempt to alter Taiwan's status by force as a threat to regional peace. We endorse, with enthusiasm, President Reagan's affirmation that it is the policy of the United States to support and fully implement the provisions of the Taiwan Relations Act. In addition, we fully support self determination for the people of Hong Kong.

South Africa. . . . We reaffirm our commitment to the rights of all South Africans. Apartheid is repugnant. In South Africa, as elsewhere on the continent, we support well-conceived efforts to foster peace, prosperity, and stability.

International Organizations. . . . We will not support international organizations inconsistent with our interests. In particular, we will work to eliminate their funding of Communist states.

Prominent among American ideals is the sanctity of the family. Decisions on family size should be made freely by each family. We support efforts to enhance the freedom of such family decisions. We will endeavor to assure that those who are responsible for our programs are more sensitive to the cultural needs of the countries to which we give assistance.

As part of our commitment to the family and our opposition to abortion, we will eliminate all U.S. funding for organizations which in any way support abortion or research on abortion methods. . . .

Americans cannot count on the international organizations to guarantee our security or adequately protect our interests. The United States hosts the headquarters of the United Nations, pays a fourth of its budget, and is proportionally the largest contributor to most international organizations; but many members consistently vote against us. As Soviet influence in these organizations has grown, cynicism and the double standard have become their way of life.

This is why President Reagan announced that we will leave the worst of these organizations, UNESCO. He has put the U.N. on notice that the U.S. will strongly oppose the use of the U.N. to foster anti-semitism, Soviet espionage, and hostility to the United States. The President decisively rejected the U.N. Convention on the Law of the Sea and embarked instead on a dynamic national oceans policy, animated by our traditional commitment to freedom of the seas. That pattern will be followed with regard to U.N. meddling in Antarctica and outer space. Enthusiastically endorsing those steps, we will apply the same standards to all international organizations. We will monitor their votes and activities, and particularly the votes of member states which receive U.S. aid. Americans will no longer silently suffer the hypocrisy of many of these organizations.

Human Rights. The American people believe that United States foreign policy should be animated by the cause of human rights for all the world's peoples.

A well-rounded human rights policy is concerned with specific individuals whose rights are denied by governments of the right or left, and with entire peoples whose Communist governments deny their claim to human rights as

individuals and acknowledge only the "rights" derived from membership in an economic class. Republicans support a human rights policy which includes both these concerns. . . .

By focusing solely on the shortcomings of non-Communist governments, Democrats have missed the forest for the trees, failing to recognize that the greatest threat to human rights is the Communist system itself. . . .

Arms Control. The prospect for peace is excellent because America is strong again. America's defenses have only one purpose: to assure that our people and free institutions survive and flourish.

Our security requires both the capability to defend against aggression and the will to do so. Together, will and capability deter aggression. That is why the danger of war has grown more remote under President Reagan. . . .

We are proud of a strong America. Our military strength exists for the high moral purpose of deterring conflict, not initiating war. The deterrence of aggression is ethically imperative. . . . We reaffirm the principle that the national security policy of the United States should be based upon a strategy of peace through strength, a goal of the 1980 Republican Platform.

Maintaining a technological superiority, the historical foundation of our policy of deterrence, remains essential. In other areas, such as our maritime forces, we should continue to strive for qualitative superiority.

President Reagan committed our nation to a modernized strategic and theater nuclear force sufficient to deter attack against the United States and our allies, while pursuing negotiations for balanced, verifiable reductions of nuclear weapons under arms control agreements. . . .

We will continue to modernize our deterrent capability while negotiating for verifiable arms control. We will continue the policies that have given fresh confidence and new hope to freedom-loving people everywhere. . . .

The Soviet Union has rejected every invitation by President Reagan to resume talks, refusing to return unless we remove the Pershing II and Cruise missiles which we have placed in Europe at the request of our NATO allies. Soviet intransigence is designed to force concessions from the United States even before negotiations begin. We will not succumb to this strategy. The Soviet Union will return to the bargaining table only when it recognizes that the United States will not make unilateral concessions or allow the Soviet Union to achieve nuclear superiority. . . .

To deter Soviet violations of arms control agreements, the United States must maintain the capability to verify, display a willingness to respond to Soviet violations which have military significance, and adopt a policy whereby the defense of the United States is not constrained by arms control agreements violated by the Soviet Union.

We support the President's efforts to curb the spread of nuclear weapons and to improve international controls and safeguards over sensitive nuclear technologies. The President's non-proliferation policy has emphasized results, rather than rhetoric, as symbolized by the successful meeting of nuclear supplier states in Luxembourg in July of this year. We endorse the President's initiative on comprehensive safeguards and his efforts to encourage other supplier states to support such measures.

The first duty of government is to provide for the common defense. . . . We must continue to devote the resources essential to deter a Soviet threat — a threat which has grown and should be met by an improved and modernized U.S. defense capability. . . .

We will continue to strengthen our intelligence services. We will remove statutory obstacles to the effective management, performance, and security of intelligence sources and methods. We will further improve our ability to influence international events in support of our foreign policy objectives, and we will strengthen our counterintelligence facilities. . . .

. . . Republicans understood that our nuclear deterrent

forces are the ultimate military guarantor of America's security and that of our allies. That is why we will continue to support the programs necessary to modernize our strategic forces and reduce the vulnerabilities. This includes the earliest possible deployment of a new small mobile ICBM. . . .

President Reagan has launched a bold new Strategic Defense Initiative to defend against nuclear attack. We enthusiastically support President Reagan's Strategic Defense Initiative. We enthusiastically support the development of non-nuclear, space-based defensive systems to protect the United States by destroying incoming missiles.

Recognizing the need for close consultation with our allies, we support a comprehensive and intensive effort to render obsolete the doctrine of Mutual Assured Destruction (MAD). The Democratic Party embraces Mutual Assured Destruction. The Republican Party rejects the strategy of despair and supports instead the strategy of hope and survival.

We will begin to eliminate the threat posed by strategic nuclear missiles as soon as possible. Our only purpose (one all people share) is to reduce the danger of nuclear war. To that end, we will use superior American technology to achieve space-based and ground-based defensive systems as soon as possible to protect the lives of the American people and our allies.

1988 Conventions

Presidential Candidates

Michael S. Dukakis
Democrat

George Bush
Republican

Democrats

After years of internal warfare, the Democrats staged a remarkable show of unity at their 1988 national convention, held July 18-21 in Atlanta, Ga. For once, the issue-oriented activists who dominated the Democratic nominating process for nearly two decades subordinated their agendas to the goal of party victory, thus avoiding the self-inflicted wounds that had marred so many conventions since the 1968 Chicago debacle.

Massachusetts governor Michael S. Dukakis arrived at the convention with enough delegate support to ensure his nomination as the Democratic presidential candidate. Earlier, on July 12, he had announced his choice of running mate, Sen. Lloyd Bentsen of Texas.

The only risk of serious political conflict at the convention came from Jesse Jackson, who finished second in the delegate race. The convention approached with some of Jackson's hard-core supporters threatening boycotts, protest marches and walkouts. Some saw Dukakis' selection of Bentsen as a snub to Jackson. A breakthrough, however, came at a three-hour morning meeting July 18 of Dukakis, Jackson and Bentsen.

At an ensuing news conference, Dukakis praised Jackson for his voter-registration accomplishments and for his efforts to reach out to constituent groups beyond his black base. He then stated, "I want Jesse Jackson to play a major role in this campaign. . . . He is going to be involved actively, and fully."

Jackson appeared to concur, though he said he would follow through on his plan to have his name placed in nomination the night of July 20 and even joked that he was still hoping for a "Chicago miracle." But he did agree that he and Dukakis had discussed "a relationship of substance . . . the commitment to help build a team that will expand our party and carry us to victory in November." In answer to a reporter's question, he said he no longer sought the vice presidency.

With the Dukakis-Jackson agreement reached, the atmosphere inside Atlanta's Omni Coliseum on opening night of the convention was remarkably fraternal. Democratic National Committee Chairman Paul G. Kirk Jr. persistently underlined the theme of unity, pointing to the fact that the credentials and rules reports — sources of numerous battles and test votes at past conventions — had been previously ratified by the Dukakis and Jackson campaigns. Both were adopted without discussion.

Texas state treasurer Ann Richards delivered the keynote address, which centered on a critique of the Republicans' alleged lack of concern for the interests of working

Americans. While Richards did not outline a bold new Democratic vision, she won widespread praise for her folksy, personalized delivery and her trademark sense of humor.

But any excitement that Richards generated was sapped by a series of less-than-enthralling events that followed, which culminated in an address by former president Jimmy Carter. Although the convention gave Carter an enthusiastic greeting — symbolic of the resurrection of his image within the party — many delegates became distracted during his litany of Democratic party virtues.

In the afternoon of the second day of the convention, the candidates' campaigns eliminated their last major grounds for argument — the minority planks of the Democratic platform — with a minimum of rancor.

In the debate on what the Jackson campaign called the "fair tax" plank, Manhattan Borough president David Dinkins said that "the rich and the corporations" received the bulk of the Reagan administration tax cuts, which he blamed for the large federal deficits. He echoed Jackson's line that, in closing the deficit, those tax-cut beneficiaries would now "have to pay for the party."

But Denver mayor Federico Pena called for delegates to reject the plank, warning that its passage would be campaign fodder for Republicans, who persistently portrayed the Democrats as the "tax-and-spend" party. The measure was defeated by a delegate vote of 1,091.5 to 2,499. *(Chart, p. 255)*

More emotion was expressed over the nuclear-strategy plank, with Jackson supporters waving placards and changing, "No first use!" Supporters of the plank said it would show Democratic commitment to world peace. But Dukakis supporters, while expressing solidarity with the cause of nuclear disarmament, said the defense strategy that called for use of nuclear weapons in the event of an invasion of Western Europe was a bedrock of the NATO alliance. They also said that, should Dukakis be elected president, the plank could deprive him of a key tool to force the Soviets to the bargaining table.

The minority plank was defeated, 1,220.59 to 2,474.13. *(Chart, p. 255)*

The most divisive issue was that of Palestinian rights. Arab-American activist James Zogby said that while they had agreed not to bring the subject to a vote, supporters of Palestinian self-determination had won a victory by getting the party to debate the issue openly.

Without debate the delegates adopted a compromise package of nine other amendments pressed by the Jackson camp and accepted by Dukakis. These embodied much of the spirit and some of the specifics that Jackson had tried to insert into the platform all along — a denunciation of aid to "irregular" forces in Central America, a national health program, sharply higher spending for education and a moratorium on missile flight testing.

Notwithstanding the compromise language inserted into the platform at Jackson's insistence, the overall platform debate represented a victory for the Dukakis forces. From the beginning, they had been bent on keeping the platform a document of general party themes, free of the kinds of commitments to programs and constituency groups that had aided past Republican efforts to label the Democrats the "party of special interests."

If the afternoon session was symbolic of the Democratic party's effort to moderate its national image, the evening session was a tribute to the liberalism that had been the dominant party thread for two decades. The

schedule featured leading figures of the party's liberal wing and was capped by an electrifying speech by Jackson.

Edward M. Kennedy, introduced by his nephew John F. Kennedy Jr., warmed up the crowd with rousing political rhetoric. The Massachusetts senator accused Bush of "burying his head in his hands and hiding from the record of Reagan-Bush mistakes." Kennedy then listed a series of issues — Iran-contra, the Noriega drug connection, domestic budget cuts, civil rights — on which he said the Reagan administration had made wrong choices, following each example with the refrain, "Where was George?" The delegates spontaneously picked up the slogan as a chant.

In anticipation of Jackson's speech, delegates, guests, reporters and photographers filled the narrow aisles of the arena. The Omni was so packed that convention officials were compelled to close the doors at the suggestion of the fire marshal, shutting out a number of infuriated delegates and media representatives in the process.

Jackson entered the auditorium at 10:55 p.m. to a roaring ovation and a sea of red-and-white "Jesse!" placards. As an expression of unity, virtually all of the Dukakis delegates had kept their banners out of sight, and many had given up their passes so Jackson alternates could be on the floor to cheer.

Many party professionals had wondered whether Jackson's address might become a vehicle for venting whatever resentment lingered from the rift over the running-mate selection. But while his speech stopped short of an outright endorsement of Dukakis, Jackson expressed his solidarity with the Democratic effort to regain the White House. He praised Dukakis for resisting the "temptation to stoop to demagoguery" and said he had demonstrated "a good mind, fast at work, with steel nerves, guiding his campaign out of the crowded field without appeal to the worst in us."

In his 55-minute speech, Jackson invoked the heroes of the civil rights movement, including Martin Luther King Jr., and briefly shared the stage with Rosa Parks, heroine of the 1955 Montgomery, Ala., bus boycott. He said that his campaign was a historic culmination of earlier black struggles. "As a tribute to the endurance, the patience, the courage of our forefathers and mothers . . . tomorrow night my name will go into nomination for the presidency of the United States of America," Jackson declared.

Jackson called for liberal and conservative Democrats to find "common ground" of agreement on issues of social welfare, human rights and world peace; for U.S. allies to pay a greater share of their defense burden so that American resources could be shifted to housing, health care and other social needs; for the government to act to protect the family farm and to promote domestic oil production; and for youths to avoid the temptations of illegal drugs.

Jackson received the most emotional response with a paean to the struggles of the low-income working American. The speech was climaxed by Jackson's call for Americans to "never surrender" to poverty, drugs, malnutrition, inequality, disease or physical handicaps.

The evening session of the next day, July 20, featured the presidential nominating process and balloting. Jackson's name was placed in nomination by a trio intended to symbolize the candidate's concept of the "Rainbow Coalition." International Association of Machinists President William Winpisinger, who is white, made the nominating speech; he was seconded by state senator Olga Mendez of New York, a Puerto Rican, and by black state representative Maxine Waters of California.

Arkansas governor Bill Clinton was the personal choice

of Dukakis, his friend and fellow governor, to be his nominator. In a speech that will be remembered for its duration — 35 minutes — rather than its content, he emphasized Dukakis' personal qualities and praised Dukakis as a political leader, describing him as "a man with vision, a shining vision for this country."

The roll call, marked by the usual "Great State of . . ." boosterism, went as predetermined by the primary-and-caucus process. The one surprise came from Minnesota, where three anti-abortion delegates registered support for Rep. Richard H. Stallings, Idaho, who shared their opposition to abortion.

The only apparent suspense was which state would put Dukakis over the 2,082-vote total he needed to clinch the nomination. But the Dukakis campaign — cognizant of California's importance in November — had even taken care of that detail. They arranged for several delegations to pass on the first call to ensure that California would have the honor. The final tally was Dukakis 2,876.25 delegate votes; Jackson, 1,218.5. *(Chart, p. 255)*

Following the roll call, Speaker Willie Brown Jr., of the California House and Jackson's national campaign chairman, announced that Jackson had phoned to ask that Dukakis be endorsed by acclamation. A near-unanimous chorus of "ayes" followed.

Party officials created a Hollywood-style show for the convention finale July 21. The schedule was crafted with prime-time television foremost in mind, and, in an unusual achievement for the traditionally unruly Democrats, the program went off like clockwork.

Rep. Dan Rostenkowski, Ill., gave a rousing nominating speech for Bentsen. He got his strongest response with a passage urging working-class Americans to "come home to your party . . . the party that has contributed so much to our social progress."

Following Rostenkowski, Sen. Thomas A. Daschle, S.D., lauded Bentsen's commitment to rural America. The delegates then gave a long ovation to former Texas Rep. Barbara C. Jordan, a major figure in the 1974 Judiciary Committee impeachment hearings on President Richard Nixon and the 1976 Democratic convention keynoter.

Jordan praised her longtime ally Bentsen in remarks seemingly aimed at Jackson delegates. Saying that it was a mistake to label him a conservative, Jordan said, "Lloyd Bentsen . . . believes in the principles of the Democratic party just like you do."

The compelling need for a defense of Bentsen already had been removed, though. Talk of a challenge to his nomination, so rife early in the week, had been silenced by the Dukakis-Jackson agreement and the ensuing push for unity. Jackson selected Rep. Mickey Leland of Texas to call for Bentsen's nomination by acclamation. The motion was passed overwhelmingly, with just a scattering of "no" votes.

Bentsen made a restrained address, true to his image as a dignified, formal and somewhat patrician figure. Shortly into his acceptance speech, Bentsen extended an olive branch to the Jackson supporters who had been deeply offended by Dukakis's vice presidential decision. He told the convention that "equality of opportunity is the ultimate civil right." He then hailed Jackson for "leadership and achievements [that] transcend pride of party and inspire a nation."

Bentsen received his strongest applause by calling for a plant-closing-notification law. He indicted the Reagan presidency as "an eight-year coma in which slogans were confused with solutions and rhetoric passed for reality."

Invoking a familiar Democratic theme, he said that many Americans had missed out on the prosperity of the Reagan years. He accused Reagan of financing prosperity by writing "hot checks for $200 billion a year." Dukakis, Bentsen said, was "talking about putting the American dream," including home ownership and a college education, "back in the reach of all the American people."

Though his speech was no rouser, Bentsen, who defeated Bush in a 1970 Senate contest, left the podium to a chant of "Beat Bush Again."

A series of theatrical touches primed the delegates for Dukakis. A specially commissioned musical piece, written by Boston Pops Orchestra Director John Williams and conducted by Dukakis's father-in-law, Harry Ellis Dickson, was performed. Dukakis was then introduced by his cousin, Olympia Dukakis, an Oscar-winning actress and New Jersey delegate.

Dukakis described himself as a product of the American dream. He paid tribute to his immigrant parents, and tears welled in his eyes when he talked about how proud his father would have been of his son, and of his adopted country. He cited individuals who represented America's cultural diversity, including Jackson.

Dukakis continued to feed the convention's celebratory mood, stating that "the Reagan era is over, and a new era is about to begin." He said it is time "to exchange voodoo economics for can-do economics," adding, "This election isn't about ideology. It's about competence."

Throughout the speech, Dukakis managed to hit buttons that energized the partisan audience, while avoiding contentious issues, such as tax increases and abortion, that had hurt the Democrats in recent presidential elections. The issues he emphasized were more popular Democratic stands on education, universal health care and plant-closing notification.

Dukakis's speech was interrupted several times by chants from the crowd. When he referred to Bush's failure to intercede to stop the Iran arms sales, the convention delegates reprised their "Where was George?" theme. And in a wave of optimism not seen since the post-Watergate 1976 convention, the delegates chanted, "We're gonna win."

Following are excerpts from the Democratic platform of 1988:

Economy. . . . We believe that all Americans have a fundamental right to economic justice in a stronger, surer national economy, an economy that must grow steadily without inflation, that can generate a rising standard of living for all and fulfill the desire of all to work in dignity up to their full potential in good health with good jobs at good wages, an economy that is prosperous in every region, from coast to coast, including our rural towns and our older industrial communities, our mining towns, our energy producing areas and the urban areas that have been neglected for the past seven years.

Employment, Child Care. We believe that, as a first-rate world power moving into the 21st century, we can have a first-rate full employment economy, with an indexed minimum wage that can help lift and keep families out of poverty, with training and employment programs — including child care and health care — that can help people move from welfare to work, with portable pensions and an adequate Social Security System, safeguarded against emasculation and privatization, that can help assure a comfortable and fulfilling old age, with opportunities for voluntary national public service, above and beyond current services, that can enrich our communities, and with all workers assured the protection of an effective law that guarantees their rights to organize, join the union of their choice, and bargain collectively with their employer, free from anti-union tactics....

We believe that Government should set the standard in recognizing that worker productivity is enhanced by the principle of pay equity for working women and no substandard wage competition for public contracts; by family leave policies that no longer force employees to choose between their jobs and their children or ailing parents; by safe and healthy work places, now jeopardized by seven callous years of lowered and unenforced occupational safety standards for American workers; and by major increases in assistance making child care more available and affordable to low and middle income families, helping states build a strong child care infrastructure, setting minimum standards for health, safety, and quality, and thereby enabling parents to work and their children to get an early start on their education and personal fulfillment. We believe that the strength of our families is enhanced by programs to prevent abuse and malnutrition among children, crime, dropouts and pregnancy among teenagers and violence in the family; by aggressive child support enforcement; and by emphasizing family preservation and quality foster care. We further believe that our nation faces a crisis of under-investment in our children, particularly in the early years of life. Strong, healthy babies with early opportunities that foster intellectual, emotional and physical growth begin school with an enhanced foundation for learning. There are few better investments for this country than prenatal care, infant nutrition and preschool education, and there are few more successful programs than WIC, Head Start, and prenatal care.

Trade. ... America needs more trade, fair trade, an administration willing to use all the tools available to better manage our trade in order to export more American goods and fewer American jobs, an administration willing to recognize in the formulation and enforcement of our trade laws that workers' rights are important human rights abroad as well as at home, and that advance notice of plant closings and major layoffs is not only fundamentally right but also economically sound.... [W]e ... can and must improve our competitiveness in the world economy, using our best minds to create the most advanced technology in the world through a greater commitment to civilian research and development and to science, engineering and mathematics training, through more public-private and business-labor cooperation and mutual respect, through more intergovernmental partnerships, and through a better balance between fiscal and monetary policy and between military and civilian research and development. We further believe in halting such irresponsible corporate conduct as unproductive takeovers, monopolistic mergers, insider trading, and golden parachutes for executives by reinvigorating our anti-trust and securities laws, reviewing large mergers, and discouraging short-term speculation taking place at the expense of long-term investment.

Education. ... [T]he education of our citizens, from Head Start to institutions of higher learning, deserves our highest priority.... We pledge to better balance our national priorities by significantly increasing federal funding for education. We believe that this nation needs to invest in its children on the front side of life by expanding the availability of pre-school education for children at risk; to invest in its teachers through training and enrichment programs, including a National Teacher Corps to recruit teachers for tomorrow, especially minorities, with scholarships today; to commit itself for the first time to the principle that no one should be denied the opportunity to attend college for financial reasons; to ensure equal access

to education by providing incentives and mechanisms for the equalization of financing among local school districts within each state; to reverse cuts made in compensatory reading, math and enrichment services to low income children; and to expand support for bilingual education, historically Black and Hispanic institutions, the education of those with special needs, the arts and humanities, and an aggressive campaign to end illiteracy.

Drugs. ... [I]llegal drugs pose a direct threat to the security of our nation from coast to coast.... [E]very arm and agency of government at every federal, state and local level — including every useful diplomatic, military, educational, medical and law enforcement effort necessary — should at long last be mobilized and coordinated with private efforts under the direction of a National Drug "Czar" to halt both the international supply and the domestic demand for illegal drugs now ravaging our country; and that the legalization of illicit drugs would represent a tragic surrender in a war we intend to win. We believe that this effort should include comprehensive programs to educate our children at the earliest ages on the dangers of alcohol and drug abuse, readily available treatment and counseling for those who seek to address their dependency, the strengthening of vital interdiction agencies such as the U.S. Coast Guard and Customs, a summit of Western Hemispheric nations to coordinate efforts to cut off drugs at the source, and foreign development assistance to reform drug-based economies by promoting crop substitution.

Criminal Justice. ... [T]he federal government should provide increased assistance to local criminal justice agencies, enforce a ban on "cop killer" bullets that have no purpose other than the killing and maiming of law enforcement officers, reinforce our commitment to help crime victims, and assume a leadership role in securing the safety of our neighborhoods and homes.

Individual Rights. ... [W]e honor our multicultural heritage by assuring equal access to government services, employment, housing, business enterprise and education to every citizen regardless of race, sex, national origin, religion, age, handicapping condition or sexual orientation; that these rights are without exception too precious to be jeopardized by Federal Judges and Justice Department officials chosen during the past seven years — by a political party increasingly monolithic both racially and culturally — more for their unenlightened ideological views than for their respect for the rule of law.... [W]e must work for the adoption of the Equal Rights Amendment to the Constitution; that the fundamental right of reproductive choice should be guaranteed regardless of ability to pay; that our machinery for civil rights enforcement and legal services to the poor should be rebuilt and vigorously utilized; and that our immigration policy should be reformed to promote fairness, non-discrimination and family reunification and to reflect our constitutional freedoms of speech, association and travel. We further believe that the voting rights of all minorities should be protected, the recent surge in hate violence and negative stereotyping combatted, the discriminatory English-only pressure groups resisted, our treaty commitments with Native Americans enforced by culturally sensitive officials, and the lingering effects of past discrimination eliminated by affirmative action, including goals, timetables, and procurement set-asides.

Housing. ... [T]he housing crisis of the 1980s must be halted — a crisis that has left this country battered by a rising tide of homelessness unprecedented since the Great Depression, by a tightening squeeze on low and moderate income families that is projected to leave seven million people without affordable housing by 1993, and by a bleak outlook for young working families who cannot afford to buy their first home.... We believe that homelessness — a national shame — should be ended in America; that the supply of affordable housing should be expanded in order to avoid the projected shortfall; that employer-assisted housing and development by community-based non-profit organizations should be encouraged; that the inventory of public and subsidized housing should be renovated, preserved and increased; that foreclosed government property should be restored to productive use; and that first-time home buyers should be assisted.

Infrastructure. . . . [W]e can rebuild America, creating jobs at good wages through a national reinvestment strategy to construct new housing, repair our sewers, rebuild our roads and replace our bridges. We believe that we must pursue needed investment through innovative partnerships and creative financing mechanisms such as a voluntary program to invest a portion of public and private pension funds as a steady source of investment capital by guaranteeing security and a fair rate of return and assuring sound project management.

Health Care. . . . We believe that all Americans should enjoy access to affordable, comprehensive health services for both the physically and mentally ill, from prenatal care for pregnant women at risk to more adequate care for our Vietnam and other veterans, from well-baby care to childhood immunization to Medicare; that a national health program providing federal coordination and leadership is necessary to restrain health care costs while assuring quality care and advanced medical research; that quality, affordable, long-term home and health care should be available to all senior and disabled citizens, allowing them to live with dignity in the most appropriate setting; that an important first step toward comprehensive health services is to ensure that every family should have the security of basic health insurance; and that the HIV/AIDS epidemic is an unprecedented public health emergency requiring increased support for accelerated research on, and expedited FDA approval of, treatments and vaccines, comprehensive education and prevention, compassionate patient care, adoption of the public health community consensus on voluntary and confidential testing and counseling, and protection of the civil rights of those suffering from AIDS or AIDS-Related Complex or testing positive for the HIV antibody.

Environment. . . . [P]ollution must be stopped at the source by shifting to new, environmentally sound manufacturing and farming technologies. . . . [T]he federal government must promote recycling as the best, least costly way to solve the trash crisis, aggressively enforce toxic waste laws and require polluters to be responsible for future clean-up costs. . . . [T]his nation must redouble its efforts to provide clean waterways, sound water management and safe drinkable ground water throughout the country. . . . [O]ur national parks, forests, wildlife refuges, and coastal zones must be protected and used only in an environmentally sound manner. . . . [A]ll offshore oil drilling in environmentally sensitive areas should be opposed. . . . [R]egular world environmental summits should be convened by the United States to address the depletion of the ozone layer, the "greenhouse effect," the destruction of tropical forests and other global threats and to create a global action plan for environmental restoration.

Agriculture. . . . [A]ll Americans, producers and consumers alike, benefit when food and fiber are produced not by a few large corporations and conglomerates but by hundreds of thousands of family farmers obtaining a fair price for their product. . . . [A] workable agricultural policy should include supply management, reasonable price supports, soil conservation and protection of rural water quality, credit and foreclosure relief, the return of federally held foreclosed lands to minority, beginning and restarting farmers, the development of new uses and markets for American farm products, improved disaster relief, and the revitalization of rural America through new sources of capital for

rural business and new federal support for rural health care, housing, education, water supply and infrastructure. . . .

Energy. We believe that a balanced, coherent energy policy, based on dependable supplies at reasonable prices, is necessary to protect our national security, ensure a clean environment, and promote stable economic growth and prosperity, both nationally and in our energy producing regions; that the inevitable transition from our present, nearly total dependence on increasingly scarce and environmentally damaging non-renewable sources to renewable sources should begin now; that such a policy includes increased cooperation with our hemispheric neighbors, filling the Strategic Petroleum Reserve, promoting the use of natural gas, methanol and ethanol as alternative transportation fuels, encouraging the use of our vast natural gas and coal reserves while aggressively developing clean coal technology to combat acid rain, and providing targeted new incentives for new oil and gas drilling and development, for the development of renewable and alternative sources of energy, and for promotion of energy conservation. We believe that with these changes the country could reduce its reliance on nuclear power while insisting that all plants are safe, environmentally sound, and assured of safe waste disposal.

Voting Rights. . . . [T]his country's democratic processes must be revitalized: by securing universal, same day and mail-in voter registration as well as registration on the premises of appropriate government agencies; by preventing the misuse of at-large elections, the abuse of election day challenges and registration roll purges, any undercounting in the national census, and any dilution of the one-person, one-vote principle; by ending discrimination against public employees who are denied the right to full political participation; by supporting statehood for the District of Columbia; by treating the offshore territories under our flag equitably and sensitively under federal policies, assisting their economic and social development and respecting their right to decide their future in their relationship with the United States; by empowering the commonwealth of Puerto Rico with greater autonomy within its relationship with the United States to achieve the economic, social and political goals of its people, and by giving it just and fair participation in federal programs; by assuring and pledging the full and equal access of women and minorities to elective office and party endorsement; and by minimizing the domination and distortion of our elections by moneyed interests. . . .

Foreign Policy. We believe in a clear-headed, tough-minded, decisive American foreign policy that will reflect the changing nature of threats to our security and respond to them in a way that reflects our values and the support of our people, a foreign policy that will respect our Constitution, our Congress and our traditional democratic principles and will in turn be respected for its quiet strength, its bipartisan goals, and its steadfast attention to the concerns and contributions of our allies and international organizations. We believe that we must reassume a role of responsible active international leadership based upon our commitment to democracy, human rights and a more secure world; that this nation, as the world power with the broadest global interests and concerns, has a greater stake than any in building a world at peace and governed by law; that we can neither police the world nor retreat from it; and that to have reliable allies we must be a reliable ally.

Defense. We believe that our national strength has been sapped by a defense establishment wasting money on duplicative and dubious new weapons instead of investing more in readiness and mobility; that our national strength will be enhanced by more stable defense budgets and by a commitment from our allies to assume a greater share of the costs and responsibilities required to maintain peace and liberty; and that as military spending and priorities change, government should encourage the conversion of affected military facilities and the retraining of workers to facilitate the creation of new forms of communication, space development and new peacetime growth and productivity.

We believe in an America that will promote peace and prevent war ... by maintaining a stable nuclear deterrent sufficient to counter any Soviet threat, by standing up to any American adversary whenever necessary and sitting down with him whenever possible, by making clear our readiness to use force when force is required to protect our essential security commitments, by testing the intentions of the new Soviet leaders about arms control, emigration, human rights and other issues, and by matching them not merely in rhetoric but in reciprocal initiatives and innovation, which takes advantage of what may be the greatest opportunity of our lifetime to establish a new, mutually beneficial relationship with the Soviet Union, in which we engage in joint efforts to combat environmental threats, explore peaceful uses of space and eradicate disease and poverty in the developing world, and in a mutual effort to transform the arms race that neither side can win into a contest for people's minds, a contest we know our side will win.

Arms Control. We believe in following up the INF [intermediate-range nuclear force] Treaty, a commendable first step, with mutual, verifiable and enforceable agreements that will make significant reductions in strategic weapons in a way that diminishes the risk of nuclear attack by either superpower; reduce conventional forces to lower and equivalent levels in Europe, requiring deeper cuts on the Warsaw Pact side; ban chemical and space weapons in their entirety; promptly initiate a mutual moratorium on missile flight testing and halt all nuclear weapons testing while strengthening our efforts to prevent the spread of these weapons to other nations before the nightmare of nuclear terrorism engulfs us all.

International Relations. We believe in an America that recognizes not only the realities of East-West relations, but the challenges and opportunities of the developing world; that will support and strengthen international law and institutions, promote human and political rights and measure them by one yardstick, and work for economic growth and development. We believe that we must provide leadership, compassion and economic assistance to those nations stunted by overwhelming debt, deprivation and austerity, and that we must work to promote active agreements between developing and industrial countries, and the major public and commercial lenders, to provide debt relief and rekindle and sustain economic growth and democracy in Latin America, Asia, and the poorest continent, Africa, which deserves special attention. We further believe that we must enlist the trade surplus nations to join with us in supporting new aid initiatives to fuel growth in developing countries that, though economically depressed, are rich in human and natural potential.

We believe this country should work harder to stop the supplies of arms, from both East and West, that fuel conflict in regions such as the Persian Gulf and Angola.... [W]e believe that this country, maintaining the special relationship with Israel founded upon mutually shared values and strategic interests, should provide new leadership to deliver the promise of peace and security through negotiations that has been held out to Israel and its neighbors by the Camp David Accords. We support the sovereignty, independence, and territorial integrity of Lebanon with a central government strong enough to unite its people, maintain order and live in peace in the region. We are committed to Persian Gulf security and freedom of navigation of international waters, and to an end to the Iran-Iraq war by promoting United Nations efforts to achieve a ceasefire and a negotiated settlement, through an arms embargo on the combatants. We further believe that

the United States must fully support the Arias Peace Plan, which calls for an end to the fighting, national reconciliation, guarantees of justice, freedom, human rights and democracy, an end to support for irregular forces, and a commitment by the Central American governments to prevent the use of their territory to destabilize others in the region. Instead of the current emphasis on military solutions we will use negotiations and incentives to encourage free and fair elections and security for all nations in the region. We will cease dealing with drug smugglers and seek to reconcile our differences with countries in Central America, enabling the United States and other countries to focus on the pressing social and economic needs of the people of that region. We further believe in pursuing a policy of economic cooperation instead of confrontation with Mexico and our other hemispheric friends; in helping all developing countries build their own peaceful democratic institutions free from foreign troops, subversion and domination and free from domestic dictators and aggressors; in honoring our treaty obligations; and in using all the tools at our disposal, including diplomacy, trade, aid, food, ideas, and ideals, to defend and enlarge the horizons of freedom on this planet.

Human Rights. We believe in an America that will promote human rights, human dignity and human opportunity in every country on earth; that will fight discrimination, encourage free speech and association and decry oppression in nations friendly and unfriendly, communist and non-communist; that will encourage our European friends to respect human rights and resolve their long-standing differences over Northern Ireland and Cyprus; that will encourage wherever possible the forces of pluralism and democracy in Eastern Europe and that will support the struggle for human rights in Asia.

South Africa. We believe the apartheid regime in South Africa to be a uniquely repressive regime, ruthlessly deciding every aspect of public and private life by skin color, engaging in unrelenting violence against its citizens at home and promoting naked aggression against its neighbors in Africa. We believe the time has come to end all vestiges of the failed policy of constructive engagement, to declare South Africa a terrorist state, to impose comprehensive sanctions upon its economy, to lead the international community in participation in these actions, and to determine a certain date by which United States corporations must leave South Africa. We further believe that to achieve regional security in Southern Africa, we must press forcefully for Namibia's independence by calling for the end of South Africa's illegal occupation, a cease fire and elections, must end our counterproductive policy in Angola and must offer support and further assistance to Mozambique and other frontline states....

Republicans

On the opening day of the Republican national convention, held Aug. 15-18 in New Orleans' Lousiana Superdome, the delegates hailed Ronald Reagan's valedictory, a swan song from a politician who had carried GOP conservatives to unprecedented levels of power. The delegates greeted Reagan as a conquering hero, and they cheered enthusiastically at many of his applause lines. But the mood was tempered by the poignancy of the moment — a realization that Reagan was making his last convention speech as leader of his party and his country, and that the future for Republicans was uncertain.

For his part, Reagan was firm if slightly subdued in his speech. He offered again his optimistic vision of America and took some predictable jabs at his Democratic critics. But the most pertinent symbol of Reagan's role in the 1988 campaign was his strong praise of Vice President George Bush as a key player in his administration. Stating that a regulatory task force headed by Bush had resulted in a reduction in bureaucratic paperwork, Reagan responded to the Democrats' "Where was George?" chant by intoning, "George was there." He also credited Bush with persuading NATO allies to accept American medium-range missiles, a move he said forced the Soviet Union to negotiate the intermediate-range nuclear force (INF) treaty.

Reagan's promise of campaign assistance and his call for Bush to "win one for the Gipper" was a lift for Bush supporters, who were disturbed by Reagan's previously pallid endorsement of their candidate. But the adulation afforded the president by the delegates was a reminder of why the party, fearing that the less charismatic Bush could be overshadowed, scheduled Reagan to speak on Aug. 15.

The Republicans had plenty of theater scheduled for Aug. 16, with an agenda that included New Jersey governor Thomas H. Kean's keynote address and speeches by evangelist and former GOP presidential candidate Pat Robertson, former United Nations Representative Jeane J. Kirkpatrick and former President Gerald R. Ford. But Bush himself stole the show with his midafternoon announcement that he had selected dark-horse prospect Sen. Dan Quayle of Indiana as his running mate.

Bush aides had said the candidate would not announce his choice until Aug. 18, to maintain some suspense and keep the television-viewing public focused on the convention. But after being greeted by the departing Reagan at the Belle Chasse Naval Air Station the morning of Aug. 16, Bush told reporters that he had settled on his choice.

Bush made the choice public at a welcoming ceremony on the New Orleans riverfront. He praised Quayle, who was a generation younger than Bush, as "a man of the future."

News reporters, meanwhile, had little to distract them from their rounds on the vice presidential rumor circuit as the reports of the credentials, rules, and platform committees were approved without debate in the morning session.

Though the delegates spent much of the evening session discussing what they knew about Quayle, a parade of speakers tried to engage their attention. A series of governors praised the GOP platform and compared its specifics with the generalities in the Democratic platform. The governors signaled the evening's theme, a portrayal of Massachusetts governor and Democratic presidential candidate Michael S. Dukakis and the Democrats as extreme liberals. California governor George Deukmejian, noting that Dukakis belonged to the American Civil Liberties Union (ACLU), said ACLU actually meant "Allowing Criminals to Leave Unsupervised" (a reference to a favorite GOP target, the longtime Massachusetts policy of prison furloughs).

Kirkpatrick's attack on Dukakis' foreign policy stances was warmly received. She said the contest between Dukakis and Bush was a choice between a "policy of unilateral concessions and wishful thinking or a policy of clarity and strength."

Much of keynoter speaker Kean's address was a traditional Republican assault on Democratic liberalism. Referring to the light shades of red, white, and blue used by the Democrats in Atlanta (lighting conditions at the Omni would have made bright colors look garish on television), Kean said that Americans "have no use for pastel patriotism."

Anti-abortion activists and religious conservatives, a large bloc within the Republican convention, had their moment with the appearance of Robertson. Insurgencies by Robertson supporters had led to intraparty divisions in several states. But Robertson officially released his delegates and pledged his support for the Republican ticket.

The session ended with Ford's speech. Ford hit hard at the Democrats for presenting themselves as the party of the American dream. He also reviewed Bush's extensive résumé, including his service as emissary to the People's Republic of China and CIA director under Ford.

There was no press "honeymoon" for the prospective vice presidential nominee. A series of tough questions about his background made Aug. 17 difficult for Quayle — and, by extension, for Bush.

At an afternoon news conference, their first formal appearance as the GOP team, Bush defended his choice of Quayle, who was much younger and had less government experience than many of the bypassed vice presidential prospects.

However, Quayle's answers to some of the questions he faced were not so deft. His first problem was with a question about a 1980 Florida incident in which Quayle, then a House member, and two colleagues were seen in the company of lobbyist Paula Parkinson, who later posed nude in *Playboy* magazine and said she had had sexual relationships with members of Congress. Quayle's defense at the time, that he had no involvement with Parkinson, never was refuted. But when asked if a version of the events that appeared to back up his story was true, he said, "No." When pressed, he said, "That has been covered, and there's nothing to it."

Quayle, a member of Indiana's Pulliam publishing family and one of the heirs to a family trust, also sought to deflect rumors about his wealth. He denied that his net worth was as high as $200 million.

The most potentially explosive issue raised at the news conference was whether Quayle had used family influence to gain enlistment in the Indiana National Guard in 1969 to avoid service in the Vietnam War. Quayle first referred to the question as "a cheap shot." But his answers did not defend his choice of the Guard over the combat services, and he said his thoughts at the time centered on plans for law school, marriage and family. He raised eyebrows with the off-the-cuff rejoinder, "I did not know in 1969 that I would be in this room today [as a vice presidential candidate], I confess."

The controversy, however, did not subdue the enthusiasm of convention delegates — for their soon-to-be presidential nominee George Bush or his choice of vice president.

In the evening session, Texas senator Phil Gramm took the podium to nominate Bush, lambasting the Democrats and praising Bush. The nomination was seconded by celebrities such as actress Helen Hayes, Pennsylvania State University football coach Joe Paterno, and Bush's Mexican-American daughter-in-law, Columba Bush.

The ensuing roll call turned into a frenzy of state self-promotion that took an hour and a half to complete. At 11:08 p.m. Central Daylight Time, George W. Bush announced the Texas delegation votes that put his father over the top. *(Chart, p. 256)*

With concerns about Quayle not abating, damage control became the major priority for Bush's new campaign chairman, James A. Baker III. Quayle was to address the Texas and Ohio delegations Aug. 18, but he canceled the campaign appearances, saying he had to rehearse his acceptance speech. That fueled rumors that he was to be dropped from the ticket. Late in the day, Baker, too, canceled several TV interviews. But he emerged early in the evening and trekked between network anchor booths to defend Quayle and roundly reject the rumors that the campaign considered dumping him.

During convention walk-throughs earlier in the day, Bush and Quayle had ignored a barrage of questions about the situation, allowing the convention proceedings to provide their response to the speculation. The answer came quickly. Shortly after a brief address by Barbara Bush, Quayle was placed in nomination and anointed with praise by a series of congressional colleagues, including several who had been considered for the vice presidential spot.

The Indiana senator was nominated by acclamation. A new party rule had eliminated the necessity of a roll call and made it difficult for dissident delegates to call for one if there was opposition to Bush's choice.

If Quayle was burdened with concerns over the military service issue, he checked those emotions backstage before giving his acceptance speech. The youthful-looking senator tackled his first appearance on the national stage with the cheerleader-like élan for which he was known.

Early on, Quayle confronted the National Guard issue briefly and with a somewhat defiant tone. After expressing pride in his congressional service, he said, "As a young man, I served six years in the National Guard, and like the millions of Americans who have served in the Guard ... I am proud of it."

Stating that "the future under George Bush means peace and economic opportunity," Quayle lumped Dukakis in with other Democratic figures who were frequent targets of GOP criticism. "We do not need the future the Democratic party sees, the party of George McGovern, Jimmy Carter, Walter Mondale ... Ted Kennedy, and his buddy, Michael Dukakis," Quayle said, as the delegates lustily booed each name.

Elucidating his own record, Quayle took credit for authoring the 1982 Job Training Partnership Act and discussed his membership on the Senate Armed Services Committee. He then proclaimed the "profound debt" that his generation — of which he was the first major-party national candidate — owed to Bush's generation "for bringing us to an era of peace and freedom and opportunity."

With Bush trailing Dukakis in public opinion polls, media commentators and Bush supporters alike said he had to make the "speech of his life" on the night of Aug. 18. Bush did not waste the opportunity.

"I mean to run hard, to fight hard, to stand on the issues — and I mean to win," Bush said early in his speech. And near its conclusion Bush said his experience as vice president had made him the candidate who was prepared to deal with the critical issues that came across the president's desk. "I am that man," Bush said emphatically, as the partisan crowd roared its approval.

Bush affirmed his vice presidential choice. "Born in the middle of the century, in the middle of America, and holding the promise of the future, I'm proud to have Dan Quayle at my side," Bush said.

Bush acknowledged the necessity of establishing his own identity. "Ronald Reagan asked for, and received, my candor; he never asked for, but he did receive, my loyalty," Bush said. "But now you must see me for what I am: the Republican candidate for president.... And now I turn to the American people to share my hopes and intentions, and why and where I wish to lead."

Bush hit on the conservative hot-button issues — the Pledge of Allegiance (Dukakis had vetoed, on constitutional grounds, a bill requiring Massachusetts public school students to recite the pledge), the death penalty, voluntary school prayer, gun ownership, opposition to abortion, prison furloughs — that had been raised by speaker after speaker during the convention.

But Bush prominently listed several social policy areas that had not ranked high in the conservative Republican rhetoric in the 1980s. He called for mainstreaming the disabled, ending ocean garbage-dumping, reducing acid rain, extending racial harmony and restoring pride and ethics to public service. He seemed to temper the anti-government sentiment so prominent in Reagan's politics.

While pledging "to be a patient friend to anyone ... who will fight for freedom," he made no mention of aid to the Nicaraguan contras. He did not discuss the appointment of conservative judges to the federal judiciary.

Restating his promise not to raise taxes, which he said Dukakis would not rule out, Bush said he would tell persistent tax proponents to "Read my lips. 'No new taxes.'"

Like Reagan, who ended his 1980 acceptance speech with a moment of silent prayer, Bush finished with a flourish. He led the convention in the Pledge of Allegiance, ending a week in which a record may have been set for mentions of the pledge.

Following are excerpts from the Republican platform of 1988:

Jobs. ... The Republican Party puts the creation of jobs and opportunity first....

We will use new technologies, such as computer data bases and telecommunications, to strengthen and streamline job banks matching people who want work with available jobs.

We advocate incentives for educating, training, and retraining workers for new and better jobs — through programs like the Job Training Partnership Act, which provides for a public/private partnership....

With its message of economic growth and opportunity, the GOP is the natural champion of blacks, minorities, women and ethnic Americans....

We are the party of real social progress. Republicans welcome the millions of forward-looking Americans who want an "opportunity society," not a welfare state....

● Families struggling near the poverty line are always hurt most by tax increases.... We will continue to reduce their burden.

● We advocate a youth training wage to expand opportunities and enable unskilled young people to enter the work force.

● As an alternative to inflationary — and job-destroying — increases in the minimum wage, we will work to boost the incomes of the working poor through the Earned Income Tax Credit....

● We will reform welfare to encourage work as the ticket that guarantees full participation in American life.

● We will undertake a long overdue reform of the unemployment insurance program to reward workers who find new jobs quickly.

● We insist upon the right of Americans to work at home. The Home Work Rule, banning sale of certain items made at home, must go....

● We will fight to end the Social Security earnings limitation for the elderly.... As a first step, we will remove the earnings limitation for those whose income is from child care.

We will continue our efforts ... to revitalize our cities. We support, on the federal, State and local levels, enterprise zones to promote investment and job creation in beleaguered neighborhoods....

Small Business. Republicans encourage the women and men in small businesses to think big. To help them create jobs, we will cut to 15% the current counterproductive capital gains tax. This will foster investment in new and untried ventures. . . . It will also build the retirement value of workers' pension funds and raise revenues for the federal government. . . .

Taxes. *We oppose any attempts to increase taxes.* Tax increases harm the economic expansion and reverse the trend to restoring control of the economy to individual Americans.

We reject calls for higher taxes from all quarters — including "bipartisan commissions." The decisions of our government should not be left to a body of unelected officials. . . .

Republicans know that sustaining the American economic miracle requires a growing pool of private savings. . . . To keep it going:

• We support incentives for private savings, such as our deductibility for IRA contributions.

• We oppose tax withholding on savings. . . .

• We will reduce to 15 percent the tax rates for long-term capital gains to promote investment in jobs and to raise revenue for the federal government by touching off another surge of economic expansion. . . .

Public Services. We resolve to defederalize, denationalize, and decentralize government monopolies that poorly serve the public and waste the taxpayer's dollars. To that end, we will foster competition wherever possible.

We advocate privatizing those government assets which would be more productive and better maintained in private ownership. . . .

Housing. The best housing policy is sound economic policy. Low interest rates, low inflation rates, and the availability of a job with a good paycheck that makes a mortgage affordable are the best housing programs of all. . . .

We want to foster greater choice in housing for all:

• First and foremost, Republicans stand united in defense of the homeowner's deduction for mortgage interest. . . .

• We will continue our successful drive for lower interest rates.

• We support the efforts of those in the States who fight to lower property taxes that strike hardest at the poor, the elderly, large families, and family farmers.

• We support programs to allow low-income families to earn possession of their homes through urban and rural homesteading, cooperative ventures in construction and rehabilitation, and other pioneering projects that demonstrate the vitality of the private sector and individual initiative. . . .

• We call for repeal of rent control laws. . . .

Federal Spending. We call for structural changes to control government waste, including a two-year budget cycle, a super-majority requirement for raising taxes, a legislatively enacted line-item veto, individual transmission of spending bills, greater rescission authority for the chief executive and other reforms.

• We call for a flexible freeze on current government spending. . . . We oppose any increase in taxes. . . .

• We believe the Grace Commission report to eliminate waste, inefficiency, and mismanagement in the federal government must be re-examined; its recommendations should be given a high profile by public policy officials.

• We call for a balanced budget amendment to the Constitution. If congressional Democrats continue to block it, we urge the States to renew their calls for a constitutional convention limited to consideration of such an amendment.

• We will use all constitutional authority to control congressional spending. This will include consideration of the inherent line-item veto power of the president. . . .

Trade. We will not accept the loss of American jobs to nationalized, subsidized, protected foreign industries and will continue to negotiate assertively the destruction of trade barriers. . . .

We will not tolerate unfair trade and will use free trade as a weapon against it. To ensure that rapid progress is forthcoming from our work through GATT [General Agreement on Tariffs and Trade], we stand ready to pursue special arrangements with nations which share our commitment to free trade. . . . We are prepared to negotiate free trade agreements with partners like the Republic of China on Taiwan and the Association of Southeast Asian Nations (ASEAN) countries if they are willing to open their markets to U.S. products. . . .

We will use U.S. economic aid, whether bilateral or through international organizations, to promote free market reforms: lower marginal tax rates, less regulation, reduced trade barriers. We will work with developing nations to make their economies attractive to private investment — both domestic and foreign — the only lasting way to ensure that these nations can secure capital for growth. We support innovations to facilitate repayment of loans, including "debt for equity" swaps. We urge our representatives in all multilateral organizations such as the World Bank to support conditionality with all loans to encourage democracy, private sector development, and individual enterprise. . . .

Child Care. The family's most important function is to raise the next generation of Americans, handing on to them the Judeo-Christian values of western civilization and our ideals of liberty. . . .

Republicans affirm these commonsense principles of child care:

• The more options families have in child care, the better. Government must not constrain their decisions. Individual choice should determine child care arrangements for the family.

• The best care for most children, especially in the early years, is parental. Government must never hinder it.

• Public policy must acknowledge the full range of family situations. Mothers or fathers who stay at home, who work part-time, or who work full-time, should all receive the same respect and consideration in public policy.

• Child care by close relatives, religious organizations, and other community groups should never be inhibited by government programs or policies. . . .

Pornography. We endorse legislative and regulatory efforts to anchor more securely a standard of decency in telecommunications and to prohibit the sale of sexually explicit materials in outlets operated on federal property. We commend those who refuse to sell pornographic material. We support the rigorous enforcement of "community standards" against pornography. . . .

Health. Republicans believe in reduced government control of health care while maintaining an unequivocal commitment to quality health care. . . .

• We will work for continuing progress in providing the most cost-effective, high-quality care.

• We will lead the fight for reform of medical malpractice laws to stop the intolerable escalation of malpractice insurance. . . .

• We are opposed to the establishment of government mandated professional practice fees and services requirements as a condition of professional licensure or license renewal.

• We will continue to seek opportunities for private and public cooperation in support of hospices.

• We are committed to improving the quality and financing of long term care. We will remove regulatory and tax burdens to encourage private health insurance policies for acute or long term care. We will work for convertibility of savings, IRAs [Individual Retirement Accounts], life insurance, and pensions to pay for long term care.

• We will encourage the trend in the private sector to expand opportunities for home health care to protect the integrity of the family and to provide a less expensive alternative to hospital stays. We want to ensure flexibility for both Medicare and Medicaid in the provision of services to those who need them at home or elsewhere.

● We will foster employee choice in selecting health plans to promote personal responsibility for wellness.

● . . . [W]e will work toward making catastrophic health care coverage available to our youngest citizens.

● Recognizing that inequities may exist in the current treatment of health insurance costs for those who are self employed, including farmers, we will study ways to more appropriately balance such costs. . . .

● We will work to assure access to health care for all Americans through public and private initiatives. . . .

AIDS. We will vigorously fight against AIDS. . . . Continued research on the virus is vital. We will continue as well to provide experimental drugs that may prolong life. We will establish within the Food and Drug Administration a process for expedited review of drugs which may benefit AIDS patients. We will allow supervised usage of experimental treatments.

We must not only marshal our scientific resources against AIDS, but must also protect those who do not have the disease. In this regard, education plays a critical role. AIDS education should emphasize that abstinence from drug abuse and sexual activity outside of marriage is the safest way to avoid infection with the AIDS virus. It is extremely important that testing and contact tracing measures be carried out and be appropriately confidential. . . .

Social Security. We pledge to preserve the integrity of the Social Security trust funds. We encourage public officials at all levels to safeguard the integrity of public and private pension funds against raiding. . . .

Homeless. Republicans are determined to help the homeless as a matter of ethical commitment, as well as sound public policy. . . .

Republicans are ready to deal with the root causes of the problem:

● Our top priority must be homeless families. As part of an overall emphasis on family responsibility, we will strongly enforce child support laws. We call for development of a model divorce reform law that will adequately safeguard the economic and social interests of mothers and children while securing fairness to fathers in decisions concerning child custody and support. . . .

● Rent controls promise housing below its market cost, but inevitably result in a shortage of decent homes. Our people should not have to underwrite any community which erodes its own housing supply by rent control. . . .

Equal Rights, Religious Rights, Abortion. "Deep in our hearts, we do believe":

● That bigotry has no place in American life. We denounce those persons, organizations, publications and movements which practice or promote racism, anti-Semitism or religious intolerance.

● That the Pledge of Allegiance should be recited daily in schools in all States. . . .

● In equal rights for all.

● In guaranteeing opportunity, not dictating the results of fair competition. We will resist efforts to replace equal rights with discriminatory quota systems and preferential treatment. . . .

● In defending religious freedom. Mindful of our religious diversity, we firmly support the right of students to engage in voluntary prayer in schools. We call for full enforcement of the Republican legislation that now guarantees equal access to school facilities by student religious groups.

● That the unborn child has a fundamental right to life which cannot be infringed. We therefore reaffirm our support for a human life amendment to the Constitution, and we endorse legislation to make clear that the Fourteenth Amendment's protections apply to unborn children. We oppose the use of public revenues for abortion and will

eliminate funding for organizations which advocate or support abortion.

● We . . . reaffirm our support for the appointment of judges at all levels of the judiciary who respect traditional family values and the sanctity of innocent human life.

● That churches, religious schools and any other religious institution should not be taxed. . . .

Disabled. We support efforts to provide disabled voters full access to the polls and opportunity to participate in all aspects of the political process. . . .

● We pledge to fight discrimination in health care. . . . [W]e insist upon full treatment for disabled infants. . . .

● We will protect the rights established under the Education for All Handicapped Children Act, Section 504 of the Rehabilitation Act of 1973, and the Civil Rights of Institutionalized Persons Act. We will balance those rights against the public's right to be protected against diseases and conditions which threaten the health and safety of others. . . .

Native Americans. We support self-determination for Indian Tribes in managing their own affairs and resources. . . .

Gun Ownership. Republicans defend the constitutional right to keep and bear arms. . . .

Workers' Rights. We affirm the right of all freely to form, join or assist labor organizations to bargain collectively, consistent with state laws. . . . We renew our longstanding support for the right of states to enact "Right-to-Work" laws. To protect the political rights of every worker, we oppose the use of compulsory dues or fees for partisan purposes. . . .

The Republican Party supports legislation to amend the Hobbs Act, so that union officials, like all other Americans, are once again subject to the law's prohibition against extortion and violence in labor disputes.

We also support amendments to the National Labor Relations Act to provide greater protection from labor violence for workers who choose to work during strikes.

Immigration. We welcome those from other lands who bring to America their ideals and industry. At the same time, we insist upon our country's absolute right to control its borders. . . .

Education. We will continue to . . . expand horizons for learning, teaching, and mastering the future:

● We will use federal programs to foster excellence, rewarding "Merit Schools" which significantly improve education for their students.

● We will urge our local school districts to recognize the value of kindergarten and pre-kindergarten programs.

● We will direct federal matching funds to promote magnet schools that turn students toward the challenges of the future rather than the failures of the past.

● We will support laboratories of educational excellence in every State by refocusing federal funds for educational research.

● We will increase funding for the Head Start program. . . .

● We will work with local schools and the private sector to develop models for evaluating teachers and other school officials.

● We will continue to support tuition tax credits for parents who choose to educate their children in private educational institutions. . . .

In higher education, Republicans want to promote both opportunity and responsibility:

● We will keep resources focused on low-income students and address the barriers that discourage minority students from entering and succeeding in institutions of higher education. . . .

● We will create a College Savings Bond program, with tax-exempt interest, to help families save for their children's higher education. . . .

Arts and Humanitites. [W]e will:

● Continue the Republican economic renaissance which has made possible a tremendous outpouring of support for arts and humanities.

● Support full deductibility for donations to tax-exempt cultural institutions in order to encourage the private support of arts and humanities.

● Support the National Endowments for the Arts and Humanities and the Institute of Museum Services in their effort to support America's cultural institutions, artists, and scholars.

● Guard against the misuse of governmental grants by those who attack or derogate any race or creed and oppose the politicization of the National Endowments for the Arts and Humanities....

Science and Technology. We will ensure that tax policy gives optimum incentive for the private sector to fund a high level of advanced research. Toward that end, we will make permanent the current tax credit for research and development and extend it to cooperative research ventures.

● We will strengthen the role of science and engineering in national policy by reinforcing the Office of the President's Science Advisor with the addition of a Science Advisory Council.

● We will encourage exchange of scientific information, especially between business and academic institutions, to speed up the application of research to benefit the public.

● We will improve the acquisition of scientific and technical information from other countries through expedited translation services and more aggressive outreach by federal agencies.

● We will include international technology flows as part of U.S. trade negotiations to ensure that the benefits of foreign advances are available to Americans.

● We will encourage innovation by strengthening protection for intellectual property at home and abroad. We will promote the public benefits that come from commercialization of research conducted under federal sponsorship by allowing private ownership of intellectual property developed in that manner.

● We will oppose regulation which stifles competition and hinders breakthroughs that can transform life for the better in areas like biotechnology....

Space. The Republican Party will re-establish U.S. preeminence in space. It is our nation's frontier, our manifest destiny...

We support further development of the space station, the National Aerospace Plane, Project Pathfinder, a replacement shuttle, and the development of alternate launch vehicles. We endorse Mission to Planet Earth for space science to advance our understanding of environmental and climatic forces....

We must commit to manned flight to Mars around the year 2000 and to continued exploration of the Moon....

Crime. We will forge ahead with the Republican anti-crime agenda:

● ...Republicans oppose furloughs for those criminals convicted of first degree murder and others who are serving a life sentence without possibility of parole. We believe that victims' rights should not be accorded less importance than those of convicted felons.

● We will re-establish the federal death penalty.

● We will reform the exclusionary rule, to prevent the release of guilty felons on technicalities.

● We will reform cumbersome habeas corpus procedures, used to delay cases and prevent punishment of the guilty.

● We support State laws implementing preventive detention to allow courts to deny bail to those considered dangerous and likely to commit additional crimes....

Drugs. The Republican Party is committed to a drug-free America. Our policy is strict accountability, for users of illegal drugs as well as for those who profit by that usage....

● The Republican Party unequivocally opposes legalizing or decriminalizing any illicit drug.

● We support strong penalties, including the death penalty for major drug traffickers....

● Conviction for any drug crime should make the offender ineligible for discretionary federal assistance, grants, loans and contracts for a period of time.

● To impress young Americans with the seriousness of our fight against drugs, we urge States to suspend eligibility for a driver's license to anyone convicted of a drug offense....

● We will strengthen interdiction of foreign drugs and expand the military's role in stopping traffickers.

● We will work with foreign governments to eradicate drug crops in their countries.

● In a summit of Western Hemisphere nations, we will seek total cooperation from other governments in wiping out the international drug empire....

● [W]e encourage drug education in our schools....

● We will encourage seizure and forfeiture programs by the Department of the Treasury and each State to take the profits out of illicit drug sales....

We recognize the need to improve the availability of drug rehabilitation and treatment....

Agriculture. Republicans will work to improve agricultural income through market returns at home and abroad, not government controls and subsidies:

● We pledge early action to renew and improve the successful farm programs set to expire in 1990.

● We pledge to continue international food assistance, including programs through the Eisenhower Food for Peace program, to feed the world's hungry and develop markets abroad.

● We will continue to provide leadership in the effort to improve standards of quality for grain and other agricultural products in order to meet international competition....

Oil. We will set an energy policy for the United States to maintain a viable core industry and to ensure greater energy self sufficiency through private initiatives. We will adopt forceful initiatives to reverse the decline of our domestic oil production. Republicans support:

● Repeal of the counterproductive Windfall Profits Tax.

● Maintenance of our schedule for filling the Strategic Petroleum Reserve to reach 750 million barrels by 1993 and encouragement of our allies to maintain similar reserves.

● Tax incentives to save marginal wells, to encourage exploration for new oil, and to improve the recovery of oil still in place....

● Exploration and development in promising areas, including federal lands and waters... in a manner that is protective of our environment and is in the best national interest....

Natural Gas. More progress must be made in deregulation of natural gas:

● We support fully decontrolling prices and providing more open access to transportation.

● We also support the flexible use of natural gas to fuel automobiles and boilers....

Coal. We should aggressively pursue the clean coal technology initiative....

● A major effort should be made to encourage coal exports....

Nuclear Power. We must preserve nuclear power as a safe and economic option to meet future electricity needs.... We will promote the adoption of standardized, cost-effective, and environmentally safe nuclear plant designs. We should enhance our efforts to manage nuclear waste and will insist on the highest standards of safety.

Energy Alternatives, Conservation. ...We will set priorities and, where cost effective, support research and development for alternative fuels such as ethanol, methanol, and compressed natural gas. . . .

Environment. Republicans propose the following program for the environment in the 1990s:

● We will work for further reductions in air and water pollution and effective actions against the threats posed by acid rain. . . .

● A top priority of our country must be the continued improvement of our National Parks and wildlife areas. . . .

● We will fight to protect endangered species and to sustain biological diversity worldwide.

● We support federal, State, and local policies, including tax code provisions, which lead to the renewal and revitalization of our environment through restoration and which encourage scenic easements designed to preserve farmland and open spaces.

● We will protect the productive capacity of our lands by minimizing erosion. . . .

Transportation. [T]he Republican Party supports comprehensive efforts to curb drug and alcohol abuse in transportation, including drug and alcohol testing of all those in safety-related positions. . . .

● We advocate greater local autonomy in decision-making concerning the Highway Trust Fund and the Airport and Airway Trust Fund, and we oppose diversion of their resources to other purposes. . . .

● A new spirit of competitive enterprise in transportation throughout all levels of government should be encouraged. We will encourage both States and cities to utilize private companies, where effective, to operate commuter bus and transit services at substantial savings over what publicly funded systems cost. . . .

● We consider a privately owned merchant fleet and domestic shipbuilding capacity necessary to carry our nation's commerce in peace and to support our defense responsibilities. We will support programs to give the American maritime industry greater flexibility and freedom in meeting foreign competition. . . .

Democracy Abroad. [O]ur nation has a compelling interest to encourage and help actively to build the conditions of democracy wherever people strive for freedom. . . .

The Americas. The Republican party reaffirms its strong support of the Monroe Doctrine as the foundation for our policy throughout the Hemisphere, and pledges to conduct foreign policy in accord with its principles. . . .

Republicans will continue to oppose any normalization of relations with the government of Cuba as long as Fidel Castro continues to oppress the Cuban people at home and to support international terrorism and drug trafficking abroad. We will vigorously continue our support for establishment of a genuinely representative government directly elected by the Cuban people. We reiterate our support of Radio Marti and urge the creation of TV Marti to better reach the oppressed people of Cuba. . . .

Republicans view the Panama Canal as a critical, strategic artery connecting the Atlantic and Pacific. We believe that U.S. access to the Panama Canal must remain free and unencumbered consistent with the foremost principle of the Canal Treaty. . . .

Soviet Union. Steady American leadership is needed now more than ever to deal with the challenges posed by a rapidly changing Soviet Union. Americans cannot afford a future administration which eagerly attempts to embrace perceived, but as yet unproven, changes in Soviet policy. Nor can we indulge naive inexperience or an overly enthusiastic endorsement of current Soviet rhetoric. . . .

Republicans will continue to work with the new Soviet leadership. But the terms of the relationship will be based upon persistent and steady attention to certain fundamental principles:

● Human and religious rights in the Soviet Union.

● Economic reform in the Soviet Union.

● Cessation of Soviet support for communist regimes, radical groups, and terrorists.

● Verified full compliance with all arms control agreements.

● The right of free emigration for all Soviet citizens.

● Reduction in the Soviets' massive offensive strategic and conventional capability. . . .

● An end to untied credits. . . .

Republicans proudly reaffirm the Reagan Doctrine: America's commitment to aid freedom-fighters against the communist oppression which destroys freedom and the human spirit. . . .

We call on the Soviet government to release political prisoners, allow free emigration for "refuseniks" and others, and introduce full religious tolerance. . . .

We support the desire for freedom and self-determination of all those living in Captive Nations. . . .

Europe, Defense of the West. American aid and European industriousness have restored West Europe to a position of global strength. In accord with this, the Republican Party believes that all members of NATO should bear their fair share of the defense burden.

Republicans consider consultation and cooperation with our allies and friends to stop the proliferation of ballistic missile technology is a crucial allied goal. . . .

Asia and the Pacific. Japan has assumed the role earned by her people as a world economic power. The GOP believes that our relations can only be strengthened by attacking trade barriers, both tariff and nontariff, which not only hurt the U.S. now but also will eventually distort Japan's own economy. We believe that it is time for Japan to assume a greater role in this region and elsewhere. This should include a greater commitment to its own defense, commitment to leading the way in alleviating Third World debt, and fostering economic growth in fragile democracies. . . .

We pledge full cooperation in mutual defense of the Philippines and South Korea and the maintenance of our troops and bases vital for deterring aggression. . . . We reaffirm our commitment to the security of Taiwan and other key friends and allies in the region. . . .

[T]he Republican Party believes that we must continue to encourage the abandonment of political repression in the People's Republic of China and movement toward a free market. . . .

The Middle East. The foundation of our policy in the Middle East has been and must remain the promotion of a stable and lasting peace, recognizing our moral and strategic relationship with Israel. . . .

We will continue to maintain Israel's qualitative advantage over any adversary or coalition of adversaries.

We will continue to solidify our strategic relationship with Israel. . . .

We oppose the creation of an independent Palestinian state; its establishment is inimical to the security interests of Israel, Jordan and the U.S. . . .

Republicans see Egypt as a catalyst in the Arab world for advancing the cause of regional peace and security. For this reason, we believe that the United States has a significant stake in Egypt's continuing economic development and growth. . . .

Africa. Republicans have three priorities in our country's relations with Africa. The first is to oppose the forces of Marxist imperialism, which sustain the march of tyranny in Africa. . . .

Our second priority is the need to develop and sustain democracies in Africa. . . .

Our third area of concern is humanitarian assistance, especially food aid, to African nations. . . .

We believe that peace in southern Africa can best be achieved by the withdrawal of all foreign forces from Angola, complete independence and self-determination for the people of Namibia, a rapid process of internal reconciliation, and free and fair elections in both places. . . .

Republicans deplore the apartheid system of South Africa and consider it morally repugnant. . . . Republicans call for an effective and coordinated policy that will promote equal rights and a peaceful transition to a truly representative constitutional form of government for all South Africans and the citizens of all nations throughout Africa. . . .

Terrorism. The Republican Party believes that, in order to prevent terrorist attacks, the United States must maintain an unsurpassed intelligence capability. In cases of terrorism where prevention and deterrence are not enough, we believe that the United States must be prepared to use an appropriate mix of diplomatic, political, and military pressure and action to defeat the terrorist attack. The United States must continue to push for a Western commitment to a "no-concessions" policy on terrorism. . . .

Defense. Republicans will . . . advance the cause of world freedom and world peace by using our military credibility as a vehicle for security at home and peace abroad. . . .

Even as we engage in dialogue with our adversaries to reduce the risks of war, we must continue to rely on nuclear weapons as our chief form of deterrence. This reliance will, however, move toward non-nuclear defensive weapon systems as we deploy the Strategic Defense System. . . .

Strategic Defense Initiative (SDI). We are committed to rapid and certain deployment of SDI as technologies permit, and we will determine the exact architecture of the system as technologies are tested and proven. . . .

Strategic Forces. Republicans will implement a strategic modernization program, emphasizing offensive and defensive strategic forces that are affordable and credible and that provide for a more stable balance. . . .

In the conventional area, we need to ensure that our ground, naval, and air forces are outfitted with the finest equipment and weapons that modern technology can provide; we must also assure that they are fully capable of meeting any threats they may face. We put special emphasis on integrating the guard and reserves into effective combat forces. We must sustain and accelerate the progress we have already made to ensure that all of our forces are prepared for special operations warfare. In addition, advances in conventional weapons technology, specifically, "smart," highly accurate weaponry, must be accelerated. . . .

Arms Control. Arms reduction can be an important aspect of our national policy only when agreements enhance the security of the United States and its allies. [T]rue arms reductions as a means to improve U.S. security, not just the perception of East-West detente. . . .

● We will consistently undertake necessary improvements in our forces to maintain the effectiveness of our deterrent.

● We will not negotiate in areas which jeopardize our security. In particular, we will not compromise plans for the research, testing, or the rapid and certain deployment of SDI.

● We will insist on effective verification of compliance with any and all treaties and will take proportional, compensatory actions in cases of non-compliance. . . .

● We will place special emphasis on negotiating asymmetrical Soviet cutbacks in those areas where a dangerous imbalance exists. . . .

Intelligence. The Republican Party endorses covert action as one method of implementing U.S. national security policy. We reject legislative measures that impinge on the President's constitutional prerogatives. . . .

1992 Conventions

Presidential Candidates

Bill Clinton
Democrat

George Bush
Republican

Democrats

The Democrats, meeting at Madison Square Garden in New York July 13-16, nominated a ticket consisting of two party moderates and adopted a platform heavily influenced by the centrist ideas of the Democratic Leadership Council (DLC) and its think tank, the Progressive Policy Institute. The convention stressed the themes Democrats planned to push in the fall campaign: redefining the party in the centrist vein, emphasizing youth, traditional family values and mainstream policy views — as desired by its nominee, Arkansas Gov. Bill Clinton. Every bit as unsubtle were the efforts to redefine his personal image. In appealing to youth, as in much else, Clinton, 45, was ably assisted by his running mate, Sen. Albert Gore, 44, of Tennessee, making their ticket the youngest in the twentieth century.

Despite former California governor Edmund G. "Jerry" Brown Jr.'s refusal to hop on the bandwagon or independent presidential candidate Ross Perot's stunning July 16 announcement from Dallas that he was bowing out (a decision he later reversed), Clinton controlled the focus and direction of the convention.

He declined to bow to the tough tactics of black activist and former presidential candidate Jesse L. Jackson, thus demonstrating a tough-mindedness and his own and signaling that he planed to put some distance between himself and Jackson's brand of urban liberalism.

There were reminders of Clinton's poor childhood, an effort to show he was in touch with the common people. There were clever and pointed attacks on President George Bush and Vice President Dan Quayle. There were consistent attempts to show that the Democratic Party had been unified and redefined in Clinton's centrist image. And there was a display of confidence, optimism and determination to end 12 years of GOP control of the White House.

The convention was marked by relatively few fractional disputes. Although Jesse Jackson was less than enthusiastic in his endorsement of the Arkansas governor, the important fact was that Clinton did not have to negotiate with Jackson the way his predecessors had. Brown remained the lone holdout, but Clinton's people never seemed overly upset by

that, and it did not prevent the Democrats from presenting an image of unity and harmony.

In their acceptance speeches, the final night, Clinton and Gore appealed to Perot supporters to recognize that Democrats could offer the change they wanted, but they otherwise stuck to the themes that had been stressed all week. Clinton used his speech to reintroduce himself to the voters. Recounting his fatherless childhood and stressing his small-town roots, Clinton summoned Americans to a "new covenant" of shared responsibility.

Controversy was almost entirely confined to the early part of the convention and involved primarily the question of whether Brown would be allowed to address the convention from the podium. Brown arrived with more than 600 delegates, enough to cause some disturbance. For most of the first session, they milled in the well beneath the main stage, heckling speakers and waving signs. Some covered their mouths with labels or duct tape.

The California delegation, although dominated by Clinton backers, united with the Brown delegates in support of their former governor's claim to address the convention from the podium. But neither Clinton nor DNC chair Ron Brown would relent in demanding an endorsement of the ticket as a condition for a prime-time speaking slot.

In the end, Jerry Brown was given the chance to give his own seconding speech on July 15. But that meant he spoke at shortly after 8 p.m. (5 p.m. in California), well before the commercial broadcast networks had switched from their regular programming to convention coverage. Gradually, the Brown delegates softened their protest and ended any serious attempt to disrupt the convention.

On July 13 a rousing welcome greeted Texas Gov. Ann W. Richards, the convention chair, who was best known nationally for her 1988 convention keynote address, in which she joked that Bush had been "born with a silver spoon in his mouth." She did not mention Bush by name this time, although she referred to her earlier speech and said: "I really hate to say it. But I told you so."

A large section of the opening program was designed to give exposure to six of the Democrats' leading female Senate candidates, all of whom spoke briefly from the convention floor. Dianne Feinstein of California, the last to speak, dismissed Republicans who referred to the wave of female candidates as "just gender politics." "It's not just about gender. It's about an agenda, an agenda of change," Feinstein said.

Heralding the "Year of the Woman," Democratic women played a major role at the convention, and issues women had highlighted — abortion rights, women's health care and the Clarence Thomas-Anita F. Hill hearings — were discussed from the podium, always to loud cheers from the floor.

Instead of the usual keynote speaker, the Democrats opted for three: Sen. Bill Bradley of New Jersey, Gov. Zell Miller of Georgia and former Texas representative Barbara Jordan. They stressed that the party had changed, blasted the Bush administration for economic policies that favored the rich and portrayed Clinton as a candidate from modest roots who was in touch with the people.

The Democrats later solidified their move to the center by adopting a platform devoid of many of the liberal planks and slogans that characterized previous documents. The debate over the party's manifesto was brief and uninspired. Clinton's overwhelming delegate strength and Democrats' frustration with three straight presidential losses helped mute any complaints over the centrist platform that clearly reflected the Clinton view of how the Democratic Party should present itself to voters.

The platform emphasized the need for economic growth, pledged to uphold law and order and to use military force overseas where necessary, called for a cutoff in welfare benefits after two years and supported the right of states to enact death penalty statutes. The platform did include more traditional Democratic viewpoints, such as protecting abortion rights, providing civil rights for homosexuals and taxing wealthy people at higher rates.

By prior agreement, delegates pledged to former senator Paul E. Tsongas of Massachusetts were allowed to offer and debate four minority planks. But it was a debate only in the loosest sense of the word. The speeches on both sides were brief, and most speakers for Clinton's position made little effort to engage in a point-by-point rebuttal.

Three of the planks ultimately were rejected by voice vote. One called for investment-related tax breaks. Another, on the deficit, called for limits on government spending, including Medicare and other politically sensitive entitlements. And a third proposed increasing the gasoline tax by 5 cents per gallon to benefit new spending on roads and bridges.

The hall's electronic voting system was to decide the fate of a fourth plank, which said that a middle-class tax cut and a tax credit for families with children ought to be delayed until the deficit was under control. This had been a key difference between Tsongas and Clinton during the campaign. But the plank was defeated, 953 to 2,287. *(Chart, p. 257)*

The real drama came later, when two activists afflicted with the AIDS virus moved delegates to tears and when Jesse Jackson's rousing speech brought the convention to a fever pitch.

Former president Jimmy Carter was warmly received as he vouched for Clinton's character. He said he had known Clinton for more than 15 years and described him as "a friend and a fine governor" who had endured "false and misleading political attacks.... He is a man of honesty and integrity."

New York Gov. Mario M. Cuomo formally nominated Clinton, bringing the convention hall to a fever pitch with

his denunciations of Bush and his salute to Clinton as the "Comeback Kid."

The final roll-call tally was Clinton, 3,372; Brown, 596; and Tsongas, 209, and subsequently the nomination was approved by acclamation. After the vote, the evening came to a dramatic and surprising end when the nominee answered chants of "we want Bill" by visiting the convention hall. Clinton, who had been watching the roll call two blocks away, walked most of the way to Madison Square Garden. His appearance a day early was unusual, but not unprecedented, and wildly welcomed by the delegates, who cheered, chanted and stomped in appreciation. Clinton likened his visit to the convention floor to that of John F. Kennedy in 1960, who he said "came to give a simple thank you."

On the fourth and final day of the convention — six months after the nation's first Democratic primary and more than four months before the election — Bill Clinton addressed the most pressing concern of his candidacy: How to define himself.

In his 54-minute speech, some 20 minutes longer than the seemingly interminable nominating speech he gave in 1988, Clinton zeroed in on the themes the campaign reflected in the party platform. He described himself as "a product of the American middle class" who would accept the nomination "in the name of all the people who do the work, pay the taxes, raise the kids and play by the rules — the hard-working Americans who make up our forgotten middle class." He talked about his own family and an "America where 'family values' live in our actions, not just our speeches."

Clinton and Gore paid respect to the intensity of women's political feeling. They endorsed abortion rights and equal rights in the workplace. Both lavished praise on their wives, receiving roars of approval from the audience. And when Clinton talked of a notional child "somewhere at this very moment ... born in America," he deliberately used female pronouns to refer to her.

Clinton often referred to himself as "the comeback kid." He claimed the title after rebounding from damaging stories about his alleged relationship with a singer and about the means by which he avoided the Vietnam War draft.

Clinton's acceptance speech was rife with references to God and faith, home and family. He twice quoted from Scripture. And a "New Covenant" was the Arkansan's successor phrase to the New Frontier and the New Deal.

Following are excerpts from the Democratic platform of 1992:

Economic Opportunity. Our party's first priority is opportunity — broad-based, non-inflationary economic growth and the opportunity that flows from it. Democrats in 1992 hold nothing more important for America than an economy that offers growth and jobs for all....

We reject both the do-nothing government of the last 12 years and the big government theory that says we can hamstring business and tax and spend our way to prosperity. Instead we offer a third way. Just as we have always viewed working men and women as the bedrock of our economy, we honor business as a noble endeavor and vow to create a far better climate for firms and independent contractors of all sizes that empower their workers, revolutionize their workplaces, respect the environment, and serve their communities well.

Investment in America. The only way to lay the foundation for renewed American prosperity is to spur both public and private investment. We must strive to close both the budget deficit and the investment gap. Our major competitors invest far more than we do in roads, bridges, and the information networks and technologies of the future. We will rebuild America by investing more in transportation, environmental technologies, defense conversion and a national information network.

To begin making our economy grow, the president and Congress should agree that savings from defense must be reinvested productively at home, including research, education and training, and other productive investments. This will sharply increase the meager 9 percent of the national budget now devoted to the future. We will create a "future budget" for investments that make us richer, to be kept separate from those parts of the budget that pay for the past and present. For the private sector, instead of a sweeping capital gains windfall to the wealthy and those who speculate, we will create an investment tax credit and a capital gains reduction for patient investors in emerging technologies and new business.

Technological Innovation. We will take back the advantage now ceded to Japan and Germany, which invest in new technologies at higher rates than the U.S. and have the growth to show for it. We will make the R&D tax credit permanent, double basic research in the key technologies for our future and create a civilian research agency to fast-forward their development.

The Deficit. Addressing the deficit requires fair and shared sacrifice of all Americans for the common good.... In place of the Republican supply side disaster, the Democratic investment, economic conversion and growth strategy will generate more revenues from a growing economy. We must also tackle spending by putting everything on the table; eliminate non-productive programs; achieve defense savings; reform entitlement programs to control soaring health-care costs; cut federal administrative costs by 3 percent annually for four years; limit increases in the "present budget" to the rate of growth in the average American's paycheck; apply a strict "pay as you go" rule to new non-investment spending; and make the rich pay their fair share in taxes. These choices will be made while protecting senior citizens and without further victimizing the poor....

Defense Conversion. Our economy needs both the people and the funds released from defense at the Cold War's end. We will help the stalwarts of that struggle — the men and women who served in our armed forces and who work in our defense industries — make the most of a new era. We will provide early notice of program changes to give communities, business and workers enough time to plan. We will honor and support our veterans. Departing military personnel, defense workers and defense support personnel will have access to job retraining, continuing education, placement and relocation assistance, early retirement benefits for military personnel, and incentives to enter teaching, law enforcement and other vital civilian fields. Redirected national laboratories and a new civilian research agency will put defense scientists, engineers and technicians to work at critical civilian technologies. Small business defense firms will have technical assistance and transition grants and loans to help convert to civilian markets, and defense-dependent communities will have similar aid in planning and implementing conversion. We will strongly support our civilian space program, particularly environmental missions.

Cities. Only a robust economy will revitalize our cities. It is in all Americans' interest that the cities once again be places where hard-working families can put down roots and find good jobs, quality health care, affordable housing and decent schools. Democrats will create a new partnership to rebuild America's cities after 12 years of Republican neglect. This partnership will include consideration of the seven economic growth initiatives set forth by our nation's mayors. We will create jobs by investing significant resources to put people back to work, beginning with a summer jobs initiative and training programs for inner-city youth. We support a stronger community development program and targeted fis-

cal assistance to cities that need it most. A national public works investment and infrastructure program will provide jobs and strengthen our cities, suburbs, rural communities and country. We will encourage the flow of investment to inner-city development and housing through targeted enterprise zones and incentives for private and public pension funds to invest in urban and rural projects. While cracking down on redlining and housing discrimination, we also support and will enforce a revitalized Community Reinvestment Act that challenges banks to lend to entrepreneurs and development projects; a national network of Community Development Banks to invest in urban and rural small businesses; and microenterprise lending for poor people seeking self-employment as an alternative to welfare.

Agriculture. A sufficient and sustainable agricultural economy can be achieved through fiscally responsible programs. It is time to re-establish the private/public partnership to ensure that family farmers get a fair return for their labor and investment, that consumers receive safe and nutritious foods, and that needed investments are made in basic research, education, rural business development, market development and infrastructure to sustain rural communities.

Workers' Rights. Our workplaces must be revolutionized to make them more flexible and productive. We will reform the job safety laws to empower workers with greater rights and to hold employers accountable for dangers on the job. We will act against sexual harassment in the workplace. We will honor the work ethic — by expanding the earned-income tax credit so no one with children at home who works full time is still in poverty, by fighting on the side of family farmers to ensure they get a fair price for their hard work and working to sustain rural communities; by making work more valuable than welfare; and by supporting the right of workers to organize and bargain collectively without fear of intimidation or permanent replacement during labor disputes.

Education. A competitive American economy requires the global market's best-educated, best-trained, most flexible work force. It's not enough to spend more on our schools; we must insist on results. We oppose the Bush administration's efforts to bankrupt the public school system — the bedrock of democracy — through private school vouchers. To help children reach school ready to learn, we will expand child health and nutrition programs and extend Head Start to all eligible children, and guarantee all children access to quality, affordable child care. We deplore the savage inequalities among public schools across the land and believe every child deserves an equal chance to a world-class education. Reallocating resources toward this goal must be a priority. We support education reforms such as site-based decision-making and public school choice, with strong protections against discrimination. We support the goal of a 90 percent graduation rate and programs to end dropouts. We will invest in educational technology and establish world-class standards in math, science and other core subjects, and support effective tests of progress to meet them. In areas where there are no registered apprenticeship programs, we will adopt a national apprenticeship-style program to ease the transition from school to work for non-college-bound students, so they can acquire skills that lead to high-wage jobs. In the new economy, opportunity will depend on lifelong learning. We will support the goal of literacy for all Americans. We will ask firms to invest in the training of all workers, not just corporate management.

A Domestic GI Bill. It is time to revolutionize the way student loan programs are run. We will make college affordable to *all* students who are qualified to attend, *regardless of family income*. A Domestic GI Bill will enable all Americans to borrow money for college, so long as they are willing to pay it back as a percentage of their income over time or through national service addressing unmet community needs.

Health Care. All Americans should have universal access to quality, affordable health care — not as a privilege but as a right. That requires tough controls on health costs, which are rising at two to three times the rate of inflation, terrorizing American families and businesses and depriving millions of the care they need. We will enact a uniquely American reform of the health-care system to control costs and make health care affordable; ensure quality and choice of health-care providers; cover all Americans regardless of pre-existing conditions; squeeze out waste, bureaucracy and abuse; improve primary and preventive care including child immunization and prevention of diseases like tuberculosis now becoming rampant in our cities; provide expanded education on the relationship between diet and health; expand access to mental health treatment services; provide a safety net through support of public hospitals; provide for the full range of reproductive choice — education, counseling, access to contraceptives and the right to a safe, legal abortion; expand medical research; and provide more long-term care, including home health care. We will make ending the epidemic in breast cancer a major priority, and expand reproductive health services and other special health needs of women. We must be united in declaring war on AIDS and HIV disease, implement the recommendations of the National Commission on AIDS and fully fund the Ryan White Care Act; provide targeted and honest prevention campaigns; combat HIV-related discrimination; make drug treatment available for all addicts who seek it; guarantee access to quality care; expand clinical trials for treatments and vaccines; and speed up the FDA [Food and Drug Administration] drug approval process.

Energy. We reject the Republican myth that energy efficiency and environmental protection are enemies of economic growth. We will make our economy more efficient, using less energy, reducing our dependence on foreign oil, and producing less solid and toxic waste. We will adopt a coordinated transportation policy, with a strong commitment to mass transit; encourage efficient alternative-fueled vehicles; increase our reliance on clean natural gas; promote clean coal technology; invest in R&D [research and development] on renewable energy sources; strengthen efforts to prevent air and water pollution; support incentives for domestic oil and gas operations; and push for revenue-neutral incentives that reward conservation, prevent pollution and encourage recycling.

Civil and Equal Rights. We don't have an American to waste. Democrats will continue to lead the fight to ensure that no Americans suffer discrimination or deprivation of rights on the basis of race, gender, language, national origin, religion, age, disability, sexual orientation or other characteristics irrelevant to ability. We support ratification of the Equal Rights Amendment, affirmative action, stronger protection of voting rights for racial and ethnic minorities, including language access to voting, and continued resistance to discriminatory English-only pressure groups. We will reverse the Bush administration's assault on civil rights enforcement, and instead work to rebuild and vigorously use machinery for civil rights enforcement; support comparable remedies for women; aggressively prosecute hate crimes; strengthen legal services for the poor; deal with other nations in a way that Americans of any origin do not become scapegoats or victims of foreign policy disputes; provide civil rights protection for gay men and lesbians and an end to Defense Department discrimination; respect Native American culture and our treaty commitments; require the United States government to recognize its trustee obligations to the inhabitants of Hawaii generally and to Native Hawaiians in particular; and fully enforce the Americans with Disability Act to enable people with disabilities to achieve independence and function at their highest possible level.

Strengthening the Family. Governments don't raise children, people do. People who bring children into this world have a responsibility to care for them and give them values, motivation and discipline. Children should not have children. We need a national crackdown on deadbeat parents, an effective system of child-support enforcement nationwide and a systematic effort to establish paternity for every child. We must also make it easier for parents to build strong families through pay equity. Family and medical leave will ensure that workers don't have to choose between family and work. We support a family preservation program to reduce child and spousal abuse by providing preventive services and foster care to families in crisis. We favor ensuring quality and affordable child-care opportunities for working parents, and a fair and healthy start for every child, including essential prenatal and well-baby care. We support the needs of our senior citizens for productive and healthy lives including hunger prevention, income adequacy, transportation access and abuse prevention.

Welfare Reform. Welfare should be a second chance, not a way of life. We want to break the cycle of welfare by adhering to two simple principles: No one who is able to work can stay on welfare forever, and no one who works should live in poverty. We will continue to help those who cannot help themselves. We will offer people on welfare a new social contract. We'll invest in education and job training, and provide the child care and health care they need to go to work and achieve long-term self-sufficiency. We will give them the help they need to make the transition from welfare to work, and require people who can work to go to work within two years in available jobs either in the private sector or in community service to meet unmet needs. That will restore the covenant that welfare was meant to be: A promise of temporary help for people who have fallen on hard times.

Abortion. Democrats stand behind the right of every woman to choose, consistent with *Roe v. Wade*, regardless of ability to pay, and support a national law to protect that right. It is a fundamental constitutional liberty that individual Americans — not government — can best take responsibility for making the most difficult and intensely personal decisions regarding reproduction. The goal of our nation must be to make abortion less necessary, not more difficult or more dangerous. We pledge to support contraceptive research, family planning, comprehensive family life education, and policies that support healthy childbearing and enable parents to care most effectively for their children.

Management and Labor. The private sector is the engine of our economy and the main source of national wealth.... America's corporate leaders have a responsibility to invest in their country.... If a company wants to overpay its executives and underinvest in the future or transfer jobs overseas, it shouldn't get special treatment and tax breaks from the Treasury. Managers must work with employees to make the workplace safer, more satisfying and more efficient.

Workers must also accept added responsibilities in the new economy. In return for an increased voice and a greater stake in the success of their enterprises, workers should be prepared to join in cooperative efforts to increase productivity, flexibility and quality. Government's neutrality between labor and management cannot mean neutrality about the collective bargaining process, which has been purposely crippled by Republican administrations. Our economic growth depends on processes, including collective bargaining, that permit labor and management to work together on their common interests, even as they work out their conflicts.

Environment. For ourselves and future generations, we must protect our environment. We will protect our old-growth forests, preserve critical habitats, provide a genuine "no net loss" policy on wetlands, conserve the critical resources of soil, water and air, oppose new offshore oil drilling and mineral exploration and production in our nation's many environmentally critical areas, and address ocean pollution by reducing oil and toxic waste spills at sea. We believe America's youth can serve their country well through a civilian conservation corps. To protect the public health, we will clean up the environmental horrors at federal facilities, insist that private polluters clean up their toxic and hazardous wastes, and vigorously prosecute environmental criminals. We will oppose Republican efforts to gut the Clean Air Act in the guise of competitiveness. We will reduce the volume of solid waste and encourage the use of recycled materials while discouraging excess packaging. To avoid the mistakes of the past, we will actively support energy efficiency, recycling and pollution-prevention strategies.

Government Reform. Democrats in 1992 intend to lead a revolution in government, challenging it to act responsibly and be accountable, starting with the hardest and most urgent problems of the deficit and economic growth. Rather than throwing money at obsolete programs, we will eliminate unnecessary layers of management, cut administrative costs, give people more choices in the service they get and empower them to make those choices. To foster greater responsibility in government at every level, we support giving greater flexibility to our cities, counties and states in achieving federal mandates and carrying out existing programs.

All branches of government must live by the laws the rest of us obey, determine their pay in an open manner that builds public trust and eliminate special privileges. People in public office need to be accessible to the people they represent. It's time to reform the campaign finance system, to get big money out of our politics and let the people back in. We must limit overall campaign spending and limit the disproportionate and excessive role of PACs [political action committees]. We need new voter registration laws that expand the electorate, such as universal same-day registration, along with full political rights and protections for public employees and new regulations to ensure that the airwaves truly help citizens make informed choices among candidates and policies. And we need fair political representation for all sectors of our country — including the District of Columbia, which deserves and must get statehood status.

Crime and Drugs. To empower America's communities, Democrats pledge to restore government as upholder of basic law and order for crime-ravaged communities. The simplest and most direct way to restore order in our cities is to put more police on the streets. America's police are locked in an unequal struggle with crime: Since 1951 the ratio of police officers to reported crimes has reversed, from 3-to-1 to 1-to-3. We will create a Police Corps, in which participants will receive college aid in return for several years of service after graduation in a state or local police department. As we shift people and resources from defense to the civilian economy, we will create new jobs in law enforcement for those leaving the military.

We will expand drug counseling and treatment for those who need it, intensify efforts to educate our children at the earliest ages to the dangers of drug and alcohol abuse, and curb demand from the street corner to the penthouse suite, so that the United States, with 5 percent of the world's population, no longer consumes 50 percent of the world's illegal drugs.

Neighborhoods and police should be partners in the war on crime. Democrats support more community policing, which uses foot patrols and storefront offices to make police officers visible fixtures in urban neighborhoods. We will combat street violence, and emphasize building trust and solving the problems that breed crime.

It is time to shut down the weapons bazaars in our cities. We support a reasonable waiting period to permit background checks for purchases of handguns, as well as assault weapons controls to ban the possession, sale, importation and manufacture of the most deadly assault weapons. We do not support efforts to restrict weapons used for legitimate hunt-

ing and sporting purposes. We will work for swift and certain punishment of all people who violate the country's gun laws and for stronger sentences for criminals who use guns. We will also seek to shut down the black market for guns and impose severe penalties on people who sell guns to children. . . .

Democrats also favor innovative sentencing and punishment options, including community service and boot camps for first-time offenders; tougher penalties for rapists; victim-impact statements and restitution to ensure that crime victims will not be lost in the complexities of the criminal justice system; and initiatives to make our schools safe, including alternative schools for disruptive children.

Social Services. We must further the new direction set in the Family Support Act of 1988, away from subsistence and dependence and toward work, family and personal initiative and responsibility. We advocate slower phasing out of Medicaid and other benefits to encourage work; special savings accounts to help low-income families build assets; fair lending; an indexed minimum wage; an expanded Job Corps; and an end to welfare rules that encourage family breakup and penalize individual initiative, such as the $1,000 limit on personal savings.

Immigration. Our nation of immigrants has been invigorated repeatedly as new people, ideas and ways of life have become part of the American tapestry. Democrats support immigration policies that promote fairness, non-discrimination and family reunification and that reflect our constitutional freedoms of speech, association and travel.

Housing. Safe, secure housing is essential to the institutions of community and family. We support homeownership for working families and will honor that commitment through policies to encourage affordable mortgage credit. We must also confront homelessness by renovating, preserving and expanding the stock of affordable low-income housing. We support tenant management and ownership, so public housing residents can manage their own affairs and acquire property worth protecting.

National Service. We will create new opportunities for citizens to serve each other, their communities and their country. By mobilizing hundreds of thousands of volunteers, national service will enhance the role of ordinary citizens in solving unresolved community problems.

The Arts. We believe in public support for the arts, including a National Endowment for the Arts that is free from political manipulation and firmly rooted in the First Amendment's freedom of expression guarantee.

Defense. America is the world's strongest military power, and we must remain so. A post-Cold War restructuring of American forces will produce substantial savings beyond those promised by the Bush administration, but that restructuring must be achieved without undermining our ability to meet future threats to our security. A military structure for the 1990s and beyond must be built on four pillars: *First,* a survivable nuclear force to deter any conceivable threat as we reduce our nuclear arsenals through arms control negotiations and other reciprocal action. *Second,* conventional forces shifted toward projecting power wherever our vital national interests are threatened. This means reducing the size of our forces in Europe while meeting our obligations to NATO and strengthening our rapid deployment capabilities to deal with new threats to our security posed by renegade dictators, terrorists, international drug traffickers and the local armed conflicts that can threaten the peace of entire regions. *Third,* maintenance of the two qualities that make America's military the best in the world — the superiority of our military personnel and of our technology. These qualities are vital to shortening any conflict and saving American lives. *Fourth,* intelligence capabilities redirected to develop far more sophisticated, timely and accurate analyses of the economic and political conditions that can fuel new conflicts.

The United States must be prepared to use military force decisively when necessary to defend our vital interests. The burdens of collective security in a new era must be shared fairly, and we should encourage multilateral peace-keeping through the United Nations and other international efforts.

American policy must be focused on averting military threats as well as meeting them. To halt the spread of nuclear and other weapons of mass destruction, we must lead a renewed international effort to get tough with companies that peddle nuclear and chemical warfare technologies, strengthen the International Atomic Energy Agency and enforce strong sanctions against governments that violate international restraints. A Comprehensive Test Ban would strengthen our ability to stop the spread of nuclear weapons to other countries, which may be our greatest future security threat. We must press for strong international limits on the dangerous and wasteful flow of conventional arms to troubled regions. A U.S. troop presence should be maintained in Korea as long as North Korea presents a threat to South Korea.

International Trade. The United States cannot be strong abroad if it is weak at home. Restoring America's global economic leadership must become a central element of our national security policies. The strength of nations, once defined in military terms, now is measured also by the skill of their workers, the imagination of their managers and the power of their technologies.

Either we develop and pursue a national plan for restoring our economy through a partnership of government, labor and business, or we slip behind the nations that are competing with us and growing. At stake are American jobs, our standard of living and the quality of life for ourselves and our children.

Economic strength — indeed our national security — is grounded on a healthy domestic economy. But we cannot be strong at home unless we are part of a vibrant and expanding global economy that recognizes human rights and seeks to improve the living standards of all the world's people. This is vital to achieving good quality, high-paying jobs for Americans.

Our government must work to expand trade while insisting that the conduct of world trade is fair. It must fight to uphold American interests — promoting exports, expanding trade in agricultural and other products, opening markets in major product and service sectors with our principal competitors, achieving reciprocal access. This should include renewed authority to use America's trading leverage against the most serious problems. The U.S. government also must firmly enforce U.S. laws against unfair trade.

Multilateral trade agreements can advance our economic interests by expanding the global economy. Whether negotiating the North American Free Trade Area (NAFTA) or completing the GATT [General Agreement on Tariffs and Trade] negotiations, our government must assure that our legitimate concerns about environmental, health and safety, and labor standards are included. Those American workers whose jobs are affected must have the benefit of effective adjustment assistance.

Emerging Democracies. Helping to lead an international effort to assist the emerging — and still fragile — democracies in Eastern Europe and the former Soviet Union build democratic institutions in free market settings, demilitarize their societies and integrate their economies into the world trading system. Unlike the Bush administration, which waited too long to recognize the new democratic governments in the Baltic countries and the nations of the former Soviet Union, we must act decisively with our European allies to support freedom, diminish ethnic tensions, and oppose aggression in the former communist countries, such as Bosnia-Herzegovina, which are struggling to make the transition from communism to democracy. As change sweeps through the Balkans, the United States must be sensitive to the concerns of Greece regarding the use of the name Macedonia. And in the post-Cold War era, our foreign assistance programs in Africa, the Caribbean, Latin America and elsewhere should be targeted at helping democracies rather than tyrants.

Democracy Corps. Promoting democratic institutions by creating a Democracy Corps to send American volunteers to countries that seek legal, financial and political expertise to build democratic institutions, and support groups like the National Endowment for Democracy and Asia Foundation and others.

China. Conditioning of favorable trade terms for China on respect for human rights in China and Tibet, greater market access for U.S. goods, and responsible conduct on weapons proliferation.

South Africa. Maintenance of state and local sanctions against South Africa in support of an investment code of conduct, existing limits on deductibility of taxes paid to South Africa and diplomatic pressure until there is an irreversible, full and fair accommodation with the black majority to create a democratic government with full rights for all its citizens....

Middle East Peace. Support for the peace process now under way in the Middle East, rooted in the tradition of the Camp David accords. Direct negotiations between Israel, her Arab neighbors and Palestinians, with no imposed solutions, are the only way to achieve enduring security for Israel and full peace for all parties in the region. The end of the Cold War does not alter America's deep interest in our longstanding special relationship with Israel, based on shared values, a mutual commitment to democracy and a strategic alliance that benefits both nations....

Human Rights. Standing everywhere for the rights of individuals and respect for ethnic minorities against the repressive acts of governments — against torture, political imprisonment and all attacks on civilized standards of human freedom. This is a proud tradition of the Democratic Party, which has stood for freedom in South Africa and continues to resist oppression in Cuba. Our nation should once again promote the principle of sanctuary for politically oppressed people everywhere, be they Haitian refugees, Soviet Jews seeking U.S. help in their successful absorption into Israeli society or Vietnamese fleeing communism. Forcible return of anyone fleeing political repression is a betrayal of American values.

Human Needs. Support for the struggle against poverty and disease in the developing world, including the heartbreaking famine in Africa. We must not replace the East-West conflict with one between North and South, a growing divide between the industrialized and developing world. Our development programs must be re-examined and restructured to assure that their benefits truly help those most in need to help themselves. At stake are the lives of millions of human beings who live in hunger, uprooted from their homes, too often without hope. The United States should work to establish a specific plan and timetable for the elimination of world hunger.

Global Environment. As the threat of nuclear holocaust recedes, the future of the Earth is challenged by gathering environmental crises. As governments around the world have sought the path to concerted action, the Bush administration — despite its alleged foreign policy expertise — has been more of an obstacle to progress than a leader for change, practicing isolationism on an issue that affects us all. Democrats know we must act now to save the health of the Earth and the health of our children for generations to come.

The United States must become a leader, not an impediment, in the fight against global warming. We should join our European allies in agreeing to limit carbon dioxide emissions to 1990 levels by the year 2000.

The United States must be a world leader in finding replacements for CFCs [chlorofluorocarbons] and other ozone-depleting substances.

We must work actively to protect the planet's biodiversity and preserve its forests....

We must fashion imaginative ways of engaging governments and business in the effort to encourage developing nations to preserve their environmental heritage.

Explosive population growth must be controlled by working closely with other industrialized and developing nations and private organizations to fund greater family-planning efforts.

Republicans

Five weeks after the Democratic convention, the Republicans convened in Houston Aug. 17-20 and did their best to persuade voters to remember the past and trust in experience. From the rousing opening night performance of former president Ronald Reagan to the repeated calls to honor traditional family values, the Republican National Convention looked backward as much as it looked ahead.

There were frequent references to having defeated communism and having won the Persian Gulf War. Voters were asked to ignore the Democrats' attempt to remake themselves in a more moderate image and to remember instead what life was like under Jimmy Carter, the most recent Democratic president.

There was little moderation evident in the party platform adopted for George Bush's second term. The GOP approved a hard-line approach opposing abortion rights and any attempt to increase taxes. On the social issues front, there were planks favoring school choice, school prayer and family unity.

Finally, the delegates needed little prompting to vent their frustrations at the "liberal media" for praising Democratic nominee Bill Clinton, dwelling on dissension over the GOP's anti-abortion stance and overemphasizing the weak economy. Bush sought to link Clinton to the Democratic Congress, which he blamed for the nation's problems — a refrain that would be played over and over throughout the week.

This was a homecoming of sorts for Bush. A New Englander by birth who went to Texas to work in the oil business, he retained his residency at a Houston hotel.

Party activists also sought a fresh start for Dan Quayle, widely perceived as being bumbling, gaffe-prone and ineffective. But many conservatives still viewed the vice president as a hero, and because Quayle survived attempts to dump him from the ticket during the weeks leading up to the convention, GOP strategists looked forward to remaking his image as a thoughtful, middle-class American fighting for family values.

Recognizing that a vacuum of leadership would exist after 16 years of nominating Reagan and Bush, a host of potential presidential candidates in 1996 looked forward to Houston as a place to make their mark.

By week's end, Jack F. Kemp, secretary of Housing and Urban Development, seemed to draw the widest support among the class of 1996. Television commentator and 1992 candidate Patrick J. Buchanan was the most combative and divisive. And Massachusetts governor William F. Weld, a social and economic libertarian, became the most sought-after voice for the party's moderate wing.

When the convention opened it already had become clear that efforts to force a debate on abortion had fallen short. A majority in six delegations was required to challenge the platform's call for a constitutional ban on all abortions, but abortion rights supporters said they could muster majorities in only four delegations — Maine, Massachusetts, New Mexico and the Virgin Islands. The reason, they said, was that delegates felt it was more important to avoid embarrassing Bush than to force an open debate.

In the end the platform was approved by voice vote. There were cries of "no!" when the document was put to delegates, but no public challenge.

In his speech Buchanan, who had unsuccessfully challenged Bush in the primaries, appealed to his supporters to throw their support to the president. He acknowledged the disagreements that led him to challenge Bush but said the convention marked the time to unite.

"The right place for us to be now in this presidential campaign is right beside George Bush," Buchanan said.

Buchanan had whipped the crowd into a frenzy with a bitter, scathing attack on Clinton, attacking his patriotism and charging that his view of change for America would mean abortion on demand, a litmus test for the Supreme Court, homosexual rights, women in combat and discrimination against religious schools. "That's change, all right," said Buchanan, but "it's not the kind of change we can abide in a nation that we still call God's country."

Buchanan's remarks were enthusiastically received in the hall, but the biggest response came for President Reagan, who described his speech as the "last chapter" in his political career. At 81, the grand patriarch of the Republican Party showed all the oratorical skills and political spirit that had made him the hero of GOP conservatives.

"We stood tall and proclaimed that communism was destined for the ash heap of history," he said. "We never heard so much ridicule from our liberal friends. But we knew then what the liberal Democrat leaders just couldn't figure out: The sky would not fall if America restored her strength and resolve. The sky would not fall if an American president spoke the truth. The only thing that would fall was the Berlin Wall."

House Minority Leader Robert H. Michel of Illinois, the convention chair, set the blistering tone against Congressional Democrats.

"We are here to tell the American people that this election is just as much about the Congress as it is about the presidency," he said. "The Democrats have controlled the House of Representatives now for 38 straight years, and that has to change." The Democrats "alone ... are responsible for the unholy mess Congress is in."

Congressional Democrats were used throughout as a foil to highlight the president's domestic agenda and the change he sought to implement. "The Constitution makes the president commander in chief of the Army but not commander in chief of the Congress," said keynote speaker Sen. Phil Gramm of Texas. "The Democrats who control Congress by overwhelming margins have used their majority to throttle the president's program and strangle the nation's economy in a partisan gridlock the likes of which we have not seen in this century."

Delegates heard from three governors whose successes at home had thrust them into the national spotlight and fueled speculation about a future spot on the national ticket. Tommy G. Thompson of Wisconsin and John Engler of Michigan delivered unemotional speeches, but Gov. William F. Weld of Massachusetts highlighted divisions between moderates and conservatives on abortion and homosexual rights. He said, "I happen to think that individual freedom should extend to a woman's right to choose. I want the government out of your pocketbook and your bedroom." Crowd reaction was a mixed bag of boos and cheers.

Kemp got an enthusiastic response when he credited Reagan and Bush for their roles in the demise of communism. "Ladies and gentleman," he told the assembled, "communism didn't fall. It was pushed. It was our ideas that did the pushing and our Republican presidents, Ronald Reagan and George Bush, that helped change the world."

Wednesday was family night at the Astrodome. The delegates heard from the candidates' wives, Barbara Bush and Marilyn Quayle, and speakers throughout the evening discussed family values. The evening's high point came when the entire Bush clan gathered at the podium, and the president made a cameo appearance.

Many delegates were milling about during speeches by television evangelist Pat Robertson and others; they did not settle in until the address by Mary Fisher, a victim of HIV, the virus that causes AIDS. The crowd hushed as Fisher, 44, the daughter of a Detroit multimillionaire and longtime GOP fundraiser, spoke about the AIDS virus, which she had contracted from her ex-husband.

Imploring the delegates to show people with AIDS the same sort of compassion that the president and Mrs. Bush had shown her, she said, ". . . [W]e do the president's cause no good if we praise the American family but ignore a virus that destroys it."

The mood turned more combative when Marilyn Quayle said that she and her husband, like the Democratic standard-bearers, were members of the baby boom generation, but "not everyone demonstrated, dropped out, took drugs, joined in the sexual revolution or dodged the draft."

Barbara Bush adopted a gentler theme, praising her husband as "the strongest, the most decent, the most caring, the wisest, yes, and the healthiest man I know."

Leading off the nomination speakers, Labor Secretary Lynn Martin called Democrats "whimpering naysayers" who peddle "the crass politics of fear and the false promise of change," while describing their congressmen as "aging punjabs."

The roll call was arranged so that Texas, the convention's host state and technically Bush's home, put him over the top. The final tally was 2,166 votes for Bush, 18 for Buchanan and three for others, before the nomination was approved by acclamation. New Hampshire never cast its 23 votes. (*Chart, p. 258*)

The first three days of convention week were little more than prelude for the critical closing night when Bush and Quayle would make their acceptance speeches and the convention would be pronounced a success or failure. The buildup for both addresses had been intense. Quayle's was seen as his big chance to redefine his political persona. Bush had an even greater task — to give "the speech of his life."

Neither quite lived up to the advance billing, but both delivered effective addresses that lifted the voices and spirits of the convention hall, and when both left town Friday morning, they could point to significantly better opinion polls as a sign of success. Speaking first, Quayle defiantly answered his legion of detractors. "I know my critics wish I were not standing here tonight," he said." They don't like our values. They look down on our beliefs. They're afraid of our ideas. And they know the American people stand on our side."

Bush came out fighting against the Democratic-controlled Congress and Clinton. Responding to the concerns of delegates still angry over his broken "no-new-taxes" pledge, Bush admitted that it had been a mistake but posed a question to the electorate. "Who do you trust in this election — the candidate who has raised taxes one time and regrets it, or the other candidate who raised taxes and fees 128 times and enjoyed it every time?"

Trust was again the issue as Bush highlighted his role as commander in chief in what was widely considered to be his strength — foreign policy. He spoke of Cold War triumph yet warned that "the Soviet bear may be gone, but there are still wolves in the woods."

These existing threats allowed Bush to tout his stewardship in the Persian Gulf War and raise questions about what his opponent would have done.

Quayle's entrance was preceded by a short biographical video, similar to the one that introduced Clinton to the Democratic convention.

Following are excerpts form the Republican platform of 1992:

Family Values. Our greatness starts at home — literally. So Republicans believe government should strengthen families, not replace them. Today, more than ever, the traditional family is under assault. We believe our laws should reflect what makes our nation prosperous and wholesome: faith in God, hard work, service to others and limited government. . . .

The Republican Party responds, as it has since 1980, with an unabashed commitment to the family's economic liberty and moral rights. Republicans trust parents and believe they, not courts and lawyers, know what is best for their children. That is why we will work to ensure that the Congress and the states shall enact no law abridging the rights of the family formed by blood, marriage, adoption or legal custody — rights that are anterior and superior to those of government. . . .

The demands of employment and commuting often make it hard for parents to spend time with their children. Republicans advocate maximum flexibility in working and child-care arrangements so that families can make the most of their schedules. We support pro-family policies: job-sharing, telecommuting, compressed workweeks, parental leave negotiated between employer and employees, and flextime. . . .

Most parents prefer in-home care of their children but often encounter government obstacles. Republicans will promote in-home care by allowing payment annually, instead of quarterly, of income taxes by employees and withholding taxes by employers. . . .

[W]e want to expand the Young Child Tax Credit to $500 per child and make it available to all families with children under the age of 10. . . .

Education. The Republican strategy is based on sound principle. Parents have the right to choose the best school for their children. Schools should teach right from wrong. Schools should reinforce parental authority, not replace it. We should increase flexibility from federal regulation. We should explore a new generation of break-the-mold New American Schools. Standards and assessments should be raised, not reduced to a lowest common denominator. Communities should be empowered to find what works. The pursuit of excellence in education is a fundamental goal. Good teachers should be rewarded for teaching well. Alternative certification can bring desperately needed new people into the teaching profession. America needs public, private and parochial schools. . . .

The president's proposed "GI Bill for Children" will provide $1,000 scholarships to middle- and low-income families, enabling their children to attend the school of their choice. This innovative plan will not only drive schools to excel as they compete, but will also give every parent consumer power to obtain an excellent education for his or her child....

The president has proposed allowing families to deduct the interest they pay on student loans, and penalty-free withdrawal of IRA [individual retirement account] funds for educational expenses....

We strongly support youth apprenticeships that include a year of college, to encourage a lifetime of learning and opportunity for students....

[W]e support the right of students to engage in voluntary prayer in schools and the right of the community to do so at commencements or other occasions. We will strongly enforce the law guaranteeing equal access to school facilities. We also advocate recitation of the Pledge of Allegiance in schools as a reminder of the principles that sustain us as one nation under God....

Health Care. Republicans believe government control of health care is irresponsible and ineffective. We believe health-care choices should remain in the hands of the people, not government bureaucrats. This issue truly represents a fundamental difference between the two parties.

We endorse President Bush's comprehensive health-care plan, which solves the two major problems of the current system — access and affordability — while preserving the high-quality care Americans now enjoy. The president's plan will make health care *more affordable* through tax credits and deductions that will offset insurance costs for 95 million Americans; and make health care *more accessible,* especially for small businesses, by reducing insurance costs and eliminating workers' worries of losing insurance if they change jobs. This plan will expand access to health care by:

• Creating new tax credits and deductions to help low- and middle-income Americans. These tax credits would be available in the form of vouchers for low-income people who work.

• Providing insurance security for working Americans by requiring insurers to cover pre-existing conditions.

• Making health insurance premiums fully deductible for the self-employed.

• Making it easier for small firms to purchase coverage for their employees....

• Addressing the medical malpractice problem by a cap on non-economic damage recoveries in malpractice claims and an alternative dispute resolution before going to court.

In short, the president aims to make coverage available to all, guaranteed, renewable, with no preconditions. Under his plan, no one will have to go broke to get well....

AIDS. We are committed to ensure that our nation's response to AIDS is shaped by compassion, not fear or ignorance and will oppose, as a matter of decency and honor, any discrimination against Americans who are its victims....

Above all, a cure must be found. We have committed enormous resources — $4.2 billion over the past four years for research alone, more than for any disease except cancer....

The Homeless. The Bush administration has worked vigorously to address this tragedy, believing that involuntary homelessness in America is unacceptable. Accordingly, the administration has proposed $4 billion in homeless assistance, an amount cut back by the Democrat-controlled Congress. We have also implemented a Shelter Plus Care program designed to assist homeless persons who are mentally ill, chemically dependent or stricken with AIDS....

Social Security. We reaffirm our commitment to a strong Social Security system. To stop penalizing grandparents and other seniors who care for children, we pledge to continue the Republican crusade to end the earnings limitation for Social Security recipients. More than ever, our

nation needs older Americans in its schools and workplaces. There should be no barriers to their full participation in our country's future. We pledge support for greater availability of long-term care and for research to combat Alzheimer's disease. Republicans also took the lead in expanding home health care in government programs, and we want to build on that accomplishment.

Cultural Values. We oppose any legislation or law that legally recognizes same-sex marriages and allows such couples to adopt children or provide foster care.

We must recognize that the time has come for a national crusade against pornography.... We call on federal agencies to halt the sale, under government auspices, of pornographic materials. We endorse Republican legislation, the Pornography Victims Compensation Act, allowing victims of pornography to seek damages from those who make or sell it....

Government has a responsibility, as well, to ensure that it promotes the common moral values that bind us together as a nation. We therefore condemn the use of public funds to subsidize obscenity and blasphemy masquerading as art....

Welfare Reform. Today's welfare system is anti-work and anti-marriage. It taxes families to subsidize illegitimacy. It rewards unethical behavior and penalizes initiative. It cannot be merely tinkered with by Congress; it must be re-created by states and localities. Republican governors and legislators in several states have already launched dramatic reforms, especially with workfare and learnfare. Welfare can no longer be a check in the mail with no responsibility.

We believe fathers and mothers must be held responsible for their children. We support stronger enforcement of child support laws. We call for strong enforcement and tough penalties against welfare fraud and insist that work must be a mandatory part of public assistance for all who are able to work. Because divorce, desertion and illegitimacy account for almost all the increase in child poverty over the last 20 years, we put the highest priority upon enforcement of family rights and responsibilities....

Crime. We believe in giving police the resources to do their job. Law enforcement must remain primarily a state and local responsibility. With 95 percent of all violent crimes within the jurisdiction of the states, we have led efforts to increase the number of police protecting our citizens. We also support incentives to encourage personnel leaving the armed forces to continue to defend their country — against the enemy within — by entering the law enforcement profession....

We . . . support the stiffest penalties, including the death penalty, for major drug traffickers.... Drug users must face punishment, including fines and imprisonment....

Illegal Immigration. We will build on the already announced strengthening of the Border Patrol to better coordinate interdiction of illegal entrants through greater cross-border cooperation. Specifically, we will increase the size of the Border Patrol in order to meet the increasing need to stop illegal immigration and we will equip the Border Patrol with the tools, technologies and structures necessary to secure the border....

Individual Rights. The protection of individual rights is the foundation for opportunity and security....

[W]e declare that bigotry and prejudice have no place in American life. We denounce all who practice or promote racism, anti-Semitism or religious intolerance. We believe churches and religious schools should not be taxed; we defend the right of religious leaders to speak out on public issues; and we condemn the cowardly desecration of places of worship that has shocked our country in recent years....

We renew the historic Republican commitment to the rights of women from the early days of the suffragist movement to the present. Because legal rights mean little without opportunity, we assert economic growth as the key to the continued progress of women in all fields of American life.

We believe the unborn child has a fundamental individual right to life that cannot be infringed. We therefore reaffirm our support for a human life amendment to the Constitution, and we endorse legislation to make clear that the 14th Amendment's protections apply to unborn children. We oppose using public revenues for abortion and will not fund organizations that advocate it....

We reaffirm our commitment to the Fifth Amendment to the Constitution: "No person shall be ... deprived of life, liberty, or property, without due process of law; nor shall private property be taken for public use, without just compensation." We support strong enforcement of this Takings Clause to keep citizens secure in the use and development of their property. We also seek to reduce the amount of land owned or controlled by the government, especially in the Western states. We insist upon prompt payment for private lands certified as critical for preserving essential parks and preserves.

Republicans defend the constitutional right to keep and bear arms. We call for stiff mandatory sentences for those who use firearms in a crime....

We affirm the right of individuals to form, join or assist labor organizations to bargain collectively, consistent with state laws. We support the right of states to enact right-to-work laws.

A Republican Congress will amend the Hobbs Act, so that union officials will not be exempt from the law's prohibition against extortion and violence. We call for greater legal protection from violence for workers who stay on the job during strikes.

We support self-determination for Indian tribes in managing their own affairs and resources.... Reservations and tribal lands held in trust should be free to become enterprise zones so their people can fully share in the nation's prosperity. We will work with tribal governments to improve education, health, economic opportunity and environmental conditions....

Taxes. We will oppose any attempt to increase taxes.... We believe the tax increases of 1990 should ultimately be repealed....

As the deficit comes under control, we aspire to further tax rate cuts, strengthening incentives to work, save, invest and innovate. We also support President Bush's efforts to reduce federal spending and to cap the growth of non-Social Security entitlements....

We support further tax simplification....

Business Deregulation. We support President Bush's freeze on new regulations.... We call for a permanent moratorium until our regulatory reforms are fully in place. They include market-based regulation, cost-benefit analysis of all new rule-making, and a regulatory budget that will make Congress admit — and correct — the harm it does by legislation that destroys jobs and competitiveness....

Homeownership. The best housing policy is a non-inflationary, growing economy that has produced low mortgage rates and has made housing more affordable.

We demand Congress enact President's Bush's housing program introduced as part of his pro-growth package in January.

Provide a $5,000 tax credit for first-time home buyers and allow them penalty-free IRA withdrawals.

Set a modified "passive loss rule" for active real estate investors.

Extend tax preferences for mortgage revenue bonds and low-income housing.

And allow deductions for losses on personal residences.

The average American's home is his or her primary asset. That asset should be completely shielded from federal taxation, allowing the homeowner to maintain it or access it as he or she sees fit. We call for the complete elimination of the capital gains tax on the sale of a principal residence....

Enterprise Zones. The Republican Party enthusiastically encourages the passage of federal enterprise zones. Enterprise zones have been effective programs for promoting growth in urban and rural America. Republicans believe that the concept of enterprise zones is based on unyielding faith in the entrepreneurial spirit of all Americans. Enterprise zones foster individual initiative and government deregulation....

Technology. We believe America must make technological development one of its highest priorities. We therefore support efforts to promote science and technology — providing funding for basic research, supporting investment in emerging technologies, improving education in science and engineering, enhancing tax credits for research and development, eliminating unnecessary regulation to create competitive markets, and protecting intellectual property....

Space. Republicans ... are determined to complete space station *Freedom* within this decade. Our agenda is to lower the cost of access to space, and to broaden that access to the private sector, with a family of new launchers; to build and fly sensors for the global environment; and to advance cutting-edge capabilities like the National Aerospace Plane and single stage-to-orbit rockets, so technological breakthroughs can be quickly exploited. We will promote space-based industry and ensure that space remains a frontier for private enterprise, not a restricted preserve for government....

International Trade. Economic freedom is an essential link to our foreign policy. It means expanded trade, but it also means dynamic growth based on shared values — a coming together of nations in the commonwealth of peaceful progress. To that end, U.S. aid, whether bilateral or through international organizations, should promote market reforms, limit regulation and encourage free trade.

Chief among these market reforms should be the privatization of state-owned industries such as telecommunications, power, mining and refining....

We will work with developing nations to make their economies attractive to private investment and will support innovations to guarantee repayment of their loans, including debt for equity swaps. Our experience can help them develop environmentally rational strategies for growth....

Government Reform. We reaffirm our support for a constitutional amendment to limit the number of terms House members and senators may serve....

Congress must stop exempting itself from laws such as the minimum wage and the civil rights statutes, as well as laws that apply to the executive branch. The Independent Counsel Act is a case in point.... If that act is reauthorized, it must be extended to Congress as well. Safety and health regulations, civil rights and minimum wage laws are further examples of areas where Congress has set itself apart from the people. This practice must end.

Congress must slash its own bureaucracy....

We support state-level appointment of nonpartisan redistricting commissions to apply clear standards for compactness of districts, competitiveness between the parties and protection of community interests.

Budget Reform. Republicans vigorously support a balanced budget, a balanced-budget constitutional amendment and a line-item veto for the president.

Republicans believe this balancing of the budget should be achieved, not by increasing taxes to match spending, but by cutting spending to current levels of revenue. We prefer a balanced-budget amendment that contains a supermajority requirement to raise taxes.

We also propose procedural reforms. We support legislation that would require Congress to pass a legally binding budget before it can consider spending bills. The budget's spending ceilings shall not be exceeded without a supermajority vote of both chambers. If Congress fails to pass any appropriation bill, funding for its programs will automatically be frozen at the previous year's level. The key to prosperity for the rest of this century and for the next generation of Americans is a budget strategy that restores sanity to the budget process and checks the growth of government.

Campaign Reform. We will require congressional candidates to raise most of their funds from individuals within their home constituencies. This will limit outside special-interest money and result in less expensive campaigns, with less padding for incumbents. To the same end, we will strengthen the role of political parties to remove pressure on candidates to spend so much time soliciting funds. We will eliminate political action committees supported by corporations, unions or trade associations, and restrict the practice of bundling.

To restore competition in elections by attacking the unfair advantages of incumbency, we will stop incumbents from warding off challengers merely by amassing huge war chests. Congressional candidates will be forbidden from carrying campaign funds from one election to the next. We will oppose arbitrary spending limits — cynical devices which hobble challengers to keep politicians in office.

Privatization. Privatization is an important alternative to higher taxes and reduced services. If private enterprise can perform better and more cheaply than government, let it do so....

Where it advances both efficiency and safety, we will advocate privatization of airport operation and management.

We deplore the blatant political bias of the government-sponsored radio and television networks. It is especially outrageous that taxpayers are now forced to underwrite this biased broadcasting through the Corporation for Public Broadcasting (CPB). We call for sweeping reform of CPB....

We will not initiate any federal activity that can be conducted better on the state or local level. In doing so, we reassert the crucial importance of the 10th Amendment. We oppose costly federal mandates that stifle innovation and force tax hikes upon states and localities. We require that Congress calculate the cost of mandated initiatives upon communities affected and provide adequate financial support for mandates invoked. We will continue the process of returning power to local voters by replacing federal programs with block grants.

Legal Reform. We support the Fairness Rule, to allow the winning party to a lawsuit to recover the costs of litigation from the losing party....

We believe complainants should have a choice of ways to settle problems through alternative dispute programs that will permit parties to pursue less costly and less complicated ways to resolve conflicts. We also call for greater use of judicial sanctions to stop frivolous lawsuits. We call for changes to the federal Racketeer Influenced and Corrupt Organizations (RICO) law to limit its use in civil litigation by requiring proof of all elements by clear and convincing proof.

We seek to restore fairness and predictability to punitive damages by placing appropriate limits on them, dividing trials into two phases to determine liability separately from damages and requiring clear proof of wrongdoing....

Because four-fifths of the time and cost of a lawsuit involves discovery — pretrial investigation of the facts — we will require automatic disclosure, by both sides, of basic information....

We will fight rising health-care costs — and equally important, help dedicated doctors to keep practicing in critical areas like obstetrics — by providing incentives for states to reform their liability laws. This will reduce the practice of "defensive medicine," requiring patients to be

tested for every conceivable ailment at their own enormous expense to guard against the mere possibility of a lawsuit.

Recognizing that legal reform can solve only parts of the larger problem, we support a federal product liability law. The cost of product liability protection is a great expense to the American consumer and seriously impedes our international competitiveness....

Washington, D.C. We call for closer and responsible congressional scrutiny of the city, federal oversight of its law enforcement and courts, and tighter fiscal restraints over its expenditures. We oppose statehood as inconsistent with the original intent of the framers of the Constitution and with the need for a federal city belonging to all the people as our nation's capital.

Agriculture. Agricultural prosperity is essential to the nation's global competitiveness. We will continue to expand the growth of American agriculture through exports, development of new products and new markets....

We pledge to fight unfair competition and to bring down the walls of protectionism around the world that unfairly inhibit competitiveness of U.S. farm exports. We pledge continued pressure to open world markets through the Uruguay Round, the North American Free Trade Agreement and bilateral negotiations.

We affirm that there will be no GATT agreement unless it improves opportunities for U.S. farmers to compete in world markets. We repeat our demands for cutbacks in export subsidies by the European Community and elsewhere, and we will fight the use of arbitrary health and sanitation standards to sabotage U.S. exports....

We support the widest possible use of ethanol in the U.S. motor fuel market, including in oxygenated fuels programs and as ethanol blends in reformulated gasolines.

In addition, the Republican Party supports increased research and development to reduce ethanol production costs and expand its use in motor fuel markets....

We value our nation's real wetlands habitat and the diversity of our native animal and plant life. We oppose, however, bureaucratic harassment of farm, ranch and timber families under statutes regarding endangered species and wetlands. When actions are required to protect an endangered species, we recognize that jobs can be lost, communities displaced and economic progress for all denied. Accordingly, prior to the implementation of a recovery plan for a species declared to be endangered, we will require the Congress to affirm the priority of the species on the endangered list and the specific measures to be taken in any recovery plan....

Energy. We will ... [allow] access, under environmental safeguards, to the coastal plain of the Arctic National Wildlife Refuge, possibly one of the largest petroleum reserves in our country, and to selected areas of the outer continental shelf (OCS). We support incentives to encourage domestic investment for onshore and OCS oil and gas exploration and development, including relief from the alternative minimum tax, credits for enhanced oil recovery and geological exploration under known geological oil fields and producing geological structures, and modified percentage depletion rules to benefit marginal production....

We endorse major national projects, like the superconducting super collider, which offer the promise of developing more efficient ways to store, transport and use energy.

We will hasten development of the next generation of nuclear power plants — one of the cleanest, safest energy sources of all....

We endorse development of renewable energy sources and research on fuel cells, conservation, hydro, solar, hydrogen and wind power as components of our overall plan for energy security and environmental quality.

Public Lands. The millions of acres that constitute this nation's public lands must continue to provide for a number of uses. We are committed to the multiple use of our public lands. We believe that recreation, forestry, ranching, mining, oil and gas exploration, and production on our public lands can be conducted in a way compatible with their conservation. . . .

Transportation. To keep America on the move, we assert the same principle that guides us in all other sectors of the economy: consumers benefit through competition within the private sector. That is why we will complete the job of trucking deregulation. We will also abolish the Interstate Commerce Commission, finally freeing shippers and consumers from horse-and-buggy regulation. . . .

Environment. Clearly we have led the world in investment in environmental protection. We have taught the world three vital lessons. First, environmental progress is integrally related to economic advancement. Second, economic growth generates the capital to pay for environmental gains. Third, private ownership and economic freedom are the best security against environmental degradation. . . .

However, with billions of dollars at stake in national production and jobs, not to mention our quality of life, our decisions to spend on environmental protection must not be determined by the politics of the moment. We will use scientifically respectable risk-benefit assessments to settle environmental controversies. . . .

We will legislatively overhaul the "superfund" program to speed the cleanup of hazardous waste and more efficiently use superfund dollars. . . .

NATO. [W]e reaffirm the NATO alliance. . . . The United States must remain a European power in the broadest sense, able to influence the policies and events that affect the livelihood and security of future generations of Americans. . . .

Israel. Consistent with our strategic relationship, the United States should continue to provide large-scale security assistance to Israel, maintaining Israel's qualitative military advantage over any adversary or coalition of adversaries. We also will continue to negotiate with the major arms supplying nations to reach an agreement on limiting arms sales to the Middle East and preventing the proliferation of non-conventional weapons. . . .

Middle East Peace. The basis for negotiations must be U.N. Security Council Resolutions 242 and 338. Peace must come from direct negotiations.

A meaningful peace must assure Israel's security while recognizing the legitimate rights of the Palestinian people. We oppose the creation of an independent Palestinian state. Nor will we support the creation of any political entity that would jeopardize Israel's security. . . .

Foreign Aid. We recognize that foreign aid must have a reasonable relationship to our national interests. We therefore support an ongoing review of such programs so that they can be both effectual and justified. We promote financial contribution from other democracies of the world to share the cost of the American burden for peacekeeping and foreign aid. . . .

Disarmament. We will banish the threat of nuclear annihilation from the face of the earth — not by savaging our military, as some Democrats might insist but by building on the historic diplomatic achievements of Presidents Bush and Reagan.

This means ensuring stable command and control of the former Soviet arsenal, complete acceptance and verified implementation of all treaty obligations by the successor states to the Soviet Union, and achieving the additional 50 percent reduction in strategic forces now agreed upon. We must assist in dismantling weapons, transforming the massive Soviet war machine into an engine of peace and civilian revival. We will cooperate with our former adversaries both to curtail proliferation and to move beyond the ABM Treaty toward effective ballistic missile defenses.

We will not permit the Soviet nuclear nightmare to be replaced by another one. Outlaw nations — North Korea, Iran, Iraq, Libya and others — lust for weapons of mass destruction. This is the nightmare of proliferation: nuclear, chemical and biological weapons that, together with ballistic missiles, can deliver death across whole continents, including our own.

We will renew and strengthen the Nuclear Nonproliferation Treaty. We will design security policies to counter proliferation dangers. We will reinforce multilateral accords like the Missile Technology Control Regime. And most important, we will develop and deploy global defenses against ballistic missiles. Despite the opposition of the Democratic Party and congressional Democrats, we will deploy an effective strategic defense system for the American people.

Defense. Republicans call for a controlled defense drawdown, not a free fall. That is why President Bush proposes to carefully reduce defense spending over the next four years by an additional $34 billion, including $18 billion in outlays, with a 25 percent reduction in personnel. He has already eliminated over 100 weapon systems. Around the world, American forces are coming home from the frontiers of the Cold War. More than 550 overseas bases are being closed or realigned. Yet U.S. forces retain the ability to meet the challenge of another Desert Storm with equal success. . . .

Because the United States will rely on a smaller force of offensive nuclear weapons to deter aggression in the post-Cold War era, we will maintain the triad of land, sea, and air-based strategic forces. We will continue to test the safety, reliability and effectiveness of our nuclear weapons. . . .

We will upgrade existing weapons and selectively procure those that hold the promise of dramatic forward leaps in capability. Under no circumstances will we yield our technological superiority. . . .

We applaud the president's efforts to assist all individuals and communities adversely affected by the ongoing defense build-down, with more than 30 defense adjustment programs already in place and more than $7 billion committed to the effort in just the next two years. . . .

However, we oppose liberal Democrat attempts to place women in combat positions just to make an ideological point. Unlike the Democratic Party and its candidate, we support the continued exclusion of homosexuals from the military as a matter of good order and discipline. . . .

1996 Conventions

Presidential Candidates

Bob Dole
Republican

Ross Perot
Reform Party

Bill Clinton
Democrat

Republicans

The Republican Party on Aug. 12-15 showcased its presidential nominee Bob Dole, the former Senate majority leader from Kansas, and his popular vice presidential selection, former Rep. Jack F. Kemp, R-N.Y. at its convention in San Diego, Calif. Seeking to energize loyalists while also expanding its base, the convention's carefully orchestrated moments melded the twin themes of compassion and conservatism.

The GOP organizers' efforts to tightly script the convention were successful, banishing any hint of controversy and leaving the delegates with little to do but wave their colorful Dole-Kemp placards and present a picture of enthusiastic party unity for the network television cameras. The paucity of controversy cheered Republicans, who still remembered the 1992 convention in Houston that was marked by strident speeches on abortion and other hot-button social issues. In contrast, San Diego conventioneers were treated to speech after speech that stressed inclusion and moderation.

The Republican platform — as rigidly conservative as any in recent memory — was the designated forum for the party's sharper ideological right wing. Party moderates were kept happy during convention week with prime-time speaking slots. The social conservatives — who were at least a plurality in the ranks of the delegates — were rarely on stage during prime time.

On Monday, Aug. 17, the platform was formally adopted by voice vote at the convention's sparsely attended opening morning session. The smooth and swift approval belied the fierce, prolonged struggle over the plank calling for a constitutional amendment to ban abortion.

During platform deliberations the week before the convention, multiple amendments seeking to soften the abortion plank or acknowledge differing views of the issue within the party were defeated by lopsided votes led by social conservatives who had dominated the platform-writing process. However, at the urging of the Dole campaign, the platform committee agreed to add the texts of defeated amendments to the document as an appendix headed "Minority Views." Thereafter, also at the urging of the Dole camp, abortion

rights advocates dropped their planned protest on the convention floor.

Even most of the delegates pledged to conservative commentator Patrick J. Buchanan seemed to approve of the deal. Buchanan was denied a podium speech in San Diego, and his delegates were not allowed to place his name in nomination. His supporters said they appreciated the tone of unity that prevailed and found plenty of reasons to rally around the Dole-Kemp ticket.

The program on Monday night's opening session promoted the Republicans as the party of "common sense" solutions. Both Haley Barbour, the ubiquitous chairman of the Republican National Committee, and New Jersey Gov. Christine Todd Whitman, the convention's temporary co-chairman, touted the party's "common-sense" stances.

A highlight of the first evening came when Nancy Reagan delivered a heartfelt tribute to her husband, former President Ronald Reagan, who suffering from Alzheimer's disease, did not attend the GOP convention for the first time in more than three decades. "He still sees the shining city on the hill," she said, as tears ran down many faces in the hall.

The audience barely had a chance to collect its emotions before retired Gen. Colin L. Powell appeared on stage, marched to the podium and confirmed his status as a rising GOP star. Sounding the theme of the evening — and indeed the convention itself — Powell said the GOP "must always be the party of inclusion."

In a rare acknowledgment of the party's tensions over social issues that lurked out of sight of the cameras, Powell declared his support for abortion rights and affirmative action. Such views were regarded as heresy by the rock-ribbed social conservatives in the audience.

Powell explained: "I was invited here to share my views with you because we are a big enough party — and big enough people to disagree on individual issues and still work for our common goal — restoring the American Dream." The crowd erupted with a roar, signaling that this would be a sharp departure from the open animosity of Houston.

Reflecting the party's new emphasis on diversity, female

and minority speakers dominated the podium, even though their numbers were disproportionately low among the 1,990 delegates. The convention's Tuesday night keynote speech, given by 38-year-old Rep. Susan Molinari, R-N.Y., was intended to connect with working mothers and other women, an audience that Dole had trouble reaching.

With Molinari's husband, Rep. Bill Paxon, R-N.Y., holding the couple's 3-month-old daughter, Susan Ruby Paxon, Molinari sought to empathize with the typical working mother who she said is "stretched to her limit trying to hold down a job ... while trying to hold down the fort at home, too."

Molinari tore into President Clinton's economic policies, which she said had added to the burden of such families. "Each year Bill Clinton has been in office, taxes have been higher and family incomes have been lower," she said.

The selection of Molinari, an abortion rights supporter, as keynote speaker was another signal to moderates that they were welcome in the party. However, Molinari avoided mentioning abortion in her speech.

In the convention's most intriguing role reversal, House Speaker and convention chair Newt Gingrich, who rose to power and to controversy as a partisan firebrand, used his one short speaking slot Tuesday to praise volunteer efforts — presenting a softer, warmer side of the Republican Party.

Wednesday, Aug. 14, was highlighted by what was almost certainly the most memorable part of the entire four days. Elizabeth Hanford Dole, the nominee's wife, left the podium with a hand-held microphone and went to the convention floor to praise her husband's personal and political qualities. Comfortably mixing with the delegates, stopping to embrace old acquaintances, Dole's ebullient demeanor was more reminiscent of a talk show host than a candidate's wife.

Nearly five months after he virtually wrapped up the Republican presidential nomination, Dole officially claimed the prize later that night. Sen. John McCain of Arizona gave Dole's nominating speech. "In America, we celebrate the virtues of the quiet hero," McCain began. He recalled how Dole wore a POW bracelet with McCain's name on it while McCain was a prisoner of war in Vietnam. "We fought in different wars; we keep the same faith," said McCain.

The roll call of the states followed and proved anti-climactic. It lasted about an hour and a half, yet the balloting was not unanimous. Dole ended up with 1,928 of the 1,990 delegate votes; Buchanan received 43 votes. *(Chart, p. 259)*

On the final evening, Dole and Kemp delivered acceptance speeches that laid the basis for their campaign against President Clinton. Kemp, a fervent and enthusiastic promoter of the GOP as the party of opportunity, promised Republican policies — including tax cuts and reduced regulation — would unleash a burst of economic activity benefiting all Americans.

One of the few leading conservatives who has been successful at reaching out to minorities, Kemp continued the convention's week-long theme of inclusiveness. "We will carry the word to every man, woman and child of every color and background that today, on the eve of the new American century, it is time to renew the American promise to recapture the American dream," Kemp said.

Although Dole had been among the nation's most visible national figures for a generation, he arrived in San Diego with needing to define his political persona. One goal was to bring home to the American public his rise from humble origins and recovery from a devastating World War II injury — a personal story that Dole had previously played down while establishing his better-known image as a legislative leader and Washington insider.

In his speech, Dole prominently mentioned his across-the-board, 15-percent income tax cut that had become the centerpiece of his campaign. But he was also at pains to say that "the moral and the nation's survival" took precedence over what he called "the material."

Dole also prescribed racial and ethnic tolerance as a dictum for the party. "If there is anyone who has mistakenly attached himself to our party in the belief that we are not open to citizens of every race and religion, then let me remind you," Dole said sternly. "Tonight this hall belongs to the party of Lincoln, and the exits, which are clearly marked, are for you to walk out of as I stand this ground without compromise."

As he strongly emphasized family values, Dole made an oblique criticism of First Lady Hillary Rodham Clinton. Dole denounced the communitarian concept, embodied in the title of her recent book, that "it takes a village" to raise children. "It takes a family," Dole proclaimed.

He took hard shots at Clinton, blaming him for what Dole called the largest tax increase ever and for failing to stem a tide of violent crime that the Republican nominee said had "paralyzed" the nation.

Dole drew some of his biggest cheers by pledging to rein in the Internal Revenue Service and to never place U.S. military troops under the command of the United Nations or allow U.S. trade policy to be dictated by the World Trade Organization.

Yet earlier in the speech he had candidly defended his penchant for political compromise, which has earned Dole the enmity of many in his party's right wing. Compromise is "no sin," Dole said. "It is what protects us from absolutism and intolerance."

And Dole, who earned a reputation for his dour temperament during three decades in Congress, closed by casting himself as a positive warrior. "Tonight, I stand before you tested by adversity, made sensitive by hardship, a fighter by principle, and the most optimistic man in America."

No matter how well Dole and the Republicans papered over differences at the convention, the party remained split between its traditional base of fiscal conservatives and its new base of social-issue activists who wanted to see their positions turned into policy.

Following are excerpts from the Republican platform of 1996:

> **Tax Relief.** American families are suffering from the twin burdens of stagnant incomes and near-record taxes. . . . American families deserve better. They should be allowed to keep more of their hard-earned money so they can spend on their priorities. . . .
>
> In response to this unprecedented burden confronting America, we support an across-the-board, 15-percent tax cut to marginal tax rates. . . . Another drag on family finances has been government's failure to maintain the personal and dependent exemption at historic[al] levels. . . . That is why Republicans have made the $500-per-child family tax credit one of the primary features of our tax cut package. . . . Republicans support expansion of IRAs and the establishment of spousal IRAs to encourage savings and investment. . . . To remove impediments to job creation and economic growth, we support reducing the top tax rate on capital gains by 50 percent. . . . [T]he income tax on Social Security benefits . . . must be repealed.
>
> . . . [A] tax code for the 21st century. . . . must be flatter, fairer and simpler, with a minimum of exclusions from its coverage, and one set of rules applying to all. . . . [T]oday's burdensome IRS. . . . must be dramatically downsized. . . . and made less intrusive. . . .

Balancing the Budget. . . . Republicans support a Balanced Budget Amendment to the Constitution, phased in over a short period and with appropriate safeguards for national emergencies. . . .

Creating Jobs for Americans. Our goal is to empower the American people by expanding employment and entrepreneurial opportunities. . . . The Republican Party is committed to the survival, the revival and the resurgence of small business. . . .We advocate increased access to capital for businesses. . . . We propose to consolidate federal training programs and to transfer their administration to the states and local governments. . . . [W]e will enact the TEAM Act to empower employers and employees to act as a team, rather than as adversaries, to advance their common interests. . . .

Homeownership. Homeownership is central to the American Dream. . . . Mortgage interest should remain deductible from the income tax. . . . Republicans support regulatory reform efforts that make buying a house easy, understandable, and affordable.

. . . [W]e support transforming public housing into private housing, converting low-income families into proud homeowners. Resident management of public housing is a first step toward that goal, which includes eliminating the Department of Housing and Urban Development (HUD). HUD's core functions will be turned over to the states. . . .

Promoting Trade and International Prosperity. . . . Republicans support free and fair trade. In the American Century ahead, our country will lead in international trade. . . . and we can do it better without a Department of Commerce. . . .

We should vigorously implement the North American Free Trade Agreement. . . . Republicans will not allow the World Trade Organization to undermine United States sovereignty and will support a World Trade Organization oversight commission.

Changing Washington from the Ground Up. We are the party of small, responsible and efficient government, joining our neighbors in cities and counties, rather than distant bureaucrats, to build a just society and caring communities. We therefore assert the power of the American people over government. . . . Our agenda for change . . . is based on the Tenth Amendment to the Constitution:

The powers not delegated to the United States by the Constitution, nor prohibited by it to the states, are reserved to the states respectively, or to the people.

. . . In this Information Era of uncertainty and rapid change, it is government close to home, controlled by neighborhood and community leaders, that can best respond to the needs and values of all citizens.

. . . [W]e support elimination of the Departments of Commerce, Housing and Urban Development, Education, and Energy, and the elimination, defunding or privatization of agencies which are obsolete, redundant, of limited value, or too regional in focus. Examples of agencies. . . . are the National Endowment for the Arts, the National Endowment for the Humanities, the Corporation for Public Broadcasting and the Legal Services Corporation. . . .

Government Reform. . . . True reform is indeed needed: ending taxpayer subsidies for campaigns, strengthening party structures to guard against rogue operations, requiring full and immediate disclosure of all contributions, and cracking down on the indirect support, or "soft money," by which special interest groups underwrite their favored candidates. . . .

. . . We will establish Truth in Testimony, requiring organizations which receive government funds and testify before Congress to disclose those funds. . . . A Republican administration will impose accountability on grantees, to reveal what the public is getting for its

money, and will end the process of automatic grant renewal. . . .

. . . [W]e will stop the runaway growth of entitlement spending — the programs which automatically grow without any action required by Congress or the president. . . . We will take entitlements off automatic pilot and make Congress accountable for their funding. . . .

Regulatory Reform. . . . A Republican administration will require periodic review of existing regulations to ensure they are effective and do away with obsolete and conflicting rules. We will encourage civil servants to find ways to reduce regulatory burdens on the public and will require federal agencies to disclose the costs of new regulations on individuals and small businesses. . . . We will require agencies to conduct cost-benefit analyses of their regulations. . . .

Restoring Justice to the Courts. . . . The federal judiciary, including the U.S. Supreme Court, has overstepped its authority under the Constitution. It has usurped the right of citizen legislators and popularly elected executives to make law by declaring duly enacted laws to be "unconstitutional" through the misapplication of the principle of judicial review. . . . A Republican president will ensure that a process is established to select for the federal judiciary nominees who understand that their task is first and foremost to be faithful to the Constitution and to the intent of those who framed it. . . .

. . . [W]e believe the proliferation of litigation hits the consumer with higher prices and cripples the practice of medicine. . . . We encourage state governments to. . . . Award punitive damages on a fair and reasonable basis after clear proof of wrongdoing, with limits that discourage opportunistic litigation. . . . Restore limited liability to non-profit organizations. . . . Reform medical malpractice. . . . Eliminate the use of "junk science" by opportunistic attorneys by requiring courts to verify that the science of those called as expert witnesses is reasonably acceptable within the scientific community. . . .

The Nation's Capital. . . . We reaffirm the constitutional status of the District of Columbia as the seat of government of the United States and reject calls for statehood for the District. . . . We call for structural reform of the city's government and its education system. . . .

Upholding the Rights of All. . . . We are the party of the open door. . . . [T]he Republican Party is more dedicated than ever to strengthening the social, cultural, and political ties that bind us together as a free people. . . . While our party remains steadfast in its commitment to advancing its historic principles and ideals, we also recognize that members of our party have deeply held and sometimes differing views. We view this diversity of views as a source of strength, not as a sign of weakness, and we welcome into our ranks all Americans who may hold differing positions. . . .

. . . We oppose sexual harassment in the workplace, and must ensure that no one in America is forced to choose between a job and submitting to unwelcome advances. We also oppose indoctrination in the classroom. Americans should not have to tolerate the decline of ethical standards and the collapse of behavioral norms. . . .

. . . [W]e oppose discrimination based on sex, race, age, creed, or national origin and will vigorously enforce anti-discrimination statutes. We reject the distortion of those laws to cover sexual preference, and we endorse the Defense of Marriage Act to prevent states from being forced to recognize same-sex unions. Because we believe rights inhere in individuals, not in groups, we will attain our nation's goal of equal rights without quotas or other forms of preferential treatment. . . . [W]e endorse the Dole-Canady Equal Opportunity Act to end discrimination by the federal government. We likewise endorse this year's

Proposition 209, the California Civil Rights Initiative, to restore to law the original meaning of civil rights.

We renew our historic Republican commitment to equal opportunity for women. . . . The full exercise of legal rights depends upon opportunity, and economic growth is the key to continuing progress for women in all fields of endeavor. Public policy must respect and accommodate women whether they are full-time homemakers or pursue a career. . . .

The unborn child has a fundamental individual right to life which cannot be infringed. We support a human life amendment to the Constitution and we endorse legislation to make clear that the Fourteenth Amendment's protections apply to unborn children. Our purpose is to have legislative and judicial protection of that right against those who perform abortions. We oppose using public revenues for abortion and will not fund organizations which advocate it. We support the appointment of judges who respect traditional family values and the sanctity of innocent human life.

Our goal is to ensure that women with problem pregnancies have the kind of support, material and otherwise, they need for themselves and for their babies. . . . We oppose abortion, but our pro-life agenda does not include punitive action against women who have an abortion. We salute those who provide alternatives to abortion and offer adoption services. . . .

. . . We applaud Bob Dole's commitment to revoke the Clinton executive orders concerning abortion and to sign into law an end to partial-birth abortions.

. . . We defend the constitutional right to keep and bear arms. . . . We strongly support Bob Dole's National Instant Check Initiative, which will help keep all guns out of the hands of convicted felons. . . .

We affirm the right of individuals to participate in labor organizations and to bargain collectively, consistent with state laws. . . . We support the right of States to enact Right-to-Work laws. We will restore the original scope of the Hobbs Act. . . .

A Sensible Immigration Policy. As a nation of immigrants, we welcome those who follow our laws and come to our land to seek a better life. . . . We must set immigration at manageable levels, balance the competing goals of uniting families of our citizens and admitting specially talented persons, and end asylum abuses through expedited exclusion of false claimants. . . .

Illegal aliens should not receive public benefits other than emergency aid, and those who become parents while illegally in the United States should not be qualified to claim benefits for their offspring. Legal immigrants should depend for assistance on their sponsors, who are legally responsible for their financial well-being, not the American taxpayers. . . .

From Many, One. . . . While we benefit from our differences, we must also strengthen the ties that bind us to one another. Foremost among those is the flag. Its deliberate desecration is not "free speech," but an assault against our history and our hopes. We support a constitutional amendment that will restore to the people, through their elected representatives, their right to safeguard Old Glory. . . .

. . . We support the official recognition of English as the nation's common language. We advocate foreign language training in our schools and retention of heritage languages in homes and cultural institutions. . . .

Crime. . . . We will establish no-frills prisons where prisoners are required to work productively and make the threat of jail a real deterrent to crime. . . . We will reform the Supreme Court's fanciful exclusionary rule, which has allowed a generation of criminals to get off on technicalities.

. . . We will . . . require adult trials for juveniles who commit adult crimes. . . . Recognizing that local jurisdictions have a clear and concise understanding of their problems, we encourage them to develop and enact innovative programs to address juvenile crime. We also encourage them to consider juvenile nocturnal curfews as an effective law enforcement tool. . . .

. . . Republicans propose a constitutional amendment to protect victims' rights. . . .

. . . We call for special penalties against thugs who assault or batter pregnant women and harm them or their unborn children. We endorse Bob Dole's call to bring federal penalties for child pornography in line with far tougher state penalties: ten years for a first offense, fifteen for the second, and life for a third. . . . We continue our strong support of capital punishment for those who commit heinous federal crimes; including the kingpins of the narcotics trade. . . .

Solving the Drug Crisis. . . . We support strong penalties, including mandatory minimum sentences, for drug trafficking, distribution and drug-related crimes. . . . Drug testing should be made a routine feature of the criminal justice process at every stage, including the juvenile justice system. Test results should be used in deciding pretrial release, sentencing, and probation revocation. . . .

Stronger Families. We are the party of the American family, educating children, caring for the sick, learning from the elderly, and helping the less fortunate. We believe that strengthening family life is the best way to improve the quality of life for everyone. . . . While recognizing a role for government in dealing with social ills, we look to mediating institutions — religious and community groups, private associations of all kinds — to take the lead in tackling the social ills that some government programs have only worsened. . . . We urge state legislators to review divorce laws to foster the stability of the home and protect the economic rights of the innocent spouse and children.

Improving Education. . . . [T]he federal government has no constitutional authority to be involved in school curricula or to control jobs in the workplace. That is why we will abolish the Department of Education, end federal meddling in our schools and promote family choice at all levels of learning. We therefore call for prompt repeal of the Goals 2000 program and the School-to-Work Act of 1994. . . .

. . . We encourage a reform agenda on the local level and urge state legislators to ensure quality education for all through programs of parental choice among public, private, and religious schools. That includes the option of home schooling. . . .

We will continue to work for the return of voluntary prayer to our schools. . . .

. . . We call for a national reassessment of the economics of higher education. . . . [W]e will end the Clinton administration's perverse direct lending program. We support proposals to assist families to prepare for the financial strains of higher education, like the American Dream Savings Account, passed by congressional Republicans but vetoed. . . .

Health Care. Our goal is to maintain the quality of America's health care — the best in the world, bar none — while making health care and health insurance more accessible and more affordable. . . .

● Make insurance portable from job to job;

● Ensure that persons are not denied coverage because of preexisting health conditions when changing employment;

● Crack down on Medicare and Medicaid fraud. . . .

● Reform malpractice laws. . . .

● Let individuals set up tax-free Medical Savings Accounts (MSAs. . . .

- Overhaul the Food and Drug Administration to get better products on the market faster and at less cost to consumers;
- . . . [L]et employer groups offer tax-exempt policies and make premiums 100% deductible for farmers, small businesses, and all the self-employed. . . .
- Change anti-trust laws to let health care providers cooperate in holding down charges;
- Avoid mandatory coverages that make consumers pay for more insurance than they need;
- Allow multi-employer purchasing groups and form "risk pools" in the States to make employee health insurance more affordable. . . .
- Permit families with incomes up to twice the poverty level to buy into Medicaid. . . .
- Increase funding for community and migrant health centers. . . .

We reaffirm our determination to protect Medicare. We will ensure a significant annual expansion in Medicare. That isn't "cutting Medicare." It's a projected average annual rate of growth of 7.1 percent a year — more than twice the rate of inflation — to ensure coverage for those who need it now and those who will need it in the future. . . .

. . . Medicaid should be turned over to state management with leeway for restructuring and reform. Low-income persons should have access to managed care programs and medical savings accounts, just as other persons do. . . .

. . . We remain committed to, and place a high priority on, finding a cure for HIV disease. We support increased funding for research targeted at conditions that touch the families of most Americans, like Alzheimer's, breast cancer, prostate cancer, and diabetes. We call for an increased emphasis on prevention of diseases that threaten the lives of women. . . . We call for fetal protection in biomedical research and will enforce the rights of human subjects in all federally funded studies. . . .

Renewing Hope and Opportunity. . . . The key to welfare reform is restoring personal responsibility and encouraging two-parent households. The path to that goal lies outside of official Washington. In the hands of State and local officials, and under the eye of local taxpayers. . . . All able-bodied adults must be required to work, either in private sector jobs or in community work projects. Illegal aliens must be ineligible for all but emergency benefits. And a firm time limit for receipt of welfare must be enforced.

Because illegitimacy is the most serious cause of child poverty, we will encourage States to stop cash payments to unmarried teens and set a family cap on payments for additional children. When benefits of any kind are extended to teen mothers, they must be conditioned upon their attendance at school and their living at home with a parent, adult relative or guardian. About half the children of today's teen welfare mothers were fathered in statutory rape. We echo Bob Dole's call to our nation's governors to toughen and enforce state laws in this regard, as well as those concerning enforcement of child support. . . .

Older Americans. . . . The Republican Party has always opposed the earnings limitation for Social Security benefits. . . . The Social Security system remains the cornerstone of personal security for millions of the elderly. . . . We will keep it financially sound and keep politics out of its administration. We will work to ensure the integrity and solvency of the Social Security trust funds. . . .

Environment. . . . The states and communities are the laboratories of environmental innovation. Inflexible requirements hurt the environment, add unnecessary costs, and reduce technology development. . . .

. . . [W]e will fix the broken superfund law. We will direct resources to clean-up sites where there are real risks, and cooperate with citizens, states and localities who want to help, rather than harassing them with unwarranted lawsuits. . . . as an essential component of our comprehensive superfund reform, we will remove disincentives in current federal law in order to allow states to expand their innovative "brownfields" programs. . . .

. . . [W]e recognize the current Endangered Species Act is seriously flawed and, indeed, is often counterproductive because of its reliance on federal command-and-control measures. . . . We will improve the ESA by implementing an incentive-based program in cooperation with state, local, and tribal governments and private individuals to recognize the critical relationship between a healthy environment and a healthy economy founded on private property rights and responsibilities.

Improving Public Lands. . . . We support multiple use conducted in an environmentally and economically sustainable manner. . . . We support a thorough review of the lands owned by the federal government with a goal of transferring lands that can best be managed by State, county, or municipal governments. . . . We recognize the historic use of public lands for livestock production in compliance with legal requirements. . . . Our park system needs to be rebuilt, restructured, and reinvigorated to ensure that all Americans can enjoy and be proud of their parks. . . . We stand for sustainable forestry to stabilize and provide continuity for our timber industry and to improve the health of the country's public forests. . . . We support the original intent of the Mining Law of 1872. . . . We support appropriate changes to the law to ensure the taxpayer will receive a reasonable return for the value of extracted minerals. . . .

Power for Progress. . . . We support greater competition as we move toward a market-based approach, with true and meaningful deregulation. . . .

We support elimination of the Department of Energy to emphasize the need for greater privatization and to reduce the size of the federal government. . . . We support environmentally responsible energy extraction from public and private lands. . . . We advocate environmentally sound oil production in the largest known onshore or offshore petroleum reserve in the nation — the small coastal plain portion of the 19-million acre Arctic National Wildlife Refuge. . . .

. . . Republicans deplore the arbitrary and premature abandonment of the previous policy of voluntary reductions of greenhouse gas emissions. We further deplore ceding U.S. sovereignty on environmental issues to international bureaucrats and our foreign economic competitors. . . .

The Atlantic Alliance. Our relations with the nations of Europe must continue to be based on the NATO alliance. . . . Our policy will strive to consolidate our Cold War victory in Europe and to build a firm foundation for a new century of peace. . . . [W]e call for the immediate expansion of the framework for peace to include those countries of Central Europe which demonstrate the strongest commitment to the democratic ideals NATO was created to protect. . . .

Bosnia. We support America's men and women in uniform who are serving in Bosnia and Herzegovina. However, we did not support the ill-conceived and inconsistent policies that led to their deployment. . . . We look forward to a timely withdrawal of U.S. forces from Bosnia and recognize that providing the Bosnian Federation with adequate weapons and training is the only realistic exit strategy. . . .

Russia. . . . Our foreign policy toward Russia should put American interests first and consolidate our Cold War victory in Europe. . . . [W]e will encourage Russia to respect the sovereignty and independence of its neighbors; support a special security arrangement between Russia and NATO — but not Moscow's veto over NATO enlargement; support Russian entry to the G-7 after its reforms have been achieved; and link U.S. assistance to Russian adherence to international treaty obligations.

Defending America Against Missile Attack. . . . The danger of a missile attack with nuclear, chemical, or biological weapons is the most serious threat to our national security. . . . We are determined to deploy land-based and sea-based theater missile defenses as soon as possible, and a national system thereafter. . . . We therefore endorse the Defend America Act of 1996, introduced by Senator Bob Dole, which calls for a national missile defense system for all fifty states by the year 2003. . . . This in turn will require the continuing maintenance and development of nuclear weapons and their periodic testing. The Clinton administration's proposed Comprehensive Test Ban Treaty (CTBT) is inconsistent with American security interests.

Rebuilding America's Strength. Republicans are committed to ensuring the status of the United States as the world's preeminent military power. We must reverse the decline in what our nation spends for defense. . . .

. . . Republicans will not subordinate United States sovereignty to any international authority. We oppose the commitment of American troops to U.N. "peacekeeping" operations under foreign commanders and will never compel American servicemen to wear foreign uniforms or insignia. We will insist on an end to waste, mismanagement and fraud at the United Nations. . . .

International Terrorism. . . . A Republican president will forcefully lead the world community to isolate and punish state sponsors of terrorism. . . . — through imposition and enforcement of sanctions, banning investment, and . . . effective policies. The governments of North Korea, Iran, Syria, Iraq, Libya, Sudan, and Cuba must know that America's first line of defense is not our shoreline, but their own borders. We will be proactive, not reactive, to strike the hand of terrorism before it can be raised against Americans. . . .

Asia. . . . A Republican administration will keep the mutual security treaties with Japan and with the Republic of Korea. . . . We will halt Bill Clinton's efforts to appease North Korea by rewarding treaty-breaking with American taxpayer-financed oil and nuclear reactors. We will make further improvement of relations with Vietnam and North Korea contingent upon their cooperation in achieving a full and complete accounting of our POW's and MIA's from those Asian conflicts.

China and Taiwan. We support the aspiration of the Chinese people for both economic and political liberty, which includes respect for the human rights of the people of Tibet. Our relationship with the Chinese government will be based on vigilance with regard to its military potential, proliferation activities, and its attitude toward human rights, especially in Hong Kong. . . . We reaffirm our commitment to Taiwan's security and will regard any threat to alter its status by force as a threat to our own security interests. . . .

The Middle East. . . . The Middle East remains a region vital to American security. Our enduring goals there are to promote freedom and stability, secure access to oil resources, and maintain the security of Israel, our one democratic ally in the region with whom we share moral bonds and common strategic interests. . . .

. . . Israel's security is central to U.S. interests in the region. That is why Republican administrations initiated efforts with Israel to pre-position military equipment, to conduct joint contingency planning and joint military exercises. . . .

We applaud the Republican Congress for enacting legislation to recognize Jerusalem as the undivided capital of Israel. A Republican administration will ensure that the U.S. Embassy is moved to Jerusalem by May 1999. . . .

Western Hemisphere. . . . . The Clinton administration's policy of denying most Latin American nations the opportunity to replace their obsolescent military equipment, raise the professional competence of their armed forces, and cooperate fully with the United States in joint military training and exercises will be reversed by a Republican administration.

. . . The Republican Party has not wavered and will not waver in its goal of a democratic Cuba. We affirm our policy of isolating the Castro regime, including full implementation of the Helms-Burton Act to penalize foreign firms which do business there. . . . We reject Clinton administration claims of "success" in its military intervention in Haiti. . . .

The Men and Women of Defense. . . . A Republican president will ensure a high priority for the quality of life of our military personnel and their families. . . . We affirm that homosexuality is incompatible with military service. . . . We reaffirm our support for the exemption of women from ground combat units and are concerned about the current policy of involuntarily assigning women to combat or near-combat units. . . . We will not tolerate sexual harassment or misconduct toward anyone in the uniform, but we oppose politically motivated witch-hunts that smear the innocent and destroy honorable careers. . . .

Space. . . . We consider space travel and space science a national priority. . . . We will develop the Reusable Launch Vehicle, promote markets for commercial space launch services, and push technology to its creative limits. . . . Space exploration and exploitation are a matter of national security. Our armed forces already rely on space assets to support their operations on earth, and space technology will rapidly become more critical to successful military operations. . . . [W]e cannot allow its domination by another power. . . .

Reform Party

Founded in the fall of 1995 by Texas billionaire and presidential aspirant H. Ross Perot, the Reform Party conducted its first presidential nominating convention in an unusual two-stage process. The first session convened in Long Beach, Calif., on Aug. 11, 1996, while the second session met one week later across the country at Valley Forge, Pa., on Aug. 18. During the intervening week, ballots were sent to 1.3 million Reform Party members who voted in a "national primary" for the candidate of their choice by mail, electronic mail or phone — an array of methods that party officials clearly saw as the election system of the future. *(Reform Party, p. 273)*

Perot had spent an estimated $6 million of his own money in bankrolling the party. After winning 19 percent of the popular vote in his unsuccessful independent bid against Democrat Bill Clinton and Republican President George Bush in the 1992 presidential election, Perot had formed the nonpartisan education organization, United We Stand America (UWSA), to promote his ideas on the national agenda. In 1995 Perot and UWSA supporters spun off the Reform Party as a full-fledged political party.

The California session drew roughly 2,000 members — a fairly homogeneous group demographically, overwhelmingly white and predominantly middle-aged or older. In the main, they tended to be politically disenchanted, strong proponents of the military, and strong supporters of reform in the mechanics of government and electoral politics.

Speeches by the party's two presidential candidates — Perot and former Democratic Gov. Richard D. Lamm of Colorado — highlighted the first session. While many of those in attendance in Long Beach wore either Lamm or Perot T-shirts or carried signs for one or the other, they seemed more like spectators than participants in the event (which was televised nationally on C-SPAN and CNN). "Please feel free to applaud," said Reform Party national coordinator Russell Verney at the outset. "Feel free to show emotion."

In his speech, Lamm took a number of swipes at the Democrats and Republicans. "The two major parties are not part of the solution. They're part of the problem," said Lamm. "They do not enjoy a right of perpetual existence." But he also made it clear he was an alternative to Perot. "The torch must pass," said Lamm. "The Reform Party is larger than any one individual."

Lamm echoed Perot in urging the party to build on the need for campaign reform, fiscal responsibility and increased immigration controls. The latter issue, in particular, struck a chord with the Long Beach audience, which responded with cheers when Lamm declared that "the Statue of Liberty stands for liberty, not unlimited immigration."

But if Lamm spoke politely, like an invited guest, Perot played the garrulous host. Perot had every reason to be optimistic. He led Lamm by a ratio of more than 2-to-1 in the first round of nomination balloting that determined the party's primary finalists. After a trio of introductory speakers hailed the Perot's generosity in building the party, the Texas billionaire strode onto the stage. He launched into a fast-paced speech that quickly aroused the crowd.

"I want to be your president," he declared near the outset, trying to dispel memories of 1992, when he abruptly quit the presidential race in July, only to re-enter in October. The rest of his speech was quintessential Perot, replete with folksy colloquialisms, charts and plugs for two books he had written.

During the following week, Lamm criticized the ground rules of the party's nominating process, which were devised by Perot operatives. "I don't think it has been a fair playing field or party-building endeavor as I was promised," he said.

The modern balloting system had its snags, too. Some participants, complained that they did not receive ballots in time to vote. Even Lamm had trouble obtaining a ballot for himself. In the final tally, only 5 percent of the party's declared membership voted. On Aug. 17, Verney announced that Perot had won the nomination by taking 65 percent of the primary vote to Lamm's 35 percent.

The following day the concluding session convened in the cavernous, balloon-filled convention center basement at Valley Forge. In the afternoon, as delegates milled around, ate and exchanged greetings, Reform Party congressional candidates stood on a platform meant to evoke a whistle-stop train setting and shouted out over loudspeakers their campaign messages on term limits, campaign finance reform and trade.

In the evening Lamm spoke briefly and congratulated Perot, but did not endorse him. Then a series of videotaped tributes followed to document Perot's exploits throughout his colorful career.

The convention crowd stood and cheered as Perot appeared on the stage, and a Texas flag waved conspicuously among the other signs and banners in the audience. Invok-

ing the heroism of General George Washington and the army that spent a bitter winter nearby, Perot accepted the Reform Party's presidential nomination.

In his speech he stressed the issues he has been known for — reducing the federal debt, lobbying reform, and higher ethical standards for elected officials. Perot especially ripped both parties for not following through on promising to form a task force to reform campaign finance.

Despite his earlier criticism of public financing — Perot had spent more than $60 million of his own money to self-finance his 1992 campaign — he announced that he would accept federal matching funds in 1996. But in accepting the nearly $30 million in public matching funds for which he qualified, Perot had to limit his personal funding to $50,000. At the end of his speech, Perot urged supporters to contribute to his campaign, as a telephone number flashed on screens behind him.

Perot then hastened from the stage for an appearance on CNN's *Larry King Live*, the program on which he has made many of his campaign announcements in 1996 and in 1992. The Reform Party did not have a formal platform.

Democrats

Meeting in Chicago for the eleventh time in the party's history, the Democratic Party on Aug. 26-29 jubilantly renominated President Bill Clinton and Vice President Al Gore. Democratic officials employed some smooth choreography of their own in producing a visually appealing convention designed to stir the viewing public's emotions.

Democratic speakers and videos highlighted the party's racial and ethnic diversity while drawing attention to President Clinton's efforts to ease the burdens on middle-class families. Taking advantage of meeting two weeks after the GOP convention, Democrats repeatedly hammered away at Republican nominee Bob Dole's offer to be "a bridge to the past" as proof that Republicans wanted to turn back the clock on economic, social and cultural change.

Despite the unity highlighted in Chicago, the convention also revealed the unresolved philosophical divisions between the party's liberal and centrist wings. Members of centrist Democratic Party groups such as the Blue Dogs, a group of House deficit hawks, and the Democratic Leadership Council insisted that their blueprint for smaller government was gradually becoming the dominant position in the party. They pointed to the platform adopted by the convention without dissent on Aug. 27, which was generally more conservative than past documents. "Our platform calls for a balanced budget," said Rep. Charles W. Stenholm of Texas. "That's a first."

Some veteran liberals, such as New York Rep. Charles B. Rangel, acknowledged the party's move to the center. "America has shifted on us," Rangel said. "Americans should be prepared to raise the taxes, invest in productivity and create the jobs. But they can't support that. They'd rather cut taxes, invest in defense and build jails."

Monday evening showcased speeches by prominent Democrats, such as House Minority Leader Richard A. Gephardt of Missouri and Senate Minority Leader Tom Daschle of South Dakota, the convention's co-chairmen.

However, the high point of the first evening was the appearance of a pair of lifelong Republicans: former Reagan press secretary James S. Brady, and his wife, Sarah. In a reference to the Republican convention, Sarah Brady said, "Jim, we must have made a wrong turn. This isn't San Diego." The Bradys, who had become gun control proponents after James Brady was partially paralyzed from being shot during the 1981 Reagan assassination attempt, called for increased efforts to reduce gun violence and praised Clinton for enacting the Brady bill, which imposed a seven-day waiting period for handgun purchases.

At the end of the evening, actor Christopher Reeve, paralyzed from a horse-riding accident in 1995, capped the evening's speeches with a plea for compassion and assistance to Americans with disabilities. Reeve, speaking from a wheelchair, held the hushed audience's rapt attention as he called for increased research funding for multiple sclerosis, Parkinson's disease, spinal cord injuries and AIDS.

On Tuesday former New York Gov. Mario M. Cuomo and civil rights leader Jesse Jackson from the liberal wing of the party spoke to the convention — although before the late-night portion of the broadcast by the three major television networks. While the two men agreed to disagree with the president over welfare reform, they launched some of the harshest partisan attacks of the entire convention.

Cuomo proclaimed a need to elect a Democratic majority to Congress to fend off the Republicans' conservative agenda. "They are the real threat," he said, as he urged Democrats to put aside their differences to support Clinton and other Democratic candidates.

Jackson gave an eloquent, wide-ranging address focused on the need to improve conditions in economically deprived sections of the United States. He ended his speech with chants to "keep that faith" with poor and struggling Americans, which were echoed by the rapt audience.

Much of the televised Tuesday night session was devoted to the "Families First" theme that was the platform for the national Democrats' 1996 congressional campaign. Speakers highlighted aspects of the party's centrist-oriented platform.

The keynote speaker, Indiana Gov. Evan Bayh, was joined on stage by his wife, Susan, their twin baby boys and his father, former Indiana Sen. Birch Bayh. Bayh centered his speech on his family and the record of the Clinton administration on such issues such as education. Though the youthful two-term governor is widely regarded as a rising Democratic star, he gave a mild, unstirring speech.

Rep. Tony P. Hall of Ohio spoke on the topic of families, but mentioned his anti-abortion views. "Many of us have felt left out [in the past]," he said. "This year it's different." His address held symbolic value: The party had been criticized by social conservatives since anti-abortion Gov. Robert P. Casey of Pennsylvania was not permitted to speak at the 1992 Democratic convention.

Receiving a foot-stomping welcome that lasted several minutes, first lady Hillary Rodham Clinton closed out the evening with a passionate explanation of her view of family values. She spoke about her husband and their experiences raising their daughter, and applied these anecdotes to societal concerns and family-related programs, such as the Family and Medical Leave Act, that had been embraced by the Clinton administration. Mrs. Clinton also responded to the oblique criticism Dole made at the GOP convention to her assertion that "it takes a village to raise a child."

She said parenting had taught her "that to raise a happy, healthy and hopeful child, it takes a family." But she then listed other crucial influences on a child's life, including teachers and clergy, before adding, "Yes, it takes a village, and it takes a president" who supports communitarian values such as those propounded by President Clinton.

The next day, Vice President Gore took center stage. Gore's speech broke tradition by being scheduled the day before the president's speech. Gore rallied the convention with sharp jabs at the Republican nominee. "In his speech from San Diego, Sen. Dole offered himself as a bridge to the past," said Gore. "Tonight, Bill Clinton and I offer ourselves as a bridge to the future."

Gore depicted Clinton as the last line of defense between a Republican-controlled Congress, which that he described as reckless, and its interest-group allies, which he described as greedy or working against the interests of the American people.

But the most memorable part of his speech was a deeply personal glimpse at a family tragedy. Seeking to underscore the dangers of underage smoking, Gore recounted the final, painful days and hours of his sister who began smoking at age 13 and ultimately died of lung cancer.

The nomination of Clinton followed, with Sen. Christopher J. Dodd of Connecticut, the general chairman of the DNC, hailing the president for leading the nation into an era of prosperity, while courageously taking on powerful special interests such as the gun lobby and the tobacco industry. To loud applause, Dodd called for civility in the fall campaign. "Stop attacking the president's family," he demanded of Republicans.

The formality of the presidential roll call culminated the evening. When Mississippi passed to Ohio to put Clinton over the top, Broadway singer Jennifer Holliday came to the podium to sing, "This is the Moment." Clinton waved his thanks on the overhead video screen. The final tally was announced as a unanimous 4,289 votes for Clinton, although there appeared to be roughly a dozen votes that were not cast during the roll call. *(Chart, p. 260)*

The last day's program included more than 35 local, state and federal elected officials and supporters who highlighted Clinton's efforts on a wide range of topics from crime prevention to education to reducing teen smoking. Sen. Edward M. Kennedy of Massachusetts fired up the delegates with a partisan attack against the record of Dole and congressional Republicans.

President Clinton capped the Democratic convention with a lengthy 66-minute policy address that chronicled his administration's accomplishments. The president's speech was designed to burnish his centrist image and lay the foundation for a second term. In his address, the president resolved to "build a bridge to the 21st century, to meet our values and protect our values."

Clinton promised to balance the budget without threatening Medicare and Medicaid, education programs and environmental protection. He also proposed a series of modest initiatives including deploying of 30,000 reading specialists to help enlist one million volunteer reading tutors, expanding controls on handgun sales, providing targeted tax cuts such as tax credits and deductions for college tuition and tax breaks for first-time home buyers, and increasing funding for cleaning up superfund toxic waste sites.

Clinton, who had taken heat from many liberals for signing sweeping legislation the week before that would dramatically change welfare, defended that action, insisting that the bill will provide an opportunity to "strike a new social bargain with the poor."

The only tension evident during the week came from a surprise story bursting into the news Thursday from outside the convention., Clinton's chief campaign strategist, Dick Morris, resigned amid tabloid newspaper reports of liaisons with a prostitute. Most of the delegates seemed determined not to let the flap ruin their fun. The incident was surely a distraction for the president during the day, but it did not knock him off stride during his night of celebration.

Following are excerpts from the Democratic platform of 1996:

Economic Growth. Since Bill Clinton became President, America has seen an explosion of job growth, economic renewal, and opportunity. The American people have created more than 10 million new jobs.... The combined rate of inflation, unemployment, and mortgage interest rates is the lowest in three decades. Now, 3.7 million more Americans own their own home, and Americans have started a record number of new small businesses in each of the last three years.

... In the next four years we have to make the new economy work for all Americans: balancing the budget, creating more jobs, making sure all families can count on good health care and a secure retirement, and, most of all, expanding educational opportunities so all Americans can learn the skills they need to build the best possible future.

Balancing the Budget. ... In 1992, we promised to cut the deficit in half over four years. We did. Our 1993 economic plan cut spending by over a quarter trillion dollars in five years....

Now the Democratic Party is determined to finish the job and balance the budget. President Clinton has put forward a plan to balance the budget by 2002 while living up to our commitments to our elderly and our children and maintaining strong economic growth....

Today's Democratic Party believes we have a duty to care for our parents, so they can live their lives in dignity. That duty includes securing Medicare and Medicaid, finding savings without reducing quality or benefits, and protecting Social Security for future generations....

Tax Relief. ... Today's Democratic Party is committed to targeted tax cuts that help working Americans invest in their future, and we insist that any tax cuts are completely paid for, because we are determined to balance the budget.

We want to strengthen middle-class families by providing a $500 tax cut for children. We want to cut taxes to help families pay for education after high school and to guarantee the first two years of college. We want people to be able to use their IRA's to buy a first home, deal with a medical emergency, or provide for education. We want to cut taxes for small businesses that invest in the future and set up pensions for their workers. And we want to cut taxes for people who are self-employed and self-insured so their health care is more affordable.

Foreign Trade. We believe that if we want the American economy to continue strong growth, we must continue to expand trade, and not retreat from the world.... [W]e must continue to work to lower foreign trade barriers; insist that foreign companies play by fair rules at home and abroad; strengthen rules that protect the global economy from fraud and dangerous instability; advance American commercial interests abroad; and ensure that the new global economy is directly beneficial to American working families.... [W]e must negotiate to guarantee that all trade agreements include standards to protect children, workers, public safety, and the environment....

Education. ... In the next four years, we must do even more to make sure America has the best public schools on earth.... We must hold students, teachers, and schools to the highest standards. Every child should be able to read by the end of the third grade. Students should be required to demonstrate competency and achievement for promotion or graduation. Teachers should be required to meet high standards for professional performance and be rewarded for the good jobs they do — and there should be a fair, timely, cost-effective process to remove those who do not measure up.... We should not bash teachers. We should applaud them, and find ways to keep the best teachers in the classroom. Schools should be held accountable for results. We should redesign or overhaul schools that fail. We should expand public school choice, but we should not take American tax dollars from public schools and give them to private schools. We should promote public charter schools that are held to the highest standards of accountability and access....

Technology in the Classroom. We must bring the 21st century into every classroom in America.... The only way to achieve that for every student is to give them all access to a computer, good software, trained teachers, and the Internet — and President Clinton and Vice President Gore have launched a partnership with high-tech companies, schools, state, and local governments to wire every classroom and library to the Information Superhighway by the year 2000....

Higher Education. Finally, we must make sure that every American has the opportunity to go to college.... We should expand work-study so one million students a year can work their way through college by the year 2000. We should allow people to use money from their IRA to help pay for college. We should give a $1,000 honor scholarship for the top 5 percent of graduates in every high school. And we must make 14 years of education the standard for every American. The Democratic Party wants to create a $10,000 tax deduction for families to help pay for education after high school. And we want to create a $1,500 tax cut for Americans, modeled after Georgia's successful HOPE scholarships, to guarantee the first year of tuition at a typical community college, and the second year if individuals earn it by maintaining a B average.....

Health Care. The Democratic Party is committed to ensuring that Americans have access to affordable, high-quality health care.... [W]e passed the Kennedy-Kassebaum health reform bill to stop insurance companies from denying coverage to families where one member has a preexisting condition, and to make sure that people can take their health insurance with them when they change jobs.... We have expanded the Women, Infants, and Children program that provides prenatal and early childhood nutrition.... We established a comprehensive effort to immunize children....

In the next four years, we must take further steps to ensure that Americans have access to quality, affordable health care. We should start by making sure that people get help paying premiums so they do not lose health care while they're looking for a new job. We support expanded coverage of home care, hospice, and community-based services, so the elderly and people with disabilities of all ages can live in their own communities and as independently as possible. We ... believe health insurance coverage for mental health care is vitally important and we support parity for mental health care.

Retirement. ... [W]e want ... to make sure people can carry their pensions with them when they change jobs, protect pensions even further, and expand the number of workers with pension coverage. Democrats created Social Security, we oppose efforts to dismantle it, and we will fight to save it. We must ensure that it is on firm financial footing well into the next century....

Worker Training. ... We want a G.I. Bill for Workers to transform the confusing tangle of federal training programs into a simple job-training skill grant that will go directly to unemployed workers so they will be able to get the training that is right for them. We want to strengthen training opportunities for people with disabilities, so they can learn the skills they need to live independent, productive lives.

Working Americans. We nearly doubled funding for the dislocated worker program.... We beat back efforts to undermine workers' rights to form and join unions.... We vigorously oppose Republican efforts to pass Right-to-Work legislation, and we are proud the President vetoed efforts to undermine collective bargaining through the TEAM Act....

Corporate Citizenship. Employers have a responsibility to do their part as well. President Clinton and the Democratic Party stand on the side of working families. We believe that values like loyalty, fairness, and responsibility are not inconsistent with the bottom line. We call on our corporate leaders to invest in the long-term, by providing workers with good wages and benefits, education and training, and opportunities for greater involvement in company decision making and ownership....

Fighting Crime. ... President Clinton beat back fierce Republican opposition.... to answer the call of America's police officers and pass the toughest Crime Bill in history.... And it is making a difference. In city after city and town after town, crime rates are finally coming down.

... [A]ny attempt to repeal the Brady Bill or assault weapons ban will be met with a veto. We must do everything we can to stand behind our police officers, and the first thing we should do is pass a ban on cop-killer bullets....

... We believe that people who break the law should be punished, and people who commit violent crimes should be punished severely. President Clinton made three-strikes-you're-out the law of the land.... We established the death penalty for nearly 60 violent crimes, including murder of a law enforcement officer, and we signed a law to limit appeals....

We provided almost $8 billion in new funding to help states build new prison cells so violent offenders serve their full sentences. We call on the states to.... guarantee that serious violent criminals serve at least 85 percent of their sentence....

The Democratic Party understands what the police have been saying for years: The best way to fight crime is to prevent it. That is why we fought for drug-education and gang-prevention programs in our schools.... When young people commit serious violent crimes, they should be prosecuted like adults. We established boot camps for young non-violent offenders....

Illegal Drugs. We must keep drugs off our streets and out of our schools.... We are making progress. Overall drug use in America is dropping; the number of Americans who use cocaine has dropped 30 percent since 1992. Unfortunately casual drug use by young people continues to climb. We must redouble our efforts against drug abuse everywhere, especially among our children....

Domestic Violence. ... We must do everything we can to make sure that the victims of violent crime are treated with the respect and the dignity they deserve. We support the President's call for a constitutional amendment to protect the rights of victims. We believe that when a plea bargain is entered in public, a criminal is sentenced, or a defendant is let out on bail, the victims ought to know about it, and have a say....

Immigration. ... We support a legal immigration policy that is pro-family, pro-work, pro-responsibility, and pro-citizenship, and we deplore those who blame immigrants for economic and social problems....We cannot tolerate illegal immigration and we must stop it....

We deplore those who use the need to stop illegal immigration as a pretext for discrimination. And we applaud the wisdom of Republicans.... who oppose the mean-spirited and shortsighted effort of Republicans in Congress to bar the children of illegal immigrants from schools.... Democrats want to protect American jobs by increasing criminal and civil sanctions against employers

who hire illegal workers.... We will continue to enforce labor standards to protect workers in vulnerable industries. We continue to firmly oppose welfare benefits for illegal immigrants. We believe family members who sponsor immigrants into this country should take financial responsibility for them, and be held legally responsible for supporting them.

Welfare Reform. ... Over the past four years, President Clinton has dramatically transformed the welfare system.... Welfare rolls are finally coming down — there are 1.3 million fewer people on welfare today than there were when President Clinton took office in January 1993.

... Thanks to President Clinton and the Democrats, the new welfare bill includes the health care and child care people need so they can go to work confident their children will be cared for. Thanks to President Clinton and the Democrats, the new welfare bill imposes time limits and real work requirements.... Thanks to President Clinton and the Democrats, the new welfare bill cracks down on deadbeat parents and requires minor mothers to live at home with their parents or with another responsible adult....

We know the new bill passed by Congress is far from perfect — parts of it should be fixed because they go too far and have nothing to do with welfare reform. First, Republicans cut too far into nutritional assistance for working families with children; we are committed to correcting that. Second, Republicans insisted on using welfare reform as a vehicle to cut off help to legal immigrants. That was wrong.... It is wrong to single them out for punishment just because they are immigrants. We pledge to make sure that legal immigrant families with children who fall on hard times through no fault of their own can get help when they need it....

... We challenge states to exempt battered women from time limits and other restrictions. We challenge the business community to provide more of the private sector jobs people on welfare need to build good lives and strong families.... We want to make sure welfare reform will put more people to work and move them into the economic mainstream, not take jobs away from working families....

Child Support. ... The Clinton Administration has made a determined effort to crack down on deadbeat parents.... The Clinton Administration is working to put wanted lists of parents who owe child support in the post office and on the Internet. President Clinton and Democrats in Congress insisted that the toughest possible child support enforcement be part of the new welfare reform plan — including the President's plan to deny drivers licenses and professional licenses to people who do not pay their child support....

Abortion. The Democratic Party stands behind the right of every woman to choose, consistent with *Roe v. Wade*, and regardless of ability to pay. President Clinton took executive action to make sure that the right to make such decisions is protected for all Americans. Over the last four years, we have taken action to end the gag rule and ensure safety at family planning and women's health clinics. We believe it is a fundamental constitutional liberty that individual Americans — not government — can best take responsibility for making the most difficult and intensely personal decisions regarding reproduction.

The Democratic Party is a party of inclusion. We respect the individual conscience of each American on this difficult issue, and we welcome all our members to participate at every level of our party.

Our goal is to make abortion less necessary and more rare, not more difficult and more dangerous. We support contraceptive research, family planning, comprehensive family life education, and policies that support healthy childbearing. For four years in a row, we have increased support for family planning. The abortion rate is dropping. Now we must continue to support efforts to reduce unintended pregnancies, and we call on all Americans to take personal responsibility to meet this important goal.

Political Reform. . . . The President and the Democratic Party support the bipartisan McCain-Feingold campaign finance reform bill. It will limit campaign spending, curb the influence of PACs and lobbyists, and end the soft money system. Perhaps most important of all, this bill provides free TV time for candidates, so they can talk directly to citizens about real issues and real ideas. . . . It is time to take the reins of democracy away from big money and put them back in the hands of the American people, where they belong. We applaud efforts by broadcasters and private citizens alike, to increase candidates' direct access to voters through free TV. . . .

National Security. . . . President Clinton and Vice President Gore have seized the opportunities of the post Cold War era. Over the past four years, their leadership has made America safer, more prosperous, and more engaged in solving the challenges of a new era.

Four years ago, thousands of Russian nuclear weapons were aimed at American cities. Today, not a single Russian missile points at our children. . . .

Four years ago, the forces of reform in the former Soviet Union were embattled. Today, U.S. initiatives are helping democracy and free markets take root throughout the region. . . .

Four years ago, the Middle East process had not moved beyond a set of principles, and there were no signs of peace in Northern Ireland. Today, in the Middle East we have seen real agreements toward peace, and handshakes of history, and the people of Northern Ireland have seen a 17-month cease-fire and historic negotiations among the parties. . . .

Four years ago, the North Atlantic Treaty Organization — the bulwark of Western security during the Cold War — was losing direction and support. Today, NATO is keeping the peace in Bosnia with its Partnership for Peace allies and, as a result of American leadership, preparing to welcome new members from Central Europe. . . .

Four years ago, dictators ruled in Haiti, abusing human rights and leaving thousands of its citizens desperate to flee to our shores. Today, the dictators are gone, democracy has been restored, and Haiti's mass-exodus has stopped. . . .

Strengthening Our Military. Over the past four years, the Administration has undertaken the most successful restructuring of our military forces in history. Even as the size of our forces has decreased, their capabilities, readiness and qualitative edge have increased. The Administration has ensured that America is prepared to fight alongside others when we can, and alone when we must. . . . We will continue our work to ensure that the men and women who wear American uniforms receive adequate pay and support, including: childcare, education, housing, access to quality health care for themselves and their families, and protection against discrimination and sexual harassment. . . .

Weapons of Mass Destruction. . . . The Democratic Party supports efforts to sign a Comprehensive Test Ban Treaty this year and to bring it into force as soon as possible. We support immediate ratification of the Chemical Weapons Convention. . . . We support full funding of the Nunn-Lugar Cooperative Threat Reduction program to eliminate former Soviet nuclear and chemical weapons and support funds to ensure that nuclear materials in the former Soviet Union are secure and do not fall into the wrong hands. We support vigilant efforts, in cooperation

with the Republic of Korea, Japan, and others, to ensure North Korea fully abides by its agreements to dismantle its nuclear program, and we support the Administration's vigorous efforts to prevent Iraq, Iran, and other dangerous states from acquiring or developing weapons of mass destruction.

The Democratic Party is committed to a strong and balanced National Missile Defense (NMD) program. The Administration is spending $3 billion a year on six different systems to protect our troops in the field and our allies from short and medium range missiles. To prepare for the possibility of a long range missile attack on American soil by a rogue state the Clinton Administration is committed to developing by the year 2000 a defensive system that could be deployed by 2003, well before the threat becomes real. The Democratic Party opposes the Republican NMD plan — spending up to $60 billion on a revival of the Star Wars program that would force us to choose a costly system today that could be obsolete tomorrow. . . .

Meeting New Challenges. . . . Today's Democratic Party is determined to keep the war on global terrorism, narcotics, and crime at the center of our security agenda. We will seek increased cooperation from our allies and friends abroad in fighting these threats. We will continue to work aggressively to shut off foreign drug flows, eradicate foreign drug crops, and assist countries that demonstrate active cooperation.

Europe and the Former Soviet Union. Today's Democratic Party knows that the security of Europe remains a vital American interest, and that we must remain engaged in Europe. . . . It is our vision to see, one day, a community of free, democratic, and peaceful nations, bound by political, security, cultural, and economic ties, spanning across North America and Europe. We applaud the Clinton-Gore Administration's efforts to foster a peaceful, democratic and undivided Europe — including expanded support for reform in former communist states; dramatically increased assistance to Ukraine; the Partnership for Peace program of military cooperation with Europe's new democracies; its steady, determined work to add new Central European members to NATO in the near future. . . . We support continued efforts to secure a just and lasting peace in Bosnia, Northern Ireland and Cyprus. We are committed to the success of independence in Ukraine and the Baltics. And we support the continuing evolution of a prosperous and peaceful Russia. . . .

Asia. . . . The Democratic Party applauds the important new security charter with Japan, the Administration's close cooperation with the Republic of Korea toward the goal of a unified and non-nuclear peninsula, and the deployment of an American naval task force to the Taiwan Straits to ensure that China's military exercises did not imperil the security of the region. The Party supports the Administration's policy of steady engagement to encourage a stable, secure, open and prosperous China — a China that respects human rights throughout its land and in Tibet, that joins international efforts against weapons proliferation, and that plays by the rules of free and fair trade. . . .

The Middle East. President Clinton has overseen a remarkable record of achievement toward peace and security in the Middle East — the Israeli-Palestinian accords; the peace agreement between Israel and Jordan; new regional security and investment summits; Israel's increased acceptance throughout the Middle East and the world; the dual containment of Iraq and Iran. The Democratic Party. . . . supports the efforts by the Clinton-Gore Administration to achieve a comprehensive and lasting peace among Israel and all its neighbors, including Lebanon and Syria. The Democratic Party remains committed to America's long-standing special relationship with Israel, based on shared values, a mutual commitment to democracy and a strategic alliance that benefits both nations. The United States should continue to help Israel maintain its qualitative edge. Jerusalem is the capital of Israel and should remain an undivided city accessible to people of all faiths. We are also committed to working with our Arab partners for peace to build a brighter, more secure and prosperous future for all the people of the Middle East. . . .

Putting Families First. The first and most sacred responsibility of every parent is to cherish our children and strengthen our families. The family is the foundation of American life. . . . President Clinton took office determined to put families first. We support the fundamental themes of the Families First Agenda — promoting paycheck, health care, retirement, and personal security; creating greater educational and economic opportunity; and requiring greater responsibility from individuals, businesses, and government.

Standing Up for Parents. In the first month of Bill Clinton's Presidency, the Democratic Party. . . . enacted the Family and Medical Leave Act. . . . This law is good for families, it is good for America, and it would not be the law today without the Democratic Party. . . . President Clinton fought for and secured tax credits to encourage adoption. . . . Now we want to take the next step. We believe parents should be able to take unpaid leave from work and choose flex time so they can do their job as parents: to do things like go to parent-teacher conferences or take a child to the doctor. . . .

Tobacco. . . . The President has proposed measures to cut off children's access to cigarettes, crack down on those who sell tobacco to minors illegally, and curtail advertising designed to appeal to children. Tobacco companies may market to adults if they wish, but they must take the responsibility to draw the line on children.

Community Empowerment and Cities. Today's Democratic Party understands that we cannot rebuild our poorest communities by imposing cookie-cutter solutions from Washington. We have to give communities the tools they need to create opportunity. Citizens, local government, the private sector, and civic groups must come together and take the responsibility to rebuild their communities from the bottom up.

. . . Over the next four years, we want a second round of Empowerment Zones to bring economic growth to more American communities; a significant expansion of the Community Development Financial Institutions Fund to spur more private sector investment in local economies; and a new tax incentive to encourage further cleanup and redevelopment of brownfields. Today's Democratic Party knows that the best way to bring jobs and growth back to our poorest neighborhoods is to harness the job-creating power of the private sector. . . .

Protecting Our Environment. . . . We believe America's elected officials have a responsibility to protect America's families from threats to their health, and that trust must never be abdicated — especially not by placing control of environmental safeguards in the hands of the very polluters those safeguards are meant to keep in line.

. . . We believe America should insist that toxic waste cleanup is paid for by those responsible for it in the first place — and not foisted off on the taxpayers. . . .

. . . We want to challenge businesses and communities to take more initiative in protecting the environment, and we want to make it easier for them to do it. President Clinton and Vice President Gore launched Project XL which tells businesses: If you can find a cheaper, more efficient way than government regulations require to meet even tougher pollution goals, do it — as long as you do it right. This new approach offers business flexibility, incentives, and accountability. . . .

We are committed to protecting the majestic legacy of our National Parks. . . . We will be good stewards of our old-growth forests, oppose new offshore oil drilling and mineral exploration and production in our nation's many environmentally critical areas, and protect our oceans from oil spills and the dumping of toxic and radioactive waste.

. . . We will continue to support responsible recycling, and encourage energy efficiency that makes our economy more efficient and less reliant on foreign oil. We believe that adequate investments in better mass transit, cleaner cars, and renewable energy sources are good for the environment and good for the economy.

. . . We will seek a strong international agreement to further reduce greenhouse gas emissions worldwide and protect our global climate. We are committed to preserving the planet's biodiversity, repairing the depleted ozone layer, and working with other nations to stabilize population growth. . . .

Fighting Discrimination. Today's Democratic Party knows we must renew our efforts to stamp out discrimination and hatred of every kind, wherever and whenever we see it. . . . We believe everyone in America should learn English so they can fully share in our daily life, but we strongly oppose divisive efforts like English-only legislation. . . . We continue to lead the fight to end discrimination on the basis of race, gender, religion, age, ethnicity, disability, and sexual orientation. The Democratic Party has always supported the Equal Rights Amendment, and we are committed to ensuring full equality for women and to vigorously enforce the Americans with Disabilities Act. We support continued efforts, like the Employment Non-Discrimination Act, to end discrimination against gay men and lesbians and further their full inclusion in the life of the nation.

. . . President Clinton is leading the way to reform affirmative action so that it works, it is improved, and promotes opportunity, but does not accidentally hold others back in the process. . . . When it comes to affirmative action, we should mend it, not end it.

Religious Freedom. Today's Democratic Party understands that all Americans have a right to express their faith. . . . Americans have a right to express their love of God in public, and we applaud the President's work to ensure that children are not denied private religious expression in school. . . .

Responsibility to Our Community and Our Country. Today's Democratic Party believes every American has a duty and a responsibility to give something back to their community and their country. In the past three years, 45,000 Americans have performed national service as part of the AmeriCorps program President Clinton and the Democrats fought so hard to create. . . .

We applaud the American spirit of voluntarism and charity. . . . We must shrink the government, but we cannot shrink from our challenges. We believe every school and college in America should make service a part of its basic ethic, and we want to expand national service by helping communities give scholarships to high school students for community service. We challenge Americans in all walks of life to make a new commitment to taking responsibility for themselves, their families, their communities, and their country.

Highlights of National Party Conventions, 1831-1996

1831 First national political convention held in Baltimore by Anti-Masonic Party.

1832 Democratic Party met in Baltimore for its first national convention.

1839 Whig Party held its first national convention.

1840 Democrats set up committee to select vice presidential nominees, subject to approval of convention.

1844 Democrats nominated James K. Polk — first "dark horse" candidate — after nine ballots. Silas Wright declined the vice presidential nomination. First time a convention nominee refused nomination.

1848 Democrats established continuing committee, known as "Democratic National Committee."

1852 Democrats and Whigs both adopted platforms before nominating candidates for president, setting precedent followed almost uniformly ever since.

1856 First Republican national convention held in Philadelphia.

1860 Democrats met in Charleston, S.C. After 10 days and deadlocked on a presidential nominee, delegates adjourned and reconvened in Baltimore. Benjamin Fitzpatrick, the Democrats' choice for vice president, became the first candidate to withdraw after convention adjournment and be replaced by a selection of the national committee.

First Republican credentials dispute took place over seating delegates from slave states and voting strength of delegates from states where party was comparatively weak.

1864 In attempt to close ranks during Civil War, Republicans used the name "Union Party" at convention.

1868 For the first time, Republicans gave a candidate (Ulysses S. Grant) 100 percent of vote on first ballot.
Susan B. Anthony spoke before Democratic convention urging support of women's suffrage.

1872 Victoria Clafin Woodhull, nominated by the Equal Rights Party, was first woman presidential candidate. Black leader Frederick Douglass was her running mate.

1880 Republicans nominated James A. Garfield for president on 36th ballot — party's all-time record number of ballots.

1884 Republican Rep. John Roy Lynch of Mississippi became first black elected temporary chairman of national nominating convention.

1888 Frederick Douglass was first black to receive a vote in presidential balloting at a major party political convention (Republican).

1900 Each party had one woman delegate.

1904 Florida Democrats selected delegates in first-ever presidential primary election.

1920 For first time, women attended conventions in significant numbers.

1924 Republicans adopted bonus votes for states that went Republican in previous election. GOP convention was first to be broadcast on radio.
John W. Davis was nominated by Democrats on record 103rd ballot.

1932 Republicans began tradition of appointing party leader from House of Representatives as permanent convention chairman.
Democrat Franklin D. Roosevelt became first major party candidate to accept presidential nomination in person.

1936 Democratic Party voted to end requirement of two-thirds delegate majority for nomination.

1940 Republican convention was first to be televised.

1944 Democrats adopted bonus votes for states that went Democratic in previous election.
Thomas E. Dewey became first Republican candidate to accept nomination in person.

1948 Democrats began appointing Speaker of the House as permanent chairman. Republicans renominated Thomas E. Dewey — first time GOP renominated a defeated presidential candidate.

1952 Adlai E. Stevenson was chosen as Democratic nominee in one of few genuine "drafts" in history.

1956 Democrats use party loyalty provision in selecting delegates for first time.

1960 Democrats adopted civil rights plank that was strongest in party history.
Republican nominee Richard Nixon was party's first vice president nominated for president at completion of his term.

1964 Sen. Margaret Chase Smith was nominated for presidency at Republican convention — first time a woman placed in nomination by a major party.

1968 Democratic Party voted to end unit rule. Outside the Chicago convention, anti-war protests erupt in violence.

1980 Democratic delegates were composed of an equal number of men and women.

1984 Democrats nominated Rep. Geraldine A. Ferraro of New York for vice president — the first woman placed on national ticket by a major party.

1996 The Reform Party conducted its first convention in a two-stage process that allowed balloting by mail, electronic mail or phone.

Key Convention
Ballots

Sources: Key Convention Ballots

This section (pages 195 to 260) presents the results of important balloting from the presidential nominating conventions of three major American political parties 1835 to 1996. The balloting results are arranged in chronological order by convention year. Major contenders for the respective party nominations appear in the tables by last name only. Full names and other detailed descriptions of each convention can be found in the preceding section, "Convention Chronology." Each table contains a reference indicating the page where this information appears.

The source for the balloting results for the 1835-1972 conventions is Richard C. Bain and Judith H. Parris, *Convention Decisions and Voting Records* (Washington, D.C.: Brookings Institution, 1973). Permission to use this material was granted by the Brookings Institution, which holds the copyright. The sources for the 1976 to 1996 vote totals are *The Official Proceedings of the Democratic National Convention* and the Republican National Committee. *Convention Decisions and Voting Records* contains ballots for three major parties in American history — the Democrats, the Whigs and modern Republicans. This section includes ballots from conventions of these three parties alone.

In selecting ballots to include in *National Party Conventions 1831-1996*, Congressional Quarterly followed several criteria:

- To include nominating ballots and selected other critical presidential ballots. The Democratic Party conventions of 1832, 1840, 1888, 1916, 1936 and 1964 nominated presidential candidates by acclamation without balloting.
- To include key ballots on important procedural issues, credentials contests and platform disputes.
- To exclude all ballots for vice presidential candidates.

Vote Total Discrepancies

Bain and Parris note frequent discrepancies between totals given in the published proceedings of the party conventions and the totals reached by adding up the state-by-state delegation votes. They state: "Wherever the discrepancy was obvious and the correct figure could be clearly derived, the record has been printed in corrected form. When the added totals of detailed figures listed differ from the sums printed in the proceedings, both totals are given."

Congressional Quarterly has followed this same procedure. For example, on page 198, the 49th presidential ballot of the 1852 Democratic Party convention appears. Franklin Pierce is listed as receiving 279 votes, the sum of the column. A footnote, however, indicates that the convention proceedings recorded Pierce as receiving 283 votes. Similar examples appear on pages 201, 202 and 243.

1844 Democratic

(Narrative, p. 30)

Delegation	Total Votes	Amendment Ratifying Two-Thirds Rule		First Pres. Ballot[1]		Fifth Pres. Ballot[2]		Ninth Pres. Ballot (Before shift)[3]		Ninth Pres. Ballot (After shift)
		Yea	Nay	Van Buren	Cass	Van Buren	Cass	Polk	Cass	Polk
Alabama	9	9	—	1	8	1	8	9	—	9
Arkansas	3	3	—	—	—	—	—	3	—	3
Connecticut	6	3	3	6	—	—	—	6	—	6
Delaware	3	3	—	—	3	—	3	3	—	3
Georgia	10	10	—	—	9	—	9	9	—	10
Illinois	9	9	—	5	2	2	4	9	—	9
Indiana	12	12	—	3	9	1	11	12	—	12
Kentucky	12	12	—	—	—	—	—	12	—	12
Louisiana	6	6	—	—	—	—	—	6	—	6
Maine	9	—	9	8	—	8	1	7	1	9
Maryland	8	6	2	2	4	2	6	7	1	8
Massachusetts	12	5	7	8	1	7	3	10	2	12
Michigan	5	5	—	1	4	—	5	—	5	5
Mississippi	6	6	—	—	6	—	6	6	—	6
Missouri	7	—	7	7	—	7	—	7	—	7
New Hampshire	6	—	6	6	—	2	—	6	—	6
New Jersey	7	7	—	3	2	—	4	2	5	7
New York	36	—	36	36	—	36	—	35	—	36
North Carolina	11	5	5	2	4	—	7	11	—	11
Ohio	23	—	23	23	—	20	3	18	2	23
Pennsylvania	26	12	13	26	—	16	—	19	7	26
Rhode Island	4	2	2	4	—	1	1	4	—	4
Tennessee	13	13	—	—	13	—	13	13	—	13
Vermont	6	3	3	5	1	—	6	—	6	6
Virginia	17	17	—	—	17	—	17	17	—	17
Total	266	148	118	146	83	103	107	231	29	266

1. *Other candidates: Richard M. Johnson, 24; John C. Calhoun, 6; James Buchanan, 4; Levi Woodbury, 2; Commodore Stewart, 1.*
2. *Other candidates: Johnson, 29; Buchanan, 26; not voting, 1.*
3. *Not voting, 6.*

1835 Democratic

(Narrative, p. 26)

Delegation	Total Votes	First Pres. Ballot Van Buren
Connecticut	8	8
Delaware	3	3
Georgia	11	11
Indiana	9	9
Kentucky	15	15
Louisiana	5	5
Maine	10	10
Maryland	10	10
Massachusetts	14	14
Mississippi	4	4
Missouri	4	4
New Hampshire	7	7
New Jersey	8	8
New York	42	42
North Carolina	15	15
Ohio	21	21
Pennsylvania	30	30
Rhode Island	4	4
Tennessee	15	15
Vermont	7	7
Virginia	23	23
Total	265	265

1844 Whig

(Narrative, p. 29)

Delegation	Total Votes	First Pres. Ballot Clay	Delegation	Total Votes	First Pres. Ballot Clay
Alabama	9	9	Missouri	7	7
Arkansas	3	3	New Hampshire	6	6
Connecticut	6	6	New Jersey	7	7
Delaware	3	3	New York	36	36
Georgia	10	10	North Carolina	11	11
Illinois	9	9	Ohio	23	23
Indiana	12	12	Pennsylvania	26	26
Kentucky	12	12	Rhode Island	4	4
Louisiana	6	6	South Carolina	9	9
Maine	9	9	Tennessee	13	13
Maryland	8	8	Vermont	6	6
Massachusetts	12	12	Virginia	17	17
Michigan	5	5			
Mississippi	6	6	**Total**	275	275

1848 Democratic

(Narrative, p. 31)

Delegation	Total Votes	Adoption of Two-Thirds Rule Yea	Nay	Not Voting	Amendment on N.Y. Credentials Yea	Nay	Not Voting	First Pres. Ballot[1] Cass	Buchanan	Woodbury	Fourth Pres. Ballot[2] Cass	Buchanan	Woodbury
Alabama	9	9	—	—	—	9	—	—	4	5	—	4	5
Arkansas	3	3	—	—	—	3	—	3	—	—	3	—	—
Connecticut	6	6	—	—	6	—	—	—	—	6	—	—	6
Delaware	3	2	1	—	1	2	—	3	—	—	3	—	—
Florida	3	3	—	—	—	3	—	—	—	—	—	—	3
Georgia	10	10	—	—	—	10	—	—	2	5	10	—	—
Illinois	9	9	—	—	9	—	—	9	—	—	9	—	—
Indiana	12	3	9	—	7	5	—	12	—	—	12	—	—
Iowa	4	4	—	—	4	—	—	1	3	—	4	—	—
Kentucky	12	12	—	—	10	2	—	7	1	1	8	1	1
Louisiana	6	6	—	—	—	6	—	6	—	—	6	—	—
Maine	9	9	—	—	9	—	—	—	—	9	—	—	9
Maryland	8	7	1	—	2	5	1	6	—	2	6	—	2
Massachusetts	12	10	2	—	11	1	—	—	—	12	8	—	4
Michigan	5	5	—	—	—	5	—	5	—	—	5	—	—
Mississippi	6	6	—	—	—	6	—	6	—	—	6	—	—
Missouri	7	1	6	—	1	4	2	7	—	—	7	—	—
New Hampshire	6	6	—	—	6	—	—	—	—	6	—	—	6
New Jersey	7	7	—	—	7	—	—	—	7	—	7	—	—
New York	36	—	—	36	—	—	36	—	—	—	—	—	—
North Carolina	11	11	—	—	—	11	—	—	10	1	11	—	—
Ohio	23	—	23	—	14	9	—	23	—	—	23	—	—
Pennsylvania	26	—	26	—	19	7	—	—	26	—	—	26	—
Rhode Island	4	3	1	—	2	2	—	1	—	3	4	—	—
South Carolina	9	9	—	—	—	9	—	—	—	—	9	—	—
Tennessee	13	13	—	—	9	4	—	7	2	1	7	2	2
Texas	4	4	—	—	4	—	—	4	—	—	4	—	—
Vermont	6	1	5	—	5	1	—	4	—	2	6	—	—
Virginia	17	17	—	—	—	17	—	17	—	—	17	—	—
Wisconsin	4	—	4	—	—	4	—	4	—	—	4	—	—
Total	290	176	78	36	126	125	39	125	55	53	179	33	38

1. *Other candidates: John C. Calhoun, 9; W. J. Worth, 6; George M. Dallas, 3; not voting, 39.*
2. *Other candidates: William O. Butler, 4; Worth, 1; not voting, 35.*

1848 Whig

(Narrative, p. 32)

Delegation	Total Votes	First Pres. Ballot[1]			Fourth Pres. Ballot[2]		
		Taylor	Clay	Scott	Taylor	Clay	Scott
Alabama	7	6	1	—	6	1	—
Arkansas	3	3	—	—	3	—	—
Connecticut	6	—	6	—	3	3	—
Delaware	3	—	—	—	2	—	1
Florida	3	3	—	—	3	—	—
Georgia	10	10	—	—	10	—	—
Illinois	8	4	3	1	8	—	—
Indiana	12	1	2	9	7	1	4
Iowa	4	2	1	—	4	—	—
Kentucky	12	7	5	—	11	1	—
Louisiana	6	5	1	—	6	—	—
Maine	9	5	1	—	5	—	3
Maryland	8	—	8	—	8	—	—
Massachusetts	12	—	—	—	1	—	2
Michigan	5	—	3	2	2	—	3
Mississippi	6	6	—	—	6	—	—
Missouri	7	6	—	—	7	—	—
New Hampshire	6	—	—	—	2	—	—
New Jersey	7	3	4	—	4	3	—
New York	36	—	29	5	6	13	17
North Carolina	11	6	5	—	10	1	—
Ohio	23	1	1	20	1	1	21
Pennsylvania	26	8	12	6	12	4	10
Rhode Island	4	—	4	—	4	—	—
South Carolina	2	1	1	—	1	1	—
Tennessee	13	13	—	—	13	—	—
Texas	4	4	—	—	4	—	—
Vermont	6	1	5	—	2	2	2
Virginia	17	15	2	—	16	1	—
Wisconsin	4	1	3	—	4	—	—
Total	**280**	**111**	**97**	**43**	**171**	**32**	**63**

1. *Other candidates: Daniel Webster, 22; John McLean, 2; John M. Clayton, 4.*
2. *Other candidate: Webster, 14.*

1852 Democratic

(Narrative, p. 33)

Delegation	Total Votes	First Pres. Ballot[1]		Twentieth Pres. Ballot[2]			Thirtieth Pres. Ballot[3]			Thirty-Fifth Pres. Ballot[4]				Forty-Eighth Pres. Ballot[5]				Forty-ninth Pres. Ballot[6]
		Cass	Buchanan	Buchanan	Cass	Douglas	Douglas	Buchanan	Cass	Cass	Douglas	Marcy	Buchanan	Marcy	Cass	Pierce	Douglas	Pierce
Alabama	9	—	9	9	—	—	—	9	—	—	—	—	9	9	—	—	—	9
Arkansas	4	—	4	—	—	4	4	—	—	—	4	—	—	—	—	—	4	4
California	4	—	—	1	—	3	3	1	—	2	1	—	1	—	4	—	—	4
Connecticut	6	2	2	2	2	1	6	—	—	3	3	—	—	6	—	—	—	6
Delaware	3	3	—	—	3	—	—	—	—	3	—	—	—	—	3	—	—	3
Florida	3	—	—	—	—	2	2	—	—	—	2	—	—	—	—	—	2	3
Georgia	10	—	10	10	—	—	—	10	—	—	10	—	—	10	—	—	—	10
Illinois	11	—	—	—	—	11	11	—	—	—	11	—	—	—	—	—	11	11
Indiana	13	—	—	—	—	—	—	—	—	13	—	—	—	—	13	—	—	13
Iowa	4	2	—	—	1	3	4	—	—	2	2	—	—	—	2	—	2	4
Kentucky	12	12	—	—	12	—	—	—	—	12	—	—	—	—	—	12	—	12
Louisiana	6	6	—	—	6	—	6	—	—	6	—	—	—	—	6	—	—	6
Maine	8	5	3	1	4	3	5	2	—	2	5	—	1	—	—	8	—	8
Maryland	8	8	—	—	8	—	—	—	8	8	—	—	—	1	1	5	—	5
Massachusetts	13	9	—	—	1	7	7	—	1	7	1	5	—	6	—	6	1	13
Michigan	6	6	—	—	6	—	—	—	6	6	—	—	—	—	6	—	—	6
Mississippi	7	—	7	7	—	—	—	7	—	—	—	7	—	7	—	—	—	7
Missouri	9	9	—	—	—	9	9	—	—	9	—	—	—	—	9	—	—	9
New Hampshire	5	4	—	—	5	—	—	2	—	5	—	—	—	—	—	—	5	5
New Jersey	7	7	—	7	—	—	—	7	—	7	—	—	—	7	—	—	—	7
New York	35	11	—	—	12	—	1	—	11	12	1	22	—	24	10	—	1	35
North Carolina	10	—	10	9	—	1	4	6	—	—	—	10	—	10	—	—	—	10
Ohio	23	16	—	—	13	6	9	—	7	18	3	—	—	—	15	—	4	17
Pennsylvania	27	—	27	27	—	—	—	27	—	—	—	—	27	—	—	—	—	27
Rhode Island	4	3	—	—	—	4	4	—	—	4	—	—	—	—	—	4	—	4
Tennessee	12	6	6	4	5	3	7	5	—	9	2	—	1	9	—	—	1	12
Texas	4	—	—	—	—	—	—	—	—	—	—	—	—	—	—	—	—	4
Vermont	5	5	—	—	—	5	5	—	—	—	5	—	—	—	—	—	5	5
Virginia	15	—	15	15	—	—	—	15	—	—	—	—	—	—	—	15	—	15
Wisconsin	5	2	—	—	3	2	5	—	—	3	2	—	—	—	3	—	2	5
Total	288	116	93	92	81	64	92	91	33	131	52	44	39	89	72	55	33	279[a]

1. *Other candidates: William L. Marcy, 27; Stephen A. Douglas, 20; Joseph Lane, 13; Samuel Houston, 8; J. B. Weller, 4; Henry Dodge, 3; William O. Butler, 2; Daniel S. Dickinson, 1; not voting, 1.*
2. *Other candidates: Marcy, 26; Lane, 13; Houston, 10; Butler, 1; Dickinson, 1.*
3. *Other candidates: Marcy, 26; Butler, 20; Lane, 13; Houston, 12; Dickinson, 1.*
4. *Other candidates: Franklin Pierce, 15; Houston, 5; Butler, 1; Dickinson, 1.*
5. *Other candidates: Buchanan, 28; Houston, 6; Linn Boyd, 2; Butler, 1; R. J. Ingersoll, 1; Dickinson, 1.*
6. *Other candidates: Cass, 2; Douglas, 2; Butler, 1; Houston, 1; not voting, 3.*
a. *Sum of column; proceedings record 283.*

1852 Whig

(Narrative, p. 34)

Delegation	Total Votes	First Pres. Ballot			50th Pres. Ballot			52nd Pres. Ballot			53rd Pres. Ballot		
		Scott	Fillmore	Webster	Scott	Fillmore	Webster	Scott	Fillmore	Webster	Scott	Fillmore	Webster
Alabama	9	—	9	—	—	9	—	—	9	—	—	9	—
Arkansas	4	—	4	—	—	4	—	—	4	—	—	4	—
California	4	2	1	1	3	1	—	3	—	1	3	—	1
Connecticut	6	2	1	3	2	1	3	2	1	3	2	1	3
Delaware	3	3	—	—	3	—	—	3	—	—	3	—	—
Florida	3	—	3	—	—	3	—	—	3	—	—	3	—
Georgia	10	—	10	—	—	10	—	—	10	—	—	10	—
Illinois	11	11	—	—	11	—	—	11	—	—	11	—	—
Indiana	13	13	—	—	13	—	—	13	—	—	13	—	—
Iowa	4	—	4	—	1	3	—	1	3	—	1	3	—
Kentucky	12	—	12	—	—	12	—	—	12	—	—	11	—
Louisiana	6	—	6	—	—	6	—	—	6	—	—	6	—
Maine	8	8	—	—	8	—	—	8	—	—	8	—	—
Maryland	8	—	8	—	—	8	—	—	8	—	—	8	—
Massachusetts	13	2	—	11	2	—	11	2	—	11	2	—	11
Michigan	6	6	—	—	6	—	—	6	—	—	6	—	—
Mississippi	7	—	7	—	—	7	—	—	7	—	—	7	—
Missouri	9	—	9	—	3	6	—	1	6	—	3	6	—
New Hampshire	5	1	—	4	1	—	4	1	—	4	5	—	—
New Jersey	7	7	—	—	7	—	—	7	—	—	7	—	—
New York	35	24	7	2	25	7	1	25	7	1	25	7	1
North Carolina	10	—	10	—	—	10	—	—	10	—	—	10	—
Ohio	23	22	1	—	23	—	—	23	—	—	23	—	—
Pennsylvania	27	26	1	—	26	1	—	27	—	—	27	—	—
Rhode Island	4	1	1	2	2	—	2	2	—	2	3	—	1
South Carolina	8	—	8	—	—	8	—	—	8	—	—	8	—
Tennessee	12	—	12	—	—	12	—	4	8	—	3	9	—
Texas	4	—	4	—	—	4	—	—	4	—	—	4	—
Vermont	5	1	1	3	2	—	3	2	2	1	5	—	—
Virginia	15	1	13	—	3	10	—	3	10	—	8	6	—
Wisconsin	5	1	1	3	1	1	3	2	—	2	1	—	4
Total	296	132[a]	133	29	142	122[a]	27	148[a]	118	25	159	112	21

a. The sum of the column for Scott on the first ballot is 131 votes, for Fillmore on the 50th ballot 123 votes and for Scott on the 52nd ballot is 146 votes. The source for these discrepancies is the Baltimore Sun for June 19, 1852, and June 22, 1852. The Sun reported June 19, 1852, total votes for Scott on the first ballot as 132 votes; however, the column of figures for the state-by-state ballots reported in the Sun add up to 131 votes. Similarly, on June 22, 1852, the Sun reported 122 votes for Fillmore on the 50th ballot and 148 for Scott on the 52nd ballot, but the state-by-state ballots reported in the Sun add up to 123 votes and 146 votes, respectively. Bain's Convention Decisions and Voting Records used the Baltimore Sun as its source for the 1852 Whig convention ballots.

1856 Democratic

(Narrative, p. 37)

Delegation	Total Votes	First Pres. Ballot				Tenth Pres. Ballot				Fifteenth Pres. Ballot			17th Pres. Ballot
		Buchanan	Pierce	Douglas	Other	Buchanan	Pierce	Douglas	Other	Buchanan	Douglas	Other	Buchanan
Alabama	9	—	9	—	—	—	9	—	—	—	9	—	9
Arkansas	4	—	4	—	—	—	—	4	—	—	4	—	4
California	4	—	—	—	4	—	—	—	4	—	—	4	4
Connecticut	3	6	—	—	—	6	—	—	—	6	—	—	6
Delaware	3	3	—	—	—	3	—	—	—	3	—	—	3
Florida	3	—	3	—	—	—	3	—	—	—	3	—	3
Georgia	10	—	10	—	—	3	—	7	—	3	7	—	10
Illinois	11	—	—	11	—	—	—	11	—	—	11	—	11
Indiana	13	13	—	—	—	13	—	—	—	13	—	—	13
Iowa	4	—	—	4	—	2	—	2	—	2	2	—	4
Kentucky	12	4	5	3	—	4½	—	7½	—	4	7	1	12
Louisiana	6	6	—	—	—	6	—	—	—	6	—	—	6
Maine	8	5	3	—	—	6	2	—	—	7	—	1	8
Maryland	8	6	2	—	—	7	1	—	—	8	—	—	8
Massachusetts	13	4	9	—	—	6	7	—	—	10	3	—	13
Michigan	6	6	—	—	—	6	—	—	—	6	—	—	6
Mississippi	7	—	7	—	—	—	7	—	—	—	7	—	7
Missouri	9	—	—	9	—	—	—	9	—	—	9	—	9
New Hampshire	5	—	5	—	—	—	5	—	—	—	5	—	5
New Jersey	7	7	—	—	—	7	—	—	—	7	—	—	7
New York	35	17	18	—	—	18	17	—	—	17	18	—	35
North Carolina	10	—	10	—	—	—	10	—	—	—	10	—	10
Ohio	23	13½	4½	4	1	13	3½	5	1½	13½	6½	3	23
Pennsylvania	27	27	—	—	—	27	—	—	—	27	—	—	27
Rhode Island	4	—	4	—	—	—	4	—	—	4	—	—	4
South Carolina	8	—	8	—	—	—	8	—	—	—	8	—	8
Tennessee	12	—	12	—	—	—	—	12	—	12	—	—	12
Texas	4	—	4	—	—	—	4	—	—	—	4	—	4
Vermont	5	—	5	—	—	—	—	5	—	—	5	—	5
Virginia	15	15	—	—	—	15	—	—	—	15	—	—	15
Wisconsin	5	3	—	2	—	5	—	—	—	5	—	—	5
Total	296	135½	122½	33	5[1]	147½	80½	62½	5½[2]	168½	118½	9[3]	296

1. Other candidate: Lewis Cass, 5.
2. Other candidate: Cass, 5½.
3. Other candidates: Cass, 4½; Franklin Pierce, 3½; not voting, 1.

1856 Republican

(Narrative, p. 36)

Delegation	Total Votes	Informal Pres. Ballot[1]		Formal Pres. Ballot[2]	Delegation	Total Votes	Informal Pres. Ballot[1]		Formal Pres. Ballot[2]
		Fremont	McLean	Fremont			Fremont	McLean	Fremont
California	12	12	—	12	Minnesota	2	—	—	—
Connecticut	18	18	—	18	New Hampshire	15	15	—	15
Delaware	9	—	9	9	New Jersey	21	7	14	21
Illinois	34	14	19	33	New York	105	93	3	105
Indiana	39	18	21	39	Ohio	69	30	39	55
Iowa	12	12	—	12	Pennsylvania	81	10	71	57
Kansas	10	9	—	9	Rhode Island	12	12	—	12
Kentucky	5	5	—	5	Vermont	15	15	—	15
Maine	24	13	11	24	Wisconsin	15	15	—	15
Maryland	9	4	3	7	District of Columbia	3	—	—	—
Massachusetts	39	39	—	39	**Total**	567	359	190	520
Michigan	18	18	—	18					

1. Other candidates: Nathaniel Banks, 1; Charles Sumner, 2; William Seward, 1; absent or not voting, 14.
2. Other candidates: John McLean, 37; Seward, 1; absent or not voting, 9.

1860 Democratic

(Narrative, p. 39)

Charleston Convention   Baltimore Convention

Delegation	Total Votes	Butler Amend. on 1856 platform		Minority Report on platform		First Pres. Ballot[1]			57th Pres. Ballot[2]		Minority Report on Credentials			Reconsider Louisiana Credentials			First Pres. Ballot[3]	Second Pres. Ballot[4]
		Yea	Nay	Yea	Nay	Douglas	Hunter	Guthrie	Douglas	Guthrie	Yea	Nay	Not Voting	Yea	Nay	Not Voting	Douglas	Douglas
Alabama	9	—	9	—	9	—	—	—	—	—	—	—	9	—	—	9	9	9
Arkansas	4	—	4	—	4	—	1	—	—	—	½	½	3	½	½	3	1	1½
California	4	—	4	—	4	—	—	—	—	—	4	—	—	—	4	—	—	—
Connecticut	6	2½	3½	6	—	3½	—	—	3½	2½	2½	3½	—	3½	2½	—	3½	3½
Delaware	3	3	—	—	3	—	2	—	—	—	2	—	1	—	2	1	—	—
Florida	3	—	3	—	3	—	—	—	—	—	—	—	3	—	—	3	—	—
Georgia	10	10	—	—	10	—	—	—	—	—	—	—	10	—	—	10	—	—
Illinois	11	—	11	11	—	11	—	—	11	—	—	11	—	11	—	—	11	11
Indiana	13	—	13	13	—	13	—	—	13	—	—	13	—	13	—	—	13	13
Iowa	4	—	4	4	—	4	—	—	4	—	—	4	—	4	—	—	4	4
Kentucky	12	9	3	2½	9½	—	—	12	—	12	10	2	—	2	10	—	—	3
Louisiana	6	—	6	—	6	—	—	—	—	—	—	—	6	—	—	6	6	6
Maine	8	3	5	—	—	5	—	3	5	3	2½	5½	—	5½	2½	—	5½	7
Maryland	8	5½	2½	3½	4½	2	5	—	4	4	5½	2	½	2	6	—	2½	2½
Massachusetts	13	8	5	7	6	5½	6	—	6	6	8	5	—	—	5	8	10	10
Michigan	6	—	6	6	—	6	—	—	6	—	—	6	—	6	—	—	6	6
Minnesota	4	1½	2½	4	—	4	—	—	3	—	1½	2½	—	2½	1½	—	2½	4
Mississippi	7	—	7	—	7	—	—	—	—	—	—	—	7	—	—	7	—	—
Missouri	9	4½	4½	4	5	4½	—	4½	4½	4½	5	4	—	4½	4½	—	4½	4½
New Hampshire	5	—	5	5	—	5	—	—	5	—	½	4½	—	4½	½	—	5	5
New Jersey	7	5	2	5	2	—	—	7	2	5	4	3	—	2½	4½	—	2½	2½
New York	35	—	35	35	—	35	—	—	35	—	—	35	—	35	—	—	35	35
North Carolina	10	10	—	—	10	1	9	—	1	—	9	1	—	1	8½	½	1	1
Ohio	23	—	23	23	—	23	—	—	23	—	—	23	—	23	—	—	23	23
Oregon	3	3	—	—	3	—	—	—	—	—	3	—	—	—	3	—	—	—
Pennsylvania	27	16½	10½	12	15	9	3	9	9½	17½	17	10	—	10	17	—	10	19
Rhode Island	4	—	4	4	—	4	—	—	4	—	—	4	—	4	—	—	4	4
South Carolina	8	—	8	—	8	—	1	—	—	—	—	—	8	—	—	8	—	—
Tennessee	12	11	1	1	11	—	—	—	1	11	10	1	1	2	10	—	3	3
Texas	4	—	4	—	4	—	—	—	—	—	—	—	4	—	—	4	—	—
Vermont	5	—	5	5	—	5	—	—	5	—	1½	3½	—	4½	½	—	5	5
Virginia	15	12½	2½	1	14	—	—	15	1	—	14	1	—	—	15	—	1½	3
Wisconsin	5	--	5	5	—	5	—	—	5	—	—	5	—	5	—	—	5	5
Total	303	105	198	165	138	145½	42	35½[a]	151½	65½	100½	150	52½	151[b]	100½[c]	51½	173½	190½[d]

1. Other candidates: Andrew Johnson, 12; Daniel S. Dickinson, 7; Joseph Lane, 6; Isaac Toucey, 2½; Jefferson Davis, 1½; James A. Pearce, 1; not voting, 50.
2. Other candidates: Robert M. T. Hunter, 16; Lane, 14; Dickinson, 4; Davis, 1; not voting, 51.
3. Other candidates: James Guthrie, 9; John C. Breckinridge, 5; Thomas S. Bocock, 1; Horatio Seymour, 1; Henry A. Wise, ½; Dickinson, ½; not voting, 112½.
4. Other candidates: Breckinridge, 7½; Guthrie, 5½; not voting, 99½.
a. Sum of column; proceedings record 35.
b. Sum of column; proceedings record 150½.
c. Sum of column; proceedings record 99.
d. Sum of column; proceedings record 181½.

1860 Republican

(Narrative, p. 40)

Delegation	Total Votes	First Pres. Ballot[1]					Second Pres. Ballot[2]		Third Pres. Ballot[3] (Before shift)		Third Pres. Ballot[4] (After shift)	
		Seward	Lincoln	Cameron	Bates	Chase	Seward	Lincoln	Seward	Lincoln	Seward	Lincoln
California	8	8	—	—	—	—	8	—	8	—	3	5
Connecticut	12	—	2	—	7	2	—	4	1	4	1	8
Delaware	6	—	—	—	6	—	—	6	—	6	—	6
Illinois	22	—	22	—	—	—	—	22	—	22	—	22
Indiana	26	—	26	—	—	—	—	26	—	26	—	26
Iowa	8	2	2	1	1	1	2	5	2	5½	—	8
Kansas	6	6	—	—	—	—	6	—	6	—	—	6
Kentucky	23	5	6	—	—	8	7	9	6	13	—	23
Maine	16	10	6	—	—	—	10	6	10	6	—	16
Maryland	11	3	—	—	8	—	3	—	2	9	2	9
Massachusetts	26	21	4	—	—	—	22	4	18	8	18	8
Michigan	12	12	—	—	—	—	12	—	12	—	12	—
Minnesota	8	8	—	—	—	—	8	—	8	—	—	8
Missouri	18	—	—	—	18	—	—	—	—	—	—	18
Nebraska	6	2	1	1	—	2	3	1	3	1	—	6
New Hampshire	10	—	—	—	—	1	1	9	1	9	—	10
New Jersey	14	1	7	—	—	—	4	—	5	8	5	8
New York	70	70	—	—	—	—	70	—	70	—	70	—
Ohio	46	—	8	—	—	34	—	14	—	29	—	46
Oregon	5	—	—	—	5	—	—	—	1	4	—	5
Pennsylvania	54	1½	4	47½	—	—	2½	48	—	52	½	53
Rhode Island	8	—	—	—	1	1	—	3	1	5	—	8
Texas	6	4	—	—	2	—	6	—	6	—	—	6
Vermont	10	—	—	—	—	—	—	10	—	10	—	10
Virginia	23	8	14	1	—	—	8	14	8	14	—	23
Wisconsin	10	10	—	—	—	—	10	—	10	—	10	—
District of Columbia	2	2	—	—	—	—	2	—	2	—	—	2
Total	466	173½	102	50½	48	49	184½	181	180	231½	121½	340[a]

1. Other candidates: Benjamin F. Wade, 3; John McLean, 12; John M. Reed, 1; William L. Dayton, 14; Charles Sumner, 1; John C. Fremont, 1; Jacob Collamer, 10; absent and not voting, 1.
2. Other candidates: Edward Bates, 35; Simon Cameron, 2; McLean, 8; Salmon P. Chase, 42½; Dayton, 10; Cassius M. Clay, 2; absent and not voting, 1.
3. Other candidates: Edward Bates, 22; Chase, 24½; McLean, 5; Dayton, 1; Clay, 1; absent and not voting, 1.
4. Other candidates: Chase, 2; Dayton, 1; Clay, 1; McLean, ½.
a. Sum of column; proceedings record 364.

1864 Democratic

(Narrative, p. 43)

Delegation	Total Votes	First Pres. Ballot[1] (Before shift)		First Pres. Ballot (After shift)	
		McClellan	Seymour	McClellan	Seymour
California	5	2½	2½	5	—
Connecticut	6	5½	—	6	—
Delaware	3	—	3	—	3
Illinois	16	16	—	16	—
Indiana	13	9½	3½	9½	3½
Iowa	8	3	—	8	—
Kansas	3	3	—	3	—
Kentucky	11	5½	5½	11	—
Maine	7	4	3	7	—
Maryland	7	—	7	—	7
Massachusetts	12	11½	—	12	—
Michigan	8	6½	—	8	—
Minnesota	4	4	—	4	—
Missouri	11	6½	—	7	4
New Hampshire	5	5	—	5	—
New Jersey	7	7	—	7	—
New York	33	33	—	33	—
Ohio	21	8½	10½	15	6
Oregon	3	2	1	3	—
Pennsylvania	26	26	—	26	—
Rhode Island	4	4	—	4	—
Vermont	5	4	1	5	—
Wisconsin	8	7	1	8	—
Total	226	174	38	202½	23½[a]

1. Other candidates: Horatio Seymour, 12 (votes on table are for Thomas H. Seymour); Charles O'Connor, ½; blank, 1½.
a. Sum of column; proceedings record 28½.

1864 Republican

(Narrative, p. 42)

Delegation	Total Votes	First Pres. Ballot[1]	
		Lincoln	Grant
Arkansas	10	10	—
California	10	7	—
Colorado	6	6	—
Connecticut	12	12	—
Delaware	6	6	—
Illinois	32	32	—
Indiana	26	26	—
Iowa	16	16	—
Kansas	6	6	—
Kentucky	22	22	—
Louisiana	14	14	—
Maine	14	14	—
Maryland	14	14	—
Massachusetts	24	24	—
Michigan	16	16	—
Minnesota	8	8	—
Missouri	22	—	22
Nebraska	6	6	—
Nevada	6	6	—
New Hampshire	10	10	—
New Jersey	14	14	—
New York	66	66	—
Ohio	42	42	—
Oregon	6	6	—
Pennsylvania	52	52	—
Rhode Island	8	8	—
Tennessee	15	15	—
Vermont	10	10	—
West Virginia	10	10	—
Wisconsin	16	16	—
Total	519	494[a]	22

1. Not voting, 3.
a. Sum of column; proceedings record 484.

1868 Democratic

(Narrative, p. 45)

Delegation	Total Votes	First Pres. Ballot[1]				22nd Pres. Ballot[2] (Before shift)		22nd Pres. Ballot (After shift)
		Pendleton	Hancock	Church	Johnson	Hancock	Hendricks	Seymour
Alabama	8	—	—	—	8	8	—	8
Arkansas	5	—	—	—	—	—	5	5
California	5	2	—	—	—	—	5	5
Connecticut	6	—	—	—	—	—	—	6
Delaware	3	3	—	—	—	3	—	3
Florida	3	—	—	—	3	—	3	3
Georgia	9	—	—	—	9	9	—	9
Illinois	16	16	—	—	—	—	16	16
Indiana	13	13	—	—	—	—	13	13
Iowa	8	8	—	—	—	—	8	8
Kansas	3	2	—	—	—	1	2	3
Kentucky	11	11	—	—	—	—	—	11
Louisiana	7	—	7	—	—	7	—	7
Maine	7	1½	4½	—	1	4½	2½	7
Maryland	7	4½	—	—	2½	6	1	7
Massachusetts	12	1	11	—	—	—	—	12
Michigan	8	—	—	—	—	—	8	8
Minnesota	4	4	—	—	—	—	4	4
Mississippi	7	—	7	—	—	7	—	7
Missouri	11	5	2	1	½	2	8	11
Nebraska	3	3	—	—	—	—	3	3
Nevada	3	—	—	—	—	—	3	3
New Hampshire	5	2	2	—	—	4½	½	5
New Jersey	7	—	—	—	—	—	7	7
New York	33	—	—	33	—	—	33	33
North Carolina	9	—	—	—	9	—	9	9
Ohio	21	21	—	—	—	—	—	21
Oregon	3	3	—	—	—	—	3	3
Pennsylvania	26	—	—	—	—	26	—	26
Rhode Island	4	—	—	—	—	—	—	4
South Carolina	6	—	—	—	6	6	—	6
Tennessee	10	—	—	—	10	3½	1½	10
Texas	6	—	—	—	6	6	—	6
Vermont	5	—	—	—	—	—	5	5
Virginia	10	—	—	—	10	10	—	10
West Virginia	5	5	—	—	—	—	5	5
Wisconsin	8	—	—	—	—	—	—	8
Total	317	105	33½	34	65	103½	145½	317

1. Other candidates: James E. English, 16; Joel Parker, 13; Asa Packer, 26; James R. Doolittle, 13; Thomas A. Hendricks, 2½; Frank P. Blair, ½; Reverdy Johnson, 8½.
2. Other candidates: Horatio Seymour, 22; English, 7; Doolittle, 4; Johnson, 4; not voting, 31.

1868 Republican

(Narrative, p. 44)

Delegation	Total Votes	First Pres. Ballot Grant
Alabama	18	18
Arkansas	10	10
California	10	10
Colorado	6	6
Connecticut	12	12
Delaware	6	6
Florida	6	6
Georgia	18	18
Idaho	2	2
Illinois	32	32
Indiana	26	26
Iowa	16	16
Kansas	6	6
Kentucky	22	22
Louisiana	14	14
Maine	14	14
Maryland	14	14
Massachusetts	24	24
Michigan	16	16
Minnesota	8	8
Mississippi	14	14
Missouri	22	22
Montana	2	2
Nebraska	6	6
Nevada	6	6
New Hampshire	10	10
New Jersey	14	14
New York	66	66
North Carolina	18	18
Dakota[a]	2	2
Ohio	42	42
Oregon	6	6
Pennsylvania	52	52
Rhode Island	8	8
South Carolina	12	12
Tennessee	20	20
Texas	12	12
Vermont	10	10
Virginia	20	20
West Virginia	10	10
Wisconsin	16	16
District of Columbia	2	2
Total	650	650

a. Dakota Territory, includes North and South Dakota.

1872 Democratic

(Narrative, p. 47)

Delegation	Total Votes	First Pres. Ballot[1] Greeley
Alabama	20	20
Arkansas	12	12
California	12	12
Connecticut	12	12
Delaware	6	—
Florida	8	6
Georgia	22	18
Illinois	42	42
Indiana	30	30
Iowa	22	22
Kansas	10	10
Kentucky	24	24
Louisiana	16	16
Maine	14	14
Maryland	16	16
Massachusetts	26	26
Michigan	22	22
Minnesota	10	10
Mississippi	16	16
Missouri	30	30
Nebraska	6	6
Nevada	6	6
New Hampshire	10	10
New Jersey	18	9
New York	70	70
North Carolina	20	20
Ohio	44	44
Oregon	6	6
Pennsylvania	58	35
Rhode Island	8	8
South Carolina	14	14
Tennessee	24	24
Texas	16	16
Vermont	10	10
Virginia	22	22
West Virginia	10	8
Wisconsin	20	20
Total	**732**	**686**

1. Other candidates: Thomas F. Bayard, 15; Jeremiah S. Black, 21; William S. Groesbeck, 2; blank, 8.

1872 Republican

(Narrative, p. 47)

Delegation	Total Votes	First Pres. Ballot Grant
Alabama	20	20
Arizona	2	2
Arkansas	12	12
California	12	12
Colorado	2	2
Connecticut	12	12
Delaware	6	6
Florida	8	8
Georgia	22	22
Idaho	2	2
Illinois	42	42
Indiana	30	30
Iowa	22	22
Kansas	10	10
Kentucky	24	24
Louisiana	16	16
Maine	14	14
Maryland	16	16
Massachusetts	26	26
Michigan	22	22
Minnesota	10	10
Mississippi	16	16
Missouri	30	30
Montana	2	2
Nebraska	6	6
Nevada	6	6
New Hampshire	10	10
New Jersey	18	18
New Mexico	2	2
New York	70	70
North Carolina	20	20
Dakota[a]	2	2
Ohio	44	44
Oregon	6	6
Pennsylvania	58	58
Rhode Island	8	8
South Carolina	14	14
Tennessee	24	24
Texas	16	16
Utah	2	2
Vermont	10	10
Virginia	22	22
Washington	2	2
West Virginia	10	10
Wisconsin	20	20
Wyoming	2	2
District of Columbia	2	2
Total	**752**	**752**

a. Dakota Territory, includes North and South Dakota.

1876 Democratic

(Narrative, p. 49)

Delegation	Total Votes	First Pres. Ballot[1]			Second Pres. Ballot[2]	
		Tilden	Hendricks	Hancock	Tilden	Hendricks
Alabama	20	13	5	2	20	—
Arkansas	12	12	—	—	12	—
California	12	12	—	—	12	—
Colorado	6	—	6	—	6	—
Connecticut	12	12	—	—	12	—
Delaware	6	—	—	—	6	—
Florida	8	8	—	—	8	—
Georgia	22	5	—	1	22	—
Illinois	42	19	23	—	26	16
Indiana	30	—	30	—	—	30
Iowa	22	14	6	2	22	—
Kansas	10	—	10	—	2	8
Kentucky	24	24	—	—	24	—
Louisiana	16	9	—	5	16	—
Maine	14	14	—	—	14	—
Maryland	16	11	3	—	14	2
Massachusetts	26	26	—	—	26	—
Michigan	22	14	8	—	19	3
Minnesota	10	10	—	—	10	—
Mississippi	16	16	—	—	16	—
Missouri	30	—	14	—	30	—
Nebraska	6	6	—	—	6	—
Nevada	6	3	3	—	4	—
New Hampshire	10	10	—	—	10	—
New Jersey	18	—	—	—	18	—
New York	70	70	—	—	70	—
North Carolina	20	9	4	5	20	—
Ohio	44	—	—	—	—	—
Oregon	6	6	—	—	6	—
Pennsylvania	58	—	—	58	—	—
Rhode Island	8	8	—	—	8	—
South Carolina	14	14	—	—	14	—
Tennessee	24	—	24	—	—	24
Texas	16	10½	2½	2	16	—
Vermont	10	10	—	—	10	—
Virginia	22	17	1	—	17	1
West Virginia	10	—	—	—	—	—
Wisconsin	20	19	1	—	19	1
Total	**738**	**401½[a]**	**140½**	**75**	**535**	**85**

1. Other candidates: William Allen, 54; Allen G. Thurman, 3; Thomas F. Bayard, 33; Joel Parker, 18; James O. Broadhead, 16.
2. Other candidates: Allen, 54; Bayard, 4; Winfield Scott Hancock, 58; Thurman, 2.
a. Sum of column; proceedings record 404½.

1876 Republican

(Narrative, p. 48)

Delegation	Total Votes	First Pres. Ballot[1] Blaine	Morton	Conkling	Bristow	Abolish Unit Rule Yea	Nay	Not Voting	Fifth Pres. Ballot[2] Blaine	Bristow	Conkling	Hayes	Morton	Sixth Pres. Ballot[3] Blaine	Morton	Conkling	Bristow	Hayes	Seventh Pres. Ballot[4] Blaine	Hayes
Ala.	20	10	—	—	7	20	—	—	16	4	—	—	—	15	—	—	4	1	17	—
Ariz.	2	2	—	—	—	2	—	—	2	—	—	—	—	2	—	—	—	—	2	—
Ark.	12	—	12	—	—	4	8	—	1	—	—	—	11	1	11	—	—	—	11	1
Calif.	12	9	—	1	2	11	1	—	6	—	3	3	—	6	—	2	—	4	6	6
Colo.	6	6	—	—	—	6	—	—	6	—	—	—	—	6	—	—	—	—	6	—
Conn.	12	—	—	—	2	3	9	—	2	8	—	2	—	2	—	—	7	3	2	3
Del.	6	6	—	—	—	5	1	—	6	—	—	—	—	6	—	—	—	—	6	—
Fla.	8	1	4	3	—	4	4	—	2	—	—	—	3	4	4	—	—	—	8	—
Ga.	22	5	6	8	3	9	13	—	8	2	6	—	5	9	4	6	2	—	14	7
Idaho	2	2	—	—	—	2	—	—	2	—	—	—	—	2	—	—	—	—	2	—
Ill.	42	38	—	—	3	38	4	—	33	5	—	3	—	32	—	—	5	3	35	2
Ind.	30	—	30	—	—	1	29	—	—	—	—	—	30	—	30	—	—	—	—	25
Iowa	22	22	—	—	—	22	—	—	21	—	1	—	—	21	—	—	—	1	22	—
Kan.	10	10	—	—	—	10	—	—	10	—	—	—	—	10	—	—	—	—	10	—
Ky.	24	—	—	—	24	1	23	—	—	24	—	—	—	—	—	—	24	—	—	24
La.	16	2	14	—	—	6	10	—	5	—	—	—	11	6	10	—	—	—	14	2
Maine	14	14	—	—	—	14	—	—	14	—	—	—	—	14	—	—	—	—	14	—
Md.	16	16	—	—	—	16	—	—	16	—	—	—	—	16	—	—	—	—	16	—
Mass.	26	6	—	—	17	15	7	4	5	19	—	—	—	5	—	—	19	—	5	21
Mich.	22	8	—	1	9	3	19	—	—	—	—	22	—	—	—	—	—	22	—	22
Minn.	10	10	—	—	—	7	3	—	9	—	—	—	—	9	—	—	—	—	9	1
Miss.	16	—	11	1	3	9	6	1	—	8	2	2	4	1	5	2	4	4	—	16
Mo.	30	14	12	1	2	25	5	—	20	3	—	2	5	18	7	—	3	2	20	10
Mont.	2	2	—	—	—	2	—	—	1	—	—	1	—	1	—	—	—	1	—	2
Neb.	6	6	—	—	—	6	—	—	6	—	—	—	—	6	—	—	—	—	6	—
Nev.	6	—	—	2	3	—	6	—	—	1	2	1	—	—	—	2	2	1	—	6
N.H.	10	7	—	—	3	10	—	—	7	3	—	—	—	7	—	—	3	—	7	3
N.J.	18	13	—	—	—	15	3	—	12	—	—	6	—	12	—	—	—	6	12	6
N.M.	2	2	—	—	—	2	—	—	2	—	—	—	—	2	—	—	—	1	2	—
N.Y.	70	—	—	69	1	15	54	1	—	2	68	—	—	—	—	68	2	—	9	61
N.C.	20	9	2	7	1	6	13	1	—	—	—	12	1	12	1	—	—	1	—	20
Dak.[a]	2	2	—	—	—	2	—	—	2	—	—	—	—	2	—	—	—	—	2	—
Ohio	44	—	—	—	—	14	30	—	—	—	—	44	—	—	—	—	—	44	—	44
Ore.	6	6	—	—	—	6	—	—	6	—	—	—	—	6	—	—	—	—	6	—
Pa.	58	—	—	—	—	1	57	—	5	—	—	—	—	14	—	—	—	—	30	28
R.I.	8	2	—	—	6	1	7	—	2	6	—	—	—	2	—	—	6	—	2	6
S.C.	14	—	13	—	1	2	12	—	5	3	—	1	5	10	2	—	1	1	7	7
Tenn.	24	4	10	—	10	19	5	—	7	10	—	—	7	7	1	—	12	4	6	18
Texas	16	2	5	3	6	4	12	—	3	3	—	1	8	2	4	1	1	7	1	15
Utah	2	2	—	—	—	2	—	—	2	—	—	—	—	2	—	—	—	—	2	—
Vt.	10	1	—	—	8	5	5	—	—	8	—	2	—	—	—	—	8	2	—	10
Va.	22	16	3	3	—	19	2	1	16	—	—	—	3	13	4	—	3	2	14	8
Wash.	2	2	—	—	—	2	—	—	2	—	—	—	—	2	—	—	—	—	2	—
W.Va.	10	8	—	—	—	10	—	—	7	—	—	2	—	6	—	—	—	4	6	4
Wis.	20	20	—	—	—	17	3	—	16	3	—	—	1	16	1	—	3	—	16	4
Wyo.	2	—	—	—	2	—	2	—	—	2	—	—	—	—	—	—	2	—	—	2
D.C.	2	—	2	—	—	2	—	—	1	—	—	—	1	1	1	—	—	—	2	—
Total	**756**	**285**	**124**	**99**	**113**	**395**	**353**	**8**	**286**	**114**	**82**	**104**	**95**	**308**	**85**	**81**	**111**	**113**	**351**	**384**

1. *Other candidates: Rutherford B. Hayes, 61; John F. Hartranft, 58; Marshall Jewell, 11; William A. Wheeler, 3; not voting, 2.*
2. *Other candidates: Hartranft, 69; Elihu B. Washburne, 3; Wheeler, 2; not voting, 2.*
3. *Other candidates: Hartranft, 50; Washburne, 4; Wheeler, 2; not voting, 2.*
4. *Other candidate: Benjamin H. Bristow, 21.*
a. *Dakota Territory, includes North and South Dakota.*

1880 Democratic

(Narrative, p. 52)

Delegation	Total Votes	First Pres. Ballot[1]			Second Pres. Ballot[2] (Before shift)			Second Pres. Ballot[3] (After shift)
		Bayard	Hancock	Payne	Hancock	Bayard	Randall	Hancock
Alabama	20	7	7	—	11	5	—	20
Arkansas	12	—	—	—	—	—	—	12
California	12	—	—	—	5	—	—	12
Colorado	6	—	—	—	—	—	—	6
Connecticut	12	4	—	2	—	1	—	12
Delaware	6	6	—	—	—	6	—	6
Florida	8	8	—	—	—	8	—	8
Georgia	22	5	8	—	7	5	—	22
Illinois	42	—	—	—	42	—	—	42
Indiana	30	—	—	—	—	—	—	—
Iowa	22	3	7	2	9	1	12	21
Kansas	10	—	—	—	10	—	—	10
Kentucky	24	6	1	—	8	7	—	24
Louisiana	16	—	16	—	16	—	—	16
Maine	14	—	14	—	14	—	—	14
Maryland	16	16	—	—	—	16	—	14
Massachusetts	26	11½	6	—	11	7	3½	26
Michigan	22	2	5	1	14	4	1	22
Minnesota	10	—	10	—	10	—	—	10
Mississippi	16	8	5	—	6	8	—	16
Missouri	30	4	12	—	28	2	—	30
Nebraska	6	—	—	6	—	—	6	6
Nevada	6	—	—	—	—	—	1	6
New Hampshire	10	3	4	—	5	—	5	10
New Jersey	18	10	—	—	7	4	4	18
New York	70	—	—	70	—	—	70	70
North Carolina	20	7	9	—	20	—	—	20
Ohio	44	—	—	—	—	—	—	44
Oregon	6	—	—	—	—	—	—	6
Pennsylvania	58	7	28	—	32	—	25	58
Rhode Island	8	2	2	—	6	—	1	8
South Carolina	14	14	—	—	—	14	—	14
Tennessee	24	9	11	—	14	8	—	24
Texas	16	5	9	—	11	5	—	16
Vermont	10	—	10	—	10	—	—	10
Virginia	22	10	3	—	7	8	—	22
West Virginia	10	—	3	—	7	1	—	10
Wisconsin	20	6	1	—	10	2	—	20
Total	738	153½	171	81	320	112	128½	705

1. *Other candidates: Allen G. Thurman, 68½; Stephen J. Field, 65; William R. Morrison, 62; Thomas A. Hendricks, 49½; Samuel J. Tilden, 38; Horatio Seymour, 8; W. A. H. Loveland, 5; Samuel J. Randall, 6; Thomas Ewing, 10; Joseph E. McDonald, 3; George B. McClellan, 2; Joel Parker, 1; Jeremiah Black, 1; Hugh J. Jewett, 1; James E. English, 1; Lothrop, 1; not voting, 10½.*
2. *Other candidates: Hendricks, 31; English, 19; Tilden, 6; Thurman, 50; Parker, 2; Field, 65½; Jewett, 1; not voting, 3.*
3. *Other candidates: Hendricks, 30; Bayard, 2; Tilden, 1.*

1880 Republican

(Narrative, p. 50)

Delegation	Total Votes	Minority Report Illinois 1st Dist. Yea	Nay	Not Voting	First Pres. Ballot[1] Grant	Blaine	Sherman	Other	34th Pres. Ballot[2] Grant	Blaine	Sherman	Other	35th Pres. Ballot[3] Grant	Blaine	Sherman	Garfield	Other	36th Pres. Ballot[4] Grant	Blaine	Garfield	Other
Ala.	20	16	4	—	16	1	3	—	16	4	—	—	16	4	—	—	—	16	4	—	—
Ariz.	2	—	2	—	—	2	—	—	—	2	—	—	—	2	—	—	—	—	—	2	—
Ark.	12	12	—	—	12	—	—	—	12	—	—	—	12	—	—	—	—	12	—	—	—
Calif.	12	—	12	—	—	12	—	—	—	12	—	—	—	12	—	—	—	—	12	—	—
Colo.	6	6	—	—	6	—	—	—	6	—	—	—	6	—	—	—	—	6	—	—	—
Conn.	12	—	10	2	—	3	—	9	—	3	—	9	—	3	—	—	9	—	1	11	—
Del.	6	—	6	—	—	6	—	—	—	6	—	—	—	6	—	—	—	—	6	—	—
Fla.	8	8	—	—	8	—	—	—	8	—	—	—	8	—	—	—	—	8	—	—	—
Ga.	22	6	16	—	6	8	8	—	8	9	5	—	8	9	5	—	—	8	10	1	3
Idaho	2	—	2	—	—	2	—	—	—	2	—	—	—	2	—	—	—	—	2	—	—
Ill.	42	40	—	2	24	10	—	8	24	10	—	8	24	10	—	—	8	24	6	7	5
Ind.	30	5	25	—	1	26	2	1	2	20	2	6	1	2	—	27	—	1	—	29	—
Iowa	22	—	22	—	—	22	—	—	—	22	—	—	—	22	—	—	—	—	22	—	—
Kan.	10	—	—	10	4	6	—	—	4	6	—	—	4	6	—	—	—	4	—	6	—
Ky.	24	21	3	—	20	1	3	—	20	1	3	—	20	1	3	—	—	20	1	3	—
La.	16	8	8	—	8	2	6	—	8	4	4	—	8	4	4	—	—	8	—	8	—
Maine	14	—	14	—	—	14	—	—	—	14	—	—	—	14	—	—	—	—	14	—	—
Md.	16	8	8	—	7	7	2	—	7	2	7	—	7	3	2	4	—	6	—	10	—
Mass.	26	4	22	—	3	—	2	21	4	—	21	1	4	—	21	—	1	4	—	22	—
Mich.	22	1	21	—	1	21	—	—	1	21	—	—	1	21	—	—	—	1	—	21	—
Minn.	10	4	6	—	—	—	—	10	—	6	—	4	1	6	—	—	3	2	—	8	—
Miss.	16	11	5	—	6	4	6	—	8	4	3	1	8	4	3	1	—	7	—	9	—
Mo.	30	29	1	—	29	—	—	1	29	—	—	1	29	—	—	—	1	29	—	1	—
Mont.	2	—	2	—	—	2	—	—	—	2	—	—	—	2	—	—	—	—	—	2	—
Neb.	6	—	6	—	—	6	—	—	—	6	—	—	—	6	—	—	—	—	—	6	—
Nev.	6	—	6	—	—	6	—	—	—	6	—	—	—	6	—	—	—	2	1	3	—
N.H.	10	—	10	—	—	10	—	—	—	10	—	—	—	10	—	—	—	—	—	10	—
N.J.	18	—	18	—	—	16	—	2	—	14	2	2	—	14	2	—	2	—	—	18	—
N.M.	2	—	2	—	—	2	—	—	—	2	—	—	—	2	—	—	—	—	—	2	—
N.Y.	70	47	22	1	51	17	2	—	50	18	2	—	50	18	2	—	—	50	—	20	—
N.C.	20	19	1	—	6	—	14	—	6	—	14	—	6	—	13	1	—	5	—	15	—
Dak.[a]	2	1	1	—	1	1	—	—	1	1	—	—	1	1	—	—	—	—	—	2	—
Ohio	44	16	28	—	—	9	34	1	—	9	34	1	—	9	34	—	1	—	—	43	1
Ore.	6	—	6	—	—	6	—	—	—	6	—	—	—	6	—	—	—	—	—	6	—
Pa.	58	34	24	—	32	23	3	—	35	22	—	1	36	20	—	1	1	37	—	21	—
R.I.	8	—	8	—	—	8	—	—	—	8	—	—	—	8	—	—	—	—	—	8	—
S.C.	14	10	4	—	13	—	1	—	11	1	2	—	11	1	2	—	—	8	—	6	—
Tenn.	24	16	8	—	16	6	1	1	17	4	3	—	17	4	3	—	—	15	1	8	—
Texas	16	11	4	1	11	2	2	1	13	1	1	1	13	1	1	—	1	13	—	3	—
Utah	2	—	2	—	1	1	—	—	1	1	—	—	1	1	—	—	—	—	—	2	—
Vt.	10	4	6	—	—	—	—	10	—	—	—	10	—	—	—	—	10	—	—	10	—
Va.	22	13	9	—	18	3	1	—	16	3	3	—	16	3	3	—	—	19	—	3	—
Wash.	2	—	2	—	—	2	—	—	—	2	—	—	—	2	—	—	—	—	—	2	—
W.Va.	10	—	10	—	1	8	—	1	1	8	1	—	1	8	1	—	—	1	—	9	—
Wis.	20	1	19	—	1	7	3	9	2	1	—	17	2	2	—	16	—	—	—	20	—
Wyo.	2	1	1	—	1	1	—	—	1	1	—	—	1	1	—	—	—	—	—	2	—
D.C.	2	1	1	—	1	1	—	—	1	1	—	—	1	1	—	—	—	—	—	2	—
Total	**756**	**353**	**387**	**16**	**304**	**284**	**93**	**75**	**312**	**275**	**107**	**62**	**313**	**257**	**99**	**50**	**37**	**306**	**42**	**399**	**9**

1. *Other candidates: George F. Edmunds, 34; Elihu B. Washburne, 30; William Windom, 10; not voting, 1.*
2. *Other candidates: Washburne, 30; James A. Garfield, 17; Edmunds, 11; Windom, 4.*
3. *Other candidates: Washburne, 23; Edmunds, 11; Windom, 3.*
4. *Other candidates: Washburne, 5; John Sherman, 3; not voting, 1.*
a. *Dakota Territory, includes North and South Dakota.*

1884 Democratic

(Narrative, p. 53)

Delegation	Total Votes	Unit Rule: Amendment to Permit Polling of Delegates			First Pres. Ballot[1]			Second Pres. Ballot[2] (Before shift)			Second Pres. Ballot[3] (After shift)	
		Yea	Nay	Not Voting	Cleveland	Bayard	Thurman	Cleveland	Bayard	Hendricks	Cleveland	Bayard
Alabama	20	15	5	—	4	14	1	5	14	—	5	14
Arizona	2	—	—	2	2	—	—	2	—	—	2	—
Arkansas	14	—	14	—	14	—	—	14	—	—	14	—
California	16	16	—	—	—	—	16	—	—	—	16	—
Colorado	6	4	2	—	—	—	1	6	—	—	6	—
Connecticut	12	2	10	—	12	—	—	12	—	—	12	—
Delaware	6	6	—	—	—	6	—	—	6	—	—	6
Florida	8	2	6	—	8	—	—	6	2	—	8	—
Georgia	24	12	12	—	10	12	—	14	10	—	22	2
Idaho	2	—	—	2	2	—	—	2	—	—	2	—
Illinois	44	22	22	—	28	2	1	38	3	1	43	—
Indiana	30	30	—	—	—	—	—	—	—	30	30	—
Iowa	26	6	20	—	23	1	1	22	—	4	26	—
Kansas	18	3	15	—	11	5	2	12	4	—	17	1
Kentucky	26	20	6	—	—	—	—	3	7	15	4	21
Louisiana	16	—	16	—	13	1	1	15	—	—	15	—
Maine	12	2	10	—	12	—	—	12	—	—	12	—
Maryland	16	—	16	—	6	10	—	10	6	—	16	—
Massachusetts	28	21	7	—	5	21	2	8	7½	12½	8	7½
Michigan	26	12	12	2	14	1	11	13	—	13	23	—
Minnesota	14	—	14	—	14	—	—	14	—	—	14	—
Mississippi	18	18	—	—	1	15	1	2	14	2	2	14
Missouri	32	8	24	—	15	10	3	21	5	6	32	—
Montana	2	—	—	2	2	—	—	2	—	—	2	—
Nebraska	10	5	5	—	8	1	1	9	1	—	9	1
Nevada	6	6	—	—	—	—	6	—	—	5	—	—
New Hampshire	8	—	8	—	8	—	—	8	—	—	8	—
New Jersey	18	14	4	—	4	3	—	5	2	11	5	2
New Mexico	2	—	—	2	2	—	—	1	—	—	2	—
New York	72	—	72	—	72	—	—	72	—	—	72	—
North Carolina	22	10	12	—	—	22	—	—	22	—	22	—
Dakota[a]	2	—	—	2	2	—	—	2	—	—	2	—
Ohio	46	25	21	—	21	—	23	21	—	1	46	—
Oregon	6	—	6	—	2	4	—	2	2	2	6	—
Pennsylvania	60	21	39	—	5	—	—	42	2	11	42	2
Rhode Island	8	—	8	—	6	2	—	6	2	—	7	1
South Carolina	18	3	14	1	8	10	—	8	9	1	10	8
Tennessee	24	17	7	—	2	8	9	2	10	1	24	—
Texas	26	12	10	4	11	10	4	12	12	1	26	—
Utah	2	—	—	2	—	—	—	1	—	1	2	—
Vermont	8	—	8	—	8	—	—	8	—	—	8	—
Virginia	24	6	18	—	13	9	1	13	8	2	23	—
Washington	2	—	—	2	1	—	—	2	—	—	2	—
West Virginia	12	9	3	—	7	2	2	6	3	—	10	2
Wisconsin	22	5	17	—	12	1	2	20	—	2	22	—
Wyoming	2	—	—	2	2	—	—	2	—	—	2	—
District of Columbia	2	—	—	2	2	—	—	—	—	2	2	—
Total	**820**	**332**	**463**	**25**	**392**	**170**	**88**	**475**	**151½**	**123½**	**683**	**81½**

1. *Other candidates: Joseph E. McDonald, 56; Samuel J. Randall, 78; John G. Carlisle, 27; George Hoadly, 3; Thomas A. Hendricks, 1; Samuel J. Tilden, 1; Roswell P. Flower, 4.*
2. *Other candidates: Allen G. Thurman, 60; Randall, 5; McDonald, 2; Tilden, 2; not voting, 1.*
3. *Other candidates: Hendricks, 45½; Thurman, 4; Randall, 4; McDonald, 2.*
a. *Dakota Territory, includes North and South Dakota.*

1884 Republican

(Narrative, p. 53)

Delegation	Total Votes	Temporary Chairman[1]		First Pres. Ballot[2]			Third Pres. Ballot[3]		Fourth Pres. Ballot[4]	
		Lynch	Clayton	Arthur	Blaine	Edmunds	Arthur	Blaine	Arthur	Blaine
Alabama	20	19	1	17	1	—	17	2	12	8
Arizona	2	—	2	—	2	—	—	2	—	2
Arkansas	14	1	13	4	8	2	3	11	3	11
California	16	—	16	—	16	—	—	16	—	16
Colorado	6	—	6	—	6	—	—	6	—	6
Connecticut	12	6	6	—	—	—	—	—	—	—
Delaware	6	1	5	1	5	—	1	5	1	5
Florida	8	7	1	7	1	—	7	1	5	3
Georgia	24	24	—	24	—	—	24	—	24	—
Idaho	2	2	—	2	—	—	1	1	—	2
Illinois	44	16	28	1	3	—	1	3	3	34
Indiana	30	10	20	9	18	1	10	18	—	30
Iowa	26	3	23	—	26	—	—	26	2	24
Kansas	18	4	14	4	12	—	—	15	—	18
Kentucky	26	20	6	16	5½	—	16	6	15	9
Louisiana	16	11	4	10	2	—	9	4	7	9
Maine	12	—	12	—	12	—	—	12	—	12
Maryland	16	6	10	6	10	—	4	12	1	15
Massachusetts	28	24	4	2	1	25	3	1	7	3
Michigan	26	12	14	2	15	7	4	18	—	26
Minnesota	14	6	8	1	7	6	2	7	—	14
Mississippi	18	16	2	17	1	—	16	1	16	2
Missouri	32	14	16	10	5	6	11	12	—	32
Montana	2	1	1	—	1	1	—	1	—	2
Nebraska	10	2	8	2	8	—	—	10	—	10
Nevada	6	—	6	—	6	—	—	6	—	6
New Hampshire	8	8	—	4	—	4	5	—	2	3
New Jersey	18	9	9	—	9	6	1	11	—	17
New Mexico	2	2	—	2	—	—	2	—	2	—
New York	72	46	26	31	28	12	32	28	30	29
North Carolina	22	17	3	19	2	—	18	4	12	8
Dakota[a]	2	—	2	—	2	—	—	2	—	2
Ohio	46	22	23	—	21	—	—	25	—	46
Oregon	6	—	6	—	6	—	—	6	—	6
Pennsylvania	60	13	45	11	47	1	8	50	8	51
Rhode Island	8	8	—	—	—	8	—	—	1	7
South Carolina	18	18	—	17	1	—	16	2	15	2
Tennessee	24	21	2	16	7	—	17	7	12	11
Texas	26	12	12	11	13	—	11	14	8	15
Utah	2	—	2	2	—	—	2	—	—	2
Vermont	8	8	—	—	—	8	—	—	—	—
Virginia	24	20	4	21	2	—	20	4	20	4
Washington	2	1	1	—	2	—	—	2	—	2
West Virginia	12	—	12	—	12	—	—	12	—	12
Wisconsin	22	11	10	6	10	6	10	11	—	22
Wyoming	2	2	—	2	—	—	2	—	—	2
District of Columbia	2	1	1	1	1	—	1	1	1	1
Total	820	424	384	278	334½	93	274	375	207	541

1. Not voting, 12.
2. Other candidates: John A. Logan, 63½; John Sherman, 30; Joseph R. Hawley, 13; Robert T. Lincoln, 4; William T. Sherman, 2; not voting, 2.
3. Other candidates: George F. Edmunds, 69; Logan, 53; John Sherman, 25; Hawley, 13; Lincoln, 8; William T. Sherman, 3; not voting, 1.
4. Other candidates: Edmunds, 41; Hawley, 15; Logan, 7; Lincoln, 2; not voting, 7.
a. Dakota Territory, includes North and South Dakota.

1888 Republican

(Narrative, p. 56)

Delegation	Total Votes	First Pres. Ballot[1]						Sixth Pres. Ballot[2]					Seventh Pres. Ballot[3]					Eighth Pres. Ballot[4]			
		Alger	Allison	Depew	Gresham	Harrison	Sherman	Alger	Allison	Gresham	Harrison	Sherman	Alger	Allison	Gresham	Harrison	Sherman	Alger	Gresham	Harrison	Sherman
Ala.	20	6	—	1	—	1	12	6	—	—	1	12	6	—	—	—	12	10	—	3	5
Ariz.	2	2	—	—	—	—	—	2	—	—	—	—	2	—	—	—	—	—	—	2	—
Ark.	14	—	—	—	1	1	2	14	—	—	—	—	14	—	—	—	—	14	—	—	—
Calif.	16	—	—	—	—	—	—	—	—	—	—	—	1	—	—	15	—	—	—	15	—
Colo.	6	—	1	—	3	2	—	—	—	—	5	—	—	6	—	—	—	—	—	6	—
Conn.	12	—	—	—	—	—	—	2	4	—	—	6	2	—	—	4	5	—	—	12	—
Del.	6	—	—	—	6	—	—	—	—	1	5	—	—	—	1	5	—	—	—	6	—
Fla.	8	—	—	—	—	1	4	5	—	—	1	1	3	—	—	4	1	4	—	2	2
Ga.	24	—	—	—	1	2	19	—	—	1	2	19	1	—	1	3	17	3	1	10	9
Idaho	2	—	1	—	1	—	—	—	—	2	—	—	—	—	2	—	—	—	—	2	—
Ill.	44	—	—	—	44	—	—	—	—	41	3	—	1	—	40	3	—	—	40	4	—
Ind.	30	—	—	—	1	29	—	—	—	1	29	—	—	—	1	29	—	—	1	29	—
Iowa	26	—	26	—	—	—	—	—	26	—	—	—	—	26	—	—	—	1	3	22	—
Kan.	18	—	—	—	—	—	—	2	3	3	6	1	1	3	—	12	1	1	—	16	—
Ky.	26	4	—	1	5	4	12	6	—	2	7	9	3	—	2	10	9	1	2	15	7
La.	16	2	3	1	1	—	9	3	2	2	—	9	3	2	2	—	9	4	—	9	3
Maine	12	3	2	3	1	2	1	2	1	2	1	3	1	2	2	2	1	—	1	5	3
Md.	16	—	2	1	1	5	5	—	1	—	6	6	—	—	—	9	6	—	—	11	4
Mass.	28	6	2	1	2	4	9	8	2	1	5	11	2	3	1	9	11	1	—	25	2
Mich.	26	26	—	—	—	—	—	26	—	—	—	—	26	—	—	—	—	26	—	—	—
Minn.	14	1	—	2	11	—	—	3	—	5	6	—	2	—	4	8	—	1	—	13	—
Miss.	18	—	—	1	3	—	14	—	—	3	—	14	—	—	3	—	14	—	3	4	11
Mo.	32	6	3	2	11	3	6	15	1	11	2	2	14	—	12	3	2	15	8	7	2
Mont.	2	—	1	—	1	—	—	—	1	1	—	—	—	1	1	—	—	—	—	2	—
Neb.	10	2	3	—	1	—	3	2	5	—	—	3	2	5	—	2	1	1	—	9	—
Nev.	6	3	3	—	—	—	—	5	—	—	—	—	—	6	—	—	—	2	—	4	—
N.H.	8	—	—	4	—	4	—	—	1	—	6	1	—	—	—	8	—	—	—	8	—
N.J.	18	—	—	—	—	—	—	—	1	—	14	—	1	—	1	10	—	—	—	18	—
N.M.	2	1	—	—	—	—	—	1	—	—	—	1	1	—	—	—	1	—	—	2	—
N.Y.	72	—	—	71	—	—	1	—	—	—	72	—	—	—	—	72	—	—	—	72	—
N.C.	22	2	—	1	2	1	15	9	—	—	2	11	7	—	—	3	12	3	—	8	11
Dak.[a]	10	1	1	2	1	1	1	—	—	—	10	—	—	—	—	10	—	—	—	10	—
Ohio	46	—	—	—	—	—	46	—	—	—	1	45	—	—	—	1	45	—	—	1	45
Ore.	6	—	—	—	4	1	—	—	—	5	—	—	—	—	6	—	—	—	—	6	—
Pa.	60	1	—	5	—	—	29	—	—	—	6	54	—	—	—	9	51	—	—	59	1
R.I.	8	—	8	—	—	—	—	—	8	—	—	—	—	6	—	2	—	—	—	8	—
S.C.	18	3	—	1	—	—	11	11	—	—	1	6	11	—	—	1	6	10	—	4	4
Tenn.	24	9	1	2	1	1	7	6	1	—	1	8	9	1	—	3	5	3	—	20	—
Texas	26	2	7	—	5	1	7	3	8	3	1	7	2	8	1	3	7	—	—	26	—
Utah	2	—	2	—	—	—	—	—	2	—	—	—	—	2	—	—	—	—	—	2	—
Vt.	8	—	—	—	—	8	—	—	—	—	8	—	—	—	—	8	—	—	—	8	—
Va.	24	3	3	—	1	5	11	3	5	—	6	10	3	5	—	6	10	—	—	15	9
Wash.	6	—	1	—	3	1	—	1	—	4	1	—	1	—	4	1	—	—	—	6	—
W.Va.	12	1	—	—	2	2	5	1	—	1	2	5	—	—	5	3	1	—	—	12	—
Wis.	22	—	—	—	—	—	—	—	—	1	21	—	—	—	2	20	—	—	—	22	—
Wyo.	2	—	2	—	—	—	—	—	2	—	—	—	—	2	—	—	—	—	—	2	—
D.C.	2	—	—	—	—	—	—	1	—	—	—	—	1	—	—	—	—	—	—	2	—
Total	832	84	72	99	107	85	229	137	73	91	231	244	120	76	91	279	230	100	59	544	118

1. Other candidates: James G. Blaine, 35; John J. Ingalls, 28: William W. Phelps, 25; Jeremiah M. Rusk, 25; Edwin H. Fitler, 24; Joseph R. Hawley, 13; Robert T. Lincoln, 3; William McKinley, 2; not voting, 1.
2. Other candidates: Blaine, 40; McKinley, 12; Joseph B. Foraker, 1; Frederick D. Grant, 1; not voting, 2.
3. Other candidates: McKinley, 16; Blaine, 15; Lincoln, 2; Foraker, 1; Creed Haymond, 1; not voting, 1.
4. Other candidates: Blaine, 5; McKinley, 4; not voting, 2.
a. Dakota Territory, includes North and South Dakota.

1892 Democratic

(Narrative, p. 58)

Delegation	Total Votes	First Pres. Ballot[1] Cleveland	Boies	Hill
Alabama	22	14	1	2
Arizona	6	5	—	—
Arkansas	16	16	—	—
California	18	18	—	—
Colorado	8	—	5	3
Connecticut	12	12	—	—
Delaware	6	6	—	—
Florida	8	5	—	—
Georgia	26	17	—	5
Idaho	6	—	6	—
Illinois	48	48	—	—
Indiana	30	30	—	—
Iowa	26	—	26	—
Kansas	20	20	—	—
Kentucky	26	18	2	—
Louisiana	16	3	11	1
Maine	12	9	—	1
Maryland	16	6	—	—
Massachusetts	30	24	1	4
Michigan	28	28	—	—
Minnesota	18	18	—	—
Mississippi	18	8	3	3
Missouri	34	34	—	—
Montana	6	—	6	—
Nebraska	16	15	—	—
Nevada	6	—	4	—
New Hampshire	8	8	—	—
New Jersey	20	20	—	—
New Mexico	6	4	1	1
New York	72	—	—	72
North Carolina	22	3 1/3	1	—
North Dakota	6	6	—	—
Ohio	46	14	16	6
Oklahoma[a]	4	4	—	—
Oregon	8	8	—	—
Pennsylvania	64	64	—	—
Rhode Island	8	8	—	—
South Carolina	18	2	13	3
South Dakota	8	7	1	—
Tennessee	24	24	—	—
Texas	30	23	6	1
Utah	2	2	—	—
Vermont	8	8	—	—
Virginia	24	12	—	11
Washington	8	8	—	—
West Virginia	12	7	—	1
Wisconsin	24	24	—	—
Wyoming	6	3	—	—
Alaska	2	2	—	—
District of Columbia	2	2	—	—
Total	**910**	**617 1/3**	**103**	**114**

1. Other candidates: Arthur P. Gorman, 36 1/2; John G. Carlisle, 14; Adlai E. Stevenson, 16 2/3; James E. Campbell, 2: William R. Morrison, 3; William E. Russell, 1; William C. Whitney, 1; Robert E. Pattison, 1; not voting, 1/2.
a. Including Indian Territory, 2 votes.

1892 Republican

(Narrative, p. 57)

Delegation	Total Votes	First Pres. Ballot[1] Harrison	Blaine	McKinley
Alabama	22	15	—	7
Arizona	2	1	1	—
Arkansas	16	15	—	1
California	18	8	9	1
Colorado	8	—	8	—
Connecticut	12	4	—	8
Delaware	6	4	1	1
Florida	8	8	—	—
Georgia	26	26	—	—
Idaho	6	—	6	—
Illinois	48	34	14	—
Indiana	30	30	—	—
Iowa	26	20	5	1
Kansas	20	11	—	9
Kentucky	26	22	2	1
Louisiana	16	8	8	—
Maine	12	—	12	—
Maryland	16	14	—	2
Massachusetts	30	18	1	11
Michigan	28	7	2	19
Minnesota	18	8	9	1
Mississippi	18	13 1/2	4 1/2	—
Missouri	34	28	4	2
Montana	6	5	1	—
Nebraska	16	15	—	1
Nevada	6	—	6	—
New Hampshire	8	4	2	—
New Jersey	20	18	2	—
New Mexico	6	6	—	—
New York	72	27	35	10
North Carolina	22	17 2/3	2 2/3	1
North Dakota	6	2	4	—
Ohio	46	1	—	45
Oklahoma	2	2	—	—
Oregon	8	1	—	7
Pennsylvania	64	19	3	42
Rhode Island	8	5	1	1
South Carolina	18	13	3	2
South Dakota	8	8	—	—
Tennessee	24	17	4	3
Texas	30	22	6	—
Utah	2	2	—	—
Vermont	8	8	—	—
Virginia	24	9	13	2
Washington	8	1	6	1
West Virginia	12	12	—	—
Wisconsin	24	19	2	3
Wyoming	6	4	2	—
Alaska	2	2	—	—
District of Columbia	2	—	2	—
Indian Territory	2	1	1	—
Total	**906**	**535 1/6**	**182 1/6**	**182**

1. Other candidates: Thomas B. Reed, 4; Robert T. Lincoln, 1; not voting, 1 2/3.
* Source: Official Proceeding, 10th Republican Convention.

1896 Democratic

(Narrative, p. 61)

Delegation	Total Votes	Minority Gold Standard Plank			First Pres. Ballot[1]			Fourth Pres. Ballot[2]			Fifth Pres. Ballot[3]	
		Yea	Nay	Not Voting	Bryan	Bland	Pattison	Bryan	Bland	Pattison	Bryan	Pattison
Alabama	22	—	22	—	—	—	—	22	—	—	22	—
Arizona	6	—	6	—	—	6	—	—	6	—	6	—
Arkansas	16	—	16	—	—	16	—	—	16	—	16	—
California	18	—	18	—	4	—	—	12	2	—	18	—
Colorado	8	—	8	—	—	—	—	8	—	—	8	—
Connecticut	12	12	—	—	—	—	—	—	—	2	—	2
Delaware	6	5	1	—	1	—	3	1	—	3	1	3
Florida	8	3	5	—	1	2	1	5	—	—	8	—
Georgia	26	—	26	—	26	—	—	26	—	—	26	—
Idaho	6	—	6	—	—	6	—	6	—	—	6	—
Illinois	48	—	48	—	—	48	—	—	48	—	48	—
Indiana	30	—	30	—	—	—	—	—	—	—	30	—
Iowa	26	—	26	—	—	—	—	—	—	—	26	—
Kansas	20	—	20	—	—	20	—	20	—	—	20	—
Kentucky	26	—	26	—	—	—	—	—	—	—	26	—
Louisiana	16	—	16	—	16	—	—	16	—	—	16	—
Maine	12	10	2	—	2	2	5	2	2	5	4	4
Maryland	16	12	4	—	4	—	11	5	—	10	5	10
Massachusetts	30	27	3	—	1	2	3	1	2	3	6	3
Michigan	28	—	28	—	9	4	—	28	—	—	28	—
Minnesota	18	11	6	1	2	—	2	10	1	—	11	—
Mississippi	18	—	18	—	18	—	—	18	—	—	18	—
Missouri	34	—	34	—	—	34	—	—	34	—	34	—
Montana	6	—	6	—	—	4	—	—	6	—	6	—
Nebraska	16	—	16	—	16	—	—	16	—	—	16	—
Nevada	6	—	6	—	—	—	—	6	—	—	6	—
New Hampshire	8	8	—	—	—	—	1	—	—	1	—	1
New Jersey	20	20	—	—	—	—	—	—	—	2	—	2
New Mexico	6	—	6	—	—	6	—	—	6	—	6	—
New York	72	72	—	—	—	—	—	—	—	—	—	—
North Carolina	22	—	22	—	22	—	—	22	—	—	22	—
North Dakota	6	—	6	—	—	—	—	—	—	—	4	—
Ohio	46	—	46	—	—	—	—	—	—	—	46	—
Oklahoma [a]	12	—	12	—	—	12	—	—	12	—	12	—
Oregon	8	—	8	—	—	—	—	8	—	—	8	—
Pennsylvania	64	64	—	—	—	—	64	—	—	64	—	64
Rhode Island	8	8	—	—	—	—	6	—	—	6	—	6
South Carolina	18	—	18	—	—	—	—	18	—	—	18	—
South Dakota	8	8	—	—	6	—	1	7	—	1	8	—
Tennessee	24	—	24	—	—	24	—	—	24	—	24	—
Texas	30	—	30	—	—	30	—	—	30	—	30	—
Utah	6	—	6	—	—	6	—	—	6	—	6	—
Vermont	8	8	—	—	4	—	—	4	—	—	4	—
Virginia	24	—	24	—	—	—	—	—	24	—	24	—
Washington	8	3	5	—	1	7	—	2	6	—	4	—
West Virginia	12	—	12	—	—	—	—	1	10	—	2	—
Wisconsin	24	24	—	—	4	—	—	5	—	—	5	—
Wyoming	6	—	6	—	—	—	—	6	—	—	6	—
Alaska	6	6	—	—	—	6	—	—	6	—	6	—
District of Columbia	6	2	4	—	—	—	—	5	—	—	6	—
Total	930	303	626	1	137	235	97	280	241	97	652	95

1. *Other candidates: Horace Boies, 67; Claude Matthews, 37; John R. McLean, 54; Joseph S. C. Blackburn, 82; Adlai E. Stevenson, 6; Henry M. Teller, 8; William E. Russell, 2; Benjamin R. Tillman, 17; James E. Campbell, 1; Sylvester Pennoyer, 8; David B. Hill, 1; not voting, 178.*
2. *Other candidates: Boies, 33; Mathews, 36; Blackburn, 27; McLean, 46; Stevenson, 8; Hill, 1; not voting, 161.*
3. *Other candidates: Richard P. Bland, 11; Stevenson, 8; Hill, 1; David Turpie, 1; not voting, 162.*
a. *Including Indian Territory, 6 votes.*

1896 Republican

(Narrative, p. 60)

Delegation	Total Votes	McKinley	Reed	Morton	Allison	Quay
		First Pres. Ballot[1]				
Alabama	22	19	2	1	—	—
Arizona	6	6	—	—	—	—
Arkansas	16	16	—	—	—	—
California	18	18	—	—	—	—
Colorado	8	—	—	—	—	—
Connecticut	12	7	5	—	—	—
Delaware	6	6	—	—	—	—
Florida	8	6	—	2	—	—
Georgia	26	22	2	—	—	2
Idaho	6	—	—	—	—	—
Illinois	48	46	2	—	—	—
Indiana	30	30	—	—	—	—
Iowa	26	—	—	—	26	—
Kansas	20	20	—	—	—	—
Kentucky	26	26	—	—	—	—
Louisiana	16	11	4	—	½	½
Maine	12	—	12	—	—	—
Maryland	16	15	1	—	—	—
Massachusetts	30	1	29	—	—	—
Michigan	28	28	—	—	—	—
Minnesota	18	18	—	—	—	—
Mississippi	18	17	—	—	—	1
Missouri	34	34	—	—	—	—
Montana	6	1	—	—	—	—
Nebraska	16	16	—	—	—	—
Nevada	6	3	—	—	—	—
New Hampshire	8	—	8	—	—	—
New Jersey	20	19	1	—	—	—
New Mexico	6	5	—	—	1	—
New York	72	17	—	55	—	—
North Carolina	22	19½	2½	—	—	—
North Dakota	6	6	—	—	—	—
Ohio	46	46	—	—	—	—
Oklahoma[a]	12	10	1	—	1	—
Oregon	8	8	—	—	—	—
Pennsylvania	64	6	—	—	—	58
Rhode Island	8	—	8	—	—	—
South Carolina	18	18	—	—	—	—
South Dakota	8	8	—	—	—	—
Tennessee	24	24	—	—	—	—
Texas	30	21	5	—	3	—
Utah	6	3	—	—	3	—
Vermont	8	8	—	—	—	—
Virginia	24	23	1	—	—	—
Washington	8	8	—	—	—	—
West Virginia	12	12	—	—	—	—
Wisconsin	24	24	—	—	—	—
Wyoming	6	6	—	—	—	—
Alaska	4	4	—	—	—	—
District of Columbia	2	—	1	—	1	—
Total	924	661½	84½	58	35½	61½

1. *Other candidates: J. Donald Cameron, 1; not voting, 22.*
a. *Including Indian Territory, 6 votes.*

1900 Democratic

(Narrative, p. 63)

Delegation	Total Votes	First Pres. Ballot Bryan
Alabama	22	22
Arizona	6	6
Arkansas	16	16
California	18	18
Colorado	8	8
Connecticut	12	12
Delaware	6	6
Florida	8	8
Georgia	26	26
Idaho	6	6
Illinois	48	48
Indiana	30	30
Iowa	26	26
Kansas	20	20
Kentucky	26	26
Louisiana	16	16
Maine	12	12
Maryland	16	16
Massachusetts	30	30
Michigan	28	28
Minnesota	18	18
Mississippi	18	18
Missouri	34	34
Montana	6	6
Nebraska	16	16
Nevada	6	6
New Hampshire	8	8
New Jersey	20	20
New Mexico	6	6
New York	72	72
North Carolina	22	22
North Dakota	6	6
Ohio	46	46
Oklahoma[a]	12	12
Oregon	8	8
Pennsylvania	64	64
Rhode Island	8	8
South Carolina	18	18
South Dakota	8	8
Tennessee	24	24
Texas	30	30
Utah	6	6
Vermont	8	8
Virginia	24	24
Washington	8	8
West Virginia	12	12
Wisconsin	24	24
Wyoming	6	6
Alaska	6	6
District of Columbia	6	6
Hawaii	6	6
Total	**936**	**936**

a. Including Indian Territory, 6 votes.

1900 Republican

(Narrative, p. 62)

Delegation	Total Votes	First Pres. Ballot McKinley
Alabama	22	22
Arizona	6	6
Arkansas	16	16
California	18	18
Colorado	8	8
Connecticut	12	12
Delaware	6	6
Florida	8	8
Georgia	26	26
Idaho	6	6
Illinois	48	48
Indiana	30	30
Iowa	26	26
Kansas	20	20
Kentucky	26	26
Louisiana	16	16
Maine	12	12
Maryland	16	16
Massachusetts	30	30
Michigan	28	28
Minnesota	18	18
Mississippi	18	18
Missouri	34	34
Montana	6	6
Nebraska	16	16
Nevada	6	6
New Hampshire	8	8
New Jersey	20	20
New Mexico	6	6
New York	72	72
North Carolina	22	22
North Dakota	6	6
Ohio	46	46
Oklahoma[a]	12	12
Oregon	8	8
Pennsylvania	64	64
Rhode Island	8	8
South Carolina	18	18
South Dakota	8	8
Tennessee	24	24
Texas	30	30
Utah	6	6
Vermont	8	8
Virginia	24	24
Washington	8	8
West Virginia	12	12
Wisconsin	24	24
Wyoming	6	6
Alaska	4	4
District of Columbia	2	2
Hawaii	2	2
Total	**926**	**926**

a. Including Indian Territory, 6 votes.

1904 Democratic

(Narrative, p. 65)

Delegation	Total Votes	First Pres. Ballot[1] (Before shift)		First Pres. Ballot[2] (After shift)		Sending Telegram to Parker		
		Parker	Hearst	Parker	Hearst	Yea	Nay	Not Voting
Alabama	22	22	—	22	—	22	—	—
Arizona	6	—	6	—	6	—	6	—
Arkansas	18	18	—	18	—	18	—	—
California	20	—	20	—	20	16	4	—
Colorado	10	4	5	4	5	4	6	—
Connecticut	14	14	—	14	—	14	—	—
Delaware	6	—	—	—	—	6	—	—
Florida	10	6	4	6	4	6	4	—
Georgia	26	26	—	26	—	26	—	—
Idaho	6	—	6	6	—	—	6	—
Illinois	54	—	54	—	54	54	—	—
Indiana	30	30	—	30	—	30	—	—
Iowa	26	—	26	—	26	—	26	—
Kansas	20	7	10	7	10	—	20	—
Kentucky	26	26	—	26	—	26	—	—
Louisiana	18	18	—	18	—	18	—	—
Maine	12	7	1	7	1	7	2	3
Maryland	16	16	—	16	—	16	—	—
Massachusetts	32	—	—	—	—	32	—	—
Michigan	28	28	—	28	—	28	—	—
Minnesota	22	9	9	9	9	9	13	—
Mississippi	20	20	—	20	—	20	—	—
Missouri	36	—	—	—	—	—	36	—
Montana	6	6	—	6	—	—	6	—
Nebraska	16	—	4	—	4	—	16	—
Nevada	6	—	6	2	4	2	4	—
New Hampshire	8	8	—	8	—	8	—	—
New Jersey	24	24	—	24	—	24	—	—
New Mexico	6	—	6	—	6	6	—	—
New York	78	78	—	78	—	78	—	—
North Carolina	24	24	—	24	—	24	—	—
North Dakota	8	—	—	—	—	—	8	—
Ohio	46	46	—	46	—	31	6	9
Oklahoma[a]	12	7	3	7	3	7	5	—
Oregon	8	4	2	4	2	4	4	—
Pennsylvania	68	68	—	68	—	68	—	—
Rhode Island	8	2	6	2	6	2	5	1
South Carolina	18	18	—	18	—	18	—	—
South Dakota	8	—	8	—	8	—	8	—
Tennessee	24	24	—	24	—	24	—	—
Texas	36	36	—	36	—	36	—	—
Utah	6	6	—	6	—	6	—	—
Vermont	8	8	—	8	—	8	—	—
Virginia	24	24	—	24	—	24	—	—
Washington	10	—	10	10	—	10	—	—
West Virginia	14	10	2	13	1	14	—	—
Wisconsin	26	—	—	—	—	26	—	—
Wyoming	6	—	6	—	6	2	2	2
Alaska	6	6	—	6	—	6	—	—
District of Columbia	6	6	—	6	—	6	—	—
Hawaii	6	—	6	—	6	2	4	—
Puerto Rico	6	2	—	2	—	6	—	—
Total	**1000**	**658**	**200**	**679**	**181**	**794**	**191**	**15**

1. Other candidates: George Gray, 12; Nelson A. Miles, 3; Francis M. Cockrell, 42; Richard Olney, 38; Edward C. Wall, 27; George B. McClellan, 3; Charles A. Towne, 2; Robert E. Pattison, 4; John S. Williams, 8; Bird S. Coler, 1; Arthur P. Gorman, 2.
2. Other candidates: Gray, 12; Miles, 3; Cockrell, 42; Olney, 38; Wall, 27; McClellan, 3; Towne, 2; Pattison, 4; Williams, 8; Coler, 1.
a. Including Indian Territory, 6 votes.

1904 Republican

(Narrative, p. 64)

Delegation	Total Votes	First Pres. Ballot Roosevelt
Alabama	22	22
Arizona	6	6
Arkansas	18	18
California	20	20
Colorado	10	10
Connecticut	14	14
Delaware	6	6
Florida	10	10
Georgia	26	26
Idaho	6	6
Illinois	54	54
Indiana	30	30
Iowa	26	26
Kansas	20	20
Kentucky	26	26
Louisiana	18	18
Maine	12	12
Maryland	16	16
Massachusetts	32	32
Michigan	28	28
Minnesota	22	22
Mississippi	20	20
Missouri	36	36
Montana	6	6
Nebraska	16	16
Nevada	6	6
New Hampshire	8	8
New Jersey	24	24
New Mexico	6	6
New York	78	78
North Carolina	24	24
North Dakota	8	8
Ohio	46	46
Oklahoma[a]	12	12
Oregon	8	8
Pennsylvania	68	68
Rhode Island	8	8
South Carolina	18	18
South Dakota	8	8
Tennessee	24	24
Texas	36	36
Utah	6	6
Vermont	8	8
Virginia	24	24
Washington	10	10
West Virginia	14	14
Wisconsin	26	26
Wyoming	6	6
Alaska	6	6
District of Columbia	2	2
Hawaii	6	6
Philippine Islands	2	2
Puerto Rico	2	2
Total	**994**	**994**

a. Including Indian Territory, 6 votes.

1908 Democratic

(Narrative, p. 67)

Delegation	Total Votes	First Pres. Ballot[1] Bryan
Alabama	22	22
Arizona	6	6
Arkansas	18	18
California	20	20
Colorado	10	10
Connecticut	14	9
Delaware	6	—
Florida	10	10
Georgia	26	4
Idaho	6	6
Illinois	54	54
Indiana	30	30
Iowa	26	26
Kansas	20	20
Kentucky	26	26
Louisiana	18	18
Maine	12	10
Maryland	16	7
Massachusetts	32	32
Michigan	28	28
Minnesota	22	—
Mississippi	20	20
Missouri	36	36
Montana	6	6
Nebraska	16	16
Nevada	6	6
New Hampshire	8	7
New Jersey	24	—
New Mexico	6	6
New York	78	78
North Carolina	24	24
North Dakota	8	8
Ohio	46	46
Oklahoma	14	14
Oregon	8	8
Pennsylvania	68	49½
Rhode Island	8	5
South Carolina	18	18
South Dakota	8	8
Tennessee	24	24
Texas	36	36
Utah	6	6
Vermont	8	7
Virginia	24	24
Washington	10	10
West Virginia	14	14
Wisconsin	26	26
Wyoming	6	6
Alaska	6	6
District of Columbia	6	6
Hawaii	6	6
Puerto Rico	6	6
Total	**1002**	**888½**

1. Other candidates: John A. Johnson, 46; George Gray, 59½; not voting, 8.

1908 Republican

(Narrative, p. 67)

Delegation	Total Votes	Minority Report on Changing Delegate Apportionment Formula			Minority Plank for Direct Election of Senators		First Pres. Ballot[1]
		Yea	Nay	Not Voting	Yea	Nay	Taft
Alabama	22	—	22	—	—	22	22
Arizona	2	—	2	—	—	2	2
Arkansas	18	—	18	—	—	18	18
California	20	—	20	—	—	20	20
Colorado	10	10	—	—	—	10	10
Connecticut	14	14	—	—	—	14	14
Delaware	6	—	6	—	—	6	6
Florida	10	—	10	—	—	10	10
Georgia	26	—	26	—	—	26	17
Idaho	6	—	6	—	3	3	6
Illinois	54	54	—	—	1	53	3
Indiana	30	30	—	—	11	19	—
Iowa	26	6	20	—	1	25	26
Kansas	20	—	20	—	—	20	20
Kentucky	26	1	25	—	2	24	24
Louisiana	18	—	18	—	—	18	18
Maine	12	12	—	—	—	12	12
Maryland	16	—	16	—	1	15	16
Massachusetts	32	32	—	—	—	32	32
Michigan	28	18	10	—	5	23	27
Minnesota	22	10	11	1	—	22	22
Mississippi	20	—	20	—	—	20	20
Missouri	36	12	24	—	4	32	36
Montana	6	—	6	—	—	6	6
Nebraska	16	7	9	—	16	—	16
Nevada	6	—	6	—	—	6	6
New Hampshire	8	8	—	—	—	8	5
New Jersey	24	23	1	—	—	24	15
New Mexico	2	—	—	2	—	2	2
New York	78	78	—	—	—	78	10
North Carolina	24	—	24	—	—	24	24
North Dakota	8	—	8	—	—	8	8
Ohio	46	8	38	—	2	44	42
Oklahoma	14	—	14	—	14	—	14
Oregon	8	3	5	—	—	8	8
Pennsylvania	68	68	—	—	13	55	1
Rhode Island	8	8	—	—	—	8	8
South Carolina	18	—	18	—	—	18	13
South Dakota	8	8	—	—	8	—	8
Tennessee	24	—	24	—	—	24	24
Texas	36	—	36	—	—	36	36
Utah	6	6	—	—	2	4	6
Vermont	8	8	—	—	—	8	8
Virginia	24	—	24	—	—	24	21
Washington	10	4	6	—	—	10	10
West Virginia	14	14	—	—	5	9	14
Wisconsin	26	26	—	—	25	1	1
Wyoming	6	—	6	—	—	6	6
Alaska	2	2	—	—	—	2	2
District of Columbia	2	1	1	—	—	2	1
Hawaii	2	—	2	—	1	1	2
Philippine Islands	2	—	2	—	—	2	2
Puerto Rico	2	—	2	—	—	2	2
Total	980	471	506	3	114	866	702

1. Other candidates: Philander C. Knox, 68; Charles E. Hughes, 67; Joseph G. Cannon, 58; Charles W. Fairbanks, 40; Robert M. La Follette, 25; Joseph B. Foraker, 16; Theodore Roosevelt, 3; not voting, 1.

1912 Democratic

(Narrative, p. 69)

Delegation	Total Votes	Temporary Chairman[1]		First Pres. Ballot[2]				Tenth Pres. Ballot[3]			Thirtieth Pres. Ballot[4]			43rd Pres. Ballot[5]		45th Pres. Ballot[6]		46th Pres. Ballot[7]
		Bryan	Parker	Clark	Wilson	Harmon	Underwood	Clark	Wilson	Underwood	Clark	Wilson	Underwood	Clark	Wilson	Clark	Wilson	Wilson
Ala.	24	1½	22½	—	—	—	24	—	—	24	—	—	24	—	—	—	—	24
Ariz.	6	4	2	6	—	—	—	6	—	—	4	2	—	3	2	3	3	6
Ark.	18	—	18	18	—	—	—	18	—	—	18	—	—	18	—	18	—	18
Calif.	26	7	18	26	—	—	—	26	—	—	26	—	—	26	—	26	—	2
Colo.	12	6	6	12	—	—	—	12	—	—	12	—	—	11	1	2	10	12
Conn.	14	2	12	—	—	—	—	7	—	7	7	3	4	1	5	2	5	14
Del.	6	6	—	—	6	—	—	—	6	—	—	6	—	—	6	—	6	6
Fla.	12	1	11	—	—	—	12	—	—	12	—	—	12	—	2	—	3	7
Ga.	28	—	28	—	—	—	28	—	—	28	—	—	28	—	—	—	—	28
Idaho	8	8	—	8	—	—	—	8	—	—	2½	5½	—	1	7	1½	6½	8
Ill.	58	—	58	58	—	—	—	58	—	—	58	—	—	—	58	—	58	58
Ind.	30	8	21	—	—	—	—	—	—	—	1	28	—	1	28	—	30	30
Iowa	26	13	13	26	—	—	—	26	—	—	12	14	—	11½	14½	9	17	26
Kan.	20	20	—	20	—	—	—	20	—	—	—	20	—	—	20	—	20	20
Ky.	26	7½	17½	26	—	—	—	26	—	—	26	—	—	26	—	26	—	26
La.	20	10	10	11	9	—	—	10	10	—	7	12	—	6	14	5	15	18
Maine	12	1	11	1	9	—	2	1	11	—	1	9	2	1	11	1	11	12
Md.	16	1½	14½	16	—	—	—	16	—	—	11	4½	—	9	5½	8½	7	16
Mass.	36	18	15	36	—	—	—	33	1	2	—	7	—	—	9	—	9	36
Mich.	30	9	21	12	10	7	—	18	9	—	18	12	—	2	28	2	28	30
Minn.	24	24	—	—	24	—	—	—	24	—	—	24	—	—	24	—	24	24
Miss.	20	—	20	—	—	—	20	—	—	20	—	—	20	—	—	—	—	20
Mo.	36	14	22	36	—	—	—	36	—	—	36	—	—	36	—	36	—	—
Mont.	8	7	1	8	—	—	—	8	—	—	2	6	—	1	7	1	7	8
Neb.	16	13	3	12	—	4	—	13	3	—	3	13	—	3	13	3	13	16
Nev.	6	6	—	6	—	—	—	6	—	—	6	—	—	6	—	6	—	—
N.H.	8	5	3	8	—	—	—	5	3	—	3	5	—	3	5	3	5	8
N.J.	28	24	4	2	24	—	2	4	24	—	4	24	—	4	24	4	24	24
N.M.	8	8	—	8	—	—	—	8	—	—	8	—	—	8	—	8	—	8
N.Y.	90	—	90	—	—	90	—	90	—	—	90	—	—	90	—	90	—	90
N.C.	24	9	15	—	16½	½	7	—	18	6	—	17½	6½	—	22	—	22	24
N.D.	10	10	—	—	10	—	—	—	10	—	—	10	—	—	10	—	10	10
Ohio	48	19	29	1	10	35	—	6	11	—	—	19	10	—	20	—	23	33
Okla.	20	20	—	10	10	—	—	10	10	—	10	10	—	10	10	10	10	20
Ore.	10	9	1	—	10	—	—	—	10	—	—	10	—	—	10	—	10	10
Pa.	76	67	9	—	71	5	—	5	71	—	4	72	—	2	74	—	76	76
R.I.	10	—	10	10	—	—	—	10	—	—	10	—	—	10	—	10	—	10
S.C.	18	18	—	—	18	—	—	—	18	—	—	18	—	—	18	—	18	18
S.D.	10	10	—	—	10	—	—	—	10	—	—	10	—	—	10	—	10	10
Tenn.	24	7	17	6	6	6	6	13	7½	3½	13½	8	2½	10	8	8	10	24
Texas	40	40	—	—	40	—	—	—	40	—	—	40	—	—	40	—	40	40
Utah	8	4	4	1½	6	½	—	1½	6½	—	1½	6½	—	1½	6½	—	8	8
Vt.	8	—	8	—	—	—	—	—	8	—	—	8	—	—	8	—	8	8
Va.	24	10	14	—	9½	—	14½	½	9½	14	3	9½	11½	—	24	—	24	24
Wash.	14	14	—	14	—	—	—	14	—	—	14	—	—	14	—	14	—	14
W.Va.	16	4½	10½	16	—	—	—	16	—	—	16	—	—	—	16	—	16	16
Wis.	26	26	—	6	19	—	—	6	20	—	6	19	—	4	22	—	26	26
Wyo.	6	6	—	6	—	—	—	6	—	—	6	—	—	—	6	—	6	6
Alaska	6	2	4	4	—	—	—	3	3	—	6	—	—	1	5	—	6	6
D.C.	6	—	6	6	—	—	—	6	—	—	6	—	—	6	—	6	—	6
Hawaii	6	2	4	2	3	—	1	2	3	1	2	3	1	2	4	2	4	6
Phil. Is.	6	2	4	—	—	—	—	—	—	—	—	—	—	—	—	—	—	—
P.R.	6	4	2	2	3	—	1	2	4	—	1½	4½	—	1	4½	1	4½	6
Total	1094	508	579	440½	324	148	117½	556	350½	117½	455	460	121½	329	602	306	633	990

1. Other candidates: James A. O'Gorman, 4; John W. Kern, 1; not voting, 2.
2. Other candidates: Simeon E. Baldwin, 22; Thomas R. Marshall, 31; William J. Bryan, 1; William Sulzer, 2; not voting, 8.
3. Other candidates: Judson Harmon, 31; Marshall, 31; Kern, 1; Bryan, 1; not voting, 6.
4. Other candidates: Eugene N. Foss, 30; Harmon, 19; Kern, 2; not voting ½.
5. Other candidates: Oscar W. Underwood, 98½; Harmon, 28; Foss, 27; Bryan, 1; Kern, 1; not voting, 7½.
6. Other candidates: Underwood, 97; Foss, 27; Harmon, 25; not voting, 6.
7. Other candidates: Champ Clark, 84; Harmon, 12; not voting, 8.

1912 Republican

(Narrative, p. 69)

Delegation	Total Votes	Temporary Chairman[1]		Table Motion Prohibiting Challenged Taft Delegates from Voting			First Pres. Ballot[2]		
		Root	McGovern	Yea	Nay	Not Voting	Taft	Roosevelt	Present, Not Voting
Alabama	24	22	2	22	2	—	22	—	2
Arizona	6	6	—	6	—	—	6	—	—
Arkansas	18	17	1	17	1	—	17	—	1
California	26	2	24	2	24	—	2	—	24
Colorado	12	12	—	12	—	—	12	—	—
Connecticut	14	14	—	14	—	—	14	—	—
Delaware	6	6	—	6	—	—	6	—	—
Florida	12	12	—	12	—	—	12	—	—
Georgia	28	22	6	24	4	—	28	—	—
Idaho	8	—	8	—	8	—	1	—	—
Illinois	58	9	49	7	51	—	2	53	1
Indiana	30	20	10	20	9	1	20	3	7
Iowa	26	16	10	16	10	—	16	—	—
Kansas	20	2	18	2	18	—	2	—	18
Kentucky	26	23	3	24	2	—	24	2	—
Louisiana	20	20	—	20	—	—	20	—	—
Maine	12	—	12	—	12	—	—	—	12
Maryland	16	8	8	9	7	—	1	9	5
Massachusetts	36	18	18	18	18	—	15	—	21
Michigan	30	19	10	20	10	—	20	9	1
Minnesota	24	—	24	—	24	—	—	—	24
Mississippi	20	16	4	16	4	—	17	—	3
Missouri	36	16	20	16	20	—	16	—	20
Montana	8	8	—	8	—	—	8	—	—
Nebraska	16	—	16	—	16	—	—	2	14
Nevada	6	6	—	6	—	—	6	—	—
New Hampshire	8	8	—	8	—	—	8	—	—
New Jersey	28	—	28	—	28	—	—	2	26
New Mexico	8	6	2	7	1	—	7	1	—
New York	90	76	13	75	15	—	76	8	6
North Carolina	24	3	21	2	22	—	1	1	22
North Dakota	10	—	9	2	8	—	—	—	—
Ohio	48	14	34	14	34	—	14	—	34
Oklahoma	20	4	16	4	16	—	4	1	15
Oregon	10	3	6	5	5	—	—	8	2
Pennsylvania	76	12	64	12	64	—	9	2	62
Rhode Island	10	10	—	10	—	—	10	—	—
South Carolina	18	11	7	11	6	1	16	—	1
South Dakota	10	—	10	—	10	—	—	5	—
Tennessee	24	23	1	23	1	—	23	1	—
Texas	40	31	8	29	9	2	31	—	8
Utah	8	7	1	7	1	—	8	—	—
Vermont	8	6	2	6	2	—	6	—	2
Virginia	24	22	2	21	3	—	22	—	1
Washington	14	14	—	14	—	—	14	—	—
West Virginia	16	—	16	—	16	—	—	—	16
Wisconsin	26	—	12	—	26	—	—	—	—
Wyoming	6	6	—	6	—	—	6	—	—
Alaska	2	2	—	2	—	—	2	—	—
District of Columbia	2	2	—	2	—	—	2	—	—
Hawaii	6	—	6	6	—	—	6	—	—
Philippine Islands	2	2	—	2	—	—	2	—	—
Puerto Rico	2	2	—	2	—	—	2	—	—
Total	**1078**	**558**	**501**	**567**	**507**	**4**	**556**[a]	**107**	**348**[b]

1. Other candidates: W. S. Lauder, 12; Asle J. Gronna, 1; not voting, 6.
2. Other candidates: Robert M. La Follette, 41; Albert B. Cummins, 17; Charles E. Hughes, 2; absent and not voting, 7.
a. Sum of column; proceedings record 561.
b. Sum of column; proceedings record 349.

1916 Democratic

(Narrative, p. 73)

Delegation	Total Votes	Minority Plank on Women's Suffrage		
		Yea	Nay	Not Voting
Alabama	24	1	23	—
Arizona	6	—	6	—
Arkansas	18	—	18	—
California	26	—	26	—
Colorado	12	—	12	—
Connecticut	14	1	13	—
Delaware	6	—	6	—
Florida	12	4	8	—
Georgia	28	23½	4½	—
Idaho	8	—	8	—
Illinois	58	1	57	—
Indiana	30	24	6	—
Iowa	26	—	26	—
Kansas	20	—	20	—
Kentucky	26	—	26	—
Louisiana	20	8	12	—
Maine	12	—	6	6
Maryland	16	16	—	—
Massachusetts	36	6	30	—
Michigan	30	—	30	—
Minnesota	24	9	15	—
Mississippi	20	—	20	—
Missouri	36	4	24	8
Montana	8	—	8	—
Nebraska	16	—	16	—
Nevada	6	—	6	—
New Hampshire	8	1	7	—
New Jersey	28	10	11	7
New Mexico	6	—	6	—
New York	90	—	90	—
North Carolina	24	11	13	—
North Dakota	10	—	10	—
Ohio	48	20	28	—
Oklahoma	20	—	20	—
Oregon	10	—	10	—
Pennsylvania	76	—	76	—
Rhode Island	10	1	9	—
South Carolina	18	—	18	—
South Dakota	10	—	10	—
Tennessee	24	—	24	—
Texas	40	32	8	—
Utah	8	—	8	—
Vermont	8	—	8	—
Virginia	24	—	24	—
Washington	14	—	14	—
West Virginia	16	8	8	—
Wisconsin	26	—	26	—
Wyoming	6	—	6	—
Alaska	6	—	6	—
District of Columbia	6	—	6	—
Hawaii	6	—	6	—
Philippine Islands	6	1	4	1
Puerto Rico	6	—	6	—
Total	1092	181½	888½	22

1916 Republican

(Narrative, p. 72)

Delegation	Total Votes	First Pres. Ballot[1]			Second Pres. Ballot[2]		Third Pres. Ballot[3]
		Hughes	Root	Weeks	Hughes	Root	Hughes
Alabama	16	8	—	3	9	—	16
Arizona	6	4	—	—	4	—	6
Arkansas	15	1	3	3	—	2	15
California	26	9	8	3	11	12	26
Colorado	12	—	5	—	—	5	12
Connecticut	14	5	5	1	5	7	14
Delaware	6	—	—	—	—	—	6
Florida	8	8	—	—	8	—	8
Georgia	17	5	—	6	6	—	17
Idaho	8	4	—	—	4	1	8
Illinois	58	—	—	—	—	—	58
Indiana	30	—	—	—	—	—	30
Iowa	26	—	—	—	—	—	26
Kansas	20	10	2	3	10	2	20
Kentucky	26	10	—	—	11	—	26
Louisiana	12	4	1	3	6	1	12
Maine	12	6	1	3	8	1	12
Maryland	16	7	1	5	7	1	15
Massachusetts	36	4	—	28	12	—	32
Michigan	30	—	—	—	28	—	30
Minnesota	24	—	—	—	—	—	24
Mississippi	12	4	—	1½	4	—	8½
Missouri	36	18	—	8	22	—	34
Montana	8	—	—	—	—	—	7
Nebraska	16	—	—	—	2	—	16
Nevada	6	4	2	—	4	2	6
New Hampshire	8	—	—	8	3	3	8
New Jersey	28	12	12	1	16	3	27
New Mexico	6	2	—	2	2	—	5
New York	87	42	43	—	43	42	87
North Carolina	21	6	2	3	6	2	14
North Dakota	10	—	—	—	—	—	10
Ohio	48	—	—	—	—	—	48
Oklahoma	20	5	1	6	5	1	19
Oregon	10	10	—	—	10	—	10
Pennsylvania	76	2	—	—	8	1	72
Rhode Island	10	10	—	—	10	—	10
South Carolina	11	2	1	3	4	—	6
South Dakota	10	—	—	—	—	—	10
Tennessee	21	9	—	3½	8	½	18
Texas	26	1	1	1	3	3	26
Utah	8	4	3	—	5	2	7
Vermont	8	8	—	—	8	—	8
Virginia	15	5½	3	3	8½	5	15
Washington	14	5	8	—	5	—	14
West Virginia	16	1	—	5	4	1	16
Wisconsin	26	11	—	—	11	—	23
Wyoming	6	6	—	—	6	—	6
Alaska	2	1	—	1	1	—	2
Hawaii	2	—	—	1	1	—	2
Philippine Islands	2	—	1	—	—	1	2
Total	**987**	**253½**	**103**	**105**	**328½**	**98½**	**949½**

1. Other candidates: Albert B. Cummins, 85; Theodore E. Burton, 77½; Charles W. Fairbanks, 74½; Lawrence Y. Sherman, 66; Theodore Roosevelt, 65; Philander C. Knox, 36; Henry Ford, 32; Martin G. Brumbaugh, 29; Robert M. La Follette, 25; William H. Taft, 14; Coleman du Pont, 12; Frank B. Willis, 4; William E. Borah, 2; Samuel W. McCall, 1; not voting, 2½.
2. Other candidates: Fairbanks, 88½; Cummins, 85; Roosevelt, 81; John W. Weeks, 79; Burton, 76½; Sherman, 65; Knox, 36; La Follette, 25; du Pont, 13; John Wanamaker, 5; Willis, 1; Leonard Wood, 1; Warren G. Harding, 1; McCall, 1; not voting, 2.
3. Other candidates: Roosevelt, 18½; La Follette, 3; du Pont, 5; Henry Cabot Lodge, 7; Weeks, 3; not voting, 1.

1920 Democratic

(Narrative, p. 76)

Delegation	Total Votes	First Pres. Ballot[1]				Thirtieth Pres. Ballot[2]			39th Pres. Ballot[3]		44th Pres. Ballot[4]	
		McAdoo	Cox	Palmer	Smith	McAdoo	Cox	Palmer	McAdoo	Cox	McAdoo	Cox
Alabama	24	9	3	6	2	12	7	—	8	—	8	13
Arizona	6	4	1	—	—	3	2	—	4	2	2½	3½
Arkansas	18	3	7	2	—	3	14	1	4	14	—	18
California	26	10	4	3	1	10	13	1	14	12	13	13
Colorado	12	3	—	8	—	5	6	—	4	7	3	9
Connecticut	14	—	—	—	—	1	6	4	3	10	2	12
Delaware	6	4	—	—	—	4	2	—	4	2	3	3
Florida	12	1	—	8	—	3	9	—	3	9	—	12
Georgia	28	—	—	28	—	—	—	28	28	—	—	28
Idaho	8	8	—	—	—	8	—	—	8	—	8	—
Illinois	58	9	9	35	5	21	36	1	18	38	13	44
Indiana	30	—	—	—	—	29	—	—	11	19	—	30
Iowa	26	—	—	—	—	—	26	—	—	26	—	26
Kansas	20	20	—	—	—	20	—	—	20	—	20	—
Kentucky	26	3	23	—	—	5	20	—	5	20	—	26
Louisiana	20	5	2	2	—	4	14	—	7	12	—	20
Maine	12	5	—	5	—	7	—	5	12	—	5	5
Maryland	16	5½	5½	—	—	5½	8½	—	5½	8½	—	13½
Massachusetts	36	4	4	17	7	2	15	16	1	33	—	35
Michigan	30	15	—	12	—	15	6	9	14	12	—	30
Minnesota	24	10	2	7	—	14	4	4	16	7	15	8
Mississippi	20	—	—	—	—	—	20	—	—	20	—	20
Missouri	36	15½	2½	10	—	18	6	5	20½	11½	17	18
Montana	8	1	—	—	—	8	—	—	8	—	2	6
Nebraska	16	—	—	—	—	7	—	—	7	—	2	5
Nevada	6	—	6	—	—	—	6	—	—	6	—	6
New Hampshire	8	4	—	1	—	5	2	1	5	2	6	2
New Jersey	28	—	—	—	—	—	28	—	—	28	—	28
New Mexico	6	2	—	1	—	6	—	—	6	—	6	—
New York	90	—	—	—	90	20	70	—	20	70	20	70
North Carolina	24	—	—	—	—	24	—	—	24	—	24	—
North Dakota	10	6	1	2	—	8	2	—	9	1	4	2
Ohio	48	—	48	—	—	—	48	—	—	48	—	48
Oklahoma	20	—	—	—	—	—	—	—	—	—	—	—
Oregon	10	10	—	—	—	10	—	—	10	—	10	—
Pennsylvania	76	2	—	73	—	2	1	73	2	1	4	68
Rhode Island	10	2	—	5	2	3	4	3	1	7	1	9
South Carolina	18	18	—	—	—	18	—	—	18	—	18	—
South Dakota	10	—	—	—	—	6	4	—	6	3	3	5
Tennessee	24	2	8	9	—	—	—	—	—	—	—	—
Texas	40	40	—	—	—	40	—	—	40	—	40	—
Utah	8	8	—	—	—	8	—	—	8	—	7	1
Vermont	8	4	2	1	1	1	6	1	4	4	—	8
Virginia	24	—	—	—	—	—	—	—	10	11	2½	18½
Washington	14	10	—	—	—	14	—	—	11	2½	—	13
West Virginia	16	—	—	—	—	—	—	—	—	—	—	—
Wisconsin	26	11	5	3	1	19	7	—	19	7	3	23
Wyoming	6	6	—	—	—	6	—	—	6	—	3	3
Alaska	6	2	1	3	—	2	1	3	4	2	—	6
Canal Zone	2	1	—	1	—	1	—	1	2	—	2	—
District of Columbia	6	—	—	6	—	—	—	6	—	6	—	6
Hawaii	6	2	—	4	—	1	5	—	1	5	—	6
Philippine Islands	6	—	—	—	—	3	2	1	3	2	2	4
Puerto Rico	6	1	—	2	—	2	—	2	6	—	1	5
Total	1094	266	134	254[a]	109	403½	400½	165	440	468½	270	699½

1. Other candidates: Homer S. Cummings, 25; James W. Gerard, 21; Robert L. Owen, 33; Gilbert M. Hitchcock, 18; Edwin T. Meredith, 27; Edward I. Edwards, 42; John W. Davis, 32; Carter Glass, 26½; Furnifold M. Simmons, 24; Francis B. Harrison, 6; John S. Williams, 20; Thomas R. Marshall, 37; Champ Clark, 9; Oscar W. Underwood, ½; William R. Hearst, 1; William J. Bryan, 1; Bainbridge Colby, 1; Josephus Daniels, 1; Wood, 4.
2. Other candidates: Cummings, 4; Owen, 33; Davis, 58; Glass, 24; Clark, 2; Underwood, 2; not voting, 2.
3. Other candidates: A. Mitchell Palmer, 74; Davis, 71½; Owen, 32; Cummings, 2; Clark, 2; Colby, 1; not voting, 3.
4. Other candidates: Palmer, 1; Davis, 52; Owen, 34; Glass, 1½; Colby, 1; not voting, 36.
a. Sum of column; proceedings record 256.

1920 Republican

(Narrative, p. 75)

Delegation	Total Votes	First Pres. Ballot[1]			Fourth Pres. Ballot[2]			Eighth Pres. Ballot[3]			Ninth Pres. Ballot[4]			Tenth Pres. Ballot[5] (Before shift)		Tenth Pres. Ballot[6] (After shift)	
		Wood	Lowden	Johnson	Wood	Lowden	Johnson	Wood	Lowden	Harding	Wood	Lowden	Harding	Wood	Harding	Wood	Harding
Alabama	14	4	6	3	4	6	4	4	6	4	4	6	4	3	8	3	8
Arizona	6	6	—	—	6	—	—	6	—	—	6	—	—	6	—	—	6
Arkansas	13	6	6	—	2½	10½	—	1½	11½	—	1½	10½	1	—	13	—	13
California	26	—	—	26	—	—	26	—	—	—	—	—	—	—	—	—	—
Colorado	12	9	2	—	9	2	—	6	3	3	6	1	5	6	5	—	12
Connecticut	14	—	14	—	—	13	1	1	11	—	—	—	13	—	13	—	13
Delaware	6	—	—	—	—	2	—	—	—	3	—	—	3	—	6	—	6
Florida	8	4½	2½	—	6½	1½	—	7	1	—	1	—	7	½	7½	½	7½
Georgia	17	8	9	—	8	9	—	8	9	—	8	8	1	7	10	7	10
Idaho	8	5	—	1	5	1	1	4	2	1	5	1	1	3	2	3	2
Illinois	58	14	41	3	—	41	17	—	41	—	—	41	—	—	22.2	—	38.2
Indiana	30	22	—	8	18	3	6	15	4	11	15	4	11	8	20	9	21
Iowa	26	—	26	—	—	26	—	—	26	—	—	26	—	—	26	—	26
Kansas	20	14	6	—	14	6	—	10	6	4	—	—	20	1	18	1	18
Kentucky	26	—	20	1	—	26	—	—	26	—	—	26	—	—	26	—	26
Louisiana	12	3	3	1	3	6	—	3	7	2	—	—	12	—	12	—	12
Maine	12	11	—	—	11	—	—	12	—	—	12	—	—	12	—	12	—
Maryland	16	16	—	—	16	—	—	16	—	—	16	—	—	10	5	10	5
Massachusetts	35	7	—	—	16	—	—	11	—	—	11	1	1	17	17	17	17
Michigan	30	—	—	30	—	—	30	13	7	—	15	6	1	1	25	1	25
Minnesota	24	19	3	2	17	5	2	16	5	—	17	5	—	21	2	21	2
Mississippi	12	4½	2	2	7½	2½	—	8½	1½	2	7½	—	4½	2½	9½	—	12
Missouri	36	4½	18	3	8½	19	1	2½	15½	17	—	—	36	—	36	—	36
Montana	8	—	—	8	—	—	8	—	—	—	—	—	—	—	—	—	—
Nebraska	16	3	—	13	6	—	10	14	—	—	16	—	—	5	4	5	4
Nevada	6	2	1½	2	2½	2	1½	1½	—	3½	1½	—	3½	—	3½	—	3½
New Hampshire	8	8	—	—	8	—	—	8	—	—	8	—	—	8	—	8	—
New Jersey	28	17	—	11	17	—	11	16	—	2	15	—	4	15	5	15	5
New Mexico	6	6	—	—	6	—	—	6	—	—	6	—	—	6	—	—	6
New York	88	10	2	—	20	32	5	23	45	8	5	4	66	6	68	6	68
North Carolina	22	—	—	1	3	15	2	2	16	4	3	—	18	2	20	2	20
North Dakota	10	2	—	8	3	1	6	3	4	—	3	4	—	1	9	—	10
Ohio	48	9	—	—	9	—	—	9	—	39	9	—	39	—	48	—	48
Oklahoma	20	1½	18½	—	2	18	—	2	18	—	½	—	18	½	18	½	18
Oregon	10	1	—	9	5	—	5	4	—	1	4	—	1	3	2	3	2
Pennsylvania	76	—	—	—	—	—	—	—	—	—	—	—	—	14	60	14	60
Rhode Island	10	10	—	—	10	—	—	10	—	—	10	—	—	—	10	—	10
South Carolina	11	—	8	—	—	11	—	—	11	—	—	—	11	—	11	—	11
South Dakota	10	10	—	—	10	—	—	10	—	—	10	—	—	6	4	6	4
Tennessee	20	20	—	—	19	1	—	10	7	3	6	1	13	—	20	—	20
Texas	23	8½	5	1½	8	9½	1	5	8½	8½	1	1	19½	—	23	—	23
Utah	8	5	2	—	5	2	—	4	2	2	2	2	4	1	5	1	5
Vermont	8	8	—	—	8	—	—	8	—	—	8	—	—	8	—	8	—
Virginia	15	3	12	—	3	12	—	3	10	—	4	—	11	1	14	1	14
Washington	14	—	—	—	—	—	—	—	—	—	—	—	—	5	6	—	14
West Virginia	16	—	—	—	8	—	1	9	—	7	8	—	7	—	16	—	16
Wisconsin	26	1	—	—	1	—	2	1	—	—	1	—	—	—	1	—	1
Wyoming	6	—	3	—	3	3	—	—	—	—	—	—	6	—	6	—	6
Alaska	2	—	—	—	1	—	—	1	—	—	1	—	1	—	2	—	2
District of Columbia	2	2	—	—	2	—	—	2	—	—	—	—	2	—	2	—	2
Hawaii	2	—	—	—	—	—	—	—	2	—	—	—	2	—	2	—	2
Philippine Islands	2	2	—	—	2	—	—	2	—	—	2	—	—	2	—	2	—
Puerto Rico	2	1	1	—	1	1	—	1	1	—	—	—	2	—	2	—	2
Total	**984**	**287½**	**211½**	**133½**	**314½**	**289**	**140½**	**299**	**307**	**133[a]**	**249**	**121½**	**374½**	**181½**	**644.7**	**156**	**692.2**

1. Other candidates: Warren G. Harding, 65½; William C. Sproul, 84; Calvin Coolidge, 34; Herbert Hoover, 5½; Coleman du Pont, 7; Jeter C. Pritchard, 21; Robert M. La Follette, 24; Howard Sutherland, 17; William E. Borah, 2; Charles B. Warren, 1; Miles Poindexter, 20; Nicholas M. Butler, 69½; not voting, 1.
2. Other candidates: Harding, 61½; Sproul, 79½; Coolidge, 25; Hoover, 5; du Pont, 2; La Follette, 22; Sutherland, 3; Borah, 1; Poindexter, 15; Butler, 20; James E. Watson, 4; Knox, 2.
3. Other candidates: Haram W. Johnson, 87; Coolidge, 30; du Pont, 3; Frank B. Kellogg, 1; La Follette, 24; Poindexter, 15; Irving L. Lenroot, 1; Hoover, 5; Butler, 2; Knox, 1; Sproul, 76.
4. Other candidates: Johnson, 82; Sproul, 78; Coolidge, 28; Hoover, 6; Lenroot, 1; Butler, 2; Knox, 1; La Follette, 24; Poindexter, 14; Will H. Hays, 1; H. F. MacGregor, 1; not voting, 1.
5. Other candidates: Frank Lowden, 28; Johnson, 80 4/5; Hoover, 10½; Coolidge, 5; Butler, 2; Lenroot, 1; Hays, 1; Knox, 1; La Follette, 24; Poindexter, 2; not voting, 2½.
6. Other candidates: Lowden, 11; Johnson, 80 4/5; Hoover, 9½; Coolidge, 5; Butler, 2; Lenroot, 1; Hays, 1; Knox, 1; La Follette, 24; not voting, ½.
a. Sum of column; proceedings record 133½.

1924 Republican

(Narrative, p. 78)

Delegation	Total Votes	First Pres. Ballot[1] Coolidge
Alabama	16	16
Arizona	9	9
Arkansas	14	14
California	29	29
Colorado	15	15
Connecticut	17	17
Delaware	9	9
Florida	10	10
Georgia	18	18
Idaho	11	11
Illinois	61	61
Indiana	33	33
Iowa	29	29
Kansas	23	23
Kentucky	26	26
Louisiana	13	13
Maine	15	15
Maryland	19	19
Massachusetts	39	39
Michigan	33	33
Minnesota	27	27
Mississippi	12	12
Missouri	39	39
Montana	11	11
Nebraska	19	19
Nevada	9	9
New Hampshire	11	11
New Jersey	31	31
New Mexico	9	9
New York	91	91
North Carolina	22	22
North Dakota	13	7
Ohio	51	51
Oklahoma	23	23
Oregon	13	13
Pennsylvania	79	79
Rhode Island	13	13
South Carolina	11	11
South Dakota	13	3
Tennessee	27	27
Texas	23	23
Utah	11	11
Vermont	11	11
Virginia	17	17
Washington	17	17
West Virginia	19	19
Wisconsin	29	1
Wyoming	9	9
Alaska	2	2
District of Columbia	2	2
Hawaii	2	2
Philippine Islands	2	2
Puerto Rico	2	2
Total	**1109**	**1065**

1. Other candidates: Robert M. La Follette, 34; Hiram W. Johnson, 10.

1924 Democratic

(Narrative, p. 79)

Delegation	Total Votes	Minority Report on League of Nations			Minority Report on Ku Klux Klan			First Pres. Ballot[1]		Fiftieth Pres. Ballot[2]		Ninetieth Pres. Ballot[3]		
		Yea	Nay	Not Voting	Yea	Nay	Not Voting	McAdoo	Smith	McAdoo	Smith	McAdoo	Smith	Ralston
Alabama	24	12½	11½	—	24	—	—	—	—	—	—	—	—	—
Arizona	6	1½	4½	—	1	5	—	4½	—	3½	—	3½	—	—
Arkansas	18	3	15	—	—	18	—	—	—	—	—	—	—	—
California	26	4	22	—	7	19	—	26	—	26	—	26	—	—
Colorado	12	9½	2½	—	6	6	—	—	—	4	3	1	3	½
Connecticut	14	5	9	—	13	1	—	—	6	4	10	2	12	—
Delaware	6	6	—	—	6	—	—	—	—	—	—	—	—	—
Florida	12	5	7	—	1	11	—	12	—	10	1	9	—	3
Georgia	28	—	28	—	1	19½	7½	28	—	28	—	28	—	—
Idaho	8	8	—	—	—	8	—	8	—	8	—	8	—	—
Illinois	58	10	48	—	45	13	—	12	15	13	20	12	36	6
Indiana	30	—	30	—	5	25	—	—	—	—	—	—	—	30
Iowa	26	—	26	—	13½	12½	—	26	—	26	—	—	—	—
Kansas	20	—	20	—	—	20	—	—	—	—	—	—	—	—
Kentucky	26	9½	16½	—	9½	16½	—	26	—	26	—	26	—	—
Louisiana	20	—	20	—	—	20	—	—	—	—	—	—	—	—
Maine	12	11	1	—	8	4	—	2	3½	2½	4½	1½	4½	—
Maryland	16	—	16	—	16	—	—	—	—	—	—	—	—	—
Massachusetts	36	8	28	—	35½	½	—	1½	33	2½	33½	2½	33½	—
Michigan	30	6	24	—	12½	16½	1	—	—	15	15	—	10	20
Minnesota	24	10	14	—	17	7	—	5	10	6	15	6	15	—
Mississippi	20	—	20	—	—	20	—	—	—	—	—	—	—	20
Missouri	36	2	34	—	10½	25½	—	36	—	36	—	—	—	36
Montana	8	—	8	—	1	7	—	7	1	7	—	7	1	—
Nebraska	16	—	16	—	3	13	—	1	—	13	3	1	—	—
Nevada	6	—	6	—	—	6	—	6	—	6	—	—	—	6
New Hampshire	8	8	—	—	2½	5½	—	—	—	4½	3½	3	3½	—
New Jersey	28	—	28	—	28	—	—	—	—	—	28	—	28	—
New Mexico	6	—	6	—	1	5	—	6	—	6	—	6	—	—
New York	90	35	55	—	90	—	—	—	90	2	88	2	88	—
North Carolina	24	6	18	—	3 17/20	20 3/20	—	24	—	17	—	3	—	—
North Dakota	10	1	9	—	10	—	—	10	—	5	5	5	5	—
Ohio	48	48	—	—	32½	15½	—	—	—	—	—	—	20½	17
Oklahoma	20	—	20	—	—	20	—	20	—	20	—	—	—	20
Oregon	10	1	9	—	—	10	—	10	—	10	—	10	—	—
Pennsylvania	76	52	22	2	49½	24½	2	25½	35½	25½	38½	25½	39½	—
Rhode Island	10	—	10	—	10	—	—	—	10	—	10	—	10	—
South Carolina	18	18	—	—	—	18	—	18	—	18	—	18	—	—
South Dakota	10	—	10	—	6	4	—	10	—	9	—	9	—	—
Tennessee	24	15	9	—	3	21	—	24	—	24	—	24	—	—
Texas	40	—	40	—	—	40	—	40	—	40	—	40	—	—
Utah	8	5½	2½	—	4	4	—	8	—	8	—	8	—	—
Vermont	8	2	6	—	8	—	—	1	7	1	7	—	8	—
Virginia	24	24	—	—	2½	21½	—	—	—	—	—	—	—	—
Washington	14	—	14	—	—	14	—	14	—	14	—	14	—	—
West Virginia	16	16	—	—	7	9	—	—	—	—	—	—	—	1
Wisconsin	26	4	22	—	25	1	—	3	23	3	23	1	23	—
Wyoming	6	3	3	—	2	4	—	—	—	1	4½	—	3	—
Alaska	6	—	5	—	6	—	—	1	3	1	3	—	5	—
Canal Zone	6	—	6	—	2	4	—	6	—	6	—	3	3	—
District of Columbia	6	—	6	—	6	—	—	6	—	6	—	6	—	—
Hawaii	6	—	6	—	4	2	—	1	1	1	1	1	—	—
Philippine Islands	6	2	4	—	2	2	2	3	3	3	3	2	2	—
Puerto Rico	6	1	5	—	2	4	—	—	—	—	—	—	1	—
Virgin Islands		—	—	—	—	—	—	—	—	—	—	—	—	—
Total	1098	353½	742½	2	542 7/20	543 3/20	12½	431½	241	461½	320½	314	354½	159½

1. *Other candidates: Oscar W. Underwood, 42½; Joseph T. Robinson, 21; Willard Saulsbury, 7; Samuel M. Ralston, 30; Jonathan M. Davis, 20; Albert C. Ritchie, 22½; Woodbridge N. Ferris, 30; James M. Cox, 59; Charles W. Bryan, 18; Fred H. Brown, 17; George S. Silzer, 38; Carter Glass, 25; John W. Davis, 31; William E. Sweet, 12; Patrick Harrison, 43½; Houston Thompson, 1; John B. Kendrick, 6.*

2. *Other candidates: John W. Davis, 64; Ralston, 58; Underwood, 42½; Robinson, 44; Glass, 24; Cox, 54; Ritchie, 16½; Saulsbury, 6; Thomas J. Walsh, 1; Jonathan M. Davis, 2; Owen, 4.*

3. *Other candidates: Underwood, 42½; Robinson, 20; John W. Davis, 65½; Glass, 30½; Ritchie, 16½; Saulsbury, 6; Walsh, 5; Bryan, 15; Jonathan M. Davis, 22; Josephus Daniels, 19; Edwin T. Meredith, 26; not voting, 2.*

1924 Democratic

(Narrative, p. 79)

Delegation	100th Pres. Ballot[4] McAdoo	Smith	Davis	101st Pres. Ballot[5] Underwood	Smith	Davis	Meredith	102nd Pres. Ballot[6] Underwood	Davis	Walsh	103rd Pres. Ballot[7] (Before shift) Underwood	Davis	103rd Pres. Ballot[8] (After shift) Underwood	Davis
Alabama	—	—	—	24	—	—	—	24	—	—	24	—	—	24
Arizona	3	—	—	3	—	—	—	3	—	—	3	—	3	—
Arkansas	—	—	—	—	—	—	—	—	—	—	—	—	—	—
California	16½	—	—	—	—	1	3	—	—	26	2	2	—	26
Colorado	½	3½	1½	1	3	2½	1	6½	1½	—	5	3	5	3
Connecticut	2	12	—	11	—	1	—	11	—	3	11	—	—	14
Delaware	—	—	—	—	—	6	—	—	—	—	6	—	6	—
Florida	9	—	3	—	—	3	—	—	5	4	—	6	—	6
Georgia	28	—	—	—	—	5	12	1	13	—	—	27	—	27
Idaho	—	—	—	—	—	—	—	—	—	8	—	8	—	8
Illinois	—	35	6	20	—	4	13	20	3	13	19	19	—	58
Indiana	—	—	14	3	—	10	6	10	10	—	5	25	5	25
Iowa	—	—	—	—	—	—	26	—	—	—	—	26	—	26
Kansas	—	—	20	—	—	20	—	—	20	—	—	20	—	20
Kentucky	12	—	8½	1	1	9	½	1	9	6½	1	22½	—	26
Louisiana	—	—	20	—	—	20	—	—	20	—	—	20	—	20
Maine	1	2	8	5	—	6	—	8	4	—	10	2	10	2
Maryland	—	—	—	—	—	16	—	—	16	—	—	16	—	16
Massachusetts	2½	33½	—	—	33	—	—	8	½	2	23½	2	23½	2
Michigan	—	10	15	10	—	12	1	14	16	—	—	29½	—	29½
Minnesota	6	15	1	—	15	1	—	14	2	1	16	3	16	3
Mississippi	—	—	—	—	—	20	—	—	20	—	—	20	—	20
Missouri	—	—	36	—	—	36	—	—	36	—	—	36	—	36
Montana	1	—	—	—	—	—	—	—	—	8	—	—	—	—
Nebraska	—	2	—	—	—	1	11	2	—	4	2	1	2	1
Nevada	—	6	—	—	—	—	—	—	—	6	—	6	—	6
New Hampshire	—	1	2	—	1	1	1½	—	3½	4½	—	3½	—	3½
New Jersey	—	28	—	16	—	—	—	16	2	—	16	1	16	1
New Mexico	6	—	—	—	1½	1	1	—	2½	—	—	2	—	2
New York	2	88	—	86½	—	—	—	84	1	1	44	4	—	60
North Carolina	—	—	—	1	—	20	1	—	23	—	5½	18½	—	24
North Dakota	3	5	—	—	5	—	—	5	—	5	—	—	—	—
Ohio	—	15	23	5	10	23	5	7	25	—	4	41	1	46
Oklahoma	—	—	—	—	—	—	—	—	20	—	—	20	—	20
Oregon	10	—	—	1	—	2	1	1	2	—	1	5	1	5
Pennsylvania	17½	39½	9	6	36½	19½	1	32½	29½	4	31½	37½	—	76
Rhode Island	—	10	—	10	—	—	—	10	—	—	—	10	—	10
South Carolina	18	—	—	—	—	18	—	—	18	—	—	18	—	18
South Dakota	—	—	—	—	—	15	—	2	—	—	2	—	2	—
Tennessee	6	—	8	1	—	15	—	—	19	—	—	19	—	19
Texas	40	—	—	—	—	—	40	—	40	—	—	40	—	40
Utah	—	—	4	—	—	—	—	—	4	4	—	8	—	8
Vermont	—	8	—	4	—	4	—	4	4	—	—	8	—	8
Virginia	—	—	—	—	—	12	—	—	12	—	—	12	—	24
Washington	—	—	—	—	—	—	—	—	—	14	—	14	—	14
West Virginia	—	—	16	—	—	16	—	—	16	—	—	16	—	16
Wisconsin	—	22	—	8	9	—	1	11	—	9	8	1	1	22
Wyoming	—	3	½	—	3	3	—	—	6	—	—	6	—	6
Alaska	—	6	—	6	—	—	—	6	—	—	2	4	2	4
Canal Zone	3	3	—	—	—	1	3	3	3	—	—	6	—	6
District of Columbia	—	—	—	—	—	—	—	6	—	—	6	—	6	—
Hawaii	1	1	3	1	1	4	—	1	4	—	1	4	1	4
Philippine Islands	2	2	—	5	—	—	1	5	—	—	1	4	1	4
Puerto Rico	—	1	5	1	—	5	—	1	5	—	1	5	1	5
Virgin Islands	—	—	—	—	—	—	—	—	—	—	—	—	—	—
Total	190	351½	203½	229½	121	316	130	317	415½	123	250½	575½	102½	844

4. Other candidates: Underwood, 41½; Robinson, 46; Bryan, 2; Saulsbury, 6; Walsh, 52½; Owen, 20; Ritchie, 17½; Meredith, 75½; David F. Houston, 9; Glass, 35; Daniels, 24; Newton D. Baker, 4; George L. Berry, 1; James W. Gerard, 19; not voting, 9.

5. Other candidates: Robinson, 22½; William G. McAdoo, 52; Walsh, 98; Ritchie, ½; Berry, 1; A. A. Murphree, 4; Houston, 9; Owen, 23; Cummings, 9; Glass, 59; Gerard, 16; Baker, 1; Daniels, 24; Cordell Hull, 2; not voting, 3½.

6. Other candidates: Robinson, 21; McAdoo, 21; Alfred E. Smith, 44; Thompson, 1; Ritchie, ½; Bryan, 1; Gerard, 7; Glass, 67; Cordell Daniels, 2; Berry, 1½; Meredith, 66½; Henry T. Allen, 1; Hull, 1; not voting, 8.

7. Other candidates: McAdoo, 14½; Robinson, 21; Meredith, 42½; Glass, 79; Hull, 1; Smith, 10½; Daniels, 1; Gerard, 8; Thompson, 1; Walsh, 84½; not voting, 9.

8. Other candidates: Robinson, 20; McAdoo, 11½; Smith, 7½; Walsh, 58; Meredith, 15½; Glass, 23; Gerard, 7; Hull, 1; not voting, 8.

1928 Democratic

(Narrative, p. 82)

Delegation	Total Votes	First Pres. Ballot[1] (Before shift) Smith	First Pres. Ballot[2] (After shift) Smith
Alabama	24	1	1
Arizona	6	6	6
Arkansas	17	17	17
California	26	26	26
Colorado	12	12	12
Connecticut	14	14	14
Delaware	6	6	6
Florida	12	—	—
Georgia	28	—	—
Idaho	8	8	8
Illinois	58	56	56
Indiana	30	—	25
Iowa	26	26	26
Kansas	20	—	11½
Kentucky	26	26	26
Louisiana	20	20	20
Maine	12	12	12
Maryland	16	16	16
Massachusetts	36	36	36
Michigan	30	30	30
Minnesota	24	24	24
Mississippi	20	—	9½
Missouri	36	—	—
Montana	8	8	8
Nebraska	16	—	12
Nevada	6	6	6
New Hampshire	8	8	8
New Jersey	28	28	28
New Mexico	6	6	6
New York	90	90	90
North Carolina	24	4 2/3	4 2/3
North Dakota	10	10	10
Ohio	48	1	45
Oklahoma	20	10	10
Oregon	10	10	10
Pennsylvania	76	70½	70½
Rhode Island	10	10	10
South Carolina	18	—	—
South Dakota	10	10	10
Tennessee	24	—	23
Texas	40	—	—
Utah	8	8	8
Vermont	8	8	8
Virginia	24	6	6
Washington	14	14	14
West Virginia	16	10½	10½
Wisconsin	26	26	26
Wyoming	6	6	6
Alaska	6	6	6
Canal Zone	6	6	6
District of Columbia	6	6	6
Hawaii	6	6	6
Philippine Islands	6	6	6
Puerto Rico	6	6	6
Virgin Islands	2	2	2
Total	**1100**	**724 2/3**	**849 1/6**

1. Other candidates: Cordell Hull, 71 5/6; Walter F. George, 52½; James A. Reed, 48; Atlee Pomerene, 47; Jesse H. Jones, 43; Evans Woollen, 32; Patrick Harrison, 20; William A. Ayres, 20; Richard C. Watts, 18; Gilbert M. Hitchcock, 16; Vic Donahey, 5; Houston Thompson, 2.
2. Other candidates: George, 52½; Reed, 52; Hull, 50 5/6; Jones, 43; Watts, 18; Harrison, 8½; Woollen, 7; Donahey, 5; Ayres, 3; Pomerene, 3; Hitchcock, 2; Thompson, 2; Theodore G. Bilbo, 1; not voting, 2½.

1928 Republican

(Narrative, p. 81)

Delegation	Total Votes	First Pres. Ballot[1] Hoover
Alabama	15	15
Arizona	9	9
Arkansas	11	11
California	29	29
Colorado	15	15
Connecticut	17	17
Delaware	9	9
Florida	10	9
Georgia	16	15
Idaho	11	11
Illinois	61	24
Indiana	33	—
Iowa	29	7
Kansas	23	—
Kentucky	29	29
Louisiana	12	11
Maine	15	15
Maryland	19	19
Massachusetts	39	39
Michigan	33	33
Minnesota	27	11
Mississippi	12	12
Missouri	39	28
Montana	11	10
Nebraska	19	11
Nevada	9	9
New Hampshire	11	11
New Jersey	31	31
New Mexico	9	7
New York	90	90
North Carolina	20	17
North Dakota	13	4
Ohio	51	36
Oklahoma	20	—
Oregon	13	13
Pennsylvania	79	79
Rhode Island	13	12
South Carolina	11	11
South Dakota	13	2
Tennessee	19	19
Texas	26	26
Utah	11	9
Vermont	11	11
Virginia	15	15
Washington	17	17
West Virginia	19	1
Wisconsin	26	9
Wyoming	9	9
Alaska	2	2
District of Columbia	2	2
Hawaii	2	2
Philippine Islands	2	2
Puerto Rico	2	2
Total	**1089**	**837**

1. Other candidates: Frank O. Lowden, 74; Charles Curtis, 64; James E. Watson, 45; George W. Norris, 24; Guy D. Goff, 18; Calvin Coolidge, 17; Charles G. Dawes, 4; Charles E. Hughes, 1; not voting, 5.

1932 Democratic

(Narrative, p. 84)

Delegation	Total Votes	Louisiana Credentials Yea	Nay	Not Voting	Minnesota Credentials Yea	Nay	Not Voting	Permanent Organization Yea	Nay	First Pres. Ballot[1] Roosevelt	Smith	Second Pres. Ballot[2] Roosevelt	Smith	Third Pres. Ballot[3] Roosevelt	Smith	Fourth Pres. Ballot[4] Roosevelt	Smith
Ala.	24	—	24	—	—	24	—	4½	19½	24	—	24	—	24	—	24	—
Ariz.	6	—	6	—	—	6	—	—	6	6	—	6	—	6	—	6	—
Ark.	18	—	18	—	—	18	—	—	18	18	—	18	—	18	—	18	—
Calif.	44	44	—	—	44	—	—	44	—	—	—	—	—	—	—	44	—
Colo.	12	—	12	—	—	12	—	—	12	12	—	12	—	12	—	12	—
Conn.	16	9½	6½	—	9¼	6¾	—	9½	6½	—	16	—	16	—	16	—	16
Del.	6	1	5	—	—	6	—	1	5	6	—	6	—	6	—	6	—
Fla.	14	3	11	—	—	14	—	—	14	14	—	14	—	14	—	14	—
Ga.	28	—	28	—	—	28	—	—	28	28	—	28	—	28	—	28	—
Idaho	8	—	8	—	—	8	—	—	8	8	—	8	—	8	—	8	—
Ill.	58	50¼	7¾	—	48	10	—	42	16	15¼	2¼	15¼	2¼	15¼	2¼	58	—
Ind.	30	30	—	—	30	—	—	30	—	14	2	16	2	16	2	30	—
Iowa	26	13	13	—	—	26	—	10	16	26	—	26	—	26	—	26	—
Kan.	20	—	20	—	—	20	—	6½	13½	20	—	20	—	20	—	20	—
Ky.	26	—	26	—	—	26	—	—	26	26	—	26	—	26	—	26	—
La.	20	—	20	—	—	20	—	—	20	20	—	20	—	20	—	20	—
Maine	12	6	6	—	6	6	—	7	5	12	—	12	—	12	—	12	—
Md.	16	16	—	—	16	—	—	16	—	—	—	—	—	—	—	16	—
Mass.	36	36	—	—	36	—	—	36	—	—	36	—	36	—	36	—	36
Mich.	38	—	38	—	—	38	—	—	38	38	—	38	—	38	—	38	—
Minn.	24	1	23	—	1	23	—	3	21	24	—	24	—	24	—	24	—
Miss.	20	—	20	—	—	20	—	—	20	20	—	20	—	20	—	20	—
Mo.	36	19½	19½	—	16½	19½	—	16½	10½	12	—	18	—	20½	—	36	—
Mont.	8	—	8	—	—	8	—	—	8	8	—	8	—	8	—	8	—
Neb.	16	—	16	—	—	16	—	1	15	16	—	16	—	16	—	16	—
Nev.	6	—	6	—	—	6	—	—	6	6	—	6	—	6	—	6	—
N.H.	8	—	8	—	—	8	—	—	8	8	—	8	—	8	—	8	—
N.J.	32	32	—	—	32	—	—	32	—	—	32	—	32	—	32	—	32
N.M.	6	—	6	—	—	6	—	3	3	6	—	6	—	6	—	6	—
N.Y.	94	65	29	—	65	29	—	67	27	28½	65½	29½	64½	31	63	31	63
N.C.	26	20½	5½	—	—	26	—	4	22	26	—	26	—	25 4/100	—	26	—
N.D.	10	—	10	—	2½	7½	—	1	9	9	—	10	—	9	—	10	—
Ohio	52	40	11	1	48½	2½	1	49½	2½	—	—	½	—	2½	—	29	17
Okla.	22	22	—	—	22	—	—	22	—	—	—	—	—	—	—	22	—
Ore.	10	—	10	—	—	10	—	1	9	10	—	10	—	10	—	10	—
Pa.	76	20½	55½	—	25	49	2	27½	48½	44½	30	44½	23½	45½	21	49	14½
R.I.	10	10	—	—	10	—	—	10	—	—	10	—	10	—	10	—	10
S.C.	18	—	18	—	—	18	—	—	18	18	—	18	—	18	—	18	—
S.D.	10	—	10	—	—	10	—	—	10	10	—	10	—	10	—	10	—
Tenn.	24	—	24	—	—	24	—	—	24	24	—	24	—	24	—	24	—
Texas	46	46	—	—	46	—	—	46	—	—	—	—	—	—	—	46	—
Utah	8	—	8	—	—	8	—	—	8	8	—	8	—	8	—	8	—
Vt.	8	—	8	—	—	8	—	—	8	8	—	8	—	8	—	8	—
Va.	24	24	—	—	24	—	—	24	—	—	—	—	—	—	—	24	—
Wash.	16	—	16	—	—	16	—	—	16	16	—	16	—	16	—	16	—
W.Va.	16	—	16	—	3	13	—	—	16	16	—	16	—	16	—	16	—
Wis.	26	2	24	—	2	24	—	2	24	24	2	24	2	24	2	24	2
Wyo.	6	—	6	—	—	6	—	—	6	6	—	6	—	6	—	6	—
Alaska	6	—	6	—	—	6	—	6	—	5	—	6	—	6	—	6	—
Canal Z.	6	—	6	—	—	6	—	—	6	6	—	6	—	6	—	6	—
D.C.	6	—	6	—	—	6	—	—	6	6	—	6	—	6	—	6	—
Hawaii	6	—	6	—	—	6	—	—	6	6	—	6	—	6	—	6	—
Phil. Is.	6	6	—	—	6	—	—	6	—	—	6	—	6	—	6	6	—
P.R.	6	—	6	—	—	6	—	—	6	6	—	6	—	6	—	6	—
Vir. Is.	2	—	2	—	—	2	—	—	2	2	—	2	—	2	—	2	—
Total	1154	514¼	638¾	1	492¾	658¼	3	528	626	666¼	201¾	677¾	194¼	682 79/100	190¼	945	190½

1. *Other candidates: John N. Garner, 90¼; Harry F. Byrd, 25; Melvin A. Traylor, 42¼; Albert C. Ritchie, 21; James A. Reed, 24; George White, 52; William H. Murray, 23; Newton D. Baker, 8½.*
2. *Other candidates: Garner, 90¼; Byrd, 24; Traylor, 40¼; Ritchie, 23½; Reed, 18; White, 50½; Baker, 8; Will Rogers, 22; not voting, 5½.*
3. *Other candidates: Garner, 101¼; Byrd, 24 96/100; Traylor, 40¼; Ritchie, 23½; Reed, 27½; White, 52½; Baker, 8½; not voting, 2½.*
4. *Other candidates: Ritchie, 3½; White, 3; Baker, 5½; James M. Cox, 1; not voting, 5½.*

1932 Republican

(Narrative, p. 84)

Delegation	Total Votes	Repeal of Prohibition Plank		First Pres. Ballot[1]
		Yea	Nay	Hoover
Alabama	19	—	19	19
Arizona	9	9	—	9
Arkansas	15	—	15	15
California	47	6	41	47
Colorado	15	1	14	15
Connecticut	19	19	—	19
Delaware	9	—	9	9
Florida	16	—	16	16
Georgia	16	2	14	16
Idaho	11	—	11	11
Illinois	61	45	15½	54½
Indiana	31	28	3	31
Iowa	25	3	22	25
Kansas	21	4	17	21
Kentucky	25	15	10	25
Louisiana	12	—	12	12
Maine	13	5	8	13
Maryland	19	—	19	19
Massachusetts	34	16	17	34
Michigan	41	25½	15½	41
Minnesota	25	—	25	25
Mississippi	11	11	—	11
Missouri	33	8½	23¾	33
Montana	11	—	11	11
Nebraska	17	1	16	17
Nevada	9	8	1	9
New Hampshire	11	—	11	11
New Jersey	35	35	—	35
New Mexico	9	2	7	8
New York	97	76	21	97
North Carolina	28	3	25	28
North Dakota	11	—	11	9
Ohio	55	12 2/9	42 2/9	55
Oklahoma	25	—	25	25
Oregon	13	3	10	9
Pennsylvania	75	51	23	73
Rhode Island	8	8	—	8
South Carolina	10	—	10	10
South Dakota	11	3	8	11
Tennessee	24	1	23	24
Texas	49	—	49	49
Utah	11	1	10	11
Vermont	9	9	—	9
Virginia	25	—	25	25
Washington	19	11	8	19
West Virginia	19	4	15	19
Wisconsin	27	22	5	15
Wyoming	9	9	—	9
Alaska	2	—	2	2
District of Columbia	2	—	2	2
Hawaii	2	2	—	2
Philippine Islands	2	1	1	2
Puerto Rico	2	—	2	2
Total	**1154**	**460 2/9**	**690 19/36**	**1126½**

1. Other candidates: John J. Blaine, 13; Calvin Coolidge, 4½; Joseph I. France, 4; Charles G. Dawes, 1; James W. Wadsworth, 1; not voting, 4.

1936 Republican

(Narrative, p. 86)

Delegation	Total Votes	First Pres. Ballot[1] Landon
Alabama	13	13
Arizona	6	6
Arkansas	11	11
California	44	44
Colorado	12	12
Connecticut	19	19
Delaware	9	9
Florida	12	12
Georgia	14	14
Idaho	8	8
Illinois	57	57
Indiana	28	28
Iowa	22	22
Kansas	18	18
Kentucky	22	22
Louisiana	12	12
Maine	13	13
Maryland	16	16
Massachusetts	33	33
Michigan	38	38
Minnesota	22	22
Mississippi	11	11
Missouri	30	30
Montana	8	8
Nebraska	14	14
Nevada	6	6
New Hampshire	11	11
New Jersey	32	32
New Mexico	6	6
New York	90	90
North Carolina	23	23
North Dakota	8	8
Ohio	52	52
Oklahoma	21	21
Oregon	10	10
Pennsylvania	75	75
Rhode Island	8	8
South Carolina	10	10
South Dakota	8	8
Tennessee	17	17
Texas	25	25
Utah	8	8
Vermont	9	9
Virginia	17	17
Washington	16	16
West Virginia	16	15
Wisconsin	24	6
Wyoming	6	6
Alaska	3	3
District of Columbia	3	3
Hawaii	3	3
Philippine Islands	2	2
Puerto Rico	2	2
Total	**1003**	**984**

1. Other candidates: William E. Borah, 19.

1940 Democratic

(Narrative, p. 89)

Delegation	Total Votes	First Pres. Ballot[1] Roosevelt
Alabama	22	20
Arizona	6	6
Arkansas	18	18
California	44	43
Colorado	12	12
Connecticut	16	16
Delaware	6	6
Florida	14	12½
Georgia	24	24
Idaho	8	8
Illinois	58	58
Indiana	28	28
Iowa	22	22
Kansas	18	18
Kentucky	22	22
Louisiana	20	20
Maine	10	10
Maryland	16	7½
Massachusetts	34	21½
Michigan	38	38
Minnesota	22	22
Mississippi	18	18
Missouri	30	26½
Montana	8	8
Nebraska	14	13
Nevada	6	2
New Hampshire	8	8
New Jersey	32	32
New Mexico	6	6
New York	94	64½
North Carolina	26	26
North Dakota	8	8
Ohio	52	52
Oklahoma	22	22
Oregon	10	10
Pennsylvania	72	72
Rhode Island	8	8
South Carolina	16	16
South Dakota	8	3
Tennessee	22	22
Texas	46	—
Utah	8	8
Vermont	6	6
Virginia	22	5 14/15
Washington	16	15
West Virginia	16	12
Wisconsin	24	21
Wyoming	6	6
Alaska	6	—
Canal Zone	6	—
District of Columbia	6	6
Hawaii	6	6
Philippine Islands	6	6
Puerto Rico	6	3
Virgin Islands	2	2
Total	**1100**	**946** 13/30

1. Other candidates: James A. Farley, 72 9/10; John N. Garner; 61; Millard E. Tydings, 9½; Cordell Hull, 5 2/3; not voting, 4½.

1940 Republican

(Narrative, p. 88)

Delegation	Total Votes	First Pres. Ballot[1] Dewey	Taft	Willkie	Fourth Pres. Ballot[2] Dewey	Taft	Willkie	Fifth Pres. Ballot[3] Taft	Willkie	Sixth (before shift)[4] Taft	Willkie	Sixth (after shift)[5] Willkie
Alabama	13	7	6	—	7	5	1	7	5	7	6	13
Arizona	6	—	—	—	—	—	6	—	6	—	6	6
Arkansas	12	2	7	2	3	7	2	10	2	10	2	12
California	44	7	7	7	9	11	10	12	9	22	17	44
Colorado	12	1	4	3	1	4	3	4	4	6	5	12
Connecticut	16	—	—	16	—	—	16	—	16	—	16	16
Delaware	6	—	1	3	—	—	6	—	6	—	6	6
Florida	12	6	1	—	9	2	—	3	7	2	10	12
Georgia	14	7	3	—	6	3	2	7	6	7	6	14
Idaho	8	8	—	—	8	—	—	7	—	6	2	8
Illinois	58	52	2	4	17	27	10	30	17	33	24	58
Indiana	28	7	7	9	5	6	15	7	20	5	23	28
Iowa	22	—	—	—	2	—	—	13	7	15	7	22
Kansas	18	—	—	—	11	2	5	—	18	—	18	18
Kentucky	22	12	8	—	9	13	—	22	—	22	—	22
Louisiana	12	5	5	—	6	6	—	12	—	12	—	12
Maine	13	—	—	—	2	2	9	—	13	—	13	13
Maryland	16	16	—	—	—	—	14	1	14	1	15	16
Massachusetts	34	—	—	1	—	2	28	2	28	2	30	34
Michigan	38	—	—	—	2	—	—	—	—	2	35	38
Minnesota	22	3	4	6	2	9	9	12	9	11	10	22
Mississippi	11	3	8	—	2	9	—	11	—	9	2	11
Missouri	30	10	3	6	4	3	18	7	21	4	26	30
Montana	8	8	—	—	3	3	2	4	4	4	4	8
Nebraska	14	14	—	—	2	5	5	9	5	6	8	14
Nevada	6	—	2	2	—	1	4	2	4	2	4	6
New Hampshire	8	—	—	—	—	—	4	2	6	2	6	8
New Jersey	32	20	—	12	6	1	23	1	26	—	32	32
New Mexico	6	3	1	2	1	1	4	2	4	1	5	6
New York	92	61	—	8	48	5	35	10	75	7	78	92
North Carolina	23	9	7	2	6	6	9	11	12	8	15	23
North Dakota	8	2	1	1	2	1	3	4	4	4	4	8
Ohio	52	—	52	—	—	52	—	52	—	52	—	52
Oklahoma	22	22	—	—	10	6	3	18	4	5	17	22
Oregon	10	—	—	—	1	—	1	—	1	3	7	10
Pennsylvania	72	1	—	1	—	—	19	—	21	—	72	72
Rhode Island	8	1	3	3	—	4	4	4	4	3	5	8
South Carolina	10	10	—	—	8	—	2	—	9	—	10	10
South Dakota	8	—	—	—	4	1	—	7	1	2	6	8
Tennessee	18	8	3	2	5	6	5	9	6	5	10	17
Texas	26	—	26	—	—	26	—	26	—	26	—	26
Utah	8	2	2	1	2	2	1	3	5	1	7	8
Vermont	9	1	3	3	1	3	5	3	6	2	7	9
Virginia	18	2	9	5	—	7	11	7	11	2	16	18
Washington	16	13	3	—	12	3	—	16	—	4	10	16
West Virginia	16	8	5	3	6	3	7	9	6	—	15	15
Wisconsin	24	24	—	—	24	—	—	—	—	2	20	24
Wyoming	6	1	1	2	3	2	1	3	3	—	6	6
Alaska	3	1	2	—	—	2	1	3	—	1	2	3
District of Columbia	3	2	1	—	—	1	2	1	2	—	3	3
Hawaii	3	—	—	—	—	—	—	1	1	—	3	3
Philippine Islands	2	—	1	1	—	1	1	1	1	—	2	2
Puerto Rico	2	1	1	—	1	1	—	2	—	—	2	2
Total	1000	360	189	105	250	254	306	377	429	318	655	998

1. Other candidate: Arthur H. Vandenberg, 76; Arthur H. James, 74; Joseph W. Martin, 44; Hanford MacNider, 34; Frank E. Gannett, 33; H. Styles Bridges, 28; Arthur Capper, 18; Herbert Hoover, 17; Charles L. McNary, 13; Harlan J. Bushfield, 9.
2. Other candidates: Vandenberg, 61; James, 56; Hoover, 31; NacNider, 26; McNary, 8; Gannett, 4; Bridges, 1; not voting, 3.
3. Other candidates: James, 59; Thomas E. Dewey, 57; Vandenberg, 42; Hoover, 20; McNary, 9; MacNider, 4; Gannett, 1; not voting, 2.
4. Other candidates: Dewey, 11; Hoover, 10; Gannett, 1; McNary, 1; not voting, 4.
5. Not voting, 2.

1944 Democratic

(Narrative, p. 91)

Delegation	Total Votes	First Pres. Ballot[1] Roosevelt
Alabama	24	22
Arizona	10	10
Arkansas	20	20
California	52	52
Colorado	12	12
Connecticut	18	18
Delaware	8	8
Florida	18	14
Georgia	26	26
Idaho	10	10
Illinois	58	58
Indiana	26	26
Iowa	20	20
Kansas	16	16
Kentucky	24	24
Louisiana	22	—
Maine	10	10
Maryland	18	18
Massachusetts	34	34
Michigan	38	38
Minnesota	24	24
Mississippi	20	—
Missouri	32	32
Montana	10	10
Nebraska	12	12
Nevada	8	8
New Hampshire	10	10
New Jersey	34	34
New Mexico	10	10
New York	96	94½
North Carolina	30	30
North Dakota	8	8
Ohio	52	52
Oklahoma	22	22
Oregon	14	14
Pennsylvania	72	72
Rhode Island	10	10
South Carolina	18	14½
South Dakota	8	8
Tennessee	26	26
Texas	48	36
Utah	10	10
Vermont	6	6
Virginia	24	—
Washington	18	18
West Virginia	18	17
Wisconsin	26	26
Wyoming	8	8
Alaska	6	6
Canal Zone	6	6
District of Columbia	6	6
Hawaii	6	6
Philippine Islands	6	6
Puerto Rico	6	6
Virgin Islands	2	2
Total	1176	1086

1. Other candidates: Harry F. Byrd, 89; James A. Farley, 1.

1944 Republican

(Narrative, p. 90)

Delegation	Total Votes	First Pres. Ballot[1] Dewey
Alabama	14	14
Arizona	8	8
Arkansas	12	12
California	50	50
Colorado	15	15
Connecticut	16	16
Delaware	9	9
Florida	15	15
Georgia	14	14
Idaho	11	11
Illinois	59	59
Indiana	29	29
Iowa	23	23
Kansas	19	19
Kentucky	22	22
Louisiana	13	13
Maine	13	13
Maryland	16	16
Massachusetts	35	35
Michigan	41	41
Minnesota	25	25
Mississippi	6	6
Missouri	30	30
Montana	8	8
Nebraska	15	15
Nevada	6	6
New Hampshire	11	11
New Jersey	35	35
New Mexico	8	8
New York	93	93
North Carolina	25	25
North Dakota	11	11
Ohio	50	50
Oklahoma	23	23
Oregon	15	15
Pennsylvania	70	70
Rhode Island	8	8
South Carolina	4	4
South Dakota	11	11
Tennessee	19	19
Texas	33	33
Utah	8	8
Vermont	9	9
Virginia	19	19
Washington	16	16
West Virginia	19	19
Wisconsin	24	23
Wyoming	9	9
Alaska	3	3
District of Columbia	3	3
Hawaii	5	5
Philippine Islands	2	—
Puerto Rico	2	2
Total	1059	1056

1. Other candidates: Douglas MacArthur, 1; absent, 2.

1948 Democratic

(Narrative, p. 94)

Delegation	Total Votes	Pro-Southern Amendment to Civil Rights Plank		Plank Endorsing Truman's Civil Rights Policy		First Pres. Ballot[1] (Before shift)		First Pres. Ballot[2] (After shift)	
		Yea	Nay	Yea	Nay	Truman	Russell	Truman	Russell
Alabama	26	26	—	—	26	—	26	—	26
Arizona	12	—	12	—	12	12	—	12	—
Arkansas	22	22	—	—	22	—	22	—	22
California	54	1½	52½	53	1	53½	—	54	—
Colorado	12	3	9	10	2	12	—	12	—
Connecticut	20	—	20	20	—	20	—	20	—
Delaware	10	—	10	—	10	10	—	10	—
Florida	20	20	—	—	20	—	19	—	20
Georgia	28	28	—	—	28	—	28	—	28
Idaho	12	—	12	—	12	12	—	12	—
Illinois	60	—	60	60	—	60	—	60	—
Indiana	26	—	26	17	9	25	—	26	—
Iowa	20	—	20	18	2	20	—	20	—
Kansas	16	—	16	16	—	16	—	16	—
Kentucky	26	—	26	—	26	26	—	26	—
Louisiana	24	24	—	—	24	—	24	—	24
Maine	10	—	10	3	7	10	—	10	—
Maryland	20	—	20	—	20	20	—	20	—
Massachusetts	36	—	36	36	—	36	—	36	—
Michigan	42	—	42	42	—	42	—	42	—
Minnesota	26	—	26	26	—	26	—	26	—
Mississippi	22	22	—	—	22	—	—	—	—
Missouri	34	—	34	—	34	34	—	34	—
Montana	12	—	12	1½	10½	12	—	12	—
Nebraska	12	—	12	3	9	12	—	12	—
Nevada	10	—	10	—	10	10	—	10	—
New Hampshire	12	—	12	1	11	11	—	11	—
New Jersey	36	—	36	36	—	36	—	36	—
New Mexico	12	—	12	—	12	12	—	12	—
New York	98	—	98	98	—	83	—	98	—
North Carolina	32	32	—	—	32	13	19	13	19
North Dakota	8	—	8	—	8	8	—	8	—
Ohio	50	—	50	39	11	50	—	50	—
Oklahoma	24	—	24	—	24	24	—	24	—
Oregon	16	3	13	7	9	16	—	16	—
Pennsylvania	74	—	74	74	—	74	—	74	—
Rhode Island	12	—	12	—	12	12	—	12	—
South Carolina	20	20	—	—	20	—	20	—	20
South Dakota	8	—	8	8	—	8	—	8	—
Tennessee	28	28	—	—	28	—	28	—	28
Texas	50	50	—	—	50	—	50	—	50
Utah	12	—	12	—	12	12	—	12	—
Vermont	6	—	6	6	—	5½	—	5½	—
Virginia	26	26	—	—	26	—	26	—	26
Washington	20	—	20	20	—	20	—	20	—
West Virginia	20	—	20	7	13	15	4	20	—
Wisconsin	24	—	24	24	—	24	—	24	—
Wyoming	6	1½	4½	4	2	6	—	6	—
Alaska	6	3	3	2	4	6	—	6	—
Canal Zone	2	—	2	—	2	2	—	2	—
District of Columbia	6	—	6	6	—	6	—	6	—
Hawaii	6	—	6	6	—	6	—	6	—
Puerto Rico	6	—	6	6	—	6	—	6	—
Virgin Islands	2	—	2	2	—	2	—	2	—
Total	**1234**	**310**[a]	**924**[b]	**651½**	**582½**	**926**	**266**	**947½**	**263**

1. *Other candidates: Paul V. McNutt, 2½; James A. Roe, 15; Alben W. Barkley, 1; not voting, 23½.*
2. *Other candidates: McNutt, ½; not voting, 23.*
a. *Sum of column; proceedings record 309.*
b. *Sum of column; proceedings record 925.*

1948 Republican

(Narrative, p. 93)

Delegation	Total Votes	First Pres. Ballot[1]			Second Pres. Ballot[2]			Third Pres. Ballot
		Dewey	Stassen	Taft	Dewey	Stassen	Taft	Dewey
Alabama	14	9	—	5	9	—	5	14
Arizona	8	3	2	3	4	2	2	8
Arkansas	14	3	4	7	3	4	7	14
California	53	—	—	—	—	—	—	53
Colorado	15	3	5	7	3	8	4	15
Connecticut	19	—	—	—	—	—	—	19
Delaware	9	5	1	2	6	1	2	9
Florida	16	6	4	6	6	4	6	16
Georgia	16	12	1	—	13	1	—	16
Idaho	11	11	—	—	11	—	—	11
Illinois	56	—	—	—	5	—	50	56
Indiana	29	29	—	—	29	—	—	29
Iowa	23	3	13	5	13	7	2	23
Kansas	19	12	1	2	14	1	2	19
Kentucky	25	10	1	11	11	1	11	25
Louisiana	13	6	—	7	6	—	7	13
Maine	13	5	4	1	5	7	—	13
Maryland	16	8	3	5	13	—	3	16
Massachusetts	35	17	1	2	18	1	3	35
Michigan	41	—	—	—	—	—	—	41
Minnesota	25	—	25	—	—	25	—	25
Mississippi	8	—	—	8	—	—	8	8
Missouri	33	17	6	8	18	6	7	33
Montana	11	5	3	3	6	2	3	11
Nebraska	15	2	13	—	6	9	—	15
Nevada	9	6	1	2	6	1	2	9
New Hampshire	8	6	2	—	6	2	—	8
New Jersey	35	—	—	—	24	6	2	35
New Mexico	8	3	2	3	3	2	3	8
New York	97	96	—	1	96	—	1	97
North Carolina	26	16	2	5	17	2	4	26
North Dakota	11	—	11	—	—	11	—	11
Ohio	53	—	9	44	1	8	44	53
Oklahoma	20	18	—	1	19	—	1	20
Oregon	12	12	—	—	12	—	—	12
Pennsylvania	73	41	1	28	40	1	29	73
Rhode Island	8	1	—	1	4	—	2	8
South Carolina	6	—	—	6	—	—	6	6
South Dakota	11	3	8	—	7	4	—	11
Tennessee	22	6	—	—	8	—	13	22
Texas	33	2	1	30	2	2	29	33
Utah	11	5	2	4	6	2	3	11
Vermont	9	7	2	—	7	2	—	9
Virginia	21	10	—	10	13	—	7	21
Washington	19	14	2	1	14	2	3	19
West Virginia	16	11	5	—	13	3	—	16
Wisconsin	27	—	19	—	2	19	—	27
Wyoming	9	4	3	2	6	3	—	9
Alaska	3	2	—	1	3	—	—	3
District of Columbia	3	2	—	—	3	—	—	3
Hawaii	5	3	—	1	3	—	2	5
Puerto Rico	2	—	—	2	1	—	1	2
Total	1094	434	157	224	515	149	274	1094

1. Other candidates: Arthur H. Vandenberg, 62; Earl Warren, 59; Dwight H. Green, 56; Alfred E. Driscoll, 35; Raymond E. Baldwin, 19; Joseph W. Martin, 18; B. Carroll Reece, 15; Douglas MacArthur, 11; Everett M. Dirksen, 1; not voting, 3.
2. Other candidates: Vandenberg, 62; Warren, 57; Baldwin, 19; Martin, 10; MacArthur, 7; Reece, 1.

1952 Democratic

(Narrative, p. 98)

Delegation	Total Votes	Seating Virginia Delegation Yea	Nay	Not Voting	Table Motion to Adjourn Yea	Nay	Not Voting	First Pres. Ballot[1] Harriman	Kefauver	Russell	Stevenson	Second Pres. Ballot[2] Harriman	Kefauver	Russell	Stevenson	Third Pres. Ballot[3] Kefauver	Russell	Stevenson
Alabama	22	22	—	—	13½	8½	—	—	8	13	½	—	7½	14	½	7½	14	½
Arizona	12	12	—	—	12	—	—	—	—	—	—	—	—	12	—	—	12	—
Arkansas	22	22	—	—	19	3	—	—	—	—	—	1	1½	18	1½	1½	—	20½
California	68	4	61	3	—	68	—	—	68	—	—	—	68	—	—	68	—	—
Colorado	16	4½	11½	—	4	12	—	5	2	8½	½	5	5	2½	3½	4	3½	8½
Connecticut	16	—	16	—	16	—	—	—	—	—	16	—	—	—	16	—	—	16
Delaware	6	6	—	—	6	—	—	—	—	—	6	—	—	—	6	—	—	6
Florida	24	24	—	—	19	5	—	—	5	19	—	—	5	19	—	5	19	—
Georgia	28	28	—	—	28	—	—	—	—	28	—	—	—	28	—	—	28	—
Idaho	12	12	—	—	—	12	—	3½	3	1	1½	—	—	—	12	—	—	12
Illinois	60	52	8	—	53	7	—	1	3	—	53	—	3	—	54	3	—	54
Indiana	25	14½	6½	5	25	1	—	—	1	—	25	—	1	—	25	1	—	25
Iowa	24	17	7	—	8	15	1	½	8	2	8	½	8½	3	9½	8	3	10
Kansas	16	—	16	—	16	—	—	—	—	—	16	—	—	—	16	—	—	16
Kentucky	26	26	—	—	26	—	—	—	—	—	—	—	—	—	—	—	—	—
Louisiana	20	20	—	—	20	—	—	—	—	20	—	—	—	20	—	—	20	—
Maine	10	2½	7½	—	4½	5½	—	1½	1½	2½	3½	1	1	2½	4½	½	2½	7
Maryland	18	18	—	—	18	—	—	—	18	—	—	—	15½	2	—	8½	2½	6
Massachusetts	36	16	19	1	30	4½	1½	—	—	—	—	—	2½	—	—	5	1	25
Michigan	40	—	40	—	—	40	—	—	40	—	—	—	40	—	—	—	—	40
Minnesota	26	—	26	—	—	26	—	—	—	—	—	1½	17	—	7½	13	—	13
Mississippi	18	18	—	—	18	—	—	—	—	18	—	—	—	18	—	13	18	—
Missouri	34	34	—	—	29	5	—	1½	2	—	18	1½	2	—	19½	2	—	22
Montana	12	—	12	—	12	—	—	—	—	—	—	3	3	3	—	—	—	12
Nebraska	12	8	3	1	—	12	—	—	5	1	2	—	5	1	2	3	1	8
Nevada	10	10	—	—	9½	½	—	—	½	8	1	—	½	7½	2	½	7½	2
New Hampshire	8	1	7	—	—	8	—	—	8	—	—	—	8	—	—	8	—	—
New Jersey	32	—	32	—	24	8	—	1	3	—	28	—	4	—	28	4	—	28
New Mexico	12	12	—	—	12	—	—	1	1½	4	1	—	1½	6	4½	1½	3½	7
New York	94	7	87	—	5	89	—	83½	1	—	6½	84½	—	1	6½	4	—	86½
North Carolina	32	32	—	—	32	—	—	—	—	26	5½	—	—	24	7	—	24	7½
North Dakota	8	8	—	—	8	—	—	—	2	2	2	—	—	—	—	—	—	8
Ohio	54	33½	14½	6	26	28	—	1	29½	7	13	1	27½	8	17½	27	1	26
Oklahoma	24	24	—	—	24	—	—	—	—	—	—	—	—	—	—	—	—	—
Oregon	12	4	8	—	—	12	—	—	12	—	—	—	12	—	—	11	—	1
Pennsylvania	70	57	13	—	35	35	—	4½	22½	—	36	2½	21½	—	40	—	—	70
Rhode Island	12	10	2	—	10	2	—	1½	3½	—	5½	—	4	—	8	—	—	12
South Carolina	16	—	—	16	—	—	16	—	—	16	—	—	—	16	—	—	16	—
South Dakota	8	—	8	—	—	8	—	—	8	—	—	—	8	—	—	8	—	—
Tennessee	28	—	28	—	—	28	—	—	28	—	—	—	28	—	—	28	—	—
Texas	52	52	—	—	52	—	—	—	—	52	—	—	—	52	—	—	52	—
Utah	12	3	9	—	—	12	—	6½	½	2	½	9	1½	—	½	—	—	12
Vermont	6	—	6	—	6	—	—	—	½	—	5	—	½	½	5	—	½	5½
Virginia	28	—	—	28	28	—	—	—	—	28	—	—	—	28	—	—	28	—
Washington	22	12½	9½	—	3	10	—	—	12	½	6	2	12½	½	6	11	½	10½
West Virginia	20	13½	5	1½	10	9	1	—	5½	7	1	—	7½	6½	5½	7½	3½	9
Wisconsin	28	1	27	—	—	28	—	—	28	—	—	—	28	—	—	28	—	—
Wyoming	10	5½	4½	—	2½	7½	—	3½	1½	½	3	2½	3	—	4½	—	—	10
Alaska	6	—	6	—	—	6	—	—	6	—	—	—	6	—	—	6	—	—
Canal Zone	2	2	—	—	2	—	—	—	—	2	—	—	—	2	—	—	—	2
D.C.	6	—	6	—	—	6	—	6	—	—	—	6	—	—	—	—	—	6
Hawaii	6	—	6	—	4	2	—	1	1	—	2	—	1	—	5	1	—	5
Puerto Rico	6	2	4	—	1	5	—	—	—	—	6	—	—	—	6	—	—	6
Virgin Islands	2	—	2	—	—	2	—	—	1	—	1	—	1	—	1	—	—	2
Total	**1230**	**650½**	**518**	**61½**	**671**	**539½ᵃ**	**19½**	**123½**	**340**	**268**	**273**	**121**	**362½**	**294**	**324½**	**275½**	**261**	**617½**

1. *Other candidates: Alben W. Barkley, 48½; Robert S. Kerr, 65; J. William Fulbright, 22; Paul H. Douglas, 3; Oscar R. Ewing, 4; Paul A. Dever, 37½; Hubert H. Humphrey, 26; James E. Murray, 12; Harry S. Truman, 6; William O. Douglas, ½; not voting, 1.*
2. *Other candidates: Barkley, 78½; Paul H. Douglas, 3; Kerr, 5½; Ewing, 3; Dever, 30½; Truman, 6; not voting, 1½.*
3. *Other candidates: Barkley, 67½; Paul H. Douglas, 3; Dever, ½; Ewing, 3; not voting, 2.*
a. *Sum of column; proceedings record 534.*

1952 Republican

(Narrative, p. 97)

Delegation	Total Votes	Pro-Taft Amendment on Louisiana Delegates Yea	Nay	Pro-Eisenhower Report on Georgia Delegates Yea	Nay	First Pres. Ballot[1] (Before shift) Eisenhower	Taft	First Pres. Ballot[2] (After shift) Eisenhower	Taft
Alabama	14	9	5	5	9	5	9	14	—
Arizona	14	12	2	3	11	4	10	4	10
Arkansas	11	11	—	3	8	4	6	11	—
California	70	—	70	62	8	—	—	—	—
Colorado	18	1	17	17	1	15	2	17	1
Connecticut	22	2	20	21	1	21	1	22	—
Delaware	12	5	7	8	4	7	5	12	—
Florida	18	15	3	5	13	6	12	18	—
Georgia	17	17	—	—	—	14	2	16	1
Idaho	14	14	—	—	14	—	14	14	—
Illinois	60	58	2	1	59	1	59	1	59
Indiana	32	31	1	3	29	2	30	2	30
Iowa	26	11	15	16	10	16	10	20	6
Kansas	22	2	20	20	2	20	2	22	—
Kentucky	20	18	2	2	18	1	19	13	7
Louisiana	15	13	2	—	2	13	2	15	—
Maine	16	5	11	11	5	11	5	15	1
Maryland	24	5	19	15	9	16	8	24	—
Massachusetts	38	5	33	33	5	34	4	38	—
Michigan	46	1	45	32	14	35	11	35	11
Minnesota	28	—	28	28	—	9	—	28	—
Mississippi	5	5	—	—	5	—	5	5	—
Missouri	26	4	22	21	5	21	5	26	—
Montana	8	7	1	1	7	1	7	1	7
Nebraska	18	13	5	7	11	4	13	7	11
Nevada	12	7	5	2	10	5	7	10	2
New Hampshire	14	—	14	14	—	14	—	14	—
New Jersey	38	5	33	32	6	33	5	38	—
New Mexico	14	8	6	5	9	6	8	6	8
New York	96	1	95	92	4	92	4	95	1
North Carolina	26	14	12	10	16	12	14	26	—
North Dakota	14	11	3	3	11	4	8	5	8
Ohio	56	56	—	—	56	—	56	—	56
Oklahoma	16	10	6	4	12	4	7	8	4
Oregon	18	—	18	18	—	18	—	18	—
Pennsylvania	70	13	57	52	18	53	15	70	—
Rhode Island	8	2	6	6	2	6	1	8	—
South Carolina	6	5	1	1	5	2	4	6	—
South Dakota	14	14	—	—	14	—	14	7	7
Tennessee	20	20	—	—	20	—	20	20	—
Texas	38	22	16	—	—	33	5	38	—
Utah	14	14	—	—	14	—	14	14	—
Vermont	12	—	12	12	—	12	—	12	—
Virginia	23	13	10	7	16	9	14	19	4
Washington	24	4	20	19	5	20	4	21	3
West Virginia	16	15	1	1	15	1	14	3	13
Wisconsin	30	24	6	6	24	—	24	—	24
Wyoming	12	8	4	4	8	6	6	12	—
Alaska	3	3	—	—	3	1	2	3	—
Canal Zone	—	—	—	—	—	—	—	—	—
District of Columbia	6	6	—	—	6	—	6	6	—
Hawaii	8	7	1	3	5	3	4	4	4
Puerto Rico	3	2	1	1	2	—	3	1	2
Virgin Islands	1	—	1	1	—	1	—	1	—
Total	**1206**	**548**	**658**	**607**	**531**	**595**	**500**	**845**	**280**

1. Other candidates: Earl Warren, 81; Harold E. Stassen, 20; Douglas MacArthur, 10.
2. Other candidates: Warren, 77; MacArthur, 4.

1956 Democratic

(Narrative, p. 100)

Delegation	Total Votes	First Pres. Ballot[1]		
		Stevenson	Harriman	Other
Alabama	26	15½	—	10½
Arizona	16	16	—	—
Arkansas	26	26	—	—
California	68	68	—	—
Colorado	20	13½	6	½
Connecticut	20	20	—	—
Delaware	10	10	—	—
Florida	28	25	—	3
Georgia	32	—	—	32
Idaho	12	12	—	—
Illinois	64	53½	8½	2
Indiana	26	21½	3	1½
Iowa	24	16½	7	½
Kansas	16	16	—	—
Kentucky	30	—	—	30
Louisiana	24	24	—	—
Maine	14	10½	3½	—
Maryland	18	18	—	—
Massachusetts	40	32	7½	½
Michigan	44	39	5	—
Minnesota	30	19	11	—
Mississippi	22	—	—	22
Missouri	38	—	—	38
Montana	16	10	6	—
Nebraska	12	12	—	—
Nevada	14	5½	7	1½
New Hampshire	8	5½	1½	1
New Jersey	36	36	—	—
New Mexico	16	12	3½	½
New York	98	5½	92½	—
North Carolina	36	34½	1	½
North Dakota	8	8	—	—
Ohio	58	52	½	5½
Oklahoma	28	—	28	—
Oregon	16	16	—	—
Pennsylvania	74	67	7	—
Rhode Island	16	16	—	—
South Carolina	20	2	—	18
South Dakota	8	8	—	—
Tennessee	32	32	—	—
Texas	56	—	—	56
Utah	12	12	—	—
Vermont	6	5½	½	—
Virginia	32	—	—	32
Washington	26	19½	6	½
West Virginia	24	24	—	—
Wisconsin	28	22½	5	½
Wyoming	14	14	—	—
Alaska	6	6	—	—
Canal Zone	3	3	—	—
District of Columbia	6	6	—	—
Hawaii	6	6	—	—
Puerto Rico	6	6	—	—
Virgin Islands	3	3	—	—
Total	1372	905½	210	256½

1. *Other candidates: Lyndon B. Johnson, 80; James C. Davis, 33; Albert B. Chandler, 36½; John S. Battle, 32½; George B. Timmerman, 23½; W. Stuart Symington, 45½; Frank Lausche, 5½.*

1956 Republican

(Narrative, p. 101)

Delegation	Total Votes	First Pres. Ballot Eisenhower
Alabama	21	21
Arizona	14	14
Arkansas	16	16
California	70	70
Colorado	18	18
Connecticut	22	22
Delaware	12	12
Florida	26	26
Georgia	23	23
Idaho	14	14
Illinois	60	60
Indiana	32	32
Iowa	26	26
Kansas	22	22
Kentucky	26	26
Louisiana	20	20
Maine	16	16
Maryland	24	24
Massachusetts	38	38
Michigan	46	46
Minnesota	28	28
Mississippi	15	15
Missouri	32	32
Montana	14	14
Nebraska	18	18
Nevada	12	12
New Hampshire	14	14
New Jersey	38	38
New Mexico	14	14
New York	96	96
North Carolina	28	28
North Dakota	14	14
Ohio	56	56
Oklahoma	22	22
Oregon	18	18
Pennsylvania	70	70
Rhode Island	14	14
South Carolina	16	16
South Dakota	14	14
Tennessee	28	28
Texas	54	54
Utah	14	14
Vermont	12	12
Virginia	30	30
Washington	24	24
West Virginia	16	16
Wisconsin	30	30
Wyoming	12	12
Alaska	4	4
District of Columbia	6	6
Hawaii	10	10
Puerto Rico	3	3
Virgin Islands	1	1
Total	1323	1323

1960 Democratic

(Narrative, p. 103)

Delegation	Total Votes	Kennedy	Johnson	Stevenson	Symington
Alabama	29	3	20	½	3½
Alaska	9	9	—	—	—
Arizona	17	17	—	—	—
Arkansas	27	—	27	—	—
California	81	33½	7½	31½	8
Colorado	21	13½	—	5½	2
Connecticut	21	21	—	—	—
Delaware	11	—	11	—	—
Florida	29	—	—	—	—
Georgia	33	—	33	—	—
Hawaii	9	1½	3	3½	1
Idaho	13	6	4½	½	2
Illinois	69	61½	—	2	5½
Indiana	34	34	—	—	—
Iowa	26	21½	½	2	½
Kansas	21	21	—	—	—
Kentucky	31	3½	25½	1½	½
Louisiana	26	—	26	—	—
Maine	15	15	—	—	—
Maryland	24	24	—	—	—
Massachusetts	41	41	—	—	—
Michigan	51	42½	—	2½	6
Minnesota	31	—	—	—	—
Mississippi	23	—	—	—	—
Missouri	39	—	—	—	39
Montana	17	10	2	2½	2½
Nebraska	16	11	½	—	4
Nevada	15	5½	6½	2½	½
New Hampshire	11	11	—	—	—
New Jersey	41	—	—	—	—
New Mexico	17	4	13	—	—
New York	114	104½	3½	3½	2½
North Carolina	37	6	27½	3	—
North Dakota	11	11	—	—	—
Ohio	64	64	—	—	—
Oklahoma	29	—	29	—	—
Oregon	17	16½	—	½	—
Pennsylvania	81	68	4	7½	—
Rhode Island	17	17	—	—	—
South Carolina	21	—	21	—	—
South Dakota	11	4	2	1	2½
Tennessee	33	—	33	—	—
Texas	61	—	61	—	—
Utah	13	8	3	—	1½
Vermont	9	9	—	—	—
Virginia	33	—	33	—	—
Washington	27	14½	2½	6½	3
West Virginia	25	15	5½	3	1½
Wisconsin	31	23	—	—	—
Wyoming	15	15	—	—	—
Canal Zone	4	—	4	—	—
District of Columbia	9	9	—	—	—
Puerto Rico	7	7	—	—	—
Virgin Islands	4	4	—	—	—
Total	**1521**	**806**	**409**	**79½**	**86**

The header "First Pres. Ballot[1]" appears above the candidate columns.

1. Other candidates: Ross R. Barnett, 23 (Mississippi); George A. Smathers, 30 (29 in Florida, ½ in Alabama, ½ in North Carolina); Hubert H. Humphrey, 42½ (31 in Minnesota, 8 in Wisconsin, 1½ in South Dakota, ½ in Nebraska, ½ in Utah); Robert B. Meyner, 43 (41 in New Jersey, 1½ in Pennsylvania, ½ in Alabama); Herschel C. Loveless, 1½ (Iowa); Orval E. Faubus, ½ (Alabama); Edmund G. Brown, ½ (California); Albert D. Rosellini, ½ (Washington).

1960 Republican

(Narrative, p. 104)

First Pres. Ballot

Delegation	Total Votes	Nixon	Goldwater
Alabama	22	22	—
Alaska	6	6	—
Arizona	14	14	—
Arkansas	16	16	—
California	70	70	—
Colorado	18	18	—
Connecticut	22	22	—
Delaware	12	12	—
Florida	26	26	—
Georgia	24	24	—
Hawaii	12	12	—
Idaho	14	14	—
Illinois	60	60	—
Indiana	32	32	—
Iowa	26	26	—
Kansas	22	22	—
Kentucky	26	26	—
Louisiana	26	16	10
Maine	16	16	—
Maryland	24	24	—
Massachusetts	38	38	—
Michigan	46	46	—
Minnesota	28	28	—
Mississippi	12	12	—
Missouri	26	26	—
Montana	14	14	—
Nebraska	18	18	—
Nevada	12	12	—
New Hampshire	14	14	—
New Jersey	38	38	—
New Mexico	14	14	—
New York	96	96	—
North Carolina	28	28	—
North Dakota	14	14	—
Ohio	56	56	—
Oklahoma	22	22	—
Oregon	18	18	—
Pennsylvania	70	70	—
Rhode Island	14	14	—
South Carolina	13	13	—
South Dakota	14	14	—
Tennessee	28	28	—
Texas	54	54	—
Utah	14	14	—
Vermont	12	12	—
Virginia	30	30	—
Washington	24	24	—
West Virginia	22	22	—
Wisconsin	30	30	—
Wyoming	12	12	—
District of Columbia	8	8	—
Puerto Rico	3	3	—
Virgin Islands	1	1	—
Total	**1331**	**1321**	**10**

1964 Republican

(Narrative, p. 107)

Delegation	Total Votes	Minority Amendment on Civil Rights[1]		First Pres. Ballot[2] (Before shift)			First Pres. Ballot[3] (After shift)		
		Yea	Nay	Goldwater	Rockefeller	Scranton	Goldwater	Rockefeller	Scranton
Alabama	20	—	20	20	—	—	20	—	—
Alaska	12	12	—	—	—	8	—	—	8
Arizona	16	—	16	16	—	—	16	—	—
Arkansas	12	—	12	9	1	2	12	—	—
California	86	—	86	86	—	—	86	—	—
Colorado	18	—	18	15	—	3	18	—	—
Connecticut	16	11	5	4	—	12	16	—	—
Delaware	12	11	1	7	—	5	10	—	2
Florida	34	—	34	34	—	2	34	—	—
Georgia	24	—	24	22	—	2	24	—	—
Hawaii	8	4	4	4	—	—	8	—	—
Idaho	14	—	14	14	—	—	14	—	—
Illinois	58	4	54	56	2	—	56	2	—
Indiana	32	—	32	32	—	—	32	—	—
Iowa	24	2	22	14	—	10	24	—	—
Kansas	20	2	18	18	—	1	18	—	1
Kentucky	24	1	23	21	—	3	22	—	2
Louisiana	20	—	20	20	—	—	20	—	—
Maine	14	11	3	—	—	—	—	—	—
Maryland	20	17	3	6	1	13	7	1	12
Massachusetts	34	27	7	5	—	26	34	—	—
Michigan	48	37	9	8	—	—	48	—	—
Minnesota	26	17	9	8	—	—	26	—	—
Mississippi	13	—	13	13	—	—	13	—	—
Missouri	24	1	23	23	—	1	24	—	—
Montana	14	—	14	14	—	—	14	—	—
Nebraska	16	—	16	16	—	—	16	—	—
Nevada	6	—	6	6	—	—	6	—	—
New Hampshire	14	14	—	—	—	14	—	—	14
New Jersey	40	40	—	20	—	20	38	—	2
New Mexico	14	—	14	14	—	—	14	—	—
New York	92	86	6	5	87	—	87	—	—
North Carolina	26	—	26	26	—	—	26	—	—
North Dakota	14	1	13	7	1	—	14	—	—
Ohio	58	—	58	57	—	—	58	—	—
Oklahoma	22	—	22	22	—	—	22	—	—
Oregon	18	10	8	—	18	—	16	—	—
Pennsylvania	64	62	2	4	—	60	64	—	—
Rhode Island	14	11	3	3	—	11	14	—	—
South Carolina	16	—	16	16	—	—	16	—	—
South Dakota	14	—	14	12	—	2	14	—	—
Tennessee	28	—	28	28	—	—	28	—	—
Texas	56	—	56	56	—	—	56	—	—
Utah	14	—	14	14	—	—	14	—	—
Vermont	12	8	4	3	2	2	3	2	2
Virginia	30	—	30	29	—	1	30	—	—
Washington	24	1	23	22	—	1	22	—	1
West Virginia	14	4	10	10	2	2	12	1	1
Wisconsin	30	—	30	30	—	—	30	—	—
Wyoming	12	—	12	12	—	—	12	—	—
District of Columbia	9	7	2	4	—	5	4	—	5
Puerto Rico	5	5	—	—	—	5	5	—	—
Virgin Islands	3	3	—	—	—	3	3	—	—
Total	**1308**	**409**	**897**	**883**	**114**	**214**	**1220**	**6**	**50**

1. Not voting, 2.
2. Other candidates: George Romney, 41 (40 in Michigan, 1 in Kansas); Margaret C. Smith, 27 (14 in Maine, 5 in Vermont, 3 in North Dakota, 2 in Alaska, 1 in Massachusetts, 1 in Ohio, 1 in Washington); Walter H. Judd, 22 (18 in Minnesota, 3 in North Dakota, 1 in Alaska); Hiram L. Fong, 5 (4 in Hawaii, 1 in Alaska); Henry C. Lodge, 2 (Massachusetts).
3. Other candidates: Smith, 22 (14 in Maine, 5 in Vermont, 2 in Alaska, 1 in Washington); Fong, 1 (Alaska); Judd, 1 (Alaska); Romney, 1 (Kansas); not voting, 7 (5 in New York, 2 in Oregon).

1968 Democratic

Key Convention Ballots

(Narrative, p. 113)

Delegation	Total Votes	Texas Credentials[1] Yea	Nay	Georgia Credentials[2] Yea	Nay	Alabama Credentials[3] Yea	Nay	End Unit Rule[4] Yea	Nay	Report on Vietnam[5] Yea	Nay	First Pres. Ballot[6] Humphrey	McCarthy	McGovern	Phillips
Ala.	32	32	—	10	22	—	—	5½	24½	1½	30½	23	—	—	—
Alaska	22	17	5	5	17	14	8	22	—	10	12	17	2	3	—
Ariz.	19	1½	17	17	2	7½	11½	—	19	6½	12½	14½	2½	2	—
Ark.	33	33	—	3	29	8	23	—	32	7	25	30	2	—	—
Calif.	174	1	173	173	1	173	1	173	1	166	6	14	91	51	17
Colo.	35	—	35	30	5	34	1	35	—	21	14	16½	10	5½	3
Conn.	44	30	12	13	27	21	21	9	30	13	30	35	8	—	1
Del.	22	21	—	3	18	2	19	—	21	—	21	21	—	—	—
Fla.	63	58	4	9	54	6	57	11	52	7	56	58	5	—	—
Ga.	43	—	—	—	—	25	17½	39	4	19½	23½	19½	13½	1	3
Hawaii	26	26	—	4	22	—	26	3	23	—	26	26	—	—	—
Idaho	25	22½	2½	4½	20½	2	23	1	24	10	15	21	3½	½	—
Ill.	118	114	4	12	83	18	100	3	115	13	105	112	3	3	—
Ind.	63	34	10	25	38	13	41½	63	—	15	47½	49	11	2	1
Iowa	46	37½	8½	32	12	24½	21½	46	—	36	10	18½	19½	5	—
Kan.	38	38	—	3½	34½	5½	31½	6	20	4½	33½	34	1	3	—
Ky.	46	40½	5½	6	40	6½	39½	6½	39½	7	39	41	5	—	—
La.	36	32	4	7	29	—	36	—	36	2½	33½	35	—	—	—
Maine	27	25	1	5	22	—	26	27	—	4½	22½	23	4	—	—
Md.	49	46	3	3	46	2	47	49	—	12	37	45	2	2	—
Mass.	72	16	47	39	24	29	29	37	31	56	16	2	70	—	—
Mich.	96	70	23	35	58	26	67	43½	44½	52	44	72½	9½	7½	6½
Minn.	52	34½	14½	16	33	23½	28½	16	33½	16½	34½	38	11½	—	2½
Miss.	24	2	18½	18	2	12½	8½	21½	½	19½	2½	9½	6½	4	2
Mo.	60	48	12	12	48	8	52	60	—	10	50	56	3½	—	½
Mont.	26	20	4	2½	21½	3½	22½	12½	12	6	20	23½	2½	—	—
Neb.	30	12	16	11	18	13	15	26	2	19	11	15	6	9	—
Nev.	22	13	7	14	8	12½	9½	22	—	3½	18½	18½	2½	1	—
N.H.	26	6	20	23	2	25	—	23	3	23	3	6	20	—	—
N.J.	82	43	25	22	51	21	61	21	61	24	57	62	19	—	1
N.M.	26	13	13	11	15	11	15	11	15	11½	14½	15	11	—	—
N.Y.	190	—	190	190	—	80e	82e	190	—	148	42	96½	87	1½	2
N.C.	59	54½	4½	3½	55½	1	58	2	57	7	51	44½	2	½	—
N.D.	25	17	5	5	17	7	18	17	5	6	19	18	7	—	—
Ohio	115	37½	27	21	80	30½	65	23	92	48	67	94	18	2	—
Okla.	41	40	1	1	40	6½	34	6	35	4	37	37½	2½	½	½
Ore.	35	10	23	32	—	31	—	31	—	29	6	—	35	—	—
Pa.	130	80¾	42¼	31½	90½	22¼	100½	39¾	79¼	35¼	92¼	103¾	21½	2½	1½
R.I.	27	24½	2½	12	11	2½	24½	3½	23½	5	22	23½	2½	—	—
S.C.	28	28	—	4	22	—	28	4½	23½	1	27	28	—	—	—
S.D.	26	1	25	26	—	24	2	26	—	26	—	2	—	24	—
Tenn.	51	48½	1	—	51	½	49½	2½	46½	2	49	49½	½	1	—
Texas	104	—	—	2.55	101.45	—	104	5	99	—	104	100½	2½	—	1
Utah	26	18	8	7	19	5	21	26	—	6	20	23	2	—	1
Vt.	22	5	13	17	4	14	7	22	—	17	5	8	6	7	—
Va.	54	21½	22½	8½	35½	1	53	9½	43½	8	46	42½	5½	—	2
Wash.	47	31½	15½	18	29	16	28	21½	25½	15½	31½	32½	8½	6	—
W.Va.	38	19	12	8	22	9	29	38	—	8	30	34	3	—	—
Wis.	59	5	54	52	7	54	4	58	1	52	7	8	49	1	1
Wyo.	22	18½	3½	2	20	6½	15½	3	19	3½	18½	18½	3½	—	—
Canal Z.	5	4	—	2	3	—	4	1	4	1½	3½	4	—	1	—
D.C.	23	—	22	22	—	23	—	23	—	21	2	2	—	—	21
Guam	5	4½	½	—	5	—	5	½	4½	½	4½	5	—	—	—
P.R.	8	8	—	7½	—	—	8	1	7	—	8	8	—	—	—
Vir. Is.	5	5	—	2½	—	—	5	5	—	—	5	5	—	—	—
Total	**2622**	**1368¼a**	**956¾b**	**1043.55c**	**1415.45d**	**880¾f**	**1607g**	**1351¼h**	**1209**	**1041¼**	**1567¾**	**1759¼j**	**601**	**146½**	**67½**

1. Not voting, 297.
2. Not voting, 163.
3. Not voting, 134½.
4. Not voting, 61¾.
5. Not voting, 13.
6. Other candidates: Dan K. Moore, 17½ (12 in North Carolina, 3 in Virginia, 2 in Georgia, ½ in Alabama); Edward M. Kennedy, 12¾ (proceedings record, 12½) (3½ in Alabama, 3 in Iowa, 3 in New York, 1 in Ohio, 1 in West Virginia, ¾ in Pennsylvania; ½ in Georgia); Bryant, 1½ (Alabama); George C. Wallace, ½ (Alabama); James H. Gray, ½ (Georgia); not voting, 15 (3 in Alabama, 3 in Georgia, 2 in Mississippi, 1 in Arkansas, 1 in California, 1 in Delaware, 1 in Louisiana, 1 in Rhode Island, 1 in Vermont, 1 in Virginia).

a. Sum of column; proceedings record, 1368.
b. Sum of column; proceedings record, 955.
c. Sum of column; proceedings record, 1041½.
d. Sum of column; proceedings record, 1413.
e. New York vote announced after outcome of roll call.
f. Sum of column; proceedings record (without New York vote), 801½.
g. Sum of column; proceedings record (without New York), 1525.
h. Sum of column; proceedings record, 1350.
i. Sum of column; proceedings record, 1206.
j. Sum of column; proceedings record, 1761¾.

1968 Republican

(Narrative, p. 111)

Delegation	Total Votes	First Pres. Ballot[1] (Before shift)			First Pres. Ballot (After shift)		
		Nixon	Rockefeller	Reagan	Nixon	Rockefeller	Reagan
Alabama	26	14	—	12	26	—	—
Alaska	12	11	1	—	12	—	—
Arizona	16	16	—	—	16	—	—
Arkansas	18	—	—	—	18	—	—
California	86	—	—	86	86	—	—
Colorado	18	14	3	1	18	—	—
Connecticut	16	4	12	—	16	—	—
Delaware	12	9	3	—	12	—	—
Florida	34	32	1	1	34	—	—
Georgia	30	21	2	7	30	—	—
Hawaii	14	—	—	—	14	—	—
Idaho	14	9	—	5	14	—	—
Illinois	58	50	5	3	58	—	—
Indiana	26	26	—	—	26	—	—
Iowa	24	13	8	3	24	—	—
Kansas	20	—	—	—	19	1	—
Kentucky	24	22	2	—	24	—	—
Louisiana	26	19	—	7	26	—	—
Maine	14	7	7	—	14	—	—
Maryland	26	18	8	—	26	—	—
Massachusetts	34	—	34	—	34	—	—
Michigan	48	4	—	—	48	—	—
Minnesota	26	9	15	—	26	—	—
Mississippi	20	20	—	—	20	—	—
Missouri	24	16	5	3	24	—	—
Montana	14	11	—	3	14	—	—
Nebraska	16	16	—	—	16	—	—
Nevada	12	9	3	—	12	—	—
New Hampshire	8	8	—	—	8	—	—
New Jersey	40	18	—	—	40	—	—
New Mexico	14	8	1	5	14	—	—
New York	92	4	88	—	4	88	—
North Carolina	26	9	1	16	26	—	—
North Dakota	8	5	2	1	8	—	—
Ohio	58	2	—	—	58	—	—
Oklahoma	22	14	1	7	22	—	—
Oregon	18	18	—	—	18	—	—
Pennsylvania	64	22	41	1	64	—	—
Rhode Island	14	—	14	—	14	—	—
South Carolina	22	22	—	—	22	—	—
South Dakota	14	14	—	—	14	—	—
Tennessee	28	28	—	—	28	—	—
Texas	56	41	—	15	54	—	2
Utah	8	2	—	—	8	—	—
Vermont	12	9	3	—	12	—	—
Virginia	24	22	2	—	24	—	—
Washington	24	15	3	6	24	—	—
West Virginia	14	11	3	—	13	1	—
Wisconsin	30	30	—	—	30	—	—
Wyoming	12	12	—	—	12	—	—
District of Columbia	9	6	3	—	6	3	—
Puerto Rico	5	—	5	—	5	—	—
Virgin Islands	3	2	1	—	3	—	—
Total	1333	692	277	182	1238	93	2

1. Other candidates: James A. Rhodes, 55 (Ohio); George Romney, 50 (44 in Michigan, 6 in Utah); Clifford P. Case, 22 (New Jersey); Frank Carlson, 20 (Kansas); Winthrop Rockefeller, 18 (Arkansas); Hiram L. Fong, 14 (Hawaii); Harold Stassen, 2 (1 in Minnesota, 1 in Ohio); John V. Lindsay, 1 (Minnesota).

1972 Republican

(Narrative, p. 120)

Delegation	Total Votes	First Pres. Ballot	
		Nixon	McCloskey
Alabama	18	18	—
Alaska	12	12	—
Arizona	18	18	—
Arkansas	18	18	—
California	96	96	—
Colorado	20	20	—
Connecticut	22	22	—
Delaware	12	12	—
Florida	40	40	—
Georgia	24	24	—
Hawaii	14	14	—
Idaho	14	14	—
Illinois	58	58	—
Indiana	32	32	—
Iowa	22	22	—
Kansas	20	20	—
Kentucky	24	24	—
Louisiana	20	20	—
Maine	8	8	—
Maryland	26	26	—
Massachusetts	34	34	—
Michigan	48	48	—
Minnesota	26	26	—
Mississippi	14	14	—
Missouri	30	30	—
Montana	14	14	—
Nebraska	16	16	—
Nevada	12	12	—
New Hampshire	14	14	—
New Jersey	40	40	—
New Mexico	14	13	1
New York	88	88	—
North Carolina	32	32	—
North Dakota	12	12	—
Ohio	56	56	—
Oklahoma	22	22	—
Oregon	18	18	—
Pennsylvania	60	60	—
Rhode Island	8	8	—
South Carolina	22	22	—
South Dakota	14	14	—
Tennessee	26	26	—
Texas	52	52	—
Utah	14	14	—
Vermont	12	12	—
Virginia	30	30	—
Washington	24	24	—
West Virginia	18	18	—
Wisconsin	28	28	—
Wyoming	12	12	—
District of Columbia	9	9	—
Guam	3	3	—
Puerto Rico	5	5	—
Virgin Islands	3	3	—
Total	1348	1347	1

1972 Democratic

(Narrative, p. 117)

Delegation[1]	Total Votes	Minority Report South Carolina Credentials			Minority Report California Credentials			Minority Report Illinois Credentials		
		Yea	Nay	Not Voting	Yea	Nay	Not Voting	Yea	Nay	Not Voting
California	271	120	151	—	120	—	151	84	136	51
South Carolina	32	—	9	23	3	29	—	31	1	—
Ohio	153	63	87	3	75	78	—	69	70	14
Canal Zone	3	1.50	1.50	—	3	—	—	1	2	—
Utah	19	10	8	1	13	6	—	5	14	—
Delaware	13	5.85	7.15	—	6.50	6.50	—	6.50	6.50	—
Rhode Island	22	20	2	—	22	—	—	7.09	14.91	—
Texas	130	34	96	—	34	96	—	96	34	—
West Virginia	35	13	22	—	15	20	—	24	11	—
South Dakota	17	17	—	—	17	—	—	—	17	—
Kansas	35	17	18	—	18	17	—	18	17	—
New York	278	269	9	—	267	11	—	20	256	2
Virginia	53	34.50	18.50	—	38.50	14.50	—	16.50	35.50	1
Wyoming	11	2.20	8.80	—	4.40	6.60	—	7.70	3.30	—
Arkansas	27	13	14	—	8	19	—	13	14	—
Indiana	76	18	58	—	33	43	—	53	23	—
Puerto Rico	7	6.50	0.50	—	6.50	0.50	—	0.50	6.50	—
Tennessee	49	22	27	—	23	26	—	20	29	—
Pennsylvania	182	55.50	126	0.50	72	105	5	106.50	62	13.50
Mississippi	25	20	5	—	19	6	—	—	25	—
Wisconsin	67	39	28	—	55	12	—	12	55	—
Illinois	170	79	90	1	114.50	55.50	—	76	30	64
Maine	20	1	19	—	—	20	—	13	7	—
Florida	81	1	80	—	3	78	—	80	1	—
New Hampshire	18	13.50	4.50	—	9.90	8.10	—	9	8.10	0.90
Arizona	25	15	10	—	12	13	—	4	21	—
North Carolina	64	6	58	—	21	43	—	39	23	2
Massachusetts	102	97	5	—	97	5	—	11	91	—
Nebraska	24	14	9	1	20	4	—	13	11	—
Georgia	53	5.50	47.50	—	21.75	31.25	—	24	27.50	1.50
North Dakota	14	7	6.30	0.70	8.40	5.60	—	2.10	11.90	—
Maryland	53	24	29	—	27.83	25.17	—	28.67	24.33	—
New Jersey	109	79	29	1	85.50	22.50	1	30	75.50	3.50
Vermont	12	7	5	—	11	1	—	2	10	—
Nevada	11	5.75	5.25	—	5.75	5.25	—	6.75	4.25	—
Michigan	132	51	81	—	55	76	1	85	47	—
Iowa	46	23	23	—	27	19	—	20	26	—
Colorado	36	23	13	—	27	9	—	5	31	—
Alabama	37	1	36	—	1	36	—	32	5	—
Alaska	10	6.75	3.25	—	7.25	2.75	—	4.75	5.25	—
Hawaii	17	2	15	—	7	10	—	17	—	—
Washington	52	—	52	—	—	52	—	52	—	—
Minnesota	64	56	8	—	29	35	—	32	32	—
Louisiana	44	25	19	—	22.50	21.50	—	9.50	32.50	2
Idaho	17	12.50	4.50	—	11.50	5.50	—	4	13	—
Montana	17	10	7	—	14.50	1	1.50	2.50	14.50	—
Connecticut	51	8	43	—	21	30	—	40	11	—
District of Columbia	15	12	3	—	13.50	1.50	—	1.50	13.50	—
Virgin Islands	3	1	2	—	2.50	0.50	—	3	—	—
Kentucky	47	10	37	—	11	36	—	36	10	1
Missouri	73	13.50	59.50	—	22.50	50.50	—	59	13	1
New Mexico	18	10	8	—	10	8	—	8	10	—
Guam	3	1.50	1.50	—	1.50	1.50	—	—	3	—
Oregon	34	16	18	—	33	1	—	2	32	—
Oklahoma	39	11	28	—	11	28	—	29	9	1
Total	**3016**	**1429.05**	**1555.75**	**31.20**	**1618.28**	**1238.22**	**159.50**	**1371.56**[a]	**1486.04**[b]	**158.40**

1. Delegations at this convention are listed in the order in which they voted. All fractional votes are expressed in decimals for consistency.
a. Sum of column; proceedings record, 1371.55.
b. Sum of column; proceedings record, 1486.05.

1972 Democratic

(Narrative, p. 117)

Minority Report Guaranteed Income			First Pres. Ballot[2] (Before shift)					First Pres. Ballot[3] (After shift)				
Yea	Nay	Not Voting	McGovern	Jackson	Wallace	Chisholm	Sanford	McGovern	Jackson	Wallace	Chisholm	Sanford
131	114	26	271	—	—	—	—	271	—	—	—	—
4	21	7	6	10	6	4	6	10	9	6	—	6
39	86	28	77	39	—	23	3	77	39	—	23	3
2.50	0.50	—	3	—	—	—	—	3	—	—	—	—
8	11	—	14	1	—	—	3	14	1	—	—	3
4.55	8.45	—	5.85	6.50	—	0.65	—	5.85	5.85	—	0.65	—
10.86	11.14	—	22	—	—	—	—	22	—	—	—	—
15	115	—	54	23	48	4	—	54	23	48	4	—
3	32	—	16	14	1	—	4	16	14	1	—	4
1	16	—	17	—	—	—	—	17	—	—	—	—
5	30	—	20	10	—	2	1	20	10	—	2	1
152	118	8	263	9	—	6	—	278	—	—	—	—
30	21	2	33.50	4	1	5.50	9	37	5	—	2.50	8.50
0.55	10.45	—	3.30	6.05	—	1.10	—	3.30	6.05	—	1.10	—
10	16	1	1	1	—	—	—	1	1	—	—	—
17	56	3	26	20	26	1	—	28	19	25	—	—
4	3	—	7	—	—	—	—	7	—	—	—	—
21	27	1	—	—	33	10	—	5	—	32	7	—
49.50	117.50	15	81	86.50	2	9.50	1	81	86.50	2	9.50	1
22	—	3	10	—	—	12	3	23	—	—	2	—
29	38	—	55	3	—	5	—	55	3	—	5	—
59	95	16	119	30.50	0.50	4.50	2	155	6	—	1	—
1	19	—	5	—	—	—	—	5	—	—	—	—
4	77	—	2	—	75	2	—	4	—	75	1	—
0.90	14.40	2.70	10.80	5.40	—	—	—	10.80	5.40	—	—	—
6	19	—	21	3	—	—	1	22	3	—	—	—
17	47	—	—	—	37	—	27	—	—	37	—	27
60	40	2	102	—	—	—	—	102	—	—	—	—
2	22	—	21	3	—	—	—	21	3	—	—	—
10.50	34	8.50	14.50	14.50	11	12	1	14.50	14.50	11	12	1
1.40	10.50	2.10	8.40	2.80	0.70	0.70	—	10.50	2.10	—	0.70	—
14.33	38.67	—	13	—	38	2	—	13	—	38	2	—
61.50	35.50	12	89	11.50	—	4	1.50	92.50	11	—	3.50	—
4	8	—	12	—	—	—	—	12	—	—	—	—
2.75	8.25	—	5.75	5.25	—	—	—	5.75	5.25	—	—	—
30.50	96.50	5	50.50	7	67.50	3	1	51.50	7	67.50	2	1
6	39	1	35	—	—	3	4	35	—	—	3	4
15	21	—	27	—	—	7	—	29	2	—	5	—
10	27	—	9	1	24	—	1	9	1	24	—	1
3	5.50	1.50	6.50	3.25	—	—	—	6.50	3.25	—	—	—
1.50	15.50	—	6.50	8.50	—	1	—	6.50	8.50	—	1	—
1	51	—	—	52	—	—	—	—	52	—	—	—
28	33	3	11	—	—	6	—	43	—	—	4	1
22	20	2	10.25	10.25	3	18.50	2	25.75	5.25	3	4	1
5	12	—	12.50	2.50	—	2	—	12.50	2.50	—	2	—
2	14	1	16	—	—	1	—	16	—	—	1	—
22	29	—	30	20	—	—	1	30	20	—	—	1
15	—	—	13.50	1.50	—	—	—	13.50	1.50	—	—	—
2.50	0.50	—	1	1.50	—	0.50	—	1	1.50	—	0.50	—
1	41	5	10	35	—	—	2	10	35	—	—	2
12	55	6	24.50	48.50	—	—	—	24.50	48.50	—	—	—
3	15	—	10	—	8	—	—	10	—	8	—	—
—	3	—	1.50	1.50	—	—	—	1.50	1.50	—	—	—
11	23	—	34	—	—	—	—	34	—	—	—	—
5.50	31.50	2	10.50	23.50	—	1	4	9.50	23.50	—	2	4
999.34	1852.86	163.80	1728.35	525.00	381.70	151.95	77.50	1864.95	485.65	377.50	101.45	69.50

2. *Other candidates: Hubert H. Humphrey, 66.70 (46 in Minnesota, 4 in Ohio, 4 in Wisconsin, 3 in Michigan, 2 in Indiana, 2 in Pennsylvania, 2 in Florida, 1 in Utah, 1 in Colorado, 1 in Hawaii, 0.70 in North Dakota); Wilbur D. Mills, 33.80 (25 in Arkansas, 3 in Illinois, 3 in New Jersey, 2 in Alabama, 0.55 in Wyoming, 0.25 in Alaska); Edmund S. Muskie, 24.30 (15 in Maine, 5.50 in Illinois, 1.80 in New Hampshire, 1 in Texas, 1 in Colorado); Edward M. Kennedy, 12.70 (4 in Iowa, 3 in Illinois, 2 in Ohio, 1 in Kansas, 1 in Indiana, 1 in Tennessee, 0.70 in North Dakota); Wayne L. Hays, 5 (Ohio); Eugene J. McCarthy, 2 (Illinois); Mondale, 1 (Kansas); Clark, 1 (Minnesota); not voting, 5 (Tennessee).*

3. *Humphrey, 35 (16 in Minnesota, 4 in Ohio, 4 in Wisconsin, 3 in Indiana, 3 in Michigan, 2 in Pennsylvania, 1 in Utah, 1 in Florida, 1 in Hawaii); Mills, 32.80 (25 in Arkansas, 2 in Illinois, 2 in New Jersey, 2 in South Carolina, 0.55 in Wyoming, 0.25 in Alaska); Muskie, 20.80 (15 in Maine, 3 in Illinois, 1.80 in New Hampshire, 1 in Texas); Kennedy, 10.65 (4 in Iowa, 2 in Ohio, 1 in Kansas, 1 in Indiana, 1 in Tennessee, 1 in Illinois, 0.65 in Delaware); Hays, 5 (Ohio); McCarthy, 2 (Illinois); Mondale, 1 (Kansas).*

1976 Democratic

(Narrative, p. 123)

Delegation	Total Votes	First Pres. Ballot[1] (Before shift)				First Pres. Ballot[2] (After shift)			
		Carter	Udall	Brown	Wallace	Carter	Udall	Brown	Wallace
Alabama	35	30	—	—	5	30	—	—	5
Alaska	10	10	—	—	—	10	—	—	—
Arizona	25	6	19	—	—	6	19	—	—
Arkansas	26	25	1	—	—	25	1	—	—
California	280	73	2	205	—	278	2	—	—
Colorado	35	15	6	11	—	15	6	11	—
Connecticut	51	35	16	—	—	35	16	—	—
Delaware	12	10.50	—	1.50	—	10.50	—	1.50	—
Florida	81	70	—	1	10	70	—	1	10
Georgia	50	50	—	—	—	50	—	—	—
Hawaii	17	17	—	—	—	17	—	—	—
Idaho	16	16	—	—	—	16	—	—	—
Illinois	169	164	1	2	1	164	1	2	1
Indiana	75	72	—	—	3	72	—	...	3
Iowa	47	25	20	1	—	25	20	1	—
Kansas	34	32	2	—	—	32	2	—	—
Kentucky	46	39	2	—	5	29	2	—	5
Louisiana	41	18	—	18	5	35	—	1	5
Maine	20	15	5	—	—	15	5	—	—
Maryland	53	44	6	3	—	44	6	3	—
Massachusetts[3]	104	65	21	—	11	65	21	—	11
Michigan	133	75	58	—	—	75	58	—	—
Minnesota	65	37	2	1	—	37	2	1	—
Mississippi	24	23	—	—	—	23	—	—	—
Missouri	71	58	4	2	—	58	4	2	—
Montana	17	11	2	—	—	11	2	—	—
Nebraska	23	20	—	3	—	20	—	3	—
Nevada	11	3	—	6.50	—	3	—	6.50	—
New Hampshire	17	15	2	—	—	15	2	—	—
New Jersey	108	108	—	—	—	108	—	—	—
New Mexico	18	14	4	—	—	14	4	—	—
New York	274	209.50	56.50	4	—	209.50	56.50	4	—
North Carolina	61	56	—	—	3	56	—	—	3
North Dakota	13	13	—	—	—	13	—	—	—
Ohio	152	132	20	—	—	132	20	—	—
Oklahoma	37	32	1	—	—	32	1	—	—
Oregon	34	16	—	10	—	16	—	10	—
Pennsylvania	178	151	21	6	—	151	21	6	—
Rhode Island	22	14	—	8	—	22	—	—	—
South Carolina	31	28	—	1	2	28	—	1	2
South Dakota	17	11	5	—	—	11	5	—	—
Tennessee	46	45	—	—	1	45	—	—	1
Texas	130	124	—	4	1	124	—	4	1
Utah	18	10	—	5	—	10	—	5	—
Vermont	12	5	4	3	—	5	4	3	—
Virginia	54	48	6	—	—	48	6	—	—
Washington	53	36	11	3	—	36	11	3	—
West Virginia	33	30	1	—	—	30	1	—	—
Wisconsin	68	29	25	—	10	29	25	—	10
Wyoming	10	8	1	1	—	8	1	1	—
District of Columbia	17	12	5	—	—	12	5	—	—
Puerto Rico	22	22	—	—	—	22	—	—	—
Canal Zone	3	3	—	—	—	3	—	—	—
Guam	3	3	—	—	—	3	—	—	—
Virgin Islands	3	3	—	—	—	3	—	—	—
Democrats Abroad	3	2.50	—	0.50	—	2.50	—	0.50	—
Total	**3008**	**2238.50**	**329.50**	**300.50**	**57.00**	**2468.50**	**329.50**	**70.50**	**57.00**

1. *Other candidates: Ellen McCormack, 22 (1 in Illinois, 2 in Massachusetts, 11 in Minnesota, 7 in Missouri, 1 in Wisconsin); Frank Church, 19 (3 in Colorado, 4 in Montana, 1 in Nevada, 8 in Oregon, 1 in Utah, 2 in Washington); Hubert H. Humphrey, 10 (9 in Minnesota, 1 in South Dakota); Henry M. Jackson, 10 (2 in Massachusetts, 4 in New York, 1 in Washington, 3 in Wisconsin); Fred Harris, 9 (2 in Massachusetts, 4 in Minnesota, 3 in Oklahoma); Milton J. Shapp, 2 (1 in Massachusetts, 1 in Utah); receiving one vote each Robert C. Byrd (West Virginia); Cesar Chavez (Utah); Leon Jaworski (Texas); Barbara C. Jordan (Oklahoma); Edward M. Kennedy (Iowa); Jennings Randolph (West Virginia); Fred Stover (Minnesota); "nobody" (0.5 in Nevada); not voting, 3 (1 in Mississippi, 2 in North Carolina).*
2. *The rules were suspended after the switches and Carter was nominated by acclamation.*
3. *Massachusetts passed when originally called on and cast its votes at the end of the roll call, after vote switches.*

1976 Republican

(Narrative, p. 127)

Delegation	Total Votes	Rule 16C[1]		First Pres. Ballot[2]	
		Yes	Nay	Ford	Reagan
Alabama	37	37	—	—	37
Alaska	19	2	17	17	2
Arizona	29	25	4	2	27
Arkansas	27	17	10	10	17
California	167	166	1	—	167
Colorado	31	26	5	5	26
Connecticut	35	—	35	35	—
Delaware	17	1	16	15	2
Florida	66	28	38	43	23
Georgia	48	39	7	—	48
Hawaii	19	1	18	18	1
Idaho	21	17	4	4	17
Illinois	101	20	79	86	14
Indiana	54	27	27	9	45
Iowa	36	18	18	19	17
Kansas	34	4	30	30	4
Kentucky	37	26	10	19	18
Louisiana	41	34	6	5	36
Maine	20	5	15	15	5
Maryland	43	8	35	43	—
Massachusetts	43	15	28	28	15
Michigan	84	29	55	55	29
Minnesota	42	5	35	32	10
Mississippi	30	—	30	16	14
Missouri	49	30	18	18	31
Montana	20	20	—	—	20
Nebraska	25	18	7	7	18
Nevada	18	15	3	5	13
New Hampshire	21	3	18	18	3
New Jersey	67	4	62	63	4
New Mexico	21	20	1	—	21
New York	154	20	134	133	20
North Carolina	54	51	3	25	29
North Dakota	18	6	12	11	7
Ohio	97	7	90	91	6
Oklahoma	36	36	—	—	36
Oregon	30	14	16	16	14
Pennsylvania	103	14	89	93	10
Rhode Island	19	—	19	19	—
South Carolina	36	25	11	9	27
South Dakota	20	11	9	9	11
Tennessee	43	17	26	21	22
Texas	100	100	—	—	100
Utah	20	20	—	—	20
Vermont	18	—	18	18	—
Virginia	51	36	15	16	35
Washington	38	31	7	7	31
West Virginia	28	12	16	20	8
Wisconsin	45	—	45	45	—
Wyoming	17	9	8	7	10
District of Columbia	14	—	14	14	—
Puerto Rico	8	—	8	8	—
Guam	4	—	4	4	—
Virgin Islands	4	—	4	4	—
Total	2259	1069	1180	1187	1070

1. Not voting, 10.
2. Other candidate: Elliot L. Richardson, 1 (New York); not voting, 1 (Illinois). The nomination was made unanimous at the end of the balloting.

1980 Democratic

(Narrative, p. 136)

Delegation	Total Votes	Minority Rule #5[1]		First Pres. Ballot[3] (Before shift)		First Pres. Ballot[4] (After shift)	
		Yea	Nay	Carter	Kennedy	Carter	Kennedy
Alabama	45	3	42	43	2	43	2
Alaska	11	6.11	4.89	8.40	2.60	8.40	2.60
Arizona	29	16	13	13	16	13	16
Arkansas	33	9	24	25	6	25	6
California	306	171	132[2]	140	166	140	166
Colorado	40	24	16	27	10	27	10
Connecticut	54	28	26	26	28	26	28
Delaware	14	6.50	7.50	10	4	14	—
District of Columbia	19	12	7	12	5	12	5
Florida	100	25	75	75	25	75	25
Georgia	63	1	62	62	—	62	—
Hawaii	19	4	15	16	2	16	2
Idaho	17	9	8	9	7	9	7
Illinois	179	26	153	163	16	163	16
Indiana	80	27	53	53	27	53	27
Iowa	50	21	29	31	17	33	17
Kansas	37	17	20	23	14	23	14
Kentucky	50	12	38	45	5	45	5
Louisiana	51	15	36	50	1	50	1
Maine	22	12	10	11	11	11	11
Maryland	59	27	32	34	24	34	24
Massachusetts	111	81	30	34	77	34	77
Michigan	141	71	70	102	38	102	38
Minnesota	75	30	45	41	14	41	14
Mississippi	32	—	32	32	—	32	—
Missouri	77	20	57	58	19	58	19
Montana	19	9	10	13	6	13	6
Nebraska	24	11	13	14	10	14	10
Nevada	12	6.47	5.53	8.12	3.88	8.12	3.88
New Hampshire	19	9	10	10	9	10	9
New Jersey	113	68	45	45	68	45	68
New Mexico	20	11	9	10	10	10	10
New York	282	163	118	129	151	129	151
North Carolina	69	13	56	66	3	66	3
North Dakota	14	10	4	5	7	5	7
Ohio	161	81	80	89	72	89	72
Oklahoma	42	9	33	36	3	36	3
Oregon	39	14	25	26	13	26	13
Pennsylvania	185	102	83	95	90	95	90
Puerto Rico	41	20	21	21	20	21	20
Rhode Island	23	17	6	6	17	6	17
South Carolina	37	6	31	37	—	37	—
South Dakota	19	10	9	9	10	9	10
Tennessee	55	8	47	51	4	51	4
Texas	152	47	105	108	38	108	38
Utah	20	12	8	11	4	11	4
Vermont	12	7.50	4.50	5	7	5	7
Virginia	64	7	57	59	5	59	5
Washington	58	24	34	36	22	36	22
West Virginia	35	16	19	21	10	21	10
Wisconsin	75	26	49	48	26	48	26
Wyoming	11	3.50	7.50	8	3	8	3
Virgin Islands	4	—	4	4	—	4	—
Guam	4	—	4	4	—	4	—
Latin America	4	4	—	4	—	4	—
Democrats Abroad	4	2.50	1.50	1.50	2	1.50	2
Total	3331	1390.58	1936.42	2123.02	1150.48	2129.02	1150.48

1. The vote was on a minority report by supporters of Sen. Edward M. Kennedy to overturn a proposed rule that would bind all delegates to vote on the first ballot for the presidential candidate under whose banner they were elected. A "yes" vote supported the Kennedy position while a "no" supported the Carter view that delegates should be bound.

2. Not voting, 1.

3. Other candidates: William Proxmire, 10 (Minnesota); Scott M. Matheson, 5 (Utah); Koryne Horbal, 5 (Minnesota); Ronald V. Dellums, 2.5 (2 in New York, 0.5 from Democrats Abroad); receiving 2 votes each: John C. Culver (Iowa); Warren Spannous (Minnesota); Alice Tripp (Minnesota); Kent Hance (Texas); Robert C. Byrd (West Virginia); receiving 1 vote each: Dale Bumpers (Arkansas); Edmund S. Muskie (Colorado); Walter F. Mondale (Minnesota); Hugh L. Carey (Oklahoma); Tom Steed (Oklahoma); Edmund G. Brown (Wisconsin); uncommitted, 10; not voting, 5; absent, 2.

4. Votes for other candidates remained the same except that Iowa switched its 2 votes for Culver to Carter. After the switches Carter was nominated by acclamation.

1980 Republican

(Narrative, p. 132)

Delegation	Total Votes	First Pres. Ballot[1]		
		Reagan	Anderson	Bush
Alabama	27	27	—	—
Alaska	19	19	—	—
Arizona	28	28	—	—
Arkansas	19	19	—	—
California	168	168	—	—
Colorado	31	31	—	—
Connecticut	35	35	—	—
Delaware	12	12	—	—
District of Columbia	14	14	—	—
Florida	51	51	—	—
Georgia	36	36	—	—
Guam	4	4	—	—
Hawaii	14	14	—	—
Idaho	21	21	—	—
Illinois	102	81	21	—
Indiana	54	54	—	—
Iowa	37	37	—	—
Kansas	32	32	—	—
Kentucky	27	27	—	—
Louisiana	31	31	—	—
Maine	21	21	—	—
Maryland	30	30	—	—
Massachusetts	42	33	9	—
Michigan	82	67	—	13
Minnesota	34	33	—	—
Mississippi	22	22	—	—
Missouri	37	37	—	—
Montana	20	20	—	—
Nebraska	25	25	—	—
Nevada	17	17	—	—
New Hampshire	22	22	—	—
New Jersey	66	66	—	—
New Mexico	22	22	—	—
New York	123	121	—	—
North Carolina	40	40	—	—
North Dakota	17	17	—	—
Ohio	77	77	—	—
Oklahoma	34	34	—	—
Oregon	29	29	—	—
Pennsylvania	83	83	—	—
Puerto Rico	14	14	—	—
Rhode Island	13	13	—	—
South Carolina	25	25	—	—
South Dakota	22	22	—	—
Tennessee	32	32	—	—
Texas	80	80	—	—
Utah	21	21	—	—
Vermont	19	19	—	—
Virginia	51	51	—	—
Virgin Islands	4	4	—	—
Washington	37	36	1	—
West Virginia	18	18	—	—
Wisconsin	34	28	6	—
Wyoming	19	19	—	—
Total	**1994**	**1939**	**37**	**13**

1. Other candidates: Anne Armstrong, 1 (Michigan); not voting, 4.

1984 Democratic

(Narrative, p. 143)

Delegation	Total Votes	No First Use of Nuclear Weapons			Defense Spending			Dual Primaries			Military Force Restrictions		
		Yea	Nay	Not Voting	Yea	Nay	Not Voting	Yea	Nay	Not Voting	Yea	Nay	Not Voting
Alabama	62	15	46	1	11	49	2	13	49	—	61	1	—
Alaska	14	7	7	—	1	13	—	2	12	—	13	1	—
Arizona	40	20	19	—	18	21	—	20	19	—	39	—	—
Arkansas	42	13	29	—	12	30	—	7	33	2	39	2	1
California	345	149	84	—	99	170	—	129	128	—	285	31	—
Colorado	51	31	16	4	5	45	1	26	24	1	51	—	—
Connecticut	60	28	24	8	32	27	1	27	33	—	60	—	—
Delaware	18	1	17	—	1	17	—	1	17	—	18	—	—
D.C.	19	15	4	—	17	2	—	14	5	—	6	12	—
Florida	143	47	76	20	42	81	20	27	110	6	95	25	23
Georgia	84	40	33	—	38	45	—	39	42	—	67	1	2
Hawaii	27	1	26	—	—	27	—	—	27	—	—	—	—
Idaho	22	9	—	—	10	11	—	9	13	—	22	—	—
Illinois	194	42	145	—	40	147	—	48	143	—	191	—	3
Indiana	88	31	46	—	18	64	—	23	64	—	88	—	—
Iowa	58	22	36	—	7	51	—	5	53	—	58	—	—
Kansas	44	14	29	1	6	38	—	10	34	—	44	—	—
Kentucky	63	14	48	—	10	52	—	15	47	—	55	8	—
Louisiana	69	24	32	—	30	39	—	44	22	—	44	22	—
Maine	27	7	16	—	3	23	—	10	16	—	23	1	—
Maryland	74	20	51	3	20	54	—	18	56	—	51	19	4
Massachusetts	116	89	24	—	69	43	1	82	31	1	112	—	—
Michigan	155	43	105	7	32	118	5	37	111	7	137	—	18
Minnesota	86	37	41	8	30	48	8	25	57	4	73	2	11
Mississippi	43	15	26	2	16	26	1	13	29	1	33	8	2
Missouri	86	20	62	4	22	62	2	24	61	1	70	—	16
Montana	25	8	15	2	4	21	—	5	20	—	25	—	—
Nebraska	30	2	25	3	2	25	3	10	17	3	24	—	6
Nevada	20	6	14	—	3	17	—	5	15	—	19	—	—
New Hampshire	22	10	12	—	5	17	—	1	21	—	22	—	—
New Jersey	122	9	113	—	9	113	—	7	115	—	116	6	—
New Mexico	28	7	19	2	2	26	—	3	25	—	27	1	—
New York	285	134	140	—	131	139	7	125	146	3	196	57	—
North Carolina	88	28	56	—	19	66	—	32	55	—	73	3	—
North Dakota	18	13	5	—	8	10	—	8	10	—	18	—	—
Ohio	175	71	103	—	47	122	6	40	133	2	173	—	2
Oklahoma	53	16	35	2	3	47	3	3	49	1	49	3	1
Oregon	50	32	13	5	26	21	3	24	24	2	49	—	1
Pennsylvania	195	42	153	—	39	156	—	53	142	—	195	—	—
Puerto Rico	53	—	53	—	—	53	—	—	53	—	10	43	—
Rhode Island	27	11	15	1	11	15	1	8	18	1	24	—	2
South Carolina	48	21	23	4	23	19	6	21	25	2	21	19	8
South Dakota	19	7	12	—	7	12	—	7	12	—	—	6	—
Tennessee	76	31	41	4	29	41	6	34	39	3	72	1	3
Texas	200	53	137	10	47	141	12	39	150	11	152	38	10
Utah	27	17	10	—	11	15	1	13	14	—	19	7	1
Vermont	17	11	4	—	10	4	—	10	4	—	12	3	—
Virginia	78	29	48	—	29	48	—	33	43	—	50	23	4
Washington	70	49	18	—	29	39	1	35	35	—	67	—	—
West Virginia	44	12	27	5	12	29	3	17	24	3	—	—	—
Wisconsin	89	28	45	16	26	57	6	31	54	4	83	6	—
Wyoming	15	2	12	—	2	12	—	13	1	—	13	1	—
Latin America	5	—	5	—	.5	4.5	—	—	5	—	5	—	—
Democrats Abroad	5	1.5	3.5	—	1.5	3.5	—	—	5	—	5	—	—
Virgin Islands	6	1.2	4.8	—	2.6	2.6	.6	1.2	4.8	—	4.8	1.2	—
American Samoa	6	—	6	—	—	6	—	—	6	—	6	—	—
Guam	7	—	7	—	—	7	—	7	—	—	7	—	—
Total	3933	1405.7	2216.3	112	1127.6	2591.6	99.6	1253.2	2500.8	58	3271.8	351.2	118

1984 Democratic

(Narrative, p. 143)

	Total	First Pres. Ballot[1]		
Delegation	Votes	Mondale	Hart	Jackson
Alabama	62	39	13	9
Alaska	14	9	4	1
Arizona	40	20	16	2
Arkansas	42	26	9	7
California	345	95	190	33
Colorado	51	1	42	1
Connecticut	60	23	36	1
Delaware	18	13	5	0
D.C.	19	5	—	14
Florida	143	82	55	3
Georgia	84	40	24	20
Hawaii	27	27	—	0
Idaho	22	10	12	0
Illinois	194	114	41	39
Indiana	88	42	38	8
Iowa	58	37	18	2
Kansas	44	25	16	3
Kentucky	63	51	5	7
Louisiana	69	26	19	24
Maine	27	13	13	0
Maryland	74	54	3	17
Massachusetts	116	59	49	5
Michigan	155	96	49	10
Minnesota	86	63	3	4
Mississippi	43	26	4	13
Missouri	86	55	14	16
Montana	25	11	13	1
Nebraska	30	12	17	1
Nevada	20	9	10	1
New Hampshire	22	12	10	0
New Jersey	122	115	—	7
New Mexico	28	13	13	2
New York	285	156	75	52
North Carolina	88	53	19	16
North Dakota	18	10	5	1
Ohio	175	84	80	11
Oklahoma	53	24	26	3
Oregon	50	16	31	2
Pennsylvania	195	177	—	18
Puerto Rico	53	53	—	0
Rhode Island	27	14	12	0
South Carolina	48	16	13	19
South Dakota	19	9	10	0
Tennessee	76	39	20	17
Texas	200	119	40	36
Utah	27	8	19	0
Vermont	17	5	8	3
Virginia	78	34	18	25
Washington	70	31	36	3
West Virginia	44	30	14	0
Wisconsin	89	58	25	6
Wyoming	15	7	7	0
Latin America	5	5	—	0
Democrats Abroad	5	3	1.5	0.5
Virgin Islands	6	4	—	2
American Samoa	6	6	—	0
Guam	7	7	—	0
Total	3933	2191	1200.5	465.5

1. Other candidates: Thomas F. Eagleton, 18 (16 in Minnesota, 2 in North Dakota); George McGovern, 4 (3 in Massachusetts, 1 in Iowa); John Glenn, 2 (Texas); Joseph R. Biden Jr., 1 (Maine); Martha Kirkland, 1 (Alabama); not voting, 40 (27 in California, 7 in Connecticut, 2 in Arizona, 2 in Florida, 1 in Vermont, 1 in Wyoming); absent, 10.

1984 Republican

(Narrative, p. 148)

Delegation	Total Votes	First Pres. Ballot[1] Reagan
Alabama	38	38
Alaska	18	18
Arizona	32	32
Arkansas	29	29
California	176	176
Colorado	35	35
Connecticut	35	35
Delaware	19	19
District of Columbia	14	14
Florida	82	82
Georgia	37	37
Guam	4	4
Hawaii	14	14
Idaho	21	21
Illinois	93	92
Indiana	52	52
Iowa	37	37
Kansas	32	32
Kentucky	37	37
Louisiana	41	41
Maine	20	20
Maryland	31	31
Massachusetts	52	52
Michigan	77	77
Minnesota	32	32
Mississippi	30	30
Missouri	47	47
Montana	20	20
Nebraska	24	24
Nevada	22	22
New Hampshire	22	22
New Jersey	64	64
New Mexico	24	24
New York	136	136
North Carolina	53	53
North Dakota	18	18
Ohio	89	89
Oklahoma	35	35
Oregon	32	32
Pennsylvania	98	97
Puerto Rico	14	14
Rhode Island	14	14
South Carolina	35	35
South Dakota	19	19
Tennessee	46	46
Texas	109	109
Utah	26	26
Vermont	19	19
Virginia	50	50
Virgin Islands	4	4
Washington	44	44
West Virginia	19	19
Wisconsin	46	46
Wyoming	18	18
Total	2235	2233

1. Not voting, 2.

1988 Democratic

(Narrative, p. 155)

Delegation	Total Votes	Fair Tax[1]		No First Use of Nuclear Weapons[2]		First Pres. Ballot[3]	
		Yea	Nay	Yea	Nay	Dukakis	Jackson
Alabama	65	14	35	19	38	37	28
Alaska	17	5	7	8	8	9	7
Arizona	43	15	21	15	25	28	14
Arkansas	48	11	27	9	25	31	11
California	363	104	240	119.09	192.63	235	122
Colorado	55	20	31	20	32	37	18
Connecticut	63	16	42	21	39	47	16
Delaware	19	8	11	8	11	9	7
Florida	154	33	89	33	100	116	35
Georgia	94	30	43	36	43	50	42
Hawaii	28	8	19	8	19	19	8
Idaho	24	3	18	3	18	20	3
Illinois	200	28	75	40	62	138	57
Indiana	89	18	68	19	66	69.50	18
Iowa	61	11	48	21	38	49	12
Kansas	45	12	29.50	14.50	28.50	30	15
Kentucky	65	6	43	6	46	59	6
Louisiana	76	23	11	26	13	41	33
Maine	29	11	15	11	14	17	12
Maryland	84	21	58	21	58	59	25
Massachusetts	119	20	79	23	86	99	19
Michigan	162	78	77	78	77	80	80
Minnesota	91	36	45	42	46	57	29
Mississippi	47	24	15	27	16	19	26
Missouri	88	31	49	33	50	50	37
Montana	28	5	21	7	19	22	5
Nebraska	30	7	23	7	23	22	8
Nevada	23	5	15	6	15	16	5
New Hampshire	22	0	22	1	21	22	0
New Jersey	126	19	39	19	64	107	19
New Mexico	30	7	19	7	20	22	8
New York	292	90	181	108	173	194	97
North Carolina	95	36	51	37	51	58	35
North Dakota	22	46	131	5	11	17	3
Ohio	183	46	131	48	132	136	46
Oklahoma	56	4	44	4	46	52	4
Oregon	54	18	31	18	34	35	18
Pennsylvania	202	22	177	22	179	179	23
Rhode Island	28	3	15	4	16	24	3
South Carolina	53	29	19	30	23	22	31
South Dakota	20	2	16	2	17	19	1
Tennessee	84	12	54	15	57	63	20
Texas	211	72	123	72	121	135	71
Utah	28	3	18	5	20	25	3
Vermont	20	10	9	11	9	9	9
Virginia	86	37	46	41	44	42	42
Washington	77	27	46	29	42	50	27
West Virginia	47	0	44	1	43	47	0
Wisconsin	91	24	59	25	59	65	25
Wyoming	18	4	12	6	10	14	4
District of Columbia	25	13	6	16	8	7	18
Puerto Rico	57	3	53	8	48	48.50	8
Virgin Islands	5	5	0	5	0	0	5
American Samoa	6	0	6	0	6	6	0
Guam	4	0	4	0	4	4	0
Democrats Abroad	9	0.50	8.50	1	8	8.25	0.50
Total	4,162	1,091.50	2,499.00	1,220.59	2,474.13	2,876.25	1,218.50

1. Not voting, 90.
2. Not voting, 67.
3. Other candidates: Lloyd Bentsen, 1 (Alaska); Joseph R. Biden Jr., 2 (Delaware); Richard A. Gephardt, 2 (1 in Louisiana, 1 in Texas); Richard H. Stallings, 3 (Minnesota); Gary Hart, 1 (Vermont), absent, 44.25.

1988 Republican

(Narrative, p. 160)

Delegation	Total Votes	First Pres. Ballot Bush
Alabama	38	38
Alaska	19	19
Arizona	33	33
Arkansas	27	27
California	175	175
Colorado	36	36
Connecticut	35	35
Delaware	17	17
Florida	82	82
Georgia	48	48
Hawaii	20	20
Idaho	22	22
Illinois	92	92
Indiana	51	51
Iowa	37	37
Kansas	34	34
Kentucky	38	38
Louisiana	41	41
Maine	22	22
Maryland	41	41
Massachusetts	52	52
Michigan	77	77
Minnesota	31	31
Mississippi	31	31
Missouri	47	47
Montana	20	20
Nebraska	25	25
Nevada	20	20
New Hampshire	23	23
New Jersey	64	64
New Mexico	26	26
New York	136	136
North Carolina	54	54
North Dakota	16	16
Ohio	88	88
Oklahoma	36	36
Oregon	32	32
Pennsylvania	96	96
Rhode Island	21	21
South Carolina	37	37
South Dakota	18	18
Tennessee	45	45
Texas	111	111
Utah	26	26
Vermont	17	17
Virginia	50	50
Washington	41	41
West Virginia	28	28
Wisconsin	47	47
Wyoming	18	18
District of Columbia	14	14
Puerto Rico	14	14
Virgin Islands	4	4
Guam	4	4
Total	2,277	2,277

1992 Democratic

(Narrative, p. 168)

Delegation	Total Votes	Tax Fairness [1]		First Pres. Ballot [2]		
		Yes	Nay	Clinton	Brown	Tsongas
Alabama	67	0	67	67	0	0
Alaska	18	0	16	18	0	0
Arizona	49	29	15	23	12	14
Arkansas	48	0	48	48	0	0
California	406	96	176	211	160	0
Colorado	58	31	23	26	19	13
Connecticut	66	23	30	45	21	0
Delaware	21	8	8	17	3	1
Florida	167	50	71	141	3	15
Georgia	96	14	50	96	0	0
Hawaii	28	5	17	24	2	0
Idaho	26	5	17	22	0	1
Illinois	195	51	76	155	9	29
Indiana	93	21	68	73	20	0
Iowa	59	7	43	55	2	0
Kansas	44	5	38	43	0	0
Kentucky	64	3	53	63	0	0
Louisiana	75	0	75	75	0	0
Maine	31	18	2	14	13	4
Maryland	85	27	23	83	0	2
Massachusetts	119	97	0	109	6	1
Michigan	159	43	82	120	35	0
Minnesota	92	23	43	61	8	2
Mississippi	46	0	46	46	0	0
Missouri	92	6	46	91	1	0
Montana	24	0	19	21	2	0
Nebraska	33	10	14	24	9	0
Nevada	27	0	25	23	4	0
New Hampshire	24	10	10	17	0	7
New Jersey	126	12	76	102	24	0
New Mexico	34	3	27	30	3	0
New York	290	116	109	155	67	64
North Carolina	99	0	64	95	1	0
North Dakota	22	3	14	18	0	0
Ohio	178	37	141	144	34	0
Oklahoma	58	0	53	56	2	0
Oregon	57	14	38	38	19	0
Pennsylvania	194	21	78	139	43	4
Rhode Island	29	7	9	27	2	0
South Carolina	54	7	40	54	0	0
South Dakota	21	1	16	21	0	0
Tennessee	85	6	38	85	0	0
Texas	232	33	112	204	4	20
Utah	29	25	0	20	9	0
Vermont	21	11	6	14	7	0
Virginia	97	11	43	94	3	0
Washington	84	30	29	49	18	14
West Virginia	41	0	13	41	0	0
Wisconsin	94	29	61	46	30	18
Wyoming	19	5	8	18	1	0
District of Columbia	31	0	30	31	0	0
Puerto Rico	58	0	58	57	0	0
Virgin Islands	5	0	5	5	0	0
American Samoa	5	0	5	5	0	0
Guam	4	0	4	4	0	0
Democrats Abroad	9	0	8.75	9	0	0
Total	4,288	953.00	2,286.75	3,372	596	209

1. Not voting, 177.
2. Other candidates: Larry Agran, 3 (1 in Idaho, 2 in Minnesota); Robert P. Casey, 10 (Minnesota); Patricia Schroeder, 8 (Colorado); Albert Gore Jr., 1 (Pennsylvania); Joseph Simonetti, 1 (Pennsylvania); Others, 2 (1 in New Mexico, 1 in North Dakota). Not voting, 86.

1992 Republican

(Narrative, p. 174)

Delegation	Total Votes	First Pres. Ballot [1]	
		Bush	Buchanan
Alabama	38	38	0
Alaska	19	19	0
Arizona	37	37	0
Arkansas	27	27	0
California	201	201	0
Colorado	37	31	5
Connecticut	35	35	0
Delaware	19	19	0
Florida	97	97	0
Georgia	52	52	0
Hawaii	14	14	0
Idaho	22	22	0
Illinois	85	85	0
Indiana	51	51	0
Iowa	23	23	0
Kansas	30	30	0
Kentucky	35	35	0
Louisiana	38	38	0
Maine	22	22	0
Maryland	42	42	0
Massachusetts	38	35	1
Michigan	72	72	0
Minnesota	32	32	0
Mississippi	34	34	0
Missouri	47	47	0
Montana	20	20	0
Nebraska	24	24	0
Nevada	21	21	0
New Hampshire [2]	23	—	0
New Jersey	60	60	0
New Mexico	25	25	0
New York	100	100	0
North Carolina	57	57	0
North Dakota	17	17	0
Ohio	83	83	0
Oklahoma	34	34	0
Oregon	23	23	0
Pennsylvania	91	90	1
Rhode Island	15	15	0
South Carolina	36	36	0
South Dakota	19	19	0
Tennessee	45	34	11
Texas	121	121	0
Utah	27	27	0
Vermont	19	19	0
Virginia	55	55	0
Washington	35	35	0
West Virginia	18	18	0
Wisconsin	35	35	0
Wyoming	20	20	0
District of Columbia	14	14	0
Puerto Rico	14	14	0
Virgin Islands	4	4	0
American Samoa	4	4	0
Guam	4	4	0
Total	2,210	2,166	18

1. Other candidates: Howard Phillips, 2 (1 in Colorado; 1 in Massachusetts), Alan Keyes, 1 (Massachusetts).
2. Never voted.

1996 Republican

(Narrative, p. 180)

Delegation	Total Votes	First Pres. Ballot[1]	
		Dole	Buchanan
Alabama	40	40	0
Alaska	19	16	0
Arizona	39	37	0
Arkansas	20	16	0
California	165	165	0
Colorado	27	27	0
Connecticut	27	27	0
Delaware	12	12	0
Florida	98	98	0
Georgia	42	42	0
Hawaii	14	14	0
Idaho	23	19	0
Illinois	69	69	0
Indiana	52	52	0
Iowa	25	25	0
Kansas	31	31	0
Kentucky	26	26	0
Louisiana	30	17	10
Maine	15	15	0
Maryland	32	32	0
Massachusetts	37	37	0
Michigan	57	52	5
Minnesota	33	33	0
Mississippi	33	33	0
Missouri	36	24	11
Montana	14	14	0
Nebraska	24	24	0
Nevada	14	14	0
New Hampshire	16	16	0
New Jersey	48	48	0
New Mexico	18	18	0
New York	102	102	0
North Carolina	58	58	0
North Dakota	18	17	0
Ohio	67	67	0
Oklahoma	38	38	0
Oregon	23	18	5
Pennsylvania	73	73	0
Rhode Island	16	16	0
South Carolina	37	37	0
South Dakota	18	18	0
Tennessee	38	37	0
Texas	123	121	2
Utah	28	27	1
Vermont	12	12	0
Virginia	53	53	0
Washington	36	27	9
West Virginia	18	18	0
Wisconsin	36	36	0
Wyoming	20	20	0
District of Columbia	14	14	0
Puerto Rico	14	14	0
Virgin Islands	4	4	0
American Samoa	4	4	0
Guam	4	4	0
Total	1,990	1,928	43

1. *Other candidates: Phil Gramm, 2 (Louisiana); Alan Keyes, 1(Missouri); Robert Bork, 1 (Louisiana); not voting, 15.*

1996 Democratic

(Narrative, p. 186)

Delegation	Total Votes	First Pres. Ballot[1] Clinton
Alabama	66	66
Alaska	19	19
Arizona	59	59
Arkansas	47	47
California	422	416
Colorado	56	56
Connecticut	67	67
Delaware	21	21
Florida	178	178
Georgia	91	91
Hawaii	30	29
Idaho	23	23
Illinois	193	193
Indiana	88	88
Iowa	56	56
Kansas	42	42
Kentucky	61	61
Louisiana	71	71
Maine	32	32
Maryland	88	88
Massachusetts	114	114
Michigan	156	156
Minnesota	92	92
Mississippi	47	47
Missouri	93	93
Montana	24	24
Nebraska	34	34
Nevada	26	26
New Hampshire	26	26
New Jersey	122	122
New Mexico	34	34
New York	289	289
North Carolina	99	99
North Dakota	22	21
Ohio	172	172
Oklahoma	52	52
Oregon	57	54
Pennsylvania	195	195
Rhode Island	32	31
South Carolina	51	51
South Dakota	22	22
Tennessee	80	80
Texas	229	229
Utah	31	31
Vermont	22	22
Virginia	97	97
Washington	90	90
West Virginia	43	43
Wisconsin	93	93
Wyoming	19	19
District of Columbia	33	33
Puerto Rico	58	58
Virgin Islands	4	4
American Samoa	6	6
Guam	6	6
Democrats Abroad	9	9
Total	4,289	4,277

1. Not voting, 12.

Political Parties
and Candidates

U.S. Presidents and Vice Presidents

President and Political Party	Born	Died	Age at Inauguration	Native of	Elected from	Term of Service	Vice President
George Washington (F)	1732	1799	57	Va.	Va.	April 30, 1789-March 4, 1793	John Adams
George Washington (F)			61			March 4, 1793-March 4, 1797	John Adams
John Adams (F)	1735	1826	61	Mass.	Mass.	March 4, 1797-March 4, 1801	Thomas Jefferson
Thomas Jefferson (DR)	1743	1826	57	Va.	Va.	March 4, 1801-March 4, 1805	Aaron Burr
Thomas Jefferson (DR)			61			March 4, 1805-March 4, 1809	George Clinton
James Madison (DR)	1751	1836	57	Va.	Va.	March 4, 1809-March 4, 1813	George Clinton
James Madison (DR)			61			March 4, 1813-March 4, 1817	Elbridge Gerry
James Monroe (DR)	1758	1831	58	Va.	Va.	March 4, 1817-March 4, 1821	Daniel D. Tompkins
James Monroe (DR)			62			March 4, 1821-March 4, 1825	Daniel D. Tompkins
John Q. Adams (DR)	1767	1848	57	Mass.	Mass.	March 4, 1825-March 4, 1829	John C. Calhoun
Andrew Jackson (D)	1767	1845	61	S.C.	Tenn.	March 4, 1829-March 4, 1833	John C. Calhoun
Andrew Jackson (D)			65			March 4, 1833-March 4, 1837	Martin Van Buren
Martin Van Buren (D)	1782	1862	54	N.Y.	N.Y.	March 4, 1837-March 4, 1841	Richard M. Johnson
W. H. Harrison (W)	1773	1841	68	Va.	Ohio	March 4, 1841-April 4, 1841	John Tyler
John Tyler (W)	1790	1862	51	Va.	Va.	April 6, 1841-March 4, 1845	
James K. Polk (D)	1795	1849	49	N.C.	Tenn.	March 4, 1985-March 4, 1849	George M. Dallas
Zachary Taylor (W)	1784	1850	64	Va.	La.	March 4, 1849-July 9, 1850	Millard Fillmore
Millard Fillmore (W)	1800	1874	50	N.Y.	N.Y.	July 10, 1850-March 4, 1853	
Franklin Pierce (D)	1804	1869	48	N.H.	N.H.	March 4, 1853-March 4, 1857	William R. King
James Buchanan (D)	1791	1868	65	Pa.	Pa.	March 4, 1857-March 4, 1861	John C. Breckinridge
Abraham Lincoln (R)	1809	1865	52	Ky.	Ill.	March 4, 1861-March 4, 1865	Hannibal Hamlin
Abraham Lincoln (R)			56			March 4, 1865-April 15, 1865	Andrew Johnson
Andrew Johnson (R)	1808	1875	56	N.C.	Tenn.	April 15, 1865-March 4, 1869	
Ulysses S. Grant (R)	1822	1885	46	Ohio	Ill.	March 4, 1869-March 4, 1873	Schuyler Colfax
Ulysses S. Grant (R)			50			March 4, 1873-March 4, 1877	Henry Wilson
Rutherford B. Hayes (R)	1822	1893	54	Ohio	Ohio	March 4, 1877-March 4, 1881	William A. Wheeler
James A. Garfield (R)	1831	1881	49	Ohio	Ohio	March 4, 1881-Sept. 19, 1881	Chester A. Arthur
Chester A. Arthur (R)	1830	1886	50	Vt.	N.Y.	Sept. 20, 1881-March 4, 1885	
Grover Cleveland (D)	1837	1908	47	N.J.	N.Y.	March 4, 1885-March 4, 1889	Thomas A. Hendricks
Benjamin Harrison (R)	1833	1901	55	Ohio	Ind.	March 4, 1889-March 4, 1893	Levi P. Morton
Grover Cleveland (D)	1837	1908	55	N.J.	N.Y.	March 4, 1893-March 4, 1897	Adlai E. Stevenson
William McKinley (R)	1843	1901	54	Ohio	Ohio	March 4, 1897-March 4, 1901	Garret A. Hobart
William McKinley (R)			58			March 4, 1901-Sept. 14, 1901	Theodore Roosevelt
Theodore Roosevelt (R)	1858	1919	42	N.Y.	N.Y.	Sept. 14, 1901-March 4, 1905	
Theodore Roosevelt (R)			46			March 4, 1905-March 4, 1909	Charles W. Fairbanks
William H. Taft (R)	1857	1930	51	Ohio	Ohio	March 4, 1909-March 4, 1913	James S. Sherman
Woodrow Wilson (D)	1856	1924	56	Va.	N.J.	March 4, 1913-March 4, 1917	Thomas R. Marshall
Woodrow Wilson (D)			60			March 4, 1917-March 4, 1921	Thomas R. Marshall
Warren G. Harding (R)	1865	1923	55	Ohio	Ohio	March 4, 1921-Aug. 2, 1923	Calvin Coolidge
Calvin Coolidge (R)	1872	1933	51	Vt.	Mass.	Aug. 3, 1923-March 4, 1925	
Calvin Coolidge (R)			52			March 4, 1925-March 4, 1929	Charles G. Dawes
Herbert Hoover (R)	1874	1964	54	Iowa	Calif.	March 4, 1929-March 4, 1933	Charles Curtis
Franklin D. Roosevelt (D)	1882	1945	51	N.Y.	N.Y.	March 4, 1933-Jan. 20, 1937	John N. Garner
Franklin D. Roosevelt (D)			55			Jan. 20, 1937-Jan. 20, 1941	John N. Garner
Franklin D. Roosevelt (D)			59			Jan. 20, 1941-Jan. 20, 1945	Henry A. Wallace
Franklin D. Roosevelt (D)			63			Jan. 20, 1945-April 12, 1945	Harry S. Truman
Harry S. Truman (D)	1884	1972	60	Mo.	Mo.	April 12, 1945-Jan. 20, 1949	
Harry S. Truman (D)			64			Jan. 20, 1949-Jan. 20, 1953	Alben W. Barkley
Dwight D. Eisenhower (R)	1890	1969	62	Texas	N.Y.	Jan. 20, 1953-Jan. 20, 1957	Richard Nixon
Dwight D. Eisenhower (R)			66		Pa.	Jan. 20, 1957-Jan. 20, 1961	Richard Nixon
John F. Kennedy (D)	1917	1963	43	Mass.	Mass.	Jan. 20, 1961-Nov. 22, 1963	Lyndon B. Johnson
Lyndon B. Johnson (D)	1908	1973	55	Texas	Texas	Nov. 22, 1963-Jan. 20, 1965	
Lyndon B. Johnson (D)			56			Jan. 20, 1965-Jan. 20, 1969	Hubert H. Humphrey
Richard Nixon (R)	1913	1994	56	Calif.	N.Y.	Jan. 20, 1969-Jan. 20, 1973	Spiro T. Agnew
Richard Nixon (R)			60		Calif.	Jan. 20, 1973-Aug. 9, 1974	Spiro T. Agnew
							Gerald R. Ford
Gerald R. Ford (R)	1913		61	Neb.	Mich.	Aug. 9, 1974-Jan. 20, 1977	Nelson A. Rockefeller
Jimmy Carter (D)	1924		52	Ga.	Ga.	Jan. 20, 1977-Jan. 20, 1981	Walter F. Mondale
Ronald Reagan (R)	1911		69	Ill.	Calif.	Jan. 20, 1981-Jan. 20, 1985	George Bush
Ronald Reagan (R)			73			Jan. 20, 1985-Jan. 20, 1989	George Bush
George Bush (R)	1924		64	Mass.	Texas	Jan. 20, 1989-Jan. 20, 1993	Dan Quayle
Bill Clinton (D)	1946		46	Ark.	Ark.	Jan. 20, 1993-Jan. 20, 1997	Albert Gore Jr.
Bill Clinton (D)			50			Jan. 20, 1997-	Albert Gore Jr.

Note: *D—Democrat; DR—Democratic-Republican; F—Federalist; R—Republican; W—Whig.*

Historical Profiles
Of American Political Parties

America First Party (1992-)

(See People's Party-Populists.)

American Independent Party (1968-) and American Party (1972-)

Both the American Party and the American Independent Party descended from the American Independent Party that served as the vehicle for George C. Wallace's third party presidential candidacy in 1968.

Wallace, governor of Alabama (1963-67; 1971-79), burst onto the national scene in 1964 as a Democratic presidential candidate opposed to the 1964 Civil Rights Act. Entering three Northern primaries — Wisconsin, Indiana and Maryland — he surprised political observers by winning between 30 percent and 43 percent of the popular vote in the three primaries. His unexpectedly strong showing brought the term "white backlash" into the political vocabulary as a description of the racial undertone of the Wallace vote.

In 1968 Wallace broke with the Democrats and launched his second presidential bid under the American Independent Party label. His candidacy capitalized on the bitter reactions of millions of voters, especially whites and blue-collar workers, to the civil rights activism, urban riots, antiwar demonstrations and heavy federal spending on Johnson administration "Great Society" programs that marked the mid-1960s. With the help of volunteer groups, Wallace was able to get on the ballot in all fifty states.

The former governor did not hold a convention for his party, but in October he announced his vice presidential running mate (retired air force general Curtis LeMay) and released a platform. In the November election the Wallace ticket received 9,906,473 votes (13.5 percent of the popular vote), carried five Southern states and won forty-six electoral votes. The party's showing was the best by a third party since 1924, when Robert M. La Follette collected 16.6 percent of the vote on the Progressive Party ticket.

After his defeat in that election, Wallace returned to the Democratic Party, competing in Democratic presidential primaries in 1972 and 1976. Wallace's American Independent Party began to break into factions after the 1968 election but in 1972 united behind John G. Schmitz, a Republican U.S. representative from California (1970-73), as its presidential nominee. Thomas J. Anderson, a farm magazine and syndicated news features publisher from Tennessee, was the party's vice presidential candidate. In many states, the party shortened its name to American Party. In the November election, the Schmitz ticket won 1,099,482 votes (1.4 percent of the popular vote) but failed to win any electoral votes.

In December 1972 a bitter fight occurred for the chairmanship of the American Independent Party between Anderson and William K. Shearer, the California chairman of the party. Anderson defeated Shearer, retaining control of the party but renaming it the American Party. Shearer, over the following four years, expanded his California-based group into a new national party. He had kept the name American Independent Party in California and made that the name of the new nationwide group.

By 1976 there were two distinct entities: the American Party headed by Anderson and the American Independent Party headed by Shearer.

The 1976 American Party convention was held in Salt Lake City, Utah, from June 17 to 20. Anderson was nominated for president and Rufus Shackleford of Florida for vice president.

The party's nomination of Anderson followed its failure to enlist a prominent conservative to lead the ticket. Both Gov. Meldrim Thomson Jr. of New Hampshire and Sen. Jesse Helms of North Carolina were approached, but both decided to remain in the Republican Party. With well-known conservatives declining the party's overtures, the convention turned to Anderson. He easily won the nomination on the first ballot by defeating six party workers.

Anderson's campaign stressed the "permanent principles" of the party, augmented by the 1976 platform. These principles included opposition to foreign aid, U.S. withdrawal from the United Nations and an end to trade with or recognition of communist nations. The platform included planks opposing abortion, gun control, the Equal Rights Amendment and government-sponsored health care and welfare programs. In general, the party favored limits on federal power and was against budget deficits except in wartime.

The American Party was on the ballot in eighteen states, including eight states where the American Independent Party was also. In seven of those eight states, Anderson ran ahead of the American Independent Party ticket. Anderson's strength was spread fairly evenly across the country. His best showings were in Utah (2.5 percent of the vote) and Montana (1.8 percent). He received more than 0.5 percent of the vote

---

Sources

This sections profiles all major and minor political parties that received a substantial presidential vote at some point in their history, generally 1 percent or more. The following sources were used: Congressional Quarterly, *Congressional Quarterly Weekly Report* (Washington, D.C.: Congressional Quarterly); *Dictionary of American History*, 8 vols. (New York: Scribner's, 1976); *Encyclopaedia Britannica* (Chicago: Encyclopaedia Britannica, 1980); *Encyclopedia Americana*, 30 vols. (Danbury, Conn.: Grolier Education, 1982); J. David Gillespie, *Politics at the Periphery: Third Parties in Two-Party America* (Columbia: University of South Carolina Press, 1993); Earl R. Kruschke, *Encyclopedia of Third Parties in the United States* (Santa Barbara, Calif.: ABC-CLIO, 1991); Arthur M. Schlesinger Jr., *History of U.S. Political Parties*, 1973 Reprint, (New York: Chelsea House, 1981); George W. Stimpson, *A Book About American Politics* (New York: Harper, 1952).

in Virginia (1.0), Mississippi (0.9), Minnesota (0.7) and Kentucky (0.7). Anderson's total of 160,773 popular votes (0.2 percent) placed him almost 10,000 votes behind the American Independent Party candidate nationally.

The American Independent Party convention met in Chicago, August 24-27, 1976, and chose former Georgia governor Lester Maddox (1967-71), a Democrat, as its presidential nominee and former Madison, Wis., mayor William Dyke, a Republican, as its vice presidential candidate. Maddox won a first-ballot nomination over Dallas columnist Robert Morris and former representative John R. Rarick, a Democrat of Louisiana (1967-75).

At the convention, a group of nationally prominent conservatives made a bid to take over the party and use it as a vehicle to build a new conservative coalition. Richard Viguerie, a fund raiser for Wallace and a nationally known direct mail expert, was the leader of the group. He was joined at the convention by two leading conservatives — William Rusher, publisher of the *National Review*, and Howard Phillips, the former head of the Office of Economic Opportunity (1973) and leader of the Conservative Caucus, an activist conservative group. Viguerie, Phillips and Rusher all argued that the American Independent Party should be overhauled, changed from a fringe group to a philosophical home for believers in free enterprise and traditional moral values. They also hoped they could attract Senator Helms, Governor Thomson or Rep. Philip M. Crane, R-Ill. When none of these men agreed to run on the American Independent Party ticket, Viguerie and his allies found themselves unable to promote Morris, a lesser-known substitute, successfully.

Many American Independent Party members favored Maddox because they saw him as a colorful personality, one capable of drawing media attention and perhaps of picking up the 5 percent of the national vote needed to qualify the party for federal funding. Maddox never came close to that goal, however, achieving only 0.2 percent of the national vote (170,531). It was 51,098 votes in California, where American Party nominee Anderson was not on the ballot, that enabled Maddox to run slightly ahead of Anderson nationally.

Despite the power struggle between Anderson and Shearer, there was little difference between their two party platforms. Like the American Party, the American Independent Party opposed abortion, gun control, forced busing, foreign aid and membership in the United Nations.

By 1980 neither party was much of a force in American politics. Both retained the same basic platforms, but each was on the ballot in only a handful of states. The American Independent Party's nominee, former Democrat Rarick, ran in only eight states. Economist Percy L. Greaves Jr., the American Party candidate, was listed in just seven.

The American Independent Party did not field candidates in 1984, while the American Party placed Delmar Dennis, a book publisher from Pigeon Forge, Tenn., on the ballot in six states.

Dennis also ran under the American Party banner in 1988 and, with his running mate, Earl Jeppson, received 3,475 votes. The American Independent Party did better with their candidates, presidential nominee James C. Griffin and vice presidential nominee Charles J. Morsa, receiving 27,818 votes.

By 1992 fortunes for both parties had dwindled. American Party presidential nominee Robert J. Smith and running mate Doris Feimer were on the ballot only in Utah, where they received 292 votes. The American Independent Party did not appear on any presidential ballots.

American Party-"Know-Nothings" (1856)

The American Party politicized the nativist, anti-immigrant movement in the mid-1850s, a peak period of European immigration to the United States in the pre-Civil War years. In the decade before the rise of a formal party, the movement took the form of local, secret organizations whose members were sworn to secrecy about their elaborate rituals. To questions about their affiliation, they pleaded ignorance. Hence, the party's popular name: the Know-Nothings.

Many of the millions of immigrants in the mid-19th century were Catholic, and the Know-Nothings were hostile to Catholics. They advocated nominating only native American Protestants for political office and requiring a twenty-one-year waiting period before naturalization.

In addition to the great waves of immigrants, the party's meteoric rise was spurred by the increasing polarization of the Democrats and Whigs over the volatile slavery issue. The Know-Nothings benefited from the political situation and attracted members from both of the older parties. In the party's peak years 1854 and 1855, the Know-Nothings elected governors in California, Connecticut, Delaware, Kentucky, Massachusetts, New Hampshire and Rhode Island, and elected five senators and forty-three members of the House.

But as a national party the Know-Nothings, like the Democrats and Whigs, were split eventually by the slavery issue. When a party convention in June 1855 adopted a pro-Southern position on slavery, antislavery elements bolted, dividing the party and setting the stage for its downfall.

The Know-Nothings held their first and only national nominating convention in February 1856 and selected as their candidate former Whig president Millard Fillmore (1850-53). The antislavery wing of the party convened separately and endorsed the Republican nominee, John C. Fremont. Fillmore finished third in the three-way race, receiving 21.5 percent of the popular vote and carrying only one state, Maryland.

Within a year, the bulk of the Northern Know-Nothings had joined the Republican Party. By the end of the decade, the party existed only in the Border States, where it formed the basis for the unsuccessful, antiwar Constitutional Union Party. *(Constitutional Union Party, p. 265)*

Anti-Federalists (1789-96)

Never a formal party, the Anti-Federalists were a loosely organized group opposed to ratification of the Constitution. With the adoption of the Constitution in 1788, the Anti-Federalists served as the opposition to the Federalists in the early years of Congress.

Anti-Federalists were primarily rural, agrarian men from inland regions who favored individual freedom and states' rights, which they felt would be jeopardized by the new Constitution. After ratification, the efforts of the Anti-Federalists led to adoption of the first ten amendments, the Bill of Rights, which spelled out the major limitations of federal power.

As the opposition faction in Congress during the formative years of the Republic, the Anti-Federalists basically held to a strict interpretation of the Constitution, particularly in regard to the various economic proposals of Treasury Secretary Alexander Hamilton to centralize more power in the federal government.

Although never the majority faction in Congress, the Anti-Federalists were a forerunner of Thomas Jefferson's Democratic-Republican Party, which came into existence in the 1790s and dominated American politics for the first quarter of the 19th century. *(Democratic-Republican Party, p. 267)*

Anti-Masonic Party (1832-36)

Born in the late 1820s in upstate New York, the Anti-Masonic Party focused the strong, antielitist mood of the period on a conspicuous symbol of privilege, the Masons. The Masons were a secret fraternal organization with membership drawn largely from the upper class. Conversely, the appeal of the Anti-Masonic movement was to the common man — poor farmers and laborers especially — who resented the secrecy and privilege of the Masons.

The spark that created the party came in 1826, when William Morgan, a dissident Mason from Batavia, N.Y., allegedly on the verge of exposing the inner workings of the order, mysteriously disappeared and never was seen again. Refusal of Masonic leaders to cooperate in the inconclusive investigation of Morgan's disappearance led to suspicions that Masons had kidnapped and murdered him and were suppressing the inquiry.

From 1828 through 1831, the new Anti-Masonic Party spread through New England and the Middle Atlantic states, in many places establishing itself as the primary opposition to the Democrats. In addition to its appeal to the working classes, particularly in Northern rural areas, and its opposition to Masonry, the Anti-Masons displayed a fervor against immorality, as seen not only in secret societies but also in slavery, intemperance and urban life.

In September 1831 the party held the first national nominating convention in American history. One hundred and sixteen delegates from thirteen states gathered in Baltimore, Md., and nominated former attorney general William Wirt of Maryland for the presidency. While Wirt received only 100,715 votes (7.8 percent of the popular vote) and carried just one state, Vermont, the Anti-Masons did reasonably well at other levels, winning two governorships and fifty-three House seats.

But the decline of Masonry, especially in New York, where the number of lodges dropped from 507 in 1826 to 48 six years later, robbed the Anti-Masons of an emotional issue and hastened their decline. The 1832 election was the high point for the Anti-Masons as a national party. In the 1836 campaign the party endorsed Whig candidate William Henry Harrison. Subsequently, the bulk of the Anti-Masonic constituency moved into the Whig Party.

Citizens Party (1979-84)

Organized in 1979 as a coalition of dissident liberals and populists, the first Citizens Party convention chose author and environmental scientist Barry Commoner as its 1980 presidential candidate and La Donna Harris, wife of former Democratic senator Fred R. Harris of Oklahoma, as his running mate. The Citizens Party ticket ran on the central theme that major decisions in America were made to benefit corporations and not the average citizen. The party proposed public control of energy industries and multinational corporations, a halt to the use of nuclear power, a sharp cut in military spending and price controls on food, fuel, housing and health care.

Commoner ran in all of the large electoral vote states except Florida and Texas. He made his biggest push in California, Illinois, Michigan, New York and Pennsylvania, where party leaders believed they could tap a "sophisticated working-class population" and appeal to political activists who had been involved in the environmental and antinuclear movements that sprang up in the late 1970s.

The Commoner/Harris ticket was on the ballot in twenty-nine states and the District of Columbia in 1980. Party leaders asserted that it was the largest number of ballot positions attained by any third party in its first campaign. In addition to its presidential ticket, the Citizens Party also fielded twenty-two candidates for other offices, including two for the U.S. Senate and seven for the House. The Citizens Party won 234,294 votes, or 0.3 percent of the 1980 vote.

As its 1984 presidential nominee the Citizens Party chose outspoken feminist Sonia Johnson of Virginia. Johnson first attracted national attention in 1979, when the Mormon Church excommunicated her for supporting the Equal Rights Amendment. In 1982 she staged a thirty-seven-day hunger strike in an unsuccessful effort to pressure the Illinois legislature to approve the ERA. The Citizens Party selected party activist Richard J. Walton of Rhode Island to accompany Johnson on the ticket. Winning 72,200 votes in 1984, the ticket garnered 0.1 percent of the vote.

Communist Party (1924-)

In 1919, shortly after the Russian Revolution, Soviet communists encouraged American left-wing groups to withdraw from the Socialist Party and to form a communist party in the United States. After several years of internal dissension, a new political organization named the Workers' Party of America was established in 1921 at the insistence of Moscow. The goal of the new party was revolutionary — to overthrow capitalism and to create a communist state ruled by the working classes.

William Z. Foster, a labor organizer, was the party's first presidential candidate, in 1924. National tickets were run every four years through 1940 and from 1968 through 1984, but the party's peak year at the polls was 1932, when Foster received 103,253 votes (0.3 percent of the popular vote).

The communists have a distinctive place in American political history as the only party to have had international ties. In 1929 a party split brought the formal creation of the Communist Party of the United States, with acknowledged status as a part of the worldwide communist movement (the Communist International).

The Communist International terminated during World War II, and in 1944 the party's leader in America, Earl Browder, dissolved the party and committed the movement to operate within the two-party system. In the 1944 campaign the communists endorsed President Franklin D. Roosevelt, who repudiated their support.

However, with the breakup of the U.S.-Soviet alliance after World War II, the Communists reconstituted themselves as a political party. They supported Henry Wallace's Progressive Party candidacy in 1948, but they were limited in the Cold War period of the 1950s by restrictive federal and state legislation that virtually outlawed the party.

With the gradual easing of restrictive measures, the Communist Party resumed electoral activities in the late 1960s. In a policy statement written in 1966, the party described itself as "a revolutionary party whose aim is the fundamental transformation of society."

The party's success at the polls, however, continued to be minimal. Its presidential candidates in 1968, 1972, 1976, 1980 and 1984 — the last year that they appeared on the ballot — each received less than one-tenth of 1 percent of the vote.

Constitutional Union Party (1860)

The short-lived Constitutional Union Party was formed in 1859 to promote national conciliation in the face of rampant sectionalism, which included Southern threats of secession. The party appealed to conservative remnants of the

American (Know-Nothing) and Whig parties, who viewed preservation of the Union as their primary goal.

The Constitutional Union Party held its first and only national convention in Baltimore in May 1860. For president the party nominated John Bell of Tennessee, a former senator and Speaker of the House of Representatives, who previously had been both a Democrat and a Whig. The convention adopted a short platform, which intentionally avoided controversial subjects, most notably the divisive slavery issue. Instead, the platform simply urged support for "the Constitution, the Union and the Laws."

In the fall election, Bell received 590,901 votes (12.6 percent of the popular vote) and won Kentucky, Tennessee and Virginia. However, the Bell ticket finished last in the four-way presidential race and, together with the sectional split in the Democratic Party, was a prominent factor in the victory of Republican Abraham Lincoln.

In the months after the 1860 election the Constitutional Union Party continued to urge national conciliation, but with the outbreak of the Civil War the party disappeared.

Democratic Party (1832-)

There is no precise birth date for the Democratic Party. It developed as an outgrowth of Thomas Jefferson's Democratic-Republican Party, which splintered into factions in the 1820s. The faction led by Andrew Jackson took the name Democratic-Republican, but after 1830 dropped the last half of this label and became simply the Democratic Party. The new party encouraged and benefited from the increasing democratization of American politics that began in the 1820s. Andrew Jackson became a symbol of this mass democracy, and when he was elected in 1828 a period of Democratic dominance began that lasted until the Civil War.

The Democrats were a national party, with a particular appeal among workers, immigrants and settlers west of the Alleghenies. The success of the party in the pre-Civil War period was due in part to a national organization stronger than that of its rivals. In 1832 the Democrats were the first major party to hold a national nominating convention, and they in 1848 became the first party to establish an ongoing national committee.

Between 1828 and 1860 the party held the White House for twenty-four years, controlled the Senate for twenty-six years and controlled the House of Representatives for twenty-four years. Leadership in the party generally resided in Congress. The Democrats' two-thirds nominating rule, adopted at the 1832 convention and retained for a century, gave the South veto power over the choice of a national ticket. The result, not only in the pre-Civil War years but until the rule was eliminated in 1936, was the frequent selection of conservative candidates for president.

The early philosophy of the Democratic Party stressed a belief in a strict interpretation of the Constitution, states' rights and limited spending by the federal government. While party members throughout the nation accepted these basic tenets, there was no national consensus on the volatile slavery issue, which strained the party in the mid-19th century and finally divided it geographically in 1860. Two separate Democratic tickets were run in the 1860 election — one Northern, one Southern. The party division aided the election of the candidate of the new antislavery Republican Party, Abraham Lincoln, who received less than 40 percent of the popular vote.

During the Civil War the Northern wing of the party was factionalized, with one wing, the Copperheads, hostile to the Union war effort and favoring a negotiated peace with the Confederacy. The stance of the Copperheads, coupled with the involvement of many Southern Democrats in the Confederate government, enabled the Republicans for a generation after the Civil War to denounce the reunified Democratic Party as the "party of treason."

The Democrats were a national party after the Civil War, but they were displaced as the majority party by the Republicans. The strength of the Democrats was in the South, which voted in large majorities for Democratic candidates. Party strength outside the South was scattered, being most noticeable among urban ethnics and voters in the Border States. The period of Republican dominance lasted for nearly three-quarters of a century, 1860 to 1932. The Democrats occupied the White House for sixteen of these seventy-two years, controlled the House of Representatives for twenty-six years, and controlled the Senate for ten years.

The Depression, which began in 1929, dramatically altered American politics and provided the opportunity for the Democrats to reemerge as the majority party. The Democrats swept to victory behind Franklin D. Roosevelt in 1932 and with widespread popular acceptance of his New Deal programs a new coalition was formed, which has remained largely intact. The new majority coalition combined the bulk of the black electorate, the academic community and organized labor with the party's core strength among urban ethnic and Southern voters.

Between 1932 and 1980 the Democrats occupied the presidency thirty-two of forty-eight years and controlled both houses of Congress for forty-four years. The acceptance of Roosevelt's New Deal, coupled with the abolishment of the two-thirds rule for nominating candidates and the decline of Southern power, resulted in more liberal party leadership. The liberal stance of most party leaders included belief in a broad interpretation of the Constitution and increased use of federal power and government spending to combat the problems of society.

From time to time since 1932 the party's unity has been threatened from both the inside and outside. As a party of diverse elements, its strength traditionally was undermined by Southern Democrats' loose alliance with Republicans. More recently the South, once solidly Democratic, has voted Republican in congressional and presidential elections. At the national level the party has been split by explosive issues such as the Vietnam War, which prompted violent protest demonstrations at the 1968 Democratic convention in Chicago.

In the 1970s the party began revising its delegate-selection rules to give minorities and women more representation in the party's national nominating convention. The effect of the rules changes was largely negated, however, by the growth of primaries and the resultant evolution of the convention into an event where nominations are merely formalized.

The Democrats remained the majority party during the 1970s, despite the impact of divisive issues and conservative members' defections to the Republicans, particularly in presidential elections. The 1980 election brought signs of a power shift, however, as the Republicans regained the presidency and won control of the Senate for the first time in twenty-eight years. The 1982 mid-term elections swept twenty-six new Democrats into the House and strengthened the Democrats' control of that chamber. According to a Gallup poll taken in spring 1983, when the nation was beginning to recover from the most serious recession since the Great Depression of the 1930s, more than twice as many people described themselves as Democrats (46 percent) than as Republicans (23 percent).

As the economy rebounded under the leadership of Republican president Ronald Reagan, the Democratic Party lost ground, according to a Gallup poll taken in August 1984. By this time the percentage of people who identified themselves as Democrats had dropped to 42 percent, while the Republican share increased to 28 percent. In the 1984 election Democratic presidential nominee Walter F. Mondale won 40.6 percent of the popular vote and only 13 of the 538 electoral votes. Mondale's running mate, Rep. Geraldine A. Ferraro, New York, was the first woman to receive a major party nomination for national office.

By late 1986 the Democratic Party rejuvenated. Congressional elections gave the Senate back to the Democrats with a 55-45 majority. Some experts speculated that the "forgotten middle class" and other groups that suffered from federal budget cuts voted Democratic in hope of finding a voice there. A Democratic Congress paired with a Republican president limited the GOP's power.

The Democrats were not able to rally enough support in 1988 to elect their candidates — Michael S. Dukakis and Lloyd Bentsen. The Democratic ticket received 45.6 percent of the popular vote and 111 electoral votes. In Congress, meanwhile, the Democrats held on to their majority. In the mid-term elections of 1990, they even picked up eight seats in the House and one seat in the Senate.

In 1992 the Democrats paired for the first time two Southern moderates, Bill Clinton of Arkansas and Albert Gore Jr. of Tennessee, on the presidential ticket. Widespread dissatisfaction with government and the lingering effects of the recession of 1990-91 helped the Democrats regain the presidency after twelve years. Clinton campaigned as a "new Democrat" who declared that "the era of big government is over." The presence of a major third party candidate, Ross Perot, although not substantially affecting the outcome, did result in Clinton's being elected without a majority. The Clinton-Gore ticket took 43.0 percent of the popular vote and received 370 electoral votes.

The flush of victory was short-lived, however. While the Democrats were winning back the White House they were losing ten seats in the House. Party strength in the Senate remained unchanged. Two years later the midterm elections were even more disastrous for the party. It lost control of Congress, ending forty years of Democratic rule in the House and eight in the Senate. From 1995 to 1996, as the Republican Congress led by Speaker Newt Gingrich tried to dismantle decades-old social programs, President Clinton adopted more moderate positions and fought successfully to maintain his budget priorities.

Boosted by his budget stand against the Republican Congress and buoyed by continued good economic news, Clinton defeated his Republican challenger, former Senate majority leader Robert J. Dole in the 1996 presidential race. Clinton won reelection with 49.2 percent of the popular vote and 379 electoral votes. Although Perot was again a candidate, he won only 8.4 percent of the popular vote — less than half of what he won four years earlier. Despite holding onto the White House, the Democrats did not regain control of Congress. In the congressional elections, the Democratic Party lost two seats in the Senate while picking up nine seats in the House.

Democratic-Republican Party (1796-1828)

The Democratic-Republican Party developed in the early 1790s as the organized opposition to the incumbent Federalists and successor to the Anti-Federalists, who were a loose alliance of elements initially opposed to the ratifica-tion of the Constitution and subsequently to the policies of the George Washington administration, which were designed to centralize power in the federal government.

Thomas Jefferson was the leader of the new party, whose members as early as 1792 referred to themselves as Republicans. This remained their primary name throughout the party's history, although in some states they became known as Democratic-Republicans, the label used frequently by historians to avoid confusing Jefferson's party with the later Republican Party, which began in 1854. Party members were called Jeffersonian Republicans as well.

The Democratic-Republicans favored states' rights, a literal interpretation of the Constitution and expanded democracy through extension of suffrage and popular control of the government. The party was dominated by rural, agrarian interests, intent on maintaining their dominance over the growing commercial and industrial interests of the Northeast. The principal strength of the party came from the Southern and Middle Atlantic states.

The Democratic-Republicans first gained control of the federal government in 1800, when Jefferson was elected president and the party won majorities in both houses of Congress. For the next twenty-four years the party controlled both the White House and Congress, the last eight years virtually without opposition. For all but four years during this twenty-four-year period, there was a Virginia-New York alliance controlling the executive branch, with all three presidents from Virginia — Jefferson, James Madison and James Monroe — and three of the four vice presidents from New York. Lacking an opposition party, the Democratic-Republicans in the 1820s became increasingly divided. In 1824, when four party leaders ran for president, John Quincy Adams won the election in the House of Representatives, although Andrew Jackson had received more popular votes.

The deep factionalism evident in the 1824 election doomed the Democratic-Republican Party. The two-party system revived shortly thereafter with the emergence of the National Republican Party, an outgrowth of the Adams faction, and the Democratic-Republican Party, the political organization of the Jackson faction. After 1830 the Jacksonians adopted the name Democratic Party.

Federalist Party (1789-1816)

The Federalist Party grew out of the movement that drafted and worked for the ratification of the Constitution of 1787, which established a stronger national government than that in operation under the existing Articles of Confederation. Supporters of the new constitutional government were known as Federalists, and in the formative first decade of the Republic they controlled the national government. With President Washington staying aloof from the development of political parties, leadership of the Federalists was exercised by Alexander Hamilton and John Adams. The party's basic strength was among urban, commercial interests, who were particularly drawn to the Federalists by the party's belief in a strong federal economic policy and the maintenance of domestic order — viewpoints based on a broad interpretation of the Constitution.

The Federalists were perceived widely as a party of the aristocracy, a decided liability in the late 18th and early 19th centuries when the right to vote was being widely extended to members of the middle and lower classes. Never so well organized as the Democratic-Republicans, the Federalists were unable to compete for support of the important rural, agrarian elements that composed a majority of the electorate.

The election of Jefferson in 1800 ended Federalist control of both the White House and Congress. After 1800 the Federalists did not elect a president or win a majority in either house of Congress. The party's strength was largely limited to commercial New England, where Federalists advocated states' rights and were involved in threats of regional secession in 1808 and again during the War of 1812.

The party soon began to lose its energy, and in 1812 the Federalists held their last meeting of party leaders to field a presidential ticket. Four years later there were no nominations, but Federalist electors were chosen in three states. Although this marked the last appearance of the party at the national level, the Federalists remained in existence at the local level until the mid-1820s.

Free Soil Party (1848-52)

Born as a result of opposition to the extension of slavery into the newly acquired Southwest territories, the Free Soil Party was launched formally at a convention in Buffalo, N.Y., in August 1848. The Free Soilers were composed of antislavery elements from the Democratic and Whig parties as well as remnants of the Liberal Party. Representatives from all the Northern states and three Border States attended the Buffalo convention, where the slogan "free soil, free speech, free labor and free men" was adopted. This slogan expressed the antislavery sentiment of the Free Soilers as well as the desire for cheap Western land.

Former Democratic president Martin Van Buren (1837-41) was selected by the convention as the party's presidential candidate and Charles Francis Adams, the son of President John Quincy Adams (1825-29), was chosen as his running mate.

In the 1848 election the Free Soil ticket received 291,501 votes (10.1 percent of the popular vote) but was unable to carry a single state. The party did better at the congressional level, winning nine House seats and holding the balance of power in the organization of the closely divided new Congress.

The 1848 election marked the peak of the party's influence. With the passage of compromise legislation on slavery in 1850, the Free Soilers lost their basic issue and began a rapid decline. The party ran its second and last national ticket in 1852, headed by John Hale, who received 155,210 votes (4.9 percent of the popular vote). As in 1848 the Free Soil national ticket failed to carry a single state.

Although the party went out of existence shortly thereafter, its program and constituency were absorbed by the Republican Party, whose birth and growth dramatically paralleled the resurgence of the slavery issue in the mid-1850s.

Green Party (1996-)

With famed consumer activist Ralph Nader heading its ticket, the Green Party made an impressive debut in U.S. presidential politics in 1996. Nader received 684,872 votes to finish a distant fourth behind the Reform Party's Ross Perot, the most successful third party candidate in 84 years.

Nader was on the ballot in twenty-two states, including California and several other Western states. His running mate was Winona LaDuke, thirty-seven, of the White Earth reservation in Minnesota. A Harvard graduate, LaDuke was active as an advocate and writer on human rights and Native American environmental causes.

Although new to the United States, the Green Party was part of a decentralized worldwide movement for peace, social justice and the environment. Until the collapse of international communism and the fall of the Berlin Wall, the

Greens were best known for their political inroads in Germany. But the party lost ground after opposing reunification and it only recently has returned to the German parliament.

Nader spoke at the Green Party convention in Los Angeles in August 1996 and agreed to be its candidate. He refused campaign contributions, however, and left the organizational work to the party.

Greenback Party (1876-84)

The National Independent or Greenback-Labor Party, commonly known as the Greenback Party, was launched in Indianapolis, Ind., in November 1874 at a meeting organized by the Indiana Grange. The party grew out of the Panic of 1873, a post-Civil War economic depression, which hit farmers and industrial workers particularly hard. Currency was the basic issue of the new party, which opposed return to the gold standard and favored retention of the inflationary paper money (known as greenbacks), first introduced as an emergency measure during the Civil War.

In the 1876 presidential election the party ran Peter Cooper, a New York philanthropist, and drafted a platform that focused entirely on the currency issue. Cooper received 75,973 votes (0.9 percent of the popular vote), mainly from agrarian voters. Aided by the continuing depression, a Greenback national convention in 1878 effected the merger of the party with various labor reform groups and adopted a platform that addressed labor and currency issues. Showing voting strength in the industrial East as well as in the agrarian South and Midwest, the Greenbacks polled more than one million votes in the 1878 congressional races and won fourteen seats in the U.S. House of Representatives. This marked the high point of the party's strength.

Returning prosperity, the prospect of fusion with one of the major parties, and a split between the party's agrarian and labor leadership served to undermine the Greenback Party. In the 1880 election the party elected only eight representatives and its presidential candidate, Rep. James B. Weaver of Iowa, received 305,997 votes (3.3 percent of the popular vote), far less than party leaders expected.

The party slipped further four years later, when the Greenbacks' candidate for president, former Massachusetts governor Benjamin F. Butler, received 175,096 votes (1.7 percent of the popular vote). With the demise of the Greenbacks, most of the party's constituency moved into the Populist Party, the agrarian reform movement that swept the South and Midwest in the 1890s.

Liberal Republican Party (1872)

A faction of the Republican Party, dissatisfied with President Ulysses S. Grant's first term in office, withdrew from the party in 1872 to form a new party. Composed of party reformers, as well as anti-Grant politicians and newspaper editors, the new party focused on the corruption of the Grant administration and the need for civil service reform and for an end to the Reconstruction policy in the South.

The call for the Liberal Republican national convention came from the state party in Missouri, the birthplace of the reform movement. The convention, meeting in Cincinnati, Ohio, in May 1872, nominated Horace Greeley, editor of the *New York Tribune*, for president and Missouri governor B. Gratz Brown as his running mate. Greeley, the choice of anti-Grant politicians but suspect among reformers, was not popular among many Democrats either, who recalled his longtime criticism of the Democratic Party.

With the hope of victory in the fall election, however, the Democratic national convention, meeting in July, endorsed the Liberal Republican ticket and platform. The coalition was an unsuccessful one, as many Democrats refused to vote for Greeley. He received 2,834,761 votes (43.8 percent of the popular vote) but carried only six states and lost to Grant by more than 750,000 votes out of nearly 6.5 million cast. Greeley died shortly after the election.

Underfinanced, poorly organized and dependent on the Democrats for their success, the Liberal Republicans went out of existence after the 1872 election.

Libertarian Party (1971-)

In the brief period of four years, 1972 to 1976, the Libertarian Party leaped from a fledgling organization on the presidential ballot in only two states to the nation's largest third party. As of 1996, although its candidate ran fifth in the presidential race, the Libertarians still claimed to be the largest third party, with more than twenty-one thousand paying members nationwide.

Formed in Colorado in 1971, the party nominated John Hospers of California for president in 1972. On the ballot only in Colorado and Washington, Hospers garnered 3,673 votes (including write-in votes from other states). But he received a measure of national attention when a Republican presidential elector from Virginia, Roger MacBride, cast his electoral vote for the Libertarian presidential nominee.

MacBride's action made him a hero in Libertarian circles, and the party chose him as its 1976 standard-bearer at its August 1975 convention in New York City. MacBride had served in the Vermont legislature in the 1960s and was defeated for the Republican gubernatorial nomination in that state in 1964. In the 1970s he settled on a farm near Charlottesville, Va., and devoted himself to writing and party affairs. He was cocreator of the television series *Little House on the Prairie*.

Making a major effort in 1976, the Libertarians got on the ballot in thirty-two states, more than Eugene J. McCarthy — who ran independent of any political party — or any other third party candidate. The reward was a vote of 173,011, more than for any other minor party candidate but far below McCarthy's total and only 0.2 percent of the national vote. MacBride's strength was centered in the West; he received 5.5 percent of the vote in Alaska and 1.0 percent or more in Arizona, Hawaii and Idaho. He also ran well ahead of his national average in California (0.7 percent) and Nevada (0.8 percent). His running mate was David P. Bergland, a California lawyer.

In 1980 the Libertarian Party appeared on the ballot in all fifty states and the District of Columbia for the first time. The party also fielded about 550 candidates for other offices, a number that dwarfed other third party efforts. The party nominees, Edward E. Clark of California for president and David Koch of New York for vice president, garnered 921,299 votes or 1.1 percent of the vote nationwide. Again, the major support for the Libertarians came from Western states.

Of all minor party presidential candidates running in 1984, the Libertarians appeared on the greatest number of ballots: thirty-eight states and the District of Columbia. David Bergland, who had run in 1976 for the second slot, was the party's presidential candidate, and Jim Lewis, a Connecticut business executive, his running mate. In 1988 the Libertarian presidential and vice presidential nominees — Ron Paul and Andre V. Marrou, respectively — were on the ballot in all fifty-one jurisdictions save four and received 432,179 votes.

In 1992 Nevada real estate broker Marrou was the presidential nominee with running mate Nancy Lord, a Georgia lawyer. The pair was on the ballot in all states and the District of Columbia and had a campaign budget of $1 million. Marrou received 291,627 votes in a fourth-place finish behind Ross Perot, who stole most of the third party candidates' thunder that year. The Libertarians maintained their strong Western base, especially in California, Nevada and Hawaii, where they also ran candidates for most House seats.

In 1996 the Libertarians regained voting strength but nevertheless dropped to fifth place in the presidential race behind Ralph Nader of the new Green Party. The Libertarian candidate, financial analyst Harry Browne of Lafayette, Calif., and running mate Jo Anne Jorgensen of Greenville, S.C., drew 485,120 votes or 0.50 percent of the total. It was the party's best showing since 1980. Besides being on the presidential ballot in all states, Libertarians were congressional candidates in thirty-three states.

Individual responsibility and minimal government interference were the hallmarks of the Libertarian philosophy. The party favored repeal of laws against so-called victimless crimes — such as pornography, drug use and homosexual activity — the abolition of all federal police agencies, and the elimination of all government subsidies to private enterprise. In foreign and military affairs, the Libertarians advocated the removal of U.S. troops from abroad, a cut in the defense budget, and the emergence of the United States as a "giant Switzerland," with no international treaty obligations. Libertarians also favored repeal of legislation that they believe hindered individual or corporate action. They opposed gun control, civil rights laws, price controls on oil and gas, labor protection laws, federal welfare and poverty programs, forced busing, compulsory education, Social Security, national medical care and federal land-use restrictions.

Liberty Party (1840-48)

Born in 1839, the Liberty Party was the product of a split in the antislavery movement between a faction led by William Lloyd Garrison that favored action outside the political process and a second led by James G. Birney that proposed action within the political system through the establishment of an independent antislavery party. The Birney faction launched the Liberty Party in November 1839. The following April a national convention with delegates from six states nominated Birney for the presidency.

Although the Liberty Party was the first political party to take an antislavery position, and the only one at the time to do so, most abolitionist voters in the 1840 election supported the Democratic or Whig presidential candidates. Birney received only 6,797 votes (0.3 percent of the popular vote).

Aided by the controversy over the annexation of slaveholding Texas, the Liberty Party's popularity increased in 1844. Birney, again the party's presidential nominee, received 62,103 votes (2.3 percent of the popular vote) but again as in 1840 carried no states. The peak strength of the party was reached two years later in 1846, when in various state elections Liberty Party candidates received 74,017 votes.

In October 1847 the party nominated New Hampshire senator John P. Hale for the presidency, but his candidacy was withdrawn the following year when the Liberty Party joined the broader-based Free Soil Party. (*Free Soil Party, p. 268*)

National Democratic Party (1896)

A conservative faction in favor of the gold standard, the National Democrats bolted from the Democratic Party after the 1896 convention adopted a pro-silver platform and nominated William Jennings Bryan. With the nation in the midst of a depression and the Populists in the agrarian Midwest and South demanding monetary reform, currency was the dominant issue of the 1896 campaign. This produced a brief realignment in American politics.

The Republican Party was controlled by leaders who favored maintenance of the gold standard, a noninflationary currency. Agrarian Midwestern and Southern Democrats, reflecting a Populist philosophy, gained control of the Democratic Party in 1896 and committed it to the free coinage of silver, an inflationary currency demanded by rural elements threatened by debts. The Democrats attracted pro-silver bolters from the Republican Party, but gold standard Democrats, opposed to the Republicans' protectionist position on the tariff issue, established an independent party.

Meeting in Indianapolis in September 1896, the National Democrats adopted a platform favoring maintenance of the gold standard and selected a ticket headed by seventy-nine-year-old Illinois senator John M. Palmer.

Democratic president Grover Cleveland and leading members of his administration, repudiated by the convention that chose Bryan, supported the National Democrats. During the campaign the National Democrats encouraged conservative Democrats to vote either for the National Democratic ticket or for the Republican candidate, William McKinley. The Palmer ticket received 133,435 votes (1.0 percent of the popular vote), and McKinley defeated Bryan.

In the 1890s returning prosperity and the Spanish-American War overshadowed the currency issue, and the intense Democratic Party factionalism that produced the National Democratic Party ended.

National Republican Party (1828-32)

The Democratic-Republican Party splintered after the 1824 election into two factions. The group led by Andrew Jackson retained the name Democratic-Republicans, which eventually was shortened to Democrats; the other faction, headed by President John Quincy Adams, assumed the name National Republicans. Reflecting the belief of President Adams in the establishment of a national policy by the federal government, the new party supported a protective tariff, the Bank of the United States, federal overview of public lands and national programs of internal improvements. But Adams's belief in a strong national government contrasted with the prevailing mood of populism and states' rights.

The Adams forces controlled Congress for two years, 1825 to 1827, but as party structures formalized the National Republicans became a minority in Congress and suffered a decisive loss in the 1828 presidential election. Running for reelection, Adams was beaten by Jackson. Adams received 43.6 percent of the popular vote and carried eight states, none in the South. Henry Clay, the party's candidate against Jackson four years later, had even less success. He received only 37.4 percent of the popular vote and carried just six states, none of which, again, were in the South.

Poorly organized, with dwindling support and a heritage of defeat, the National Republicans went out of existence after the 1832 election, but their members provided the base for a new anti-Jackson party, the Whigs, which came into being in 1834. *(Whig Party, p. 278)*

National Unity Party
(Independent John B. Anderson) (1980-88)

Republican representative John B. Anderson of Illinois formed the National Unity Campaign as the vehicle for his independent presidential campaign in 1980. Anderson began

his quest for the presidency by trying to win the Republican Party nomination. But, as a liberal in a party coming under conservative control, he won no primaries and could claim only fifty-seven convention delegates by April 1980. Anderson withdrew from the Republican race and declared his independent candidacy.

Anderson focused his campaign on the need to establish a viable third party as an alternative to domination of the political scene by the Republican and Democratic parties. The National Unity Campaign platform touted the Anderson program as a "new public philosophy" — more innovative than that of the Democrats, who "cling to the policies of the New Deal," and more enlightened than that of the Republicans, who talk "incessantly about freedom, but hardly ever about justice." Generally the group took positions that were fiscally conservative and socially liberal. Anderson and his running mate, former Democratic Wisconsin governor Patrick J. Lucey, tried to appeal to Republican and Democratic voters disenchanted with their parties and to the growing bloc of voters who classified themselves as independents.

The National Unity Campaign ticket was on the ballot in all fifty states in 1980, although Anderson had to wage costly legal battles in some states to ensure that result. In the end, the party won 6.6 percent of the presidential vote, well over the 5 percent necessary to qualify for retroactive federal campaign funding.

In April 1984 Anderson announced that he would not seek the presidency in that year. He said that instead he would focus his energies on building the National Unity Party, which he established officially in December 1983. He planned to concentrate initially on running candidates at the local level. On August 28 Anderson endorsed Walter F. Mondale, the Democratic nominee for president, and his running mate, Geraldine A. Ferraro.

The National Unity Party did not run a presidential candidate in the 1988 race and by 1992 was no longer a political party.

Natural Law Party (1992-)

Improving on its first outing, the Natural Law Party claimed more than 2 million votes nationwide for its candidates in 1996. The presidential candidate, John Hagelin of Fairfield, Iowa, received 113,659 votes, almost tripling his 1992 total of 39,179. Among third parties, Hagelin's vote was fifth highest in 1996.

Hagelin was on the ballot in forty-four states. In all, the party had some four hundred candidates in federal, state and local races. Because it fulfilled the necessary requirements, Natural Law was assured automatic ballot access in ten states in the next election.

Hagelin, a Harvard-trained quantum physicist, was born in Pittsburgh in 1954 and grew up in Connecticut. He became associated with Maharishi International University in Iowa in 1983. His running mate was fellow Maharishi scientist Mike Tompkins, a Harvard graduate and specialist in crime prevention programs.

Natural Law described itself as "the fastest growing grassroots party," standing for the environment, education, economic growth, job creation and lower taxes. Despite its title, the party seemed to have little connection with the philosophic concept of natural law, which holds that some rules of society — such as the prohibition against murder — are so basic and inherent that they must be obeyed whether or not they are legislated.

Hagelin and the party advocated prevention-oriented government and meditative, tension-relieving programs "designed to bring national life into harmony with natural law."

New Alliance Party (1988-)

The New Alliance Party formed in the late 1980s to promote a combination of minority interests. Self-described as "black-led, multiracial, pro-gay and pro-socialist," the party aggressively filed lawsuits to attain ballot access. In 1988 presidential candidate Lenora B. Fulani, a New York psychologist, drew 217,219 votes nationwide for a fourth-place finish. Her best showing was in the District of Columbia, where she received more than 1 percent of the vote.

In 1992, with the party qualifying for $1.8 million in federal matching funds, Fulani ran again, this time with California teacher Maria Munoz as a running mate. Fulani campaigned for equal employment for all. "I believe that a job at a union wage is the right of all Americans," she said. The New Alliance ticket appeared on the ballot in thirty-nine states and the District of Columbia and received 73,714 votes, slightly less than 0.1 percent nationwide.

The New Alliance Party fielded no candidates in 1996.

Peace and Freedom Party (1967-)

Although founded in Michigan, the radical Peace and Freedom Party has been active largely in California — the only state where it appeared on the ballot in 1996.

From the outset, the party worked with the California Black Panther Party to oppose U.S. involvement in the Vietnam War and espouse black nationalism and other so-called New Left causes. The first Peace and Freedom nominee for president, in 1968, was Black Panther leader Eldridge Cleaver. Running with various vice-presidential candidates, Cleaver received 36,563 votes.

Cleaver's autobiographical, antiracist polemic, *Soul on Ice*, was published in 1968. After the election Cleaver, a paroled convict awaiting trial for murder, went into exile. On his return years later he became a born-again Christian.

Before the 1968 election, black activist-comedian Dick Gregory broke with the Peace and Freedom Party and set up the similarly named Freedom and Peace Party with himself as the presidential nominee. He received 47,133 votes.

After 1968 no Peace and Freedom candidate attracted significant numbers of presidential votes until 1980, when Maureen Smith and Elizabeth Barron received 18,116. In 1972, however, noted pacifist and pediatrician Benjamin Spock, the People's Party nominee, ran under the Peace and Freedom banner in California. He received 55,167 votes there and 23,589 votes in other states.

In 1974 the California Peace and Freedom Party declared itself to be socialist. In recent elections its presidential ticket has received at least ten thousand votes: 1988, Herbert Lewin and Vikki Murdock, 10,370; 1992, Ron Daniels and Asiba Tupahache, 27,961; and 1996, Marsha Feinland, 25,332.

People's Party (1971-)

Delegates from activist and peace groups established the People's Party at a November 1971 convention held in Dallas, Texas. The initial cochairmen were pediatrician Benjamin Spock and author Gore Vidal.

The People's Party first ran a presidential candidate in 1972. They chose Dr. Spock for president and black activist Julius Hobson of Washington, D.C., for vice president. Despite hopes for widespread backing from the poor and social activists, the ticket received only 78,756 votes, 0.1 percent of the national total. A total of 55,167 of those votes came from California alone.

At its convention, held in St. Louis, Missouri, August 31, 1975, the People's Party chose black civil rights activist Margaret Wright of California for president and Maggie Kuhn of Pennsylvania, a leader in the Gray Panthers movement for rights for the elderly, for vice president. Kuhn, however, declined the nomination and was replaced on the ticket by Spock.

The party platform focused on cutting the defense budget, closing tax loopholes, and making that money available for social programs. Other planks included redistribution of land and wealth, unconditional amnesty for war objectors and free health care. In her campaign, Wright stressed the necessity for active participation by citizens in the governmental process, so that institutions and programs could be run from the roots up rather than from the top down.

As in 1972 the party's main backing came in California, where it was supported by the state Peace and Freedom Party. Wright's total national vote in 1976 was 49,024, and 85.1 percent (41,731 votes) of those votes came from California. The party has not fielded presidential candidates since 1976.

People's Party-Populists (1892-1908, 1984-)

The People's Party, also called the Populist Party, was organized at a convention in Cincinnati, Ohio, in May 1891 and climaxed several decades of farm protest against deteriorating economic conditions. Chronically depressed commodity prices, caused by over-production and world competition, had spurred the politicization of farmers.

Most of the Populist leaders came from the defunct Greenback movement and Southern and Midwestern farm cooperative associations. The Populists tended to blame their problems on the most visible causes, primarily the high railroad rates and shrinking currency supply, but the platform they adopted at their first national nominating convention in 1892 was a wide-reaching one. As well as advocating the government ownership of railroads and the free coinage of silver, the Populists proposed institution of a graduated income tax and the direct election of senators. Although the Populists proposed labor reforms, such as reducing the working day to eight hours, the party never gained appreciable support among industrial workers.

The Populists ran James B. Weaver, the former Greenback candidate, as their presidential nominee in 1892. Weaver received 1,024,280 votes (8.5 percent of the popular vote) and carried five states in the Midwest and West. Increasingly tied to the silver issue, the party showed growing strength in the 1894 congressional races. Especially strong west of the Mississippi River, party congressional candidates polled nearly 1.5 million votes. After the election the Populists had six senators and seven representatives in Congress.

The Democrats surprised Populist leaders in 1896 by writing a free silver platform and nominating a free silver candidate, William Jennings Bryan. The Populists were faced with the dilemma of either endorsing Bryan and losing their party identity or running a separate ticket and splitting the free silver vote. The Populist convention endorsed Bryan but ran a separate candidate for vice president, Thomas E. Watson.

After this initial fusion with the Democrats, most Populists remained within the Democratic Party after the 1896 election. The Populist Party remained in existence, running presidential candidates until 1908, but never received more than 0.8 percent of the popular vote. The party did not expand its voter appeal beyond an agrarian reform movement, but many of its proposals, particularly in the areas of government and electoral reform, were espoused by progressive politicians in the early 20th century and enacted into law.

After being absent from the political scene for nearly three-quarters of a century, the Populist Party revived in early 1984 to place former Olympic pole vaulter Bob Richards as a candidate on the presidential ballot in fourteen states. Backers of the new party advocated wiping out the Federal Reserve System, repealing the federal income tax and protecting U.S. industry from imports. Richards received 66,336 votes. In 1988 the Populists nominated David Duke, a former member of the Ku Klux Klan, who received 47,047 votes nationwide.

In 1992 the Populist Party nominated former Green Beret commander James "Bo" Gritz for president and Cyril Minett for vice president. On the ballot as the America First Party in eighteen states, the Populists received 107,014 votes or 0.1 percent nationwide. Gritz performed especially well in the West, where he received 3.8 percent of the vote in Utah and 2.1 percent in Idaho.

The 1996 America First candidate, Ralph Forbes of Arkansas, received 932 votes.

Progressive Party-Bull Moose (1912)

A split in Republican ranks, spurred by the bitter personal and ideological dispute between President William Howard Taft (1909-13) and former president Theodore Roosevelt (1901-09), resulted in the withdrawal of the Roosevelt forces from the Republican Party after the June 1912 convention and the creation of the Progressive Party two months later. The new party was known popularly as the Bull Moose Party, a name resulting from Roosevelt's assertion early in the campaign that he felt as fit as a bull moose. While the Taft-Roosevelt split was the immediate reason for the new party, the Bull Moosers were an outgrowth of the progressive movement that was a powerful force in both major parties in the early years of the 20th century.

Although in 1908 Roosevelt had handpicked Taft as his successor, his disillusionment with Taft's conservative philosophy came quickly, and with the support of progressive Republicans Roosevelt challenged the incumbent for the 1912 Republican presidential nomination. Roosevelt outpolled Taft in the presidential primary states. Taft nevertheless won the nomination with nearly solid support in the South and among party conservatives, providing the narrow majority of delegates that enabled him to win the bulk of the key credentials challenges.

Although few Republican politicians followed Roosevelt in his bolt, the new party demonstrated a popular base at its convention in Chicago in August 1912. Thousands of delegates, basically middle- and upper-class reformers from small towns and cities, attended the convention that launched the party and nominated Roosevelt for president and California governor Hiram Johnson as his running mate. Roosevelt appeared in person to deliver his "Confession of Faith," a speech detailing his nationalistic philosophy and progressive reform ideas. The Bull Moose platform reflected key tenets of the Progressive movement, calling for more extensive government antitrust action and for labor, social, government and electoral reform.

Roosevelt was wounded in an assassination attempt while campaigning in Milwaukee, Wis., in October, but he finished the campaign. In the general election Roosevelt received more than 4 million votes (27.4 percent of the popular vote) and carried six states. His percentage of the vote was the highest ever received by a third party candidate in American history, but his candidacy split the Republican vote and enabled the Democrats' nominee, Woodrow Wilson, to win the election. The Progressive Party had minimal success at the state and local levels, winning thirteen House seats but electing no senators or governors.

Roosevelt declined the Progressive nomination in 1916 and endorsed the Republican candidate, Charles Evans Hughes. With the defection of its leader, the decline of the progressive movement, and the lack of an effective party organization, the Bull Moose Party ceased to exist.

Progressive Party (1924)

Like the Bull Moose Party of Theodore Roosevelt, the Progressive Party that emerged in the mid-1920s was a reform effort led by a Republican. Wisconsin senator Robert M. La Follette led the new Progressive Party, a separate entity from the Bull Moosers, which, unlike the middle- and upper-class Roosevelt party of the previous decade, had its greatest appeal among farmers and organized labor.

The La Follette Progressive Party grew out of the Conference for Progressive Political Action (CPPA), a coalition of railway union leaders and a remnant of the Bull Moose effort that was formed in 1922. The Socialist Party joined the coalition the following year. Throughout 1923 the Socialists and labor unions argued over whether their coalition should form a third party, with the Socialists in favor and the labor unions against it. It was finally decided to run an independent presidential candidate, La Follette, in the 1924 election but not to field candidates at the state and local levels. La Follette was given the power to choose his running mate and selected Montana senator Burton K. Wheeler, a Democrat.

Opposition to corporate monopolies was the major issue of the La Follette campaign, although the party advocated various other reforms, particularly aimed at farmers and workers, which were proposed earlier by either the Populists or Bull Moosers. But the Progressive Party itself was a major issue in the 1924 campaign, as the Republicans attacked the alleged radicalism of the party.

Although La Follette had its endorsement, the American Federation of Labor (AFL) provided minimal support. The basic strength of the Progressives, like that of the Populists in the 1890s, derived from agrarian voters west of the Mississippi River. La Follette received 4,832,532 votes (16.6 percent of the popular vote) but carried just one state, his native Wisconsin. When La Follette died in 1925, the party collapsed as a national force. It was revived by La Follette's sons on a statewide level in Wisconsin in the mid-1930s.

Progressive Party (1948)

Henry A. Wallace's Progressive Party resulted from the dissatisfaction of liberal elements in the Democratic Party with the leadership of President Harry S. Truman, particularly in the realm of foreign policy. The Progressive Party was one of two bolting groups from the Democratic Party in 1948; conservative Southern elements withdrew to form the States' Rights Party.

Henry Wallace, the founder of the Progressive Party, was secretary of agriculture, vice president and finally secretary of commerce under President Franklin Roosevelt. He carried the reputation of one of the most liberal idealists in the Roosevelt administration. Fired from the Truman cabinet in 1946 after breaking with administration policy and publicly advocating peaceful coexistence with the Soviet Union, Wallace began to consider the idea of a liberal third party candidacy. Supported by the American Labor Party, the Progressive Citizens of America and other progressive organizations in California and Illinois, Wallace announced his third party candidacy in December 1947.

The Progressive Party was launched formally the following July at a convention in Philadelphia, which ratified the selection of Wallace for president and Sen. Glen H. Taylor, D-Idaho, as his running mate. The party adopted a platform that emphasized foreign policy — opposing the Cold War anticommunism of the Truman administration and specifically urging abandonment of the Truman Doctrine and the Marshall Plan. These measures were designed to contain the spread of communism and bolster noncommunist nations. On domestic issues the Progressives stressed humanitarian concerns and equal rights for both sexes and all races.

Minority groups — women, youth, African Americans, Jews, Hispanic-Americans — were active in the new party, but the openness of the Progressives brought Wallace a damaging endorsement from the Communist Party. Believing the two parties could work together, Wallace accepted the endorsement while characterizing his philosophy as "progressive capitalism."

In 1948 the Progressives appeared on the presidential ballot in forty-five states, but the Communist endorsement helped keep the party on the defensive the entire campaign. In the November election Wallace received only 1,157,326 votes (2.4 percent of the national popular vote), with nearly half of the votes from the state of New York. Not only were the Progressives unable to carry a single state, but in spite of their defection from the Democratic Party President Truman won reelection. The Progressives had poor results in the congressional races, failing to elect one representative or senator.

The Progressive Party's opposition to the Korean War in 1950 drove many moderate elements out of the party, including Henry Wallace. The party ran a national ticket in 1952, but received only 140,023 votes nationwide or 0.2 percent of the national popular vote. The party crumbled completely after the election.

Prohibition Party (1869-)

The Prohibition Party existed longer than any third party in American history. It was formed in September 1869 at a convention in Chicago, which attracted approximately five hundred delegates from twenty states. For the first time in U.S. politics, women had equal status with men as delegates. By a narrow majority the convention decided to form an independent party, and three years later the new party put forth its first national ticket. The party's basic goal was enactment of laws prohibiting the manufacture and sale of intoxicating liquor, but its platforms have included other reform proposals. The 1872 Prohibition Party platform included the first women's suffrage plank.

For all but one election between 1884 and 1916, the party's presidential candidate received at least 1.0 percent of the popular vote. The party's best showing came in 1892, when its presidential nominee, John Bidwell, received 270,770 votes (2.2 percent of the popular vote). The party has run a national ticket in every presidential election since 1872, but its candidates have never carried a single state. After the 1976 election the Prohibition Party changed its name to the National Statesman Party, and its 1980 candidate registered using that party name. The 1984 candidate, Earl F. Dodge of Colorado, emphasized that his party — on the ballots once again as Prohibitionists — no longer focused on a single issue: the party backed religious freedom and an antiabortion amendment. Dodge again was the party's standard-bearer in 1988, 1992 and 1996. In 1992 the

party could muster only 961 votes nationwide. It did slightly better in 1996, receiving 1,298 votes. The temperance movement succeeded in gaining prohibition legislation in numerous states in the late nineteenth and early twentieth centuries, and its efforts were capped in 1919 by passage of national prohibition legislation (the 18th Amendment to the U.S. Constitution, repealed fourteen years later by the 21st Amendment). The achievements of the temperance movement were due as much to independent organizations, such as the Women's Christian Temperance Union (WCTU) and the Anti-Saloon League, as to the Prohibition Party, which had limited success at the polls. These organizations allowed active Democrats and Republicans to remain in their parties while working for prohibition.

Reform Party (1995-)

The Reform Party emerged almost full grown from independent H. Ross Perot's self-financed presidential candidacy of 1992. Unlike that campaign, in which the Dallas billionaire spurned public funding to avoid federal campaign spending limits, the Reform Party effort of 1996 qualified for federal funding and went along with the limitations that acceptance of the money entailed. By garnering more than 5 percent of the 1992 presidential vote, Perot qualified in 1996 for some $30 million, less than half the amount he spent from his own pocket four years earlier. *(United We Stand America, p. 277.)*

Perot was challenged for the Reform Party nomination by Richard D. Lamm, a former Democratic governor of Colorado who had shown a willingness to risk voter displeasure. Lamm had called, for example, for deep cuts in Medicare, the popular health care program for the elderly.

Perot defeated Lamm in an unusual two-stage procedure, with a preliminary vote after nominating speeches at a convention in Long Beach, Calif., followed by a mail and electronic vote with the winner announced a week later in Valley Forge, Pa. Ballots had been sent to 1.3 million voters who were registered party members or signers of its ballot access petitions.

Perot again was on the ballot in all states. He chose as his running mate Pat Choate, a native Texan and economist who had coached Perot in his unsuccessful fight against NAFTA (the North American Free Trade Agreement). The Reform Party also had congressional candidates in ten states.

Locked out of the presidential debates, Perot spent much of his campaign money on television "infomercials" espousing the party's principles. Besides a balanced budget these included higher ethical standards for the White House and Congress, campaign and elections reforms, a new tax system and lobbying restrictions.

Even with the restricted budget, Perot again placed third in the national election after the two major party candidates. However, his 8,085,285 votes, 8.4 percent of the total, came to less than half of his 1992 achievement of 18.9 percent, a third party figure surpassed in the 20th century only by former president Theodore Roosevelt and his Bull Moose candidacy of 1912. Perot had his best showing in Maine, where he received 14.2 percent of the vote. He won no electoral votes.

At a postelection convention in Nashville in early 1997 the Reform Party began the task of building a permanent new political party rivaling the two major parties. An unresolved issue was the future role of Perot, with many stalwarts arguing that the party needed to emerge from what Lamm termed Perot's "dominating shadow." Denying that

Reform had become "the party of personality," Perot nevertheless declined to rule out another try for the presidency in 2000. The Nashville convention ended with Perot supporters still firmly in control of the Reform Party.

Republican Party (1854-)

Born in 1854 in the upper Midwest, the Republican Party grew out of the antislavery forces' bitter dissatisfaction with the Kansas-Nebraska Act. The act overturned earlier legislation (the Missouri Compromise of 1820 and the Compromise of 1850), limiting the extension of slavery into the territories, and instituted the concept of popular sovereignty, by which each territory decided its position on slavery. While historians generally credit residents of Ripon, Wis., with holding the party's first organizational meeting in March 1854 and citizens of Jackson, Mich., with running the party's first electoral ticket in July 1854, the birth of the party was nearly simultaneous in many communities throughout the Northern states. The volatile slavery issue was the catalyst that brought the party's birth, but the political vacuum caused by the decline of the Whigs and the failure of the Know-Nothing and Free Soil parties to gain a stable national following allowed the Republicans to grow with dramatic rapidity.

The constituency of the new party was limited to the Northern states, since opposition to slavery was the basic issue of the Republicans. But the party did attract diverse elements in the political spectrum — former Whigs, Know-Nothings, Free Soilers and dissident Democrats.

In its first year the party took the name Republican. Horace Greeley is credited with initiating the name in a June 1854 issue of his newspaper, the *New York Tribune.* In pushing the name, he referred to the Jeffersonian Republicans of the early 19th century and Henry Clay's National Republican Party of the 1830s, an early rival of the Democrats.

The Republicans ran candidates throughout the North in 1854 and, in combination with other candidates opposed to the Kansas-Nebraska Act, won a majority in the House of Representatives. Two years later the Republicans ran their first national ticket. Although their presidential candidate, John C. Fremont, did not win, he polled one-third of the vote in a three-man race and carried eleven states. The Republicans were established as a major party.

While the party was built on the slavery question, the Republicans were far from a one-issue party. They presented a nationalistic platform with appeal to business and commercial interests as well as rural antislavery elements. The Republicans proposed legislation for homesteading (free land), the construction of a transcontinental railroad, and the institution of a protective tariff.

Firmly established by the late 1850s, the Republican Party benefited from the increasing sectional factionalism in the Democratic Party over the slavery issue. In 1858 the party won control of the House of Representatives. Two years later, with Abraham Lincoln as its candidate, the Republicans won the White House and retained control of the House. Lincoln, benefiting from a sectional split in the Democratic Party, won an unusual four-way race and captured the presidency with 39.9 percent of the popular, vote.

Lincoln was a wartime president, and his success in preserving the Union helped the party for the next generation. After the Civil War the Republicans projected a patriotic image, which, coupled with the party's belief in national expansion and limited federal involvement in the free enterprise system, helped make it the dominant party over the next three-quarters of a century. For most of the seventy-two years between 1860 and 1932, the Republicans were the majority party, occupying the White House for fifty-six years and controlling the Senate for sixty years and the House for fifty years. Except for the South, where the party basically was limited to the small number of black voters, the Republicans were strong throughout the nation.

Congressional leaders exercised the dominant power during this period of Republican hegemony. Presidents had little success in challenging the authority wielded by the GOP's congressional leadership.

Just as the party vaulted to power on the divisive slavery issue, its history was altered by another traumatic event — the Great Depression, which began in 1929. As the incumbent party during the economic collapse, the Republicans suffered the political blame; their fall from power was rapid. In 1928 the Republican presidential candidate (Herbert Hoover) carried forty states; in 1936, during Franklin D. Roosevelt's New Deal days, the Republican standard-bearer (Alfred M. Landon) won just two states. In 1928 the party held a clear majority of seats in both the House and Senate, 267 and 56 respectively; but eight years later the party's numbers had shrunk dramatically, the Republicans holding only 89 seats in the House and 17 in the Senate.

The party eventually made a comeback from this low point but remained the minority party in Congress through the 1980 elections. Between 1932 and 1988 the Republicans won seven of fifteen presidential elections but controlled both chambers of Congress for just four years.

While the Republicans struggled to find the formula for a new majority, the party's basic conservatism made it increasingly appealing, especially in presidential races, to segments of the electorate that previously were firm parts of the Democratic coalition — notably blue-collar workers and the once-Democratic South. Beginning in 1952 the party was able to attract a winning combination when it ran presidential candidates with a moderate conservative image, such as Dwight D. Eisenhower, Richard Nixon or Ronald Reagan. However, the GOP enjoyed less success at the state and local levels where Democratic majorities, established during the New Deal, remained largely intact.

The Republican difficulties in establishing a new majority were compounded after the 1972 election by the Watergate scandal, which brought down the Nixon administration. Gerald R. Ford, who became president after Nixon resigned August 9, 1974, lost his 1976 election bid to former Georgia governor Jimmy Carter, giving the Democrats control of the White House as well as Congress.

Republican fortunes improved dramatically in 1980 when former California governor Reagan won a landslide electoral vote victory over Carter. Republicans also took control of the Senate for the first time in twenty-eight years and made substantial gains in the House. Although a resurgence of Democratic political strength in the 1982 midterm elections swept more Democrats into the House, the Republicans retained control of the Senate.

In a Gallup poll taken shortly before the 1984 national elections, 28 percent of the respondents identified themselves as Republicans. Although Republicans remained the minority party (the Democrats had captured 42 percent of the voters in this survey), the party clearly was recovering from the lows it had experienced during the Watergate era. Not since the Eisenhower presidency had more voters identified themselves as Republicans. The party enjoyed a second landslide victory for Reagan, gaining even more strength and making Reagan one of the most popular presidents of the 20th century.

But the Republicans' cycle of misfortune repeated itself in late 1986. Congressional elections saw the Democrats regain control of the Senate — despite a nationwide campaign by Reagan to promote Republican senatorial candidates — giving the Democrats full control of Congress and the GOP a sizable obstacle in policy making. A few weeks later the Iran-contra scandal broke. A special prosecutor was appointed, and congressional investigations, including months of public hearings, lasted for almost all of 1987.

The setback to the party, if any, did not keep Reagan's vice president, George Bush, from winning big in 1988 — 53.4 percent of the vote and 426 electoral votes. Bush became the first sitting vice president to win the White House since Martin Van Buren in 1836. Bush also was the first candidate since John F. Kennedy to win the presidential election while his party lost seats in the House. His inability to carry others into office may have been partly due to his message, which was essentially a call to "stay the course."

In seeking a second term in 1992, Bush was burdened with an economy slowly recovering from the recession of 1990-91. Bush took only 37.4 percent of the nationwide vote and received 168 electoral votes. But while the Democrats regained the White House after twelve years, the Republicans posted victories elsewhere, gaining ten seats in the House in 1992 and one Senate seat and two gubernatorial seats in 1993. In 1994 the Democratic setbacks turned into a rout, with the GOP taking control of both houses of Congress. Grateful House Republicans elected as Speaker Newt Gingrich of Georgia, who had engineered their victory with a ten-point "Contract with America" setting forth conservative goals for the GOP Congress. For the next two years the Republican Congress tried to dismantle decades-old social programs, with repercussions for both parties in the following presidential election.

As the "out" party in 1996, the Republicans faced a wide-open race for its presidential nomination. After a shaky start in which he lost the New Hampshire primary to columnist Pat Buchanan, Senate majority leader Robert J. Dole of Kansas emerged as the front-runner among several major candidates. Despite some questions about his age (at seventy-three he would have been the oldest new president), Dole clinched the nomination and launched an energetic campaign against the incumbent Clinton. Dole chose an ex-rival as his running mate, former House member Jack F. Kemp of New York.

Clinton nevertheless stayed far ahead in the preelection polls. The president appeared to benefit from a public opinion backlash against the Republican Congress for its attacks on cherished Democratic programs. Although he narrowed the expected margin of defeat, Dole lost to Clinton with 39.2 million votes or 40.7 percent of the total. He won 159 electoral votes.

Despite the voters' reservations about Congress, and particularly House Speaker Newt Gingrich of Georgia, the GOP kept control of Congress while losing nine seats in the House but gaining two in the Senate. Under an ethics cloud for which he was later reprimanded, Gingrich in 1997 nevertheless became the first Republican Speaker reelected since 1929.

Socialist Labor Party (1888-)

The Socialist Labor Party, the first national socialist party in the United States, ranks second only to the Prohibitionists among third parties in longevity. Formed in 1874 by elements of the Socialist International in New York, it was first known as the Social Democratic Workingmen's Party. In

1877 the group adopted the name Socialist Labor Party. Throughout the 1880s the party worked in concert with other left-wing third parties, including the Greenbacks.

The Socialist Labor Party ran national tickets in every presidential election from 1892 through 1976. The party collected its highest proportion of the national vote in 1896, when its candidate received 36,356 votes (0.3 percent of the popular vote).

Led by the autocratic Daniel DeLeon (1852-1914), a former Columbia University law lecturer, the Socialist Labor Party became increasingly militant and made its best showing in local races in 1898. But DeLeon's insistence on rigid party discipline and his opposition to the organized labor movement created a feeling of alienation among many members. Moderate elements bolted from the party, joining the Socialist Party of Eugene V. Debs, which formed in 1901.

The Socialist Labor Party continued as a small, tightly organized far-left group bound to DeLeon's uncompromising belief in revolution. As late as 1976 the party advocated direct worker action to take over control of production and claimed five thousand members nationwide.

Socialist Party (1901-)

The Socialist Party was born officially in July 1901 at a convention in Indianapolis, Indiana, which joined together former American Railway Union president Eugene V. Debs' Social Democratic Party with a moderate faction of the Socialist Labor Party. The two groups had begun discussions a year before and in the 1900 presidential campaign jointly supported a ticket headed by Debs that received 86,935 votes (0.6 percent of the popular vote).

The 1901 unity convention identified the new Socialist Party with the working class and described the party's goal as "collective ownership . . . of the means of production and distribution." The party grew rapidly in the early 20th century, reaching a peak membership of approximately 118,000 in 1912. That year also proved to be the party's best at the polls. Debs, a presidential candidate five times between 1900 and 1920, received 900,369 votes (6.0 percent of the popular vote). The Socialists elected 1,200 candidates to local offices, including seventy-nine candidates for mayor.

With the outbreak of World War I, the party became a vehicle for antiwar protest. In 1917 pacifist Socialists converted a number of mayoral elections into referendums on the war, winning 34 percent of the vote in Chicago, more than 25 percent in Buffalo and 22 percent in New York City.

The following year Debs was convicted of sedition for making an antiwar speech and was sentenced to a term in the Atlanta federal penitentiary, from which he ran for president in 1920 and received 915,490 votes (3.4 percent of the popular vote).

Four years later the Socialists endorsed Wisconsin senator Robert M. La Follette's presidential candidacy, an unsuccessful attempt to establish a farm-labor coalition. In 1928 the Socialists resumed running a presidential ticket. With the death of Debs in 1926, the party selected Norman Thomas, a former minister and social worker, to be the party's standard-bearer for the next six elections. The Depression brought a brief surge for the Socialists in 1932, with Thomas polling 884,649 votes (2.2 percent of the popular vote).

But 1932 proved to be only a temporary revival for the Socialists. Roosevelt's New Deal stole their thunder, and the Socialist Party failed to attract even one-half of 1 percent of the vote in any succeeding presidential election. In 1976 the party ran its first presidential ticket in two decades. The candidates received 6,038 votes, 0.01 percent of the popular vote.

Although Socialist Party candidates received a few more votes in the 1980 elections, 6,898, their percentage share of the total vote remained 0.01 percent. The old-line Socialist Party faded again from the presidential candidate scene in 1984 but reappeared in 1988, 1992 and 1996. The Socialist candidates, Willa Kenoyer and Ron Ehrenreich in 1988 and J. Quinn Brisben and Barbara Garson in 1992, however, experienced a precipitous drop in support, receiving only 3,882 nationwide votes in 1988 and 3,057 in 1992. The 1996 candidate, Mary Cal Hollis of Colorado, did slightly better with 4,764 votes.

Socialist Workers Party (1938-)

The Socialist Workers Party was formed in 1938 by followers of the Russian revolutionary Leon Trotsky. Originally a faction within the U.S. Communist Party, the Trotskyites were expelled in 1936 on instructions from Soviet leader Joseph Stalin. A brief Trotskyite coalition with the Socialist Party ended in 1938 when the dissidents decided to organize independently as the Socialist Workers Party. Through its youth arm, the Young Socialist Alliance, the Socialist Workers Party was active in the anti-Vietnam War movement and contributed activists to civil rights protests.

Since 1948 the party has run a presidential candidate, but its entries have never received more than 0.1 percent of the popular vote. In 1992 presidential candidate James Warren was on the ballot in thirteen states and the District of Columbia and drew 23,096 votes nationwide. The party's 1996 candidate, James Harris of Georgia, received 8,463 votes.

Southern Democrats (1860)

Agitation over the slavery issue, building for a generation, reached a climax in 1860 and produced a sectional split in the Democratic Party. Throughout the mid-19th century the Democrats had remained unified by supporting the various pieces of compromise legislation that both protected slavery in the Southern states and endorsed the policy of popular sovereignty in the territories. But in 1860 Southern Democrats wanted the Democratic convention (meeting in Charleston, S.C.) to insert a plank specifically protecting slavery in the territories. When their plank was defeated, delegates from most of the Southern states walked out.

The Charleston convention stalemated over a presidential choice and, after recessing for six weeks, reconvened in Baltimore, where Illinois senator Stephen A. Douglas was nominated. Most of the Southern delegates, plus those from California and Oregon, bolted the convention and nominated their own ticket in a rump convention held after Douglas's selection. Vice President John C. Breckinridge of Kentucky was chosen for president, and Joseph Lane, a states' rights advocate from Oregon, was selected as his running mate. A platform was adopted that recognized the right of slavery to exist in the territories. After the formation of the two sectional tickets, two separate Democratic national committees operated in Washington, D.C., to oversee their campaigns.

Although in the 1860 election the combined Douglas-Breckinridge vote comprised a majority of the ballots cast, the split in Democratic ranks was a boon to the campaign of the Republican candidate, Abraham Lincoln, who won with a plurality of the vote. The Breckinridge ticket received 848,019 votes (18.1 percent of the popular vote) and carried nine Southern and Border states.

During the Civil War the Southern Democrats provided much of the leadership for the Confederate government, including its president, Jefferson Davis. At the end of the conflict the Southern Democrats made no attempt to continue as a separate sectional entity and rejoined the national Democratic Party.

States' Rights Democratic Party (1948)

The States' Rights Democratic Party was a conservative Southern faction that bolted from the Democrats in 1948. The immediate reason for the new party, popularly known as the Dixiecrats, was dissatisfaction with President Harry Truman's civil rights program. But the Dixiecrat effort to maintain a segregated way of life was also an attempt to demonstrate the political power of the 20th century Southern Democrats and to reestablish their importance in the Democratic Party.

The Mississippi Democratic Party's state executive committee met in Jackson in May 1948 to lay the groundwork for the Dixiecrat secession. The meeting called for a bolt by Southern delegates if the Democratic National Convention endorsed Truman's civil rights program. When the convention did approve a strong civil rights plank, the entire Mississippi delegation and half the Alabama delegation left the convention. Gov. Fielding L. Wright of Mississippi invited all anti-Truman delegates to meet in Birmingham three days after the close of the Democratic convention to select a states' rights ticket.

Most Southern Democrats with something at stake — national prominence, seniority in Congress, patronage privileges — shunned the new Dixiecrat Party. The party's leaders came from the ranks of Southern governors and other state and local officials. The Birmingham convention chose two governors to lead the party: J. Strom Thurmond of South Carolina for president and Wright of Mississippi for vice president.

Other than the presidential ticket, the Dixiecrats did not run candidates for any office. Rather than try to develop an independent party organization, the Dixiecrats, whenever possible, used existing Democratic Party apparatus.

The party was on the ballot in only one state outside the South and in the November election received only 1,157,326 votes (2.4 percent of the popular vote). The Thurmond ticket carried four Deep South states where it ran under the Democratic Party label, but it failed in its basic objective to prevent the reelection of President Truman.

After the election the party ceased to exist almost as abruptly as it had begun, with most of its members returning to the Democratic Party. In a statement upon reentering the Democratic fold, Thurmond characterized the Dixiecrat episode as "a fight within our family." (While serving in the U.S. Senate sixteen years later, Thurmond switched to the Republican Party.)

Union Party (1936)

Advocating more radical economic measures in light of the Great Depression, several early supporters of President Franklin D. Roosevelt broke with him and ran their own ticket in 1936 under the Union Party label. Largely an outgrowth of the Rev. Charles E. Coughlin's National Union for Social Justice, the new party also had the support of Dr. Francis E. Townsend, leader of a movement for government-supported old-age pensions, and Gerald L. K. Smith, self-appointed heir of Louisiana senator Huey P. Long's share-the-wealth program.

Father Coughlin was the keystone of the Union Party and was instrumental in choosing its presidential ticket in June 1936 — Rep. William Lemke, R-N.D., for president and Thomas O'Brien, a Massachusetts railroad union lawyer, for vice president. The new party did not hold a convention. The party's platform reportedly was written by Coughlin, Lemke and O'Brien and was similar to the program espoused by Coughlin's National Union. Among the features of the Union Party platform were proposals for banking and currency reform, a guaranteed income for workers, restrictions on wealth, and an isolationist foreign policy.

Lacking organization and finances during the campaign, the party further suffered from the increasingly violent and often anti-Semitic tone of the oratory of both Coughlin and Smith.

The Union Party failed miserably in its primary goal of defeating Roosevelt. Roosevelt won a landslide victory and the Lemke ticket received only 892,267 votes (2 percent of the popular vote). The party standard-bearers were unable to carry a single state, and the Union Party's candidates for the House and Senate all were defeated. The party continued on a local level until it was finally dissolved in 1939.

United We Stand America
(Independent H. Ross Perot) (1992-)

The presidential campaign of Texas billionaire H. Ross Perot in 1992 drew the highest vote share of any independent or third party candidate in eighty years. Relying heavily on his wealth and on grass-roots volunteer efforts to get his name on the ballot in all fifty states and the District of Columbia, Perot received 19,741,657 votes or 18.9 percent of the nationwide vote. He did not win any sizable constituency or receive any electoral votes, but he drew a respectable 10 percent to 30 percent in popular voting across the nation. He ran best in the West, New England, the Plains states, around his Dallas base, in economically distressed parts of the Rust Belt and in high-growth districts on Florida's coasts.

Perot, who announced the possibility of his candidacy in February 1992, ran his early unofficial campaign mainly on one issue — eliminating the federal deficit. He had the luxury of funding his entire campaign, which included buying huge amounts of television time. Drawing on the disenchantment of voters, Perot and his folksy, no-nonsense approach to government reform struck a populist chord. But he also demonstrated his quirkiness by bizarrely withdrawing from the presidential race in mid-July and then reversing himself and reentering in October. He chose as his running mate retired admiral James B. Stockdale, who as a navy flier had been a prisoner during much of the Vietnam War.

United We Stand America (UWSA), formed from the ashes of Perot's candidacy, did not bill itself as an official political party. Promoting itself instead as a nonpartisan educational organization, UWSA called for a balanced budget, government reform and health care reform. While the group's leaders did not endorse candidates or offer them financial assistance, the leaders attempted to influence elections and hold incumbents accountable through election forums and voter guides ranking candidates on selected issues.

After the election Ross Perot, rather than UWSA, commanded considerable attention on Capitol Hill. From marshaling grass-roots support for congressional reform to unsuccessfully opposing the North American Free Trade Agreement (NAFTA), Perot remained highly visible on the political scene. Democrats and Republicans were unable to co-opt his following as they had those of major third party movements in the past. And Perot continued to use his supporters' anger with government and the political process to sustain himself as an independent political force. In the fall of 1995 Perot created a full-fledged political party, the

Reform Party, and ran as its nominee in a campaign financed with federal funds. *(Reform Party, p. 273.)*

U.S. Labor Party
(Independent Lyndon LaRouche) (1973-)

Formed in 1973 as the political arm of the National Caucus of Labor Committees (NCLC), the U.S. Labor Party made its debut in national politics in 1976. The NCLC, a Marxist group, was organized in 1968 by splinters of the radical movements of the 1960s. New Yorker Lyndon LaRouche, the party's chairman and a self-taught economist who worked in the management and computer fields, became its 1976 presidential nominee and Wayne Evans, a Detroit steelworker, his running mate.

The party directed much of its fire at the Rockefeller family. It charged that banks controlled by the Rockefellers were strangling the U.S. and world economies. In an apocalyptic vein, the party predicted a world monetary collapse by election day and the destruction of the country by thermonuclear war by the summer of 1977.

LaRouche's party developed a reputation for harassment because of its shouted interruptions and demonstrations against its political foes, including the Communist Party and the United Auto Workers. It accused some left-wing organizations and individuals, such as linguist Noam Chomsky and Marcus Raskin and his Institute for Policy Studies, of conspiring with the Rockefellers and the Central Intelligence Agency.

During the 1976 campaign, LaRouche was more critical of challenger Jimmy Carter than President Gerald R. Ford. He depicted Ford as a well-meaning man out of his depth in the presidency, but Carter as a pawn of nuclear war advocates and a disgracefully unqualified presidential candidate. LaRouche captured only 40,043 votes, less than 0.1 percent of the national vote. He was on the ballot in twenty-three states and the District of Columbia.

Although the U.S. Labor Party did not run a presidential candidate in the 1980 election, LaRouche ran a strident campaign — as a Democrat. By this time, LaRouche's politics had shifted to the right, and his speeches were fraught with warnings of conspiracy.

He continued his crusade in 1984 but as an "independent Democrat," dismissing Democratic presidential nominee Walter F. Mondale as an "agent of Soviet influence." LaRouche received 78,807 votes, or 0.1 percent of the vote.

In 1988 LaRouche again attempted to run as a Democrat but, failing the nomination, garnered 25,562 votes under the banner of the National Economic Recovery Party. On December 16, 1988, LaRouche and six of his associates were convicted on 47 counts of mail fraud and conspiracy to commit mail fraud. LaRouche was sentenced to fifteen years in prison.

In 1992 the unflagging LaRouche ran again for president from his jail cell. As a convicted felon, he no longer had the right to vote himself. LaRouche ran as an independent although his name appeared on several state ballots under various party names, including Economic Recovery. His supporters, experienced in winning ballot access, placed him on the ballot in seventeen states and the District of Columbia. He received 26,333 votes nationwide. In 1996 LaRouche's name disappeared from general election ballots.

U.S. Taxpayers Party (1992-)

Making its second appearance in a presidential election, the U.S. Taxpayers Party was on the ballot in thirty-nine states in 1996. Its nominee, Howard Phillips of Vienna, Va., drew 184,359 votes or almost five times more than his 1992 total of 43,434. Of the eighteen minor parties receiving at least 750 votes in 1996, the Taxpayers Party received the fourth highest total.

Phillips, longtime chairman of the Conservative Caucus, founded the party to counter what he perceived to be a left-to-center movement by the Republican Party under George Bush. Failing to recruit rightist icons such as Pat Buchanan, Oliver North or Jesse Helms to be the party's nominee, Phillips ran himself as its standard bearer. In addition to taxes the party opposed welfare, abortion and affirmative action.

Whig Party (1834-56)

Organized in 1834 during the administration of President Andrew Jackson, the Whig Party was an amalgam of forces opposed to Jackson administration policies. Even the name "Whig" was symbolic of the intense anti-Jackson feeling among the party's adherents. The name was taken from the earlier British Whig Party, founded in the 17th century in opposition to the tyranny of the Stuart monarchs. Likewise, the term was popular during the American Revolution, as the colonists opposed what they considered the tyranny of King George III. The new Whig Party was opposed to "King Andrew," the Whig characterization of President Jackson and his strong executive actions.

Southerners, enraged over Jackson's stand against states' rights in the South Carolina nullification dispute, joined the coalition early. Then came businessmen, merchants and conservatives, shocked and fearful of Jackson's war on the Bank of the United States. This group, basically a remnant of the National Republican Party, espoused Henry Clay's American Plan, a program of federal action to aid the economy and tie together the sections of the country. The plan included tariff protection for business, a national bank, public works and distribution to the states of money received for the sale of public lands. The Clay plan became the basis for the Whigs' nationalistic economic program.

Another influential group joining the Whig coalition was the Anti-Masons, an egalitarian movement strong in parts of New England, New York and Pennsylvania.

Throughout its life, the Whig Party was plagued by factionalism and disunity. In 1836, the first presidential election in which the Whigs took part, the party had no national presidential candidate. Rather, three different candidates ran in different parts of the country — Gen. William Henry Harrison, Hugh L. White and Daniel Webster — each hoping to carry Whig electors in states where they were popular. Then the Whig electors, if a majority, could combine in the electoral college on one candidate or, if that proved impossible, throw the election into the House. But Van Buren, the Democratic nominee, won a majority of the electors.

Befitting their lack of unity, the Whigs adopted no platform in 1840 and nominated Harrison, a military hero, for the presidency. His campaign, emphasizing an apocryphal log cabin and hard cider home life in Ohio, resulted in a landslide victory.

But Harrison died only a month after taking office (April 4, 1841). The new president, John Tyler of Virginia, proceeded to veto most elements of the Whig economic program, including the tariff and reestablishment of the national bank. Given Tyler's well-known states' rights posi-

tion — ignored by the Whigs in 1840 when they capitalized on his Southern appeal — the vetoes were inevitable. The cabinet resigned in outrage, and for the rest of his term Tyler remained a president without a party. Since his first two years in office were the only ones in which the Whigs controlled the presidency and both houses of Congress, Tyler's vetoes spoiled the only chance the Whigs ever had of implementing their program.

The Whigs won the White House for the second and last time in 1848 by running another military hero, Gen. Zachary Taylor. Like Harrison, Taylor was a nonideological candidate who died in office. He was succeeded by Vice President Millard Fillmore.

The development of the slavery question in the 1840s and its intensification in the 1850s proved to be the death knell for the Whig Party. A party containing antislavery New Englanders and Southern plantation owners was simply unable to bridge the gap between them. The Compromise of 1850, forged by Clay, only briefly allayed the controversy over extension of slavery into the Western territories. Many Southern Whigs gravitated toward the Democrats, whom they believed more responsive to their interests. In the North, new parties specifically dedicated to opposing the expansion of slavery (Free Soilers, Anti-Nebraskans, Republicans) attracted Whig voters.

The last Whig national convention, in 1856, adopted a platform but endorsed former president Millard Fillmore, already the nominee of the Know-Nothing Party. The Whig platform deplored sectional strife and called for compromise to save the Union. But it was a futile campaign, with Fillmore carrying only Maryland and winning only 21.5 percent of the national vote.

Workers World Party (1959-)

With the Hungarian citizen revolt and other developments in Eastern Europe providing some impetus, the Workers World Party in 1959 split off from the Socialist Workers Party. The party theoretically supports worker uprisings in all parts of the world. Yet it backed the communist governments that put down rebellions in Hungary during the 1950s, Czechoslovakia in the 1960s, and Poland in the 1980s. Workers World is an activist revolutionary group that, up until 1980, concentrated its efforts on specific issues, such as the antiwar and civil rights demonstrations during the 1960s and 1970s. The party has an active youth organization, Youth Against War and Fascism.

In 1980 party leaders saw an opportunity, created by the weakness of the U.S. economy and the related high unemployment, to interest voters in its revolutionary ideas. That year it placed Deirdre Griswold, the editor of the party's newspaper and one of its founding members, on the presidential ballot in ten states. Together with her running mate Larry Holmes, a twenty-seven-year-old black activist, Griswold received 13,300 votes. In 1984 Holmes ran as the presidential candidate, getting on the ballot in eight states and receiving 15,329 votes. In 1988 Holmes ran with Gloria La Riva, and they garnered 7,846 votes. La Riva ran as the presidential candidate in 1992 and was on the ballot only in New Mexico, where she received 181 votes.

The Workers World Party dramatically improved its electoral fortunes in 1996. Its candidate, Monica Moorehead of New Jersey, was on the ballot in twelve states and received 29,082 votes.

Political Party Nominees, 1831-1996

Following is a comprehensive list of major and minor party nominees for president and vice president since 1831, when the first nominating convention was held by the Anti-Masonic Party. In many cases, minor parties made only token efforts at a presidential campaign. Often, third-party candidates declined to run after being nominated by the convention, or their names appeared on the ballots of only a few states. In some cases the names of minor candidates did not appear on any state ballots and they received only a scattering of write-in votes, if any.

The basic source for the 1832 to 1972 elections was Joseph Nathan Kane, *Facts About the Presidents*, 6th ed. (New York: H. W. Wilson Co., 1993). To verify the names appearing in Kane, Congressional Quarterly consulted the following additional sources: Richard M. Scammon, *America at the Polls* (Pittsburgh: University of Pittsburgh Press, 1965); Richard M. Scammon, *America Votes 8* (Washington, D.C.: Congressional

Quarterly, 1969); Richard M. Scammon, *America Votes 10* (Washington, D.C.: Congressional Quarterly, 1973); Richard B. Morris, ed. *Encyclopedia of American History*, (New York: Harper and Row, 1965); *Dictionary of American Biography*, (New York: Scribner's, 1928-1936); *Facts on File* (New York: Facts on File Inc., 1945-1975); Arthur M. Schlesinger, ed., *History of U.S. Political Parties*, Vols. I-IV, (New York: McGraw Hill, 1971); and *Who Was Who in America, 1607-1968*, Vols. I-V (Chicago: Marquis Co., 1943-1968). The source for the 1976 to 1996 elections was Congressional Quarterly's *America Votes* series, Vols. 12 (1977), 14 (1981), 16 (1985), 18 (1989), 20 (1993) and 22 (1997) published in Washington, D.C.

In cases where these sources contain information in conflict with Kane, the conflicting information is included in a footnote. Where a candidate appears in Kane *but could not be verified in another source*, an asterisk appears beside the candidate's name on the list.

1832 Election

Democratic Party
President: Andrew Jackson, Tennessee
Vice president: Martin Van Buren, New York
National Republican Party
President: Henry Clay, Kentucky
Vice president: John Sergeant, Pennsylvania
Independent Party
President: John Floyd, Virginia
Vice president: Henry Lee, Massachusetts
Anti-Masonic Party
President: William Wirt, Maryland
Vice president: Amos Ellmaker, Pennsylvania

1836 Election

Democratic Party
President: Martin Van Buren, New York
Vice president: Richard Mentor Johnson, Kentucky
Whig Party
President: William Henry Harrison, Hugh Lawson White, Daniel Webster
Vice president: Francis Granger, John Tyler
  The Whigs nominated regional candidates in 1836 hoping that each candidate would carry his region and deny Democrat Van Buren an electoral vote majority. Webster was the Whig candidate in Massachusetts; Harrison in the rest of New England, the Middle Atlantic states, and the West; and White in the South.
  Granger was the running mate of Harrison and Webster. Tyler was White's running mate.

1840 Election

Whig Party
President: William Henry Harrison, Ohio
Vice president: John Tyler, Virginia

Democratic Party
President: Martin Van Buren, New York
  The Democratic convention adopted a resolution that left the choice of vice-presidential candidates to the states. Democratic electors divided their vice-presidential votes among incumbent Richard M. Johnson (forty-eight votes), Littleton W. Tazewell (eleven votes), and James K. Polk (one vote).
Liberty Party
President: James Gillespie Birney, New York
Vice president: Thomas Earle, Pennsylvania

1844 Election

Democratic Party
President: James Knox Polk, Tennessee
Vice president: George Mifflin Dallas, Pennsylvania
Whig Party
President: Henry Clay, Kentucky
Vice president: Theodore Frelinghuysen, New Jersey
Liberty Party
President: James Gillespie Birney, New York
Vice president: Thomas Morris, Ohio
National Democratic Party
President: John Tyler, Virginia
Vice president: None
  Tyler withdrew in favor of the Democrat, Polk.

1848 Election

Whig Party
President: Zachary Taylor, Louisiana
Vice president: Millard Fillmore, New York
Democratic Party
President: Lewis Cass, Michigan
Vice president: William Orlando Butler, Kentucky
Free Soil Party
President: Martin Van Buren, New York
Vice president: Charles Francis Adams, Massachusetts

Political Party Nominees

Free Soil (Barnburners—Liberty Party)
President: John Parker Hale, New Hampshire
Vice president: Leicester King, Ohio
Later John Parker Hale relinquished the nomination.
National Liberty Party
President: Gerrit Smith, New York
Vice president: Charles C. Foote, Michigan

1852 Election

Democratic Party
President: Franklin Pierce, New Hampshire
Vice president: William Rufus De Vane King, Alabama
Whig Party
President: Winfield Scott, New Jersey
Vice president: William Alexander Graham, North Carolina
Free Soil
President: John Parker Hale, New Hampshire
Vice president: George Washington Julian, Indiana

1856 Election

Democratic Party
President: James Buchanan, Pennsylvania
Vice president: John Cabell Breckinridge, Kentucky
Republican Party
President: John Charles Fremont, California
Vice president: William Lewis Dayton, New Jersey
American (Know-Nothing) Party
President: Millard Fillmore, New York
Vice president: Andrew Jackson Donelson, Tennessee
Whig Party (the "Silver Grays")
President: Millard Fillmore, New York
Vice president: Andrew Jackson Donelson, Tennessee
North American Party
President: Nathaniel Prentice Banks, Massachusetts
Vice president: William Freame Johnson, Pennsylvania
Banks and Johnson declined the nominations and gave their support to the Republicans.

1860 Election

Republican Party
President: Abraham Lincoln, Illinois
Vice president: Hannibal Hamlin, Maine
Democratic Party
President: Stephen Arnold Douglas, Illinois
Vice president: Herschel Vespasian Johnson, Georgia
Southern Democratic Party
President: John Cabell Breckinridge, Kentucky
Vice president: Joseph Lane, Oregon
Constitutional Union Party
President: John Bell, Tennessee
Vice president: Edward Everett, Massachusetts

1864 Election

Republican Party
President: Abraham Lincoln, Illinois
Vice president: Andrew Johnson, Tennessee
Democratic Party
President: George Brinton McClellan, New York
Vice president: George Hunt Pendleton, Ohio
Independent Republican Party
President: John Charles Fremont, California
Vice president: John Cochrane, New York
Fremont and Cochrane declined the nominations and gave their support to the Republicans.

1868 Election

Republican Party
President: Ulysses Simpson Grant, Illinois
Vice president: Schuyler Colfax, Indiana
Democratic Party
President: Horatio Seymour, New York
Vice president: Francis Preston Blair Jr., Missouri

1872 Election

Republican Party
President: Ulysses Simpson Grant, Illinois
Vice president: Henry Wilson, Massachusetts
Liberal Republican Party
President: Horace Greeley, New York
Vice president: Benjamin Gratz Brown, Missouri
Independent Liberal Republican Party (Opposition Party)
President: William Slocum Groesbeck, Ohio
Vice president: Frederick Law Olmsted, New York
Democratic Party
President: Horace Greeley, New York
Vice president: Benjamin Gratz Brown, Missouri
Straight-Out Democratic Party
President: Charles O'Conor, New York
Vice president: John Quincy Adams, Massachusetts
Prohibition Party
President: James Black, Pennsylvania
Vice president: John Russell, Michigan
People's Party (Equal Rights Party)
President: Victoria Claflin Woodhull, New York
Vice president: Frederick Douglass
Labor Reform Party
President: David Davis, Illinois
Vice president: Joel Parker, New Jersey
Liberal Republican Party of Colored Men
President: Horace Greeley, New York
Vice president: Benjamin Gratz Brown, Missouri
National Working Men's Party
President: Ulysses Simpson Grant, Illinois
Vice president: Henry Wilson, Massachusetts

1876 Election

Republican Party
President: Rutherford Birchard Hayes, Ohio
Vice president: William Almon Wheeler, New York
Democratic Party
President: Samuel Jones Tilden, New York
Vice president: Thomas Andrews Hendricks, Indiana
Greenback Party
President: Peter Cooper, New York
Vice president: Samuel Fenton Cary, Ohio
Prohibition Party
President: Green Clay Smith, Kentucky
Vice president: Gideon Tabor Stewart, Ohio
American National Party
President: James B. Walker, Illinois
Vice president: Donald Kirkpatrick, New York

1880 Election

Republican Party
President: James Abram Garfield, Ohio
Vice president: Chester Alan Arthur, New York
Democratic Party
President: Winfield Scott Hancock, Pennsylvania
Vice president: William Hayden English, Indiana
Greenback Labor Party
President: James Baird Weaver, Iowa
Vice president: Benjamin J. Chambers, Texas

Prohibition Party
President: Neal Dow, Maine
Vice president: Henry Adams Thompson, Ohio
American Party
President: John Wolcott Phelps, Vermont
Vice president: Samuel Clarke Pomeroy, Kansas *

1884 Election

Democratic Party
President: Grover Cleveland, New York
Vice president: Thomas Andrews Hendricks, Indiana
Republican Party
President: James Gillespie Blaine, Maine
Vice president: John Alexander Logan, Illinois
Anti-Monopoly Party
President: Benjamin Franklin Butler, Massachusetts
Vice president: Absolom Madden West, Mississippi
Greenback Party
President: Benjamin Franklin Butler, Massachusetts
Vice president: Absolom Madden West, Mississippi
Prohibition Party
President: John Pierce St. John, Kansas
Vice president: William Daniel, Maryland
American Prohibition Party
President: Samuel Clark Pomeroy, Kansas
Vice president: John A. Conant, Connecticut
Equal Rights Party
President: Belva Ann Bennett Lockwood, District of Columbia
Vice president: Marietta Lizzie Bell Stow, California

1888 Election

Republican Party
President: Benjamin Harrison, Indiana
Vice president: Levi Parsons Morton, New York
Democratic Party
President: Grover Cleveland, New York
Vice president: Allen Granberry Thurman, Ohio
Prohibition Party
President: Clinton Bowen Fisk, New Jersey
Vice president: John Anderson Brooks, Missouri *
Union Labor Party
President: Alson Jenness Streeter, Illinois
Vice president: Charles E. Cunningham, Arkansas *
United Labor Party
President: Robert Hall Cowdrey, Illinois
Vice president: William H. T. Wakefield, Kansas *
American Party
President: James Langdon Curtis, New York
Vice president: Peter Dinwiddie Wigginton, California *
Equal Rights Party
President: Belva Ann Bennett Lockwood, District of Columbia
Vice president: Alfred Henry Love, Pennsylvania *
Industrial Reform Party
President: Albert E. Redstone, California *
Vice president: John Colvin, Kansas *

1892 Election

Democratic Party
President: Grover Cleveland, New York
Vice president: Adlai Ewing Stevenson, Illinois
Republican Party
President: Benjamin Harrison, Indiana
Vice president: Whitelaw Reid, New York
People's Party of America
President: James Baird Weaver, Iowa
Vice president: James Gaven Field, Virginia

Prohibition Party
President: John Bidwell, California
Vice president: James Britton Cranfill, Texas
Socialist Labor Party
President: Simon Wing, Massachusetts
Vice president: Charles Horatio Matchett, New York *

1896 Election

Republican Party
President: William McKinley, Ohio
Vice president: Garret Augustus Hobart, New Jersey
Democratic Party
President: William Jennings Bryan, Nebraska
Vice president: Arthur Sewall, Maine
People's Party (Populist)
President: William Jennings Bryan, Nebraska
Vice president: Thomas Edward Watson, Georgia
National Democratic Party
President: John McAuley Palmer, Illinois
Vice president: Simon Bolivar Buckner, Kentucky
Prohibition Party
President: Joshua Levering, Maryland
Vice president: Hale Johnson, Illinois *
Socialist Labor Party
President: Charles Horatio Matchett, New York
Vice president: Matthew Maguire, New Jersey
National Party
President: Charles Eugene Bentley, Nebraska
Vice president: James Haywood Southgate, North Carolina *
National Silver Party (Bi-Metallic League)
President: William Jennings Bryan, Nebraska
Vice president: Arthur Sewall, Maine

1900 Election

Republican Party
President: William McKinley, Ohio
Vice president: Theodore Roosevelt, New York
Democratic Party
President: William Jennings Bryan, Nebraska
Vice president: Adlai Ewing Stevenson, Illinois
Prohibition Party
President: John Granville Wooley, Illinois
Vice president: Henry Brewer Metcalf, Rhode Island
Social-Democratic Party
President: Eugene Victor Debs, Indiana
Vice president: Job Harriman, California
People's Party (Populist—Anti-Fusionist faction)
President: Wharton Barker, Pennsylvania
Vice president: Ignatius Donnelly, Minnesota
Socialist Labor Party
President: Joseph Francis Malloney, Massachusetts
Vice president: Valentine Remmel, Pennsylvania
Union Reform Party
President: Seth Hockett Ellis, Ohio
Vice president: Samuel T. Nicholson, Pennsylvania
United Christian Party
President: Jonah Fitz Randolph Leonard, Iowa
Vice president: David H. Martin, Pennsylvania
People's Party (Populist—Fusionist faction)
President: William Jennings Bryan, Nebraska
Vice president: Adlai Ewing Stevenson, Illinois
Silver Republican Party
President: William Jennings Bryan, Nebraska
Vice president: Adlai Ewing Stevenson, Illinois
National Party
President: Donelson Caffery, Louisiana
Vice president: Archibald Murray Howe, Massachusetts *

Political Party Nominees

1904 Election

Republican Party
President: Theodore Roosevelt, New York
Vice president: Charles Warren Fairbanks, Indiana
Democratic Party
President: Alton Brooks Parker, New York
Vice president: Henry Gassaway Davis, West Virginia
Socialist Party
President: Eugene Victor Debs, Indiana
Vice president: Benjamin Hanford, New York
Prohibition Party
President: Silas Comfort Swallow, Pennsylvania
Vice president: George W. Carroll, Texas
People's Party (Populist)
President: Thomas Edward Watson, Georgia
Vice president: Thomas Henry Tibbles, Nebraska
Socialist Labor Party
President: Charles Hunter Corregan, New York
Vice president: William Wesley Cox, Illinois
Continental Party
President: Austin Holcomb
Vice president: A. King, Missouri

1908 Election

Republican Party
President: William Howard Taft, Ohio
Vice president: James Schoolcraft Sherman, New York
Democratic Party
President: William Jennings Bryan, Nebraska
Vice president: John Worth Kern, Indiana
Socialist Party
President: Eugene Victor Debs
Vice president: Benjamin Hanford
Prohibition Party
President: Eugene Wilder Chafin, Illinois
Vice president: Aaron Sherman Watkins, Ohio
Independence Party
President: Thomas Louis Hisgen, Massachusetts
Vice president: John Temple Graves, Georgia
People's Party (Populist)
President: Thomas Edward Watson, Georgia
Vice president: Samuel Williams, Indiana
Socialist Labor Party
President: August Gillhaus, New York
Vice president: Donald L. Munro, Virginia
United Christian Party
President: Daniel Braxton Turney, Illinois
Vice president: Lorenzo S. Coffin, Iowa

1912 Election

Democratic Party
President: Woodrow Wilson, New Jersey
Vice president: Thomas Riley Marshall, Indiana
Progressive Party ("Bull Moose" Party)
President: Theodore Roosevelt, New York
Vice president: Hiram Warren Johnson, California
Republican Party
President: William Howard Taft, Ohio
Vice president: James Schoolcraft Sherman, New York
    Sherman died October 30; he was replaced by Nicholas
    Murray Butler, New York.
Socialist Party
President: Eugene Victor Debs, Indiana
Vice president: Emil Seidel, Wisconsin
Prohibition Party
President: Eugene Wilder Chafin, Illinois
Vice president: Aaron Sherman Watkins, Ohio

Socialist Labor Party
President: Arthur Elmer Reimer, Massachusetts
Vice president: August Gillhaus, New York[1]

1916 Election

Democratic Party
President: Woodrow Wilson, New Jersey
Vice president: Thomas Riley Marshall, Indiana
Republican Party
President: Charles Evans Hughes, New York
Vice president: Charles Warren Fairbanks, Indiana
Socialist Party
President: Allan Louis Benson, New York
Vice president: George Ross Kirkpatrick, New Jersey
Prohibition Party
President: James Franklin Hanly, Indiana
Vice president: Ira Landrith, Tennessee
Socialist Labor Party
President: Arthur Elmer Reimer, Massachusetts *
Vice president: Caleb Harrison, Illinois *
Progressive Party
President: Theodore Roosevelt, New York
Vice president: John Milliken Parker, Louisiana

1920 Election

Republican Party
President: Warren Gamaliel Harding, Ohio
Vice president: Calvin Coolidge, Massachusetts
Democratic Party
President: James Middleton Cox, Ohio
Vice president: Franklin Delano Roosevelt, New York
Socialist Party
President: Eugene Victor Debs, Indiana
Vice president: Seymour Stedman, Illinois
Farmer Labor Party
President: Parley Parker Christensen, Utah
Vice president: Maximilian Sebastian Hayes, Ohio
Prohibition Party
President: Aaron Sherman Watkins, Ohio
Vice president: David Leigh Colvin, New York
Socialist Labor Party
President: William Wesley Cox, Missouri
Vice president: August Gillhaus, New York
Single Tax Party
President: Robert Colvin Macauley, Pennsylvania
Vice president: R. G. Barnum, Ohio
American Party
President: James Edward Ferguson, Texas
Vice president: William J. Hough

1924 Election

Republican Party
President: Calvin Coolidge, Massachusetts
Vice president: Charles Gates Dawes, Illinois
Democratic Party
President: John William Davis, West Virginia
Vice president: Charles Wayland Bryan, Nebraska
Progressive Party
President: Robert La Follette, Wisconsin
Vice president: Burton Kendall Wheeler, Montana
Prohibition Party
President: Herman Preston Faris, Missouri
Vice president: Marie Caroline Brehm, California
Socialist Labor Party
President: Frank T. Johns, Oregon
Vice president: Verne L. Reynolds, New York

Socialist Party
President: Robert La Follette, New York
Vice president: Burton Kendall Wheeler, Montana
Workers Party (Communist Party)
President: William Zebulon Foster, Illinois
Vice president: Benjamin Gitlow, New York
American Party
President: Gilbert Owen Nations, District of Columbia
Vice president: Charles Hiram Randall, California[2]
Commonwealth Land Party
President: William J. Wallace, New Jersey
Vice president: John Cromwell Lincoln, Ohio
Farmer Labor Party
President: Duncan McDonald, Illinois *
Vice president: William Bouck, Washington *
Greenback Party
President: John Zahnd, Indiana *
Vice president: Roy M. Harrop, Nebraska *

1928 Election

Republican Party
President: Herbert Clark Hoover, California
Vice president: Charles Curtis, Kansas
Democratic Party
President: Alfred Emanuel Smith, New York
Vice president: Joseph Taylor Robinson, Arkansas
Socialist Party
President: Norman Mattoon Thomas, New York
Vice president: James Hudson Maurer, Pennsylvania
Workers Party (Communist Party)
President: William Zebulon Foster, Illinois
Vice president: Benjamin Gitlow, New York
Socialist Labor Party
President: Verne L. Reynolds, Michigan
Vice president: Jeremiah D. Crowley, New York
Prohibition Party
President: William Frederick Varney, New York
Vice president: James Arthur Edgerton, Virginia
Farmer Labor Party
President: Frank Elbridge Webb, California
Vice president: Will Vereen, Georgia[3]
Greenback Party
President: John Zahnd, Indiana *
Vice president: Wesley Henry Bennington, Ohio *

1932 Election

Democratic Party
President: Franklin Delano Roosevelt, New York
Vice president: John Nance Garner, Texas
Republican Party
President: Herbert Clark Hoover, California
Vice president: Charles Curtis, Kansas
Socialist Party
President: Norman Mattoon Thomas, New York
Vice president: James Hudson Maurer, Pennsylvania
Communist Party
President: William Zebulon Foster, Illinois
Vice president: James William Ford, New York
Prohibition Party
President: William David Upshaw, Georgia
Vice president: Frank Stewart Regan, Illinois
Liberty Party
President: William Hope Harvey, Arkansas
Vice president: Frank B. Hemenway, Washington
Socialist Labor Party
President: Verne L. Reynolds, New York
Vice president: John W. Aiken, Massachusetts
Farmer Labor Party
President: Jacob Sechler Coxey, Ohio
Vice president: Julius J. Reiter, Minnesota

Jobless Party
President: James Renshaw Cox, Pennsylvania
Vice president: V. C. Tisdal, Oklahoma
National Party
President: Seymour E. Allen, Massachusetts

1936 Election

Democratic Party
President: Franklin Delano Roosevelt, New York
Vice president: John Nance Garner, Texas
Republican Party
President: Alfred Mossman Landon, Kansas
Vice president: Frank Knox, Illinois
Union Party
President: William Lemke, North Dakota
Vice president: Thomas Charles O'Brien, Massachusetts
Socialist Party
President: Norman Mattoon Thomas, New York
Vice president: George A. Nelson, Wisconsin
Communist Party
President: Earl Russell Browder, Kansas
Vice president: James William Ford, New York
Prohibition Party
President: David Leigh Colvin, New York
Vice president: Alvin York, Tennessee
Socialist Labor Party
President: John W. Aikin, Massachusetts
Vice president: Emil F. Teichert, New York
National Greenback Party
President: John Zahnd, Indiana *
Vice president: Florence Garvin, Rhode Island *

1940 Election

Democratic Party
President: Franklin Delano Roosevelt, New York
Vice president: Henry Agard Wallace, Iowa
Republican Party
President: Wendell Lewis Willkie, New York
Vice president: Charles Linza McNary, Oregon
Socialist Party
President: Norman Mattoon Thomas, New York
Vice president: Maynard C. Krueger, Illinois
Prohibition Party
President: Roger Ward Babson, Massachusetts
Vice president: Edgar V. Moorman, Illinois
Communist Party (Workers Party)
President: Earl Russell Browder, Kansas
Vice president: James William Ford, New York
Socialist Labor Party
President: John W. Aiken, Massachusetts
Vice president: Aaron M. Orange, New York
Greenback Party
President: John Zahnd, Indiana *
Vice president: James Elmer Yates, Arizona *

1944 Election

Democratic Party
President: Franklin Delano Roosevelt, New York
Vice president: Harry S. Truman, Missouri
Republican Party
President: Thomas Edmund Dewey, New York
Vice president: John William Bricker, Ohio
Socialist Party
President: Norman Mattoon Thomas, New York
Vice president: Darlington Hoopes, Pennsylvania
Prohibition Party
President: Claude A. Watson, California
Vice president: Andrew Johnson, Kentucky

Political Party Nominees

Socialist Labor Party
President: Edward A. Teichert, Pennsylvania
Vice president: Arla A. Albaugh, Ohio
America First Party
President: Gerald Lyman Kenneth Smith, Michigan
Vice president: Henry A. Romer, Ohio

1948 Election

Democratic Party
President: Harry S. Truman, Missouri
Vice president: Alben William Barkley, Kentucky
Republican Party
President: Thomas Edmund Dewey, New York
Vice president: Earl Warren, California
States' Rights Democratic Party
President: James Strom Thurmond, South Carolina
Vice president: Fielding Lewis Wright, Mississippi
Progressive Party
President: Henry Agard Wallace, Iowa
Vice president: Glen Hearst Taylor, Idaho
Socialist Party
President: Norman Mattoon Thomas, New York
Vice president: Tucker Powell Smith, Michigan
Prohibition Party
President: Claude A. Watson, California
Vice president: Dale Learn, Pennsylvania
Socialist Labor Party
President: Edward A. Teichert, Pennsylvania
Vice president: Stephen Emery, New York
Socialist Workers Party
President: Farrell Dobbs, New York
Vice president: Grace Carlson, Minnesota
Christian Nationalist Party
President: Gerald Lyman Kenneth Smith, Missouri
Vice president: Henry A. Romer, Ohio
Greenback Party
President: John G. Scott, New York
Vice president: Granville B. Leeke, Indiana *
Vegetarian Party
President: John Maxwell, Illinois
Vice president: Symon Gould, New York *

1952 Election

Republican Party
President: Dwight David Eisenhower, New York
Vice president: Richard Milhous Nixon, California
Democratic Party
President: Adlai Ewing Stevenson II, Illinois
Vice president: John Jackson Sparkman, Alabama
Progressive Party
President: Vincent William Hallinan, California
Vice president: Charlotta A. Bass, New York
Prohibition Party
President: Stuart Hamblen, California
Vice president: Enoch Arden Holtwick, Illinois
Socialist Labor Party
President: Eric Hass, New York
Vice president: Stephen Emery, New York
Socialist Party
President: Darlington Hoopes, Pennsylvania
Vice president: Samuel Herman Friedman, New York
Socialist Workers Party
President: Farrell Dobbs, New York
Vice president: Myra Tanner Weiss, New York
America First Party
President: Douglas MacArthur, Wisconsin
Vice president: Harry Flood Byrd, Virginia
American Labor Party
President: Vincent William Hallinan, California
Vice president: Charlotta A. Bass, New York

American Vegetarian Party
President: Daniel J. Murphy, California
Vice president: Symon Gould, New York *
Church of God Party
President: Homer Aubrey Tomlinson, New York
Vice president: Willie Isaac Bass, North Carolina *
Constitution Party
President: Douglas MacArthur, Wisconsin
Vice president: Harry Flood Byrd, Virginia
Greenback Party
President: Frederick C. Proehl, Washington
Vice president: Edward J. Bedell, Indiana
Poor Man's Party
President: Henry B. Krajewski, New Jersey
Vice president: Frank Jenkins, New Jersey

1956 Election

Republican Party
President: Dwight David Eisenhower, Pennsylvania
Vice president: Richard Milhous Nixon, California
Democratic Party
President: Adlai Ewing Stevenson II, Illinois
Vice president: Estes Kefauver, Tennessee
States' Rights Party
President: Thomas Coleman Andrews, Virginia
Vice president: Thomas Harold Werdel, California
  Ticket also favored by Constitution Party.
Prohibition Party
President: Enoch Arden Holtwick, Illinois
Vice president: Edward M. Cooper, California
Socialist Labor Party
President: Eric Hass, New York
Vice president: Georgia Cozzini, Wisconsin
Texas Constitution Party
President: William Ezra Jenner, Indiana *
Vice president: Joseph Bracken Lee, Utah *
Socialist Workers Party
President: Farrell Dobbs, New York
Vice president: Myra Tanner Weiss, New York
American Third Party
President: Henry Krajewski, New Jersey
Vice president: Ann Marie Yezo, New Jersey
Socialist Party
President: Darlington Hoopes, Pennsylvania
Vice president: Samuel Herman Friedman, New York
Pioneer Party
President: William Langer, North Dakota *
Vice president: Burr McCloskey, Illinois *
American Vegetarian Party
President: Herbert M. Shelton, California *
Vice president: Symon Gould, New York *
Greenback Party
President: Frederick C. Proehl, Washington
Vice president: Edward Kirby Meador, Massachusetts *
States' Rights Party of Kentucky
President: Harry Flood Byrd, Virginia
Vice president: William Ezra Jenner, Indiana
South Carolinians for Independent Electors
President: Harry Flood Byrd, Virginia
Christian National Party
President: Gerald Lyman Kenneth Smith
Vice president: Charles I. Robertson

1960 Election

Democratic Party
President: John Fitzgerald Kennedy, Massachusetts
Vice president: Lyndon Baines Johnson, Texas
Republican Party
President: Richard Milhous Nixon, California
Vice president: Henry Cabot Lodge, Massachusetts

National States' Rights Party
President: Orval Eugene Faubus, Arkansas
Vice president: John Geraerdt Crommelin, Alabama

Socialist Labor Party
President: Eric Hass, New York
Vice president: Georgia Cozzini, Wisconsin

Prohibition Party
President: Rutherford Losey Decker, Missouri
Vice president: Earle Harold Munn, Michigan

Socialist Workers Party
President: Farrell Dobbs, New York
Vice president: Myra Tanner Weiss, New York

Conservative Party of New Jersey
President: Joseph Bracken Lee, Utah
Vice president: Kent H. Courtney, Louisiana

Conservative Party of Virginia
President: C. Benton Coiner, Virginia
Vice president: Edward M. Silverman, Virginia

Constitution Party (Texas)
President: Charles Loten Sullivan, Mississippi
Vice president: Merritt B. Curtis, District of Columbia

Constitution Party (Washington)
President: Merritt B. Curtis, District of Columbia
Vice president: B. N. Miller

Greenback Party
President: Whitney Hart Slocomb, California *
Vice president: Edward Kirby Meador, Massachusetts *

Independent Afro-American Party
President: Clennon King, Georgia
Vice president: Reginald Carter

Tax Cut Party (America First Party; American Party)
President: Lar Daly, Illinois
Vice president: Merritt Barton Curtis, District of Columbia

Theocratic Party
President: Homer Aubrey Tomlinson, New York
Vice president: Raymond L. Teague, Alaska *

Vegetarian Party
President: Symon Gould, New York
Vice president: Christopher Gian-Cursio, Florida

1964 Election

Democratic Party
President: Lyndon Baines Johnson, Texas
Vice president: Hubert Horatio Humphrey, Minnesota

Republican Party
President: Barry Morris Goldwater, Arizona
Vice president: William Edward Miller, New York

Socialist Labor Party
President: Eric Hass, New York
Vice president: Henning A. Blomen, Massachusetts

Prohibition Party
President: Earle Harold Munn, Michigan
Vice president: Mark Shaw, Massachusetts

Socialist Workers Party
President: Clifton DeBerry, New York
Vice president: Edward Shaw, New York

National States' Rights Party
President: John Kasper, Tennessee
Vice president: J. B. Stoner, Georgia

Constitution Party
President: Joseph B. Lightburn, West Virginia
Vice president: Theodore C. Billings, Colorado

Independent States' Rights Party
President: Thomas Coleman Andrews, Virginia
Vice president: Thomas H. Werdel, California *

Theocratic Party
President: Homer Aubrey Tomlinson, New York
Vice president: William R. Rogers, Missouri *

Universal Party
President: Kirby James Hensley, California
Vice president: John O. Hopkins, Iowa

1968 Election

Republican Party
President: Richard Milhous Nixon, New York
Vice president: Spiro Theodore Agnew, Maryland

Democratic Party
President: Hubert Horatio Humphrey, Minnesota
Vice president: Edmund Sixtus Muskie, Maine

American Independent Party
President: George Corley Wallace, Alabama
Vice president: Curtis Emerson LeMay, Ohio
LeMay replaced S. Marvin Griffin, who originally had been selected.

Peace and Freedom Party
President: Eldridge Cleaver
Vice president: Judith Mage, New York

Socialist Labor Party
President: Henning A. Blomen, Massachusetts
Vice president: George Sam Taylor, Pennsylvania

Socialist Workers Party
President: Fred Halstead, New York
Vice president: Paul Boutelle, New Jersey

Prohibition Party
President: Earle Harold Munn Sr., Michigan
Vice president: Rolland E. Fisher, Kansas

Communist Party
President: Charlene Mitchell, California
Vice president: Michael Zagarell, New York

Constitution Party
President: Richard K. Troxell, Texas
Vice president: Merle Thayer, Iowa

Freedom and Peace Party
President: Richard Claxton (Dick) Gregory, Illinois
Vice president: Mark Lane, New York

Patriotic Party
President: George Corley Wallace, Alabama
Vice president: William Penn Patrick, California

Theocratic Party
President: William R. Rogers, Missouri

Universal Party
President: Kirby James Hensley, California
Vice president: Roscoe B. MacKenna

1972 Election

Republican Party
President: Richard Milhous Nixon, California
Vice president: Spiro Theodore Agnew, Maryland

Democratic Party
President: George Stanley McGovern, South Dakota
Vice president: Thomas Francis Eagleton, Missouri
Eagleton resigned and was replaced on August 8, 1972, by Robert Sargent Shriver Jr., Maryland, selected by the Democratic National Committee.

American Independent Party
President: John George Schmitz, California
Vice president: Thomas Jefferson Anderson, Tennessee

Socialist Workers Party
President: Louis Fisher, Illinois
Vice president: Genevieve Gunderson, Minnesota

Socialist Labor Party
President: Linda Jenness, Georgia
Vice president: Andrew Pulley, Illinois

Communist Party
President: Gus Hall, New York
Vice president: Jarvis Tyner

Prohibition Party
President: Earle Harold Munn Sr., Michigan
Vice president: Marshall Uncapher

Libertarian Party
President: John Hospers, California
Vice president: Theodora Nathan, Oregon

Political Party Nominees

People's Party
President: Benjamin McLane Spock
Vice president: Julius Hobson, District of Columbia
America First Party
President: John V. Mahalchik
Vice president: Irving Homer
Universal Party
President: Gabriel Green
Vice president: Daniel Fry

1976 Election

Democratic Party
President: James Earl (Jimmy) Carter Jr., Georgia
Vice president: Walter Frederick Mondale, Minnesota
Republican Party
President: Gerald Rudolph Ford, Michigan
Vice president: Robert Joseph Dole, Kansas
Independent candidate
President: Eugene Joseph McCarthy, Minnesota
Vice president: none[4]
Libertarian Party
President: Roger MacBride, Virginia
Vice president: David P. Bergland, California
American Independent Party
President: Lester Maddox, Georgia
Vice president: William Dyke, Wisconsin
American Party
President: Thomas J. Anderson, Tennessee
Vice president: Rufus Shackleford, Florida
Socialist Workers Party
President: Peter Camejo, California
Vice president: Willie Mae Reid, California
Communist Party
President: Gus Hall, New York
Vice president: Jarvis Tyner, New York
People's Party
President: Margaret Wright, California
Vice president: Benjamin Spock, New York
U.S. Labor Party
President: Lyndon H. LaRouche Jr., New York
Vice president: R. W. Evans, Michigan
Prohibition Party
President: Benjamin C. Bubar, Maine
Vice president: Earl F. Dodge, Colorado
Socialist Labor Party
President: Jules Levin, New Jersey
Vice president: Constance Blomen, Massachusetts
Socialist Party
President: Frank P. Zeidler, Wisconsin
Vice president: J. Quinn Brisben, Illinois
Restoration Party
President: Ernest L. Miller
Vice president: Roy N. Eddy
United American Party
President: Frank Taylor
Vice president: Henry Swan

1980 Election[5]

Republican Party
President: Ronald Wilson Reagan, California
Vice president: George Herbert Walker Bush, Texas
Democratic Party
President: James Earl (Jimmy) Carter Jr., Georgia
Vice president: Walter Frederick Mondale, Minnesota
National Unity Campaign
President: John B. Anderson, Illinois
Vice president: Patrick Joseph Lucey, Wisconsin
Libertarian Party
President: Edward E. Clark, California
Vice president: David Koch, New York

Citizens Party
President: Barry Commoner, New York
Vice president: LaDonna Harris, New Mexico
Communist Party
President: Gus Hall, New York
Vice president: Angela Davis, California
American Independent Party
President: John Richard Rarick, Louisiana
Vice president: Eileen M. Shearer, California
Socialist Workers Party
President: Andrew Pulley, Illinois
Vice president: Matilde Zimmermann
President: Clifton DeBerry, California
Vice president: Matilde Zimmermann
President: Richard Congress, Ohio
Vice president: Matilde Zimmermann
Right to Life Party
President: Ellen McCormack, New York
Vice president: Carroll Driscoll, New Jersey
Peace and Freedom Party
President: Maureen Smith, California
Vice president: Elizabeth Barron
Workers World Party
President: Deirdre Griswold, New Jersey
Vice president: Larry Holmes, New York
Statesman Party
President: Benjamin C. Bubar, Maine
Vice president: Earl F. Dodge, Colorado
Socialist Party
President: David McReynolds, New York
Vice president: Diane Drufenbrock, Wisconsin
American Party
President: Percy L. Greaves, New York
Vice president: Frank L. Varnum, California
President: Frank W. Shelton, Utah
Vice president: George E. Jackson
Middle Class Party
President: Kurt Lynen, New Jersey
Vice president: Harry Kieve, New Jersey
Down With Lawyers Party
President: Bill Gahres, New Jersey
Vice president: J. F. Loghlin, New Jersey
Independent Party
President: Martin E. Wendelken
Natural Peoples Party
President: Harley McLain, North Dakota
Vice president: Jewelie Goeller, North Dakota

1984 Election[6]

Republican Party
President: Ronald Wilson Reagan, California
Vice president: George Herbert Walker Bush, Texas
Democratic Party
President: Walter Fritz Mondale, Minnesota
Vice president: Geraldine Anne Ferraro, New York
Libertarian Party
President: David P. Bergland, California
Vice president: Jim Lewis, Connecticut
Independent Party
President: Lyndon H. LaRouche Jr., Virginia
Vice president: Billy Davis, Mississippi
Citizens Party
President: Sonia Johnson, Virginia
Vice president: Richard Walton, Rhode Island
Populist Party
President: Bob Richards, Texas
Vice president: Maureen Kennedy Salaman, California
Independent Alliance Party
President: Dennis L. Serrette, New Jersey
Vice president: Nancy Ross, New York

Communist Party
President: Gus Hall, New York
Vice president: Angela Davis, California
Socialist Workers Party
President: Mel Mason, California
Vice president: Andrea Gonzalez, New York
Workers World Party
President: Larry Holmes, New York
Vice president: Gloria La Riva, California
President: Gavrielle Holmes, New York
Vice president: Milton Vera
American Party
President: Delmar Dennis, Tennessee
Vice president: Traves Brownlee, Delaware
Workers League Party
President: Ed Winn, New York
Vice presidents: Jean T. Brust, Helen Halyard, Edward Bergonzi
Prohibition Party
President: Earl F. Dodge, Colorado
Vice president: Warren C. Martin, Kansas

1988 Election[7]

Republican Party
President: George Herbert Walker Bush, Texas
Vice president: James "Dan" Quayle, Indiana
Democratic Party
President: Michael Stanley Dukakis, Massachusetts
Vice president: Lloyd Millard Bentsen Jr., Texas
Libertarian Party
President: Ronald E. Paul, Texas
Vice president: Andre V. Marrou, Nevada
New Alliance Party
President: Lenora B. Fulani, New York
Vice president: Joyce Dattner
Populist Party
President: David E. Duke, Louisiana
Vice president: Floyd C. Parker
Consumer Party
President: Eugene Joseph McCarthy, Minnesota
Vice president: Florence Rice
American Independent Party
President: James C. Griffin, California
Vice president: Charles J. Morsa
National Economic Recovery Party
President: Lyndon H. LaRouche Jr., Virginia
Vice president: Debra H. Freeman
Right to Life Party
President: William A. Marra, New Jersey
Vice president: Joan Andrews
Workers League Party
President: Edward Winn, New York
Vice president: Barry Porster
Socialist Workers Party
President: James Warren, New Jersey
Vice president: Kathleen Mickells
Peace and Freedom Party
President: Herbert Lewin
Vice president: Vikki Murdock
Prohibition Party
President: Earl F. Dodge, Colorado
Vice president: George D. Ormsby
Workers World Party
President: Larry Holmes, New York
Vice president: Gloria La Riva, California
Socialist Party
President: Willa Kenoyer, Minnesota
Vice president: Ron Ehrenreich
American Party
President: Delmar Dennis, Tennessee
Vice president: Earl Jepson

Grassroots Party
President: Jack E. Herer, California
Vice president: Dana Beal
Independent Party
President: Louie Youngkeit, Utah
Third World Assembly
President: John G. Martin, District of Columbia
Vice president: Cleveland Sparrow

1992 Election[8]

Democratic Party
President: Bill Clinton, Arkansas
Vice president: Albert Gore Jr., Tennessee
Republican Party
President: George Herbert Walker Bush, Texas
Vice president: James "Dan" Quayle, Indiana
Independent
President: H. Ross Perot, Texas
Vice president: James Stockdale, California
Libertarian Party
President: Andre V. Marrou, Nevada
Vice president: Nancy Lord, Georgia
America First Party (Populist)
President: James "Bo" Gritz, Nevada
Vice president: Cyril Minett
New Alliance Party
President: Lenora B. Fulani, New York
Vice president: Maria E. Munoz, California
U.S. Taxpayers Party
President: Howard Phillips, Virginia
Vice president: Albion W. Knight, Maryland
Natural Law Party
President: John Hagelin, Iowa
Vice president: Mike Tompkins, Iowa
Peace and Freedom Party
President: Ron Daniels, California
Vice president: Asiba Tupahache
Independent
President: Lyndon H. LaRouche Jr., Virginia
Vice president: James L. Bevel
Socialist Workers Party
President: James Warren, New Jersey
Vice president: Willie Mae Reid
Independent
President: Drew Bradford
Grassroots Party
President: Jack E. Herer, California
Vice president: Derrick P. Grimmer
Socialist Party
President: J. Quinn Brisben, Illinois
Vice president: Barbara Garson
Workers League Party
President: Helen Halyard, Michigan
Vice president: Fred Mazelis, Michigan
Take Back America Party
President: John Yiamouyiannas
Vice president: Allen C. McCone
Independent
President: Delbert L. Ehlers
Vice president: Rick Wendt
Prohibition Party
President: Earl F. Dodge, Colorado
Vice president: George D. Ormsby
Apathy Party
President: Jim Boren
Vice president: Will Weidman
Third Party
President: Eugene A. Hem
Vice president: Joanne Roland
Looking Back Party
President: Isabell Masters, Oklahoma
Vice president: Walter Masters, Florida

Political Party Nominees

American Party
President: Robert J. Smith
Vice president: Doris Feimer
Workers World Party
President: Gloria La Riva, California
Vice president: Larry Holmes, New York

1996 Election[9]

Democratic Party
President: Bill Clinton, Arkansas
Vice president: Albert Gore Jr., Tennessee
Republican Party
President: Robert Dole, Kansas
Vice President: Jack Kemp, New York
Reform Party
President: H. Ross Perot, Texas
Vice President: Pat Choate, District of Columbia
Green Party
President: Ralph Nader, District of Columbia
Vice President: Winona LaDuke, Minnesota
Libertarian Party
President: Harry Browne, California
Vice President: Jo Anne Jorgensen, South Carolina
U.S. Taxpayers Party
President: Howard Phillips, Virginia
Vice President: Herbert W. Titus, Virginia
Natural Law Party
President: John Hagelin, Iowa
Vice President: Mike Tompkins, North Carolina
Workers World Party
President: Monica Moorehead, New York
Vice President: Gloria La Riva, California

Peace and Freedom Party
President: Marsha Feinland, California
Vice President: Kate McClatchy, Massachusetts
Independent
President: Charles E. Collins, Florida
Vice President: Rosemary Giumarra
Socialist Workers Party
President: James E. Harris, Georgia
Vice President: Laura Garza, New York
Grassroots Party
President: Dennis Peron, Minnesota
Vice President: Arlin Troutt, Arizona
Socialist Party
President: Mary Cal Hollis, Colorado
Vice President: Eric Chester, Massachusetts
Socialist Equality Party
President: Jerome White, Michigan
Vice President: Fred Mazelis, Michigan
American Party
President: Diane Beall Templin, California
Vice President: Gary Van Horn, Utah
Prohibition Party
President: Earl F. Dodge, Colorado
Vice President: Rachel Bubar Kelly, Maine
Independent Party of Utah
President: A. Peter Crane, Utah
Vice President: Connie Chandler, Utah
America First Party
President: Ralph Forbes, Arkansas
Independent Grassroots Party
President: John Birrenbach, Minnesota
Vice President: George McMahon, Iowa
Looking Back Party
President: Isabell Masters, Oklahoma
Vice President: Shirley Jean Masters, California
Independent
President: Steve Michael, District of Columbia

Notes
    * Candidates appeared in Joseph Nathan Kane, *Facts About the Presidents,* 4th ed. (New York: H. W. Wilson, 1981), but could not be verified in another source.
    1. *1912:* Arthur M. Schlesinger's *History of American Presidential Elections* (New York: McGraw-Hill, 1971) lists the Socialist Labor Party vice-presidential candidate as Francis. No first name is given.
    2. *1924:* Richard M. Scammon's *America at the Polls* (Pittsburgh: University of Pittsburgh Press, 1965) lists the American Party vice-presidential candidate as Leander L. Pickett.
    3. *1928:* *America at the Polls* lists the Farmer Labor Party vice-presidential candidate as L. R. Tillman.
    4. *1976:* McCarthy, who ran as an independent with no party designation, had no national running mate, favoring the elimination of the office. But as various state laws required a running mate, he had different ones in different states, amounting to nearly two dozen, all political unknowns.
    5. *1980:* In several cases vice-presidential nominees were different from those listed for most states, and the Socialist Workers and American Party nominees for president varied from state to state. For example, because Pulley, the major standard-bearer for the Socialist Workers Party was only twenty-nine years old, his name was not allowed on the ballot in some states (the Constitution requires presidential candidates to be at least thirty-five years old). Hence, the party ran other candidates in those states. In a number of states, candidates appeared on the ballot with variants of the party designations listed, without any party designation, or with entirely different party names.
    6. *1984:* Both Larry Holmes and Gavrielle Holmes were standard-bearers of the Workers World Party. Of the two, Larry Holmes was listed on more state ballots. Milton Vera was Gavrielle Holmes's vice-presidential running mate in Ohio and Rhode Island. The Workers League Party had three vice-presidential candidates: Jean T. Brust in Illinois; Helen Halyard in Michigan, New Jersey, and Pennsylvania; and Edward Bergonzi in Minnesota and Ohio.
    7. *1988:* The candidates listed include all those who appeared on the ballot in at least one state. In some cases, a party's vice-presidential candidate varied from state to state. Candidates' full names and states were not available from some parties.
    8. *1992:* The candidates listed include all those who appeared on the ballot in at least one state. In some cases a party's vice-presidential candidate varied from state to state. Candidates' states were not available from some parties.
    9. *1996:* The candidates listed include all those who appeared on the ballot in at least one state. In some cases a party's vice-presidential candidate varied from state to state. Candidates' states were not available from some parties.

Biographical Directory of Presidential And Vice Presidential Candidates

The names in the directory include all persons who have received electoral votes for president or vice president since 1789. Also included are prominent third party candidates who received popular votes but no electoral votes, and Nelson Aldrich Rockefeller, appointed vice president by Gerald Ford, who became president following the resignation of Richard M. Nixon.

The material is organized as follows: name, state of residence in the year(s) the individual received electoral votes, party or parties with which the individual identified when he or she received electoral votes, date of birth, date of death (where applicable), major offices held, and the year(s) of candidacy.

For the elections of 1789 through 1800, presidential electors did not vote separately for president or vice president. It was, therefore, difficult in many cases to determine if an individual receiving electoral votes in these elections was a candidate for the office of president or vice president. Where no determination could be made from the sources consulted by Congressional Quarterly, the year in which the individual received electoral votes is given with no specification as to whether the individual was a candidate for president or vice president.

The following sources were used: *American Leaders, 1789-1994: A Biographical Summary*, (Washington, D.C.: Congressional Quarterly, 1994); *Biographical Directory of the United States Congress, 1774-1989*, (Washington, D.C.: Government Printing Office, 1989); Rhodes Cook, *America Votes 22* (1997), (Washington, D.C.: Congressional Quarterly, 1997); *Dictionary of American Biography*, (New York: Scribner's, 1928-36); John A. Garraty, ed., *Encyclopedia of American Biography*, (New York: Harper and Row, 1974); Jaques Cattell Press, ed., *Who's Who in American Politics, 1977-78*, 6th ed. (New York: R. R. Bowker, 1977); Svend Petersen, *A Statistical History of the American Presidential Elections*, (Westport, Conn.: Greenwood Press, 1981); Richard M. Scammon, *America Votes 10* (1972), (Washington, D.C.: Congressional Quarterly, 1973); Richard M. Scammon and Alice V. McGillivray, *America Votes 12* (1976), (Washington, D.C.: Congressional Quarterly, 1977); *America Votes 14* (1980), (Washington, D.C.: Congressional Quarterly, 1981); *America Votes 18* (1988), (Washington, D.C.: Congressional Quarterly, 1989); *America Votes 20* (1992), (Washington, D.C.: Congressional Quarterly, 1993); *Who Was Who in America, 1607-1968*, (Chicago: Marquis, 1943-68).

Adams, Charles Francis - Mass. (Free Soil) Aug. 18, 1807 - Nov. 21, 1886; House, 1859-61; minister to Great Britain, 1861-68. Candidacy: VP - 1848.

Adams, John - Mass. (Federalist) Oct. 30, 1735 - July 4, 1826; Continental Congress, 1774; signer of Declaration of Independence, 1776; minister to Great Britain, 1785; U.S. vice president, 1789-97; U.S. president, 1797-1801. Candidacies: VP - 1789, 1792; P - 1796, 1800.

Adams, John Quincy - Mass. (Democratic-Republican, National Republican) July 11, 1767 - Feb. 23, 1848; Senate, 1803-08; minister to Russia, 1809-14; minister to Great Britain, 1815-17; secretary of state, 1817-25; U.S. president, 1825-29; House, 1831-48. Candidacies: P - 1820, 1824, 1828.

Adams, Samuel - Mass. (Federalist) Sept. 27, 1722 - Oct. 2, 1803; Continental Congress, 1774-81; signer of Declaration of Independence; governor, 1793-97. Candidacy: 1796.

Agnew, Spiro Theodore - Md. (Republican) Nov. 9, 1918 - Sept. 17, 1996; governor, 1967-69; U.S. vice president, 1969-73 (resigned Oct. 10, 1973). Candidacies: VP - 1968, 1972.

Anderson, John B. - Ill. (Republican, Independent) Feb. 15, 1922—; state's attorney, 1956-60; House, 1961-81. Candidacy: P - 1980.

Armstrong, James - Pa. (Federalist) Aug. 29, 1748 - May 6, 1828; House, 1793-95. Candidacy: 1789.

Arthur, Chester Alan - N.Y. (Republican) Oct. 5, 1830 - Nov. 18, 1886; collector, Port of N.Y., 1871-78; U.S. vice president, 1881; U.S. president, 1881-85. Candidacy: VP - 1880.

Banks, Nathaniel Prentice - Mass. (Liberal Republican) Jan. 30, 1816 - Sept. 1, 1894; House, 1853-57, 1865-73, 1875-79, 1889-91; governor, 1858-61. Candidacy: VP - 1872.

Barkley, Alben William - Ky. (Democratic) Nov. 24, 1877 - April 30, 1956; House, 1913-27; Senate, 1927-49, 1955-56; Senate majority leader, 1937-47; Senate minority leader, 1947-49; U.S. vice president, 1949-53. Candidacy: VP - 1948.

Bell, John - Tenn. (Constitutional Union) Feb. 15, 1797 - Sept. 10, 1869; House, 1827-41; Speaker of the House, 1834-35; secretary of war, 1841; Senate, 1847-59. Candidacy: P - 1860.

Benson, Allan Louis - N.Y. (Socialist) Nov. 6, 1871 - Aug. 19, 1940; writer, editor; founder of *Reconstruction Magazine,* 1918. Candidacy: P - 1916.

Bentsen, Lloyd Millard Jr. - Texas (Democratic) Feb. 11, 1921—; House 1948-55; Senate 1971-93; secretary of Treasury, 1993-94. Candidacy: VP - 1988.

Bidwell, John - Calif. (Prohibition) Aug. 5, 1819 - April 4, 1900; California pioneer; major in Mexican War; House, 1865-67. Candidacy: P - 1892.

Birney, James Gillespie - N.Y. (Liberty) Feb. 4, 1792 - Nov. 25, 1857; Kentucky Legislature, 1816-17; Alabama Legislature, 1819-20. Candidacies: P - 1840, 1844.

Blaine, James Gillespie - Maine (Republican) Jan. 31, 1830 - Jan. 27, 1893; House, 1863-76; Speaker of the House, 1869-75; Senate, 1876-81; secretary of state, 1881, 1889-92; president, first Pan American Congress, 1889. Candidacy: P - 1884.

Blair, Francis Preston Jr. - Mo. (Democratic) Feb. 19, 1821 - July 8, 1875; House, 1857-59, 1860, 1861-62, 1863-64; Senate, 1871-73. Candidacy: VP - 1868.

Bramlette, Thomas E. - Ky. (Democratic) Jan. 3, 1817 - Jan. 12, 1875; governor, 1863-67. Candidacy: VP - 1872.

Breckinridge, John Cabell - Ky. (Democratic, Southern Democratic) Jan. 21, 1821 - May 17, 1875; House, 1851-55; U.S. vice president, 1857-61; Senate, 1861; major general, Confederacy, 1861-65; secretary of war, Confederacy, 1865. Candidacies: VP - 1856; P - 1860.

Bricker, John William - Ohio (Republican) Sept. 6, 1893 - March 22, 1986; attorney general of Ohio, 1933-37; governor, 1939-45; Senate, 1947-59. Candidacy: VP - 1944.

Brown, Benjamin Gratz - Mo. (Democratic) May 28, 1826 - Dec. 13, 1885; Senate, 1863-67; governor, 1871-73. Candidacy: VP - 1872.

Bryan, Charles Wayland - Neb. (Democratic) Feb. 10, 1867 - March 4, 1945; governor, 1923-25, 1931-35; Candidacy: VP - 1924.

Bryan, William Jennings - Neb. (Democratic, Populist) March 19, 1860 - July 26, 1925; House, 1891-95; secretary of state, 1913-15. Candidacies: P - 1896, 1900, 1908.

Buchanan, James - Pa. (Democratic) April 23, 1791 - June 1, 1868; House, 1821-31; minister to Russia, 1832-34; Senate, 1834-45; secretary of state, 1845-49; minister to Great Britain, 1853-56; U.S. president, 1857-61. Candidacy: P - 1856.

Burr, Aaron - N.Y. (Democratic-Republican) Feb. 6, 1756 - Sept. 14, 1836; attorney general of N.Y., 1789-90; Senate, 1791-97; U.S. vice president, 1801-05. Candidacies: 1792, 1796, 1800.

Bush, George - Texas (Republican) June 12, 1924—; House, 1967-70; ambassador to the United Nations, 1971-73; chairman of the Republican National Committee, 1973-74; head of the U.S. liaison office in Peking, 1974-75; director of the Central Intelligence Agency, 1976-77; U.S. vice president, 1981-89; U.S. president, 1989-93. Candidacies: VP - 1980, 1984; P - 1988, 1992.

Butler, Benjamin Franklin - Mass. (Greenback, Anti-Monopoly) Nov. 5, 1818 - Jan. 11, 1893; House, 1867-75, 1877-79; governor, 1883-84. Candidacy: P - 1884.

Butler, Nicholas Murray - N.Y. (Republican) April 2, 1862 - Dec. 7, 1947; president, Columbia University, 1901-45; president, Carnegie Endowment for International Peace, 1925-45. Candidacy: VP - 1912. (Substituted as candidate after Oct. 30 death of nominee James S. Sherman.)

Butler, William Orlando - Ky. (Democratic) April 19, 1791 - Aug. 6, 1880; House, 1839-43. Candidacy: VP - 1848.

Byrd, Harry Flood - Va. (States' Rights Democratic, Independent Democratic) June 10, 1887 - Oct. 20, 1966; governor, 1926-30; Senate, 1933-65. Candidacies: P - 1956, 1960.

Calhoun, John Caldwell - S.C. (Democratic-Republican, Democratic) March 18, 1782 - March 31, 1850; House, 1811-17; secretary of war, 1817-25; U.S. vice president, 1825-32; Senate, 1832-43, 1845-50; secretary of state, 1844-45. Candidacies: VP - 1824, 1828.

Carter, James Earl Jr. - Ga. (Democratic) Oct. 1, 1924—; Georgia Legislature, 1963-67; governor, 1971-75; U.S. president, 1977-81. Candidacies: P - 1976, 1980.

Cass, Lewis - Mich. (Democratic) Oct. 9, 1782 - June 17, 1866; military and civil governor of Michigan Territory, 1813-31; secretary of war, 1831-36; minister to France, 1836-42; Senate, 1845-48, 1849-57; secretary of state, 1857-60. Candidacy: P - 1848.

Clay, Henry - Ky. (Democratic-Republican, National Republican, Whig) April 12, 1777 - June 29, 1852; Senate, 1806-07, 1810-11, 1831-42, 1849-52; House, 1811-14, 1815-21, 1823-25; Speaker of the House, 1811-14, 1815-20, 1823-25; secretary of state, 1825-29. Candidacies: P - 1824, 1832, 1844.

Cleveland, Stephen Grover - N.Y. (Democratic) March 18, 1837 - June 24, 1908; mayor of Buffalo, 1882; governor, 1883-85; U.S. president, 1885-89, 1893-97. Candidacies: P - 1884, 1888, 1892.

Clinton, Bill - Ark. (Democrat) Aug. 19, 1946—; attorney general of Arkansas, 1977-79; governor, 1979-81, 1983-92; U.S. president, 1993—. Candidacy: P - 1992, 1996.

Clinton, De Witt - N.Y. (Independent Democratic-Republican, Federalist) March 2, 1769 - Feb. 11, 1828; Senate, 1802-03; mayor of New York, 1803-07, 1810, 1811, 1813, 1814; governor, 1817-23, 1825-28. Candidacy: P - 1812.

Clinton, George - N.Y. (Democratic-Republican) July 26, 1739 - April 20, 1812; Continental Congress, 1775-76; governor, 1777-95, 1801-04; U.S. vice president, 1805-12. Candidacies: VP - 1789, 1792, 1796, 1804, 1808.

Colfax, Schuyler - Ind. (Republican) March 23, 1823 - Jan. 13, 1885; House, 1855-69; Speaker of the House, 1863-69; U.S. vice president, 1869-73. Candidacy: VP - 1868.

Colquitt, Alfred Holt - Ga. (Democratic) April 20, 1824 - March 26, 1894; House, 1853-55; governor, 1877-82; Senate, 1883-94. Candidacy: VP - 1872.

Coolidge, Calvin - Mass. (Republican) July 4, 1872 - Jan. 5, 1933; governor, 1919-21; U.S. vice president, 1921-23; U.S. president, 1923-29. Candidacies: VP - 1920; P - 1924.

Cox, James Middleton - Ohio (Democratic) March 31, 1870 - July 15, 1957; House, 1909-13; governor, 1913-15, 1917-21. Candidacy: P - 1920.

Crawford, William Harris - Ga. (Democratic-Republican) Feb. 24, 1772 - Sept. 15, 1834; Senate, 1807-13; president pro tempore of the Senate, 1812-13; secretary of war, 1815-16; secretary of the treasury, 1816-25. Candidacy: P - 1824.

Curtis, Charles - Kan. (Republican) Jan. 25, 1860 - Feb. 8, 1936; House, 1893-1907; Senate, 1907-13, 1915-29; president pro tempore of the Senate, 1911; Senate majority leader, 1925-29; U.S. vice president, 1929-33. Candidacies: VP - 1928, 1932.

Dallas, George Mifflin - Pa. (Democratic) July 10, 1792 - Dec. 31, 1864; Senate, 1831-33; minister to Russia, 1837-39; U.S. vice president, 1845-49; minister to Great Britain, 1856-61. Candidacy: VP - 1844.

Davis, David - Ill. (Democratic) March 9, 1815 - June 26, 1886; associate justice of U.S. Supreme Court, 1862-77; Senate, 1877-83; president pro tempore of the Senate, 1881. Candidacy: P - 1872.

Davis, Henry Gassaway - W.Va. (Democratic) Nov. 16, 1823 - March 11, 1916; Senate, 1871-83; chairman of Pan American Railway Committee, 1901-16. Candidacy: VP - 1904.

Davis, John William - W.Va., N.Y. (Democratic) April 13, 1873 - March 24, 1955; House, 1911-13; solicitor general, 1913-18; ambassador to Great Britain, 1918-21. Candidacy: P - 1924.

Dawes, Charles Gates - Ill. (Republican) Aug. 27, 1865 - April 3, 1951; U.S. comptroller of the currency, 1898-1901; first director of Bureau of the Budget, 1921-22; U.S. vice president, 1925-29; ambassador to Great Britain, 1929-32. Candidacy: VP - 1924.

Dayton, William Lewis - N.J. (Republican) Feb. 17, 1807 - Dec. 1, 1864; Senate, 1842-51; minister to France, 1861-64. Candidacy: VP - 1856.

Debs, Eugene Victor - Ind. (Socialist) Nov. 5, 1855 - Oct. 20, 1926; Indiana Legislature, 1885; president, American Railway Union, 1893-97. Candidacies: P - 1900, 1904, 1908, 1912, 1920.

Dewey, Thomas Edmund - N.Y. (Republican) March 24, 1902 - March 16, 1971; district attorney, New York County, 1937-41; governor, 1943-55. Candidacies: P - 1944, 1948.

Dole, Robert Joseph - Kan. (Republican) July 22, 1923—; House, 1961-69; Senate, 1969-96; Senate majority leader, 1985-87, 1995-96; Senate minority leader, 1987-95; chairman of the Republican National Committee, 1971-73. Candidacies: VP - 1976; P - 1996.

Donelson, Andrew Jackson - Tenn. (American "Know-Nothing") Aug. 25, 1799 - June 26, 1871; minister to Prussia, 1846-48; minister to Germany, 1848-49. Candidacy: VP - 1856.

Douglas, Stephen Arnold - Ill. (Democratic) April 23, 1813 - June 3, 1861; House, 1843-47; Senate, 1847-61. Candidacy: P - 1860.

Dukakis, Michael Stanley - Mass. (Democratic) Nov. 3, 1933—; governor, 1975-79, 1983-91. Candidacy: P - 1988.

Eagleton, Thomas Francis - Mo. (Democratic) Sept. 4, 1929—; attorney general of Missouri, 1961-65; lieutenant governor, 1965-68; Senate, 1968-87. Candidacy: VP - 1972. (Resigned from Democratic ticket July 31; replaced by R. Sargent Shriver Jr.)

Eisenhower, Dwight David - N.Y., Pa. (Republican) Oct. 14, 1890 - March 28, 1969; general of U.S. Army, 1943-48; Army chief of staff, 1945-48; president of Columbia University, 1948-51; commander of North Atlantic Treaty Organization, 1951-52; U.S. president, 1953-61. Candidacies: P - 1952, 1956.

Ellmaker, Amos - Pa. (Anti-Masonic) Feb. 2, 1787 - Nov. 28, 1851; elected to the House for the term beginning in 1815 but did not qualify; attorney general of Pennsylvania, 1816-19, 1828-29. Candidacy: VP - 1832.

Ellsworth, Oliver - Conn. (Federalist) April 29, 1745 - Nov. 26, 1807; Continental Congress, 1778-83; Senate, 1789-96; chief justice of United States, 1796-1800; minister to France, 1799. Candidacy: 1796.

English, William Hayden - Ind. (Democratic) Aug. 27, 1822 - Feb. 7, 1896; House, 1853-61. Candidacy: VP - 1880.

Everett, Edward - Mass. (Constitutional Union) April 11, 1794 - Jan. 15, 1865; House, 1825-35; governor, 1836-40; minister to Great Britain, 1841-45; president of Harvard University, 1846-49; secretary of state, 1852-53; Senate, 1853-54. Candidacy: VP - 1860.

Fairbanks, Charles Warren - Ind. (Republican) May 11, 1852 - June 4, 1918; Senate, 1897-1905; U.S. vice president, 1905-09. Candidacies: VP - 1904, 1916.

Ferraro, Geraldine Anne - N.Y. (Democratic) Aug. 26, 1935—; assistant district attorney, Queens County, 1974-78; House, 1979-85. Candidacy: VP - 1984.

Field, James Gaven - Va. (Populist) Feb. 24, 1826 - Oct. 12, 1901; major in the Confederate Army, 1861-65; attorney general of Virginia, 1877-82. Candidacy: VP - 1892.

Fillmore, Millard - N.Y. (Whig, American "Know-Nothing") Jan. 7, 1800 - March 8, 1874; House, 1833-35, 1837-43; N.Y. comptroller, 1847-49; U.S. vice president, 1849-50; U.S. president, 1850-53. Candidacies: VP - 1848; P - 1856.

Fisk, Clinton Bowen - N.J. (Prohibition) Dec. 8, 1828 - July 9, 1890; Civil War brevet major general; founder of Fisk University, 1866; member, Board of Indian Commissioners, 1874, president, 1881-90. Candidacy: P - 1888.

Floyd, John - Va. (Independent Democratic) April 24, 1783 - Aug. 17, 1837; House, 1817-29; governor, 1830-34. Candidacy: P - 1832.

Ford, Gerald Rudolph Jr. - Mich. (Republican) July 14, 1913—; House, 1949-73; House minority leader, 1965-73; U.S. vice president, 1973-74; U.S. president, 1974-77. Candidacy: P - 1976.

Frelinghuysen, Theodore - N.J. (Whig) March 28, 1787 - April 12, 1862; attorney general of New Jersey, 1817-29; Senate, 1829-35; president of Rutgers College, 1850-62. Candidacy: VP - 1844.

Fremont, John Charles - Calif. (Republican) Jan. 21, 1813 - July 13, 1890; explorer and Army officer in West before 1847; Senate, 1850-51; governor of Arizona Territory, 1878-81. Candidacy: P - 1856.

Garfield, James Abram - Ohio (Republican) Nov. 19, 1831 - Sept. 19, 1881; major general in Union Army during Civil War; House, 1863-80; U.S. president, 1881. Candidacy: P - 1880.

Garner, John Nance - Texas (Democratic) Nov. 22, 1868 - Nov. 7, 1967; House, 1903-33; House minority leader, 1929-31; Speaker of the House, 1931-33; U.S. vice president, 1933-41. Candidacies: VP - 1932, 1936.

Gerry, Elbridge - Mass. (Democratic-Republican) July 17, 1744 - Nov. 23, 1814; Continental Congress, 1776-80, 1783-85; signer of Declaration of Independence; Constitutional Convention, 1787; House, 1789-93; governor, 1810-12; U.S. vice president, 1813-14. Candidacy: VP - 1812.

Goldwater, Barry Morris - Ariz. (Republican) Jan. 1, 1909—; Senate, 1953-65, 1969-87. Candidacies: VP - 1960; P - 1964.

Gore, Albert Jr. - Tenn. (Democrat) March 31, 1948—; House, 1977-85; Senate, 1985-93; U.S. vice president, 1993—. Candidacy: VP - 1992, 1996.

Graham, William Alexander - N.C. (Whig) Sept. 5, 1804 - Aug. 11, 1875; Senate, 1840-43; governor, 1845-49; secretary of the Navy, 1850-52; Confederate Senate, 1864. Candidacy: VP - 1852.

Granger, Francis - N.Y. (Whig) Dec. 1, 1792 - Aug. 31, 1868; House, 1835-37, 1839-41, 1841-43; postmaster general, 1841. Candidacy: VP - 1836.

Grant, Ulysses Simpson - Ill. (Republican) April 27, 1822 - July 23, 1885; commander-in-chief, Union Army during Civil War; U.S. president, 1869-77. Candidacies: P - 1868, 1872.

Greeley, Horace - N.Y. (Liberal Republican, Democratic) Feb. 3, 1811 - Nov. 29, 1872; founder and editor, New York Tribune, 1841-72; House, 1848-49. Candidacy: P - 1872.

Griffin, S. Marvin - Ga. (American Independent) Sept. 4, 1907 - June 13, 1982; governor, 1955-59. Candidacy: VP - 1968. (Substituted as candidate until permanent candidate Curtis LeMay was chosen.)

Groesbeck, William Slocum - Ohio (Democratic) July 24, 1815 - July 7, 1897; House, 1857-59; delegate to International Monetary Conference in Paris, 1878. Candidacy: VP - 1872.

Hale, John Parker - N.H. (Free Soil) March 31, 1806 - Nov. 19, 1873; House, 1843-45; Senate, 1847-53, 1855-65; minister to Spain, 1865-69. Candidacy: P - 1852.

Hamlin, Hannibal - Maine (Republican) Aug. 27, 1809 - July 4, 1891; House, 1843-47; Senate, 1848-57, 1857-61, 1869-81; governor, 1857; U.S. vice president, 1861-65. Candidacy: VP - 1860.

Hancock, John - Mass. (Federalist) Jan. 23, 1737 - Oct. 8, 1793; Continental Congress, 1775-78, 1785-86; president of Continental Congress, 1775-77; governor, 1780-85, 1787-93. Candidacy: 1789.

Hancock, Winfield Scott - Pa. (Democratic) Feb. 14, 1824 - Feb. 9, 1886; brigadier general, commander of II Army Corps, Civil War. Candidacy: P - 1880.

Harding, Warren Gamaliel - Ohio (Republican) Nov. 2, 1865 - Aug. 2, 1923; lieutenant governor, 1904-05; Senate, 1915-21; U.S. president, 1921-23. Candidacy: P - 1920.

Harper, Robert Goodloe - Md. (Federalist) January 1765 - Jan. 14, 1825; House, 1795-1801; Senate, 1816. Candidacies: VP - 1816, 1820.

Harrison, Benjamin - Ind. (Republican) Aug. 20, 1833 - March 13, 1901; Union officer in Civil War; Senate, 1881-87; U.S. president, 1889-93. Candidacies: P - 1888, 1892.

Harrison, Robert H. - Md. 1745 - 1790; chief justice, General Court of Maryland, 1781. Candidacy: 1789.

Harrison, William Henry - Ohio (Whig) Feb. 9, 1773 - April 4, 1841; delegate to Congress from the Northwest Territory, 1799-1800; territorial governor of Indiana, 1801-13; House, 1816-19; Senate, 1825-28; U.S. president, 1841. Candidacies: P - 1836, 1840.

Hayes, Rutherford Birchard - Ohio (Republican) Oct. 4, 1822 - Jan. 17, 1893; major general in Union Army during Civil War; House, 1865-67; governor, 1868-72, 1876-77; U.S. president, 1877-81. Candidacy: P - 1876.

Hendricks, Thomas Andrews - Ind. (Democratic) Sept. 7, 1819 - Nov. 25, 1885; House, 1851-55; Senate, 1863-69; governor, 1873-77; U.S. vice president, 1885. Candidacies: P - 1872; VP - 1876, 1884.

Henry, John - Md. (Democratic-Republican) Nov. 1750 - Dec. 16, 1798; Continental Congress, 1778-80, 1785-86; Senate, 1789-97; governor, 1797-98. Candidacy - 1796.

Hobart, Garret Augustus - N.J. (Republican) June 3, 1844 - Nov. 21, 1899; New Jersey Senate, 1876-82; president of New Jersey Senate, 1881-82; Republican National Committee, 1884-96; U.S. vice president, 1897-99. Candidacy: VP - 1896.

Hoover, Herbert Clark - Calif. (Republican) Aug. 10, 1874 - Oct. 20, 1964; U.S. food administrator, 1917-19; secretary of commerce, 1921-28; U.S. president, 1929-33; chairman, Commission on Organization of the Executive Branch of Government, 1947-49, 1953-55. Candidacies: P - 1928, 1932.

Hospers, John - Calif. (Libertarian) June 9, 1918—; director of school of philosophy at University of Southern California. Candidacy: P - 1972.

Howard, John Eager - Md. (Federalist) June 4, 1752 - Oct. 12, 1827; Continental Congress, 1788; governor, 1788-91; Senate, 1796-1803. Candidacy: VP - 1816.

Hughes, Charles Evans - N.Y. (Republican) April 11, 1862 - Aug. 27, 1948; governor, 1907-10; associate justice of U.S. Supreme Court, 1910-16; secretary of state, 1921-25; chief justice of United States, 1930-41. Candidacy: P - 1916.

Humphrey, Hubert Horatio Jr. - Minn. (Democratic) May 27, 1911 - Jan. 13, 1978; mayor of Minneapolis, 1945-48; Senate, 1949-64, 1971-78; U.S. vice president, 1965-69. Candidacies: VP - 1964; P - 1968.

Huntington, Samuel - Conn., July 3, 1731 - Jan. 5, 1796; Continental Congress, 1776, 1778-81, 1783; president of the Continental Congress, 1779-81; governor, 1786-96. Candidacy: 1789.

Ingersoll, Jared - Pa. (Federalist) Oct. 24, 1749 - Oct. 31, 1822; Continental Congress, 1780-81; Constitutional Convention, 1787. Candidacy: VP - 1812.

Iredell, James - N.C. (Federalist) Oct. 5, 1751 - Oct. 20, 1799; associate justice of U.S. Supreme Court, 1790-99. Candidacy: 1796.

Jackson, Andrew - Tenn. (Democratic-Republican, Democratic) March 15, 1767 - June 8, 1845; House, 1796-97; Senate, 1797-98, 1823-25; territorial governor of Florida, 1821; U.S. president, 1829-37. Candidacies: P - 1824, 1828, 1832.

Jay, John - N.Y. (Federalist) Dec. 12, 1745 - May 17, 1829; Continental Congress, 1774-76, 1778-79; president of Continental Congress, 1778-79; minister to Spain, 1779; chief justice of United States, 1789-95; governor, 1795-1801. Candidacies: 1789, 1796, 1800.

Jefferson, Thomas - Va. (Democratic-Republican) April 13, 1743 - July 4, 1826; Continental Congress, 1775-76, 1783-84; author and signer of Declaration of Independence, 1776; governor, 1779-81; minister to France, 1784-89; secretary of state, 1790-93; U.S. vice president, 1797-1801; U.S. president, 1801-09. Candidacies: VP - 1792; P - 1796, 1800, 1804.

Jenkins, Charles Jones - Ga. (Democratic) Jan. 6, 1805 - June 14, 1883; governor, 1865-68. Candidacy: P - 1872.

Johnson, Andrew - Tenn. (Republican) Dec. 29, 1808 - July 31, 1875; House, 1843-53; governor, 1853-57; Senate, 1857-62, 1875; U.S. vice president, 1865; U.S. president, 1865-69. Candidacy: VP - 1864.

Johnson, Herschel Vespasian - Ga. (Democratic) Sept. 18, 1812 - Aug. 16, 1880; Senate, 1848-49; governor, 1853-57; senator, Confederate Congress, 1862-65. Candidacy: VP - 1860.

Johnson, Hiram Warren - Calif. (Progressive) Sept. 2, 1866 - Aug. 6, 1945; governor, 1911-17; Senate, 1917-45. Candidacy: VP - 1912.

Johnson, Lyndon Baines - Texas (Democratic) Aug. 27, 1908 - Jan. 22, 1973; House, 1937-49; Senate, 1949-61; Senate minority leader, 1953-55; Senate majority leader, 1955-61; U.S. vice president, 1961-63; U.S. president, 1963-69. Candidacies: VP - 1960; P - 1964.

Johnson, Richard Mentor - Ky. (Democratic) Oct. 17, 1780 - Nov. 19, 1850; House,

1807-19, 1829-37; Senate, 1819-29; U.S. vice president, 1837-41. Candidacies: VP - 1836, 1840.

Johnston, Samuel - N.C. (Federalist) Dec. 15, 1733 - Aug. 17, 1816; Continental Congress, 1780-81; governor, 1787-89; Senate, 1789-93. Candidacy: 1796.

Jones, Walter Burgwyn - Ala. (Independent Democratic) Oct. 16, 1888 - Aug. 1, 1963; Alabama Legislature, 1919-20; Alabama circuit court judge, 1920-35; presiding judge, 1935-63. Candidacy: P - 1956.

Julian, George Washington - Ind. (Free Soil, Liberal Republican) May 5, 1817 - July 7, 1899; House, 1849-51, 1861-71. Candidacies: VP - 1852, 1872.

Kefauver, Estes - Tenn. (Democratic) July 26, 1903 - Aug. 10, 1963; House, 1939-49; Senate, 1949-63. Candidacy: VP - 1956.

Kemp, Jack F. - N.Y. (Republican) July 13, 1935—; House, 1971-89; secretary of Housing and Urban Development, 1989-93. Candidacy: VP - 1996.

Kennedy, John Fitzgerald - Mass. (Democratic) May 29, 1917 - Nov. 22, 1963; House, 1947-53; Senate, 1953-60; U.S. president, 1961-63. Candidacy: P - 1960.

Kern, John Worth - Ind. (Democratic) Dec. 20, 1849 - Aug. 17, 1917; Senate, 1911-17; Senate majority leader, 1913-17. Candidacy: VP - 1908.

King, Rufus - N.Y. (Federalist) March 24, 1755 - April 29, 1827; Continental Congress, 1784-87; Constitutional Convention, 1787; Senate, 1789-96, 1813-25; minister to Great Britain, 1796-1803, 1825-26. Candidacies: VP - 1804, 1808; P - 1816.

King, William Rufus de Vane - Ala. (Democratic) April 7, 1786 - April 18, 1853; House, 1811-16; Senate, 1819-44, 1848-52; president pro tempore of the Senate, 1836, 1837, 1838, 1839, 1840, 1841, 1850; minister to France, 1844-46; U.S. vice president, 1853. Candidacy: VP - 1852.

Knox, Franklin - Ill. (Republican) Jan. 1, 1874 - April 28, 1944; secretary of the Navy, 1940-44. Candidacy: VP - 1936.

La Follette, Robert Marion - Wis. (Progressive) June 14, 1855 - June 18, 1925; House, 1885-91; governor, 1901-06; Senate, 1906-25. Candidacy: P - 1924.

Landon, Alfred Mossman - Kan. (Republican) Sept. 9, 1887 - Oct. 12, 1987; governor, 1933-37. Candidacy: P - 1936.

Lane, Joseph - Ore. (Southern Democratic) Dec. 14, 1801 - April 19, 1881; governor of Oregon Territory, 1849-50, 1853; House (territorial delegate), 1851-59; Senate, 1859-61. Candidacy: VP - 1860.

Langdon, John - N.H. (Democratic-Republican) June 26, 1741 - Sept. 18, 1819; Continental Congress, 1775-76, 1787; governor, 1805-09, 1810-12; Senate, 1789-1801; first president pro tempore of the Senate, 1789. Candidacy: VP - 1808.

Lee, Henry - Mass. (Independent Democratic) Feb. 4, 1782 - Feb. 6, 1867; merchant and publicist. Candidacy: VP - 1832.

LeMay, Curtis Emerson - Ohio (American Independent) Nov. 15, 1906 - Oct. 1, 1990; Air Force chief of staff, 1961-65. Candidacy: VP - 1968.

Lemke, William - N.D. (Union) Aug. 13, 1878 - May 30, 1950; House, 1933-41, 1943-50. Candidacy: P - 1936.

Lincoln, Abraham - Ill. (Republican) Feb. 12, 1809 - April 15, 1865; House, 1847-49. U.S. president, 1861-65 Candidacies: 1860, 1864.

Lincoln, Benjamin - Mass. (Federalist) Jan. 24, 1733 - May 9, 1810; major general in Continental Army, 1777-81. Candidacy: 1789.

Lodge, Henry Cabot Jr. - Mass. (Republican) July 5, 1902 - Feb. 27, 1985; Senate, 1937-44, 1947-53; ambassador to United Nations, 1953-60; ambassador to Republic of Vietnam, 1963-64, 1965-67. Candidacy: VP - 1960.

Logan, John Alexander - Ill. (Republican) Feb. 9, 1826 - Dec. 26, 1886; House, 1859-62, 1867-71; Senate, 1871-77, 1879-86. Candidacy: VP - 1884.

Machen, Willis Benson - Ky. (Democratic) April 10, 1810 - Sept. 29, 1893; Confederate Congress, 1861-65; Senate, 1872-73. Candidacy: VP - 1872.

Macon, Nathaniel - N.C. (Democratic-Republican) Dec. 17, 1757 - June 29, 1837; House, 1791-1815; Speaker of the House, 1801-07; Senate, 1815-28; president pro tempore of the Senate, 1826, 1827. Candidacy: VP - 1824.

Madison, James - Va. (Democratic-Republican) March 16, 1751 - June 28, 1836; Continental Congress, 1780-83, 1787-88; Constitutional Convention, 1787; House, 1789-97; secretary of state, 1801-09; U.S. president, 1809-17. Candidacies: P - 1808, 1812.

Mangum, Willie Person - N.C. (Independent Democrat) May 10, 1792 - Sept. 7, 1861; House, 1823-26; Senate, 1831-36, 1840-53. Candidacy: P - 1836.

Marshall, John - Va. (Federalist) Sept. 24, 1755 - July 6, 1835; House 1799-1800; secretary of state, 1800-01; chief justice of United States, 1801-35. Candidacy: VP - 1816.

Marshall, Thomas Riley - Ind. (Democratic) March 14, 1854 - June 1, 1925; governor, 1909-13; U.S. vice president, 1913-21. Candidacies: VP - 1912, 1916.

McCarthy, Eugene Joseph - Minn. (Independent) March 29, 1916—; House, 1949-59; Senate, 1959-71. Candidacy: P - 1976.

McClellan, George Brinton - N.J. (Democratic) Dec. 3, 1826 - Oct. 29, 1885; general-in-chief of Army of the Potomac, 1861; governor, 1878-81. Candidacy: P - 1864.

McGovern, George Stanley - S.D. (Democratic) July 19, 1922—; House, 1957-61; Senate, 1963-81. Candidacy: P - 1972.

McKinley, William Jr. - Ohio (Republican) Jan. 29, 1843 - Sept. 14, 1901; House, 1877, 1885-91; governor, 1892-96; U.S. president, 1897-1901. Candidacies: P - 1896, 1900.

McNary, Charles Linza - Ore. (Republican) June 12, 1874 - Feb. 25, 1944; state Supreme Court judge, 1913-15; Senate, 1917-18, 1918-44; Senate minority leader, 1933-44. Candidacy: VP - 1940.

Miller, William Edward - N.Y. (Republican) March 22, 1914 - June 24, 1983; House, 1951-65; chairman of Republican National Committee, 1960-64. Candidacy: VP - 1964.

Milton, John - Ga. circa 1740 - circa 1804; secretary of state, Georgia, circa 1778, 1781, 1783. Candidacy: 1789.

Mondale, Walter Frederick - Minn. (Democratic) Jan. 5, 1928—; Senate, 1964-76; U.S. vice president, 1977-81; ambassador to Japan, 1993-96. Candidacies: VP - 1976, 1980; P - 1984.

Monroe, James - Va. (Democratic-Republican) April 28, 1758 - July 4, 1831; Continental Congress, 1783-86; Senate, 1790-94; minister to France, 1794-96, 1803; minister to England, 1803-07; governor, 1799-1802, 1811; secretary of state, 1811-14, 1815-17; U.S. president, 1817-25. Candidacies: VP - 1808; P - 1816, 1820.

Morton, Levi Parsons - N.Y. (Republican) May 16, 1824 - May 16, 1920; House, 1879-81; minister to France, 1881-85; U.S. vice president, 1889-93; governor, 1895-97. Candidacy: VP - 1888.

Muskie, Edmund Sixtus - Maine (Democratic) March 28, 1914 - March 26, 1996; governor, 1955-59; Senate, 1959-80; secretary of state, 1980-81. Candidacy: VP - 1968.

Nathan, Theodora Nathalia - Ore. (Libertarian) Feb. 9, 1923—; broadcast journalist; National Judiciary Committee, Libertarian Party, 1972-75; vice chairperson, Oregon Libertarian Party, 1974-75. Candidacy: VP - 1972.

Nixon, Richard Milhous - Calif., N.Y. (Republican) Jan. 9, 1913 - April 22, 1994; House, 1947-50; Senate, 1950-53; U.S. vice president, 1953-61; U.S. president, 1969-74. Candidacies: VP - 1952, 1956; P - 1960, 1968, 1972.

Palmer, John McAuley - Ill. (Democratic, National Democratic) Sept. 13, 1817 - Sept. 25, 1900; governor, 1869-73; Senate, 1891-97. Candidacies: VP - 1872; P - 1896.

Parker, Alton Brooks - N.Y. (Democratic) May 14, 1852 - May 10, 1926; chief justice of N.Y. Court of Appeals, 1898-1904. Candidacy: P - 1904.

Pendleton, George Hunt - Ohio (Democratic) July 19, 1825 - Nov. 24, 1889; House, 1857-65; Senate, 1879-85; minister to Germany, 1885-89. Candidacy: VP - 1864.

Perot, H. Ross - Texas (Independent, Reform) June 27, 1930—; business executive and owner. Candidacy: P - 1992, 1996.

Pierce, Franklin - N.H. (Democratic) Nov. 23, 1804 - Oct. 8, 1869; House, 1833-37; Senate, 1837-42; U.S. president, 1853-57. Candidacy: P - 1852.

Pinckney, Charles Cotesworth - S.C. (Federalist) Feb. 25, 1746 - Aug. 16, 1825; president, state senate, 1779; minister to France, 1796. Candidacies: VP - 1800; P - 1804, 1808.

Pinckney, Thomas - S.C. (Federalist) Oct. 23, 1750 - Nov. 2, 1828; governor, 1787-89; minister to Great Britain, 1792-96; envoy to Spain, 1794-95; House, 1797-1801. Candidacy: 1796.

Polk, James Knox - Tenn. (Democratic) Nov. 2, 1795 - June 15, 1849; House, 1825-39; Speaker of the House, 1835-39; governor, 1839-41; U.S. president, 1845-49. Candidacies: VP - 1840; P - 1844.

Quayle, Dan - Ind. (Republican) Feb. 4, 1947—;House, 1977-81; Senate, 1981-89; U.S. vice president, 1989-93. Candidacies; VP - 1988, 1992.

Reagan, Ronald Wilson - Calif. (Republican) Feb. 6, 1911—; governor, 1967-75; U.S. president, 1981-89. Candidacies: P - 1980, 1984.

Reid, Whitelaw - N.Y. (Republican) Oct. 27, 1837 - Dec. 15, 1912; minister to France, 1889-92; editor-in-chief, *New York Tribune*, 1872-1905. Candidacy: VP - 1892.

Robinson, Joseph Taylor - Ark. (Democratic) Aug. 26, 1872 - July 14, 1937; House,

1903-13; governor, 1913; Senate, 1913-37; Senate minority leader, 1923-33; Senate majority leader, 1933-37. Candidacy: VP - 1928.

Rockefeller, Nelson Aldrich - N.Y. (Republican) July 8, 1908 - Jan. 26, 1979; governor, 1959-73; U.S. vice president, 1974-77 (nominated under the provisions of the 25th Amendment).

Rodney, Daniel - Del. (Federalist) Sept. 10, 1764 - Sept. 2, 1846; governor, 1814-17; House, 1822-23; Senate, 1826-27. Candidacy: VP - 1820.

Roosevelt, Franklin Delano - N.Y. (Democratic) Jan. 30, 1882 - April 12, 1945; assistant secretary of the Navy, 1913-20; governor, 1929-33; U.S. president, 1933-45. Candidacies: VP - 1920; P - 1932, 1936, 1940, 1944.

Roosevelt, Theodore - N.Y. (Republican, Progressive) Oct. 27, 1858 - Jan. 6, 1919; assistant secretary of the Navy, 1897-98; governor, 1899-1901; U.S. vice president, 1901; U.S. president, 1901-09. Candidacies: VP - 1900; P - 1904, 1912.

Ross, James - Pa. (Federalist) July 12, 1762 - Nov. 27, 1847; Senate, 1794-1803. Candidacy: VP - 1816.

Rush, Richard - Pa. (Democratic-Republican, National-Republican) Aug. 29, 1780 - July 30, 1859; attorney general, 1814-17; minister to Great Britain, 1817-24; secretary of the Treasury, 1825-29. Candidacies: VP - 1820, 1828.

Rutledge, John - S.C. (Federalist) Sept. 1739 - July 23, 1800; Continental Congress, 1774-75, 1782-83; governor, 1779-82; Constitutional Convention, 1787; associate justice of U.S. Supreme Court, 1789-91; chief justice of United States, 1795. Candidacy: 1789.

Sanford, Nathan - N.Y. (Democratic-Republican) Nov. 5, 1777 - Oct. 17, 1838; Senate, 1815-21, 1826-31. Candidacy: VP - 1824.

Schmitz, John George - Calif. (American Independent) Aug. 12, 1930—; House, 1970-73. Candidacy: P - 1972.

Scott, Winfield - N.J. (Whig) June 13, 1786 - May 29, 1866; general-in-chief of U.S. Army, 1841-61. Candidacy: P - 1852.

Sergeant, John - Pa. (National-Republican) Dec. 5, 1779 - Nov. 23, 1852; House, 1815-23, 1827-29, 1837-41. Candidacy: VP - 1832.

Sewall, Arthur - Maine (Democratic) Nov. 25, 1835 - Sept. 5, 1900; Democratic National Committee member, 1888-96. Candidacy: VP - 1896.

Seymour, Horatio - N.Y. (Democratic) May 31, 1810 - Feb. 12, 1886; governor, 1853-55, 1863-65. Candidacy: P - 1868.

Sherman, James Schoolcraft - N.Y. (Republican) Oct. 24, 1855 - Oct. 30, 1912; House, 1887-91, 1893-1909; U.S. vice president, 1909-12. Candidacies: VP - 1908, 1912. (Died during 1912 campaign; Nicholas Murray Butler replaced Sherman on the Republican ticket.)

Shriver, Robert Sargent Jr. - Md. (Democratic) Nov. 9, 1915—; director, Peace Corps, 1961-66; director, Office of Economic Opportunity, 1964-68; ambassador to France, 1968-70. Candidacy: VP - 1972. (Replaced Thomas F. Eagleton on Democratic ticket Aug. 8.)

Smith, Alfred Emanuel - N.Y. (Democratic) Dec. 30, 1873 - Oct. 4, 1944; governor, 1919-21, 1923-29. Candidacy: P - 1928.

Smith, William - S.C., Ala. (Independent Democratic-Republican) Sept. 6, 1762 - June 26, 1840; Senate, 1816-23, 1826-31. Candidacies: VP - 1828, 1836.

Sparkman, John Jackson - Ala. (Democratic) Dec. 20, 1899 - Nov. 16, 1985; House, 1937-46; Senate, 1946-79. Candidacy: VP - 1952.

Stevenson, Adlai Ewing - Ill. (Democratic) Oct. 23, 1835 - June 14, 1914; House, 1875-77, 1879-81; assistant postmaster general, 1885-89; U.S. vice president, 1893-97. Candidacies: VP - 1892, 1900.

Stevenson, Adlai Ewing II - Ill. (Democratic) Feb. 5, 1900 - July 14, 1965; assistant to the secretary of Navy, 1941-44; assistant to the secretary of state, 1945; governor, 1949-53; ambassador to United Nations, 1961-65. Candidacies: P - 1952, 1956.

Stockton, Richard - N.J. (Federalist) April 17, 1764 - March 7, 1828; Senate, 1796-99; House, 1813-15. Candidacy: VP - 1820.

Taft, William Howard - Ohio (Republican) Sept. 15, 1857 - March 8, 1930; secretary of war, 1904-08; U.S. president, 1909-13; chief justice of United States, 1921-30. Candidacies: P - 1908, 1912.

Talmadge, Herman Eugene - Ga. (Independent Democratic) Aug. 9, 1913—; governor, 1947, 1948-55; Senate, 1957-81. Candidacy: VP - 1956.

Taylor, Glen Hearst - Idaho (Progressive) April 12, 1904 - April 28, 1984; Senate, 1945-51. Candidacy: VP - 1948.

Taylor, Zachary - La. (Whig) Nov. 24, 1784 - July 9, 1850; major general, U.S. Army; U.S. president, 1849-50. Candidacy: P - 1848.

Tazewell, Littleton Waller - Va. (Democratic) Dec. 17, 1774 - May 6, 1860; House, 1800-01; Senate, 1824-32; president pro tempore of the Senate, 1832; governor, 1834-36. Candidacy: VP - 1840.

Telfair, Edward - Ga. (Democratic-Republican) 1735 - Sept. 17, 1807; Continental Congress, 1778, 1780-82; governor, 1789-93. Candidacy: 1789.

Thomas, Norman Mattoon - N.Y. (Socialist) Nov. 20, 1884 - Dec. 19, 1968; Presbyterian minister, 1911-31; author and editor. Candidacies: P - 1928, 1932, 1936, 1940, 1944, 1948.

Thurman, Allen Granberry - Ohio (Democratic) Nov. 13, 1813 - Dec. 12, 1895; House, 1845-47; Ohio Supreme Court, 1851-56; Senate, 1869-81; president pro tempore of the Senate, 1879, 1880. Candidacy: VP - 1888.

Thurmond, James Strom - S.C. (States' Rights Democrat) Dec. 5, 1902—; governor, 1947-51; Senate, 1954-56, 1956—; president pro tempore of the Senate, 1981-87; 1995—. Candidacies: P - 1948.

Tilden, Samuel Jones - N.Y. (Democratic) Feb. 9, 1814 - Aug. 4, 1886; governor, 1875-77. Candidacy: P - 1876.

Tompkins, Daniel D. - N.Y. (Democratic-Republican) June 21, 1774 - June 11, 1825; elected to the House for the term beginning in 1805 but resigned before taking seat; governor, 1807-17; U.S. vice president, 1817-25. Candidacies: VP - 1816, 1820.

Truman, Harry S. - Mo. (Democratic) May 8, 1884 - Dec. 26, 1972; Senate, 1935-45; U.S. vice president, 1945; U.S. president, 1945-53. Candidacies: VP - 1944; P - 1948.

Tyler, John - Va. (Whig) March 29, 1790 - Jan. 18, 1862; governor, 1825-27; Senate, 1827-36; U.S. vice president, 1841; U.S. president, 1841-45. Candidacies: VP - 1836, 1840.

Van Buren, Martin - N.Y. (Democratic, Free Soil) Dec. 5, 1782 - July 24, 1862; Senate, 1821-28; governor, 1829; secretary of state, 1829-31; U.S. vice president, 1833-37; U.S. president, 1837-41. Candidacies: VP - 1824, 1832; P - 1836, 1840, 1848.

Wallace, George Corley - Ala. (American Independent) Aug. 25, 1919—; governor, 1963-67, 1971-79, 1983-89. Candidacy: P - 1968.

Wallace, Henry Agard - Iowa (Democratic, Progressive) Oct. 7, 1888 - Nov. 18, 1965; secretary of agriculture, 1933-40; U.S. vice president, 1941-45; secretary of commerce, 1945-46. Candidacies: VP - 1940; P - 1948.

Warren, Earl - Calif. (Republican) March 19, 1891 - July 9, 1974; governor, 1943-53; chief justice of United States, 1953-69. Candidacy: VP - 1948.

Washington, George - Va. (Federalist) Feb. 22, 1732 - Dec. 14, 1799; First and Second Continental Congresses, 1774, 1775; commander-in-chief of armed forces, 1775-83; president of Constitutional Convention, 1787; U.S. president, 1789-97. Candidacies: P - 1789, 1792, 1796.

Watson, Thomas Edward - Ga. (Populist) Sept. 5, 1856 - Sept. 26, 1922; House, 1891-93; Senate, 1921-22. Candidacies: VP - 1896; P - 1904, 1908.

Weaver, James Baird - Iowa (Greenback, Populist) June 12, 1833 - Feb. 6, 1912; House, 1879-81, 1885-89; Candidacies: P - 1880, 1892.

Webster, Daniel - Mass. (Whig) Jan. 18, 1782 - Oct. 24, 1852; House, 1813-17, 1823-27; Senate, 1827-41, 1845-50; secretary of state, 1841-43, 1850-52. Candidacy: P - 1836.

Wheeler, Burton Kendall - Mont. (Progressive) Feb. 27, 1882 - Jan. 6, 1975; Senate, 1923-47. Candidacy: VP - 1924.

Wheeler, William Almon - N.Y. (Republican) June 30, 1819 - June 4, 1887; House, 1861-63, 1869-77; U.S. vice president, 1877-81. Candidacy: VP - 1876.

White, Hugh Lawson - Tenn. (Whig) Oct. 30, 1773 - April 10, 1840; Senate, 1825-35, 1835-40. Candidacy: P - 1836.

Wilkins, William - Pa. (Democratic) Dec. 20, 1779 - June 23, 1865; Senate, 1831-34; minister to Russia, 1834-35; House, 1843-44; secretary of war, 1844-45. Candidacy: VP - 1832.

Willkie, Wendell Lewis - N.Y. (Republican) Feb. 18, 1892 - Oct. 8, 1944; utility executive, 1933-40. Candidacy: P - 1940.

Wilson, Henry - Mass. (Republican) Feb. 16, 1812 - Nov. 22, 1875; Senate, 1855-73; U.S. vice president, 1873-75. Candidacy: VP - 1872.

Wilson, Woodrow - N.J. (Democratic) Dec. 28, 1856 - Feb. 3, 1924; governor, 1911-13; U.S. president, 1913-21. Candidacies: P - 1912, 1916.

Wirt, William - Md. (Anti-Masonic) Nov. 8, 1772 - Feb. 18, 1834; attorney general, 1817-29. Candidacy: P - 1832.

Wright, Fielding Lewis - Miss. (States' Rights Democratic) May 16, 1895 - May 4, 1956; governor, 1946-52. Candidacy: VP - 1948.

Bibliography

Books

Alexander, Herbert E., and Monica Bauer. *Financing the 1988 Election.* Boulder, Colo.: Westview, 1991.

Alexander, Herbert E., and Anthony Corrado. *Financing the 1992 Election.* Armonk, N.Y.: M. E. Sharpe, 1995.

Aldrich, John H. *Before the Convention: Strategies and Choices in Presidential Nomination Campaigns.* Chicago: University of Chicago Press, 1980.

Arnett, A. M. *The Populist Movement in Georgia.* 1922. Reprint. New York: Columbia University Press, 1971.

Bain, Richard C., and Judith H. Parris. *Convention Decisions and Voting Records.* 2nd ed. Washington, D.C.: Brookings, 1975.

Bibby, John F. *Governing by Consent: An Introduction to American Politics.* 2nd ed. Washington, D.C.: CQ Press, 1995.

___. *Politics, Parties, and Elections in America.* 3rd ed. Chicago: Nelson-Hall, 1996.

Blue, Frederick J. *The Free Soilers: Third Party Politics, 1848-1854.* Urbana: University of Illinois Press, 1973.

Borden, Morton. *Parties and Politics in the Early Republic, 1789-1815.* Arlington Heights, Ill.: Davidson, Harlan, 1967.

Brock, William. *Parties and Political Conscience: American Dilemmas, 1840-1850.* Millwood, N.Y.: Kraus International Publications, 1979.

Brown, Stuart G. *First Republicans: Political Philosophy and Public Policy in the Party of Jefferson and Madison.* 1954. Reprint. Westport, Conn.: Greenwood Press, 1977.

Buell, Emmett H., Jr., and Lee Sigelman. *Nominating the President.* Knoxville: University of Tennessee Press, 1991.

Burner, David. *The Politics of Provincialism: The Democratic Party in Transition, 1918-1932.* 1968. Reprint. Cambridge: Harvard University Press, 1986.

Byrne, Gary C., and Paul Marx. *The Great American Convention: A Political History of Presidential Elections.* Palo Alto, Calif.: Pacific Books, 1977.

Cannon, James P. *The History of American Trotskyism from Its Origin in 1928 to the Founding of the Socialist Labor Workers Party.* New York: Pathfinders Press, 1972.

Chambers, William N., and Walter D. Burnham, eds. *The American Party Systems: Stages of Political Development.* 2nd ed. New York: Oxford University Press, 1975.

Chase, James S. *Emergence of the Presidential Nominating Convention: 1789-1832.* Urbana: University of Illinois Press, 1973.

Congressional Quarterly. *Presidential Elections 1789-1996.* Washington, D.C.: Congressional Quarterly, 1997.

Congressional Quarterly. *Selecting the President: From 1789-1996.* Washington, D.C.: Congressional Quarterly, 1997.

Conway, M. Margaret. *Political Participation in the United States.* 2nd ed. Washington, D.C.: CQ Press, 1991.

Cotter, Cornelius P. *Party Organization in American Politics.* Pittsburgh: University of Pittsburgh Press, 1989.

Cunningham, Noble E. *Jeffersonian Republicans: The Formation of Party Organization, 1789-1801.* Chapel Hill: University of North Carolina Press, 1967.

Davis, James W. *National Conventions: Nominations Under the Big Top.* Woodbury, N.Y.: Barron Educational Series, 1972.

___. *National Conventions in an Age of Party Reform.* Westport, Conn.: Greenwood Press, 1983.

de Tocqueville, Alexis. *Democracy in America.* Reprint. New York: Vintage, 1990.

Dinkin, Robert J. *Voting in Revolutionary America: A Study of Elections in the Original Thirteen States, 1776-1789.* Westport, Conn.: Greenwood Press, 1982.

Durbin, Thomas, ed. *Nomination and Election of the President and Vice President of the United States, 1992, Including the Manner of Selecting Delegates to National Party Conventions.* Washington, D.C.: U.S. Government Printing Office, 1992.

Eldersveld, Samuel J. *Political Parties in American Society.* New York: Basic Books, 1982.

Fairlie, Henry. *The Parties: Republicans and Democrats in this Century.* New York: St. Martin's Press, 1978.

Farley, James A. *Behind the Ballots: the Personal History of a Politician.* 1938. Reprint. New York: Da Capo Press, 1973.

Fleishman, Joel L. *The Future of American Political Parties.* Englewood Cliffs, N.J.: Prentice-Hall, 1982.

Foner, Eric. *Free Soil, Free Labor, Free Men: The Ideology of the Republican Party Before the Civil War.* Rev. ed. New York: Oxford University Press, 1995.

Gillespie, J. David. *Politics at the Periphery: Third Parties in Two-Party America.* Columbia: University of South Carolina Press, 1993.

Halstead, Murat. *Trimmers, Trucklers and Temporizers: Notes of Murat Halstead from the Political Convention of 1856.* Madison: Wisconsin Historical Society Press, 1961.

Hertzke, Allen D. *Echoes of Discontent: Jesse Jackson, Pat Robertson, and the Resurgence of Populism.* Washington, D.C.: CQ Press, 1993.

Hicks, John D. *The Populist Revolt: A History of the Farmer's Alliance in the People's Party.* Reprint. Minneapolis: University of Minnesota Press, 1981.

Hofstadter, Richard. *The Idea of a Party System: The Rise of Legitimate Opposition in the United States, 1780-1840.* Berkeley: University of California Press, 1969.

Holcombe, Arthur N. *Political Parties of Today: A Study in Republican and Democratic Politics.* New York: Harper and Row, 1974.

Jackson, John S., and William Crotty. *The Politics of Presidential Selection.* New York: HarperCollins, 1996.

Jones, Charles O. *The Republican Party in American Politics.* New York: Macmillan, 1965.

Keech, William R., and Donald R. Matthews. *The Party's Choice: With an Epilogue on the 1976 Nominations.* Washington, D.C.: Brookings, 1977.

Keefe, William J. *Parties, Politics, and Public Policy in America.* 7th ed. Washington, D.C.: CQ Press, 1994.

Kent, Frank R. *The Democratic Party: A History.* 1928. Reprint. New York: Johnson Reprint, 1968.

Kessel, John H. *Presidential Campaign Politics.* 4th ed. Pacific Grove, Calif.: Brooks-Cole, 1992.

Kipnis, Ira. *American Socialist Movement, 1897-1912.* Westport, Conn.: Greenwood Press, 1968.

Kraut, Alan M., ed. *Crusaders and Compromisers: Essays on the Relationship of Antislavery Struggle to the Antebellum Party System.* Westport, Conn.: Greenwood Press, 1983.

Kruschke, Earl R. *Encyclopedia of Third Parties in the United States.* Santa Barbara, Calif.: ABC-CLIO, 1991.

Ladd, Everett C., Jr. *Where Have All the Voters Gone? The Fracturing of American Political Parties.* 2nd ed. New York: Norton, 1982.

Ladd, Everett C., Jr., and Charles D. Hadley. *Transformations of the American Party System: Political Coalitions from the New Deal to the 1970s.* 2nd ed. New York: Norton, 1978.

Lamis, Alexander P. *The Two-Party South.* 2nd ed. New York: Oxford University Press, 1990.

Lee, John H. *The Origin and Progress of the American Party in Politics: Embracing a Complete History of the Philadelphia Riots in May and July, 1844.* Reprint. Salem, N.H.: Ayer, 1977.

Livermore, Shaw, Jr. *Twilight of Federalism: The Disintegration of the Federalist Party, 1815-1830.* Staten Island, N.Y.: Gordian Press, 1972.

Main, Jackson T. *Political Parties Before the Constitution.* New York: Norton, 1974.

Maisel, L. Sandy. *The Parties Respond: Changes in American Parties and Campaigns.* Boulder, Colo.: Westview, 1994.

Matthews, Donald R. *Perspectives on Presidential Selection.* Washington, D.C.: Brookings, 1973.

McCormick, Richard P. *The Second American Party System: Party Formulation in the Jacksonian Era.* Chapel Hill: University of North Carolina Press, 1973.

McKay, Kenneth. *The Progressive Movement of 1924.* New York: Octagon Books, 1966.

McKee, Thomas H. *The National Conventions and Platforms of All Political Parties, 1789-1905: Convention, Popular and Electoral Vote.* New York: AMS Press, 1971.

Milkis, Sidney M. *The President and the Parties: The Transformation of the American Party System Since the New Deal.* New York: Oxford University Press, 1993.

Morgan, Wayne. *From Hayes to McKinley: National Party Politics, 1877-1896.* Syracuse, N.Y.: Syracuse University Press, 1969.

Morris, Richard B., and Jeffrey B. Morris, eds. *Encyclopedia of American History.* 7th ed. New York: Harper and Row, 1996.

Nichols, Roy F. *The Invention of the American Political Parties: A Study of Political Improvisation.* New York: Free Press, 1972.

Parris, Judith H. *The Convention Problem: Issues in Reform of Presidential Nominating Procedures.* Washington, D.C.: Brookings, 1972.

Pika, Joseph H., and Richard Watson. *The Presidential Contest.* 5th ed. Washington, D.C.: CQ Press, 1995.

Pinchot, Amos R. E. *History of the Progressive Party, 1912-1916.* 1958. Reprint. New York: Westport, Conn.: Greenwood Press, 1978.

Pomper, Gerald M. *Nominating the President: The Politics of Convention Choice.* New York: Dodd, Mead, 1975.

___. *Voters, Elections, and Parties: The Practice of Democratic Theory.* New Brunswick, N.J.: Transaction Books, 1988.

Porter, Kirk H., and Donald Bruce Johnson. *National Party Platforms, 1840-1972.* Urbana: University of Illinois Press, 1973.

Reichley, A. James. *The Life of the Parties: A History of American Political Parties.* New York: Free Press, 1992.

Reeves, Richard. *Convention.* New York: Harcourt Brace Jovanovich, 1977.

Robinson, Edgar E. *The Evolution of American Political Parties.* 1924. Reprint. New York: Harcourt Brace Jovanovich, 1971.

Roseboom, Eugene H. *A History of Presidential Elections: From George Washington to Jimmy Carter.* 4th ed. New York: Macmillan, 1979.

Rosenstone, Steven J., Ray L. Behr and Edward H. Lazarus. *Third Parties in America: Citizen Response to Major Party Failure.* Princeton, N.J.: Princeton University Press, 1984.

Ross, Earle D. *The Liberal Republican Movement.* New York: AMS Press, 1971.

Rossiter, Clinton. *Parties and Politics in America.* Ithaca, N.Y.: Cornell University Press, 1960.

Sanford, Terry. *A Danger of Democracy: The Presidential Nominating Process.* Boulder, Colo.: Westview, 1981.

Schefter, Martin. *Political Parties and the State: The American Historical Experience.* Princeton, N.J.: Princeton University Press, 1994.

Schlesinger, Arthur M., Jr. *History of U.S. Political Parties.* 4 vols. 1973. Reprint. New York: Chelsea House, 1981.

———, ed. *The Coming to Power: Critical Presidential Elections in American History.* New York: Chelsea House, 1981.

Schlesinger, Joseph A. *Political Parties and the Winning of Office.* Ann Arbor: University of Michigan Press, 1991.

Shafer, Byron. *Bifurcated Politics: Evolution and Reform in the National Party Convention.* Cambridge, Mass.: Harvard University Press, 1988.

Shafritz, Jay M. *The Dorsey Dictionary of American Government and Politics.* Chicago: Dorsey Press, 1988.

Shannon, David A. *The Decline of American Communism: A History of the Communist Party in the United States Since 1945.* Chatham, N.J.: Chatham Booksellers, 1971.

Smallwood, Frank. *The Other Candidates: Third Parties in Presidential Elections.* Hanover, N.H.: University Press of New England, 1983.

Smith, Theodore C. *Liberty and Free Soil Parties in the Northwest.* Reprint. New York: Arno Press, 1970.

Stedman, Murray S., Jr., and Susan W. Stedman. *Discontent at the Polls: A Study of Farmer and Labor Parties, 1827-1948.* New York: Russell and Russell Publishers, 1967.

Sundquist, James L. *Dynamics of the Party System: Alignment and Realignment of Political Parties in the United States.* Rev. ed. Washington, D.C.: Brookings, 1983.

Timberlake, James H. *Prohibition and the Progressive Movement, 1912-1925.* New York: Random House, 1969.

Van Buren, Martin. *Inquiry into the Origin and Course of Political Parties in the United States.* 1867. Reprint. New York: A. M. Kelley, 1967.

Wattenberg, Martin P. *The Decline of the American Political Parties 1952 to 1992.* Boston: Harvard University Press, 1994.

White, Theodore H. *America in Search of Itself: The Making of the President, 1956-1980.* New York: Harper and Row, 1982.

___. *The Making of the President, 1960.* New York: Atheneum, 1961.

___. *The Making of the President, 1964.* New York: Atheneum, 1965.

___. *The Making of the President, 1968.* New York: Atheneum, 1969.

___. *The Making of the President, 1972.* New York: Atheneum, 1973.

Articles

Adkinson, Denny M. "The Electoral Significance of the Vice Presidency." *Presidential Studies Quarterly* 12 (Summer 1982): 330-336.

Angle, Paul M. "The Republican Convention of 1860." *Chicago History* (Spring 1960): 341.

Aldrich, John H. "A Dynamic Model of Presidential Nomination Campaigns." *American Political Science Review* 74 (September 1980): 651-669.

Democratic National Committee, Research Department. "General Information about the DNC." December 1988.

Hurley, Patricia A. "Partisan Representation and the Failure of Realignment in the 1980s." *American Journal of Political Science* 33 (February 1989): 240-261.

Maisel, L. Sandy. "The Platform-Writing Process: Candidate-Centered Platforms in 1992," *Political Science Quarterly* (Winter 1993-94): 671.

McNitt, Andrew D. "The Effect of Preprimary Endorsement on Competition for Nominations: An Examination of Different Nominating Systems." *Journal of Politics* 42 (February 1980): 257-266.

Miller, Warren E. "Party Identification, Realignment, and Party Voting: Back to the Basics." *American Political Science Review* 85 (June 1991): 557-568.

Paletz, David L., and Martha Elson. "Television Coverage of Presidential Conventions: Now You See It, Now You Don't." *Political Science Quarterly* 91 (Spring 1976).

Polsby, Nelson W. "Decision Making at the National Conventions." *Western Political Quarterly* (September 1960): 609-619.

Schlesinger, Joseph A. "The New American Political Party." *American Political Science Review* 79 (December 1985): 1152-1169.

Stanley, Harold W., and Richard G. Niemi. "Partisanship and Group Support, 1952-1988." *American Politics Quarterly* 19 (April 1991): 189-210.

Wildavsky, Aaron B. "On the Superiority of National Conventions." *Review of Politics* (July 1962): 307-319.

Wilson, Woodrow. "There Ought Never to Be Another Presidential Nominating Convention: Excerpts from a Letter, February 5, 1913." *U.S. News & World Report,* Oct. 23, 1967, 124.

Index

Note: Italic numbers refer to photographs or illustrations.

5605